To:

Tam Ramsby

May this text help in your sales career. Good luck!

December 1956

SALESMANSHIP
PRACTICES AND PROBLEMS

SALESMANSHIP
PRACTICES AND PROBLEMS

BY

BERTRAND R. CANFIELD

Salesmanship, Babson Institute
Of Business Administration

SECOND EDITION
SECOND IMPRESSION

New York Toronto London
McGRAW-HILL BOOK COMPANY, INC.
1950

SALESMANSHIP

PREFACE

So many books have been written about salesmanship that the only justification for another book is that it presents a new approach to the subject. This volume is a departure from the usual text on salesmanship in that it contains a minimum of inspirational, anecdotal, psychological, and economic material.

It is also unique in that it combines a discussion of the 20 fundamental problems commonly encountered in selling goods and services and the practices of successful salesmen in dealing with those problems. Selling is essentially a task of dealing with problems which are created by a salesman himself, his product, and his prospects.

These fundamental problems are experienced in selling every variety of product and service and all types of buyers. Some problems arise before a salesman comes face to face with a prospective customer and they persist long after an order has been secured. Many of the problems confronting a salesman are a product of his personality, knowledge, skill, habits, health, education, and attitude. Other problems are created by prospective purchasers and are a result of their experience, personality, education, needs, ability to buy, and authority.

Twenty of the most common problems encountered in selling were selected as representative of the difficulties met by salesmen in selling all kinds of products and services. The problems were selected after field observation of the work of many salesmen, analysis of the sales training courses of many corporations, and conferences with salesmen, sales executives, and buyers. Each of these problems is represented by a chapter in this book.

Sales interviews illustrating the 20 basic problems of salesmen are included at the end of each chapter. These interviews realistically exemplify the practices of salesmen in dealing with these problems. They provide a concrete basis for study and discussion of sales practice.

Several unique methods were employed in procuring many of these interviews between salesmen and prospects. Microphones were installed in the offices of buyers and the actual conversations between salesmen and buyers were recorded on wax cylinders in adjoining offices. These records were obtained without knowledge of the salesmen. Transcriptions from these records produced several hundred pages of verbatim sales conversations. In addition, investigators, equipped with dictographs and earphones, listened in on sales interviews and rated the problems of salesmen on 80 separate points, including opening remarks, personality factors, objections encountered, strategy in dealing with price, competition, closing the sale, etc.

Observers also accompanied salesmen on the job to record their remarks, methods, time employment, and problems encountered. Investigators shopped in retail stores and made verbatim records of the presentations of retail salesmen and the problems involved in consumer selling. Many of these interviews are the first actual records of what salesmen say to buyers that have been published in book form.

In this revised edition are included unique recorded interviews with consumers which reveal the buying motives and process, a matter of fundamental importance in the study of salesmanship. Salesmen and students of selling will find that analysis and discussion of these interviews dispel the impractical aspect of a purely theoretical approach to the study of salesmanship. These interviews challenge the imagination and, since they are susceptible of several interpretations, readily provoke group discussion and exchange of opinion, thus stimulating constructive thinking. In a few instances interviews are fictitious. Each interview is followed by a list of questions to guide the reader in arriving at a sound solution of the problem in each sales interview.

In conjunction with a knowledge of the problems encountered in selling, it is equally important that the practices of successful salesmen in dealing with these problems be understood. Accordingly, the interviews at the end of each chapter are preceded by a description of the practices of outstanding salesmen in dealing with the specific selling problem illustrated in each interview. To secure the best methods of dealing with sales problems, field observers watched salesmen at work and recorded their methods, and purchasing agents rated the performance of salesmen calling upon them. Time studies were made of salesmen traveling by automobile, and foot travel also was measured by salesmen over a period of several months.

In addition to this extensive field research carried on over a period of several years, the practices of successful salesmen in solving these problems were determined through interviews with salesmen, from the writings of outstanding salesmen and sales executives, and from the sales training programs of progressive sales organizations. Many of these practices used successfully by salesmen of one product apply equally well to selling every type of product or service.

To aid salesmen in applying the practices described in each chapter, simple outlines or "routines" are included at the end of each chapter. This unique feature of the book makes it possible for a salesman to apply quickly the practices of successful salesmen in dealing with each of the 20 principal problems. By memorizing these routines and practicing them in interviews with buyers, a salesman can effectively dispose of problems which arise in every sales presentation. When confronted with a basic sales problem, a salesman who has familiarized himself with the routine for attacking that problem has no hesitancy in dealing with it. Selling proficiency comes from developing good selling habits which can be quickly acquired by following the "routines" at the end of each chapter. They provide the "how" to use the "what" discussed in each chapter. Here, for the first time, is a complete description of the practices of outstanding salesmen illustrated by interviews with buyers.

Each chapter is followed by a list of reading references to supplement the material in the chapter and to serve as a source of additional information bearing on the problems included therein.

In the revised edition, two new chapters have been added: one on the field of salesmanship to orient the student to the subject; and a second on the customer to discuss the motives and viewpoints of consumers. In addition, much new material from the sales training of large corporations has been included, and numerous changes to simplify and clarify the text have been made as a result of eight years of teaching experience with the original edition.

This book is designed to enable salesmen who want to improve their performance and earnings to profit from the practices of successful salesmen; to aid sales executives in the development of their own sales training programs; and to serve as a textbook for courses in salesmanship in schools and colleges.

The author is indebted to numerous students who have aided in the field research; to sales executives who have cooperated in investigating the problems and methods of their salesmen; to the purchasing agents of numerous corporations; to consumers who have cooperated in the research of buying processes; to the publishers of sales magazines, particularly *Printers' Ink,* and The Dartnell Corporation; to the authors of books on sales and advertising; and to his wife, who has given invaluable aid in the preparation of the manuscript.

Bertrand R. Canfield

Babson Park, Mass.
    March, 1950

CONTENTS

CHAPTER I

THE FIELD OF SALESMANSHIP

What Is Salesmanship? There are many definitions of salesmanship. They range from the cynical description of selling as, "The art of persuading you to spend money you do not have for something you do not need for more than it is worth," to the definition attributed to the late John Wanamaker, "Salesmanship is the art of so successfully demonstrating the merits of the goods and services of a house that a permanent customer is made." Another definition of modern salesmanship is, "The art of providing products that won't come back to customers who will."

The function of a salesman, in general, is to seek out an individual who has a need and ability to buy and bring him into contact with a supplier who can best satisfy that need to the mutual advantage of the customer, the salesman, and his company.

Salesmanship is difficult to define adequately because of the many types of products, services, customers, distributing organizations, and functions involved in getting goods from the producer to the ultimate consumer.

Types of Selling. Salesmanship may be classified in the following ways:

1. *Type of product or service sold*, according to the nature of the commodity, whether it be tangible or intangible. Selling tangibles, such as automobiles, refrigerators, typewriters, or oil burners, is quite different from selling intangibles, such as life insurance, investments, or advertising. The desire for intangibles must usually be created, and as their benefits are often deferred, their sale requires more imagination and skill than is needed in selling products which can be seen and the benefits of which can be enjoyed immediately.

Of the tangible commodities, distinction is made between the staples and specialties, and closely allied to the latter are the luxuries or novelties. Staples, such as nails, wire, bread, sugar, milk, and muslin, are necessities bought on a price or utility basis, with few distinguishing characteristics and limited brand appeal. Selling of staples is

1

largely automatic and requires a minimum of selling skill. Luxuries and novelties possess some original or unique feature, such as costume jewelry, evening dresses, or perfume, and require high selling ability.

Specialties, such as automobiles, major electric appliances, and office machines, subordinate price and emphasize quality; are in irregular demand; enjoy individuality by special process of feature, patent right, or packaging; are usually branded and offer broader profit. Specialties, luxuries, and novelties are more difficult to sell and call for more initiative, knowledge, persuasiveness, and effort on the part of the salesman than staples or necessities for which the need is recognized. Wants must be created for specialties, particularly those which are pioneering the market, such as personal aircraft, home air conditioning, and television receivers.

Selling of tangibles is also classified according to the market, as individual consumer goods or industrial or capital goods. Individual consumer goods include staples as well as specialties, luxuries, and novelties which are sold through wholesale and retail establishments or direct to the homes of consumers. Industrial or capital goods include raw materials; installation equipment, such as presses, boilers, and air conditioners; accessory goods, such as desks or typewriters; fabricating materials and parts, such as batteries and bearings; and operating supplies, such as stationery and fuel oil.

A salesman of consumer goods has many potential customers, makes numerous contacts, and makes sales more or less frequently, but the size of his average order is often small. An industrial goods salesman, on the other hand, usually has a limited number of customers; makes sales infrequently but for more sizable amounts; is technically trained and serves as well as sells. Industrial buyers are better informed than most consumers and put a higher requirement on a salesman's ability to solve the buyer's problems with the product.

Selling of commodities is also classified according to the frequency of sales. Products which have a long life, such as pianos, home insulation, and heating equipment, offer little or no possibilities for repeat sales. Once a salesman has sold a steam boiler, it will be many years before the customer may be in the market again. The unit-of-sale price is high, and a large number of prospects must be contacted in nonrepeat selling. However, repeat products, such as fuel, food, and beverages, require frequent sales contacts with a more or less limited number of customers.

Selling is also frequently described by the nature of the service or commodities sold, such as hardware, food, drug, implement, insurance, or investment selling. The functions of a salesman vary widely depending upon the nature of the product which he is selling.

2. *Type of customer,* according to whether the buyer is an individual consumer, an industrial concern or institution buying for its own use, or a distributor, wholesaler, or retail dealer buying for resale to ultimate consumers.

A salesman selling the ultimate consumer may be employed by a retail merchant or by a manufacturer selling direct to the ultimate consumer. Or he may be an inside salesman to whom the customer comes for satisfaction of his wants.

Salesmen selling to industrial concerns or institutions, such as hospitals, hotels, and schools, usually have a limited number of prospects and sell large quantities of staples. In the case of technical products and specialties sold to industry, salesmen often have technical training, are skilled in locating and solving technical problems, and are more concerned with service than actual selling. This is usually known as sales engineering and is done chiefly by graduate engineers.

Salesmen representing wholesalers sell to retailers while those representing manufacturers sell to wholesalers, chain, individual, or department stores and mail-order houses for resale to ultimate consumers.

3. *Type of function.* Several functional types of salesmen are used in selling to distributors and dealers: *Specialty selling* by men who specialize on a new product or on reviving the sale of an established item. This type of selling calls for initiative, aggressiveness, and a high degree of persuasiveness. *Missionary selling* by men who sell a full line and call on established dealers at regular intervals to insure fresh, adequate stocks, proper display, and pricing. They also persuade dealers to use local advertising in newspapers, and to use direct mail, window, counter, and floor displays. These salesmen, sometimes called detail, service, or merchandising men, train dealers and their salespeople and give counsel in store system, stock control, arrangement, credit, and service. This type of selling calls for energy, persistence, enthusiasm, and helpfulness and is widely used in the food, drug, hardware, and tobacco industries.

Another type of customer sold to largely by detail men representing manufacturers is the professional buyer, such as a doctor, dentist, architect, contractor, or engineer, who is an ultimate consumer of technical equipment and operating supplies. These customers are also specifiers of equipment and supplies for their clients. This type of selling is often indirect, service, or missionary work calling for knowledge of product and its applications.

4. *Type of distributor,* according to whom the salesman represents—a manufacturer, wholesaler, retailer, broker, selling agent, or other functional middleman.

The manufacturer's salesmen sell to institutions, wholesalers, distributors, retailers, or direct to the ultimate consumer. These salesmen may do either specialty, missionary, detail, service, or merchandising selling, as described previously.

The wholesaler, jobber, or distributor salesmen sell to retailers, institutions, or industrial consumers and do specialty, missionary, or merchandising selling, as described previously. This type of selling involves calling at regular intervals on an established group of customers who usually keep "want lists" which the salesman uses in making up an order. Or he may check the merchant's stock and suggest needed items. As they carry from 5,000 to 10,000 items and make collections, wholesale salesmen usually have little time for creative selling. They are often "order takers" who rely on friendship and merchandising service to get business. Specialty wholesale salesmen, on the other hand, who pioneer new products or revive the sale of established items must be more aggressive and resourceful, and their task requires more knowledge and ability.

Retail selling in small quantities to individual consumers includes both inside and outside selling. The latter largely involves the sale of home appliances and automobiles, although brushes, hosiery, and corsets are also sold house-to-house. Many inside salespeople are little more than clerks who display, make change, and wrap merchandise for customers who know what they want. This kind of inside selling requires little intelligence, knowledge, or skill and promises to be eventually supplanted by self-service or automatic vending. However, there is a definite place in service stores for a salesperson who is a merchandise adviser interested in helping customers to buy and stimulating their desires for merchandise which they need.

Manufacturer's agent selling to wholesalers, retailers, institutions, and chain or department stores is done by brokers, selling agents, manufacturers' agents who represent a number of noncompeting manufacturers and call at regular intervals on established customers soliciting wholesale orders for their principals. This type of selling is similar to "side-line" selling by salesmen who sell the products of several manufacturers.

5. *Type of territory,* according to the geographical area in which a salesman operates. Export selling is done in foreign markets as contrasted with domestic selling done in this country. Foreign selling demands a special knowledge of foreign exchange, tariffs, laws, shipping regulations, political and market conditions abroad. Export salesmen are frequently promoted from the domestic force and are given greater responsibility and higher compensation.

City selling, wherein the activities of a salesman are confined to the city or suburb in which the headquarters of the salesman is located, is often distinguished from country or field selling, where a salesman travels in rural areas or from town to village throughout the country.

6. *Other specialized types of salesmen,* according to the duties of the salesman—specialty, missionary, and engineering or technical, which have been described previously. Further specialization in selling is practical in some companies which employ junior salesmen or sales assistants to conserve the time of salesmen in prospecting, planning sales, analyzing needs, studying product application, making appointments, preparing surveys, gathering information, and other routine work required by salesmen, except making sales presentations and demonstrations.

A large office-systems manufacturer uses sales assistants to study office routines and to prepare proposals. A vacuum cleaner manufacturer uses "planters" to get cleaners into houses for trial use, and later salesmen follow up the trials and close sales. A large casualty insurance organization has divided its selling into two parts—new business procurement and service selling—using two separate sales organizations, one for securing new customers and another for following up policyholders.

SCOPE AND DEVELOPMENT OF SALESMANSHIP

Salesmanship, in the sense of persuasion, is as old as history. Marco Polo, the Venetian traveler, sold the Orient to the Occident; Christopher Columbus sold Ferdinand and Isabella on a new World; the Wright brothers sold air travel. All of the famous leaders of history—statesmen, scientists, churchmen, and businessmen—have used salesmanship to exploit their genius.

In the broadest meaning of the word, everyone is a salesman from birth to death. The baby in his cradle cries for attention; the young man sells his proposal of marriage to the girl of his choice; the doctor uses salesmanship to gain the confidence of his patient; the lawyer sells his client to the jury; and the minister sells religion to his congregation. These people sell ideas. Salesmen sell goods and services.

Selling of commodities began in the barter of primitive peoples. Later, buyers and sellers came to meet at convenient places for the purpose of trading. Markets were established in France in Roman times. There were 758 market towns in England and Wales in 1720.

As it was impossible for everyone to visit the market towns to buy, itinerant merchants or peddlers visited the markets, bought goods, and carried them to people in their homes. The first salesmen in this country were the Yankee peddlers who, beginning in 1790, sold clocks, tinware, woolens, notions from packs on their backs and later from wagons. Unscrupulous tricksters, believing in the philosophy of "let the buyer beware," these peddlers created much ill will and aroused the resistance of consumers.

America at the opening of the nineteenth century was a land of craftsmen, carpenters, shoemakers, saddlers, and blacksmiths, who made their own goods and sold them to their neighbors.

Then came the wilderness trading post and general store where the sharp practices of the peddlers were followed by the merchants who put sand in the sugar, chicory in the coffee, and dust in the pepper. In Bethel, Connecticut, a young salesman named P. T. Barnum, who was later to be known as the "Prince of Humbugs" worked in his father's general store and described the salesmanship of that period as follows: "Our cottons were sold for wool, our wool and cotton for silk and linen; in fact, nearly everything was different from what it was represented to be. The factories cheated us in their fabrics; we cheated the customers with our goods. Each party expected to be cheated if it was possible. We believed little that we saw and less that we heard."

In the decade preceding the Civil War, the growing number of retailers stimulated competition between wholesalers who employed men to "drum-up" trade by inducing retailers to visit their establishments. These "drummers" met the country retailers at their hotels when they came to the wholesale markets once or twice a year to buy merchandise. Their functions have been described by a contemporary, as follows: "They watch for customers as a cunning animal watches for prey. The country merchant is hooked on his arrival, captivated by insincere courtesy, attracted by appeals to his appetite, is coaxed, decoyed and finally ensnared or captured."

Following the panic of 1837, so many wholesalers lost money that drummers were sent on the road to gather credit information, as well as to sell, and became the first traveling salesmen. The total number of these salesmen in 1861 has been estimated at not more than 1,000.

By 1870 the government Census found 7,000, and by 1900 there were 93,000 traveling salesmen.

In the 1870's, the department store began to develop, pioneered by Jordan Marsh in Boston, John Wanamaker in Philadelphia, and Marshall Field in Chicago, and followed by the first mail-order house, Montgomery Ward and Company, in 1872. F. W. Woolworth opened the first chain of variety stores in 1879. By 1900, there were 611,000 salesmen and saleswomen, mostly in retail stores.

Until the turn of the century, demand exceeded supply, and the seller had the advantage. When the customer bought, it was at his own risk. Selling was a battle of wits. Few articles were marked with plain prices, and buying was a matter of haggling over price. Salesmen outtalked, browbeat, and outtricked customers. The pitch-man with his card tricks circulated profitably over the land selling snake oil in the light of his gasoline flare.

But a great change gradually occurred in selling as production caught up with demand and many new articles—electrical appliances, automobiles, prepared foods in packages, automatic heating and plumbing equipment were produced. To sell these modern articles, manufacturers began to brand them with their own names, advertise them at one price to all, and back them with a money-back guarantee. A new consciousness of the consumer permeated selling, a sense of obligation to serve the buyer, which spelled the death of the old philosophy of "let the buyer beware." Modern professional salesmanship began slowly to emerge.

Salesmen have made an important contribution to the attainment of our present high standard of living. They have played a significant part in pioneering acceptance of modern developments in transportation, housing, foods, manufacturing, and agriculture in the face of strong resistance to change. The appliances which are recognized as necessities in most modern homes today were introduced by salesmen who overcame the indifference and antagonism of consumers and by courageous persistence made possible the volume production of millions of time and laborsaving devices at prices within the means of nearly everyone.

THE RISE OF MODERN PROFESSIONAL SALESMANSHIP

The lush years from 1914 to 1929 marked the "high-pressure" era in salesmanship, when salesmen swarmed from home to home, and to offices, obsessed with the aim of making an immediate sale regardless of the needs, interests, or purchasing power of the customer. Sell-

ing was called a game—like stalking wild animals. Even more persistence and high-powered sales ammunition was used by these high-
pressure salesmen than was employed by peddlers and hucksters not
many years before. Salesmen were referred to as "go-getters" and
were driven by their managers with inspirational meetings and prizes
to "go out and get the business—and use any tactics you like so long
as you stay out of jail."

But the depression of the early 1930's completely discredited pressure selling. It ushered in the buyers' market and showed the fallacy
of bullying and tricking customers into buying. A new ethical concept
of customer relations emerged—a philosophy of helpfulness and service to consumers—a new viewpoint of aiding customers to recognize
their needs and showing them how to solve their problems through the
purchase of merchandise or services.

Webster's Dictionary defines a profession as "a calling in which one
professes to have acquired some special knowledge used by way
either of instructing, guiding, or advising others or of serving them
in some art." This definition aptly describes the vocation of the
modern professional salesman, who obtains his principal compensation
from his interest in learning more about his product and its applications and the contribution which, by reason of his knowledge, he can
make to satisfying the need of his customers.

There are still many salesmen, who gained their experience in the
days of "let the buyer beware," who are little more than peddlers and
hucksters. But there is a growing number of professional salesmen
who pride themselves on being able to serve their customers well.

A professional salesman, according to Robert S. Wilson, vice-president in charge of sales, the Goodyear Tire and Rubber Company, is
one who has made selling his chosen calling—his life work; a man
who is constantly studying to improve his proficiency and recognizes
that there is no substitute for hard work; who maintains his own self-
respect, integrity and independence and who puts a true value on
his services.

He must be activated by a true and militant spirit of service;
imbued with a burning zeal for his product or his service and a love
for his work.

The salesmen who have made the greatest progress toward professional status are a select group of life insurance underwriters who
are graduates of the American College of Life Underwriters which
confers the Chartered Life Underwriter degree after four years of

study and passing exhaustive tests on life insurance fundamentals, general education, laws, trusts, taxes, and finance.

This fundamental training compares favorably with that given in some of the recognized professions. A C.L.U. salesman diagnoses a prospect's financial needs in a manner comparable to a physical examination of a patient by a physician; writes a remedy for the prospect's financial problem as a doctor writes a prescription; and sells the prospect on accepting the recommendations.

Successful sales engineers selling technical products to industry also qualify as professional salesmen by helping their customers to understand their needs, diagnosing their production problems, and showing them how their difficulties can be satisfied through the purchase of technical equipment and supplies.

There is a great need for professional salesmen with retail training to study the problems of merchants and prescribe better methods of handling store personnel, accounting, buying, merchandise control, advertising, display, lighting, and other phases of store operation which contribute to increased sales of the products which wholesale and manufacturer's salesmen sell.

STANDARDS OF PROFESSIONAL SALESMANSHIP

Establishment of professional standards for selling is fundamental to the future progress of salesmanship. In the life insurance business the demand for higher standards of selling has resulted in 10 states passing laws requiring a fundamental knowledge of the business before a license to sell is issued. Similar, recognized, state-controlled examinations, such as those required to practice medicine, law, or the ministry, are needed for selling. Basic education, selection, training, and apprenticeship requirements must be established to qualify salesmen for professional status, as in other professions. Collegiate training for selling, including courses in advertising, marketing, salesmanship, retailing, public relations, psychology, accounting, public speaking, and English, leading to a degree in salesmanship, is just as essential as the major areas of study which have been established for law, medicine, and education.

The professional attitude in selling needs definition and recognition by both business and consumers. Through joint action of producers, wholesalers, distributors, retailers, and consumers in those industries where the need for professional salesmanship is greatest, professional standards can be established for the mutual profit of buyer and seller.

The need for professional status for salesmen grows with the rising importance of selling as a vital factor in our industrial and commercial prosperity.

GROWING IMPORTANCE OF SALESMANSHIP

The growth of selling activity in the past 70 years clearly illustrates the importance of the role of selling in modern business. In 1870, 24 per cent of the population worked in distribution, but by 1930 this number had nearly doubled to 47 per cent.

The 1940 Census classified 3,188,854 persons as salesmen and saleswomen of whom 2,320,435 were men and 868,419 were women. Included are 525,591 retail inside salespeople.

In wholesale selling, the latest available count, taken in 1939, was 361,500 salesmen, of whom 226,500 were employed by wholesale merchants and 109,000 by manufacturers' sales branches; 11,000 sold for petroleum bulk tank stations and 15,000 were agents and brokers.

As our industrial economy has developed through the introduction of new machinery, and the improvement of production methods and inventions, manufacturers have been forced to create a demand for their products in order to dispose of the high volume of goods which they are able to produce. Salesmanship has grown in importance with the increasing number and variety of products available.

During the Second World War, we doubled our capacity to produce, but high production is impossible without continuous consumption stimulated by sound salesmanship. Full employment of more than twenty million workers in factories depends on the sale of the goods which they produce.

"Until someone sells somebody else something, nothing happens," says A. H. Motley, sales executive. Without salesmen, mass distribution of manufactured goods would be impossible, and without distribution, factories would close and widespread unemployment would result.

It has been estimated that an average salesman provides a livelihood for 59 people by producing orders which create work for 15 wage earners. More than 15 men and women in factories, offices, and farms depend on the average salesman for their pay checks.

National prosperity depends on full employment resulting from high-level consumption inspired by good salesmanship.

The need for salesmen to maintain high postwar production has been estimated at 8,000,000 men—nearly four times as many as were engaged in selling before the war. The major appliance industry required 250,000 retail salesmen after the Second World War or four times as many as sold appliances in the prewar years. With no selling during the war years, there are 500,000 fewer men in sales and service than in 1940, according to reliable estimates. The number of retail automobile salesmen declined from 125,000 in 1941 to 25,000 in 1945.

OPPORTUNITIES IN SELLING

In view of the growing importance of selling and the need for competent salesmen, it is significant that salesmanship is looked down upon by those considering a business or a profession. Numerous surveys among high-school and college graduates confirm the fact that only 5 per cent are interested in selling as a career. Many people would rather do anything but sell. An investigation among more than 15,000 men and women employed in Evansville, Indiana, war plants showed that only 200 had the slightest interest in selling; while out of 437 who had been salesmen before the war, only 138 were interested in going back into selling.

Why is salesmanship held in such low esteem? Many people still cling to the conception of selling as practiced early in the century by peddlers, hucksters, and high-pressure drummers. There still are salesmen who do not subscribe to the ethics of professional salesmanship, just as there are quacks and shysters in every profession. Many persons, particularly young people, have never been exposed to professional salesmanship. They class all salesmen with peddlers and untrained house-to-house vendors. The professional salesman equipped with knowledge of his product and its applications and motivated with a sincere desire to help buyers satisfy their needs is still a rarity, and few people have had an opportunity to observe this type of salesman at work.

Many have a poor opinion of selling because sales have come so easily during the postwar years when demand so far outran supply of most commodities that the quality of selling deteriorated into mere order taking. Those who advocate a controlled economy rather than free enterprise preach the waste and futility of salesmanship.

Failure on the part of many business organizations to train and supervise their salesmen, to give them adequate knowledge of their product, company, policies, needs of customers, and a sound professional approach has resulted in lowered prestige for salesmen and their work. A leading sales training executive says that fewer than one out of every six applicants for sales work is qualified to sell, and only one in ten is qualified to sell when the filling of future district managerships is in mind. Lack of proper selection and lack of training are chiefly responsible for the turnover of salesmen, which from 1925 to 1939 averaged over 380 per cent and of house-to-house canvassers up to 1,400 per cent, according to Dr. S. N. Stevens, president of Grinnell College.

However, the caliber of salesmanship is slowly but steadily improving under the growing recognition of employers and their salesmen that training is essential to good selling and that a professional attitude toward sales work pays big dividends in sales and prestige.

THE SATISFACTIONS OF SELLING

Salesmanship offers many satisfactions to qualified men and women. Competent salesmen normally enjoy greater job security than any other vocational group in full-time employment. Even in periods of depression, a salesman's services are more essential than in good times. A salesman who has proven his ability to make sales at a profit is always sure of his job, as the operation of his company depends on the orders which he produces.

Opportunity for Advancement. The opportunities for advancement in selling are numerous, as sales operations are divided into many classifications of selling and supervision. These classifications provide a wide variety of jobs suited to various degrees of experience and ability. Beginners may start as junior or assistant salesmen and advance to positions of senior salesman, district representative, branch manager, zone manager, assistant sales manager, division sales manager, up to general sales manager or vice-president in charge of sales. A survey of 300 companies by the Chicago Sales Managers Club showed that 38 per cent of their presidents were formerly salesmen; while another 10 per cent had sales, or sales and financial, backgrounds. Furthermore, promotion in selling usually depends on proven performance rather than on seniority or length of service as in many occupations.

Adequate Compensation. According to the U.S. Department of Commerce, a higher percentage of salesmen than any other vocational group earned $5,000 a year or more in 1940. The earnings of manufacturers' salesmen reported by 487 companies to The Dartnell Corporation in 1946 averaged $6,177 annually compared with $3,008 in 1940, an increase of about 60 per cent. Starting salaries reported in the same survey ranged from $175 to $250 a month.

A study of the average incomes of salesmen by age groups in varied fields of business in 1940 showed that in the twenty- to twenty-nine-year age group accountants earned $1,858 annually, production workers, $2,014, and salesmen, $2,700; in the thirty- to thirty-nine-year age group accountants earned $4,066, production men, $4,105, and salesmen, $4,515; and in the forty- to forty-nine-year age group accountants earned $4,600, production men, $4,862, and salesmen, $5,952 annually.

Salesmen representing wholesalers and jobbers before the Second World War earned an average of $45 a week up to $70 or $80 a week. Inside retail salesmen averaged $21.82 a week, although outside retail salesmen averaged $35 a week before the war and $40 to $60 a week in the postwar period.

Some life insurance, specialty, and technical salesmen earn from $8,000 to $10,000 a year with outstanding men averaging $15,000 to $25,000 annually.

Satisfaction of Service. The satisfaction which comes from serving others is one of the great compensations of sales work. The insurance salesman makes it possible for men to have financial independence, freedom from want and fear in their old age. The heating equipment salesman brings comfort, health, and satisfaction to the homes of his customers. The electrical appliance salesman makes it possible for housewives to enjoy more leisure and freedom from labor. By making life fuller and happier for others, a salesman derives real enjoyment himself.

Recognition of Achievement. The accomplishments of salesmen are readily recognized by the accepted standard of sales volume. A salesman has always before him a gauge of his performance in the number and amount of orders booked. Sales ability cannot go undiscovered for long, and achievement is often rewarded by incentives in the form of bonuses, prizes, or promotion. If a salesman's own company fails to appreciate his ability, alert competitors are always aware of his accomplishments and not slow to make him attractive offers.

Freedom from Boredom. Sales work is never monotonous, as each call, every customer, presents a new situation and problem. There is infinite variety in the types of customers served and the nature of their needs. The many different tasks which a salesman must perform, from locating new prospects to following up old customers, include investigation, analysis, planning, demonstrating, and reporting and add variety to the work. Salesmen who travel widely see new places daily and enjoy interesting experiences.

Opportunity for Self-expression. Selling affords an unusual opportunity for self-expression through creative, original thinking in respect to sales strategy, sales presentations, and in the organization and employment of time and effort. Most salesmen are practically in business for themselves in the sense that they usually have the liberty to plan their own work and develop their plans in their own way with a minimum of interference and supervision by their managers. This freedom of action and thought is one of the big compensations of sales work.

A Healthful Vocation. Outside salesmen work in a healthful environment where they get plenty of exercise and can enjoy the physical stimulation of an active life. Salesmen probably more than other workers operate under most favorable working conditions.

Training and Cooperation. Salesmen in progressive companies are given more training and assistance than workers in other vocations. Because of the essential nature of selling, millions are spent in educational programs to provide salesmen with a knowledge of product or service, company, policies, advertising, service, and selling strategy. It costs $4,500 to train a new man to sell the products of a leading beverage manufacturer. As a result of this training, salesmen are in a position to advance more rapidly and increase their incomes faster than other workers.

WEAKNESSES OF MODERN SELLING

Modern salesmanship is of such recent origin that it is not surprising it is suffering the customary "growing pains" of all infant developments. Selling is still in the pioneering stage of its evolution, characterized by the raw, unpolished practices and customs of a pioneering era. There is a lack of the standards of practice, ethics, and manners which are common in established professions.

Shortage of Qualified Personnel. Selling is primarily suffering from an acute shortage of qualified personnel. Too many men have taken selling jobs as a mere substitute for idleness or from inability to succeed in other vocations. Salesmanship has been looked upon as a last resort before going on relief. It is a common assumption that anybody with a pleasant smile and affable manner could succeed in selling. Because educational and professional standards for selling have been lacking, it is understandable that it would attract many who have no aptitude for sales work. As demand has often exceeded supply in the past, it is clear why unqualified persons have been able to earn a living selling.

Ample evidence of the lack of qualified salesmen is the high turnover rate and the obvious absence of even fundamental traits of good salesmanship in the work of many of those employed as salesmen.

The popular misconception that almost anyone is qualified to sell has been encouraged by employers, many of whom have had no standards for selecting salesmen or have relied upon graphology or astrology to guide them in picking sales representatives. In the keen competition for sales man power, many concerns have been satisfied to accept almost anyone willing to give them sales representation. This has been particularly true of those companies seeking straight commission salesmen who have been willing to assume all of the risk by financing their activities.

Fortunately there is a growing interest in better selection of qualified salesmen by more scientific methods of testing and the establishment of qualifications by progressive companies. One life insurance company, after improving selection, found that 500 well-selected salesmen sold three times as much life insurance as 1,500 men sold before selection was improved.

Inadequate Knowledge and Skill. Second only to the shortage of qualified sales personnel is the inadequate knowledge and skill of persons employed as salesmen. In order to help customers understand their needs and to show them how products and services will bring them profit or satisfaction, it is essential that salesmen have a sound knowledge of the design, construction, materials, distinctive features, processes of manufacture, as well as the various applications of the products which they sell. In addition, salesmen need the skill to seek out possible buyers, make sales presentations, conduct demonstrations, meet objections, and close sales. Few salesmen possess the fundamental information about their products or services to enable them to render a professional service to customers. In all of the established trades and professions, members are required to spend a specified time in study and training as apprentices or internes before they are permitted to practice. Until such requirements are established for salesmen, there will be many employed as salesmen who do not have the knowledge or skill essential to success.

While a few companies invest substantial sums in sales training programs, the majority simply supply new salesmen with sales literature, catalogue, and order book and turn them loose with a blessing into a competitive world to sink or swim by their own efforts. The persistent man eventually educates himself and acquires skill by trial and error, but the majority never learn more than a few superficial things about what they are selling. Until management recognizes its responsibility to train not only beginners but experienced salesmen as well, sales performance must be mediocre.

Ineffective Management. Salesmen must necessarily be left largely to their own devices. Yet, comparatively few salesmen have the ability to manage their time and efforts effectively with the result that there is a great deal of lost motion in selling. Only about 15 per cent of the average salesman's time is spent face to face with customers. The balance of his time is devoted to traveling, waiting, or doing routine work. Time is a salesman's capital and few have learned to budget this important asset. More salesmen fail because of inability to use their time properly than for any other reason.

Nor has management in many cases been conspicuously successful in supervising salesmen. Salesmen's compensation is often unsatisfactory, particularly with respect to arbitrary limitation of earnings, unwarranted changes in compensation method, establishment of "house" or no-commission accounts, inadequate remuneration of beginners—all of which have created dissatisfaction among salesmen. Indefinite agreements; arbitrary quotas; failure to give salesmen the same vacation, retirement, or other benefits enjoyed by other employees in comparable positions; threatening loss of employment to achieve results; and excessive paper work have contributed to lowering the morale and efficiency of salesmen.

INDUCTION AND ADVANCEMENT OF OUTSIDE SALESMEN

Beginners in sales work, as a part of their training, sometimes start with inside work at the home office, factory, or a branch to give them a good working knowledge of the business before permitting them to contact customers. The candidate for sales work is usually assigned to one of three types of inside jobs: (1) Sales-clerical as order clerk, stock clerk, sales statistician, or sales correspondent; (2) Factory as laborer, machine operator, assembler, truck driver, mechanical helper, or serviceman; (3) Inside selling as telephone salesman or floor salesman.

Another induction method is to start inexperienced salesmen outside contacting prospects and customers in two ways: (1) direct selling to buyers or (2) missionary or nonselling service work including collecting, servicing, advertising, or sales-promotion work as an assistant or junior salesman. About 40 per cent of all concerns induct new salesmen in this way.

This is the induction process usually followed for salesmen of non-technical goods or services sold to individual consumers or to whole-sale or retail merchants. In selling technical products, however, be-ginner salesmen undergo a more or less lengthy apprenticeship ranging from one to several years in factory, laboratory, and office to acquaint them with the more complex features and applications of machines or equipment sold to industry.

The following progress charts show the starting job and successive advancements to terminal positions held by salesmen of various types of products.

Induction process of beginner industrial salesman, employed by a large producer of heavy chemicals, solvents, and industrial alcohol, follows:

Starting Job: Laboratory Re-search Assistant.

Duties: Works in laboratory studying product uses and composition.

Second Job: Application Labora-tory.

Duties: Works in application labora-tory studying uses and making tests of products with a view to sales.

Third Job: Sales Service Depart-ment.

Duties: Works in sales service depart-ment answering inquiries, cor-respondence, and serving cus-tomers.

Fourth Job: Fundamental Busi-ness Training.

Duties: Works in various departments to secure fundamental business training lacking in highly spe-cialized technical education.

Fifth Job: Sales Correspondent.

Duties: Taking and acknowledging tel-ephone orders, answering ques-tions, handling complaints. Cor-responding on various products.

Sixth Job: Sales Serviceman.

Duties: Calling on customers, giving information, aiding in solution of customers' problems.

Seventh Job: Senior Salesman.

Duties: Assumes full responsibility for a sales territory.

Induction process of candidates for sales work for a large confec-tionery manufacturer, showing the jobs en route to the terminal position of senior salesmen:

Starting Job: Factory Work.   Duties: Rotating from department to
                                     department in the factory to
                                     learn the products and reveal
                                     ability to work.

Second Job: Office Work.   Duties: Rotating from department to
                                     department in the home office
                                     doing clerical work to learn
                                     company policies.

Third Job: Wholesale Inside   Duties: Inside selling to jobbers who
     Work.   call at factory wholesale store
                                     for stock to get over-the-
                                     counter sales experience.

Fourth Job: Missionary Sales-   Duties: Calling on retail trade, doing
     man.   missionary work, and some-
                                     times taking orders to be filled
                                     by jobbers.

Fifth Job: Senior Salesman.   Duties: Selling candy jobbers through-
                                     out the United States.

Candidates for sales work hold the following jobs en route to the
terminal position of senior salesman in a large meat-packing corporation:

Starting Job: Plant Work.   Duties: Rotating through eight plant
                                     departments cutting meat, fish,
                                     dressing poultry, sorting and
                                     grading meat, to get acquainted
                                     with the products in the line.

Second Job: Order Board.   Duties: Taking telephone orders from
                                     salesmen and customers.

Third Job: Relief Salesman.   Duties: Relieving salesmen who are
                                     sick or on vacation, calling
                                     upon and selling customers in
                                     the field.

Fourth Job: Senior Salesman.   Duties: Direct responsibility for a ter-
                                     ritory and full line selling.

The rate of progress from first to terminal sales jobs varies widely
according to the ability of the man, complexity of the product, the
turnover in the sales force, and expansion in the organization. In
some companies men attain senior rank in a few months while in
others it takes several years.

A comparatively limited number of salesmen go into executive or
administrative jobs as supervisors or junior and senior sales execu-

tives, as well as into related jobs in advertising, sales promotion, public relations, service, and general administration.

Reading References

C. H. FERNALD, "Salesmanship," pp. 1–28, Prentice-Hall, Inc., New York, 1945.

J. M. HILL and R. G. WALTERS, "Success through Salesmanship," pp. 1–16, South-Western Publishing Company, Cincinnati, 1940.

PAUL W. IVEY, "Salesmanship Applied," pp. 3–48, McGraw-Hill Book Company, Inc., New York, 1937.

O. P. and C. H. ROBINSON, "Successful Retail Salesmanship," pp. 1–19, Prentice-Hall, Inc., New York, 1942.

F. A. RUSSELL and F. H. BEACH, "Textbook of Salesmanship," pp. 3–51, McGraw-Hill Book Company, Inc., New York, 1949.

HARRY SIMMONS, "A Practical Course in Successful Selling," pp. 1–21, Harper & Brothers, New York, 1939.

CHAPTER II

THE SALESMAN'S JOB

What Is a Salesman's Job? In general, the job of a salesman is to locate individuals or organizations that have legitimate needs for, as well as the ability to buy, his product or service; to aid such prospective purchasers in reaching a decision to buy by telling and showing them how the product or service meets their needs; and to see that the customer obtains the satisfaction from the purchase to which he is entitled.

Types of Salesmen's Jobs. Sales jobs may be classified in numerous ways, but the generally accepted types described in Chap. I are:

I. *Type of Product or Service.*
    1. Tangibles.
    2. Intangibles or services.
    3. Specialties.
    4. Staples or necessities.
    5. Luxuries.
    6. Novelties.
    7. Individual consumer goods.
    8. Industrial or capital goods.
    9. Frequency of sale.
    10. Nature of the product itself.

II. *Type of Customer.*
    1. Individual consumer.
    2. Industrial consumer.
    3. Institution.
    4. Distributor or wholesaler.
    5. Retail dealer.

III. *Type of Function.*
    1. Specialty selling.
    2. Missionary, detail, service, or merchandising selling.
    3. Engineering.
    4. Junior selling.

IV. *Type of Distributor.*
    1. Manufacturer.

    2. Wholesaler or wholesale distributor.
    3. Retailer.
    4. Manufacturer's agent, including brokers and selling agents.
V. *Type of Territory.*
    1. Domestic.
    2. Export or foreign.
    3. City.
    4. Country.

Profiting by the experience of industrial engineers, progressive sales executives have made studies of the duties of outstanding salesmen engaged in various types of selling so that all salesmen may know exactly what duties must be performed in a specific sales job and poor salesmen may profit by executing the same duties as successful salesmen. Unfortunately, many salesmen have little more than a general impression of the duties required of them. A salesman's conception of his specific duties often differs from that of his manager, who may have only a mental picture of the sales job. Salesmen in the same organization frequently perform widely different duties.

Salesmen who have an exact statement of their responsibilities will work harder and more happily because they know exactly what is expected of them. They can locate their weaknesses by checking their operations against their job description to discover those duties which are being neglected.

SALES-JOB DESCRIPTIONS

To show the specific duties of salesmen engaged in various types of sales activity, the following job descriptions have been prepared with the cooperation of well-known sales organizations. Although these descriptions omit obvious and minor duties, they include all the major tasks involved in the following principal types of sales jobs: (1) house-to-house, direct-to-consumer salesman, representing a manufacturer of food products; (2) wholesale salesman of specialty food products selling for a manufacturer to retail food merchants; (3) retail salesman of automobiles selling for a retailer direct to consumers; (4) export salesman of rubber tires and sundries selling for a domestic manufacturer to distributors abroad; (5) industrial salesman representing a manufacturer of accounting machines selling direct to business organizations; (6) wholesale salesman of surgical dressings and packaged drug sundries representing a manufacturer selling direct to retail druggists; (7) retail salesman selling to ultimate consumers in a retail department store; (8) typical inside retail salesperson; (9)

wholesale salesmen of perishable food products selling for a manufacturer direct to retail grocery and delicatessen merchants, industrial and institutional users.

These sales-job descriptions were obtained by interviewing salesmen, asking them questions as to how, why, and what they do; interviewing field sales supervisors, branch managers, and general sales managers; observing salesmen at work; reviewing printed sales training material; and examining salesmen's reports of field work.

Experienced salesmen may profit from study of these job descriptions by checking their methods with those of successful salesmen in in the various lines. Beginner salesmen should find in them a comprehensive picture of their duties and responsibilities and a guide to profitable activity.

1. House-to-house, Direct-to-consumer Salesman, Representing a Manufacturer of Food Products. The salesman of a national manufacturer of packaged food products, sold and delivered direct to ultimate consumers, performs the following duties:

I. *Selling duties.*
  A. Procedure with active customers.
    1. Deliver previous order; collect; post customer's house card; post route book.
    2. Sell order for future delivery.
    3. Sell coffee.
    4. Sell bargain group of products.
    5. Discuss premium offer; show premium; deliver company advertisement; ask for prospect.
  B. Procedure for securing new customer.
    1. Describe premium offer.
    2. Show premiums.
    3. Show company house organ.
    4. Demonstrate coffee mortar.
    5. Give calendar house card.
  C. Procedure for getting back inactive customers.
    1. Review inactive accounts before going on territory.
    2. Determine objections that may be encountered.
    3. Decide on approach to be used.
  D. Procedure for house calls.
    1. Carry neat, clean display basket with fresh samples.
    2. Set basket and premium on floor.
    3. Pick up one article at a time and hand to customer.
    4. Be sure customer knows how to use product.
    5. Make coffee once for every customer.

II. *Routine duties.*
    A. Post route book and house card after each sale.
    B. Balance cash.
    C. Record collections.
    D. Prepare remittance to district office.
    E. Perform sales-car duties.
        1. Load.
        2. Check performance.
        3. Wipe clean.
        4. Fill tires.
        5. Refuel.
III. *Executive duties.*
    A. Make first call at 8 A.M.
    B. Average 60 calls, 40 deliveries daily.
    C. Prepare route to call every two weeks on each customer.
    D. Keep informed on merits of each product.
    E. Spend minimum of eight productive hours daily in field.
IV. *Good-will duties.*
    A. Adjust complaints.
    B. Be punctual and regular on calls.

This analysis of a house-to-house salesman's duties reveals that nothing has been left to chance to ensure a thorough selling job. Instead of relying upon the momentary inspiration or skill of the salesman to obtain good interviews, this company made an analysis of the work of their best salesmen in dealing with active, inactive, and new customers. The practices of these outstanding men were incorporated in procedures or routines for handling each type of buyer. All salesmen are trained to perform the specific routines and their performance is judged by the way they carry out the various steps as outlined in the description.

The least imaginative and unresourceful salesman is sure to conduct an acceptable interview if he adheres to the procedures that have been established. Standard selling talks have also been prepared to accompany each step in the procedures.

While the character of selling in this case obviously lends itself to standard procedures, the profitable performance of salesmen of this company proves the merit of organizing and regularizing the salesman's job for this type of sales work.

Definite daily objectives are set for these salesmen, based on the number of calls, deliveries, and hours spent in the field, which guarantee a greater measure of accomplishment.

2. Wholesale Salesman of Specialty Food Products Selling for a Manufacturer to Retail Food Merchants. The salesman of a national manufacturer and distributor of packaged specialty food products, who calls upon food retailers and takes order for delivery by food wholesalers, performs the following duties in addition to the obvious customary functions of selling volume, getting orders, and making contacts:

I. *Primary duties.*
1. Build floor, counter, and window displays.
2. Price stock correctly.
3. Prepare advertising for handbill or newspaper.
4. Hold consumer sales in retail store.
5. Know retail merchant's problems and be able to give helpful suggestions about his store.
6. Check stock in the retail store.
7. Interest salespeople in the company's products.
8. Be firm with merchant when refusing a request.
9. Plan sales work.
10. Know company policies and guarantees.
11. Study company publication.

II. *Secondary duties.*
1. Contact printers for dealer advertising.
2. Call on wholesalers.
3. Call on army posts.
4. Call on hotels and restaurants.
5. Conduct food shows.
6. Drive a company car.
7. Purchase stock from wholesalers when necessary.
8. Fill orders for cash from company car.
9. Care for company automobile.
10. Handle damaged merchandise.
11. Adjust consumer complaints.
12. Know all company products and discuss them intelligently.
13. Know direct prices on all company products.
14. Know and discuss percentage of profit to merchant on company products at retailers' prices.
15. Arrange material in company sales car for most efficient operation.
16. Know and read code dates on packages of company products.
17. Know company and competitive merchandising activities in territory.
18. Know prices of all competitive products.
19. Know voluntary chain operations in territory.
20. Know retailers' objections to premiums for consumers.
21. Check wholesalers' stocks of company products.

III. *Reporting duties.*
    1. Prepare a report on each call.
    2. Prepare a daily summary report on all calls.
    3. Answer correspondence from supervisors and district offices.
    4. Prepare a weekly route list.
    5. Prepare reports on store sales.
    6. Prepare weekly expense and automobile-operation **report**.
    7. Write automobile accident reports, when necessary.
    8. Write automobile fire and theft reports, when necessary.

This description of the duties of a salesman of specialty food products sold through retail merchants indicates the growing amount of missionary or service selling to promote the resale of nationally advertised products. Salesmen to dealers are no longer chiefly concerned with writing orders; they perform a multiplicity of merchandising duties for retailers, such as building displays, preparing advertising, holding consumer sales, training salespeople, and advising on management problems.

Further evidence of greater sales service to retailers is the practice of this company's salesmen in purchasing company products from wholesalers and reselling them for cash to retailers as an accommodation.

SALES INTERVIEW OBSERVATION RECORD

  I. *Observer check interview on following points.*
    A. Original or follow-up call.
    B. Salesman—known or unknown to buyer.
    C. Product or service offered.
    D. Appointment—by phone.   By letter
    E. Cold canvass.   Referred to buyer
    F. Immediately heard.   Waited   (time)
    G. Was business card used?
 II. *Opening interview—technique.*
    A. Verify buyer's identity.
    B. Announce name and company.
    C. Initiative in shaking hands.
    D. Handling of seating.
    E. "Breaking ice," how?
    F. Does salesman divert buyer from previous work? How?
    G. How does salesman handle buyer who continues working?
    H. Opening statement of salesman.
    I. How does salesman handle third party at interview?
    J. Does salesman use entering wedge of clipping, picture, etc.?
III. *Interview technique.*
    A. Does salesman have apparent purpose in calling? Why?
    B. Does he know needs of buyer?
    C. Does he seek to discover needs? How?

D. Does he interrupt buyer?

E. Does he do all the talking?

F. Does he engage in irrelevant conversation?

G. Does he argue?

H. Does he apparently have a standard story?

IV. *Visual material technique.*

    A. Does he use visual material? What?

    B. Does he introduce it naturally?

    C. Does he keep control of it?

    D. Does he use it mechanically?

V. *Demonstration technique.*

    A. Did salesman demonstrate all or any feature of product?

    B. Did buyer take part in demonstration?

    C. Was it introduced naturally?

    D. Was talk mechanical—too rapid?

    E. Was demonstration directly related to buyer's needs and interests?

    F. Were materials in good order?

    G. What questions were asked by buyer?

VI. *Meeting objections technique.*

    A. Did salesman apparently forestall objections in sales talk?

    B. Were objections met calmly, respectfully?

    C. What were principal objections of buyer?

    D. How did salesman answer each objection?

    E. Were objections disposed of immediately or answers deferred?

    F. Did salesman seek to minimize objection? How?

    G. Did salesman ascertain that his answer was satisfactory? How?

    H. Was salesman "thrown off the track" by the objection or did he swing back on his story?

    I. Did salesman distinguish between real obstacles and excuses?

VII. *Closing technique.*

    A. Did salesman test prospect's interest in his proposition? How?

    B. Did he try to secure an order? How?

    C. Was the trial premature?

    D. How many closing attempts were made?

    E. If sale was not closed, why?

    F. Was further effort planned?

    G. Was order blank introduced naturally?

    H. Did buyer take initiative in buying?

    I. Was a payment required with order? How was payment obtained?

    J. Was buyer's signature secured? How?

    K. Was a trial order secured?

Sales interview observation record used by a sales supervisor in checking the performance of a salesman before a prospect. This form lists the general duties that must be performed by salesmen in presenting products or services to prospects. A salesman can discover his weaknesses and take the first step toward improving his interviewing methods by having his presentation rated on these points.

The considerable amount of paper work to be done by salesmen is revealed in this job description. There are eight types of reports ranging from individual call reports to accounts of fire and theft of sales cars. Although these reports may be necessary to good supervision in this case, a job description indicates records that may be eliminated or combined with a saving in time for the salesmen.

The general use of automobiles in transporting salesmen creates added responsibilities for them in the operation and care of their cars and the arrangement of stock and promotion materials therein.

3. Retail Salesman of Automobiles Selling for a Retailer Direct to Consumers. Analysis of the methods of outstanding salesmen by a well-known manufacturer provided material for the following job description of automobile selling.

The salesmen whose work is described are employed by successful retail automobile dealers in all parts of the country.

I. *Selling duties.*
  A. Locate prospect's needs.
    1. Discover number in family; which members drive; how car is used; approximate price prospect can afford.
    2. Use portfolio, catalogue, or other visual sales aid to help prospect clarify in his mind the qualities in a car that are most important to him, such as appearance, safety, comfort, and economy.
    3. Ask questions to discover facts that bear on fitting car to prospect's needs.
  B. Tell how product fits needs of prospect.
    1. Use portfolio or visual material.
    2. Discuss each need and get a decision on one quality at a time.
  C. Show how product fits needs of prospect.
    1. Demonstrate.
      a. Have a plan for demonstration.
        (1) Get car in condition.
        (2) Plan demonstration route.
  D. Get prospect's agreement on each point *as it is made, i.e.,* "close" the sale on *that* point.
  E. Answer or, preferably, forestall objections, including those growing out of competition.
  F. Take first opportunity to get an order; seek an order in *every* interview.
  G. Handle trade-ins.
    1. Sell new car thoroughly, including demonstration, before making a trade-in offer.
    2. Examine used car thoroughly in prospect's presence to avoid suspicion of guessing at price.
  H. Sell accessories.

II. *Routine duties.*

    A. Report, daily, *names of new prospects* with address, telephone number, car owned, model interested in, and sources.

    B. Report, daily, *calls on prospects, owners, suspects,* with names, addresses, telephone numbers, result of calls, time spent with each, date for next work, and remarks.

    C. Prepare *summary of daily sales efforts* classified as productive and nonproductive work.

    D. Prepare *file card* for each prospect secured and file by days of month for follow-up.

    E. Prepare daily call schedule of prospects, owners, and suspects, listing addresses and telephone numbers.

III. *Executive duties.*

    A. Mail advertising to prospects in advance of calls.

    B. Secure names of prospects from customers and friends, and by canvassing, observation, and consulting registration list.

    C. Set a daily objective of calls, demonstrations, appraisals, and hours in the field.

    D. Make a daily work plan each night for the succeeding day.

    E. Qualify prospects by telephone and in person.

    F. Keep informed about the industry, company, product, buyer's motives, company advertising, and competitive products.

    G. Attend sales meetings.

IV. *Service duties.*

    A. Deliver service policy in person or be present when it is delivered and explained by service manager.

    B. Show and discuss service policy during sales interview.

    C. Make follow-up call in person and by telephone once a month to remind customers to get service provided in policy.

V. *Good-will duties.*

    A. Call on owners several times during the first three weeks after delivery, and at least once a month thereafter.

The trend toward "planned selling" of specialties is emphasized in this job description of automobile selling. The eight steps outlined in detail organize a salesman's presentation with sufficient flexibility for the first call on every type of automobile prospect. Definite objectives are given the salesman to enable him to control the interview, to focus discussion on the features of the product of greatest interest to the prospect, to test his interest, and to seek action. This plan provides an orderly presentation, yet leaves the salesman free to adjust his story to the individual prospect.

A salesman following this procedure is not guided largely by questions asked by the prospects. This plan keeps him on the track and saves the time of both parties to the interview. Unplanned interviews often lead into "dead ends" or time-wasting side trips leading to a vague promise to "think it over."

The emphasis in this sales specification is on the prospect, his needs and interests, rather than on the salesman and the car. This "flank attack" strategy is superseding the traditional "frontal attack" in selling specialties. Salesmen using it seldom talk about what their product *is*, its specifications and construction; they get enthusiastic about what it *does*, its comfort, safety, economy, or performance, for the owner.

The importance of planned activity as well as planned interviews is emphasized by this job description. To make the best use of selling time, the duties of the salesman call for the preparation of a daily work plan each night. A daily call schedule of prospects and owners is required and a daily objective of calls, demonstrations, and appraisals, based on a definite number of hours in the field. Such a systematic program reduces waste time and helps to increase sales.

4. Export Salesman of Rubber Tires and Sundries Selling for a Domestic Manufacturer to Distributors Abroad. The export salesman of a large domestic producer of tires and rubber goods, who sells to distributors located in foreign countries, performs the following duties:

I. *Selecting distributors.*
    1. Study qualifications of interested firms.
    2. Secure complete information about them.
    3. Recommend to factory, firms to be approached.
II. *Contacting distributors.*
    1. Provide distributor with product information.
    2. See that personnel is of right type and organized efficiently.
    3. Make consumer and dealer calls with distributor's salesmen.
    4. Aid distributor in analyzing market and establishing quotas.
    5. Aid distributor in getting prompt service from factory on shipments, documents, credit, etc.
    6. Act as buffer between factory and distributor.
    7. Create good spirit in distributor's organization.
    8. Check distributor's contract to ensure
        a. Proper execution.
        b. Clear understanding.
        c. Satisfactory execution.
    9. Check distributor's stock and take monthly orders to avoid shortages.

III. *Contacting dealers.*
1. Secure new dealers for distributors.
2. Identify dealer with advertising.
3. Keep dealers adequately stocked.
4. See that dealer's prices, terms, service are competitive.
5. Check character of distributor's service.
6. Aid dealer in promoting consumer sales.
7. Give dealers product information.
8. Secure dealer's preferred attention to line.
9. Create good will of dealer.
10. See that automobile importers specify company tires.

IV. *Competitor relations.*
1. Analyze competitive situation to ensure that prices, discounts, terms, advertising are competitive.
2. Cooperate with reciprocating competitors to ensure that distributors do not undersell competitors and that dealer terms are exchanged with cooperating competitors.

V. *Advertising.*
1. Check advertising expenditures of distributors in approved media in specified period.
2. See that dealers have store and window displays.
3. Secure publication of publicity stories.
4. Aid distributor in erecting outdoor signs.
5. Induce distributor to match company appropriation for retail advertising.
6. Supply distributor with advertising material.
7. See that distributor sends in proofs and bills for advertising.
8. Aid dealers and distributors in preparing mailing lists.
9. Report on competitors' advertising.

VI. *Shipping duties, charges, taxes, laws.*
1. Investigate shipping charges periodically.
2. Notify company of changes in shipping charges.
3. Provide company with copy of freight tariffs in native language.
4. Examine consular declarations to ensure that importations are classified to secure minimum rates.
5. Supply company with pamphlets covering local laws and taxes.

VII. *Credit and financial.*
1. Report on credit standing of new and old customers.
2. Make credit reports on history, type of business, character of managers, references, and reputation of customers.

VIII. *Claims and adjustments.*
1. Inspect each article submitted for adjustment.
2. Determine amount to be charged in replacement.
3. Report on adjustments to home office.
4. Check distributor's willingness to make adjustments.

IX. *Reporting duties.*
    1. Be sure that correspondence
        a. Is clear and brief.
        b. Has a separate letter for each subject.
        c. Refers to previous correspondence.
    2. Report on competition, monthly.
    3. Report on expenses, weekly.
    4. Report in general, annually.
    5. Report on estimated sales, annually.
    6. Report itinerary.
    7. Report on advertising to advertising department.
    8. Make special reports as required.

The complex responsibilities of salesmen in foreign markets are illustrated by the job description of a rubber-tire export salesman. Not only do overseas salesmen perform the same duties as domestic salesmen, but in addition they are held accountable for shipments and must watch import duties, tariffs, taxes, shipping charges, and laws in the countries in which they are operating. Their duties include contacts with retail dealers as well as wholesale distributors. Settlement of claims is in their hands, as well as an important credit responsibility. Operating at long distances from their domestic headquarters, export salesmen usually have a large measure of supervision of all phases of distribution in their territories, not shared by salesmen in this country.

Much attention must be paid by salesmen abroad to the competitive situation as indicated by this job specification. The employing company in this case is a member of a combination export association authorized under the Webb-Pomerene Act which permits cooperation among competitors to fix prices and standardize sales terms in foreign markets. Accordingly, the salesmen of this company cooperate closely with competitors.

The advertising functions of foreign salesmen are more numerous than those of domestic salesmen. Wholesale as well as retail, advertising must be run and distributors given aid in establishing appropriations, controlling expenditures, and using the manufacturer's advertising helps. Competitors' advertising efforts must also be reported.

5. Industrial Salesman Representing a Manufacturer of Accounting Machines Selling Direct to Business Organizations.

I. *Securing interviews.*
    1. Select right man to see.
    2. Prepare for interview.

II. *Conducting interviews.*
   1. Gain attention of prospect.
   2. Arouse interest of prospect.
   3. Obtain a knowledge of the prospect's problem.
   4. Secure facts from the prospect.
   5. Explain principle of machines clearly.
   6. Discuss machines with prospect.
   7. Obtain the confidence of the prospect.
   8. Establish prestige for the company.
   9. Create a desire in the prospect for the machines.
   10. Show examples of satisfied customers by means of the classified users' list.
   11. Establish conviction of prospects.
   12. Secure permission to make survey.
   13. Secure permission to demonstrate.
   14. Meet objections.
   15. Secure orders.
III. *Conducting demonstrations.*
   1. Demonstrate to prospects by appointment at company office.
   2. Demonstrate to prospects by appointment at prospect's office.
   3. Demonstrate applications to prospect after a survey.
   4. Demonstrate after a survey to sell the idea originally presented.
   5. Demonstrate additional applications to customers.
   6. Make a standard demonstration.
   7. Prepare for demonstration.
   8. Explain principle of company's machines.
   9. Know machines.
   10. Create desire for the equipment.
   11. Obtain conviction of the prospect.
   12. Establish prestige of the company.
   13. Obtain action following demonstration.
IV. *Conducting surveys.*
   1. Make survey at proper time.
   2. Contact right individual for survey.
   3. Secure receptivity of prospect to survey.
   4. Obtain cooperation of prospect in survey.
   5. Obtain an accurate understanding of the prospect's situation.
   6. Get the facts about the prospect's problem.
   7. Obtain the prospect's confirmation to the facts obtained.
   8. Talk the prospect's language.
   9. Prepare for the survey.
   10. Create the confidence of the prospect in the survey.
   11. Obtain the cooperation of the prospect's employees.
   12. Analyze the prospect's present situation.

13. Keep the ultimate objective of the survey in view.
14. Determine fruitful results.
15. Develop a definite plan.
16. Check the plan with the known needs of the prospect.

V. *Presenting the proposition.*
    1. Make preliminary oral presentation.
    2. Present proposition during first approach; demonstrate, while getting facts, checking facts, developing plan, or establishing a prospect's needs.
    3. Use exhibits.
    4. Determine proper executive to get proposition.
    5. Forestall delay to take action.
    6. Use list of users of product.
    7. Explain company policies.
    8. Explain contract.
    9. Show results with pictures rather than technical details.
    10. Close the sale.

VI. *Servicing customers.*
    1. Know customer responsibilities and company policies.
    2. Provide new customers with detailed write-up of directions for using machines.
    3. Supervise preparation of proper codes by customer.
    4. Establish proper control.
    5. Aid customer in selection of proper personnel.
    6. Educate customer's personnel.
    7. Supervise primary operation of equipment including source of data, flow of documents, coding, punching, verifying, and scheduling production.
    8. Aid customer in scheduling reports and determining their number, sequence, distribution.
    9. Review reports with executives.
    10. Aid customer in providing filing facilities.
    11. Continuously check up with customers' executives.
    12. Make a continual study of customer's business.
    13. Advise customers of latest equipment and methods, users in competitive industries, company publications, and accessory services.

VII. *Performing routine and executive duties.*
    1. Prepare call reports and special customer reports.
    2. Schedule work and make proper use of time.
    3. Get acquainted with several key men in each business.
    4. Analyze territory opportunities.
    5. Use files for call reports, surveys, and correspondence.
    6. Learn manufacturing processes, products, and problems of prospects.

7. Capitalize on reputation of company executives.
8. Pursue outside activities which will contribute to business success and participate in civic and community affairs.
9. Consult newspapers for leads.
10. Maintain list of active prospects.
11. Study continuously to learn all possible about every prospect and customer.
12. Study company machines, applications, executive talks, educational material, publications, sales helps.
13. Know proper use of salesman's equipment.
14. Contact former and competitive product users.
15. Make a monthly schedule of calls.
16. Know the company's creed for salesmen.
17. Know how to organize work to make it automatic.
18. Know competitive products, their limitations, and the claims of competitors.
19. Attend company sales meetings.
20. Attend National Association of Cost Accountants meetings and keep posted on their activities.
21. Prepare forecasts of sales.
22. Prepare machine specifications.
23. Know company policies, contracts, and prices.
24. Know company sales plans.
25. Know factory organization.
26. Attend group meetings of C.P.A., Comptrollers' Institute, Business clubs, and associations.

VIII. *Using company advertising and sales aids.*
1. Know operations of company's educational department.
2. Know company's customer training program.
3. Use reprints of executives' speeches.
4. Use classified list of users.
5. Know and use company publications.
6. Know services of company's commercial research department.
7. Know functions of special representatives on national accounts.

The above description of the job of a salesman of business machines emphasizes the importance of adequate preparation in advance of a sales interview through the medium of a thorough survey of a prospect's needs. Although the numerous applications for this type of product demand that a salesman be conversant with a prospect's business problems in order to adapt the product to his needs, the desirability of advance knowledge of a prospect's situation gained through a survey is becoming recognized as fundamental to the successful selling of many commodities. In this case, a salesman must perform

16 operations in making a survey from the proper timing of the survey to the formulation of a complete plan checked against the known needs of the prospect. Such a survey must be sold to a prospect and his cooperation secured in carrying it out. Possessed of the facts disclosed by the investigation, a salesman is in an excellent position to present his product, from the standpoint of the prospect's problem, and meet objections effectively. The salesman's time and expense involved in making a preliminary survey are justified by increased sales resulting from the use of the facts obtained.

The importance of showing advantages by means of demonstration in addition to telling about them is emphasized in this job description. In the sale of all types of mechanical equipment a demonstration is a most effective selling tool. The 13 demonstrating duties required of salesmen of this company ensure that prospects shall understand the applications of the product to the solution of their problems.

The growing necessity for salesmen to study is indicated here. Salesmen must study not only the processes, products, and problems of their prospects, but the machines, applications, executive talks, educational material, publications, and sales helps of their company. The importance of study of company policies, products, plans, and organization is emphasized by this company in common with other progressive sales organizations.

6. Wholesale Salesman of Surgical Dressings and Drug Sundries Representing a Manufacturer Selling Direct to Retail Druggists.

I. *Maintain sales of established items.*
    1. Remind buyer of all items in line which he can possibly carry by
        a. Showing photograph album.
        b. Describing the line and enumerating all classes as well as prominent individual items.
    2. Check dealer's stock, if he does not do so himself.
    3. Use inventory check sheet.
    4. Write order for items not stocked.

II. *Sell items not now stocked by buyer.*
    1. Show one or more pocket samples.
    2. Get one item not now stocked started in each store every trip.
    3. Discover items which buyer should order but does not.
    4. Present item not now stocked.
    5. Use this item as a "call leader," "feature item," "opener," or "finisher."

III. *Present dealer fixed or flexible merchandising assortments, units, deals, or offers.*
    1. Work these into order before or after review of the line.

    2. Study sales arguments on these features.

    3. Secure coaching on presentation.

IV. *Introduce sales helps.*

    1. Carry selling helps in sales car.

    2. Set up counter displays.

    3. Use sales promotional material list.

    4. Call dealer's attention to company advertising.

    5. Order sales helps to be shipped to dealer.

    6. Set up mass merchandising displays.

    7. Introduce counter cards, price tickets, window displays, etc.

V. *Sell company merchandising plan.*

    1. Sell stock rotation sale idea.

    2. Sell value of open mass display with price tickets.

    3. Emphasize many uses for company's products.

    4. Stress importance of turnover in earning profits.

    5. Get products out in front where they will sell.

    6. Sell large quantities or case lots of fastest moving merchandising sizes.

VI. *Make adjustments.*

    1. Correct errors and misunderstandings.

    2. Arrange for return of merchandise for replacement.

    3. Know adjustment policy of company.

    4. Leave no loose threads in customer relationships after calls.

VII. *Make collections.*

    1. Collect from dealers who buy direct when they have not remitted within 60 days of invoice date.

VIII. *Call on distributors.*

    1. Contact wholesalers, surgical supply dealers, hospitals, institutions, industrials, and miscellaneous retailers.

    2. Employ tact, polish, and a thorough knowledge of items and prices in this work.

The above instructions for a salesman of surgical dressings emphasize the importance of maintaining sales of items already stocked by dealer customers. In their desire to sell new items or those not stocked by a buyer, salesmen often ignore products that have been previously stocked by a dealer customer. Sales of established items should not be taken for granted; a salesman selling regularly to a dealer should check the dealer's stock, use an inventory check sheet, and seek a reorder for items previously stocked.

The resale of established items is also stressed by this company by selling dealers on stock rotation, open mass display, preferred display position, and the importance of turnover in earning profits.

The duty of a salesman to make adjustments and correct misunderstandings with customers is included in this sales-job description.

Knowledge of the customer and his problems enables a salesman to handle adjustments to the mutual satisfaction of both buyer and seller.

In this case, salesmen make collections from dealers who buy direct from the manufacturer. This is customary for salesmen representing direct sellers.

Salesmen who call principally upon retailers also frequently contact wholesalers and institutions, particularly in lines distributing through a limited number of outlets.

7. Retail Salesman Selling to Ultimate Consumers in a Retail Department Store. This description of the selling duties of a retail salesperson is a composite description resulting from observations of more than 1,200 department store salespersons made by the Research Bureau for Retail Training.

I. *Sizing up the customer.*
   1. Notice the customer's carriage.
   2. Notice the customer's actions and expressions.
   3. Notice the customer's conversation.
   4. Notice the customer's general appearance.
   5. Watch and listen attentively.
   6. Act friendly and interested.
II. *Approaching the customer.*
   1. Be alert; show the customer you are ready to wait upon him.
   2. Smile and look good-natured.
   3. Look at the customer.
   4. Stop all care of stock and go up to customer.
   5. Leave other salespeople and go up to customer.
   6. Ask the customer to be seated when possible.
   7. Avoid using same phrases over and over; make words of greeting cordial.
   8. Call the customer by name, if possible.
III. *Finding out what the customer wants.*
   1. Ask question about use or purpose of article wanted.
   2. Display merchandise and watch expressions and action of customer as he looks at goods.
   3. Listen attentively to what customer asks for.
   4. Listen to customer's questions and comments about merchandise.
IV. *Displaying merchandise.*
   1. Make room to display merchandise.
   2. Select merchandise to be shown *first* which should be that which has been requested or is particularly suited to customer or has been advertised or is on display or is medium-priced.
   3. Display enough merchandise to afford sufficient selection.
   4. Show only a few samples at one time.

    5. Stop showing merchandise as soon as customer shows interest.

    6. Show how the merchandise would look in use.

    7. Get merchandise to customer quickly.

    8. Handle merchandise to create impression of value.

V. *Presenting sales arguments.*

    1. Know the merchandise thoroughly.

    2. Make concrete statements about the merchandise.

    3. Call attention to interesting facts about the goods.

    4. Meet customer's objections and answer questions.

    5. Avoid talking too much.

    6. Emphasize most suitable features for customer.

    7. See what qualities customer is interested in and discuss them.

VI. *Closing the sale.*

    1. Center attention on one or two articles.

    2. Review the selling points of the articles under consideration.

    3. Meet objections.

    4. Create good will for future, through courtesy, alertness.

    5. Make out sales check.

    6. Deliver package.

    7. Return change.

    8. Answer questions about delivery and holding goods.

    9. Handle two customers at once.

VII. *Practicing suggestive selling.*

    1. Offer a substitute when article requested is out.

    2. Suggest buying in larger quantities.

    3. Suggest other merchandise in the same department.

    4. Suggest merchandise in other departments.

    5. Suggest merchandise to meet customer's needs.

In this description of the duties of a retail department store salesperson, it is significant that nearly half of the duties outlined require the salesman to get the customer's viewpoint. This practice of "sizing up the customer," "approaching the customer," and "finding out what the customer wants," is rightfully placing the emphasis in selling on the buyer and his problem rather than upon the salesman and his offering.

Many of the duties of store salespeople are also assumed by consumer salesmen of specialties such as automobiles, refrigerators, radios, when engaged in showroom selling; particularly, those duties involving the display of merchandise may be effectively applied to the work of salesmen in the display room.

The desirability of suggestive selling of related items, which has long been practiced by aggressive retail merchandisers, is recognized in this outline and several ways in which this selling strategy may be applied are suggested.

8. An Inside Salesperson. This outline of typical duties performed by salespersons is based on information gathered by trained field analysts employed by the U.S. Employment Service, the Job Analysis and Information Section, from actual observation of typical retail inside-selling jobs. This description, when combined with the preceding one, gives a complete description of store-selling duties.

I. Determines merchandise desired by customer; ascertains make, type, size, pattern or design, quantity wanted, and approximate price the customer is willing to pay.

II. Displays merchandise and assists customer to make a selection by suggestions and explanations; emphasizes the chief selling point of the article, be it quality, style, durability, popularity, utility, taste, appearance, freshness, or price; may tell or show customer how to use the article; attempts to encourage the sale of higher priced articles.

As it is usually to the worker's interest to sell as much as possible, every attempt is made to suggest articles that might be used in connection with the article purchased and to consummate each sale in a minimum of time.

III. Writes out sales slip in duplicate or triplicate (store policies vary) designating the merchandise and its price, his own identifying number, and sometimes the name and address of the customer; if the sale is to be charged or sent C.O.D., procures customer's signature on sales slip. In some establishments, no sales slip is used for cash sales. In establishments where merchandise is sold on a time payment plan, the worker may fill out a sales contract for the customer's signature instead of a sales slip.

IV. Receives payment or secures credit authorization, and gives wrapped article to customer or arranges for its delivery.

    A. If sale is cash, receives money and

        1. Wraps article, rings up sale on cash register, and makes change, **or**

        2. Gives article to a cashier-wrapper who makes change and wraps article, **or**

        3. Sends money and sales slips to a central (cashier's office) via a pneumatic tube system or overhead carrier. Cashier's office returns receipted sales slips and change (merchandise may be sent with the sales slips and money to the office).

    B. If a sale is to be charged, either

        1. Sends sales slips to credit department via a pneumatic tube system or overhead carrier for approval of account and return, **or**

        2. Places sales slips in holder of charge phone, presses signal button to call credit authorizer, verbally gives name and address of customer, and removes sales slips from holder when they have been stamped and perforated (by a stamp and punch actuated by credit authorizer) to indicate credit approval, **or**

        3. Procures written approval of account by floorman or department manager.

The original copy of the sales slip goes to the credit office if the sale is charge, or to the cashier's office if the sale is cash or C.O.D.; the duplicate is wrapped with the merchandise; and the triplicate is retained until the end of the day when it is sent, together with an itemized list of the day's sales, to the store accounting office. In stores where sales slips are written in duplicate, the original copy is sent at the end of the day to the accounting office. Merchandise that is to be delivered is wrapped and routed to the delivery department. Usually the portion of the duplicate sales slip bearing the customer's name and address is detached and used as an address label.

V. Cares for stock on sales floor; places new merchandise on shelves, racks, or stands according to a predetermined order; keeps stock neat, orderly, and dusted during the day, requisitioning replacements of staple articles of merchandise from stockroom as necessary or informing buyer or department head of shortages as they occur; may cover stock or remove it from counters at night; at end of day fills out a merchandise order slip or want slip recording, for the information of the buyer, articles of merchandise called for by customers but not carried in stock, and merchandise, the stock of which is running low.

VI. Writes out accommodation slips (in cases where merchandise is returned by the customer for alteration, repair, or some other reason, but where the customer retains ownership of the merchandise) indicating the disposition of the merchandise and whether the alteration or repair is a free service or will be charged to the customer.

VII. May trim showcases on sales floor according to directions of department head or window trimmer.

VIII. Takes periodic inventories of stock, calling out items to another worker who records them on an inventory sheet.

This general job description is supplemented by specific descriptions of work of salespersons in the principal departments in retail stores including books, china and glassware, floor coverings, furniture, flowers, furs, groceries, jewelry, in the U.S. Employment Service study of sales occupations.

9. Wholesale Salesman of Perishable Food Products Selling for a Manufacturer Direct to Retail Grocery and Delicatessen Merchants, for Resale to Consumers and to Industrial and Institutional Users. The sales representatives of a well-known manufacturer and national advertiser of perishable, packaged food products sell to individual and chain grocers and delicatessen merchants, for resale to consumers and to industrial and institutional users. Merchandise sold is distributed direct from the manufacturer's branch warehouses, located in various parts of the country, to dealers and consumers. These salesmen perform 14 major tasks:

1. Selling merchandise.
2. Handling sales promotion.

3. Building and servicing merchandise displays.
4. Checking stock and improving shelf position.
5. Instructing retailer and his help on pushing company merchandise.
6. Instructing industrial and institutional users and their employees on the correct use of company merchandise.
7. Handling collections.
8. Keeping records and making reports.
9. Utilizing and working company advertising.
10. Maintaining personal effectiveness.
11. Keeping informed on company and its policies.
12. Handling adjustments and complaints.
13. Keeping informed on market potential and customer characteristics in the territory.
14. Travel between calls and caring for company automobile.

The task of selling merchandise is detailed as follows:

Duties and Responsibilities (What he does)	*Special Knowledge* (What he must know)
I. Contact customers regularly.	

1. Call on independent retailers.
  2. Call on chain-store outlets.
  3. Call on industrial users.
  4. Call on institutional users.
	Who and where his customers are and who does the buying.
	Importance of regular contacts.
	Personal likes and dislikes of buyer.
	Buying hours.
	How to keep record of past contacts, appointments, special services requested, or favors promised.

II. Determine customer's needs.	

1. Check customer's record (route) book or previous invoice.
  2. Check stock still on hand and note quantity sold since previous trip.
  3. Check merchandise in outlet to avoid excessive overloading.
	Nature of customer's business and what he can use from company line.
	The proper use (nontechnical) of each item in line.
	How to estimate needs of customers.

III. Develop customer's interests.	
1. Get buyer's interest and attention. 2. "Set the stage" to help you make the sale.	How to approach and greet the customer. How to use what he says to meet the situation.

Duties and Responsibilities (What he does)	*Special Knowledge* (What he must know)
	How to create a favorable selling atmosphere.
	Importance of speech and personal appearance.

IV. Reorder regulars.

1. Suggest to buyer what he needs to replenish stock, selling full company line.
2. Suggest increases to meet seasonal and special demands.
3. After completing regular refill sales, suggest new items or push items.

Sales advantages of a full stock.

How to estimate quantity needs.

Timing for seasonal or other volume campaigns.

How to write an order, quota, or volume goal.

Know other lines of outside merchandise to tie-in with company line for combination sales.

Do not assume that a merchant cannot sell a certain item, with possible exception of fancy varieties, in a very poor neighborhood.

V. Make the sales talk.

1. Discuss customer's obligation to his customers.
2. Present new or special items.
3. Use price list.
4. Use carry-in kit.
5. Explain and demonstrate tie-in sales possibilities.
6. Suggest, tactfully, improvements in operation.
7. Discuss possible volume and profits.

How to express himself.

Principles of selling.

Psychology of dealing with people.

When and how to highlight special items.

How to write the order while making the sales talk.

How each item is packaged and priced.

Use of price list and discount system.

Company policies governing selling and advertising.

Competitive products and prices.

Sales points on each item in line.

VI. Answer questions and handle objections.

1. Consider the customer's questions as a salesman's opportunity.
2. Invite questions from customer.

How to distinguish between a real question, a stall, and an objection.

That both expressed and unexpressed questions influence the thinking and action of the customer.

Duties and Responsibilities (What he does)	*Special Knowledge* (What he must know)
3. Handle objections as points you failed to make clear in your presentation.	How to make use of an answered objection as a selling point. How to analyze objections as clues of what may be in the mind of the next customer.

VII. Close sale.

1. Make sure that customer feels that all his needs are covered by the order.	Importance of having the customer feel that you have helped him consider and fill all his needs.
2. Arrange for payment.	Necessity of making sure customer understands exactly the price he is paying and the arrangements for payment.
3. Thank customer for his business.	

VIII. Make appointment for next call.

1. Indicate approximate date and time (exact date if possible).	How to schedule and plan calls so as to utilize time effectively (consider avoidance of congested areas and backtracking).
2. Explain and arrange details of delivery.	How to "keep the customer's door open" to the company.

The above description of the task of selling merchandise is typical of the duties of manufacturer's and wholesaler's salesmen engaged in well-planned repeat selling to retailers and large consumers. The special knowledge required to perform each task indicates what a salesman must know to handle this job effectively.

In this type of selling, as well as in consumer salesmanship, modern emphasis is on the determination of a customer's needs which requires a knowledge, in this case, of a customer's business and how to estimate his needs.

The replenishment of stock or reorders of regularly purchased merchandise is an important task of salesmen representing manufacturers and wholesalers selling to retailers and institutions. To suggest reorders, salesmen must be able to estimate dealers' quantity needs as affected by seasonal demand or special campaigns featuring the merchandise.

Explanation by the salesman of tie-in sales possibilities for combination sales with the merchandise of other manufacturers is an important feature of this type of selling.

The advisability of "keeping the customer's door open" to the salesman by making an appointment for future contacts at a specific time is good selling strategy pointed out in this job description.

SALES DIFFICULTIES ALSO REVEAL SALESMAN'S TASK

Selling is not a repetitive activity; each new situation contains a different combination of common operations. A description of the duties of a salesman as detailed in the preceding descriptions does not give a complete picture of the actual mental and physical activities of a salesman since these operations vary according to the circumstances encountered in each sales interview.

Even if a salesman follows faithfully the duties outlined in a sales-job description as for example, "Suggest buying in larger quantities," he still must be prepared to meet the objections of the prospect to that suggestion. Such objections or problems which must be met and overcome by a salesman form the heart of his job; the fact that they differ in every sales interview makes his work a complex occupation.

Success in selling is measured not so much by the routine performance of definite duties as by the ability to solve variable problems. Good salesmen experience few such problems; poor salesmen encounter numerous insurmountable problems or difficulties. Accordingly the picture of a salesman's job cannot be complete until it includes a list of the principal difficulties encountered by salesmen and the methods used in meeting those difficulties.

These difficulties may be classified as:

1. *Personality difficulties,* including lack of confidence, poor appearance, lack of self-control, discourtesy, indifference, laziness, poor voice, and tactlessness.

2. *Knowledge difficulties,* created by ignorance of product features and applications, company history, organization, personnel, policies, competition.

3. *System difficulties,* resulting from failure to keep records of sales activities, promises to customers, routing, time control, etc.

4. *Selling-technique difficulties,* resulting from lack of plan, no information about prospect, failure to answer objections, faulty demonstration, weakness in closing.

5. *Trade difficulties,* arising out of preferential treatment, price cutting, special concessions, competition between distributors.

6. *Product difficulties,* including deterioration, poor construction, spoilage, improper packaging.

SALESMAN'S DIFFICULTY ANALYSIS FORM

	Excellent 10-9	Good 8-7	Fair 6-5	Poor 4-3	Bad 2-1
A. *Personality difficulties:*					
Confidence					
Self-control					
Aggressiveness					
Appearance					
Physique					
Alertness					
Tact					
Sociability					
Sincerity					
Enthusiasm					
Voice quality					
Courtesy					
Sense of humor					
B. *Knowledge difficulties:*					
Product knowledge					
Company knowledge					
Price knowledge					
Advertising knowledge					
Service knowledge					
Competition knowledge					
Customer needs					
Delivery knowledge					
C. *System difficulties:*					
Reports					
Time employment					
Planning work					
D. *Sales-technique difficulties:*					
Contact with prospect					
Description of product					
Comparison					
Demonstration of product					
Meeting objections					
Getting decision					
Arranging details					
E. *Miscellaneous difficulties:*					
Product difficulties					
Price difficulties					
Customer personality problems					
Competition problems					
Delivery difficulties					
Service problems					
Credit difficulties					

Sales-difficulty-analysis form used in rating the personality, knowledge, system, and sales-technique difficulties of a salesman. This form may be used by a salesman in checking his technique; or a salesman's manager, customers, or friends may be asked to rate his work on this form.

SOLUTIONS TO SALES DIFFICULTIES REVEAL SALES TASK

To obtain a full understanding of a salesman's job, the methods employed in meeting the difficulties as described above should be considered.

A typical "difficulty" and its solution by a good salesman illustrate how methods used by salesmen to handle difficulties also reveal the nature of the sales task.

The difficulty: Salesman not prepared for interview with facts concerning prospect's problem.

A solution to this problem described by a successful salesman:

In working out an interview in advance of a call, I first review all correspondence and other information available concerning the matter to be discussed in the interview.

The next thing is to determine what object, or objects, I wish to accomplish in making the call. These I fix firmly in mind so that they can be introduced at the proper time and in sequence.

I then collect and organize such supporting data as I shall need and take with me also such literature as is pertinent to the subject to be discussed.

Lastly I endeavor to put myself in the place of the person I am about to call upon and imagine what arguments or objections he may interpose and how those may best be met and overcome.

A statement of a salesman's difficulties and methods of solving them as well as his duties is essential to a full description of a salesman's job.

IMPORTANCE OF KNOWLEDGE OF SALESMAN'S JOB

If a salesman is to be successful, it is obvious that he should know in detail all the duties he is expected to perform, the difficulties commonly encountered in carrying them out, and the best methods of meeting such difficulties.

Nor is it sufficient to know *what* to do; a good salesman also knows *why* he is called upon to do the things that his job demands. A knowledge of the reasons for doing a task and the implications or consequences of the action should be fully understood if he is to carry on his work with an intelligent understanding of his job and a cheerful compliance with its requirements.

Problem I

PERFORMANCE OF SALESMAN'S JOB

Frederick C. Dayton, representing Bedford Tire and Rubber Corporation

Frederick C. Dayton has been employed as general-line salesman of the Bedford Tire and Rubber Corporation, Akron, Ohio, with headquarters at Philadelphia, since 1938. He is one of 200 salesmen selling Bedford tractor, truck, and passenger-car tires, tubes, and automobile accessories, lawn hose, and rubber soles and heels direct to retailers of automobile accessories, automobiles, implements, gasoline and oil, hardware, and large industrial concerns. Dayton's territory includes eastern Pennsylvania.

The Bedford Company has made a thorough analysis of the work of its general-line salesmen and has prepared the following job description. Dayton was given these definite written instructions in regard to his duties when he was engaged by the company:

DUTIES OF BEDFORD GENERAL-LINE SALESMAN

I. *In retaining present volume and improving dealer's merchandising methods.*
   1. Call on dealers regularly.
   2. Discuss new products, and products that require frequent follow-up.
   3. Explain Bedford advertising and promotion plans.
   4. Help dealer work out local advertising program.
   5. Review Bedford's outstanding advantages regularly.
   6. See that *Bedford Retailer's Merchandising Manual* is used in the following seven ways:
      a. Analysis of possibilities.
      b. Store location, layout, equipment.
      c. Man power.
      d. Inside selling.
      e. Outside selling.
      f. Advertising.
      g. Recording results.
   7. Discuss management problems, credits, collections, resale program, etc.
   8. Discuss new selling features, like time payments, farm tractor sales, tubes, accessories, and campaigns on new products.
   9. Inventory dealer's stocks specified by district manager.
      a. Point out to dealer what is needed to balance stock.
      b. Take orders for stock dealer requires.
  10. Develop associate dealer and petroleum outlets.
  11. Hold dealer meetings.
II. *In securing new dealer where no representation exists.*
   1. Make territory analysis on form provided.
   2. Select important problem towns.
   3. Observe active competing dealers.
   4. Select most desirable dealer prospect.
      a. Estimate number of tires sold in town, annually.
      b. Determine who is selling them.

      c. Rank dealer prospects as to desirability.

      d. Decide which should be obtained.

   5. Get acquainted with dealer prospects.

      a. Make preliminary call.

      b. Determine what interests prospect.

      c. Throw out "teaser" information.

      d. List advantages of dealer's present deal vs. Bedford advantages.

      e. Decide vulnerable points.

      f. Plan your attack.

   6. Present Bedford franchise.

      a. Arrange uninterrupted meeting.

      b. Use company advertising.

      c. Cover advantages thoroughly.

   7. Ask for prospect's business; get contract.

III. *In contacting car, truck, and implement dealers and obtaining specifications.*

   1. Keep above, using original equipment, posted on new developments in Bedford products.

   2. Establish good-will contact and relationship with local Bedford dealer.

   3. Obtain specifications where advisable.

IV. *Contacting consumer accounts.*

   1. Have limited list of most important consumer accounts in territory; call on these.

   2. Sell important consumers.

V. *In knowing competing practices and dealers.*

   1. Know and call upon competitive dealers.

   2. Check their resale practices.

   3. Be familiar with new activities of competitors, sales plans, products, advertising, etc.

VI. *About miscellaneous functions.*

   1. Check delivery service on orders placed; be familiar with back-order situation.

   2. Contact company store, if any.

   3. Contact newspaper offices, keeping their good will and getting publicity.

   4. Keep dealer informed and enthusiastic on newspaper and billboard advertising.

   5. Check current dealer campaigns advocated by Bedford.

VII. *In making reports and carrying on correspondence.*

   1. Daily reports.

   2. Route lists.

   3. Expense reports.

   4. Specifications.

   5. Reports on sales campaigns.

6. Study of reports received.

7. Analysis of time employment.

During the past year, sales in the territory have declined, and the district sales manager has made a study of Dayton's daily call reports on dealers, a typical number of which follow:

January 15. Call No. 1. Martin Auto Supply Co., dealer. Discussed new safety tubes. Took order for three batteries. Made adjustment on a 5.00-16 four-ply casing. Checked delivery on last order.

Call No. 2. Wilson Department Store. Tried to close sale for 10 truck casings and tubes as a trial order. Must call back later.

Call No. 3. Lane Oil Co. Operates four stations. Tried to interest manager in distributing our tires. Call interrupted.

Call No. 4. Jones & Bates, dealer. Discussed our time payment plan. Took order for dozen new safety tubes. Talked to their salesmen.

Call No. 5. Mudge & Mitchell, prospective dealer. First call. Presented our franchise.

Call No. 6. Bainter & Mason, a competitive dealer. Live wires. Not interested in taking on other line.

Four calls. Buyers out.

January 16. Call No. 1. Johnson Perry, dealer. Discussed time-payment plan. Complaining about poor business. Secured no business.

Call No. 2. Tom Watson, dealer. Overstocked. See on next trip.

Call No. 3. Newton Smith, competitive dealer. Is enthusiastic about present line, not interested in making a change. However, may take on battery line in spring.

Call No. 4. David Miller, dealer. Placed order for tires and tubes, amounting to $180. Inquired about advertising.

Call No. 5. Allen Manufacturing Co. Discussed truck tires with purchasing agent. May consider later.

Call No. 6. Blake County Bus Lines. Satisfied with bus tires now using. Five calls, buyers out.

January 18. Call No. 1. T. L. Jefferson, possible dealer. Discussed our line. Not financed adequately to give us volume.

Call No. 2. Morgan & Co., dealer. Reviewed advantages of our line. Stocked up. May buy later.

Call No. 3. Bruce McCormick, competing dealer. May consider our line later.

Call No. 4. Y. K. Yount, dealer. Ordered two motorcycle casings, five passenger casings, and two all-solid tires.

Call No. 5. Spring & McCutchinson, dealers. Sales poor. Complaining no business. May liquidate tires and concentrate on gas and oil business.

Call No. 6. Bounter Oil Co., prospective dealer. Presented company franchise. Will consider and I shall call back later.

Call No. 7. McArthur & Co. Moving and trucking concern. Now using competitor's tires. Not interested in changing.

Three calls, buyers out.

Salesman Dayton maintains that he is making a good number of calls, is securing some business, and is attempting to locate new dealers as well as maintain the volume of present dealers. He claims that he is contacting important consumer tire accounts in his territory. Declining sales are caused by poor business conditions, he believes.

The district sales manager believes that Dayton is not doing a thorough job in developing present dealers and has not followed the duties outlined in his job description.

Questions

1. Is salesman Dayton doing a thorough job of selling as indicated by the typical call reports compared with the job description quoted in the problem?

2. Compare Dayton's call reports with his job description and list the duties required which are not being performed.

3. What other duties should be included in the Bedford sales-job description?

Problem II

PERFORMANCE OF SALESMAN'S JOB

Howard R. Parker, representing Larson, Baker Automobile Sales Corporation

Howard R. Parker, representing Larson, Baker Automobile Sales Corporation, Los Angeles, Calif., sells the Carter Motor Car, a well-known make of eight-cylinder automobile ranging in price from $2,500 to $3,500, to motorists in southern California. Howard Parker, one of 15 commission salesmen who represent his company, has been given a description of his selling presentation duties which was prepared by the Carter Motor Car Company after analysis of the work of hundreds of Carter salesmen. This job description is typical of the presentation task of all automobile salesmen.

DUTIES OF CARTER MOTOR CAR SALESMEN

I. *Create willingness to listen.*
   1. Through national advertising.
   2. Through direct mail.
   3. Through sales associates.
   4. Through direct approach.

II. *Know your product.*
    1. Know why it is better.
    2. Know your competitor's product.
III. *Create a desire to own a Carter.*
    1. Stimulate buying motives.
        a. Pride of possession.
        b. Protection and safety.
        c. Economy.
        d. Utility.
        e. Comfort and convenience.
    2. Make showroom presentation.
    3. Make road demonstration.
IV. *Remove objections.*
    1. Determine objections.
    2. Respect prospect's thinking.
    3. Sell around objections.
        a. Through tact.
        b. The "yes, but" technique.
    4. Sell through strong points.
V. *Close the sale.*
    1. Aim at it constantly.
    2. Direct prospect to say "yes" often.
    3. Ask for the order often.
    4. Assume the prospect will buy.
VI. *Sell accessories.*
    1. Use accessory display.
    2. Through display car.

Salesman Parker's sales manager has had a wire recording made of one of Parker's presentations to a prospect in the showroom in order to analyze the strengths and weaknesses of his salesmanship. Parker has followed up a mailing and made an appointment by telephone with the prospect, Arthur Warren, to visit the Larson, Baker showroom to see the Carter Car. Their conversation follows:

SALESMAN PARKER: Good morning, Mr. Warren. I'm glad you came in.

PROSPECT WARREN: Well, I got your letter and booklet telling about the new Carter and I was curious to have a look at it.

SALESMAN PARKER: What make of car are you driving now, Mr. Warren?

PROSPECT WARREN: Why, it's an old Speedwell. Bought it in 1942 and have driven it about 80,000 miles. It has been a fine car.

SALESMAN PARKER: Just what have you liked about your Speedwell, Mr. Warren?

PROSPECT WARREN: It's a mighty comfortable car to drive—you hardly feel the bumps in the road.

SALESMAN PARKER: Yes, I am familiar with the Speedwell floating-coil front
springs and their long vitaflex rear springs built parallel to the frame. But
if it's comfort you want, Carter's exclusive spring suspension system automatically compensates for variations in load and road to give you boulevard smoothness even on a rough detour. It is a "self-controlling" system
that gives you soft but firm cushioning, up and down, side to side, front to
rear, for the life of the car. Our owners call it a "limousine ride." When I
demonstrate the Carter, you'll appreciate its smooth and level ride.

Also you have plenty of hip and shoulder room for six on the new sofa-
wide seats which are deep-cushioned with foam rubber to fit the curve of
your seat and back and give you comfort as satisfying as stretching out in
your favorite easy chair. The rear seats are lowered and cradled ahead of
the rear wheels which gives you more headroom than most cars, as you can
see if you will sit in the rear seat. That's roomy, isn't it?

PROSPECT WARREN: It sure is.

SALESMAN PARKER: If you add the extra cushioning of the new-type, large
air-chamber and low-pressure tires, our Carter rides as smooth as a bird.
Also, you have no gears to shift with our new "Liquaflow" drive which uses
liquid to do the job of both the clutch and the usual low, second, and high
gears. There is no clutch pedal and driving is mighty smooth and easy.
Does your wife drive?

PROSPECT WARREN: Yes, she drives more than I do.

SALESMAN PARKER: Then she will appreciate how easy the Carter handles
with no gears needing shifting.

The low center of gravity also makes possible greater stability and easier
handling for maximum comfort. The car hugs the road and takes even the
sharpest curves without side sway. That means balance and comfort, don't
you think?

PROSPECT WARREN: That's all well and good but I can't afford all that luxury.
I'm afraid the Carter is too expensive for us.

SALESMAN PARKER: Yes, I can see why you would think the Carter would
be expensive, but you can expect up to 10 per cent more miles to the gallon
because of our new type of cooling system, new lubrication system, and special type of manifold. The new fourth-gear drive cuts engine speed 23 per
cent and saves about 15 per cent of your gas at ordinary speeds as well as
giving longer engine life. That makes for operating economy, doesn't it?

PROSPECT WARREN: It sounds good.

SALESMAN PARKER: I want to show you the over-all beauty of the car. Notice the graceful design of the grill, headlights, hood lines, and radiator
ornament. See that big windshield, almost a square foot bigger than most
cars; there's more than 20 square feet of window area in the new Carter.
The trunk compartment is the most convenient to get into you've ever seen,
and it has nearly 60 per cent more luggage space than prewar models.
That's convenient, isn't it?

PROSPECT WARREN: Yes, it certainly is.

SALESMAN PARKER: Let's take a ride so you can feel for yourself how comfortably the Carter rides.

(Here the prospect and salesman went out for a demonstration during which the salesman emphasized the roominess and comfort to be found in the front seat—the leg room, hip room, headroom, and shoulder room. The salesman got the prospect to agree on each point. The salesman discussed balanced springing, unsprung weight, and the leaf spring. The ease of steering and parking was demonstrated. The salesman and prospect returned to the showroom where the buyer was seated in the private office.)

SALESMAN PARKER: Mr. Warren, you've experienced for yourself the effortless riding, easy shifting, ample body room of the new Carter. Do you want me to deliver your car Saturday or the first of next week?

PROSPECT WARREN: You might give me an appraisal of my old car and drop in at the house some evening and let Mrs. Warren look over the new Carter.

SALESMAN PARKER: I'll be glad to, but before you go I'd like to show you our accessory display in our service department. You'll probably be wanting a new radio and heater and can pick them out while you're here. These smart accessories were developed just for your personal convenience.

Questions

1. Compare salesman Parker's sales presentation with his job description on each of the six major duties and criticize his performance.

a. Create willingness to listen.

b. Know your product.

c. Create a desire to own a Carter.

d. Remove objections.

e. Close the sale.

2. Which duties did salesman Parker perform most effectively? Explain.

3. What required duties were not being performed by the salesman?

4. What other duties should be included in the Carter job description?

Reading References

E. J. BENGE, "Manpower in Marketing," pp. 12–18, Harper & Brothers, New York, 1945.

J. R. Daubman, "Salemanship and Types of Selling," pp. 60–62, F. S. Crofts & Co., New York, 1939.

"It Pays to Blue Print Salesmen's Jobs," *Advertising & Selling,* April, 1940, Robbins Publishing Co., New York.

BERNARD LESTER, "Sales Engineering," pp. 3–18, John Wiley & Sons, Inc., New York, 1940.

F. A. RUSSELL and F. H. BEACH, "Textbook of Salesmanship," pp. 52–86, McGraw-Hill Book Company, Inc., New York, 1949.

CHAPTER III

PERSONAL QUALIFICATIONS FOR SELLING

Recognition of the close relationship between the personal qualifications of an individual and his success as a salesman is one of the most significant developments in salesmanship in recent years. Today, age, education, experience, and marital status have a definitely predictable bearing on a man's success or failure in the sale of numerous products and services.

Heretofore, salesmen and sales managers have had no standard, other than their personal opinion, by which to judge the relation of personal traits and experience to sales success. However, through analyses of the traits of outstanding salesmen and through the development of aptitude tests and psychological measures, much progress has been made in evaluating personal qualifications for this work. Standard qualifications are being established for specific sales jobs and a more critical examination of the qualities that make for sales achievement is supplementing individual opinion as the sole determining factor in judging the fitness of an individual for sales work. Trial-and-error methods are gradually being displaced by a more scientific approach to qualifying salesmen. On account of the many variable personality factors involved, progress in the exact measurement and testing of personal qualifications for selling must necessarily be slow, but the time may not be far distant when the traits and experience of a salesman can be weighed and measured with as much exactness as are raw materials, iron and coal, used in manufacturing. Until that time arrives, individual judgment must largely dictate the qualifications for selling.

THE SALES JOB DETERMINES THE QUALIFICATIONS OF THE SALESMAN

Personal qualifications must be considered in relation to the sale of a specific product or service and a definite sales job. The qualifications of a competent insurance salesman are unlikely to be the same as those of a good automobile salesman, as the duties and responsibilities of the two men are not comparable. Little is to be gained by generalizing qualifications. The specific demands of the individual job dictate the qualities necessary for succeeding in it.

An analysis should first be made of the job for which the salesman is to be qualified, and written job specifications prepared detailing the activities involved. Several job descriptions appear in Chap. II. To illustrate how the personal qualifications, necessary to perform a certain sales job successfully, may be drawn from such descriptions, the following table shows in the first column the activities to be performed and in the second column the personal qualities necessary in performing those activities.

DUTIES AND PARALLEL QUALIFICATIONS OF A RETAIL AUTOMOBILE SALESMAN

Salesman's Duties	*Salesman's Qualifications*
I. Locate prospect's needs by	Initiative.
a. Getting information about prospect's car and driving habits.	Tact.
	Curiosity.
b. Using visual sales material.	Imagination.
c. Questioning prospect.	Resourcefulness.
	Analysis.
II. Tell how product fits needs of prospect.	Voice.
	Use of English.
	Enthusiasm.
	Knowledge.
III. Show how product fits needs of prospect.	Enthusiasm.
	Sincerity.
	Imagination.
	Knowledge.
IV. Get prospect's agreement on each point as it is made.	Sincerity.
	Tact.
	Persistency.
	Resourcefulness.
V. Answer or forestall objections.	Self-control.
	Alertness.
	Confidence.
	Patience.
	Knowledge.
	Tact.
	Loyalty.
VI. Close sales.	Aggressiveness.
	Determination.
	Persistence.
	Sincerity.

DUTIES AND PARALLEL QUALIFICATIONS OF A RETAIL AUTOMOBILE SALESMAN

Salesman's Duties	*Salesman's Qualifications*
VII. Handle trade-ins.	Tact. Honesty. Knowledge.
VIII. Routine reports daily on calls, interviews, prospects; prepare daily call schedule.	Honesty. System. Accuracy.
IX. Executive duties; mail advertising to prospects; set daily call quota; make daily work plan; keep informed about industry, company, product, competition.	Industry. System. Organization.
X. Create good will by following up customers to see that they get service.	Friendliness. Health-energy. Unselfishness. Courtesy.

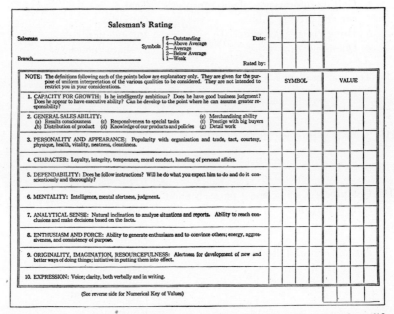

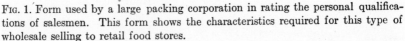

FIG. 1. Form used by a large packing corporation in rating the personal qualifications of salesmen. This form shows the characteristics required for this type of wholesale selling to retail food stores.

The 30 personal traits required by a retail automobile salesman in carrying out the duties described above may be classified as follows: *Hard traits:* industry, persistency, aggressiveness, determination, loyalty, confidence, alertness, honesty, knowledge. *Soft qualities:* tact, patience, friendliness, unselfishness, sincerity, imagination, curiosity, self-control. *Business traits:* system, organization, resourcefulness, accuracy, analysis.

These traits may also be considered from the standpoint of the development of a salesman's personality as tangible traits, or those which lie within the power of the salesman to determine; and intangible traits, or those which in some degree must be possessed as natural characteristics. Tangible traits are largely the hard qualities of honesty, industry, knowledge, determination, confidence, all of which can be cultivated. Intangible traits are such soft qualities as friendliness, patience, tact, sincerity, unselfishness, which are largely natural characteristics and not so easily developed.

To illustrate the personal characteristics demanded by another type of selling job, the duties of a wholesale salesman of tires and rubber goods are paralleled by the personal qualifications required for this specific work, as follows:

DUTIES AND PARALLEL QUALIFICATIONS OF A WHOLESALE SALESMAN OF TIRES AND RUBBER GOODS, SELLING TO RETAIL MERCHANTS

Salesman's Duties	*Salesman's Qualifications*
I. Call on dealers regularly.	Industry.
II. Discuss new products.	Knowledge of product.
III. Explain advertising and promotion plans.	Knowledge of advertising.
IV. Help dealer with local advertising.	Unselfishness.
V. Aid dealers in:	
1. Analyzing market posibilities.	Analysis.
2. Evaluating store location, layout, equipment.	Knowledge of retailing.
3. Inside and outside selling.	Retail sales experience.
VI. Discuss retail credits, collections.	Knowledge of credits and collections.
VII. Explain new selling features of line.	Voice; use of English. Enthusiasm. Knowledge.
VIII. Inventory dealers' stocks.	System. Detail, attention to.
IX. Develop associate dealer outlets.	Initiative.
X. Hold dealer meetings.	Leadership. Voice. Helpfulness.
XI. Secure new dealers.	
1. Make territory analysis.	Analysis.

Duties and Parallel Qualifications of a Wholesale Salesman of
Tires and Rubber Goods, Selling to Retail Merchants

Salesman's Duties	*Salesman's Qualifications*
2. Select important problem towns.	Discernment.
3. Observe competing dealers.	Observation.
4. Select desirable dealer prospects.	Judgment.
5. Get acquainted with prospects.	Sociability.
a. Determine prospect's interests.	Curiosity.
b. List advantages of present dealers vs. your advantages.	System.
c. Plan attack.	Organization.
	Knowledge.
6. Present company franchise.	Persuasiveness.
7. Close contract.	Sincerity.
	Forcefulness.
	Persistency.
XII. Get dealers of cars, trucks, implements to specify tires as original equipment.	Friendliness. Persuasiveness.
XIII. Sell important consumers.	Knowledge.
	Sincerity.
	Alertness.
	Convincingness.
XIV. Know competing practices and dealers.	Knowledge.
	Observation.
XV. Check delivery service.	Thoroughness.
XVI. Contact newspapers for publicity.	Tact.
XVII. Make reports and correspond.	System.
	Detail, attention to.
	Organization.
	Method.

QUALIFICATIONS FOR SELLING DETERMINED BY PSYCHOLOGICAL TESTS

While no psychological or aptitude test has yet been devised that can conclusively indicate whether a person will succeed or fail in selling, numerous tests have been developed that reveal personal traits closely associated with proficiency in selling. The fact that many large employers of salesmen use these tests to check their other measures for determining a prospective salesman's capacity is evidence that they have merit.

Tests are available for measuring the personality factors that contribute to success in selling, such as intelligence, selling aptitude, dominance, social intelligence, introversion, extroversion, confidence, observation, memory, and vocabulary.

Candidates for sales work may check their qualifications for selling as well as their interest in and aptitude for the work by taking the tests under the supervision of a vocational counsel or psychologist. The tests may be procured from the Psychological Corporation, New York, or the Cooperative Test Service, New York. Executives may also use these tests in measuring the qualifications of applicants for sales work.

The authors of many of these tests frankly state that the scores obtained should be regarded as suggestive rather than conclusive. However, the individual who desires a better understanding of himself and an evaluation of his traits in respect to sales work may profit from taking them. The results must, of course, be supplemented by interviews with sales executives, by other objective opinions, or by the experience records of employers in the field in which the individual is interested.

QUALIFICATIONS SOUGHT BY EMPLOYERS OF SALESMEN

The personal qualifications considered most significant by employers in selecting men for various types of sales work are indicative of the traits essential to success in selling.

QUALIFICATIONS FOR RETAIL APPLIANCE SELLING

The qualifications of a good retail appliance salesman can be reduced to these five essential requirements, according to the appliance and merchandise department of the General Electric Company: (1) good personality, (2) good appearance, (3) loyalty, (4) industry, (5) average intelligence.

QUALIFICATIONS FOR RETAIL AUTOMOBILE SELLING

The eight personal traits essential in retail automobile selling, according to the Packard Motor Car Company, are: (1) enthusiasm, (2) appearance, (3) self-discipline, (4) perseverance, (5) knowledge of product, (6) personality, (7) speech, (8) selling ability.

QUALIFICATIONS FOR MOTOR TRUCK SELLING

Seven basic traits are fundamental to success in motor truck selling, according to the White Motor Company, and are as follows: (1) stability, (2) industry, (3) perseverance, (4) loyalty, (5) ability to get along with others, (6) leadership, and (7) self-reliance. In addition, the company emphasizes the importance of maturity and of motivation for providing for personal and family needs.

Qualifications for Life Insurance Selling

The greatest opportunity for success in life insurance selling, according to the Phoenix Mutual Life Insurance Company, is for a man who is a college graduate; married, with two or three other dependents; who has earned $400 or more per month; who owns $15,000 or more life insurance; who has held an executive position; who has had five to six years of selling experience; who has minimum living expenses of $200 to $399 per month; who has lived in the community five years or more; and who belongs to six social or fraternal organizations.

Qualifications for Wholesale Drug Selling

A salesman of wholesale drugs, according to a study made by James H. Davis for the National Wholesale Druggists Association in 1948, should preferably have the following personal characteristics: age, twenty-three to thirty-two years; college graduate in business administration; experience in retail drugstore, wholesale drug house, or selling to the drug trade; honesty and dependability; leadership; initiative; resourcefulness; intelligence; interest in selling; and good appearance.

Qualifications for Manufacturer's Salesmen of Paper Specialties

An important manufacturer of paper specialties whose salesmen sell the retail stationery and notions trade requires salesmen with the following 12 characteristics: (1) good physical condition, (2) good education, (3) good bearing, (4) attractive personal appearance, (5) previous experience, (6) high character, (7) resourcefulness and imagination, (8) cheerfulness, (9) courtesy, (10) industry, (11) sense of humor, (12) tact.

Qualifications for Manufacturer's Salesmen of Soap

Salesmen representing a large soap manufacturer are selected for the following traits: (1) facial expression, (2) determination, (3) character and integrity, (4) manners, (5) initiative, (6) physical fitness, (7) voice, (8) knowledge of retailing merchandising problems, (9) use of English, (10) decisiveness.

Characteristics Sought by Employers of Inside Retail Salespersons

An investigation made by the National Vocational Guidance Association of the qualifications of salespersons in retail stores showed that a majority of the employers preferred salespersons with the following qualifications:

Age: minimum, eighteen to twenty-one years.

Education: minimum, high-school graduate.

Experience: not required.

Physical qualities: good health; average height and weight.

Personal qualities: courtesy, helpfulness, interest in people, honesty.

SALESMAN'S QUALIFICATIONS JUDGED BY BUYERS

The buyer is the final judge of a salesman's personal qualifications. The traits that make favorable impressions on buyers are those characteristics whose possession contributes to the success of salesmen and whose absence accounts to a great extent for their failure. An evaluation of the traits of successful salesmen of industrial products was made by the professional purchasing agents of seven large industrial corporations who rated 141 salesmen representing producers of metals, machine tools, machinery, rubber goods, leather products, oil, chemicals, and a wide variety of industrial supplies.

Eleven factors of personality were rated by these buyers, including self-confidence, appearance, voice control, aggressiveness, tact, sincerity, courtesy, use of English, enthusiasm, and alertness, in addition to 13 other factors of the salesman's presentation. Each quality of the 74 successful and 67 unsuccessful salesmen was rated on a scale of 100 points.

The personal characteristics of the 74 successful salesmen, rated by buyers and arranged in order of importance, were as follows:

Rank	Quality	Rating
1	Sincerity	82
1	Courtesy	82
3	Enthusiasm	80
4	Self-confidence	79
5	Self-control	77
5	Alertness	77
7	Appearance	76
8	Tact	75
9	Use of English	74
10	Aggressiveness	73
11	Voice quality	69

The strongest personal qualities of able industrial salesmen, according to these ratings, are sincerity, courtesy, and enthusiasm; their weakest traits are voice quality, aggressiveness, and use of English.

Customers Rate Inside Retail Salespersons

The characteristics of retail salespersons were similarly rated by customers of large retail stores in a study made by the Research Bureau for Retail Training to determine which qualities were considered most important. In order of importance they rated as follows: (1) courtesy; (2) friendliness; (3) willingness; (4) appearance; (5) serviceableness; (6) tact; (7) intelligence; (8) adaptability; (9) sincerity; (10) imagination; (11) patience; (12) memory; (13) alertness; (14) enthusiasm; (15) forcefulness; (16) honesty; (17) industriousness; (18) concentration; (19) loyalty; (20) self-confidence; (21) initiative; (22) health; (23) ambition; (24) cooperation; (25) dependability.

In another study of the characteristics of retail salespersons, conducted by Cook and Manson, customers rated personal traits in the following order of importance: (1) interest in customer; (2) ability to display merchandise; (3) alertness; (4) knowledge of merchandise; (5) courtesy.

SALESMAN'S QUALIFICATIONS AS DETERMINED BY ANALYSIS OF SUCCESSFUL AND UNSUCCESSFUL MEN

Progressive employers of salesmen have made analyses of the characteristics of their successful and unsuccessful salesmen, revealing those traits possessed by good men engaged in certain types of selling.

The Monarch Life Insurance Company asked its general agents to rate the character, mental ability, dominant qualities, persuasive qualities, staying qualities, and appearance of their successful and unsuccessful agents.

Of the successful salesmen, 54 per cent possessed the dominant qualities of courage, aggressiveness, confidence, persistency, and determination; 22 per cent possessed the persuasive qualities of sincerity, enthusiasm, tact, self-control, and friendliness; 10 per cent possessed the staying qualities of energy, patience, endurance, health, and concentration. The three factors of dominance, persuasiveness, and persistance represented 86 per cent of the total reasons given for the success of the salesmen analyzed.

Analysis of the failures in the same company showed that 11 per cent of the salesmen failed because of lack of character including honesty, reliability, morals; 14 per cent because of lack of incentive to work; 16 per cent because of the financial factors of indebtedness, extravagance, etc.; 45 per cent because of the lack of dominant, persuasive, and staying qualities.

A similar analysis of the reasons why salesmen fail was made by J. C. Aspley, who asked 103 members of the Chicago Sales Executives Club why some of their salesmen did not succeed. The principal reason for failure among the 624 men reported upon was "lack of industry," which accounted for 196, or 31 per cent, of the failures. Next in importance was "failure to follow instructions," for which reason 72, or 12 per cent, were discharged. "Inadequate knowledge" was responsible for the failure of 72, or 12 per cent of the total. Ten per cent lost out for "lack of fighting spirit." Lack of determination" was the reason for dropping 65, or 10 per cent of the men. Eight per cent, or 52, of the salesmen were dishonest. A similar number failed through "lack of enthusiasm." "Lack of tact and courtesy" accounted for the failure of 4 per cent and drinking and gambling for a similar number.

PERSONAL MANNERISMS

Because personal contact is essential in selling, a salesman's mannerisms play an important part in his relationship with customers. A mannerism is excessive adherence to a peculiar behavior, such as a recurrent movement of the body, limbs, or face of which the possessor is more or less unconscious. They indicate embarrassment, fear, nervousness, or mental conflicts which seriously handicap many salesmen in making sales presentations by distracting and annoying buyers.

To learn how significant these mannerisms may be in sales interviews, Dr. James F. Bender asked a group of 50 buyers to list those annoying mannerisms most frequently observed among salesmen. The 10 most irritating mannerisms of salesmen reported were: (1) continuous blinking of the eyelids, (2) nose-picking, (3) twitching the eyebrows, (4) cracking the knuckles, (5) biting the lips, (6) scratching the head, (7) shrugging the shoulders, (8) smacking the lips, (9) protruding the tongue, (10) licking the lips.

Buyers reported that these mannerisms were noticed more than twice as often among young as among seasoned salesmen and three times as often among mediocre as among successful salesmen.

To avoid these annoying mannerisms, they must first be identified and suppressed by conscious physical control of the body, limbs, and face. Richard C. Borden compares the delivery of a sales presentation with pitching a baseball, "When a baseball pitcher delivers a ball, he does not deliver with his fingers alone. He delivers with his legs, his shoulders, the muscles of his back—his entire body. The same thing is true of you when you make a sales presentation. You don't deliver what you say with your tongue alone but with your head, hands, arms, fingers—your whole body speaks for you whether you like it or not.

"To please your prospect's eyes—look alert—this does not mean look stiff and uncomfortable or pompous—like a stuffed shirt as if you were trying to be your own monument. It does mean look alive as if you considered the substance of your sales presentation vital."

By sitting forward in your chair, your body inclined toward the customer, your eyes on his face, your hands relaxed in your lap ready to emphasize an important point in your presentation, you give the impression that your mission is important and merits the favorable attention of the buyer. The salesman who slumps in his chair with vacant and evasive eyes, hands in pockets or scratching his head, rubbing his chin, or cracking his knuckles distracts, annoys, and loses the attention of customers.

By rehearsing sales presentations before a mirror or to an associate, negative personal mannerisms can be discovered and suppressed.

MAINTAINING PERSONAL EFFECTIVENESS

Because of the importance of personal effectiveness in sales work, it is essential that a salesman make continuous effort to improve his personal efficiency. A salesman's effectiveness is tested continuously by the nature of his tasks. He must meet keen sales resistance, overcome stiff competition, deal with objections and indifference without becoming discouraged, pessimistic, or losing confidence in himself, his company, and his product. To maintain cheerful enthusiasm and a confident attitude requires character, determination, and adherence to a program of self-improvement and morale building.

Every salesman must train himself to meet the rigorous demands of his work by reading his company and industry publications, by attending meetings, checking his own mistakes and correcting them, watching his health, living within his income, establishing social contacts, and by taking every opportunity to make himself a better informed, more effective salesman.

The following plan devised by a leading food-product manufacturer to aid his salesmen in improving their personal effectiveness is a model which might well be adopted by a salesman of any product or service:

I. *Keep self mentally fit.*
   1. Keep growing on the job by:

      a. Attending meetings and discussion groups.

      b. Studying manuals and company bulletins carefully.

      c. Reading trade journals and keeping informed on the product and industry.

  2. Learn the job thoroughly.

      a. Read, observe, ask questions, try your hand.

      b. Follow company training plan.

  3. Analyze own mistakes and try to avoid repeating.

  4. Keep teachable and interested in personal improvement.

  5. Maintain interest outside of the job.

  6. Form habit of reading to know what is "being done and said."

  7. Engage in activities that will provide mental challenge (dealing with ideas).

II. *Keep self emotionally balanced.*

  1. Analyze and know yourself.

  2. Maintain balance between elation and depression.

  3. Avoid financial and legal difficulties.

  4. Avoid family and marital difficulties.

  5. Maintain personal pride.

  6. Maintain pride in job and business.

  7. Control conduct.

  8. Work with and be friendly with women employees but conduct yourself in good taste.

  9. Be a salesman, not a "playboy."

  10. Control temper and strong biases and opinions.

  11. At all costs avoid political, religious, and racial arguments.

III. *Develop healthy group relationships.*

  1. Be a "good man" on the team.

  2. Work for interest of employer.

  3. Cooperate with fellow salesmen, deliverymen and all co-workers.

IV. *Keep self physically fit.*

  1. Avoid illness and personal injury.

  2. Give prompt attention to symptoms of physical disabilities.

  3. Provide for regular physical exercise.

  4. Watch your eyesight, heart, and blood pressure.

V. *Maintain good personal appearance.*

  1. Keep yourself looking like a quality product.

  2. Form the habit of "seeing yourself as others see you."

  3. Proper care of your wardrobe will make you a better dressed man. Cleanliness is more important than expensive clothes.

VI. *Coordinate job, home, community, and personal activities.*

  1. Set up personal schedules that will provide for time with your family.

  2. Be a real member of the community and its activities.

SALES PERFORMANCE RATING FORM

Personal Qualifications of Salesman

Salesman_____   Date_____

Rated by_____   Over-all Rating_____

Score

I. *Physical Qualities of the Salesman*	Excellent 90–100	Good 80–90	Fair 70–80	Poor 60–70	Failure Below 60
1. Health					
2. Posture					
3. Bearing					
4. Nerve control					
5. Voice					
6. Vitality					
7. Neatness					
8. Cleanliness					
9. Grooming					
10. Dress					

II. *Mental Qualities of the Salesman*	Excellent 90–100	Good 80–90	Fair 70–80	Poor 60–70	Failure Below 60
1. Confidence					
2. Enthusiasm					
3. Aggressiveness					
4. Sincerity					
5. Courtesy					
6. Self-control					
7. Alertness					
8. Tact					
9. Resourcefulness					
10. Patience					
11. Friendliness					
12. Persistence					
13. Imagination					
14. Sense of humor					
15. Vocabulary					

Miscellaneous Qualities_____

_____

_____

SUMMARY

The material in this chapter shows that there is no single characteristic or group of characteristics that ensures success in selling. There are, however, certain outstanding traits common to practically all kinds of sales work which may be considered essentials. These may be classified as mental and physical qualities. The principal physical qualities are health and appearance; the chief mental attributes are self-confidence, enthusiasm, sincerity, courtesy, iniative, and tact.

Physical Qualities. Health is the basic physical quality for salesmen since it affects not only the physical but the mental attitudes of a man, particularly his industry, confidence, enthusiasm, and initiative. Poor appearance, posture, and bearing are directly related to health. Selling is hard physical work and demands that a salesman eat proper food, secure adequate sleep, and get relaxation.

A good personal appearance is also fundamental. It means neat, clean, and inconspicuous dress, clean linen, shoes shined, hair cut, and bearing erect. An unknown salesman is only what he seems to be in the mind's eye of the prospect. If a salesman looks well, the prospect is willing to listen.

Mental Qualities. Confidence is one of the primary mental attributes of a successful salesman. Salesmen are constantly subjected to rebuffs, discouragement, and opposition; unless they are fortified with a good measure of courage and confidence, they will succumb to fear and failure. Knowledge of the market, the product, and the prospect's problem is the surest developer of confidence in a salesman.

Enthusiasm is an indispensable characteristic. Unless a salesman is emotionally aroused about his product, service, company, and proposition, he cannot make others interested in his offerings. Enthusiasm coupled with sincerity converts a monotonous recitation into a glowing, energized story which commands attention and arouses interest.

The insincerity of many poor salesmen has created a general skepticism, in the minds of many buyers, of the veracity of all salesmen's statements. The sincere salesman wins the confidence of customers and secures their business because they know where he stands. Sincerity creates that confidence which is the foundation of permanent buyer-seller relations.

Courtesy and good manners characterize successful salesmen who listen attentively, speak considerately, and defer respectfully to the opinions of others. Courtesy is indispensable in creating good will through friendliness and unselfish service.

Initiative or self-reliance is indispensable to success in selling. Salesmen must be self-starters since they have no one constantly by their side to supervise and motivate them, as in the case of office and factory workers. They must seek out new customers, discover new ways to sell old customers, and pioneer new markets by employing new methods.

Tact is the ability to deal with others without giving offense and a vital characteristic of salesmen who must see each sales problem from the buyer's viewpoint. Differences of opinion arise in every sales interview; unless a salesman adjusts his thinking to that of his prospect, tension develops, friction results, and the sales presentation stalls.

Problem I

Personal Qualifications of Salesman

Clifford K. Greene, representing Lustre-Sheen Hosiery Company

Clifford K. Greene, representing the Lustre-Sheen Hosiery Company, Philadelphia, Pa., manufacturers and distributors of women's silk hosiery, men's silk hose, silk underwear, nightwear, and neckties, sells direct to individual consumers in Portland, Me. Greene is one of 5,000 salesmen employed by his company. He is twenty-five years of age and earned $2,597.77 in commissions during the past year, which is above average for men in his organization. He began work with his company five years ago as its youngest representative.

Salesman Greene keeps a diary of his daily activities, recording informally the prospects interviewed, sales made, and customers serviced. Two typical days from his diary are quoted verbatim here to illustrate his personal qualifications for this type of sales work.

Friday: Left home at 9 A.M.

1. Called on Mr. C., but reached his office ahead of him. Waited 10 minutes until he came in. He didn't want a thing except money, so no sale was made. Saw a girl going into an apartment house wearing a white uniform of a nurse. I watched the door she went into and in about half an hour called back at the same house. Called on a first-floor apartment and found out where she lived and got her name, and went up three flights of stairs and knocked at the door. A figure clad in a negligee answered. She was embarrassed to be caught so, but I asked her if I might step in now after telling her who I was. I got in, and sold her an order of stockings, and also got about four names of her friends, as leads. One was going to be married soon.

2. Saw the first lead she had given me. Made a sale. I went up the street to call on the girl who is to be married. She was in bed but her mother came to the door. She was a very sweet person and told me all about her daughter and her future son-in-law. She was very happy over the whole thing. I complimented her on having such a charming daughter—I had seen her picture in the paper. She finally told me to call Saturday, and she would make the appointment for me.

3. Called on Mr. B. He will want something later. Mr. S. was out, call back. Mr. L. was out, call back. Miss H. C., another one of the nurses. Call back as she will be in at 7 P.M.

4. Mrs. H. wanted me to call back Saturday to see her about 9 A.M.

5. Called back at 7 P.M. on Miss H. C. Sold. So far two of my four leads were good for sales, and I have an appointment with the other for Saturday.

6. Saturday: Having an appointment at 9 A.M. with Miss F., I was sure to be on time. Rang the bell at 9 A.M. exactly. Her mother came to the door again. She said that she was very sorry, but she guessed that her daughter wouldn't need a thing. While she was out she had bought everything that she needed, including one dozen pairs of hosiery. Well, things looked bad here. I thought I would have a sure appointment, and now I haven't even met the girl.

7. So, I said to her mother, "You wouldn't mind if I met your daughter, would you? I've heard so much about her." She could see no reason not to, so in I went. In a few minutes out came the young lady. I could see that she was as lovely as her mother had described her. I began to talk of her coming marriage and edged over to my product. She became interested and wanted to see the hosiery. I finally ended up by selling three dozen pairs of our best hosiery, eight slips, six nightgowns, and two dozen pieces of other lingerie garments. It totaled $197.67—paying me a very good commission. So that was the third lead from the same nurse of the day before. I went directly to the office, quite determined to have special care taken in sending this order so as to have no mistake made.

8. In the afternoon, I went to Sandy Beach and looked over my summer territory. Came back in town and made some calls. Made some appointments for Monday night and also collected a deposit from a nurse.

Questions

1. What desirable personal characteristics are revealed by the preceding quotation from the sales diary of salesman Greene? What undesirable personal characteristics?

2. What personal characteristics are necessary for the successful performance of the type of sales work in which Greene is engaged?

3. Do you consider Greene qualified for the sales work he is doing? Give your reasons.

4. How can an individual determine his fitness for this type of sales work?

Problem II

PERSONAL QUALIFICATIONS OF SALESMAN

Guy T. Morgan, representing Industrial Supply Corporation

Guy T. Morgan, representing the Industrial Supply Corporation, Boston, Mass., wholesale distributors of pipe, valves, and fittings, sells direct to large industrial corporations and plumbing contractors in New England. The company employs five salesmen operating out of the Boston office.

To gain a more complete knowledge of their salesmen's methods with the intention of aiding them in improving their techniques, the Industrial Supply Corporation has placed microphones and sound-recording equipment in the offices of purchasing agents of industrial concerns who have agreed to cooperate with the company in securing verbatim records of salesmen's presentations. Every word of the salesman is intercepted by the microphone hidden on the buyer's desk and transmitted to the recording equipment in an adjoining room where it is recorded on wax cylinders and later transcribed into type-written form.

The following is an authentic transcription of the conversation of salesman Guy Morgan with the purchasing agent of a large transportation company:

1. SALESMAN: How do you do, sir?
2. BUYER: Good morning.
3. SALESMAN: Well, you're a busy man this morning I take it.
4. BUYER: Yes, I am.
5. SALESMAN: I'm with Industrial Supply Corporation.
6. BUYER: Yeh.
7. SALESMAN: We did business with you this quarter and also last quarter and you suggested that I come in in January some time. Thought it possible that you might be able to give us some business.
8. BUYER: Well, you quoted on fittings?
9. SALESMAN: Yes.
10. BUYER: And valves?
11. SALESMAN: Yes.
12. BUYER: I see. Well, your prices on fittings were not attractive. We couldn't do anything on them. We got a better proposition from a manufacturer or jobber or what not. That's the way the thing stands at the minute. It's up to you to have the right price.
13. SALESMAN: On fittings? Yes, I suppose that's so. And I just thought

that from time to time you could pick up some fittings from us. We have that in mind. We'd like to get some of those pickups.

14. BUYER: Yeh, we have an occasional pickup, but they're not the rule.

15. SALESMAN: No, I don't suppose so. But we hope that you might be able to find some way to give us some business. We're using your service, but we wouldn't cause you to declare any extra dividends. All business or half business, we would like a little of it. We're located near you and can give you as good service as the next fellow.

16. BUYER: Well, it's a terrible job for us to try to satisfy everybody because we've only got a limited amount of business, and it's difficult for us to spread it around thin enough to take in everybody. We've got eight or ten different people now and they're all kicking because they aren't getting enough. They're all getting something.

17. SALESMAN: Well, we'd like a little of that something. We're looking for business and if we can use more of your service, we'd like to have a little business.

18. BUYER: I'll keep the thing in mind.

19. SALESMAN: All right, thanks, good-by.

Questions

1. What desirable personal characteristics are revealed by the preceding sales interview of salesman Morgan? What undesirable traits?

2. What personal characteristics are necessary for the successful performance of the type of sales work in which Morgan is engaged?

3. Do you consider Morgan qualified from the standpoint of personality for the sales work he is doing?

4. How can Morgan improve his personal impression on prospects?

Reading References

E. C. BUEHLER and M. MALONEY, "You Sell with Your Voice," The Ronald Press Company, New York, 1939. .

J. R. DAUBMAN, "Salesmanship and Types of Selling," Chap. VII, F. S. Crofts & Co., New York, 1939.

CHARLES H. FERNALD, "Salesmanship," 3d ed. Chap. V, Prentice-Hall, Inc., New York, 1945.

J. GEORGE FREDERICK, "Modern Salesmanship," Chap. I, Garden City Publishing Company, Inc., New York, 1937.

HAROLD M. HAAS, "A Short Course in Salesmanship," Chap. XV, Prentice-Hall, Inc., New York, 1939.

PAUL W. IVEY, "Salesmanship Applied," Chaps. XI–XIV, McGraw-Hill Book Company, Inc., New York, 1937.

PAUL W. IVEY, "Successful Salesmanship," Sec. 7, Prentice-Hall, Inc., New York, 1937.

DONALD A. LAIRD, "What Makes People Buy?" Chap. XV, McGraw-Hill Book Company, Inc., New York, 1935.

C. W. Lewis, ed., "Essentials of Selling," Chap. I, II, Prentice-Hall, Inc., New York, 1945.

David R. Osborne, "Salesmanship for Today for Salesmanagers of Tomorrow," Chap. II, Harper & Brothers, New York, 1939.

O. P. and C. H. Robinson, "Successful Retail Salesmanship," Chap. II, Prentice-Hall, Inc., New York, 1942.

Frederic A. Russell and F. H. Beach, "Textbook of Salesmanship," pp. 89–113, McGraw-Hill Book Company, Inc., New York, 1949.

D. B. Tansill, "So You're Going to Sell," Chap. II, John C. Winston Company, Philadelphia, 1939.

CHAPTER IV

THE CUSTOMER

A salesman must know how a customer buys before he can sell him successfully. In other words: "To sell John Smith what John Smith buys, we must see John Smith with John Smith's eyes." While customers differ widely in many respects, at the same time they have much in common in their attitudes and buying processes. This similarity of buying viewpoint, thoroughly understood and skillfully appealed to, can be of great assistance to a salesman. Knowledge of customers' buying psychology makes it possible for a salesman to understand their motives and apply his product or service more effectively to the satisfaction of their needs—the basis of modern professional salesmanship.

TYPES OF CUSTOMERS

Customers differ in viewpoints, interests, and attitudes toward buying according to whether they are purchasing for use or for resale. Individual consumers buying for personal or family use make up the largest group of customers. Industrial concerns or institutions purchasing installations, accessory equipment, operating supplies or parts for use in manufactured goods compose another group of ultimate consumers with different buying motives and experience.

Another group of customers comprising wholesalers, jobbers, distributors, and retailers buy for resale to ultimate consumers rather than for use. Their motives for buying differ widely from those of either individual consumers or industries, although their purchasing processes are similar in many respects.

The professional customer, who not only buys for his own use but also specifies or prescribes products for his clients, has a somewhat different viewpoint but conforms to the buying customs of ultimate consumers in other ways as will be discussed in the following pages.

NUMBER AND PURCHASING POWER OF CUSTOMERS

The number of customers in this country in the ultimate consumer group is increasing rapidly, numbering 143,382,000 persons, according to the last U.S. Census estimate in 1947. In little more than seven years, our population increased by 12,500,000 and is expected to reach a total of 162,000,000 by 1975.

Not only is the number of individual customers increasing rapidly, but the number of older customers is growing; while the younger customers are declining in number. Buyers sixty years of age and over comprised 10.3 per cent of the population in 1940 and 11.4 per cent in 1948.

The number of women customers, fourteen years and over, who control the bulk of individual purchases, is expected to increase from 50,549,176 in 1940 to 55,835,000 by 1950.

New families indicated by the number of marriages are also multiplying rapidly and reached a new annual high of 2,314,491 in 1946, an increase of 68 per cent over 1935. It is estimated that the total marriages from 1940 through 1950 will exceed 17,000,000. As the average bride will buy an estimated $2,000 worth of housekeeping equipment, the potential sales to this type of customer alone is tremendous.

The number of births in the United States has also reached a new peak with an average of 314,375 a month in 1947 compared with a monthly average of 188,799 in 1939. With an estimated expenditure of $50 a baby, sales to this market promise to break all records.

Not only have the number of individual customers increased greatly since 1940, but the purchasing power of consumers has increased more than three times from a total of $45,700,000,000 liquid assets in 1939 to $150,000,000,000 in 1948. By 1950 total wages and salaries, according to assumptions of the Bureau of Labor Statistics, should exceed $122,000,000,000 compared with $60,800,000,000 in 1940.

The most important group of individual customers is composed of women, who, according to a study made by Hearst Magazines in 1948, influence over 84 per cent of all purchases of consumer goods. While this figure varies widely according to particular items, it indicates that a large share of the purchasing power is at the disposal of women. Among the commodities purchased largely by women are: foods and food products, 97 per cent; furniture, 98 per cent; rugs and carpets, 98 per cent; soaps, 98 per cent; men's shirts and neckties, 75 per cent; men's shoes, 68 per cent; and electrical appliances, 80 per cent.

Another important group of customers includes the three hundred thousand industrial concerns which are ultimate consumers of a wide range of raw materials, parts, semifinished commodities, as well as installation and accessory equipment and operating supplies.

Those merchant customers who buy for resale to consumers include 1,670,400 retailers, 166,200 wholesalers, and 677,500 service organizations, such as laundries, barber and beauty shops, shoe repairmen, and others.

QUALIFICATIONS OF CUSTOMERS

To qualify as a potential customer for a product or service, an individual, firm, or institution should have certain qualities. The five characteristics of a good prospective customer are: (1) a need, (2) ability to pay, (3) authority to buy, (4) accessibility, (5) right type for the salesman. The success of a salesman depends to a large extent upon his ability to recognize and appraise these qualities in individuals or business firms. The important work of qualifying prospects is discussed in detail in Chap. XII.

1. A Need. According to Webster's dictionary, "need" is "a condition requiring supply." The primary qualification of a good prospective customer is that the person or organization have an actual need for the salesman's product or service. To sell someone something for which he has no real need is sure to create dissatisfaction and to result in returned goods or defaulted payments and a lost customer when the buyer discovers that he has been sold something which he cannot use to advantage.

In respect to need, customers are one of three types: (1) Those who have a need, recognize it, and know how to satisfy it; (2) those who have a need, recognize it, and do not know how to satisfy it; (3) those who have a need but do not recognize it.

These three types of customers present widely different sales situations which must be recognized by a salesman and dealt with accordingly. The first type, who know their needs and how to satisfy them, do not require and may even resent advice and suggestions by a salesman. Most purchases of low-priced staples are made by buyers in this situation and the function of the salesman is merely order taking.

On the other hand, buyers who recognize their needs but do not know how to satisfy them require the counsel of a salesman, who has an excellent opportunity to use his knowledge and skill in telling and showing how his products satisfy the buyer's needs. This type of buyer is partially sold because he is convinced of his need before he meets a salesman, but he still must be convinced that the salesman's product or service, price, and company can supply his need.

Buyers who have a need but do not recognize it present an opportunity for the exercise of the highest type of creative salesmanship which establishes a need in the mind of the buyer for the benefits which the salesman's product or service provides. Salesmen who can sell buyers of this type receive the greatest money rewards and satisfaction. Many prospective customers for life insurance, investments, home, office, and industrial specialties and luxuries are in this class.

A customer's needs are of two sorts: Physical such as food, drugs, shelter, clothing, transportation; or mental, such as a need for the psychological satisfactions of love, beauty, comfort, style, recognition, sociability, which are often as real and sometimes more important to buyers than their physical requirements.

The degree of need of customers varies widely according to their standards of living, income, responsibilities. The greatest sales opportunities are found with those buyers, other things being equal, who have the greatest needs for the products or services which the salesman sells.

The emphasis in modern selling is primarily on the needs of customers. The features of design, materials, or construction of products are of significance only as they contribute to the satisfaction of needs. It is just as important that a salesman know needs or applications of his product or service as that he know the construction and operation of the product itself.

Methods of qualifying buyers' needs, as well as other characteristics, will be discussed in detail in Chap. XII.

2. Ability to Pay. The second and most important qualification of a customer is his ability to pay for the product or service that a salesman is selling. Although an individual or concern may have a real need for something, a person or organization must have either the cash or credit to pay for the purchase. While liberal credit terms have made it possible for many to buy products and services which they otherwise could not own, the fact remains that insufficient funds to satisfy the needs of buyers is one of the greatest limitations to sales. Many salesmen waste valuable selling time trying to sell buyers who are not financially qualified. However, ability to buy may not mean willingness to spend, and salesmen must recognize that the customer with the most money may be least willing to spend it to satisfy his needs.

3. Authority to Buy. An individual may admit his need, have the ability to pay, and still lack the legal or moral authority to contract for a product or service. A person whose income is held in trust by a guardian must get this guardian's consent to enter into a sales contract. The same requirement applies in the case of minor persons. Only certain employees of a corporation have legal authority to make purchases in the name of the concern.

Aside from legal authority, the question of moral authority most frequently affects an individual's decision to buy. While an individual may have legal authority, he often feels morally obligated to consult with one or more persons in his immediate family, business or partnership, corporation or social organization, before making a purchase. The extent to which authority to buy is shared by several individuals in a family or business organization is a matter of considerable importance to a salesman confronted with the question of who shares the authority to buy and who are the persons to be sold.

Much selling effort is wasted by salesmen who fail to recognize the authority of a prospective customer and devote their time selling persons who are unable to make buying decisions.

4. Accessibility. A person or firm may have a need, the ability to buy, and authority to buy but at the same time be so unapproachable or distant that a salesman may not be justified in devoting the time and effort to attempting a sale. Busy business executives or housewives usually conserve their time by surrounding themselves with secretaries, clerks, or maids to exclude salesmen who are not entitled to a hearing. Persons or concerns situated in remote areas often cost more to reach than the return to the salesman or his company unless the amount of the sale is large or profits considerable. Much selling time and effort is wasted by salesmen attempting to sell inaccessible buyers. The achievement of getting past barriers to interview unapproachable persons or traveling long distances to make sales appeals to many salesmen so strongly that they waste time trying to sell inaccessible customers.

5. Right Type for the Salesman. A customer should be of the sort that a salesman can meet and deal with agreeably. Similarity of interests, age, race, religion, and education create mutual understanding, respect, and confidence between a salesman and a customer. This is particularly true in the sale of intangibles or specialties when the confidence of the customer in the salesman is an essential factor in the transaction. The salesman who seeks customers with a similar background to his own will usually find them more receptive.

Analysis of the personal characteristics of customers whom a salesman is successful in selling will indicate the types of individuals with whom he can deal most successfully. While it may be necessary for a salesman to sell persons whose backgrounds do not correspond with his own, when a salesman has a free choice of prospective customers, he should select a type who is most suitable to him.

6. Other Qualifications. Other special qualifications are essential for customers of particular products depending on the nature of the goods. Some home appliances operate only on gas; others, only on alternate electric current. Customers must accordingly be equipped with the type of service required by these products. Legal restrictions limit the number of customers for alcoholic beverages and certain foods and drugs in various states. Life insurance can be sold only to persons able to qualify according to health and occupational requirements established by the life insurance companies. Various other factors such as age, sex, and training determine the qualifications for other types of customers. Only attorneys or students of law are logical customers for law books, and clerical robes are only sold to ministers of the gospel.

ATTITUDES OF CUSTOMERS

A salesman who knows the attitudes of customers and their viewpoints toward buying is better able to understand and deal with problems which arise in his work.

The attitude of a typical individual customer toward a salesman is often one of indifference, defense, and sometimes even antagonism. This viewpoint, usually referred to as sales resistance, arises from fear that the salesman will persuade the buyer to purchase something which he does not need and which he cannot afford. Most persons instinctively resist new ideas and changes in their customs and habits which purchases may involve. Others are satisfied with their present sources of supply or are, for various reasons, committed to buying elsewhere. Those who do not recognize a need for a salesman's product or service are naturally indifferent to his proposition. Unpleasant experiences with pressure salesmen often prejudice buyers against salesmen as a class and make it more difficult for a professional salesman to serve a buyer. A salesman may approach a buyer at an inopportune time and the customer may resent the intrusion. A salesman who recognizes these reasons for sales resistance is not disconcerted by the attitude of the customer.

Most persons, however, enjoy the experience of buying or spending money for goods and services which they believe will bring them satisfactions or enable them to reduce costs or increase profits. Wise salesmen appeal to this fundamental trait of human nature by making it easy for customers to buy. Because people like to buy, to spend rather than save, salesmanship is simply a way of aiding people to do the thing they like to do—spend their money wisely.

Although people like to buy, they do not like to be sold. Nearly everyone is proud of his purchases and likes to show and discuss them with others. But no one cares to admit that he was sold something. To say, "I was sold a new hat today," is considered a reflection on the judgment of the buyer and an admission that he was persuaded to buy a hat that was unbecoming, that he did not need, or could not afford.

By recognizing that customers like to buy but resent being sold, successful salesmen give buyers every opportunity to express themselves, exercise their buying judgment, and feel that they are making their own buying decisions. Good salesmen make every effort to dispel the impression that they are selling by avoiding the appearance, manner, voice, and strategy of a typical salesman. Retiring in dress, soft-spoken, slow in speech, listening, asking questions, never arguing or being too positive, the modern salesman makes the customer feel that he is buying and not being sold. By getting a customer to talk about his needs and by avoiding overemphasis on his product, company, and policies, a wise salesman gains the confidence of the buyer who feels that he is buying and not being sold.

Customer Attitude on Price, Quality, and Other Factors. Customer reactions to price, quality, variety, service, and advertised merchandise are of significance to salesmen, who should understand buyers' attitudes in order to be able to deal with them efficiently.

In regard to price, customers expect to pay the same price as others for the same quantity and quality of merchandise. They also believe that price should be comparable with that charged for similar goods by other suppliers. Most buyers are price-conscious, particularly so in periods of depression, and those with fixed incomes are concerned with price in periods of inflation. Customers are inclined to shop around or compare prices of competing products to get lower prices. Some buyers match one competitor against another in their effort to get a lower price. Customers, except in rare instances, are not concerned that a seller's price represents a loss or a profit to him. Special prices or bargains are particularly attractive to customers. In most transactions, price is not the only consideration, as buyers are also interested in quality and service. Buyers are usually not interested or informed on what cost elements constitute the price which they pay.

The highest quality at the lowest possible price is expected by customers. Usually consumers are not familiar with the elements which constitute quality and often assume that price is indicative of quality. While professional buyers purchase many commodities on the basis of quality standards, individual consumers have shown little interest in quality grades established for their protection in buying. Customers expect that the quality should be exactly as represented by sellers. There is a growing interest on the part of customers in the composition, materials, or ingredients of the products which they buy, and large buyers scientifically test the quality of the materials of products purchased. Federal laws now protect quality for consumers of many products.

Many customers want to make selections from a variety of goods affording a wide choice of style, color, type, and materials. Distinctive characteristics in merchandise are demanded to satisfy individual tastes and preferences or to meet manufacturing requirements. This attitude forces sellers to maintain extensive inventories and produce a diversified line to satisfy customer needs.

Customers have grown to expect an increasing amount of service from sellers, including delivery, credit, adjustment, and mechanical services. The cost of these services is reflected in the price. Some customers believe that price should reflect the amount of service provided the buyer. Customers are often willing to serve themselves in return for lower prices. When quality is identical and price quoted by competitors is similar, service becomes a major sales attraction.

Most individual customers prefer advertised goods, as advertising is a means of identifying product quality. However, many believe that advertised merchandise costs more than unbranded goods. Branded items are often considered of superior quality to unbranded goods. Industrial customers on the other hand are able to determine scientifically the quality of the goods they buy and rely less on advertised brands as a gauge of quality.

THE BUYING PROCESS

1. How Customers Buy. A knowledge of the mental processes involved in buying is essential for salesmen to enable them to understand and aid customers in reaching decisions to buy. Psychologists have described the four mental steps preceding a purchase as: (1)

recognition of a need, (2) search for a means of satisfying the need, (3) consideration of the available means, (4) adoption of a means to satisfy the need. The term "need" is used here in the sense of not only the basic necessities of life—food, clothing, shelter—but also the emotional wants and desire for comfort, beauty, protection, and love.

In taking these four steps to a purchase, every customer makes five buying decisions: (1) the need decision, (2) the means decision, (3) the source decision, (4) the price decision, (5) the time decision.

The time involved in making these decisions is highly variable. Sometimes a customer will take months to come to a recognition of his need or in searching for a means to satisfy the need. Or the five steps may be taken in a few seconds.

In some cases, a customer may have made all of the five buying decisions before seeing a salesman who, therefore, becomes merely an order taker since he has taken no part in aiding the buyer in making the decisions to purchase. Salesmanship means aiding customers in making buying decisions. The highest type of selling is that which convinces the customer of his need; persuades him that the salesman's product is the best means of satisfying his need; that the salesman's company is the best source; that the price is fair; and that now is the time to buy.

The following example illustrates the four mental steps and five decisions which must be made in a sales transaction:

A man and his wife are sitting in their living room on a winter evening when the man remarks that he is cool and his wife agrees that the house is never warm. Both persons have recognized their need for more heat and the first step in a sale has been taken.

The man says that the heating plant has worn out and should be replaced. He remarks that he will consult a heating engineer in regard to their heating problem. This is the second step in the buying process, the search for a means of satisfying the need.

The heating engineer discusses the merits of oil, gas, and coal heating with the customer, who says that he will consult with his friends who use these various methods of heating to secure their opinions. Here the third step toward buying has been taken by considering the available heating methods.

After consultation with his friends, the customer confers again with his heating engineer and decides to install gas heat. The fourth buying step and second decision to buy, the means decision, has been made by the buyer.

The customer next calls in salesmen representing various manufacturers of gas heating equipment, and the salesman of Company A persuades the customer that his firm is the most reliable and sells the best equipment. Here the source decision has been secured by the salesman.

The price quoted by Company A is next compared with the quotations of other gas equipment manufacturers, and the salesman persuades the customer his price is fair. The price decision has now been made by the buyer.

After considering the question of delaying the installation several months with the expectation of lower prices, the customer is persuaded by the salesman that prices will not decline and now is the best time to buy. This is the time decision and the fifth and last decision to be made in the sales transaction.

In the foregoing example, the need decision and the means to satisfy the need decision were made by the customer before consultation with the salesman. The source, price, and time decisions were secured by the salesman.

Salesmen must be alert to discover buying decisions which have not been made so that they can help customers make them and close the sale. Failure of customers to buy is evidence that one or more of the five buying decisions is missing. Until all decisions have been made, the sale has not been completed.

Missing decisions can be discovered by listening to comments of the customer, such as, "I think the price is too high," which indicates that the price decision is missing; or by asking the customer direct decision-checking questions, such as, "Are you ready to buy now?" whereby a salesman can determine whether a buyer has made the time decision.

Another theory of the buying process is held by psychologists who believe that there are four mental steps taken by a customer in making a purchase: (1) attention, (2) interest, (3) desire, (4) action. First, the attention of the buyer is attracted to a need and a product or service to satisfy the need. Second, the customer's interest in the article is attracted by some feature or benefits applying to the need. Third, the desire of the customer is aroused by evidence or proof that the product will provide the advantages promised; and fourth, the buyer takes action by making a buying decision.

This buying process, similar to the previously described four mental steps of: (1) recognition, (2) search, (3) consideration and (4) adoption, and the five buying decisions: (1) need, (2) means, (3) source, (4) price, (5) time, may take place in all or in part before a buyer is interviewed by a salesman or enters a store. The time involved in each of these steps varies widely from a few seconds to several years. Each step is not a separate activity but merges indistinguishably into the preceding and following steps of the process.

While many salesmen are not actually conscious of the preceding step-by-step progress of the buyer's mind during the course of a sales interview, knowledge of the buying process enables a salesman to understand a customer's viewpoint and improve the effectiveness of his sales presentation. By looking for missing buying decisions, a salesman can aid customers in making these decisions and at the same time determine his progress toward a sale.

Impulse Buying. Every purchase is a result of: (1) premeditation or advance planning, in which a customer makes most of the buying decisions before seeing a salesman or visiting a retail store, or (2) impulsive action, when buying decisions on need, source, the product, price, and time are made by a customer, without previous consideration, when he first sees and hears about a product or service.

Durable industrial goods, specialties, and luxuries involving sizable expenditures are usually premeditated purchases. Buying decisions are made only after consideration and planning by customers. A factory usually buys a machine or an individual buys an automobile after much deliberation.

Purchases of staples and low-priced necessities are often made by individuals on impulse as a result of suggestion by a salesman, display, or advertising at the point of purchase. Surveys made by E. I. DuPont de Nemours & Company show that 86 per cent of all purchases made in syndicate stores, 58 per cent of all sales in chain drugstores, and 24.6 per cent of all sales in food stores are made on impulse. A study of buying in super markets revealed that 48.2 per cent are planned purchases, 38.2 per cent are unplanned purchases, 11 per cent general plan purchases and 2.6 per cent substitute purchases.

Impulse purchasing may be either reminder buying, when a customer is reminded of his needs by a store display, or suggestion buying, when a salesperson suggests a need and sells a product to satisfy the need. In view of the large volume of impulse purchases in retail stores, excellent opportunities exist for suggestion selling.

Suggestion selling requires knowledge of products and customers' needs and ability to make skillful suggestions. Unless done intelligently, customers will resent suggestion selling as an attempt to pressure them into buying unwanted merchandise. This sort of suggestion

selling is sometimes referred to as "barber shop selling" and should be
avoided by salesmen.

Suggestion selling can be done in several ways: by selling several
units or a larger size to give a customer the benefits of economy and
greater convenience in using; by selling a related product, such as
shaving lotion with razor blades; by suggesting a new, improved
product or by recommending a higher quality product to give the
customer greater satisfaction.

2. Why Customers Buy. Customers buy as a result of mental,
physical, and economic forces which create needs, desires, or wants
which can be satisfied by the products or services sold by salesmen.

The older conception of customer motivation was that certain instincts present at birth dominated the behavior of a person throughout
his life. The modern psychologists, however, believe that there are
no common instincts which motivate consumers from birth, but that
buyers act as a result of their experiences and environments. Customers differ widely in the motives which impel them to buy as a
result of their training, experience, social and economic environments.
Human behavior is exceedingly complex and so full of drives that it
is impossible to predict how an individual will act in a buying situation. A customer may react in various ways at different times. The
urges to action of one customer are unlike those of any other.

In spite of the fact that the buying behavior of every customer is
different and that it is impractical for a salesman to assume that all
customers will be impelled to buy from a common motive, there are
five basic buying motives which inspire buying action: (1) comfort
and convenience, (2) safety and protection, (3) gain and economy,
(4) satisfaction of pride, (5) satisfaction of affection.

Comfort and Convenience. The motive of bodily comfort and convenience, which includes time and labor saving, is universal. Most
people wish for themselves and loved ones a life of ease, free from
the drudgery of physical and mental labor. The development of
mechanical devices to save labor and time in both home and industry
—prepared foods to save energy in cooking, speedy transportation to
save time—have stimulated the buying motive of comfort and convenience. Laborsaving products and services, such as dish-washing
machines, oil burners, power lawn mowers, and lounge chairs, are sold
by appealing to the motive of comfort and convenience.

Safety and Protection. Everyone instinctively craves safety and
protection against anything which interferes with his life, health, and
happiness. Many purchases are a result of the desire of individuals,

as well as business organizations, to protect themselves, families, or employees against physical dangers. The increasing emphasis on safety at home, on the highway, and in industry is making individuals conscious of self-preservation. A man buys life insurance to protect his family in the event of his death, or tire chains to protect himself and his passengers against automobile accidents. Most medical supplies and drugs are bought to protect health. Clothing and housing are purchased to avoid exposure and to preserve health. This motive is responsible for the sale of a wide variety of products ranging from firearms to aspirin tablets.

Gain and Economy. One of the most powerful motivating forces to sales is the universal desire to save money or make profits. It stimulates individuals to shop around in order to make their incomes go farther so they can enjoy higher standards of living. It causes industrial concerns to seek competitive bids in order to reduce costs of operation and increase profits. The motive of economy and gain involves the reason rather than emotion. Customers with limited buying power are often motivated in this way. Salesmen often make the mistake of assuming that buyers are motivated by economy whereas other motives may dominate the purchaser. The prevalence of bargains and price advertising is evidence of the power of this motive. Merchants buying for resale are mainly motivated by gain.

Satisfaction of Pride. The desire to be admired by others is strong in men and particularly so in women whose vanity is responsible for many sales. Pride in personal appearance is equaled by pride in accomplishment or attainment of high social or business position and is one of the most common motives for buying. Pride in being fashionable is a strong drive to buying of all style merchandise. Individuals seek to maintain their self-respect and prestige by wearing good clothes, driving impressive cars, or belonging to expensive clubs. The human desire for approval by others is the driving force which causes many persons to buy a wide variety of products from hair oil to shoe polish. Closely related to the motive of pride is that of emulation of others or "keeping up with the Joneses," by buying goods equal to those possessed by others.

Satisfaction of Affection. The desire for romance is a strong motivating force responsible for many purchases. Sex interest is the motive which creates a demand for much fashion merchandise—corsets, beauty preparations, perfumes, and romantic novels. This motive is particularly strong among young women. Affection for mothers and fathers and family members is also an impelling force for many purchases. A father's affection for his family motivates many purchases of life insurance. Special days for purchases for showing affection, such as St. Valentine's Day, Mother's Day, and Father's Day, indicate the importance of this motive in stimulating buying.

The problem of a salesman is to discover which one or more of the five motives happens to be the strongest buying incentive of a particular customer at a particular time so that he can discuss those features of his product or service which will satisfy the prevailing motive of the customer.

The importance of discovering a person's motive if you wish to persuade him was recognized by Baltasar Gracian in his "Art of Worldly Wisdom," written in 1653, as follows: "First, guess a man's ruling passion, appeal to it by word. Find out each man's thumb-screw. You must know where to get at anyone. All men are idolaters; some of fame, others of self-interest, most, of pleasure. Skill consists in knowing these idols in order to bring them into play. Knowing any man's mainspring of motive, you have as it were, the key to his will."

A salesman should seek to discover each prospective customer's motive early in every interview by listening to the buyer's remarks. For example, a salesman interested in buying an automobile says, "I travel by car a lot and get pretty tired by the end of the day sitting all cramped up behind the wheel." The alert salesman recognizes that one of the buying motives of this particular customer at the moment is comfort and accordingly the salesman emphasizes the features of the automobile which will give the customer comfort.

Another way to determine the motives of customers is to ask direct questions, such as, "Are you interested in color or design?" to learn if a buyer is motivated by desire for beauty. By observing a customer's appearance, environment, and the products which he owns, a salesman can often discover his buying motives.

Patronage Motives. In addition to the five basic buying motives which induce individuals to purchase are the patronage motives which cause customers to buy from one source rather than another. When a customer has recognized a need, he seeks a store or a salesman to satisfy his need, and his choice of a seller depends on such factors as:

1. *Location of seller.* For many necessities, customers choose the most convenient source of supply. This habit has caused certain types of stores which are located near customers to be known as "convenience stores" and include such neighborhood stores as grocery, drug, tobacco, and gasoline filling stations. Although a well-known

cigarette has been advertised as one for which a customer would walk a mile, most buyers prefer to trade at nearby stores. Location is just as important to the industrial buyer as to the individual consumer.

2. *Reputation of seller.* Customers are attracted to sources of supply which have a reputation for fair price, high-quality merchandise, liberal policies on credit, returns or guarantee, and dependable services. The reputation of a business concern for keeping promises and treating customers fairly attracts buyers.

3. *Personality of salesmen.* The cheerfulness, courtesy, and attentiveness of sales representatives, their knowledge of the buyers' needs and how their merchandise can satisfy those needs—a spirit of helpfulness and personal service—are strong patronage motives.

4. *Appearance of store.* Good housekeeping, cleanliness, modern fixtures, good lighting, and convenient layout—all contribute to create an atmosphere of attractiveness which causes customers to patronize one store in preference to another. Progressive filling stations recognize the business-getting power of clean washrooms.

5. *Services offered.* Some customers prefer credit and delivery services, while others would rather pay cash and carry their purchases. Many buyers prefer salesmen to call at home or office; while others like to visit the showrooms of the seller and make their own selections. A liberal credit service may cause customers to favor one supplier over another.

6. *Type of merchandise sold.* The quality of merchandise, variety of styles, types, sizes, range of prices, all are factors which cause customers to favor certain sources of supply.

Salesmen should recognize these strong patronage motives and capitalize on these factors which influence customers to favor one seller rather than another.

3. What Customers Buy. Customers are primarily buying benefits rather than goods or services which make the benefits possible. In other words, the product which a salesman is selling is merely a means to an end rather than the end itself. This principle is of fundamental importance in modern salesmanship and emphasizes the benefits of ownership rather than the construction features of a product or details of a service.

A customer who is interested in an automobile is first concerned with either comfort, safety, style, economy of operation, speed, or dependability; and only with horsepower, wheelbase, color, frame construction, or spring suspension as these or other features contribute to the benefits sought by the buyer.

When a salesman ignores the interest of buyers in benefits and emphasizes product details, customers are often unable to appreciate what technical features mean in respect to the results or advantages in which they are interested.

Accordingly, salesmen must translate product qualities into terms of benefits. For example, a mattress salesman, instead of saying, "This mattress is made of sponge, foam rubber filled with thousands of tiny air cells," should emphasize benefits by saying, "Perfect sleep, comfort, and complete body relaxation is made possible by this sponge, foam-rubber mattress filled with thousands of tiny air cells."

While individual consumers in general are interested in the benefits of use, women customers are primarily concerned with appearance, style, beauty, and price. Men, on the other hand, are often more interested in durability, performance, and dependability.

Distributor, wholesale, and retail merchant customers, who buy for resale, are mainly interested in turnover and profit on the merchandise which they buy rather than in benefits of use.

Industrial customers are usually interested in the intrinsic merits of the goods which they buy and establish definite requirements or specifications describing the characteristics of materials and products wanted.

SALES INFLUENCES ON CUSTOMERS

Many selling influences in addition to the personal efforts of salesmen are continually at work stimulating customers to buy. Customers are often convinced of their needs for products and services long before they come in contact with a salesman. As a result of sales impressions received from numerous sources, many buyers are presold, making it possible for a salesman to concentrate on closing sales. By taking advantage of these presale influences, salesmen can sell more intelligently and effectively.

Advertising is of great assistance to salesmen by aiding customers in recognizing their needs for products and services; in finding means of satisfying needs; in providing information about commodities and sources of supply; and in bringing prospective buyers and salesmen together. Advertising gets the attention of buyers and arouses interest which prompts them to visit stores to see and hear about a product. Often advertising messages lie dormant in the mind of the buyer until a salesman seeks out the buyer and establishes a need for the advertised product. When a potential customer who has been exposed to advertising comes in contact with a salesman, the work of advertising ceases and that of salesmanship begins. A salesman who is familiar with the sales messages featured in his company's advertising can coordinate his personal selling with the printed salesmanship of the advertising for maximum effectiveness.

Recommendations made voluntarily by owners are an important influence on potential customers, and successful salesmen cultivate owners to secure this valuable "word-of-mouth" sales assistance.

News items, publicity articles, and illustrations in daily papers are a valuable stimulus to sales by arousing the interest of possible customers. This "unpaid advertising" is eagerly sought by progressive salesmen who cultivate newspaper editors and seek every opportunity to get their product and themselves into print.

Ownership of a product by well-known, influential persons is a substantial sales influence on prospective customers, many of whom base their own buying decisions on the purchases of others whose judgment they respect. This influence is particularly significant in respect to style and fashion merchandise.

Participation by a salesman in community, social, political, and religious affairs is an indirect but effective method of influencing possible customers who, by becoming acquainted with the salesman, are inclined to consider his product favorably.

MENTAL AND PHYSICAL DIFFERENCES OF CUSTOMERS

Attempts have been made by numerous writers on salesmanship to classify customers according to their mental or physical characteristics with respect to behavior and reaction to sales appeals. Physical characteristics of the head and face are supposed to denote the mental response of an individual according to one theorist who has selected 10 head and face shapes as revealing the character of a customer. A square face is said to be more practical than a pear-shaped one; while incurved, outcurved, and circular faces have their respective characteristics. Other theorists have defined types of personalities as mental, motive, vital, nervous, good-natured, curious, careless, phlegmatic, know-it-all, timid, cynical, and patriotic. The color of hair and eyes; the shape and size of nose and ears; all have a bearing on a customer's buying reaction in the opinion of some character analysts.

While these pseudo-scientific theories were at one time popular, they have since been disproved by psychologists and discredited as having no merit or practical value in judging the reactions of customers. There are so many variables in human behavior and persons with mixed emotional and physical characteristics that it is not possible to classify behavior this way.

It is impractical for salesmen to attempt to distinguish the slight difference or similarity in these types and to deal with them accordingly. While it is obvious that a salesman's presentation will be affected by the mental reaction of a customer, it is a waste of time to attempt to type human nature and handle a buyer accordingly.

Instead of typing customers, a salesman should deal with the mental and physical differences of customers with sincerity, courtesy, tact, and consideration.

Problem I

The Buying Process

Mr. and Mrs. James Ives, Philadelphia, Pa.

Mr. and Mrs. James Ives considered in 1948 the purchase of a new automobile. They are in their late twenties; have two children, a boy five and a girl three. The Ives have never owned an automobile but have had the use of an old car belonging to Mrs. Ives's parents. Mr. Ives is an advertising agency executive. The Ives own their home and their estimated income is $5,000 annually.

To illustrate how, what, and why customers buy and the steps of the buying process of ultimate consumers, Mr. and Mrs. Ives were interviewed regarding their plans for buying a new car. Their views were automatically recorded, and the following transcription gives verbatim their buying reactions to various features of an automobile.

Their needs for a car, search for an automobile which will best satisfy their needs, consideration of the features of available cars leading to the selection of one to meet their needs, are all revealed in the following interview.

This interview indicates how customers make the five buying decisions on need, means, source of supply, price to pay, and time to buy. The various selling influences, such as advertising and the experience of others, which have a bearing on customers' buying decisions, are revealed in this interview. The attitudes of buyers regarding price, quality, service, style, as well as their buying motives are shown in this discussion.

Both Mr. and Mrs. Ives were urged to speak frankly about buying plans, and the interviewer consciously avoided influencing their opinions or prejudicing their thinking in order that their views would reveal the actual buying process.

This "depth interview" represents the typical attitudes and responses of two average consumers. It is a valuable aid to salesmen of automobiles and specialties as it reveals the thinking of buyers and indicates those product features which are of major interest to them. The role of a salesman in giving buyers advice and information about products is apparent in this interview. There is an obvious opportunity shown here for salesmen to render professional service to customers.

INTERVIEWER: I believe that you told me that you have thought about buying a new automobile. Now, just what sort of a car are you planning to buy? Can you give me a description of this car?

MR. IVES: We have considered several types, but have not made up our minds yet; we have considered a station wagon and a convertible four-seater and a sedan.

INTERVIEWER: Those three types are in your mind?

MR. IVES: Yes, I think offhand our choice will be between the station wagon and the convertible.

INTERVIEWER: Which of those types do you prefer?

MRS. IVES: I think my choice would be the four-door sedan. I prefer that type because we have two children under five and there is always the problem of their jumping out of a convertible. We would like a station wagon, but there are only four of us and as we are living in the city, perhaps this isn't the time to get one now.

INTERVIEWER: You think the four-door would be safer for the children?

MRS. IVES: Yes I think it might be, particularly when you consider the safety factor. That's important for you don't have to keep looking in the back seat when you have the top down.

INTERVIEWER: What do you think about this four-door idea, Mr. Ives?

MR. IVES: I don't have much choice between the two. My reason for preferring the convertible is that I like to ride with the top down.

MRS. IVES: I like a convertible, but perhaps we had better consider getting a convertible a little later when we are living in the country.

INTERVIEWER: Have you a country place?

MRS. IVES: We hope to be moving to the country. My family has a country place.

INTERVIEWER: Have you ever owned any one of these three types before?

MRS. IVES: No.

INTERVIEWER: Of the four-door type, just what have you thought about, a six- or an eight-cylinder?

MR. IVES: I have thought of a six. My impression is that a six is more economical to run.

MRS. IVES: But it has less power.

INTERVIEWER: Have you thought about the color?

MRS. IVES: I would like a black one.

INTERVIEWER: Why would you prefer a black one?

MRS. IVES: I think they look nicer than colored cars, which look nice when they are new, but they are not so pretty when they get old.

INTERVIEWER: How do you feel about the black color, Mr. Ives?

MR. IVES: I prefer the black color, too, because it is a good, standard, conservative-looking car, which will wear well.

MRS. IVES: You can repaint a black car easier. With a colored car you can't retouch the fenders to match. A black car is easier to match.

INTERVIEWER: How about the interior upholstery? Have you thought about the kind of upholstery you would like?

MRS. IVES: I would like leather, but it is much more expensive.

INTERVIEWER: Have you thought about any upholstery other than leather?

MRS. IVES: I also like that rough straw stuff, which doesn't show the wear and look ratty when it wears out.

INTERVIEWER: How about accessories? Have you thought of a radio, heater, and other accessories? Would you like a clock?

MR. IVES: We have up to a certain point. I think we would both like a radio and a heater.

MRS. IVES: I wouldn't care about a radio. I don't like driving with it because it is distracting.

MR. IVES: I would prefer having a radio, but I wouldn't pay the price to get it.

INTERVIEWER: What about the heater? Is that essential?

MRS. IVES: Absolutely.

MR. IVES: Also a defroster in connection with the heater.

INTERVIEWER: Now, what about other accessories, such as a vanity mirror?

MRS. IVES: No, I am not interested in that.

INTERVIEWER: Ash trays?

MRS. IVES: Yes.

INTERVIEWER: Now, are there other features of a car which you may have heard or read about recently, such as a particular type of clutch, braking system, or wheel alignment?

MR. IVES: Well, I have always been inclined to favor the Jasper no-gearshift. That wouldn't be a major point which would make me choose one car rather than another.

INTERVIEWER: Why would you like a car with a no-gearshift?

MR. IVES: It would be more convenient.

MRS. IVES: Less trouble to drive.

MR. IVES: The only car I have ever driven is the one I use now, a 1930 Baxter which has the old-style gearshift. I like it because I feel some connection with the motor. All new cars have modern gearshifts and I don't care what kind we have. We want one that will wear well and not get out of kilter. I have seen taxicabs with wheel gearshifts that did not operate well at all.

INTERVIEWER: What about other equipment in this car? Have you thought about the trunk? Is that an important feature?

MR. IVES: Yes, it is. With children, when we go to the country, we have had trouble in the past in loading the car.

Mrs. Ives: If you are going to get a car, you should get one that will carry as much as you are going to want.

Interviewer: How would you use this car, just for city driving or do you plan long trips, or just between the city and the country?

Mr. Ives: I should say city, with some trips to the country in the summer time. Very few long trips.

Mrs. Ives: We have one reason for buying the car and that is to get our son to school. He is going to school with a car pool and it is convenient for us to have a car to arrange for his transportation.

Interviewer: You would drive him back and forth to school?

Mrs. Ives: I would drive him once a week and others would take him on other days.

Interviewer: How many passengers would normally ride in this car?

Mrs. Ives: As many as we could possibly cram in, about seven children, I guess. It's a neighborhood arrangement.

Interviewer: Have you thought about any of the technical features of the car other than the gearshift?

Mr. Ives: One thing that has impressed me very strongly is the Stacy's visibility.

Interviewer: Why do you like that feature?

Mr. Ives: Visibility seems to me to be very important. I haven't driven a Stacy, but I believe it has more visibility than any other car.

Mrs. Ives: I prefer to have a heavy car because it is safer.

Interviewer: Have you thought of any other safety features of the car?

Mrs. Ives: If I heard of any others, I'd be interested in them.

Mr. Ives: Of course, there is a point about the convertible, it is not safe if it turns over.

Interviewer: What about the safety of the brakes, lights, and steering? Would you be interested in knowing more about those features?

Mrs. Ives: I would, but I would never expect to get that information. All the companies say that they have good brakes. I wouldn't see how the consumer would be able to find out.

Interviewer: Would a technical explanation of the braking system be of interest to you?

Mrs. Ives: If I could get a comparison, I might be interested.

Interviewer: Would you like to have the features of one car compared with those of another?

Mrs. Ives: If I could get one company to tell me why their brakes are better than another company's, then I might be able to make an intelligent comparison, but I wouldn't know enough about it myself.

Interviewer: What about the lighting—the headlights? Have you any thoughts about the kind of headlights you would like?

Mr. Ives: No, except that I would like to have fog lights.

Interviewer: Have you used them?

Mrs. Ives: Yes.

Interviewer: What about the horn?

Mrs. Ives: All I care is that it be heard, that's all.

Interviewer: What about the locking of the car?

Mr. Ives: Do you mean that one kind is more advantageous than another?

Interviewer: Yes. Are you interested in the locks on your car?

Mr. Ives: Yes. I assume that they all have equally good locks.

Interviewer: You think that all the locks are alike?

Mrs. Ives: I don't think they are, but I don't know anything else about them.

Interviewer: What about the bumpers on the car?

Mr. Ives: I would like the kind that are fairly heavy and extend all the way across the front and back. I saw one car which was in an accident and the bumper was bent in and broke both headlights without breaking the bumper. It was the big bar type—all the way across.

Mrs. Ives: I would like a bumper that was designed for bumping and not for beauty primarily.

Interviewer: What about the trimming on this car? Would you like to have a lot of chromium trim or very little trim?

Mr. Ives: We would prefer very little.

Interviewer: Why?

Mrs. Ives: It looks better.

Mr. Ives: The same with me.

Interviewer: What about the body style? You are familiar with the body style in which the fenders are built into the front doors. Do you like that style?

Mr. Ives: No, I don't very much. It doesn't look particularly genuine. I think a car should have running boards. A car looks better without extreme streamlining.

Mrs. Ives: It looks like a lot of car.

Interviewer: You don't care for the fenders built into the door?

Mrs. Ives: No. I think it is an extreme style. I don't like style features in a car, I like functional design.

Interviewer: What do you mean by style features?

Mrs. Ives: Oh, things which are added to make it look modern.

Mr. Ives: To me, it's excessive streamlining.

Mrs. Ives: It's the modern touch.

Interviewer: You don't care for the ultramodern type of car?

Mrs. Ives: The type of car that looks like an airplane.

Interviewer: What about the height of the car from the ground?

Mr. Ives: No. I've never asked my wife about a low car.

Mrs. Ives: Just so long as it's easy to get in and out of, it's a good height. We don't care much about the height, I don't think. I have driven my mother's car—that's a 1930 Baxter—and that's a good height, but any modern car is pretty low to the ground.

Interviewer: You want a car that's easy to get in and out of?

Mrs. Ives: Yes, but I don't care much myself.

Interviewer: Have you thought about the headroom in this car?

MRS. IVES: It does except on cold mornings, but that's true of all cars. I'm much more interested in stopping than in pickup, except as it might be a safety factor.

INTERVIEWER: You're not interested in quick pickup then?

MRS. IVES: I don't care if somebody passes me at a stop light. That's all right. I think our old car has more power in second. It has a very steady pulling power in first, but no speed. But that's handy sometimes.

INTERVIEWER: Is the over-all speed of the car important?

MR. IVES: No. I only drive at moderate speeds, anyway.

MRS. IVES: I think a car should do about 60, that's enough. It should have speed for an emergency when you are in traffic and something happens and you have to get out of the way. Our old car has a cruising speed of about 45, but if you get going extra fast you get a bad ride. At 55 it begins to shake.

INTERVIEWER: What about noise? Do you mind a little noise?

MRS. IVES: No, I don't. I don't like to be shaken up badly. Our old springs get a little uncomfortable at times, especially when we are driving over rough roads.

INTERVIEWER: Is the comfort of the springs and the shock absorbers an important thing with you?

MR. IVES: Considering the paving of modern roads, I should say no.

MRS. IVES: I happened to read the other day about a farmer's wife complaining about cars so low to the ground so that they bump on country roads. That interested me very much. I would object to that thoroughly. We drive on dirt roads in the country, and I would dislike any car which was low slung for appearance. With water thrown up from puddles, I shouldn't think it would be good to have the mechanism way down near the road.

MR. IVES: Of course, they are all built about the same distance from the ground now. You don't have any choice.

MRS. IVES: I don't know. They used to be a lot higher and I think there must be a difference. If you went over a bump and knocked your transmission, how bad that would be!

INTERVIEWER: What do you think of the front radiator design? Do you like the modern fronts?

MR. IVES: No, I think they are very poor. They are unnecessarily massive looking and quite the opposite of attractive.

MRS. IVES: They are not in the least conservative.

INTERVIEWER: Do you know what sort of front you would like on a car?

MR. IVES: My favorite front was a 1939 Baxter. A rather narrow affair with a triangular grill and very small radiator. It seemed to flow into the lines of the rest of the car very well. But now they have a very massive square, heavy front, tapering off.

INTERVIEWER: What about the two-beam headlights? Do you use the double beam?

MRS. IVES: Yes, I like them very much. In the country at night there's no light at all, and you need your long distance lights for driving then. In the city, I think they ought to have a law about using the low beam. I think they should be emphasized as a safety factor. On the open road you can pick things up when you are traveling fast.

INTERVIEWER: Do you like the dual taillights? Lights wired to the brake?

MRS. IVES: I like them very much.

MR. IVES: Also the light which shows which way you are turning.

MRS. IVES: I think that's nice, particularly when you are traveling in a fast-moving stream of traffic. It is convenient and assuring to know that you can signal a turn.

INTERVIEWER: Has your present car brake or direction signals?

MRS. IVES: No. For awhile the brake light was off and it impeded my driving extremely. I had no way of signaling. No one could see my hand, and when I wanted to turn out of traffic, it was very dangerous. I also like a light on each side of the car so you can judge where a car is.

MR. IVES: I also like a directional light, like a spotlight on the rear. You can switch it on and see what is behind you when you are backing out. We have one on our car and as we live in a dead-end street, it is useful in getting out.

INTERVIEWER: I want to ask you about raising and lowering the windows. Do you favor the automatic raising of the windows?

MR. IVES: I prefer the crank.

MRS. IVES: We're just reactionary. No, with the crank you set them where you want them. It's a reflex action with a crank. The other is an intellectual process. You push the button and hope.

INTERVIEWER: What about windshield washers?

MR. IVES: I've seen those in operation and if they work, I'm all for them. I wonder sometimes if they don't get gummed up. They're too complicated.

MRS. IVES: They don't seem entirely necessary, but would be convenient at times. They are almost an affectation.

INTERVIEWER: Have you thought of any particular brand of car?

MR. IVES: I have thought of one, but only in a general way, the Stacy. I must admit that it's streamlined and has all the things that I have objected to so far, but the visibility is the main feature. That's mighty important. It has clear sides and a big windshield forward and a glass curve around the back so the rear vision is wide.

MRS. IVES: I like it, but there is a question whether it is in the heavy class or a lighter class of car. I don't know that I know which is which.

INTERVIEWER: Have you visited a showroom where it is for sale?

MR. IVES: No.

INTERVIEWER: Have you ever had a salesman solicit you to buy an automobile?

MR. IVES: No, I don't think so. We once went to price them. That's as close as we ever got to owning a car.

MRS. IVES: I wouldn't like a salesman to try to sell me, either.

INTERVIEWER: You would rather do your own buying?

MRS. IVES: When we get to the point of buying a car, we'll go look around and see.

INTERVIEWER: Then you would rather not have a salesman talk to you about buying a car?

MRS. IVES: I don't like some of the things they have to say, for one thing. They're too much salesmen. It's their job to come and talk and question and it's unnatural basically. That's what I find exhausting and unnecessary. I know the things that would matter to me, but a salesman would have to approach me on an entirely different basis.

MR. IVES: I think I would like to talk to an engineer about cars.

MRS. IVES: Yes, I would too. After all, a salesman is not disinterested about selling a car and you feel that he is not in a position to give you any kind of objective viewpoint. I would rather read something printed, go to a showroom and look at a car, and have somebody talk to me while I looked.

INTERVIEWER: Have you read any automobile advertising recently?

MR. IVES: Yes.

INTERVIEWER: What make did you read about?

MR. IVES: I saw an ad for a Mason the other day. I haven't noticed many ads lately. I was curious as to what advertising was being done so I looked through a copy of *Life* and a copy of the *New Yorker* and saw one ad for Mason.

INTERVIEWER: Did you notice any feature of it that interested you?

MR. IVES: The only feature was that they had very little to say. It seems to me that the whole emphasis in car advertising lately is to be rather vague, name advertising, rather than features of the car.

INTERVIEWER: You would like more information in the advertisements?

MR. IVES: Yes except advertising information is not reliable usually. I think that before the war, car advertising tended to be product advertising built around features, not necessarily facts of use to the buyer but points of product construction.

MRS. IVES: Also quality. You do not get an impression of quality from the advertising. The things they advertise are superficial features rather than fundamentals. I cannot remember reading any car advertising for a long time that really got down to fundamentals.

INTERVIEWER: No. Have you considered any particular make of car?

MR. IVES: Well, I can't say that we have considered any make exactly because we just began discussing it two or three days ago.

MRS. IVES: I have considered other makes. I like the Lark and Hastings, I think they are small, compact, low-priced cars. They are made for use. And I also like the Baxter.

MR. IVES: Of course, the present price is off. The Lark and Hastings have gone up into a higher price bracket out of the level of the others.

MRS. IVES: I would be interested in looking at a Lark or Hastings. I have always liked the looks of them, but that wouldn't make me buy them. Their advertising has appealed to me.

INTERVIEWER: What about their advertising has appealed to you?

MRS. IVES: The fact that it was aimed at a market which included a lot of people who need a car and aren't primarily concerned with style. The types of persons who appear in the ads are not upper-class, but middle-class persons. I like that. Perhaps it's the manufacturers—their personalities, probably.

INTERVIEWER: You speak of the manufacturer. Does the reputation of the maker have anything to do with your interest in Larks?

MRS. IVES: I once had an old-fashioned model and another model after that. They were cars built for use and lasted a long time. Perhaps that's the connection in my mind.

MR. IVES: I, myself, have no real identification of the maker with the car. I think of a lot of car manufacturers in Detroit and that's as far as it goes. One is as good as the other as far as I am concerned.

MRS. IVES: Some cars have been on the market so long that you feel that there cannot be an enormous difference between them. They have found their place in the market and that's that. In the earlier days there was much more difference, but no more. There is not much individuality today. The advertising doesn't tell you any difference today.

MR. IVES: I was interested in the Hartford because it was a new car, but now that I've seen the car, it looks much the same as the others. I have not been informed by the advertising or any other means how Hartford is different, if it is, and it goes back into the general limbo of car manufacturers in my mind.

INTERVIEWER: Is price a factor in the purchase of this new car?

MR. IVES: Yes, of course. Certainly it is. I don't think we would extend our choice into the upper brackets of car prices, and we wouldn't hold it into the lower either. I think a medium-priced car, whatever that is. Around the $2000 mark is going to be our upper limit.

MRS. IVES: Also, current prices are a very important factor. We are going to wait just as long as we can in the hope that they will go down. If we have to get one, we'll have to get it, but we'll put it off as long as we can.

INTERVIEWER: If you bought a car would you pay cash outright or prefer to pay installments?

MR. AND MRS. IVES: Installments.

INTERVIEWER: Have you a particular dealer in mind?

MR. AND MRS. IVES: No.

MRS. IVES: I'd look in the Classified, pick one to call, and if I liked him, all right.

MR. IVES: When we come to the point when we decide to buy a car, we aren't just going to a dealer, but we'd play the whole market. You see, we're vague on price and everything else.

MRS. IVES: We'd visit several dealers' showrooms. Also inquire among our friends. Also the personality of the dealer would have a lot to do with it as far as I am concerned. Whether I felt he was responsible or not. If he was primarily a salesman and his primary business was just selling cars, I would be a little wary.

INTERVIEWER: When do you expect you might purchase a car?

MR. IVES: We've thought within the next few months. In time for the children to go to school.

MRS. IVES: Also the possible collapse of the old car.

Questions

1. What caused Mr. and Mrs. Ives to recognize their need for a new automobile?

2. What type of car do they consider will best satisfy their need for a new automobile?

3. What features do they desire in an automobile?

4. What are their principal motives for purchasing a new automobile?

5. What is Mrs. Ives's attitude toward automobile salesmen?

6. What are their attitudes toward automobile advertising?

7. What is their viewpoint on price?

8. Have they decided on the make of car to buy?

9. How are they going to determine the dealer from whom they will buy a car?

10. What is their decision on the time to buy a new car?

11. Which of the four mental steps in the buying process: recognition, search, consideration, adoption, have been taken by the Ives?

12. Which of the five basic buying decisions have been made in this case?

13. What is their patronage motive in selecting a source of supply of an automobile?

14. What are some of the benefits the Ives expect to secure from ownership of a new automobile?

Problem II

THE BUYING PROCESS

Mr. and Mrs. Ralph S. Austin, Waltham, Mass.

Mr. and Mrs. Ralph S. Austin are typical of thousands of families who, following the Second World War, were seriously considering a new home. While they now own a home, they have recently inherited a large house and eight acres of land near the city and are going to build or remodel. Mr. Austin, a man in his late forties, is a retail merchant. They have a son in college.

To illustrate how, why, and what customers buy, and the steps of the buying process of ultimate consumers, Mr. and Mrs. Austin were interviewed regarding their buying plans for the heating equipment in their new house. Their reactions were automaticaly recorded, and their verbatim views, without deletion, are quoted in the following interview.

This interview reveals how their needs for home heating equipment have been recognized as well as their search for a means to satisfy those needs and their consideration of the available solutions leading to adoption of methods to satisfy the needs. It also shows how buyers reach the five buying decisions on need, means, source of supply, price, and time. The sales influences which have a bearing on customers' buying decisions are also graphically revealed in this interview, as well as the attitudes of buyers concerning price, quality, advertising, buying motives, and other factors entering into sales decisions.

The husband and wife in this case were urged to speak fully and frankly about their buying plans, and the interviewer consciously avoided influencing their views and guiding their thinking so that their remarks would reveal their true buying behavior.

This "depth interview" is an invaluable aid to salesmen of home equipment in planning interviews since it indicates product features of major interest to customers as well as their lack of knowledge and misconceptions regarding certain features.

INTERVIEWER: Mr. Austin, I would like to ask you a question about something you are planning to purchase in the near future. I understand that you are planning to build or remodel a new home. Will you tell me a little about this home?

MR. AUSTIN: We own a piece of property on which is a large 13-room house and eight acres of land. We have a son who is now in college but will be graduating in two and a half years when of course he will likely go away and have a home of his own.

INTERVIEWER: There would then be just two of you in the family?

MR. AUSTIN: Just my wife and I. We have wondered if we should fix up the old homestead. But perhaps we should build a little bungalow or semi-bungalow and have everything up to the minute in it, and it would make our future life just that much more easy. Of course, we haven't gone into this very far as yet, but she has her daydreams and I have mine. I saw a plan of a little semi-bungalow in a magazine sent me every month and I think it's really quite nice. In the plan is a bungalow which has on the second floor a recreation room, a small bedroom, and a storeroom. It would have furniture for this recreation room which you could use during the winter months in the recreation room, and that same furniture could be used during the summer months on the little garden porch.

INTERVIEWER: How many rooms would there be in this house?

MR. AUSTIN: There would be five rooms and a breakfast nook. There would be the livingroom, dining room, kitchen, breakfast nook, and two bedrooms, a master bedroom and a smaller bedroom. Then the garden porch as the plan calls for.

INTERVIEWER: What would be the construction?

MR. AUSTIN: The construction would be a stone front and the rest clapboards.

INTERVIEWER: What was the magazine you saw this in?

MR. AUSTIN: I think it was a magazine called *Popular Homes* which is sent to me every month advertising building materials and each month it carries plans showing remodeling of old homes and usually a plan of a new home. This was one I found back several months and it looks like a nice home that could be put up on our land.

INTERVIEWER: What company sends this magazine to you?

MR. AUSTIN: This is sent to me direct from the Waltham Coal Company. One month it is advertising their thermostats and another month it advertises U.S. Gypsum products, everything connected with building.

INTERVIEWER: You would sell your present home if you build this new home?

MR. AUSTIN: I would think so, yes.

INTERVIEWER: What does your wife think about this?

MRS. AUSTIN: Personally, I am not interested in a new home at all. I would prefer our old homestead which has been in my family for a hundred and seventy-five years. My reason for fixing it up is partly sentimental. I can see that there are great possibilities there. It is large, has 13 rooms, but my husband is very much interested in woodworking and has a number of large machines in our basement now. I enjoy painting and would like to have a little studio of my own. Where it is now, we both have to work together, and it isn't always convenient for me to paint when he has his jig saw going on the bench. I thought he could use one end of this home for his woodworking place and I could use the upstairs for my studio. I think by fixing over this old home of ours we really would be better off.

INTERVIEWER: Have you thought of any other features of remodeling the old place. Do you have plans?

MRS. AUSTIN: No, we haven't. We would have to build a new garage. My husband spoke of building a shop next to the garage, but the house is so large that I think we could use the two end rooms in which we could have light to work by. He just doesn't seem to see that, so I just say period to the old home.

INTERVIEWER: Well now, Mr. Austin, about your ideas for this new home you are planning to build: Will you tell us a little more about that?

MR. AUSTIN: I have done considerable daydreaming. My wife and I are not getting any younger, and my idea is to build a small home with the new automatic features. It would make the housekeeping so much easier for my wife. We could have a new home which could be built in a couple of years and would be so much better than this old home. I can see her reasons for wanting to live in this old homestead because it has been in her family for one hundred and seventy-five years and it has some wonderful features. The house is in good shape, and my wife's uncle, from whom we purchased the property, had kept it in good condition, but there are many features that would have to be changed.

INTERVIEWER: How soon would you want to build if you decided to build?

MR. AUSTIN: Not for a couple of years. Present building conditions aren't what they will be in a couple of years—lumber is far from what it should be, and the equipment and fixtures are scarce and what are available are not what you would prefer and are high.

INTERVIEWER: Have you talked to any builder or architect about this house?

MR. AUSTIN: I have a friend who is a teacher in the manual training department in the local schools who works for a contractor during the summer months. I have talked to him about it, and he too is interested in building a house on one of these lots. We have agreed that in a couple of years would be the opportune time to build rather than at present.

INTERVIEWER: Have you thought of any feature of this home—considered the type of heating?

MR. AUSTIN: I have thought about that and would like to look into a gas heater. My reason for thinking of gas is that all you have to do is to turn the button and there you have your gas. However I do not feel that gas or even oil is as even or substantial a heat as an automatic coal stoker, which we have in our present home. Either gas or oil will cost more money than a stoker, but the big feature is the even temperature from a stoker.

INTERVIEWER: You think the gas would be a little more convenient?

MR. AUSTIN: We would have to determine at the time we built which would be the most advisable heat to install.

INTERVIEWER: Have you considered any specific make of heater?

MR. AUSTIN: No. I think the Rockford is a good one, but then the Carson heater is a very good one too and there is the Henderson heater I understand is very efficient. Some of my friends seem to think that hot water would be the best heat, but I can't see but what steam is the best.

INTERVIEWER: Do you have steam in your present home?

MR. AUSTIN: Yes, with a Rockford heater or steam boiler.

MRS. AUSTIN: Gas is very expensive to heat a house by. I have a friend whose home is heated by gas, and they say it really is expensive.

MR. AUSTIN: I understand that it is considerably more expensive, but other than that you have heard people talk about the high and low seventies. That is something you don't have with a stoker. You can set your thermostat at a given point and your heat will remain at that point almost constantly. Where with either gas or oil it is very hard to get that even temperature.

MRS. AUSTIN: How about electricity? Are there any houses heated by electricity?

MR. AUSTIN: Not around here. Just a few days ago I was reading an article which advised the people of New England to harness up their waterways and obtain electricity at a much lower cost than it is being purchased today. I have heard it said that sometime there might be heating with electricity. But today it is very expensive.

Mrs. Austin: I know, but it is so clean.

Mr. Austin: True, we know that of course from the electric range which we have in our house. You couldn't sell my wife anything but an electric range. Isn't that right?

Mrs. Austin: You bet!

Interviewer: Is there a gas supply available where you might build?

Mr. Austin: There is gas there and electricity, of course. One feature of a gas heater is that your gas is piped into your house through pipes buried deep enough so that the frost will not affect them. With an oil burner or with a stoker you would have your electric power to consider. But we have never been bothered in our present home as far as the electric power is concerned.

Mrs. Austin: But don't you think eventually they will have the electric wires underground?

Mr. Austin: I think so, but in the central parts of the city it is now underground.

Interviewer: Have you thought of the price of a gas heater for your home?

Mr. Austin: I understand that the gas company has made arrangements so that your original cost in your new home is very little more than oil or stoker. To remodel a home or put gas into a present hand-fired boiler, would cost you considerable money. The gas company, I understand, insists that a house be insulated, weather-stripped, and storm windows put on. But, of course, if I were to build, I would have my little bungalow weather-stripped and insulated right up to the minute, whether I put in gas, oil, or a stoker.

Interviewer: Now, as to the matter of cost of original gas equipment as against oil or a stoker, that isn't an important consideration in your mind?

Mr. Austin: The way I figure it, building a new house with insulation would mean that the installation of the heating equipment would be much the same regardless of what is put in. I happen to know enough about that to know that gas, oil, and a good stoker would cost about the same price.

Interviewer: How about the operating cost? Would the gas furnace cost more to operate?

Mr. Austin: There is no question but that gas would cost considerably more than oil and oil will cost quite a little more than an automatic stoker. To be sure, we would have the ashes to contend with with an automatic stoker, but after all we've got to have a little exercise. So, I favor an automatic stoker because of the even temperature which is not available by the other two types of heat.

Interviewer: What do you think about that, Mrs. Austin? Do you think the automatic stoker would be better than the gas?

Mrs. Austin: Personally, I'd rather have a stoker than gas or oil. I can't say that I have been in many houses heated by gas, but I have been in houses heated by oil and I will say I don't think they are as comfortable as those heated by a stoker.

INTERVIEWER: What do you mean by comfortable?

MRS. AUSTIN: Even heat. When the system goes off with oil, the house cools right down. Whereas with a stoker there is always a fire going and the heat is more even.

INTERVIEWER: Do you know what a gas heater would cost?

MR. AUSTIN: In my line of work, I happen to know something about that. The cost of a gas installation might be just a little bit more and the oil, perhaps, would be a little higher than an automatic stoker with a complete bin-feed connection and all the automatic features. My wife says she seems to favor the stoker. Therefore, I would agree with her. Up to this point the stoker would be almost a choice.

INTERVIEWER: But you are open-minded on the subject?

MR. AUSTIN: Oh, yes, indeed. When we come to build a house, we would have to study it thoroughly at that time.

INTERVIEWER: Has anyone approached you explaining a gas heater?

MR. AUSTIN: No, not directly. I have heard of other friends of mine who have talked with gas men and they have a wonderful story excepting that point of even temperature throughout the house.

INTERVIEWER: Do you know someone who now has a gas heater in his home?

MR. AUSTIN: Yes, we know several people.

INTERVIEWER: What has been their experience? Do they like them?

MR. AUSTIN: As far as the work entailed, yes. As far as the heat is concerned, not so satisfactory. And I have had one or two people complain that the atmosphere is not so substantial and they do feel that the gas heater is apt to eat up a little of the oxygen. Whether that is in their minds, I do not know. But, I believe a complete gas installation could be so installed that it would not affect the oxygen in a home any more than oil or a stoker.

INTERVIEWER: You would not be concerned about the safety of it?

MRS. AUSTIN: I would.

MR. AUSTIN: I hadn't thought of that as far as gas is concerned. I have as far as oil is concerned. I am a firm believer that these accidents we hear about with oil burners are caused from carelessness definitely. In a stoker there is no danger. The only thing that can happen is that the fire would go out and your house would become cold. Of course, with an oil burner, I have heard of explosions and fires, but I haven't heard of a gas explosion. Possibly, such could happen.

INTERVIEWER: Are you concerned by the safety of a gas heater?

MRS. AUSTIN: Yes, I am. I don't think I would really care for gas at all. I have a friend who has gas and she says she never even thinks of danger, but she says that when the monthly bills come in, they begin to think about it, it is so expensive.

INTERVIEWER: Have you thought of any particular make of gas furnace?

MR. AUSTIN: No, I haven't. I know there are several good furnaces. The

Rockford Company makes, I think, a very good furnace. The Henderson and Carson are good and I suppose these come in both the gas-fired and the oil-burner units, as well as the stoker unit.

INTERVIEWER: It is really not important to you which make right now?

MR. AUSTIN: Not at present.

INTERVIEWER: If you decided definitely to buy a heater, you would look pretty definitely into the manufacturer?

MR. AUSTIN: Yes, I would want to study the features of these three makes and possibly more.

INTERVIEWER: Have you read any advertising recently about these makes?

MR. AUSTIN: No, I haven't.

INTERVIEWER: Have you thought of mechanical service in connection with this heater?

MR. AUSTIN That's another thing that enters into it. With a gas burner, if anything happens to it, you are definitely out of commission. It is practically the same with an oil burner, although I believe that oil service is more obtainable than gas service. With a stoker—I say this because we have one in our present home—if anything happens, if the electricity was shut off, we could fire for a little while without any change at all. We could keep the house warm, at least above freezing, so that the pipes would not freeze. And if it looked like the power would be off for a matter of days, we could arrange it in just about ten minutes so that we could hand-fire. This could not be done with either gas or oil.

INTERVIEWER: Are you acquainted with the technical features of a gas boiler?

MR. AUSTIN: No, I haven't gone into that as yet, because I didn't feel we would be building for a couple of years.

INTERVIEWER: If you did decide to build, would you rely upon the recommendation of your builder or architect?

MR. AUSTIN: Not entirely. I'd ask him to give me at least three users that I could go to and ask them their experiences. We know several people that have gas. We would go to them and ask them definitely what they would do if they were to build again.

INTERVIEWER: Is there any other piece of equipment that you would be particularly interested in in the event you build this new home?

MR. AUSTIN: We would want the kitchen fixed up to the last degree.

INTERVIEWER: What is your idea of the kitchen in this new home?

MR. AUSTIN: I think that my wife's idea is completely an electric kitchen.

INTERVIEWER: Mrs. Austin, will you tell us what you have in mind for this kitchen?

MRS. AUSTIN: I would like a kitchen just as I have in my own home today, which is all electric. I am very much pleased with it. I have had my electric stove for 15 years and it never yet has failed me in any way.

INTERVIEWER: What do you like about that stove?

MRS. AUSTIN: It's so easy to keep clean and it bakes so nicely. Many people think that things don't cook as quickly, but when you have these calrod heating units in as I have, you will find that things will cook just as quickly as on any other type of stove.

INTERVIEWER: Would you want that same make of stove in your new home?

MRS. AUSTIN: Definitely. Yes, I would like the same stove I now have.

INTERVIEWER: What make is that?

MRS. AUSTIN: It's a Brookings model and I've had it for 15 years and it never has failed me. I broke the handle on my oven and had the man out to put on a new one and I said something about the new stoves, and he said, "Madam you shouldn't say that. You ought to think you are lucky to have this stove. Many people would give anything for it because your oven is up high, and in the newer models the ovens are down low and the housewives say that they would rather have them up high so that they won't have to stoop down to look into the oven."

INTERVIEWER: What other good things do you like about that range?

MRS. AUSTIN: It has a warming oven which I use often. It has a utility drawer and cooker that I like very much. I make all of my stews and fruits that call for slow cooking in that well. There's just one thing I don't like and that is I wish it had four burners. When one is having company, they really need more than just three.

Questions

1. How did Mr. Austin get his idea for a new home?

2. What needs does Mrs. Austin recognize in remodeling her old home? What created those needs?

3. What is Mr. Austin's primary motive for building a new home?

4. What is Mrs. Austin's primary motive for remodeling her old home?

5. What is their time decision on building a new home?

6. What means have they considered to satisfy their need for heat?

7. How are they going about reaching a decision on the method of heating?

8. What are their buying motives on home heating?

9. Which of the five buying decisions would a salesman of coal stokers have to secure to sell the Austins?

10. Has Mrs. Austin recognized her need for a kitchen stove for her new home?

11. What are Mrs. Austin's buying motives for a kitchen stove?

12. Do Mr. and Mrs. Austin qualify as prospective customers for home heating equipment? On what factors?

Reading References

CHARLES H. FERNALD, "Salesmanship," Chap. VI, Prentice Hall, Inc., New York, 1945.

HAROLD M. HAAS, "A Short Course in Salesmanship," Lesson III, Prentice-Hall, Inc., New York, 1939.

PAUL W. IVEY, "Successful Salesmanship," Section 10–12, Prentice-Hall, Inc., New York, 1947.

DONALD A. LAIRD, "What Makes People Buy?" McGraw-Hill Book Company, Inc., New York, 1935.

BERNARD LESTER, "Sales Engineering," pp. 56–71, John Wiley & Sons, Inc., New York, 1940.

DAVID R. OSBORNE, "Salesmanship for Today for Salesmanagers of Tomorrow," Chap. V, Harper & Brothers, New York, 1939.

CHARLES B. ROTH, "Secrets of Closing Sales," Chaps. V–VI, Prentice-Hall, Inc., New York, 1947.

F. A. RUSSELL and F. H. BEACH, "Textbook of Salesmanship," Chap. VI, McGraw-Hill Book Company, Inc., New York, 1949.

DONALD K. SMITH, "Essentials of Selling," Chap. III, Prentice-Hall, Inc., New York, 1945.

EUGENE WHITMORE, "Helping People Buy," pp. 35–53, The Dartnell Corporation, Chicago, 1940.

CHAPTER V

PRESENTING THE COMPANY

In the process of making a sale, the reputation of the selling company is often a significant factor. Impressed by names which have become "buy-words" through the expenditure of millions of advertising dollars, customers are yielding to the magic of company prestige. Unconcerned with "reasons why" or unable to judge the intrinsic merits of a product or a service, buyers are accepting the good name of a seller as ample guarantee of future satisfaction. With price, quality, and construction of many products almost identical, the deciding factor in many sales transactions is the reputation of the seller to give satisfactory service. The expansion of delivery, maintenance, supply, repair, installation, distribution, and other services by sellers has shifted the emphasis in many cases from the intrinsic merit of the product to the ability of the selling company to provide these accommodations.

A recent survey of buyers' motives confirmed the importance of company prestige by showing that the qualities of a product entered into a sales transaction to the extent of only 15 per cent; 85 per cent of the motives that induce purchasing are the standing of the seller, good will for the company, reputation for service, and similar factors.

The sales importance of company reputation and policies varies with the type of product sold. In a sale to individual consumers, of necessities and unbranded staples of small unit sale price such as pins, cloth, and writing paper, the standing of the selling company is of little importance. However, in the sale of luxuries and specialty products, the reputation and policy of the seller are of real concern to buyers. In purchasing mechanical specialties, the reputation of the selling company for giving satisfactory mechanical service is of primary significance to the purchaser.

Intangible services are sold largely upon the reputation of the selling company for delivering the service promised. Such intangibles as insurance, investments, and advertising are sold largely through the confidence of the buyer in the offering company, its personnel and policies.

The significance of the standing of a selling company in a transaction varies also with the type of purchaser. Industrial buyers of technical goods as well as of large quantities of raw materials and supplies are vitally concerned with the resources, policies, and facilities of their principal suppliers. Individual consumers, on the other hand, are little concerned with company reputation except in the purchase of large units of sales price items.

Wholesale and retail distributors who purchase specialties from manufacturers for resale are much interested in the size, location, resources, personnel, and policies of companies whose products they distribute. Exclusive distributors of large sale price commodities are especially concerned with the responsibility of the manufacturers whom they represent.

The reputation of a company has become such an important factor in selling that many firms have established a definite book value representing the good will of their customers. The company name and prestige of a large tobacco-products concern is valued at fifty-four million dollars. A large automobile manufacturer estimates its name is worth fifty-one million dollars; another motor-car producer values its company reputation at twenty-five million dollars. These values do not represent the tangible assets of these companies, their plants, and physical equipment, but merely the worth of their corporate names. These values have been created by the confidence of buyers in the principles and policies of these organizations.

IMPORTANCE OF COMPANY KNOWLEDGE TO SALESMAN

Not only are the resources, policies, and reputation of a selling company important considerations to many buyers, but a knowledge of these company values is of equal concern to the morale and loyalty of the salesmen who represent it. The loyalty, faith, and enthusiasm of a salesman have their inception in a thorough knowledge of his company's history, policies, resources, and personnel. Until a salesman knows that his company is headed by the type of men he can trust and respect and that its success is founded on sound policies, he cannot successfully sell his house to a prospect.

The confidence of a salesman in his house comes through his knowledge that the founders of the business adhered to principles of right dealing, quality materials, fair prices, and equitable distributing policies during good times and bad for many years.

The interest of a salesman is aroused by his acquaintance with the history and personnel of his organization. His enthusiasm is stimulated by the knowledge that the business had a small beginning, experienced early failures, and finally won success. Such knowledge creates in him an intangible regard for his firm and a respect for its founders.

A salesman's familiarity with his company's progress and personnel also creates an emotional bond between the man and his organization and gives him a feeling of belonging to his firm which manifests itself in his enthusiasm and dealings with prospects and customers.

Knowledge of company organization also shows him his opportunities for advancement, reveals his relation to other personnel in the company, and creates confidence in the scope of the business.

WHAT A SALESMAN SHOULD KNOW ABOUT HIS COMPANY

Analysis of the sales training programs of America's leading sales organizations shows that these progressive companies expect their salesmen to be informed about the following features of the company: (1) history of the company and industry; (2) executive personnel; (3) personnel and labor relations; (4) plants and branches; (5) financial status; (6) management policies; (7) distributing methods; (8) organization; (9) research and inventions; (10) competitive position; (11) sales volume and prices; (12) office routines; (13) social responsibilities; (14) company services.

1. History of the Company and Industry. The history of every successful business is replete with numerous interesting incidents of the courage, initiative, and resourcefulness of the founders, which serve as excellent illustrative material in sales presentations and at the same time stimulate the morale and heighten the pride of salesmen in an organization.

Salesmen should be informed about the following features:

1. When, why, and how company was established.
2. The conditions under which the business was started, financial, territorial, trade, etc.
3. The founder and his principles.
4. Location and size of original plant.
5. Products originally made and type of trade served.
6. The difficulties encountered in establishing the business.
7. Methods of distribution first employed.
8. Labor relations.
9. Advertising and publicity campaigns.
10. Mergers and expansions.
11. Sales policies.
12. Growth and development of the business.

13. Changes in nature of business.
14. Addition of new lines and brands.
15. Changes in territories and markets covered.
16. Interesting incidents in early history.
17. Start and development of foreign trade.
18. Plant expansions.
19. Changes in official personnel.

Company history may be compiled by executives long associated with the organization, the advertising department, or professional writers and published in sales manuals or formal histories.

Incidents from the history of a company illustrate the principles of the founders which make it distinctive. An example of such an incident, from the history of the Studebaker Corporation, shows how a historical anecdote may be used to convince prospects and inspire salesmen of the soundness of company policies.

John M. Studebaker, one of the founders and for many years head of the Studebaker organization, would never read any of the thousands of letters of praise that came from the owners of Studebaker wagons and fine carriages and, later, automobiles made by the company. He instructed that they be courteously acknowledged by an assistant. On the other hand, he insisted that every letter of complaint be brought to his personal attention. The reason that he gave was that letters of congratulation were likely to make him too well satisfied with the product as it was made, and he knew that such an attitude would be fatal.

In addition to a knowledge of the history of his company, a salesman should know about the industry of which his organization is a part. The number and types of establishments, their size, sales volume, trend of consumption, the industry's scientific progress and achievements, price structure, and employee relations are facts which should be known to every salesman. This knowledge will not only give a salesman a greater appreciation of his industry but enable him to discuss his business more intelligently with buyers.

2. Executive Personnel. A hundred years ago, the head of a business was personally acquainted with all his trade and employees. The customers of the village shoemaker had respect for the man and regard for his products because they knew him intimately. However, with the expansion of business organizations, the personal relationships between seller and buyer and employer and worker, in many cases, have disappeared. In a few companies the personalities of the executive heads have not been submerged.

Henry Ford II personalizes the Ford Motor Company. Harvey S. Firestone, Jr., personalizes the Firestone Tire and Rubber Company. The reputation of Henry Kaiser creates sales of Kaiser-Frazer automobiles.

Buyers prefer to deal with individuals rather than inanimate corporations. Salesmen can individualize their organizations by interesting prospects and customers in the personalities of major executives and in this way can revive the spirit of loyalty and good will which once characterized the personal relationships between buyers and sellers.

The loyalty of salesmen may also be enhanced by acquainting them with the accomplishments of company executives. Salesmen should have the following information about them, including directors, administrative staff, field officers, and department heads:

1. Age.
2. Place of birth.
3. Education.
4. Other business connections.
5. Interests and hobbies.
6. Official position in company.
7. Progress in company, positions held.
8. Memberships in organizations.
9. Honors received.
10. Club memberships.
11. Family history.

Anecdotes about the founder or head of a business illustrate the character of the executive personnel and serve as an inspiration to salesmen and customers. An example, from the history of the George E. Keith Company, shoe manufacturers, recounts the early experience of the founder as follows:

George E. Keith, at the age of ten, began making shoes with his father in a little back room in his home. He worked at the bench until twenty-one years of age, when, having saved about $1,000, he established a business of his own, giving employment to 10 people. From this humble beginning has grown the present plant which now employs 7,000 people and manufactures more than 20,000 pairs of shoes daily.

3. Personnel and Labor Relations. The number of employees in all departments of a business and the increase in personnel during the time the company has been in existence are facts that should be known and used by salesmen as evidence of the scope and expansion of their organization.

The number of veteran employees with a company testify to the stability of the firm and fairness of its labor policies. Many companies have 25-year clubs, composed of employees who have been with the company a quarter century or more. One shoe manufacturer has 164 employees in this class, two of whom have been with the company 50 years, one for 47 years, and 21 for 40 to 45 years.

If employees are well paid, steady, and efficient, the quality of the products which they make will reflect the company's fair treatment of the workers. Profit-sharing plans, group life insurance, home-ownership plans, pension and retirement programs, relief and loan associations, and educational activities, all for the purpose of improving the welfare of employees, are excellent sales material. The facts about such programs should be known and used by salesmen.

The labor relations of a company give evidence of the soundness of its policies and the attitude of workers affects the quality of the product very materially. A fair rate of pay, regular employment, and freedom from strikes, all contribute to sound employee relations, which mean a better product, better service for customers, and substantial selling facts for salesmen.

4. Plants and Branches. The size, number, and location of the plants and branches of a company reveal not only producing and distributing resources, but also the ability to give prompt service and fair prices to customers.

Plant and branch location has a definite bearing on prices as affected by transportation charges on incoming raw materials and outgoing finished products. The factory located near the hub rather than on the rim of the market is in a position to enjoy low delivery costs— a strong sales argument. The factory located near the source of its raw materials has a cost advantage which may be reflected in lower prices. Location also gives an advantage in the rapid handling of shipments by rail, water, or truck.

An abundant supply of skilled labor is often dependent on plant location. A shoe plant located in eastern Massachusetts may make a high-quality product by employing workers whose families have made high-grade shoes for several generations. Salesmen who sell goods produced in areas where skilled labor is available have strong quality sales points.

A large food-products concern, whose plant is located in the country, has found sales advantages in manufacturing where clean air and sunshine furnish ideal sanitary conditions, where operating expenses are reduced, and where employees are freed from the difficulties of commuting to the city.

Salesmen should be familiar with plant capacities which are indicative of company size and ability to satisfy unusual demands. The total square feet of floor space occupied, the number of buildings, acreage covered, number of machines, shipping facilities, all create a favorable impression on salesmen and prove to prospects the seller's capacity to serve.

5. Financial Status. Buyers of large sale price commodities and intangible services, such as life insurance and investments, are interested in the financial responsibility of companies from which they purchase. They are concerned that a supplier may suffer financial reverses, go out of business, and fail to make deliveries to customers according to contract. Distributors and consumers may be left with an orphan product for which there is no demand, parts, or service. Salesmen must be acquainted with their company's financial condition to enable them to prove its permanence and financial soundness.

Salesmen should be informed about the following features of company finance:

1. Present capital structure.
2. Regular dividend rate.
3. Extra dividends.
4. Comparative sales, earnings, and taxes for several years.
5. Earnings per share of present stock.
6. Number of stockholders.
7. Total assets and liabilities.
8. Increase in assets by years.
9. Reserves.

6. Management Policies. The management policies of a company are definite rules which have been adopted to guide it in its dealings with employees, suppliers, distributors, and consumers. Since some of these policies are involved in every sales transaction, it is imperative that salesmen be thoroughly familiar with all of them and know how to use them to support claims, answer objections, and secure orders. Sales policies are usually found printed in policy books or manuals for the information of salesmen and executives.

The basic company policies that should be completely understood by salesmen include the following:

1. Profits.
2. Prices and terms of sale.
3. Claims and adjustments.
4. Quality of product.
5. Credits and collections.
6. Exclusive sale.
7. Method of distribution.
8. Competition.
9. Mechanical service.
10. Advertising and promotion.
11. Personnel relations.
12. Guarantee.
13. Export.
14. Brand.

An illustration of how a basic profit policy may serve as a strong sales argument is found in the case of a well-known automobile manufacturing company which for many years has had a policy of limiting its own profits in order to give greater value to the buyers of its cars. This company maintains that it has not taken more than 10.6 per cent profit from the customer's dollar while few competitors have taken less than 15 per cent. This policy is used effectively by the salesmen of this company in selling its product.

Not only is it necessary for salesmen to know company policies, but these policies must be explained to salesmen so that they will understand their merits and realize why they are superior to the policies of competitors.

7. Distributing Methods. The distribution policy of one manufacturer of household appliances is to sell exclusively direct to consumers. All competitors distribute through wholesalers and retailers. The company explains its policy of direct selling to its salesmen so that they may defend it in discussions with prospects and customers as follows:

We sell direct: (1) because there are so many items in our line which have a wide variety of uses that they require personal salesmanship and demonstration in the home; (2) because our line has proved of sufficient importance to warrant our training men to become expert in demonstrating in the home; (3) because direct selling permits an actual demonstration in the home and helps the customer to appreciate the value of the product; (4) because the past experience of the company is evidence that the public values our selling direct.

8. Organization. Business organization is necessary to ensure proper supervision, to allocate responsibility, and to prevent duplication or repetition of duties. So that salesmen may know their relationship to other members of their company organization, it is important that they be provided with company organization charts upon which are drawn the relative positions of major executives, staff officers, executive assistants, field and branch managers, supervisors, and salesmen. Detailed descriptions of the duties of each of the executives shown on the charts will clarify their functions in the organization.

Such charts also serve as an incentive to salesmen by revealing the opportunities for advancement in the company. Furthermore, salesmen are given greater confidence in their organization through a better knowledge of its scope and relationships.

A typical description of company organization published for the information of salesmen by a well-known international manufacturer of business machines is the following:

There are five principal divisions of the corporation, namely, research and service, engineering, manufacturing, financial and recording and distribution. The head of each of these divisions reports to the president and general manager.

In the research and service division are included the research department, patent department, the mechanical service departments and the department of tests, all reporting to the manager of the research and service division. The research department carries on research as to the needs of our customers and the uses of our equipment. It is constantly developing new equipment. The patent department obtains patents on all new machines and improvements. The company has been granted hundreds of patents throughout the world. The mechanical service departments supervise the servicing of machines in the offices of our customers. A corps of trained men is kept in the field to make sure that every machine sold performs satisfactorily. The department of tests is responsible for testing new products developed by the engineering division as well as all raw materials used in manufacturing.

The engineering division designs, develops, perfects and prepares for manufacturing new products and improves existing products.

The manufacturing division is responsible for manufacturing in factories in the United States, Canada, England and France.

The financial division handles the money for commissions, payrolls, salaries, expenses and purchases; and the recording division maintains the records, compiles operating reports and statements.

The distribution division markets products through an overseas division and a domestic division and the sales managements of the respective divisions direct the work of the sales agents. The advertising department is reponsible for carrying out advertising plans. The order department handles all orders from customers, foreign subsidiaries, foreign dealers and agencies. The duplicating department produces and distributes all forms and sales promotion material.

9. Research and Inventions. Research and product development are two of the most significant features of the work of progressive industrial companies today. Improved products, greater variety of uses, lower costs are all of interest to buyers and originate in company laboratories.

Every salesman should know and use the facts of his company's research and new product developments. Prospects and customers should be told the amount of the company's annual investment in research, number of research personnel, value of equipment used in experiments, experience of the technical staff, organization for product improvement, and other details of its research equipment as well as accomplishments.

The following description of the activities of a well-known manufacturer of floor coverings illustrates the facts that salesmen should know about company research activities:

A very important department in the business is called the "Planning and Developing Department." This department has two main divisions, the first of which deals with research engineering, that is, the development of entirely new types of plant machinery; and the second deals with various classes of typical research work, such as laboratory, market, and product research. The personnel of this department comprises men of inventive and investigative turn of mind. The Laboratory Research Division of the Planning and Development Department is constantly endeavoring to better existing formulas or to create entirely new ones. The production and engineering departments are also on the lookout, first, for better machinery and, secondly, for better methods of operating and controlling what we already have.

In its instructions to salesmen, a large motor-car manufacturer says,

Our engineers have in the past pioneered a great many of the improvements which are accepted as standard in most cars today. Yet during the past few years the amount spent annually for research and engineering has been trebled. Besides this, millions have been spent on engineering and research buildings, laboratories, equipment and a million-dollar proving ground.

Aside from the value of this information in closing sales, no more stimulating facts can be cited to improve the morale of the salesmen of this company and give them confidence in the product.

10. Competitive Position. To meet competition effectively, a salesman should know the competitive position of his company or its relation to other companies making similar products or rendering comparable services in the same industry.

Salesmen should be informed about the following features of competing companies:

1. Sales volume.
2. Basic sales policies.
3. Financial stability.
4. Management.

5. Methods of distribution.
6. Plants and branches.
7. Products.
8. Research and inventions.
9. Labor relations.

A knowledge of the products and policies of competing companies enables salesmen, when called upon, to answer questions about competition and make comparisons. Salesmen also acquire confidence through the recognition of their competitive advantages.

11. Sales Volume and Prices. The volume of company sales, in total and by various items over a period of several years, should be known to a salesman and discussed as evidence of company progress and product popularity. Sales volume should be expressed in dollars and cents as well as by units of sale, such as pounds, cases, or gallons.

Salesmen should be familiar with the comparative prices received for various company products over a period of years. Should these reveal that customers are getting more goods or service at lower costs, salesmen would have a significant selling argument. For example, the General Electric Company in 1921 made Mazda electric lamps which cost consumers 45 cents each. Today, a lamp of the same rating costs but 13 cents, and consumers receive 80 per cent more light for their lighting dollar than in 1921. This specific instance is excellent sales ammunition to prove the fairness of prices and the contribution of company research toward lower costs.

The increasing number of customers served by a company over a period of years is evidence of its satisfactory service. This information may be used effectively by salesmen in interviewing prospects and customers.

12. Office Routines. Salesmen should be familiar with the office routines of their company, particularly those involving the handling of an order, the invoicing system, the accounting procedure, the claim and adjustment routine, etc. Through a knowledge of these systems, they can cooperate in facilitating the clearing of office work and improving service to customers.

An example of the information that should be given to salesmen is the following procedure set up by a builders' hardware company for handling special orders:

1. Credit department approves.
2. Sales or contract department checks prices.
3. Order department, component parts inserted, order written up.

4. Stock and material purchase department.
5. Order department writes factory orders.
6. Orders cross-indexed in order department.
7. Procedure of order in factory.
8. Shipment of order.
9. Scheduling of orders.

13. Social Responsibilities. The growing social responsibility of industry in recent years has led many companies to justify to prospects and customers their existence from the standpoint of their contribution to public welfare. Salesmen should know and discuss the contribution of their company to the relief of unemployment, through increase in the number of employees over a period of years. Company aid to greater purchasing power may be expressed in steadily growing payrolls and increases in the individual earnings of employees.

Work provided by the company to employees in other industries, which supply the company with materials for manufacture, may be computed. It is estimated that every automobile sold creates from 600 to 2,000 hours of work; an electric refrigerator creates 300 hours of employment; a radio, 20 hours of labor.

A food-products manufacturer estimates that its 3,664 employees provide security for a total of 14,656 persons, a small but distinct contribution to the welfare of the country.

Salesmen should be informed of the facts regarding the contributions of business to social welfare so that they can defend their organizations, and industry as a whole, against the attacks of opponents of the capitalist system.

14. Company Services. A salesman should know the various services which his company provides customers. Intensified competition has caused many concerns to increase the number and variety of their services to secure and retain customers. Particularly when the quality and price of competing products is identical, service is the principal consideration of buyers. Information about company services may be used effectively in sales presentations.

The size and nature of a business affects the number and variety of its services to customers. A manufacturing concern performs many services foreign to a wholesaler or retailer; while a service business, such as a laundry which does not produce or distribute merchandise, provides widely different services.

Sales representatives of manufacturing concerns should be familiar with those of the following services which may be offered to customers by their companies:

I. *Manufacturing Services.*
    1. Engineering.
    2. Customer research.
    3. Mechanical service and parts.
    4. Assembly, packing, grading, and dividing.
II. *Financial Services.*
    1. Credit.
    2. Accounting.
    3. Recording.
III. *Distributing Services.*
    1. Advertising.
    2. Delivery and storage.
    3. Market information.
    4. Technical advice.
    5. Resale service.
    6. Adjustment.

Retail salespeople should be informed about the following customer services offered by their stores including:

I. *Financial Services.*
    1. Credit plans.
    2. Open account.
    3. Budget.
    4. Installment.
II. *Delivery Services.*
    1. Area served.
    2. Frequency, cost, type of goods delivered.
III. *Adjustment and Return Service.*
IV. *Special Services.*
    1. Rest and writing rooms.
    2. Children's playrooms.
    3. Fashion shows.
    4. Ticket bureau.
    5. Advice on interior decorating.
    6. Gift wrapping.
    7. Garage and parking.
    8. Checking.
    9. Alteration.
    10. Shopping.

SOURCES OF COMPANY KNOWLEDGE

Salesmen may obtain information about the 14 important company policies and activities just described, through conversations with company officials, by reading sales manuals, and through contacts with old employees. In some cases, this information is collected by progressive companies and made available currently to salesmen. However, salesmen are often obliged to gather company facts through their own initiative.

USING COMPANY KNOWLEDGE

Most beginner salesmen and students of salesmanship assume that knowledge of a company, its policies and its product, is sufficient to achieve success in selling. However, knowledge alone is but a part of the equipment of a good salesmen. *Skill* in using knowledge—the ability to apply company information—is the foundation of an individual's success in selling. Many mediocre salesmen possess much knowledge about their companies; their weakness lies in their inability to use it effectively.

Success in selling depends largely on the exercise of skill and may be compared to success in playing golf, tennis, or similar games. A golf enthusiast may read many books and have much information about the technique of a sound golf stroke, but he has not learned to play until he has taken a club in his hands and put his knowledge into practice.

Skill in selling cannot be learned from books, by listening to lectures, taking part in discussions, or even by watching a good salesman in action; the first step in acquiring this skill is to practice the methods used by successful salesmen in using their company knowledge.

The simplest, most practicable method of using company knowledge is by means of *routines* based on the practices of successful salesmen. Webster defines "routine" as "regular procedure adhered to through habit." When a need arises in a sales interview for using company knowledge, a good salesman has a habitual manner of presenting facts about his company. After acquiring an effective habit of using company information, a good salesman develops that habit by practice until he is proficient.

Outstanding salesmen habitually use their knowledge of company history, personnel, plants, finances, policies, distributing methods, research, organization, in the five following ways, which taken together form a routine for presenting the company.

In some sales interviews it may not be desirable to use any company facts. In other cases, one or two routine steps for presenting company information may be employed, while all five steps may be used as the need arises.

Routine for Presenting the Company

1. Discuss company facts in relation to the needs and motives of the buyer.
2. Use company facts to support specific claims.
3. Use company facts to answer objections.
4. Use company facts to arouse general interest of prospects.
5. Use company facts to meet competition.

1. Discuss Company Facts in Relation to the Needs and Motives of the Buyer. Company facts and history in themselves mean little to buyers. They must be related to the needs, wants, or motives of purchasers. If company information is interpreted or explained by a salesman in terms of a prospect's desire for safety, style, comfort, or profit, dull facts then become effective sales arguments.

In order that company information may be readily related to the specific motives of a prospect, a salesman should prepare in advance of interviews by collecting and grouping company facts under the headings of the common motives for his product or service. For example, the principal motives or desires that induce people to buy automobiles are comfort, performance, reputation, style, safety, economy, and service. Some buyers may be interested in style, others in economy, still others in performance. A salesman should discover the motives or needs of his prospect and discuss such company information as applies to those needs.

Selecting two of the above motives, style and safety, as examples, an automobile salesman may collect under these headings such typical facts relating to each motive as follows:

Automobile Buyer's Motives:
Style, Beauty, Smartness

Company Facts Relating to
Style Motive

Company has new department known as Designing Section manned by experienced artists and craftsmen. It designs, not only bodies, but interior trimmings, upholstery, fittings, panels, etc.

Company conducts surveys of motorists to determine preferences on style features.

Company makes annual investment of a half-million dollars in styling.

Fifty clay models made annually by company for use in selecting styles for new models.

Automobile Buyer's Motive: *Company Facts Relating to*
      Safety   *Safety Motive*

Mr. A., world-famous designer who has created streamline trains and ocean liners, heads the company's Designing Section.

A special group of company research engineers devote their efforts exclusively to the safety problem.

The company makes exhaustive tests for safety at a million-dollar proving ground.

The company made the first all-steel body. It was first to use safety glass.

The company cooperates with the national highway safety movement and has been active in promoting highway safety through the sponsorship of safe driving organizations.

Company facts should be organized under the various buying motives as just illustrated. A salesman should memorize or become familiar with company facts related to each motive so that he can use them automatically.

A salesman should seek to discover the prospect's needs or motives by tactful questioning, by observation during the interview, or by securing permission to make a detailed analysis of the prospect's situation.

2. Use Company Facts to Support Specific Claims. In supporting a claim for fair price, good quality, demand, service, performance, etc., a salesman may use pertinent details of his company's history, organization, and policies.

In preparation for interviews the principal advantages of a product or service, from the standpoint of a purchaser, should be listed with company facts supporting each of these advantages. For example, salesmen selling a popular make of fountain pen to dealers find that one of their chief selling points is the strong consumer demand for this pen. Accordingly, company facts are collected to support the claim of strong consumer demand, as follows:

1. Increasing sales volume of company over period of years by units and dollars.

2. Number of company pens in use.

3. Extent of distribution, number, and increase in distributors.

4. National advertising policy.
5. Company in business quarter of a century.
6. Competitive position; sales compared with competitors.

Another example of relating company facts to product qualities will illustrate how this should be done. An automobile-tire manufacturer claims a superior quality product. The following company facts support the salesman's argument for quality:

1. For past twenty-five years company has sold more tires than any other manufacturer.
2. Company is world's largest tire maker.
3. Company owns and operates its own rubber and cotton plantations.
4. Company operates eight complete tire factories.
5. Company guarantee and adjustment policy.
6. List of satisfied customers.

3. Answer Objections with Company Facts. As company facts may be organized and used effectively to support claims, they may be employed equally well in meeting objections of prospects. The principal objections met by the salesmen should be listed and company information collected to serve as an answer to each.

Salesmen of a shoe manufacturer, for example, meet the following objections from shoe retailer prospects: "Why should I disturb my present line, I'm satisfied with the company supplying me." Company facts may be marshaled to meet such an objection, as follows:

1. The size of the company, a daily capacity of 20,000 pairs, insures a low overhead and lowest prices.
2. The buying power of the company, over two million skins and a million yards of cloth lining annually. Dealers benefit through low prices.
3. The company is represented in over 102 countries.
4. More than 6,000 dealers carry the line.
5. Company policy of exclusive agency protects distributors.
6. Founder was first shoe manufacturer to sell direct to the retailer.

Although the objections encountered by salesmen are numerous, some type of company information may be found to refute effectively nearly every argument of prospects.

4. Arouse General Interest of Prospects with Company Facts. Some dramatic event in a company's history, a piece of original research, unusual growth, or outstanding accomplishments of executives, described by a salesman, will "break the ice," secure the attention of prospects, or arouse the interest of customers. If a company

Salesman_____   Date_____

Rated by_____   Over-all Rating_____

Score

I. *Salesman's Knowledge of Company*	Excellent 90–100	Good 80–90	Fair 70–80	Poor 60–70	Failure Below 60
A. History					
B. Executive personnel					
C. Personnel and labor relations					
D. Plants and branches					
E. Finances					
F. Management policies					
G. Distributing methods					
H. Organization					
I. Research					
J. Competitive position					
K. Sales volume and prices					
L. Office routines					
M. Social responsibilities					
N. Company services					

II. *Salesman's Use of Company Knowledge*	Excellent 90–100	Good 80–90	Fair 70–80	Poor 60–70	Failure Below 60
A. Discuss company facts in relation to needs and motives of buyer					
B. Support specific claims with company facts					
C. Answer objections with company facts					
D. Arouse prospect's interest with company facts					
E. Meet competition with company facts					

Miscellaneous Comments_____

or its products participate in a current event of national interest, if it constructs a new plant or guarantees 300 days of employment a year to its workers, there is a wealth of sales material for a skillful salesman in each of these events. Construction of a new laboratory by an electrical equipment manufacturer is of general interest to customers.

Large and small companies are daily making commercial history which is brimful of sales arguments for salesmen with the imagination and skill to employ them in sales presentation.

5. Meet Competition with Company Facts. When a prospect or customer shows preference for the resources, policies, or personnel of a competing company, the salesman should introduce his company facts to refute the claims of a competitor. A sound knowledge of competitive position is necessary in such a situation. Direct reference to the resources or policies of competitors should be avoided, but full company facts should be used to dispose of arguments of competitors for greater size, resources, or better policies.

For example, a prospect says that he prefers to buy from a competing company because of its financial stability. In this case, the salesman should present his company's financial facts to prove the soundness of its monetary position. No mention need be made of the finances of the competing company. Such facts as the company's cash on hand, inventory, accounts receivable, and property owned should be known and used by the salesman in meeting competition.

This five-point routine for presenting company information gives a salesman an organized standard procedure for employing company facts to the fullest advantage in sales presentations.

Problem I

Alfred Martin, representing the Walker-Rand Company

Alfred Martin is one of 18 salesmen representing the Walker-Rand Company, advertising printers of New York City. This company specializes in the creation and production of all forms of direct advertising including catalogues, booklets, house organs, folders, illustrated four-page letters, posters, window displays, and blotters. Their salesmen contact large users of direct advertising in New York City, seeking to interest them in the advertising research, planning, production, and distributing services of the company. This company is equipped to handle an entire direct-advertising campaign costing several thousand dollars or a single piece of printing.

One of the principal problems of the Walker-Rand salesmen is to obtain the confidence of advertising managers in the ability of the organization to render a confidential and highly specialized service to users of direct advertising. The company must become acquainted with the sales plans and policies of its clients and work in close personal relationship with them in the creation of direct advertising.

The advertising manager of a large manufacturer of boilers, radiators, and heating equipment, located in New York City is being interviewed by salesman Martin. The following is the record of Martin's conversation with the advertising manager:

1. SALESMAN: Good afternoon, sir. Martin is my name, Alfred Martin of the Walker-Rand Company, advertising printers. We have just created and printed an unusual direct advertising campaign for one of the large oil-burner manufacturers. It has several features which may be of interest to you in connection with your own advertising of boilers and radiators. I would like to show it to you and discuss some of its unique ideas.

2. BUYER: The Brown Printing Company has handled our advertising printing since 1933 in good years and in bad. They know our problems and for that reason we would not be interested in making a change. It is more convenient to work with them. Their creative department is headed by one of the smartest direct-mail men in the city. We simply hand them a sales problem and they come up with a lot of good advertising ideas. What outfit did you say you are with?

3. SALESMAN: The Walker-Rand Company. We've been specializing exclusively on planning and producing direct advertising since 1920. Today we are serving more than three hundred advertisers with a staff of 30 writers, artists, and layout men, many of whom were once associated with leading advertisers. John Cartright, former president of the Advertising Club, is our president. You may know of him?

4. BUYER: No, I've only been in the city a couple of years. Came here after the war.

5. SALESMAN: Naturally, you want an advertising printer who knows your problems. We think the most important feature of our service to customers is a thorough understanding of their needs. That's why we established our research department, five years ago, just to make a study of the sales problems of our customers. It is headed up by Tom Clark who was director of sales and advertising research for the National Heating Equipment Company for over ten years. He has a fine knowledge of the sales and advertising problems of heating equipment manufacturers. That's why we have been creating an increasing amount of advertising for noncompeting heating and air-conditioning concerns.

6. BUYER: I knew Clark when he was with National.

7. SALESMAN: He has been running an interesting test on consumer response to a series of six mailings to lists supplied by heating contractors for one of our customers, the Hopkins Thermostat Corporation. As a result of that test we have changed the format and appeal on the campaign and increased returns more than 18 per cent.

    The way Tom Clark works is to go into the sales problems of a new client thoroughly, using a questionnaire to bring out the basic information about the customer's product, market, method of distribution, sales policies, and advertising. Then he supplements this with a field investigation of key distributors and dealers and a sampling of consumers. After several weeks' investigation of a customer's sales problems, we are ready to go to work developing a direct advertising plan to fit his needs.

8. BUYER: That research is all right, but you've got to know what to do with it when you get it. After all, it's the imagination and ideas that count in advertising.

9. SALESMAN: You're right, that's why we have one of the best art and copy staffs in the East. Our copy chief is Ed Morton who was copy director for Lynch, Townson, and Potter for nine years. He wrote the famous series of ads for the Northeastern Railroad which attracted so much attention during the war. He masterminded the series of mailings for the Automatic Heating Corporation which won the Direct Mail Advertising Association award this year.

    If you saw the last exhibition of Advertising Art of the Art Director's Club at the Ad Club recently, you may have noticed some of the work of our art director, Jack Starr.

10. BUYER: Are you fellows competitive on price? We've got to watch our costs to keep within our budget, which is some job these days.

11. SALESMAN: We are in an unusually fortunate position to undersell our principal competitors because we have recently installed in our plant in Newark the latest type high-speed, four-color rotary presses which make it possible for us to cut production costs from 10 to 15 per cent on all ordinary work. That saving we pass along to our customers in lower prices. Furthermore, our plant is located just across the river so that transportation charges are at a minimum and daily delivery from our warehouse stocks saves you storage expense.

12. BUYER: Yes, everyone is buying new equipment and chiseling the price. Of course, that doesn't make us feel bad at all.

13. SALESMAN: That's true—a lot of printers are installing new presses, but few concerns have such a large capacity as we have, a half-million impressions a day—that means low overhead and low prices. Then our large buying power, over ten tons of paper a week, makes it possible for us to pass along the low prices we get to our customers.

14. BUYER: I'd be interested to look over samples of your work sometime.

15. SALESMAN: Would next Tuesday at two be convenient for you?
16. BUYER: Yes, I'll see you then.
17. SALESMAN: Fine, good-by.

Questions

1. What was the buyer's need for advertising printing service in this case? How was it revealed?

2. What are the buying motives of the customer in this case? How are they revealed?

3. Did the salesman discuss company facts in relation to the needs and motives of the buyer? What facts? Was his discussion effective on this point?

4. Did the salesman make any claims supported by company facts? If so, what company facts were used?

5. Did the salesman answer objections with company facts? If so, what company facts were used?

6. Did the salesman use company facts to meet competition? If so, what facts were used?

7. Did the salesman apply the five-point routine for using company information in this case? Was company information handled effectively? Explain.

Problem II

Peter G. Goodman, representing the Carson Stationery Company

The Carson Stationery Company, established in 1905 in Bridgeport, Conn., produces fine copperplate engraving and makes high-grade invitations, wedding announcements, and calling cards. In addition, the company lithographs commercial stationery. Two separate sales organizations are maintained: one group engaged exclusively in selling copperplate engraving to individuals, schools, and social organizations; the other selling letterheads and envelopes to commercial organizations. Plants are located in Bridgeport, New Haven, and Hartford, Conn.

Peter G. Goodman is one of 20 salesmen selling the commercial stationery to banks and purchasing agents in Connecticut, Pennsylvania, and New York state. His headquarters are in New York City.

The following interview took place in the office of the purchasing agent of a large chemical-products manufacturer located in New York City. Salesman Goodman is interviewing Mr. King, the buyer, with the intention of selling him business stationery:

1. SALESMAN: I'm with the Carson Company.
2. BUYER: I've heard of your company, but I thought they did copper-plate engraving work.
3. SALESMAN: Our work is with the supply departments of companies. Frankly, this is a cold call. I should have sent you a letter.
4. BUYER: Someone has been in from your company. Is your plant in Connecticut?
5. SALESMAN: Yes, in Bridgeport. I don't know of anyone else who could have seen you. The copperplate engraving is only a part of our business—about one-fifth. The other is the commercial stationery production. Was the man's name Jones?
6. BUYER (looking through business cards): I can't tell you his name.
7. SALESMAN: We have three plants—Bridgeport, New Haven, Hartford. One thing, Mr. King, we have a separate sales force. One man handles only copperplate engraving and he isn't at all interested in the commercial stationery.
8. BUYER: We do all of our own stationery buying on a competitive basis.
9. SALESMAN: Let me show you something which we did for the textile field—The Blank Company. (A discussion of stationery samples follows.)
10. BUYER: I am interested in the paper they use on their letterhead. I see that their plant is located in Tennessee.
11. SALESMAN: I haven't seen the plant, but I understand it is very modern. That was printed by us in Bridgeport. That is the deep-etched offset process and the Bridgeport plant is the only one where that type of work can be done. The only adverse criticism of the letterhead came from New England. They thought the job should have cost less and the difference in cost be passed along as a longer discount. Here is a series in the publishing field which has attracted considerable comment. These are the first three and there will be a series of 24.
12. BUYER: Did you design these?
13. SALESMAN: We planned some of the designs, but most firms design their own.
14. BUYER: Who designed these?
15. SALESMAN: They did. They paid us the compliment that this series is better than anything that they had ever seen. Each manufacturer, of course, has his own problems. All that we can do on the first call is to tell you what we can do and you have to do the rest. (Smiling.)
16. BUYER: As I told you, we buy our stationery on a competitive basis and it doesn't leave much room for designing organizations. It takes more time to tell an outsider what you need than it does to go ahead and do the job from here. There's no saving; there is a loss of time.
17. SALESMAN: We have a plant of our own that we would like to keep busy and our prices are certainly in line.

18. BUYER (pointing to samples): There is some of the work we turn out. We stick to the style which we have established.

19. SALESMAN: A man who is doing the same thing day in and day out is apt to get stale. An outsider who has a fresh point of view can oftentimes be of real assistance.

20. BUYER: My criticism is that I haven't the money to put into all the things I'd like to.

21. SALESMAN: Well, maybe things will change. Maybe we can go over it sometime again and you can give me some of the details of your problem. I will see you again.

Questions

1. Did salesman Goodman present his company effectively to the purchasing agent in this case? State specific weaknesses or strengths in his presentation.

2. What information should he have given to the buyer about the Carson Stationery Company?

3. Should this buyer be concerned with the reputation of the salesman's company? Why?

4. Apply the four-point procedure or routine for presenting company information to this situation. Assume company facts.

5. What was the buyer's principal motive in this case? What company facts might be related to that motive?

Reading References

C. H. FERNALD, "Salesmanship," p. 57–59, Prentice-Hall, Inc., New York, 1945.

J. GEORGE FREDERICK, "Modern Salesmanship," Chap. VII, Garden City Publishing Company, Inc., New York, 1937.

HAROLD M. HAAS, "A Short Course in Salesmanship," Chap. XIII, Prentice-Hall, Inc., New York, 1939.

J. M. HILL and R. G. WALTERS, "Success through Salesmanship," pp. 107–118, South-Western Publishing Company, Cincinnati, 1940.

PAUL W. IVEY, "Salesmanship Applied," pp. 89–97, McGraw-Hill Book Company, Inc., New York, 1937.

PAUL W. IVEY, "Successful Salesmanship," pp. 59–60, Prentice-Hall, Inc., New York, 1947.

BERNARD LESTER, "Sales Engineering," pp. 192–194, John Wiley & Sons, Inc., New York, 1940.

HARRY SIMMONS, "How to Get the Order," pp. 70–71, Harper & Brothers, New York, 1937.

CHAPTER VI

PRESENTING THE PRODUCT OR SERVICE

If a salesman is not thoroughly familiar with his product or services, if he does not know what they are and what they will do for buyers, he has no foundation for success in his work. It is sometimes said that salesmen should not know too much about what they are selling. If they know too many product facts, they will bore buyers with confusing technicalities, annoy prospects by attempting to impress them with a display of information, or fail to concentrate on the essentials. On the contrary, salesmen cannot know too much about their products and services, provided they can select the really important facts and know how to use them effectively in their presentations. Properly used, the more information a salesman possesses, the better able he is to close sales.

A salesman needs this knowledge in order to describe product features or service advantages, to overcome objections, to answer questions, and to acquire confidence in the merit of his offerings.

The importance of this knowledge, in the success of a salesman, depends first upon the nature of the product or service, its simplicity or complexity. The knowledge required by a salesman of life insurance is obviously much more extensive than that needed by a wholesale salesman of condensed milk. The number and variety of products represented by a salesman have a bearing on the amount of product information he can retain or use. No salesman can carry in his mind every fact about every one of a long line of items. He must concentrate and know the outstanding facts about his most important products. The type of buyer with whom a salesman has to deal determines also the amount and character of his information. Buyers as a whole are becoming better informed about commodity values. This places a greater knowledge requirement on salesmen. Salesmen of technical products, bought by professional purchasing agents, are called upon for much information about their goods and applications.

134

WHAT A SALESMAN SHOULD KNOW ABOUT HIS PRODUCT OR SERVICE

In considering what specific product or service information a salesman should have, it must be recognized that thousands of facts might be learned about even the simplest product, most of which would have no significance in making a sale and would merely confuse the salesman. Few salesmen could keep so many facts in mind, much less use them effectively in a presentation. Accordingly, instead of learning a large number of product facts, a selection must be made, by the salesman or the management, of the major sales points for each product and these must be firmly fixed in the salesmen's minds. The principal selling points of a product will be found in the following classifications: (1) product-buying motives and applications; (2) distinctive-product characteristics; (3) raw materials; (4) processes of manufacture; (5) development of product or service; (6) competitive position; (7) supply of product; (8) name of product; (9) container of product; (10) relation to other products in the line; (11) product performance; (12) varieties produced; (13) special handling and maintenance; (14) production policies.

1. Product-buying Motives and Applications. The various ways in which a product or service may satisfy needs and give profit and satisfaction to purchasers should be known by the salesmen. Knowledge of uses and applications is usually of greater importance to a salesman than information about product construction since purchases are made to satisfy needs rather than to acquire things.

All commodities and services are bought in response to the five basic buying motives of (1) comfort and convenience, (2) safety and protection, (3) gain and economy, (4) satisfaction of pride and (5) satisfaction of affection discussed in Chap. IV. These incentives to purchase vary with each buyer and each type of product or service sold.

Salesmen must know these motives to discover which ones induce consumers to purchase. For example, a manufacturer of high- and low-priced automobiles found that the following inducements to buy, all related to the five basic buying motives, cause buyers to purchase low-priced cars: (1) operating economy, 75.5 per cent; (2) dependability, 72.3 per cent; (3) safety, 66.1 per cent; (4) comfort, 43.6 per cent; (5) appearance, 40.4 per cent; (6) ease of control, 33 per cent; (7) smoothness, 32 per cent; (8) pickup, 14.1 per cent; (9) speed, 8.2 per cent.

The inducements for buying high-priced cars, on the other hand, are somewhat different, as follows: (1) dependability, **74.9** per cent; (2) safety, **64.8** per cent; (3) appearance, **60.2** per cent; (4) comfort, **57.2** per cent; (5) ease of control, **49.1** per cent; (6) smoothness, **34.5** per cent; (7) operating economy, **33.5** per cent; (8) pickup, **13.3** per cent; (9) speed, **12.8** per cent.

The buying motives for life insurance are safety and protection, satisfaction of affection for family, and gain. The motives involved in the purchase of an automobile tire are safety, protection, economy, comfort, and convenience.

Salesmen should list the buying motives and needs for their product and under each heading describe the product or service features that satisfy each motive and need.

In addition, full information concerning the various uses or applications of a product or service is a fundamental part of a salesman's knowledge. The number and nature of the uses of some products are limited and obvious, as in the case of a watch or a collar button. Yet, other simple commodities, such as salt, wire, and safety pins, have hundreds of uses. The greater the number of uses for product or service, the broader the sales opportunity. An imaginative brush salesman conceived such a wide variety of special uses for his wares that he built up the largest brush business in the world.

The uses or applications for some types of products, such as accounting machines, are not only numerous but complex. The electric bookkeeping machines are used for preparing sales analyses, payroll records, cash records, factory costs, income statements, preliminary general ledgers, balance sheets, general journal, and interdepartmental transfers.

There are some thirty different applications for life insurance including personal uses, family uses, business uses, and social uses.

Salesmen should have lists of such applications and know the various uses for each of the products that they sell and how to operate, wear, prepare, eat, apply, arrange, or assemble each product.

2. Distinctive-product Characteristics. Salesmen should be fully posted on the distinctive characteristics of their products, including such factors as style, workmanship, design, construction, finish, appearance, or, in the case of an intangible service, the features of the contract, policy, or certificate. Since merchandise or services are being constantly improved, study of their distinctive features must be continuous if a salesman is to be well informed.

To acquire a knowledge of the hundreds of different points of design and construction of even a single product is obviously impracticable.

The natural course, for a salesman confronted with a large number of product facts, is to select and use a few of the outstanding distinctive features. It is not difficult to assemble thirty or forty distinctive facts about a single product. From this number he should select a few outstanding points worthy of discussion and obtain additional facts on these.

A large manufacturer of floor coverings follows this method of assembling and selecting product facts for his salesmen. From an original list of sales points compiled for each product, the five or six basic features are selected. These major points are expanded with interesting side lights, examples, and experiences. Product-point outlines are prepared in this way for each product in the line.

The six distinctive points of a well-known brand of automobile tube have been selected from hundreds of facts about workmanship, construction, design, as follows: (1) inner-sealed to hold air longer; (2) rim side extra heavy, extra tough; (3) black and red rubber welded inseparably; (4) extra heavy, extra thick on road side; (5) electric weld splice; (6) water-tested.

Sales-point outlines of distinctive features should be memorized by a salesman until they become such a part of his mental processes that they can be used automatically in sales interviews. Distinctive-product sales points are basic sales material as every feature of a good sales presentation relates to one or more product or service facts. Unique product points have been the basis of outstanding sales campaigns in a score of industries, as in the case of the balloon tire, the four-wheel brake, safety glass, stainless steel, latex foam sponge, and glass building blocks. Salesmen who know distinctive-product features have taken the first step toward individual success.

3. Raw Materials. Raw materials used in the construction of a commodity determine the quality of the finished product. Salesmen will find many quality selling points in information about the source, grade, inspection, testing, unique characteristics, method of production, transportation, cost, quality, and supply of the raw materials of manufacture.

In acquiring a knowledge of raw materials, the number of facts available again make it necessary for a salesman to concentrate on the key points. If a salesman of linoleum rugs, for example, attempted to acquire complete knowledge of any one of the three basic raw materials—felt, asphalt, and paint—used in manufacturing that product, his studies would be endless and largely a waste of time. However, if he selected the major features of each of the raw materials and fixed these points firmly in his mind, he would be adequately informed about raw materials.

A good example of the character and variety of facts about raw materials which should be in the possession of a salesman is the following information, given to the salesmen of a large brush manufacturer, about Siberian bristles, the raw material used in the product:

The best white bristle is secured from wild boars inhabiting the cold climate of Russia, Siberia, and Manchuria. The Siberian hog is a long, thin animal; the thinner and older the hog, the longer and stiffer the bristles. White bristle is very scarce and costly as probably only 1 per cent of the wild boars are white. In the spring, these wild hogs shed their bristles by rubbing their bodies against the bark of trees. The natives collect these bristles and trade them for merchandise to traders who sell the bristles to exporters in Russia, England, and Japan.

A selling-point outline describing features of the raw material should be prepared for each product. An example of the raw-material sales points for a hairbrush follows: (1) We use only the best grade of Siberian white bristle. (2) The butt end of the white bristle is strong and has a spring and resilience that untangle snarly hair without breaking it. (3) The longer the bristles, the stiffer the butt ends become. (4) We use the long white bristles ranging in length from 2 to 6 inches. (5) The longer lengths must be secured from rare white boars that are from five to seven years old. (6) The price of white bristle is much higher than that of black bristle owing to its scarcity.

Salesmen representing a manufacturer of silver plated ware are informed about the composition and production of nickel silver from the time it was discovered in China and brought to Europe in the seventeenth century to the present.

Facts about raw materials may be used effectively by salesmen to stimulate the interest of prospects, support claims for quality, and answer objections.

4. Processes of Manufacture. The various steps in the process of manufacturing a product, including the preparation of the raw material, special or exclusive processes used, routing of product through the plant, character of workmanship, special equipment, inspections, laboratory tests, and production control should be known by the salesmen. This information is best obtained by direct observation; for this reason many companies assign new salesmen to work in various departments of the factory. However, in lieu of actual experience, salesmen can learn much about manufacturing methods from company publications, motion pictures, and by discussions with factory executives. Not only does this knowledge give a salesman valuable sales points, but it also increases his confidence in his product.

In acquiring information about production methods, as in the case of other product facts, it is necessary for a salesman to concentrate on the fundamentals. He need not be an expert on manufacturing, but he should know the distinctive features of his plant operations. A list of significant production features should be prepared and committed to memory by him.

An excellent example of information for salesmen on the various steps in the process of manufacturing a product is the description prepared by the sales training department of Kraft Foods Company, of the procedure for making American cheese:

Whole or partly skimmed cow's milk	Whole milk or standardized to make a legal cheese
Pasteurized or raw	Either
Starters used	Regular lactic acid producing culture
Rennet used	Yes, about 3 oz. per 100 pounds of milk
Setting temperature	86° to 88° F.
Cooking temperature	98° to 102° F.
Approximate time from set to hoop	4 to 7 hours
Method of removing whey	Drained in the vat
Condition of curd at hooping	Curd cheddared or matted in vat prior to milling into pieces about ½″ x ½″ x 2″
Type of form used	Metal hoop lined with cheesecloth
Time and method of pressing	Pressed overnight under continuous pressure. Bandage straightened once
Method of salting	Salt added to curd in vat after milling
Type of cure	Cures uniformly throughout cheese. Should be held 45° to 55° F.
Organisms responsible for cure	Many
Approximate time required for good cure	2 months to 1 year
Approximate weight of finished cheese	All bulk sizes
Composition	Fat, 32% to 33%
	Moisture, 36% to 39%
	F.O.B., 50% to 54%

Prompt shipments are also a potent selling argument in many lines. A large metal-products manufacturer has an unusually efficient method of scheduling orders for production and shipment. The salesmen of this concern are fully informed about this method so that they are able to tell customers in advance when orders will be produced and shipments made. Knowledge of production-scheduling methods enables them to make more sales because they can support their delivery promises with production facts.

Salesmen representing a manufacturer of dairy products have an effective sales point in a special process of homogenization that breaks up and emulsifies the fat globules in the ingredients and facilitates the digestion of the product.

Production tests are a major selling argument used by salesmen of an automobile manufacturer. The salesmen of this company know and discuss the fact that there is one inspector to every 13 workmen in the company's plants. They feature the facts that one battery of devices for testing crankshafts alone cost $51,000 and that gears are tested for quietness in a soundproofed room.

5. Development of Product or Service. Salesmen should be informed about the origin and invention of the product, together with any changes and improvements that have been made in its construction or design. This information is not only of general interest to many prospects and customers, but may be used to support arguments for quality, service, or performance of the product, as well as the progressiveness of the company.

An example of interesting facts about a product, typical of those which should be known by salesmen, is the development of Celastic by a shoe manufacturer:

The company was having difficulty with shoes shipped to foreign countries. The box toes, though in fine condition when packed, arrived broken down and distorted. The hot, humid atmosphere in the hold of the vessel was ruining the finest of leather boxes. Every likely compound or substance was given rigorous tests that the best of leather failed to pass. A material was sought that could be boiled in water and would be proof against uric acid, urea, alkalis, and ordinary acids. It must have great strength, coupled with light weight, and a pressure of 200 pounds must be withstood without injury to the box toe.

After a series of tests the company produced a fabric treated with celluloid and called "Celastic," tough yet flexible, very thin and very strong. It stands perspiration, urea, alkalis, and 500 pounds per square inch pressure. This material is used for box toes and counters and is strong yet light.

Similar examples of the creation of new products may be found in the experience of every progressive company and may be used effectively by salesmen.

6. Competitive Position. Not only is it necessary for a salesman to be thoroughly familiar with his own product, but he should also be fully informed .about the following features of competing products or services: (1) distinctive characteristics, (2) applications and performance, (3) construction, (4) grades, sizes, patterns, finishes, etc., (5) prices and profit, (6) materials used in construction, (7) comparative operating costs.

Such facts are sometimes collected by the sales management and made available to salesmen in the form of comparison books which list the specifications of competing products and show how they check with the company's product on each item. In the absence of such books, salesmen should write their own product comparisons, using competitive catalogues and advertisements as the principal sources of their information.

A salesman's objective in securing information about competing products or services should not be for the purpose of disparaging competitive products, but rather for forestalling competitive claims.

A complete knowledge of the features of competing products enables a salesman to anticipate claims of other sellers. Low operating costs, for example, are claimed by several manufacturers of mechanical refrigerators. Many buyers compare the various makes on this feature. A refrigerator salesman who knows the operating costs of his own product compared with those of competing makes can forestall competition by discussing his low operating costs before a prospect has had a chance to voice claims for other makes.

Sometimes buyers demand that salesmen make direct comparisons with competing products. In such cases, it is necessary for salesmen to know the characteristics of those products. When they have such knowledge, they have greater confidence in their product and are better able to meet rival claims.

Rather than ignore competition as being unworthy of consideration, salesmen should make it a practice to acquire regularly current information about the outstanding features of rival products and services. As new ones are introduced, full details of their features should be secured and analyzed.

7. Supply of Product. Salesmen should know the available supply of their products so as to be able to assure customers of regular delivery and of the ability of the company to meet the buyer's requirements. When a product is an industrial operating supply such as coal or oil, or a material used in manufacture such as steel, regularity of supply is an important consideration to purchasers.

Salesmen should be posted on conditions that may interrupt supply, such as strikes, floods, fires, war, or bankruptcy. If competitors are suffering from these interruptions, salesmen should know the situation.

The amount of time necessary to make delivery to customers in various locations should be known by salesmen. This is often an important selling argument to buyers located at long distances from the factory.

Wholesalers and retailers are especially concerned with the regularity of supply of products for which there is a regular demand from their trade.

8. Name of Product. The name of a product may be so well known that salesmen should be familiar with its origin and meaning. In an extensive line of products the family or individual product brands or private brands sold should be thoroughly familiar to the salesmen.

Interesting anecdotes may be told about the names of many of America's famous products. These stories should be known by salesmen and related to customers and prospects. An example is the account of the origin of the Walk-Over shoe, made by the George E. Keith Company. This shoe was named by Mr. Keith in the summer of 1898 when the International Yacht Races were being run. Going home from the office, Mr. Keith told his wife of his difficulty in selecting a name for his product. His wife happened to be reading the daily newspaper and staring at her was the headline, "American Boat Has a Walk-over," so she suggested that the new shoe be called the "Walk-Over."

9. Container of Product. The growing importance of packaging from the standpoint of display value, as well as utility, makes it necessary that salesmen know the numerous values of the package in which a product is packed and shipped.

In selling to wholesale and retail distributors, salesmen can find many selling points in a package which lessens sales resistance and effects economies in handling and storing.

In selling to consumers, salesmen can feature package appearance, convenience in handling, utility, keeping qualities, correct quantity, and many other factors depending upon the individual case.

Many merchandising opportunities are opened to salesmen through the introduction of a new and unique package, provided they are fully informed concerning the sales features of the container.

10. Relation to Other Products in the Line. When a salesman sells a number of products, he should be familiar with the relation of each product to the others in the line. In some cases, a manufacturer may make two lines that are in more or less direct competition with each other. If a salesman is carrying both lines, he must know why one line should receive the major share of his attention.

Sometimes a manufacturer of several products may wish to focus selling efforts on one item in the line. Salesmen should know the reasons why this product has been selected as a leader. If it has special features, unique quality, appearance, or uses that distinguish it from other items, these points should be expanded and information about them given to the salesmen.

Leftovers and by-products create a special sales problem; salesmen should know the company's policy of disposing of such irregular items without interfering with the brand identity, price, and quality reputation of the main line.

11. Product Performance. A salesman should know how his product will perform in use. Through frequent contact with users of his merchandise, a salesman learns first-hand much about the performance of his products. Many manufacturers make exhaustive tests of product qualities, and large buyers maintain testing laboratories where the commodities which they buy for use or resale are tested under actual conditions. These sources provide much valuable information on product performance for use in sales presentations.

A salesman of apparel, textiles, or products made of textile materials knows what his product will do in terms of color permanence, shrinkage or loss of shape, breaking strength, seam slippage, resistance to water, perspiration, wear, light, and heat.

A salesman of mechanical equipment should know its durability, power consumption, cost of upkeep, cost of operation, output, speed, and other performance factors of significance to users.

In selling automobiles, a salesman should know the gasoline and oil consumption, cost of maintenance, fastness of color, durability, and other features of performance of his car.

12. Varieties Produced. To satisfy the needs and wants of customers, most products are produced in a variety of sizes, types, colors, weights, finishes, weaves, designs, and special characteristics. It is essential that a salesman be familiar with these varieties and their distinguishing features in order to be able to recommend the particular type of product best suited to the requirements of the customer.

The leading cheese producer in this country makes 45 different varieties of packaged domestic cheeses in four standard sizes to suit the taste of the most discriminating cheese customer. A famous packer of baby foods sells 38 varieties. A manufacturer of foot-aids produces 40 different types. Salesmen representing these manufacturers must know their various product types completely to be able to sell effectively.

The principal sources of information on product types are the manufacturer's catalogue listing sizes, models, colors, and special characteristics and descriptions of products produced; the sales manuals and advertisements published for the information of salesmen, dealers, and users.

13. Special Handling and Maintenance. Because of their character, some products require special handling by salesmen, distributors, and users to ensure good quality and service. Perishable food and drug products, particularly, must be protected against moisture, dust, excessive heat or cold, and contamination from the time they leave the factory until they are consumed. Some commodities must be kept under refrigeration to protect their flavor or efficacy. Salesmen must be familiar with the requirements for handling their products and the proper methods of shipping, storing, and displaying them.

Mechanical equipment requires proper care to ensure its satisfactory operation. Salesmen of machines should know how to clean, adjust, store, and lubricate their equipment and to give this information to dealers and users.

14. Production Policies. Salesmen should be acquainted with the basic production policies of their plants, especially those concerning balancing production, simplification and standardization, specialization, quality, or quantity production.

A factory that works overtime a part of the year and shuts down the balance of the time suffers from high costs, idle equipment, and labor turnover. A plant that can operate 300 days a year effects economies and secures efficiencies that are excellent sales ammunition. A production policy that provides plant employees with 48 weeks of work every year reveals not only the social responsibility of the company but also production efficiency, both of which are significant facts for salesmen.

A plant that operates on a policy of simplification and standardization of output enjoys lower production costs, lower inventories, prompt deliveries, and increased turnover, all of which facts should be included in sales presentations.

Specialization in manufacture on one or two products, as contrasted with the production of an extensive, unrelated line, creates advantages that should be familiar to the salesmen.

A factory that adopts either a quality or a quantity production policy secures numerous advantages from such a course, depending upon the market that is sought. Salesmen should recognize the economies of mass production resulting in lower prices as well as the values of restricted output of a quality product.

WHAT A SALESMAN SHOULD KNOW
ABOUT AN INTANGIBLE SERVICE

While the knowledge required by a salesman of a tangible commodity is similar in many respects to the information needed by a salesman of an intangible service, there are numerous other types of information vital to sound selling of services which should be familiar to service salesmen.

A life insurance salesman, for example, should know the following features of his service: (1) use of life insurance; (2) different kinds of policies and their uses; (3) annuities and their uses; (4) provisions of policies; (5) settlement options; (6) riders and endorsements; (7) computation of premiums; (8) investment features of life insurance; (9) reserves and valuations; (10) surplus and dividends; (11) disability and indemnity features; (12) annual statements; (13) regulation and supervision of life companies; (14) life insurance trusts; (15) business life insurance; (16) legal aspects of life insurance; (17) special types of life insurance; (18) selection of risks; (19) services to policyholders. In addition, the American College of Life Underwriters requires that chartered Life Underwriters be acquainted with the following broad fields of knowledge: (1) life insurance fundamentals, including economics of life insurance, principles and practices; (2) life insurance salesmanship, principles and psychology; (3) general education, including economic problems, government, sociology; (4) law, trusts, and taxes, including general commercial law, wills, trusts, estates, taxation, and business insurance; (5) finance, including corporation finance, banking and credit, investments.

A general security salesman must know the following features of his job: (1) general nature and features of stocks, classes of stocks; (2) history and nature of bonds, types of bond issues; (3) yield on securities; (4) how to judge security values; (5) amortization; (6) real estate securities, private mortgages, real estate mortgage bonds; (7) short-term securities, notes, commercial paper, acceptances; (8)

analysis of corporation reports; (9) railroad securities; (10) public utilities; (11) the stock exchange and money market; (12) industrial securities; (13) U.S. banking system; (14) distribution of securities; (15) failures and reorganizations; (16) exchange; (17) income taxes.

From these examples of knowledge needed by salesmen of intangible services, it is evident that service knowledge is very extensive, complex, and often much more involved than information required by salesmen of tangible goods.

SOURCES OF PRODUCT AND SERVICE KNOWLEDGE

Salesmen may obtain information about product service and applications, characteristics, and other features previously described, through personal conferences with company factory executives; through group discussions in sales meetings; by reading company and competitive publications, advertising, catalogues, direct advertising, and company magazines; by observation of manufacturing processes; by experience from working in company production departments; by reading trade or technical magazines published for the industry; by questioning other company salesmen or competitive salesmen; by studying sales and service manuals, portfolios, and comparison books published by the company; by personal use of the product or service; from customers; from the merchandise itself; by consulting suppliers of raw materials or parts; from testing bureaus; and by attending company sales courses.

The acquisition of knowledge is a pleasure and comes easily to a salesman who is really interested in his work. Such a man is always asking questions and seeking information. He does not learn by slow, laborious memorizing of insignificant details, but rather by enthusiastic interest and curiosity.

USING PRODUCT OR SERVICE KNOWLEDGE

Knowledge of product or service features alone is insufficient for success in selling. The skill or ability of a salesman in putting product facts to practical use is just as important as is the acquisition of information. A man might figuratively be a walking encyclopedia of information about a product or service yet be a failure as a salesman if he did not know how to use his knowledge to interest prospects, to meet objections, or to present effective sales arguments.

Salesmen can learn to use product or service knowledge effectively by practicing an established routine similar to that for presenting the company, described in the previous chapter. The following product or service routine is based on the practices of successful salesmen. If a salesman will memorize and practice this routine until it becomes second nature to him, product and service facts discussed in this chapter can be used most effectively in sales presentations.

Routine for Presenting the Product or Service

1. Discuss product and service facts in relation to needs and motives of the buyer.
2. Use exclusive or superior product or service facts.
3. Use nontechnical terms.
4. Use specific, concrete terms, not generalities.
5. Rephrase and repeat important product and service facts.

1. Discuss Product and Service Facts in Relation to the Needs and Motives of the Buyer. Presentation of a long series of facts about a product or service which have little or no relation to a prospect's needs and motives bores most buyers. Select, from the many available product facts, those few points of special interest to a prospect and get the buyer's favorable attention. By using facts in relation to the needs and motives of the customer, a salesman also saves valuable time.

Product facts that are of greatest significance to prospects are those which relate most directly to their needs or motives. In preparation for sales interviews, list product or service facts under the headings of the five buying motives. For example, the principal motives that induce a housekeeper to purchase a dry mop are convenience, pride, and economy. A thrifty housekeeper may have one outstanding motive for buying—economy or low cost; a lazy housekeeper may buy because the mop is a convenience and will save her labor; and a neat homemaker will buy because of her pride in a clean house. A salesman must discover by inquiring, listening, or observing which of these motives dominates the prospect and give her information about the product directly related to that motive. By arranging product or service facts by motives, a salesman can present them most effectively to buyers.

To illustrate how such facts may be organized and related to motives, eight features of a simple product, a well-known brand of dry mop, have been listed under the motive of "convenience," or "laborsaving," in the following outline:

Housekeeper's Motive for Buying a Dry Mop	*Product Facts Relating to Prospect's Convenience or Labor-saving Motive*
Convenience; laborsaving.	1. Twice size of ordinary mop; does work in half time.
	2. Gets under low furniture, behind radiators, without user bending or stooping.
	3. Square shape is made to fit square corners easily.
	4. Easy to wash in soap and water; may be run through wringer.
	5. Maple handle shaped to fit hand.
	6. Cord, to hang up conveniently.
	7. Easy to push as it lies flat on floor at all times.
	8. Right weight makes it easy to handle.

Another housekeeper may be chiefly interested in the economical features of the mop. The following collection of economy facts could be presented to this prospect:

Housekeeper's Motive for Buying a Dry Mop	*Product Facts Relating to Economy Motive*
Economy; durability.	1. Reversible feature brings both sides of mop into use.
	2. Long-staple, long-wearing yarn creates long life.
	3. Chemical treatment saves cost of oil.
	4. Detachable handle will outlast several mops.
	5. Low initial cost.
	6. Saves cost of replacing yarn.

By collecting and listing product and service facts in this way, then committing them to memory and practicing the use of them until they can be called up at will to relate to the specific motives of a prospect, a salesman soon secures mastery in using them in meeting the motives of a buyer.

2. Use Exclusive or Superior Product or Service Facts. One product or service is bought in preference to another because it possesses features that are different or more desirable. The chief differences between one product and another reveal the important selling points of each.

Salesmen should check off on their lists of product facts those features which are superior or exclusive to their product. Specifications of competitive products should be examined to discover features which are identical or inferior to those found in the product of the salesman. After a salesman has compared the features of his product with those of competitors, a number of distinctive items will probably remain. These exclusive features should be memorized and additional facts about them collected, listed, and used in sales presentations.

To illustrate how exclusive points may be selected from a general list of product features, a list of the construction features of a well-known vacuum cleaner is used as an example. Twenty-two features of the X vacuum cleaner are:

Light weight.	Patented trap bag.
Made of steel, chromium plated.	Tilting device to protect edges of rug.
Insulated completely.	Free-rolling casters.
Pistol-handl grip, trigger switch.	Two-speed motor.
Streamline design.	Vibrationless motor.
Searchlight.	Three-adjustment brush.
Nonkinkable rubber cord.	Two rows of bristles in brush.
Nonoiling ball bearings.	Accordion bag top.
Air-cooled motor.	Collapsible throat.
Ball-bearing brush.	Two sizes of sprayer nozzles.
Dust escape-proof bag.	Nozzle-spray control.

Of all these features, the manufacturer claims three exclusive points of superiority: a two-speed motor, two rows of bristles in brush, and a dustproof bag. These are described in detail by salesmen in demonstrations.

Some exclusive features are obviously more important than others, but enough material should be assembled on each point to present it completely to buyers.

3. Use Nontechnical Terms. Because a salesman is familiar with the terminology of his product or service, he often wrongfully assumes that a prospect is equally conversant with its technicalities. An insurance salesman refers glibly to dividend options, double indemnities, attestation clauses, or participating nonforfeiture additions, all of which mean little to the average layman. When an automobile salesman speaks of counterweighted crankshafts, semiautomatic spark advance, dry-plate clutch, or piston displacement, few persons except automotive engineers understand him. Sometimes salesmen use technical terms to exhibit their knowledge; more often they use technicalities thoughtlessly, but the consequences are the same. Prospects become bored and disinterested because the conversation is unintelligible to them.

Salesmen must translate their technical terminology into layman's language for the majority of buyers, and reserve technicalities for the few experts familiar with mechanics. The problem of explaining, in simple terms, an involved mechanical process is difficult but may be facilitated by similes, as has been effectively done in the case of independent front-wheel suspension in automobiles which an automobile manufacturer has referred to as "knee action." Everyone can understand the meaning of "knee action," but "independent front-wheel suspension" means little to millions of American motor-car buyers.

Successful sellers not only simplify but dramatize technicalities. "Unisteel body construction" is not only abstruse but commonplace. General Motors salesmen refer to it as a "turret top," a simple, understandable term which pictures strength and protection. The compressor on a popular make of electrical refrigerator is called a "meter miser" to describe its economical operation.

"Technicalitis" is an ailment not only of many salesmen of mechanical products but also of insurance salesmen, who sometimes discuss the intricacies of an insurance contract to the perplexity of their prospects. Even a complicated service such as life insurance may be described in simple, understandable terms.

4. Use Specific, Concrete Terms, Not Generalities. One of the surest ways for a salesman to make complex facts clear to prospects is to state them concretely rather than in vague, general, or abstract words. Not only are specific terms and examples more clear, they are more interesting, also more impressive, and most important, more convincing.

For example, a fuel-oil salesman, discussing the savings effected by users of his product, said, "We have customers using our oil who achieve very large savings." This statement is not clear because it means one thing to some prospects and something else to others. A small individual consumer may be thinking of saving a few dollars; a big industrial user may think about economies of several hundred dollars.

By giving a few specific details to indicate the type of customer referred to and what is meant by "very large savings," the salesman can make his meaning clear as follows: "Last year 40 of our customers who use less than $500 worth of our oil annually reported savings running from $15 to $50 a year in their fuel costs."

Salesmen of a famous brand of soap do not claim that it is pure soap, but they state specifically that their soap is 99 and $^{44}/_{100}$ per cent pure. And the salesmen of a well-known make of coffee do not say that it is economical, but they say you get from 45 to 55 cups from each pound.

Prospects like specific examples, if they are important and interesting, but nothing can be more obscure than dull statistics. A salesman, discussing his product, said that his company produced 64,356 units during 1939. Not one prospect in 20 would remember the production figures for one minute. However, if the salesman should say that the output of his company for 1939 would make a pile of units as high as the Empire State building, every prospect would understand and remember.

5. Rephrase and Repeat Important Product and Service Facts. An important product fact is always worth repeating. An idea that may be clear to a salesman is not always grasped by the prospect. It takes time for buyers to comprehend new ideas, particularly those which are involved, and it is necessary to keep a prospect's mind focused on them.

However, prospects resent repetition of ideas in exactly the same language. For example, a refrigerator salesman who kept repeating the phrase, "It uses less electricity; it uses less electricity; it uses less electricity," would make his thought clear but would irritate his prospects. If the repetition is phrased in different words, such as, "It uses no more current than a 40-watt electric lamp," prospects will never consider that a repetition. The sales point has been made clearer.

Fix product points in the memory of your prospect more firmly with *repetition*. It is the rhythm in a good piece of music which makes it easily remembered, just as it is the restatements of a good public speaker that drive home his message.

Problem I

PRESENTING A PRODUCT

Walter T. Rockland, representing the Eastern Oil Company

The Eastern Oil Company, refiners and distributors of lubricating oil and gasoline, with headquarters in New York City, operates 1,500 company-owned service stations located in the states of New York,

Presenting the Product or Service

Salesman_____   Date_____

Rated by_____   Over-all Rating_____

				Score	
I. *Salesman's Knowledge of his Product or Service*	Excellent 90–100	Good 80–90	Fair 70–80	Poor 60–70	Failure Below 60
A. Product buying motives or application					
B. Distinctive product characteristics					
C. Raw materials					
D. Processes of manufacturing					
E. Development of product or service					
F. Competitive position of product					
G. Supply of product					
H. Name of product					
I. Container of product					
J. Relation to other company products					
K. Product performance					
L. Varieties produced					
M. Special handling					
N. Production policies					

II. *Salesman's Use of Product Knowledge*	Excellent 90–100	Good 80–90	Fair 70–80	Poor 60–70	Failure Below 60
A. Discuss product or service facts in relation to needs and motives of the buyer					
B. Using *exclusive* product or service facts					
C. Use nontechnical terms					
D. Using specific terms, not generalities, in describing product					
E. Rephrase and repeat important product and service facts					

Miscellaneous Comments_____

_____

_____

Connecticut, Rhode Island, and Massachusetts. These stations distribute not only the petroleum products of the company but also a complete line of automobile accessories including antifreeze solution, batteries, polish, electric lamps, tire chains, and tires.

Walter T. Rockland is manager of one of the company's stations located in one of the better residential districts suburban to Boston. The following interview took place in the driveway of the station between manager Rockland and a resident of the neighborhood who occasionally buys his oil and gasoline at the station:

1. SALESMAN: Hello, Mr. Jones (salesman knew buyer by name), is there anything we can help you with? You seem to be going home early today.

2. BUYER: Yes, I need a little water. I've just taken the afternoon off. (Salesman filled radiator with water. Buyer alights and begins to crank car.)

3. SALESMAN: What's the matter? Have you got a low battery?

4. BUYER: Yes, the blamed thing has gone down and I've had to crank it for about two weeks now. You know I'm getting sick and tired of this automobile. I think the best thing to do is to trade it in.

5. SALESMAN: Why don't you let me fix you up with a low-price Spark (private brand of oil company) battery?

6. BUYER: Oh, I just hate to spend the money on this old car, and then, too, I guess I can get along without it. I can have it charged occasionally and it will come back up enough to run me for a while.

7. SALESMAN: Yes, that's true, but after you have paid for several rechargings, you will have more than paid for a new battery which needs no recharging.

8. BUYER: What is the cheapest battery you have?

9. SALESMAN (pointing to battery on stand): This little 15 Spark special here on the stand should be just about what you want.

10. BUYER: How much is it?

11. SALESMAN: The price is $7.85, with 50 cents allowed you on your old battery, making it cost you $7.35. That is about as cheap or cheaper than you can get anywhere else, so why not let me go on and put it in right now?

12. BUYER: Well, I don't know. Just what does that 15 mean anyhow?

13. SALESMAN: Why, that means that it has 15 plates. The standard battery for your car has 17, but for the use to which you will put this battery and the time you are going to keep your car, you will not need anything more than this. This battery has Port Orford Cedar separators. (Here the salesman gave a complete description of the battery's construction.)

14. BUYER: I guess you're right. That's a good battery, but I could go down

to the mail-order house retail store and get one for $7 and get an allowance of 50 cents there, too. I just don't see any reason why I should pay any more than that for a battery. Both of them will do the same thing and since I'm going to get rid of this car in a couple of months, why should I waste that extra dollar?

15. SALESMAN: Mr. Jones, you will not be wasting that extra dollar. There are many things that our company can give you that the mail-order house cannot. For instance, we have fifteen hundred retail filling stations throughout the East. They are available at all times, during day or night, to give you service on your battery. Now, there is not much chance of a new battery giving you any trouble in the next five months, but in case you get out at night and have a breakdown, you would want to be able to get instant service on your battery. The guarantee which goes with our Spark battery will assure you instant adjustment from any of our stations. The mail-order store stays open only about eight hours a day and you will never be able to get service at night. We have a 13-plate battery selling for $6.95 which we use to meet the lowest competitive prices. The mail-order house battery, selling for $7 is probably a 13-plate model and, if that is the case, our battery is in the same class, sells for 5 cents less.

16. BUYER: Yes, that may be true, but any new battery would not give me any trouble in the next six months so why should I want service, or a guarantee, or anything like that?

17. SALESMAN: Mr. Jones, you will agree with me that the best policy is to play safe. (Buyer nods.) I thought you would, so why don't you let me go on and put the battery in now?

18. BUYER: My wife is waiting on me for lunch and I am just about due at home now. I'll see you later. (Buyer turns to go.)

19. SALESMAN: I can have the old one out and the new one in in less than five minutes. A new battery might keep you from being late, in fact, real late, at some other time. (Calling to another station man.) Johnny, come over here a minute.

20. BUYER: Well, I don't know. You know that it is pretty tough to go and spend a lot of money on an automobile and then trade it in and get no more for it than if you had not fixed it up in the first place.

21. SALESMAN: Do you mind if I differ with you on that point? Now, I do know how the automobile companies are appraising used cars around here. They are plenty tough. And you would be surprised at the amount of effort they go to in going over a car when you trade it in. I believe that you will find such a small thing as a good or bad battery will greatly influence the trade-in price on this old car. Since you are going to trade in this car in a couple of months, don't you think that it would be pretty good policy to have it in pretty fair shape when you go to trade it in?

22. BUYER: What makes you think that these used-car appraisers go to so much trouble?

23. SALESMAN: Just take a look at this little book here. (Salesman shows buyer booklet describing the importance of proper care of an automobile in relation to trade-in value.) Here are some of the figures and statements made by one of the local firms in regard to trade-in values. Does that go to prove the point?

24. BUYER: Yes, I guess it does. So you might as well go on and put the new battery in. I do hate to doctor up the old bus, though.

25. SALESMAN: I am sure you'll not regret it, Mr. Jones. I honestly believe it will save you money and inconvenience this summer. While you are here, is there anything else which I can do for you Let's see (examines the gasoline supply), you haven't much gas. Shall I fill it up?

26. BUYER: Yes, put me in 10 gallons of Ethyl, and you might check my tires while you're at it. The right front seems to be a little low. The oil is O.K. so don't bother with it.

27. SALESMAN: If you will just give me your courtesy card, I will fill out your ticket in order that you will not be late in getting home.

Questions

1. Did salesman Rockland present the storage battery effectively in this interview? State specific weaknesses or strengths in his presentation.

2. What were the buyer's motives in this situation? Did the salesman discuss product facts relating to these motives? What?

3. What distinctive product features were discussed by the salesman? Were these described nontechnically and specifically?

4. Did raw materials enter into the salesman's presentation? What?

Problem II

PRESENTING A SERVICE

Martin D. Wharton, representing the Assured Benefit Life Insurance Company

The Assured Benefit Life Insurance Company, established in 1860 in New York City, has more than a billion dollars' worth of life insurance in force. It it represented by 2,500 full and part-time agents operating out of 40 general agencies in the principal cities of the country.

Martin D. Wharton has been associated with the company for five years and is now connected with the William de Mille Agency of New York City. He specializes in selling life insurance to nurses and schoolteachers for retirement income purposes.

The following interview took place in the home of Miss Roberta Jones, a registered nurse, thirty-five years of age, who is meeting Martin Wharton for the first time:

1. SALESMAN: Miss Jones, my name is Wharton of the Assured Benefit Life Insurance Company. For your consideration, I wish to present a series of ideas dealing with your financial independence.
2. PROSPECT: I'm really not interested in life insurance. I have enough now.
3. SALESMAN: Yes, I assumed that you were not interested in additional life insurance, but everyone has to be interested in her own financial security and this, of course, means the acquisition of some kind of property.
4. PROSPECT: I have a small savings account.
5. SALESMAN: Yes, but regardless of the type of property you may have, whether it be savings, stocks, bonds, real estate, for each $100 a month independence income at age sixty, it is necessary that you own at least $40,000 worth of income-producing property. May I ask, do you own at least $40,000 worth of property?
6. PROSPECT: No, I do not own anywhere near that much.
7. SALESMAN: Ownership of property means little. Only when it is income producing do we acquire financial independence. At 3 per cent it takes $40,000 of income-producing property to produce $100 a month income. You will not be satisfied to have less than $100 a month when your retirement age is reached.
8. PROSPECT: I should like to have at least that much.
9. SALESMAN: Forty thousand dollars may be more than you could reasonably expect to accumulate from investing in safe property. There is an alternative, and that is the annuity. At age sixty it takes less than half of $40,000 to guarantee an annuity of $100 for life. The ideal situation is a fund of $40,000 at age sixty; the alternative is $16,500.
10. PROSPECT: How can I accumulate $16,500?
11. SALESMAN: There are two ways. The first way is through the acquisition of general property stocks, bonds, savings. The other way is the life insurance way, the ownership of guaranteed property that requires no turnover when the need for income arises at age sixty. All through the years you are relieved of doubt as to whether general property values will hold up and provide the required fund at the time needed.
12. This modern provision for retirement is easy to acquire; easy to maintain; a high collateral value of approximately 70 per cent in two years, 78 per cent in five years, 85 per cent in 10 years; absolute safety through diversification, you actually own a cross section of approximately six hundred million dollars in assets; ease of transfer, escaping court fees and delays; automatic trusteeship, providing money management for your beneficiary without cost and guaranteed yield.
13. PROSPECT: It sounds attractive.

14. SALESMAN: Compare this guaranteed property with the uncertainty of any other financial plan dependent on market values and changing conditions and you begin to appreciate the security guaranteed by a plan like this.

15. PROSPECT: I don't believe that I can afford it.

16. SALESMAN: I am assuming, Miss Jones, that the saving of $15 to $30 a month in some worth-while way is entirely within your possibilities. Am I correct in this?

17. PROSPECT: I might be able to save $20 a month.

18. SALESMAN: Yes, $20 a month would provide a fund of nearly one-half of the minimum of the $16,500 you would require at age sixty. This would be through a $5,000 contract which would provide your mother with an income of $50 a month for more than nine years should anything happen to you. That would be splendid protection to her, wouldn't it?

19. PROSPECT: Yes, that would be fine.

20. SALESMAN: And you would be taking advantage of the trusteeship provision which provides the money management, often as important as the money itself. This $5,000 contract will guarantee you a total at age sixty of $8,240 or $50 a month when you retire as long as the need lasts. This is an attractive plan. Don't you think so?

21. Yes, but I would like to think it over.

22. SALESMAN: After all what is there to think over? The Assured Benefit Life Insurance Company is eighty years old with assets in excess of a billion dollars. Here is a list of Assured Benefit property owners in this locality.

23. PROSPECT: I would like to consider it a little further.

24. SALESMAN: Yes, but while you are thinking this over we can find out whether or not the company would assume the obligation. We will arrange for Dr. Smith to see you tomorrow morning at 10 o'clock. In the meantime, here is some descriptive information which will enable us to complete the details.

Questions

1. Did salesman Wharton present life insurance effectively in this interview? State specific weaknesses or strengths in his presentation of the policy in this case.

2. What application of life insurance did the salesman discuss in this interview? Was the discussion clear and in nontechnical terms?

3. Did the salesman discuss the needs of the prospect?

4. What were the motives of the buyer? Did the salesman appeal to these motives?

5. Were specific terms used in describing insurance features? What terms?

6. Did the salesman rephrase and restate important facts?

Reading References

E. CASEY and R. L. JOHNS, "Salesmanship for Colleges," Chap. VI, H. W. Rowe Company, Baltimore, 1938.

J. R. DAUBMAN, "Salesmanship and Types of Selling," pp. 118–123, F. S. Crofts & Co., New York, 1939.

CHARLES H. FERNALD, "Salesmanship," pp. 61–75, Prentice-Hall, Inc., New York, 1945.

J. GEORGE FREDERICK, "Modern Salesmanship," Chap. VIII, Garden City Publishing Company, Inc., New York, 1937.

HAROLD M. HAAS, "A Short Course in Salesmanship," Chap. II, Prentice-Hall, Inc., New York, 1939.

J. M. HILL and R. G. WALTERS, "Success through Salesmanship," pp. 86–102, South-Western Publishing Company, Cincinnati, 1940.

PAUL W. IVEY, "Salesmanship Applied," Chap. V, pp. 83–100, McGraw-Hill Book Company, Inc., New York, 1937.

PAUL W. IVEY, "Successful Salesmanship," Chap. V, pp. 184–225, Prentice-Hall, Inc., New York, 1945.

BERNARD LESTER, "Sales Engineering," pp. 44–50, John Wiley & Sons, Inc., New York, 1940.

F. A. RUSSELL and F. H. BEACH, "Textbook of Salesmanship," pp. 115–144, McGraw-Hill Book Company, Inc., New York, 1949.

GEORGE B. SPENCER, "How to Be a Top-flight Salesman," Chap. X, Appleton-Century-Crofts, Inc., New York, 1940.

CHAPTER VII

QUOTING SELLING PRICES AND TERMS

IMPORTANCE OF PRICE IN SALES TRANSACTIONS

The question of price enters into every sales transaction. A knowledge of prices and the ability to quote them correctly is fundamental to the success of every salesman. Although most salesmen play no part in determining the prices of their products and services, they have a great deal to do in explaining, justifying, and quoting them to buyers.

The prominence of price in the work of a salesman depends first upon the price range of the product or service that he may be selling. If he is offering a luxury, his price problem is much different than if he were offering a necessity. Since necessities, normally low in price, are subject to keen competition, price is usually a major factor in selling them. In selling luxuries, on the other hand, a salesman usually subordinates price and emphasizes quality and service.

The purpose for which goods are bought greatly determines the importance of price in the sales transaction. Merchandise or raw materials bought for manufacture are usually purchased on a price basis. Commodities, such as cotton or rubber, used in the manufacture of automobile tires, are of standard grade and quality and are sold on a price basis. Raw materials lose their identity in the finished product and have no particular attraction for the consumer other than price.

In selling merchandise for equipment, price is sometimes secondary to brand name or exclusive features, as in the case of advertised tires and well-known batteries installed as original equipment in an automobile. In the sale of merchandise for individual or home consumption, price is often a secondary consideration to the buyer, who is chiefly interested in features of design, reputation of maker, brand name, color, or style.

The type of buyer also determines the extent to which price enters into a sale. Professional purchasers are usually good judges of intrinsic values and are price-conscious. These industrial buyers, representing large consumers, because of their great purchasing power are often seeking price concessions. Price is of primary importance to wholesale and retail distributors who are obliged to purchase at terms which enable them to meet competitive resale prices and at the same time cover their costs of doing business and provide a profit.

Numerous other factors make price a major consideration in a sales transaction. Unusual climatic conditions may make price a paramount problem to a salesman seeking to dispose of heavy over-coats in a mild winter. Business depression or sharp price movements may magnify price in buyers' minds. The extent of competition also exercises a great influence on price.

WHAT A SALESMAN SHOULD KNOW ABOUT PRICES AND TERMS

Salesmen must understand price policies and be able to interpret prices and terms when a question about them arises in sales negotiations. It is necessary for salesmen to know the following: (1) general company price policy; (2) established prices; (3) discounts from list price; (4) negotiated prices; (5) terms of payment; (6) terms of delivery; (7) resale price maintenance; (8) pricing below cost; (9) discriminating in price quotations; (10) price guarantees or protection against price decline; (11) special prices; (12) price advances and reductions; (13) computing prices; (14) competitive prices; (15) relation of price to product and service values; (16) a salesman's attitude toward price.

The great amount of information available on any one of these topics makes it necessary for a salesman first to acquire information about those elements of pricing that apply specifically to the sale of his product or service. The price policy and structure of some companies are so simple that a salesman can learn very quickly all that is necessary for him to know about them. In other concerns, however, these matters are so involved with numerous discounts and complex terms and prices change so frequently that salesmen must be continuously seeking information about prices and terms.

1. General Company Price Policy. The general price policy of a company is of vital importance to its sales representatives. If the selling price of a concern is too high, the opportunities of its salesmen are narrowed, competition is invited, price cutting is probable, and sales resistance is increased. A company quoting low prices, on the other hand, may deprive its representatives of the sales benefits of quality, superior service, good-will advertising, and other aids which naturally help them close sales.

Business organizations operate under one or more of these three types of general price policies: (1) pricing below the prevailing market, or at the market minus; (2) pricing at the prevailing market, or at the market par; (3) pricing above the prevailing market, or at the market plus. A salesman's discussion of price is determined by which of these general price policies is followed by his company.

If a salesman represents a company that pursues the policy of pricing below the market, price is his principal sales argument. A price salesman must contact prospects in low-income groups, emphasize economy and durability, subordinate service and quality, and seek large volume orders.

If a salesman is selling at the prevailing market price, he is usually able to give more service, more frequent deliveries, more personal attention, more liberal credit and guarantees than the low-price seller. Friendship, good will, and a salesman's personality play a more important part when prices of competing salesmen are on a parity.

Salesmen selling at prices above the market usually have an advantage over competitors in being able to discuss superior quality of product, but buyers are few and far apart, high volume cannot be expected, and in periods of business depression, sales volume is sharply curtailed by reduced purchasing power.

2. Established Prices. A company may operate on a basic price policy of either (1) established prices or (2) negotiated prices. A salesman who works under an established price policy quotes prices which are identical for all buyers of similar status and remain the same for a series of transactions. Under a negotiated policy prices are figured and quoted for each sales transaction. Established prices are usually the policy of manufacturers and distributors of standard, packaged products; while sellers of custom-made, nonstandard products or services and those on which prices fluctuate widely, usually prefer to negotiate prices for individual orders, as in the case of special-order machinery or construction.

Most manufacturers and wholesalers prefer an established price policy which has been universally adopted by all retailers. This policy permits a salesman to quote prices immediately without referring to a superior for a price quotation, preparing a price estimate, or bargaining with the buyer. Prices may be announced, featured in advertising, and used as a sales appeal.

An established price is either quoted as "net" or "list." A "net" price is the actual amount paid by the purchaser who is not obliged to figure discounts, rebates, or other allowances. It facilitates price comparisons. Most sellers under an established price policy prefer to use a "list" price, which is the published or advertised price subject to a series of discounts allowed buyers according to the quantity purchased, the buyer's status in the trade, and other factors. The "list" price remains uniform while the amount and number of the discounts may be varied by the seller. Manufacturers often establish a "list" price to suggest a resale price to wholesalers and retailers, saving them the calculation of their prices to customers.

3. Discounts from List Price. Manufacturers and wholesalers quote one or several discounts from established list prices for different classes of buyers according to their location, requirements, services rendered by the seller, promptness in paying for purchases, and other reasons. The principal types of discounts are: (1) quantity discounts, (2) financial discounts, (3) trade discounts, (4) territorial discounts, (5) advertising discounts, (6) miscellaneous discounts. Salesmen should be familiar with all types of discounts offered, in order to quote prices correctly.

Quantity Discounts. So that buyers may be induced to increase the size of their orders, sellers allow quantity discounts from the list price, which vary with the amount of merchandise purchased. There are two types of quantity discounts, the single order and the deferred or period type. A typical single-order discount is used by a manufacturer of counting machines, who allows 3 per cent off list price for the purchase of 12 machines, 5 per cent off for 25 machines, 10 per cent off for 50 machines, 15 per cent off for 100 machines.

A typical deferred or period quantity discount is used by a food-products manufacturer who allows grocery wholesalers and chains a discount of 5 per cent on total quantity purchases providing a minimum quantity of 100 cases is bought during each three-month period.

Salesmen quoting quantity discounts can offer buyers lower prices and greater profits.

Financial Discounts. To strengthen a cash position, curtail credit losses, and stimulate collections, sellers offer cash discounts, time extensions, and post and forward datings. These allowances are discussed in greater detail in Chap. X. Cash discounts are commonly allowed by sellers as an inducement to buyers to pay their bills promptly. The rate varies in different industries from 0.5 to 5 per cent, although the usual rate is 2 per cent. A cash discount is allowed to buyers for payment of accounts in from 10 to 60 days from the date of invoice or shipment, with 10 days prevailing.

Some manufacturers of seasonal goods allow buyers forward datings or deferred datings which are, in effect, additional discounts since they allow buyers longer use of their money. Under deferred dating, a shipment made after November 1 may be invoiced as of April 1 of the following year. A salesman should show buyers the money gains possible under such an arrangement. Buyers frequently seek extra price concessions from salesmen in the form of deferred datings.

Salesmen who offer cash discounts and time extensions to buyers should induce them to take advantage of these discounts to secure lower prices, improve credit standing, and obtain the benefit of lower interest rates than may be secured from a bank or other lending agency. Buyers who discount their bills are not only better credit risks but are also able to buy more merchandise. A buyer who takes a cash discount 18 times a year on terms of 2 per cent 10 days, net 30 days, is earning the equivalent of 36 per cent a year. A discount of 3 per cent 10 days, net 30 days, taken 18 times a year, will earn at the rate of 54 per cent per annum.

Salesmen who persuade buyers to take cash discounts multiply their sales opportunities. A buyer who settles his account every 60 days can be sold only six times a year; a buyer who pays his bills every 30 days can be sold as often as 12 times a year.

Trade Discounts. Manufacturers offer trade discounts from their list price to various types of distributors. Separate discounts may be established for individual retail, wholesale, chain, or department stores, or for cooperative and self-service stores. Discounts are established for each type of distributor to protect them against competition, secure their cooperation, and afford them sufficient margin to operate profitably.

Salesmen are often allowed to use their individual judgments in quoting trade discounts to various types of distributors. It is necessary for salesmen to classify outlets by type to determine the trade discount which should be quoted. A retailer, for example, may also be wholesaling a substantial portion of his volume. A salesman is confronted with the question, "Should this merchant be entitled to a retail or wholesale discount?" Many concerns classify distributors to aid salesmen in quoting trade discounts. A corporate chain, for example, may be defined as a retail organization operating two or more stores and as such be entitled to a chain trade discount.

Territorial Discounts. To quote delivered prices in various parts of the country, sellers sometimes establish geographical, territorial, or zone prices, which include the cost of transportation from the seller's shipping point to the buyer. Salesmen should be familiar with the freight allowances or discounts that may be established for a buyer's territory.

Advertising Discounts. Many manufacturers make advertising allowances to retail distributors who are able to advertise products. Advertising discounts are usually a fixed percentage of the purchase price, or they may be figured at so many cents per unit. Formerly advertising allowances were largely considered as price concessions and in many cases retailers did not attempt to advertise the products of manufacturers from whom they received allowances; also, some buyers were favored with advertising allowances which were not offered to other customers. However, the Robinson-Patman Act now requires sellers to make advertising allowances available on proportionately equal terms to all competing customers. Most manufacturers now require proof of insertion in recognized media before paying these discounts.

Salesmen who sell to retail distributors should know their company policy on such allowances, the amount of discount permitted, and the recognized media.

Miscellaneous Discounts. Numerous other types of special discounts are offered by manufacturers to distributors and dealers which are indirect price reductions. The "free deal" in which a definite amount of merchandise is given free with the purchase of a minimum quantity of goods is one of the most common special discounts. Free goods to cover stocks in the hands of dealers are also frequently given to stimulate sales. Bonuses, prizes, and premiums are often offered to distributors by manufacturers as a sales stimulant. These are, in effect, discounts from list price. In some companies these special allowances to the trade are so numerous that salesmen have difficulty in keeping account of them. Since they are often one of the principal selling arguments used by salesmen calling on retailers and wholesalers, an effective method of presenting them should be developed.

A combination offer in which two articles are sold for the price of one is an indirect price reduction and a form of discount frequently used to stimulate packaged food and drug sales.

Trade-in allowances on used merchandise, sometimes given in connection with the purchase of new articles, are a form of price discount. The amount of these allowances is determined by the salesman after appraisal of the used equipment.

4. Negotiated Prices. When every piece of merchandise or equipment produced by a manufacturer differs in some characteristics from other merchandise of the same manufacturer, prices are determined for each product and quoted individually. Some manufacturers also custom-make products to the specifications of particular customers. In both cases established prices are not practical and negotiated prices are quoted.

When selling by negotiation, a salesman determines the need and desires of the buyer and turns this information over to an estimator who figures the price of the product. In some cases, a salesman does his own estimating which involves an appraisal of the costs of labor, material, sales, and overhead involved in making and selling the product. After an estimate has been made, it is quoted to the buyer by the salesman.

Usually a quotation after estimate is a "firm" price, not subject to change, but sometimes it is merely a basis for discussion or bargaining in which the buying power of the customer, competition, economic conditions, and the circumstances of the seller all affect the final price.

Prices are negotiated in the sale of most industrial raw materials, operating equipment, and supplies, such as printing or commodities purchased in quantity on a contract basis. Construction prices are universally negotiated.

5. Term of Payment. Price quotations on either an established or a negotiated basis include a statement of the terms of payment or when and how the buyer is expected to pay for his purchase. Customers usually have a choice of two methods of making payment: (1) cash or (2) credit. Some concerns, however, sell only for cash, whereas others extend credit only to those whose credit is acceptable, while all others pay cash.

Credit terms are discussed in detail in Chap. X. Cash terms are of several types: C.W.O. terms mean cash is required with the order. This term applies to all buyers from concerns which sell for cash only and to buyers whose credit is not at all acceptable to concerns which extend credit to customers. This term is usually applied on special orders made to the specification of the customer.

If a buyer's credit is considered somewhat more desirable, the seller is willing to produce the goods and sell on C.B.D., or cash before delivery, terms.

A still more liberal cash quotation and the one most commonly used is C.O.D., or cash on delivery, which means that the seller is willing to ship the merchandise and take payment through the delivering service.

Salesmen may be given full authority in quoting terms, although some companies reserve all responsibility for setting terms of sale to their credit departments.

6. Terms of Delivery. Price quotations also include terms of delivery, or who is responsible for delivery and payment of transportation charges. As the total cost to a buyer represents not only the price of the product but also the expense of transportation, the terms of delivery are an important element in a price quotation.

Some sellers prepay the shipping cost and quote delivered prices which include transportation charges. Similar delivery terms are "transportation charges allowed," meaning that the buyer pays for delivery but deducts the cost from the price quoted.

Other sellers quote F.O.B., meaning "free on board" shipping point, under which terms the buyer pays all transportation charges which he must include in his cost.

In other cases, sellers make "freight allowances" or pay the shipping charges up to a certain amount per hundredweight to meet the prices and terms of competitors.

A fourth method employed by some sellers is to quote a uniform delivered price, which includes transportation charges, to all buyers in the same geographical area. This zone-delivered price includes cost of the product plus an average transportation expense for the area.

While the terms of delivery are often identical for all sellers in an industry, there is a wide variation in terms between industries.

7. Resale Price Maintenance. Many manufacturers of branded, advertised food and drug products, to protect the profits of their distributors and dealers, have set a minimum price below which a wholesaler or retailer may not sell the branded article. This is known as resale price maintenance and has been legalized by fair-trade laws in 45 states and in interstate contracts by the Miller-Tydings Act.

Products which are "fair-traded" or sold under resale price maintenance contracts are favored by many merchants who believe that price maintenance will prevent cut-price stores from underselling them by using well-known brands as price leaders.

Salesmen of price-maintained products have strong sales arguments that their controlled prices will eliminate price cutting, outlaw unfair competition, standardize prices, and protect merchants' profits.

On the other hand, salesmen whose products are not price maintained claim that merchants who sell fair-trade articles lose their independence in determining their own resale prices; the good will of consumers may be jeopardized by higher prices; increased prices may reduce sales volume, and large inventories may not be sold readily.

8. Pricing below Cost. Twenty-five states have passed "unfair trade acts" which prohibit pricing by merchants below cost of goods plus a markup varying from 6 to 12 per cent. These laws are similar in intent to the fair-trade laws in that they are designed to protect merchants' profits by limiting price cutting by competitors.

Salesmen should be familiar with these state laws in order to advise merchants in pricing merchandise for resale.

9. Discriminating in Price Quotations. Salesmen in interstate commerce cannot quote different prices on the same class of merchandise to buyers who are competitors unless the difference in price is based on a difference in cost of production, selling, or service. In the past, some sellers quoted large customers lower prices than smaller buyers irrespective of the quantity purchased. This practice has been outlawed by the Robinson-Patman Amendment to the Clayton Act. This law has affected the price policies of many manufacturers who have eliminated quantity discounts, advertising allowances, brokerage allowances, cumulative discounts, and unrestrained price cutting.

10. Price Guarantees or Protection against Price Decline. Manufacturers of seasonal goods, selling to distributors or contractors, sometimes guarantee purchasers, for a specified period of time, against decline in the purchase price before delivery. Price guarantees are usually offered by salesmen when price levels are declining or advance orders are being sought.

Salesmen operating under a price guarantee policy may use it as a strong selling argument in that it relieves the distributor of the risk of price declines and enables him to lower his resale prices and secure prompt delivery and an adequate supply.

Sometimes, as protection to the seller, price guarantees are given only on the unshipped portion of orders. Distributors may ask that a price guarantee also cover their inventories or that they be given a rebate on previous purchases in the event of a price decline. Buyers may be given advance notice of price declines so that they may dispose of existing stocks before the new price is effective.

11. Special Prices. Salesmen sometimes quote special prices for a seasonal clearance, to dispose of bankrupt stock, job lots, and outmoded or shopworn merchandise. Reduced prices are also quoted on combination offers when two units may be offered for the price of one or a premium may be given with the purchase of an article at the regular price.

Price leaders or merchandise specially priced to meet competition may be featured. A new brand may be introduced temporarily at a low price to undersell competition and obtain volume. In a period of low prices, a "fighting" brand is sometimes featured without sacrificing the prestige of an established high-priced quality brand.

Salesmen feature these special price offers to secure initial orders from new buyers and repeat sales from old customers.

12. Price Advances and Reductions. Salesmen are frequently obliged to discuss price increases and reductions with customers and prospects. Wholesalers and retailers oppose reduced prices that cause them to suffer losses on stocks on hand and reduce profits. In meeting objections of the trade to lower prices, salesmen use the argument that lower prices stimulate consumption and turnover, thereby increasing profits through volume sales. If advance notice of impending price reductions is given to buyers, salesmen obtain dealer good will and large advance orders. Sales advantage also may be gained by protecting buyers against price declines which may occur between the time of placing the order and the date of shipment.

Consumer salesmen, on the other hand, find that their clients welcome price reductions. Sales are usually stimulated by sharp price declines; gradual reductions cause consumers to postpone buying in expectation of further declines.

Price advances stimulate trade demand and, as greater profits are taken on inventories, salesmen enjoy larger sales, particularly when increased prices are announced in advance and dealers are given an opportunity to buy before prices change. Price speculation, by both consumers and dealers, on a rising market creates sales opportunities for aggressive salesmen.

13. Computing Prices. Manufacturers' salesmen serving wholesalers and retailers often help merchants in determining resale prices. Some manufacturers, on the other hand, suggest resale prices to the wholesale and retail trade, thus obviating the necessity for salesmen or merchants to figure them.

In computing resale prices the salesman must first determine from the merchant the per cent markup required which should cover costs of operation plus net profit. Then he must consult a markup table like the one shown on the following page to calculate the selling price.

As the most convenient way of figuring resale prices is by means of a markup table, some salesmen carry these tables to aid dealers in determining selling prices for their customers.

Since the same markup percentage cannot be used on all types of merchandise, it is sometimes necessary for a manufacturer's salesman to aid dealers in determining the correct markup percentage for the

Margin required by budget (per cent of sales)	Mark-up necessary to provide margin (per cent of cost)	Multiply invoice cost by
75.0	300.00	4.000
70.0	233.3	3.333
66.0	200.0	3.000
65.0	185.7	2.857
60.0	150.0	2.500
55.0	122.2	2.222
50.0	100.0	2.000
48.0	92.3	1.923
46.0	85.2	1.852
44.0	78.6	1.786
42.0	72.4	1.724
40.0	66.6	1.666
38.0	61.3	1.613
36.0	56.2	1.562
34.0	51.5	1.515
33.3	50.0	1.500
32.0	47.1	1.471
30.0	42.9	1.429
28.0	38.9	1.389
26.0	35.1	1.351
24.0	31.6	1.316
22.0	28.2	1.282
20.0	25.0	1.250
18.0	22.0	1.220
16.0	19.0	1.190
15.0	17.7	1.177
14.0	16.3	1.163
12.0	13.6	1.136
10.0	11.1	1.111
5.0	5.3	1.053

00.5601-49

Fig. 2. This margin and markup table saves the time of a salesman in calculating markup and in determining resale prices for wholesale and retail merchants. It was published in "Hardware Distribution in the Gulf Southwest" by the U.S. Department of Commerce.

manufacturer's goods. A merchant should be advised to keep accurate records of his sales and operating expenses, including interest and net profit, and divide that amount by his net sales to secure the percentage of margin.

14. Competitive Prices. Salesmen should keep thoroughly informed about prices and terms of competitors by reading their advertising, price-reporting services, by exchange of information with competitive salesmen, or through trade-association channels. When prices fluctuate over a wide range and change rapidly, as in the case of securities, salesmen must have daily, even hourly, market quotations to inform buyers of current prices. Price trends over periods of months or years should be understood by salesmen to enable them to discuss future prices and justify current price quotations.

15. Relation of Price to Product and Service Values. A salesman should be able to justify his price quotations. If he quotes a comparatively high price, he should know why it is high. Perhaps the high price is due to scarcity of raw materials, high labor costs, and great demand. Maybe quality of materials, skill in manufacture, or care in packaging are largely responsible for the high price. Whichever of these or other factors contribute to the cost of a product or service, they should be known by the salesman as a part of his product or service knowledge. If a product is priced below the prevailing market, the various reasons for this condition should be known by the salesman.

The subject of price is sometimes clouded in mystery by the management and full price facts are withheld from salesmen, with the result that many of them are suspicious of the validity of the prices they quote. Accordingly, it is easy for them to lack confidence in their prices and succumb to the objections of prospects.

There should be a legitimate reason for every price, barring monopoly and charging all the traffic will bear, and salesmen should be fortified with price justifications.

16. A Salesman's Attitude toward Price. Many salesmen encounter objections to price so frequently that they hesitate to quote prices for fear of meeting price resistance. This fear puts them on the defensive so that they lose confidence and become apologetic in dealing with price. To sell successfully against competition which quotes lower prices, a salesman must have the right attitude toward price.

First, a salesman must recognize that price is usually not the most important consideration of a buyer. Price differentials almost always look more important to a salesman than they do to the buyer. Customers usually buy a salesman's product at infrequent intervals and have a vague idea of price. Many salesmen assume that price is important to customers who mention price frequently. Customers usually mention price because they can think of nothing else to talk about, or to discourage the salesman. Until a buyer understands the value of a product, he is not able to appraise price fairly.

If a salesman knows the values of his product or service, he can see the justification for its price and discuss price confidently, knowing that the product is well worth the price charged. He can defend his price and quote it freely because he understands the reasons for it.

The manner in which a salesman discusses price reveals his attitude toward it and affects the buyer's reaction to the subject. By dealing with price confidently and cheerfully, a salesman gives a customer the impression that he is not afraid to discuss price.

HOW A SALESMAN SHOULD QUOTE PRICES AND TERMS

Outstanding salesmen employ a definite technique for discussing price and terms with prospects and customers. Not only do good salesmen know their prices and terms thoroughly but, more important, they have discovered simple, effective ways of putting their knowledge to the best use. These practical, proved principles for quoting prices and terms, taken from the experience of successful men selling various types of goods and services, have been combined into a five-step routine, which should be studied and practiced until it becomes second nature in price discussions.

Routine for Quoting Price and Terms

1. Establish product benefits first.
2. Avoid price until buyer mentions it.
3. Minimize price quotations.
4. Quote price for whole job rather than part.
5. Quote price clearly and completely.

1. Establish Product Benefits First. Customers buy when they believe that the benefits to be gained from the purchase of a product or service are more important than its cost. Price is always an obstacle to a sale until the value of the product overshadows price in the mind of the buyer. Accordingly, the first task of a salesman is to establish product or service benefits by discussing features which satisfy the needs and appeal to the motives of the buyer. When benefits have been recognized by a buyer, price does not seem high.

The process of building up product benefits until they outweigh the price in the mind of a buyer has been compared to using a pair of balance scales. The weight in each pan of the scales must be equal before they balance. If the price in dollars in one pan is heavier than the weight of the benefits in the other pan, the cost outweighs the benefits and the customer does not buy. But if the salesman piles up more benefits on the scale, until they overbalance the price in the mind of the buyer, a sale will result.

Failure to establish benefits early in sales interviews causes buyers to raise price objections prematurely. As a result, price becomes the center of discussion before the buyer knows enough about the product and its benefits to determine if the price is reasonable or excessive. Good salesmen make every effort to forestall discussion of price until they have fully established benefits. If a buyer brings up the matter of price before he has completely understood the benefits, a salesman defers his quotation by diverting the discussion to product values promising to take up price later. When the benefits have been accepted by the buyer, then price can be logically discussed.

2. Avoid Price Until Buyer Mentions It. In spite of the importance of price in a sales transaction, successful salesmen have found that it is not wise to open the subject with prospects. Not only are many prospects not interested in price, some are even offended at the mention of it, and others most conscious of price are often too proud to admit their concern about it.

When a prospect states frankly the amount he expects to pay or asks a question about price, there is no objection to a salesman's discussing the matter fully. Many salesmen assume that all prospects are price-conscious, that they know exactly before purchasing what they expect to pay, and that nothing else matters. On the contrary, most buyers give little previous thought to price, a majority make up their minds on the subject after they have seen the merchandise, and many are influenced by quality factors to the exclusion of price.

Even in the sale of low-priced merchandise, the buyer is looking for other values as well as economy, and a salesman who ignores price and discusses quality values often "trades up" the prospect to purchase a more expensive item.

It is never wise to ask a prospect bluntly, "What price do you expect to pay?" or "How high do you want to go in price?" In responding to such questions, many prospects are embarrassed or admit no decision. If they name a low price, it is difficult to interest them in higher priced merchandise.

It is often possible to discover a prospect's interest in price without directly opening up the subject. By asking him about the size, model, material, or use which he expects to make of a commodity in which he is interested, a salesman can get a definite indication of the price which the prospect expects to pay. A volunteered remark or the examination of a price tag will also reveal a prospect's interest in the subject.

However, when a product is offered at a special reduced price or was made to sell at a low figure, a salesman may be justified in featuring price in his sales presentation.

3. Minimize Price Quotations. When quoting price, successful salesmen often minimize the purchase price by breaking the total down into small amounts. For example, a life insurance salesman does not quote a prospect an annual premium amounting to $200; instead he discusses the cost as amounting to only a few cents a day or less than the price of two good cigars or a magazine. This strategy of comparing cost with low-priced products minimizes the price of expensive products. By quoting installment terms in small weekly or monthly payments which contrast favorably with a cash price, a salesman makes the total cost seem low. When discussing the cost of running an electric refrigerator, the salesmen of one large manufacturer do not refer to operating expense in terms of so many dollars a month but compare it with the small cost of current necessary to light a single electric lamp.

The price of a commodity or service may be minimized by comparing it with the previous cost of a similar product or service. For example, a tire salesman may minimize the price of tires today by remarking that thirty years ago a tire would run 2,500 miles at a cost of $25, or 1 cent a mile; today, a tire costing $12 runs from 25,000 to 30,000 miles, or 1/25 cent a mile.

The "per" method of minimizing price quotations is widely used by salesmen who discuss price in terms of "per day" or "per mile" or "per square foot" of cost.

4. Quote Price for Whole Job rather than Part. When a product is but one factor of a larger purchase, or one unit in an assembled job, successful salesmen have found that it is better to quote a price for the total purchase rather than for a part. For example, a linoleum salesman selling a new floor for a restaurant, should quote a price for the complete job in one lump sum rather than a price per yard.

The same principle applies in selling fuel for heating. For example, the cost of gas for home heating should be quoted as $150 for the heating season rather than so much per cubic foot. This strategy is even more desirable when an additional charge for installation is involved.

The reason for stating the price for the complete job in one lump sum is that few customers have any idea of what price means in terms of the finished job because they do not know how many yards, pounds, gallons, or units they need. Unit prices often sound high when compared with low-priced products on the same basis of unit measurement. Furthermore, customers are saved the trouble of estimating the cost of the whole job.

When a salesman does not have the exact capacity, dimensions, or knowledge of the prospect's situation, he can quote prices on the basis of a standard-size installation. This method of quoting often eliminates the competitive effectiveness of lower unit prices.

Customers often have an exaggerated impression of the importance of a price differential on a unit basis. You may quote 10 cents a gallon for your product, while a competitor quotes nine cents. This differential seems big to a customer until you point out that it only means a difference of one dollar on a 100-gallon job.

While this strategy obviously does not apply to quoting prices on merchandise or services complete in themselves, it is a very effective way to state prices for goods sold by measure.

5. Quote Price Clearly and Completely. Serious misunderstandings may easily arise over a price quotation unless the salesman makes sure that all elements of the quotation are clearly understood and accepted by the purchaser. The necessity for a clear understanding as to price is greatest in the sale of custom-made commodities or special order goods which are produced exclusively for the buyer. Salesmen are usually required to obtain signed orders stipulating in writing the terms of the sales transaction.

To avoid misunderstandings, a good salesman reads the details of the order, including quantity, size, price, terms, color, weight, and any other specifications, to the buyer before he affixes his signature. In this way a buyer has a chance to learn the price and details and make an objection then, if he is going to make it at all, before production on the order begins.

Costly returns and adjustments sought by buyers may be avoided largely by care in reaching a clear understanding with customers concerning terms at the time orders are placed.

SALES PERFORMANCE RATING FORM

Quoting Selling Prices and Terms

Salesman_____   Date_____

Rated by_____   Over-all Rating_____

Score

I. *Salesman's Knowledge of Prices and Terms*	Excellent 90–100	Good 80–90	Fair 70–80	Poor 60–70	Failure Below 60
A. General price policy of company					
B. Established prices					
C. Discounts from list price					
D. Negotiated prices					
E. Terms of payment					
F. Terms of delivery					
G. Resale price maintenance					
H. Pricing below cost					
I. Discriminating in price quotations					
J. Price guarantees					
K. Special prices					
L. Price advances					
M. Computing resale prices					
N. Competitive prices					
O. Relation of price to value					
P. Attitude toward price					

II. *Salesman's Use of Price Knowledge*	Excellent 90–100	Good 80–90	Fair 70–80	Poor 60–70	Failure Below 60
A. Establish product benefits					
B. Avoid price discussion					
C. Minimize price quotations					
D. Quote price for whole, not part					
E. Quote price clearly and completely					

Miscellaneous Comments_____

_____

_____

Problem I

Frank H. Leighton, representing Sanitary Biscuit Company

The Sanitary Biscuit Company, Chicago, Ill., manufactures and distributes direct to retail food outlets an extensive line of packaged and bulk crackers and cakes. Salesmen of the company operate company trucks, sell and deliver in one call, and contact each customer once a week. Store and counter advertising is furnished to dealers without charge.

Frank H. Leighton is one of 40 salesmen operating in Cook County, and the city of Chicago. The following interview took place in the office of the buyer of a chain of five high-grade grocery stores serving the wealthier suburban areas surrounding Chicago. The salesman has been selling the buyer "Delicious" and "Crunchy" crackers and wishes to introduce a new brand of graham crackers.

1. SALESMAN: Here is a new graham cracker (showing package) and your net on the list price of 20 cents a package is 16 cents a package or a 20 per cent trade discount. Our terms are 2 per cent 10 days, net 30 days, delivered.

2. BUYER: What is the customary retail price? We're getting 20 cents for other brands.

3. SALESMAN: If you want to run a special on them and get your girls to suggest them to customers on the telephone, you can sell them at 17 cents and still be getting a profit out of it, underselling everybody in the country.

4. BUYER: What do you want to do that for?

5. SALESMAN (laughing): Well, no—but I'm telling you what you could do. Well, you could make a swell profit on it.

6. BUYER: There is no reason in the world why they shouldn't be sold for 20 cents if they are just as good as those other standard makes which never sell for less than 20 or 21 cents.

7. SALESMAN: Of course, this cracker is so different, you'd think people would accept it as equal in quality to the higher priced brands.

8. BUYER: Oh, well, we're selling other brands of graham crackers for 20 cents a package.

9. SALESMAN: But this is very different from the other brands.

10. BUYER: We can sell a cracker that's different. I like a cracker that's richer because it's flakier. I love it with milk.

11. SALESMAN: Yeah, well, of course, we're coming on to the season now when women are going to be buying crackers and milk, graham crackers. Now is the time to start and sell them and build the business for the summer months.

12. BUYER: I'll tell you what you do. You leave a sample of your graham crackers here and between now and a week from next Monday, I'll take it up with our managers.
13. SALESMAN: Leave one here? All right.
14. BUYER: Do you get around in a week or two?
15. SALESMAN: Well, I'll bring you up one that isn't opened. Although we just got these samples the first of the week.
16. BUYER: When do you get around again?
17. SALESMAN: Next Monday, Tuesday, or Wednesday.
18. BUYER: Why don't you leave it when you come then?
19. SALESMAN: All right.

Questions

1. Criticize the salesman's handling of price in this interview on the basis of the five routine points. State specific weaknesses and strengths of his presentation of the price.
2. How does the salesman handle competitive prices?
3. What is the retailer's markup on the product in cents, in per cent, on resale?
4. Is the resale price maintained by the seller? If so, why? If not, why?
5. What price is quoted the buyer? If the buyer's trade discount is 20 per cent, and 2 per cent for cash, what is the net cost for six packages?

Problem II

Paul K. Patrick, representing United Office Supply Company

The United Office Supply Company, Buffalo, N.Y., specializes in the distribution of office furniture, equipment, and supplies sold direct by eight salesmen to leading industrial concerns. Salesmen concentrate their efforts on industrial purchasing agents. To aid them in securing business, salesmen are supported by direct advertising to buyers.

One of the five salesmen, working out of the Buffalo office of the company, is Paul K. Patrick, who in the following interview is calling on the purchasing agent of a large railroad system. The railroad bought the majority of its office equipment during the previous year from the United Office Supply Company through salesman Patrick. The following interview between Patrick and the purchasing agent ensues:

1. BUYER: Hello, Mr. Patrick, sure is hot this morning—the humidity is so high.
2. SALESMAN: Yes, it is. I don't see how you can get any work done in this hot office.

3. BUYER: You just have to sweat and bear it; you feel like a rag by four o'clock.

4. SALESMAN: What you need is a good electric fan to keep you comfortably cool, no matter how hot the weather gets. With a 12-inch Bowes Oscillator you can dissipate the hot, stagnant air so you can work and provide comfort for your visitors. The Bowes has a motor with power to spare, great big blades that whip up a strong, steady, cooling air stream.

5. BUYER: They only give me a pain in the neck.

6. SALESMAN: There's a low table-type fan that stands on the floor and circulates the air below your knees so it won't blow on your head and give you a cold. It has a table top and the sides are completely enclosed by a grill so there is no danger of getting caught in the blades. It is beautifully styled and finished in rich, new bronze to match your office furnishings.

7. BUYER: The things are so noisy, I hate to have them around.

8. SALESMAN: I can see what you mean; the fans they made before the war made a lot of racket, but these new postwar models deliver a real breeze with scarcely a sound because they have a new type of roller-bearing action that smoothes the sound. Also they're static-free around radios.

9. BUYER: What do they cost?

10. SALESMAN: You will be surprised how little the Bowes costs to own and operate. Why, for the price of a pack of cigarettes a day, the low table model will give you solid comfort all summer long. We put 30 of them in the executives' offices at the Great National Insurance Company. They ran a test on operating cost and found that you can run one of these fans a whole month for as little as the cost of your favorite magazine.

11. BUYER: Fans used to be pretty expensive.

12. SALESMAN: Yes, they were before the war. Why, 10 years ago a good 12-inch fan would cost in the neighborhood of $25, but today you can get a better fan for around $15. How many executive offices do you have here?

13. BUYER: There are 10 executives on this floor and 12 upstairs.

14. SALESMAN: You can get 22 Bowes table-top models for all of your executive offices for only $693 on terms of 2 per cent 10 days, net 30, delivery paid.

15. BUYER: Don't we get a discount for quantity?

16. SALESMAN: That $693 includes a 10 per cent discount from the retail list price of $35 on orders for 10 or more fans. That makes each fan cost you $31.50. You can have immediate delivery from our Buffalo warehouse.

17. BUYER: I'll discuss that price with our purchasing committee.

18. SALESMAN: Here is a folder describing the features of the fan we've been talking about. When will you be ready to go on with the matter?
19. BUYER: We meet on Saturday and I'll let you know our decision the first of the week.
20. SALESMAN: Thanks, I'll see you next week.

Questions

1. Did the salesman establish his product benefits? If so, what?

2. Was price discussion avoided by the salesman until the buyer mentioned it?

3. Did the salesman minimize his price quotation? How?

4. Was the price quoted for the whole job or a part? Explain.

5. Was the price quotation clear? Explain. Complete? Explain.

Reading References

E. G. BLACKSTONE, C. C. CRAWFORD, and E. GRINNELL, "Selling," pp. 244–248, D. C. Heath and Company, Boston, 1942.

B. R. CANFIELD, "Sales Administration, Principles and Problems," rev. ed., pp. 511–531, Prentice-Hall, Inc., New York, 1947.

JESSE V. COLES, "The Consumer-Buyer and the Market," pp. 323, 376, John Wiley & Sons, Inc., New York, 1938.

J. R. DAUBMAN, "Salesmanship and Types of Selling," p. 78, F. S. Crofts & Co., New York, 1939.

PAUL W. IVEY, "Successful Salesmanship," pp. 302, 306, 394, Prentice-Hall, Inc., New York, 1947.

H. C. NOLEN and H. H. MAYNARD, "Sales Management," pp. 421–427, The Ronald Press Company, New York, 1940.

HARRY SIMMONS, "How to Get the Order," Chap. XI, Harper & Brothers, New York, 1937.

D. B. TANSILL, "So You're Going to Sell," pp. 64–69, John C. Winston Company, Philadelphia, 1939.

HARRY R. TOSDAL, "Introduction to Sales Management," pp. 194–247, McGraw-Hill Book Company, Inc., New York, 1940.

EUGENE WHITMORE, "Helping People Buy," pp. 79–90, The Dartnell Coporation, Chicago, 1940.

CHAPTER VIII

PRESENTING ADVERTISING

Advertising plays an important part in the work of salesmen representing products or services sold and advertised to consumers and distributors. To help salesmen in their work, almost two billion dollars are invested annually in advertising in the United States by more than 200,000 manufacturers and more than 1,500,000 retail establishments.

Yet many salesmen fail to take advantage of this enormous investment because they look upon advertising as something apart, unrelated to their day-to-day job of securing orders. Some salesmen are indifferent about advertising because they have never learned how it can make their efforts more productive. There are still others who look upon advertising as a competitor, reducing the need for their services.

Advertising, on the contrary, may be a salesman's most valuable assistant. It takes from his shoulders much of the energy-consuming, time-taking, discouraging work of cold canvassing, or locating logical prospects, and leaves him the important, profitable work of "closing." Salesmen put their products on dealers' shelves; advertising moves the products off the shelves and creates repeat orders from distributors. By creating a demand from consumers, advertising makes it easier for retailers to sell and in this way aids salesmen in interesting dealers.

Advertising works for a salesman during his absence, or between calls on customers, by keeping business friendships alive and making it possible for him to hold his trade more easily.

Doors that would otherwise be closed to an unknown salesman, are opened when advertising has established prestige for the company and product he represents, paving the way for his call.

A salesman's time and energy are conserved by advertising, which shortens the time of interviews by giving prospects advance information and relieving salesmen of much of the task of describing construction features, method of operation, and merits of the products or

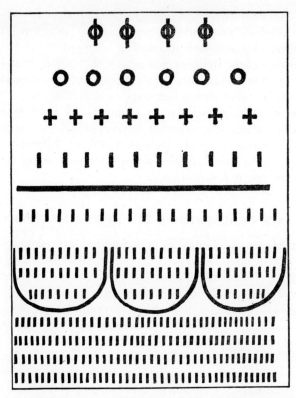

Fɪɢ. 3. This chart has been used by the General Electric Company to illustrate to salesmen the analogy between the operations of an army in action and the activities of salesmen supported by advertising.

The sales and advertising forces are shown at the bottom separated from their prospects, customers and the general public by a horizontal front line trench drawn through the center of the chart. The first figures at the bottom of the chart, represented by circles bisected with vertical lines, are the Big Berthas, or long-range artillery, representing institutional advertisements aimed at the general public, represented by the vertical lines at the top of the chart. In front of the Big Berthas, or long-range institutional advertisements, is the field artillery, represented by the circles. These stand for industrial advertisements in business magazines which are aimed at specific industries, the coal industry, steel industry, etc., represented by vertical lines surrounded by half circles. In front of the field artillery, or business magazines, are the machine guns or direct advertisements, booklets, folders, etc., represented by crosses on the chart. These concentrate on individual customers, indicated by vertical lines just above the heavy horizontal line on the chart. And in the front line trench are the individual salesmen whose activities are supported by the barrage of advertising artillery and machine guns laid down on prospects before and after sales calls.

services. More calls may be made by salesmen when advertising helps to present products and provides the names of interested prospects.

Advertising aids salesmen in meeting competition effectively as it makes possible more frequent contacts with customers and helps in following up interviews when it is impossible for salesmen to give buyers the personal attention necessary to hold business.

In many other ways, such as in winning back inactive customers, driving home arguments, securing appointments, overcoming objections, and creating prestige, various forms of advertising can be invaluable aids to salesmen who consider printed salesmanship as a sales tool and use it consistently.

IMPORTANCE OF ADVERTISING IN A SALESMAN'S PRESENTATION

The importance of advertising in a salesman's presentation depends to a large extent upon the type of buyer served as well as the amount and character of advertising done by the firm which a salesman represents. Salesmen working without benefit of advertising obviously have no occasion to refer to it in their presentations; on the other hand, those who are supported by extensive national and local advertising should make it an important part of their sales interview.

Salesmen of advertised products and services sold direct to users have little occasion to discuss advertising in their presentations to ultimate consumers. Consumers are not interested in advertising media, circulation costs, schedules, and other features of a salesman's advertising program.

ADVERTISING IN SELLING WHOLESALERS AND RETAILERS

Advertising is of much greater concern to wholesalers and retailers than it is to consumers, because wise merchants consider it indispensable in turning over a capital investment in merchandise and creating greater profits.

Merchants are concerned with two phases of a manufacturer's advertising program: the national advertising and the local advertising, both of which are related to and have an important influence on sales and profits. Each of these programs shall be considered separately in the following pages.

In the past it was sufficient for a salesman to mention that his product was advertised to secure sizable orders from wholesalers and retailers. Today, national advertisers are so numerous that there is little distinction in saying, "This product is nationally advertised." Salesmen must "sell" a national advertising program to dealers by pointing out the media used, the coverage, and the schedules, and by interpreting each of these features in terms of extra value to merchants.

Salesmen representing large advertisers are rated on their ability to secure the cooperation of their dealer customers in local advertising. Advertising plays such a prominent part in dealer selling that salesmen sometimes significantly remark that they do not sell merchandise, but advertising.

Retail merchants now depend to a large extent upon the manufacturers, whose products they sell, for assistance in planning local advertising campaigns, in determining the amount to be invested in advertising, where and when advertising should be done, and in the preparation of advertisements.

What a Salesman Should Know about His Company's National Advertising

The presentation of a salesman, selling a nationally advertised product, involves a knowledge of all the advertising done by his company. There are approximately 9,000 national advertisers investing from a few thousand to several million dollars annually in nationwide advertising. Salesmen representing these concerns explain the following features of their advertising programs to dealers in one or several interviews as the situation demands: (1) benefits of national advertising to distributors; (2) national advertising media and their values; (3) proofs of advertisements and their features; (4) schedule of national advertising; (5) coverage of advertising; (6) effectiveness of national advertising; (7) cost of national advertising.

1. Benefits of National Advertising to Distributors and Dealers. Salesmen whose firms are national advertisers must continuously educate wholesalers and retailers on the benefits of such a program. The salesman representing a consistent national advertiser has a great advantage in emphasizing the selling power which the cumulative effect of years and years of regular advertising gives to his products. The benefits derived by dealers who stock a nationally advertised line are:

a. Increased Turnover. The basic advantage of national advertising to dealers is its ability to increase stock turnover by bringing more customers into their stores. A merchant's annual profit is largely determined by the number of times he turns his stock during a year or, in other words, the earnings he makes on his capital invested in goods depends on how often he reinvests his capital or credit. If he reinvests it in nonadvertised items, on which he earns 6 per cent four times a year, his annual profit amounts to 24 per cent. However, if national advertising makes it possible for the merchant to get back his profit by selling out his stock eight times a year, he earns eight times 6 per cent, or 48 per cent—twice the amount earned before on the same margin of profit.

Merchants sometimes object to the narrow profit margins on nationally advertised goods. Granting, for example, that the profit on a nationally advertised brand is only 4 per cent, if it turns over eight times a year, contrasted with a turnover of four times on a nonadvertised brand carrying a margin of 6 per cent, the advertised item earns 32 per cent and the unadvertised goods earn 24 per cent. This example illustrates that it is not the margin of profit carried by an item that is of primary interest to a merchant, but the number of times that he can earn that profit. Furthermore, a merchant's selling costs do not increase as his rate of turnover is accelerated by national advertising.

Salesmen illustrate to dealers the principle of turnover, as promoted by national advertising, by means of charts, graphs, illustrations, and sometimes demonstrations similar to one used by a nationally advertised soft drink. Sales representatives of this company placed before dealers four small wooden shapes—a cube, a ball, a pyramid, and a hexagon. The pyramid represented an unknown soft drink; the cube stood for a drink with a few friends; the hexagon, a well-known local beverage; and the ball, the nationally advertised drink under consideration. The dealer was asked to attempt to turn over with his forefinger each of the shapes in the order mentioned. Obviously the ball representing the salesman's product, when pushed by the dealer, turned over rapidly and made a new impression of quick turnover.

b. Greater Prestige. Merchants who distribute nationally advertised wares share with the advertiser in the good will and confidence of consumers.

c. Reduced Selling Expense. Retail and wholesale salespeople spend less time selling nationally advertised merchandise and lower selling costs result. An investigation of the amount of time consumed by retail salespersons in selling advertised and nonadvertised merchandise showed that, when a customer asked for a nationally advertised article, it took the salesclerk 31 seconds to complete the transaction. To switch a customer from one advertised item to another, consumed

112 seconds, or four times as long. To switch a customer from an advertised to a private, unknown brand, took 199 seconds, or six times as long.

d. Improved Knowledge of Merchant. National advertising brings merchants valuable information about construction features, new uses, and improvements which can be used profitably in reselling to consumers.

e. Sales of Other Articles Stimulated. By bringing customers into retail stores and increasing store traffic, national advertising contributes to the sale of a much larger volume of profitable nonadvertised merchandise than would otherwise be sold. Sales of articles related in use to the advertised product are promoted by national advertising and the amounts purchased by customers are increased.

f. More Stable Inventory Values. There is less depreciation in the value of a stock of well-known, nationally advertised merchandise than in an inventory of unbranded goods. At a forced liquidation, an established brand commands a higher value by reason of the quality reputation created by the advertising.

g. Seasonal Fluctuations Overcome. National advertising tends to reduce seasonal fluctuations in demand, assuring to merchants a steady call for advertised merchandise and overcoming the irregular, spasmodic demand often experienced on unadvertised seasonal goods.

h. A Quality Requirement on Dealers. Merchants who stock nationally advertised goods are looked upon as quality outlets and are more likely to carry superior merchandise and offer higher grade service than dealers who are not identified as distributors of articles of such recognized worth.

2. National Advertising Media and Their Values. Salesmen should know not only the national publications, networks, outdoor, and car-card media in which their company's advertising appears, but also the reason why these various media are used. A salesman, for example, should not only know that his advertising is running in *The Saturday Evening Post*, but be able to give dealers facts to prove that the *Post* is the logical medium for maximum effectiveness.

Media are selected by the advertiser's agency and advertising manager after careful consideration of the following factors: number of readers or listeners, reader or listener interest, costs, coverage of market, amount of advertising carried, methods of obtaining readers, duplication of circulation, mechanical make-up, merchandising assistance. It is not necessary for a salesman to have full information on each of these factors for each medium in which his company advertises, but he should at least know those outstanding features that lead to the selection of each medium.

Dealers have definite advertising likes and dislikes; some favor one form of advertising and discount the value of another. Salesmen must be able not only to justify each publication or radio station used in their company's advertising, but also to defend the merit of each class of advertising used.

National magazines compared with other media have the advantages of a longer reading life, more thorough reading, attractive color reproduction, greater income of readers, and prestige.

When newspapers are used on a national scale as in the case of large advertisers, they have the following advantages: frequent insertion, identification of local distributors, quick action, adaptability to changing conditions, intensive local market coverage.

Radio advertising on national or regional networks has the advantages of personal appeal, high entertainment value, local dealer identification, flexibility in time, and coverage.

Outdoor advertising on a national scale has the merits of impressing with size and color, affording dealer identification, gaining power by frequent repetition, enjoying great numbers of readers, being elastic in coverage and universal in appeal. Car cards, used in advertising products of low cost and wide distribution, have, in general, the same advantages as outdoor advertising.

3. Proofs of Advertisements and Their Features. Proofs or examples of actual advertisements serve to impress merchants not only with tangible evidence of the advertising program but also with sales appeals, product features, and information about the product. A salesman who carries proofs of national advertising with him on his calls is, in effect, taking along an assistant who is ready with new talking points and fresh angles on old ideas to contribute to the interview.

Salesmen should be able to discuss the specific objective of each advertisement with dealers. Such objectives may be to increase units of purchase, to increase frequency of use, to increase length of the buying season, to increase the variety of the uses of a product, to reach specifiers who influence consumers to buy, such as architects, physicians, and dentists, to establish a trade name, and many others. Salesmen should study each of their advertisements and determine their objectives from the advertising manager.

The appeals used in a national advertisement and the reasons why these appeals are featured are talking points for a dealer salesman.

These appeals, whether they are to beauty, safety, economy, or cleanliness, should be discussed by the salesmen to give dealers the inside story of the advertising. Salesmen may suggest that pertinent paragraphs in the copy be read by dealers. One large advertiser provides his salesmen with proofs, to show to dealers, with the important paragraphs circled or phrases underlined for emphasis.

Advertising illustrations are often worthy of discussion with dealers, particularly when they feature well-known persons or have been produced by famous illustrators. Many advertisers illustrate dealers in their national advertising and bring them into the copy, which is of particular interest to merchants.

The size of the space used and the number of colors in which an advertisement is run are often excellent sales material to be used to advantage by a salesman.

The prestige of the advertising agency which prepared the copy—its size, personnel, and successful work for other well-known advertisers—is another asset that can be used to advantage in discussions with dealers.

4. Schedule of National Advertising. National advertising is planned to appear in publications, on billboards, or over the air at definite dates, determined by the sales strategy of the advertiser and the time of publication of the periodicals used or hours available on the air. Dealers should be informed of the times when advertisements are scheduled to appear so that they can tie up their local publicity with the national campaign and derive the benefits of the combined effort. Dealers will be more likely to listen to a radio program or read publications if they are told in advance when the advertising will be run. Salesmen can often obtain advance orders for specific models or patterns on the strength of advertising contemplated for appearance in the future.

Many concerns prepare charts which show the various media to be used in national advertising and the days of the week, hours of the day, or months of the year when each medium is scheduled.

5. Coverage of Advertising. Dealers are interested in the size, location, and character of the audience reached with a national advertising program. Advertising circulation, or the number of people reached by the advertising, is determined by the number of paid subscribers to periodicals or the number of radio receiving sets tuned in to the advertiser's program.

The total national circulation of all media used in a campaign is often an impressive figure, sometimes approximating the number of families in the country. A list of media in which the advertising appears and the circulation of each is a valuable sales tool.

Dealers, however, are not so much concerned with national circulation as with the number of subscribers, listeners, or observers in their immediate neighborhood or local market. Accordingly, national figures should be broken down into city, county, and state with sectional figures shown for each medium in which the advertising appears. With the aid of these breakdowns, a salesman can tell a dealer the exact number of persons exposed to a national advertising program in a local market.

The coverage of an advertising campaign, or how completely it reaches the total number of individuals or families comprising a market, is of significance to dealers. Coverage can be expressed in percentage of the total market. For example, the total number of families in a town is 2,000, while the number of magazines bought totals 3,000; therefore, the advertising has 150 per cent coverage.

The character of the advertising audience according to purchasing power and standards of living is also of primary importance to dealers in evaluating a national advertising program.

6. Effectiveness of National Advertising. In the last analysis, the worth of any advertising effort is measured by the increased sales, good will, and prestige created for the advertiser and his dealers. Definite sales increases resulting from the advertising, the volume of inquiries received, the amount of fan-mail response to a radio broadcast, and the number of new outlets secured are all factual evidence of advertising productiveness which should be discussed with dealers.

7. Cost of National Advertising. While an advertising expenditure amounting to several million dollars is impressive, dealers may feel that such a large sum would be better spent in reducing prices or increasing trade discounts. Accordingly, salesmen forestall this objection by discussing advertising expenditures in terms of single units of the product. For example, a cigarette salesman tells dealers that his company, which invests five million dollars a year in advertising, spends only $\frac{1}{2}$ cent a package for advertising. A well-known breakfast cereal spends only $\frac{3}{10}$ cent on a 15-cent package for national advertising.

The cost of one page in a national magazine should not be described as eight thousand dollars, but as $3\frac{1}{2}$ cents per reader. On the other hand, some dealers may be impressed with a large sum spent for advertising, and total expenditures may be quoted in discussing advertising costs.

What a Salesman Should Know about Local Advertising

National advertisers frequently run local advertising at their own expense, whereas others share the expense with local dealers. Salesmen secure dealer cooperation in defraying the cost of local advertising by discussing: (1) reasons why dealers should tie up their local with the manufacturer's national advertising; (2) manufacturer's local advertising; (3) local advertising media and their value; (4) the cost of local advertising; (5) planning advertising for a retail dealer; (6) aiding dealers in carrying out advertising plans.

1. Reasons Why Dealers Should Tie Up Their Local Advertising with the Manufacturer's National Advertising. Many dealers assume that since manufacturers advertise nationally, it is not necessary for them to advertise national brands locally. It is often impossible for a manufacturer to identify numerous local dealers in limited-space, national advertising. Therefore, it is necessary for retailers to inform their customers through their own local advertising of the local source of supply of the advertised article. By local advertising, merchants identify their stores with nationally advertised brands.

The prestige and reputation of a local dealer for quality merchandise are enhanced when he capitalizes on the good will created by national advertising and advertises national brands locally.

Many consumers who do not see or hear national advertising are reached by local advertising sponsored by local merchants. National advertising coverage is not as intensive as local, therefore in order to reach the majority of consumers in a city or town, local advertising is also necessary.

When manufacturers offer to share the cost of local advertising with retailers, it is to the advantage of local merchants to avail themselves of this aid and thereby increase their advertising effort.

2. The Manufacturers' Local Advertising. Some manufacturers run local newspaper or radio advertising at their own expense. The name and address of each local dealer may be included in each advertisement.

Salesmen should discuss all features of the manufacturer's local advertising program including the media used, the features of individual advertisements, schedule, circulation coverage, costs, and effectiveness as in the case of the manufacturer's national program.

Local newspapers and radio stations should be requested by the salesman to solicit local dealers for advertising to tie up with the manufacturer's local program. Sometimes manufacturers place local advertising through local dealers in order to secure a lower local rate.

3. Local Advertising Media and Their Values. Although there are numerous local advertising media such as newspapers, radio, direct advertising, sampling, premiums, novelties, and outdoor, store, counter, and window displays, manufacturers usually approve of a limited number of basic local media for use by local dealers. Certain media have been found most productive for certain types of products and services, and salesmen follow company policy in advising dealers to use these tested methods. A manufacturer of home heating equipment, for example, endorses four local media: store displays, local newspaper advertising, outdoor signs, and direct-mail advertising. A salesman's effectiveness is often judged on the basis of his ability to persuade his dealers to use one or more of these various types of advertising.

The basic medium of advertising for dealers serving a local area is the local newspaper. The advantages of newspapers for dealer advertising are low-cost, intensive local coverage, mass audience, news attraction, dealer identification, flexibility in copy, and great reader interest.

Manufacturers usually furnish, without cost, advertising copy for local newspaper advertising in matrix or electrotype form. For dealers selling a high-priced product in a restricted area or to a limited market, local direct advertising is a basic advertising medium. It may consist of letterheads, folders, booklets, blotters, mailing cards, calendars, imprinted with the dealer's name, all of which may be furnished by the manufacturer at cost of production. The advantages of direct advertising are its flexibility, personal appeal, selectivity, rapid action, and adaptability.

Local dealers may tie up with a national radio broadcast by means of short announcements made over the local stations through which a national program is broadcast. Dealers may also be furnished with radio scripts by manufacturers for broadcasting over local radio stations that cover the market served by the merchant. Electrical transcriptions may also be furnished to dealers for spot broadcasts. The entertainment value and popularity of radio make it an excellent advertising medium for the sale of low-priced, repeat mass-consumption commodities.

Store advertising including window, counter, floor, and wall displays such as cutouts, hangers, baskets, easels, stands, dummy packages, and streamers are furnished to dealers gratis or at cost by most manufacturers of low-priced articles distributed through drug, grocery, and hardware retail outlets. Some manufacturers sell dealers monthly store display services; others sell single advertising display pieces at low cost. The advantages of store displays are: they remind customers of nationally advertised goods at the point of sale and sell by suggestion; salesclerks are reminded to push the article displayed; the actual merchandise is shown. Dealers sometimes object to store displays for the following reasons: they take up valuable window or counter space; sales of a product may not justify giving space for display; small dealers do not have the time or assistance to erect and maintain large displays. Dealers should be supplied with the type of display material that they can use to the best advantage.

Local sampling campaigns are conducted by manufacturers of food and drug specialties to stimulate demand. In some cases, sample packages are supplied to merchants for distribution in the store or in outgoing orders. Occasionally, a manufacturer will distribute through his own crews of house-to-house distributors sample packages, or coupons which may be redeemed with local merchants. Merchants may provide manufacturers with lists of customers to whom samples are mailed direct from the manufacturer. Demonstrators, employed by manufacturers, are assigned to retail stores for preparation and distribution of samples to store customers. Many dealers favor sampling by manufacturers as a direct means of creating new customers and stimulating sales to old ones.

Many manufacturers supply local merchants with exterior hanging or wall signs, illuminated and unilluminated. Such signs carry the name of the manufacturer's product and sometimes the name of the dealer. Large signs are usually sold at cost by the manufacturer; small signs are supplied without charge. Twenty-four-sheet outdoor posters frequently carry the name and address of the nearest dealer and some manufacturers use three-sheet posters on panels erected on side walls of stores as a final buying suggestion to consumers near the point of purchase.

Numerous forms of novelty advertising including paper matches, ash trays, golf balls, playing cards, and mechanical pencils, imprinted with the brand of the manufacturer and the name and address of the local dealer, are made available to dealers at cost to secure prospects, to reward customers, or to feature special store events.

Publicity or short news stories describing the introduction of a new model are supplied to dealers by manufacturers for insertion in local newspapers. Such publicity is usually run by local newspapers without cost for dealers who advertise.

4. The Cost of Local Advertising. In some cases, manufacturers prefer to do all of the local advertising of their products at their own expense. Other producers prefer to produce and place all of their local advertising, but expect their dealers to cooperate in sharing its cost, usually on a per unit of product purchased basis. One motor-car manufacturer charges dealers $15 per car for local advertising handled by the maker. Dealers' names and addresses are included in the local newspaper advertisements.

The most common method of sharing the cost of local advertising is on a 50–50 basis with the manufacturer paying one-half of the cost of a dealer's local advertising up to a certain amount per unit or per cent of total purchases. For example, one manufacturer pays half of the cost of a dealer's local advertising up to 5 per cent of the dealer's dollar purchases. Dealers place the advertising and are required to submit tear sheets of local newspaper advertising accompanied by invoice for space as proof of insertion to secure credit from the manufacturer.

Local direct mail, novelties, signs, and other forms of advertising are usually supplied dealers at cost or, in some cases, are furnished gratis in controlled amounts.

A salesman should be familiar with his company's policy for assuming the cost of local advertising. Advertising order forms supplied salesmen usually state the price of various forms of advertising available to dealers.

5. Planning Advertising for a Retail Dealer. The extent to which salesmen participate in the development of dealer advertising programs depends to a large extent upon the importance of the product to the merchant from a volume and profit standpoint. If the product is but one of several hundred stocked by a small merchant, the salesman obviously will have little to do with formulating the dealer's advertising program. However, if it is the principal item in a merchant's stock, the salesman often serves as an advertising counselor, advising the dealer in regard to the media to use, when and where the publicity should be run, and how much should be invested in local promotion.

Salesmen, representing products of primary importance to dealers, aid in the development of local advertising programs by first analyzing a dealer's publicity needs through a consideration of his current advertising and its effectiveness, the volume of his past and anticipated sales, the extent of his market, his competitor's advertising, the value of local advertising media, etc. This analysis is carried out with the permission and assistance of the dealer.

After making a survey of a merchant's advertising situation, the manufacturer's salesman formulates a definite plan for the dealer. The basic advertising media recommended by the manufacturer for local use are a fundamental part of the plan. The plan details the amount of advertising that should be done, the media to be used, the time to advertise, the objectives of the program, and the copy to be run. In preparing such a plan, a salesman may have the assistance of the manufacturer's advertising department which will advise on details unfamiliar to him.

In many cases, a salesman's initial advertising plan for a dealer will be very elementary. He may make the single recommendation that an advertising sign be placed on the front of the store or that a monthly window display service be purchased from the manufacturer. In other cases, however, an extensive campaign including newspaper advertising, direct mail, outdoor posters, and window displays may be involved. Most such local advertising plans begin with a single form of publicity and expand as the sales and profits of a dealer increase.

Salesmen selling articles low in price and of little significance to merchants from a volume and profit standpoint also plan to secure a small share of the dealer's advertising program to the extent of a counter, floor, or window display at intervals, or the mention of the product in the merchant's newspaper advertisements or handbills.

After a salesman has developed an advertising plan or suggestions for a dealer, he must next present his proposal to the dealer and secure his agreement to carry it out. The objections of the dealer to features of the plan must be overcome and the advantages discussed. An order for the necessary advertising to carry out the plan should be taken by the salesman on forms provided.

6. Aiding Dealers in Carrying out Advertising Plans. When a manufacturer's salesman has sold a dealer a local advertising program, he must next follow through on the plan and see that it is carried out. Many promising advertising plans die for lack of interest on the part of the merchant; unless the salesman sees that the dealer executes the advertising program, neither the manufacturer nor the dealer benefits from the program. Several million dollars' worth of excellent retail display material gathers dust in store basements because salesmen fail to see that their advertising is used.

Salesmen frequently help dealers install window displays, exterior and interior store advertising, arrange for distribution of handbills, compile mailing lists, interview local printers and newspapers, lay out and write newspaper advertisements, and obtain mats, plates, and other advertising aids for dealers. Retail salespeople should also be

informed by the salesman about the various features of the manufacturer's advertising.

Salesman's Advertising Portfolio

So that advertising proofs, schedules, and coverage data can be
organized for convenient use in selling a national and local advertising
program to dealers, advertising departments of manufacturers prepare
advertising portfolios for salesmen. Sometimes salesmen make up
their own advertising portfolios which should include proofs of local
and national advertisements, schedules, circulation figures, statistics
of advertising effectiveness, cuts and electros, illustrations of display
material, direct-mail pieces, and novelties. When collected in a loose-
leaf leather binder, this material makes a favorable impression and
saves time in discussing the advertising program.

What a Salesman Should Know about His Company's Trade Advertising

Many companies aid their salesmen with advertisements in trade
magazines or direct mail to wholesalers and retailers. Trade advertising paves the way for salesmen by preceding their interviews,
establishing prestige, following up calls, reaching prospects whom a
salesman is unable to reach economically in person, saving selling
time, securing interviews from interested prospects, and keeping dealers and their salesmen sold on the manufacturer's product.

Salesmen can capitalize on their trade advertising by discussing the
selling points featured in the advertisements and showing proofs to
dealers to support sales arguments. Copies of the trade magazines in
which the advertising is appearing should also be shown to dealers.

Salesmen should also be familiar with the various trade publications in which their company advertising is appearing as well as the
schedule of insertions. Copies of all letters, folders, bulletins, and
other pieces of direct advertising to the trade should be included in
the salesman's portfolio of advertising.

How a Salesman Should Keep Informed about His Company's Advertising

Salesmen should be continuously conscious of their company's advertising as well as that of competitors. Every newspaper, magazine,
or trade advertisement issued by his company should be read by the
salesman, who should also listen to all company radio broadcasts.

All company outdoor posters, painted bulletins, as well as car cards, should be observed.

A salesman should be acquainted with the advertising and sales promotion managers of his company and should discuss with them his problems in presenting advertising to dealers.

Salesmen should also subscribe to one of the leading advertising publications such as *Printers' Ink* or study a good text on the subject, such as "Advertising Procedure," by Kleppner, or "Advertising," by Frey.

When seasonal or annual advertising programs are announced, a salesman should study every phase of his company's campaign, its objective, theme, method of presentation, and plan to present it effectively to dealers. Competitive advertising programs should also be studied.

A salesman should avoid a negative attitude toward his company's advertising. It is easy to criticize advertising and there are many different opinions as to what constitutes effective advertising. Even though immediate, tangible sales may not be forthcoming from advertising, that is not conclusive proof that all or part of the advertising investment is being made unwisely. Salesmen must have confidence in the experience and judgment of the executives and advertising agency responsible for the program.

How a Salesman Should Discuss Advertising with Dealers

Successful salesmen of advertised merchandise and services follow a definite plan in presenting advertising to merchants. The methods of these outstanding salesmen are included in the following four-step routine which should be used by every salesman of advertised products in discussing advertising with wholesalers and retailers.

Routine for Discussing Advertising with Dealers

1. Discover the merchant's attitude toward advertising.
2. Discuss your national advertising program.
3. Discuss your local advertising program.
4. Sell the merchant a local advertising tie-up.

1. Discover the Dealer's Attitude toward Advertising. Some dealers are opposed to advertising and advertised goods; others consider advertising one of the main inducements to stock an article. Until a salesman determines a merchant's attitude toward advertised goods, he is unable to proceed intelligently in discussion of his product advertising. Accordingly, outstanding salesmen make a definite effort, early in the interview with a merchant, to determine his attitude toward advertising.

By tactful questions, by listening to voluntary remarks, and by observation, an alert salesman can soon discover a dealer's advertising outlook. Observation of the merchandise stocked by a dealer will also indicate whether advertised or unadvertised goods are favored. If, for example, a dealer says, "We are interested in our own brands," the salesman knows that he must meet this private brand competition.

Before approaching a prospective dealer, a salesman should make inquiries about the dealer's advertising and secure as much information as possible about his attitude toward advertised brands.

If a dealer is receptive to advertising, a salesman should discuss fully the details of his national and local advertising programs. Sometimes a salesman is obliged to overcome objections to advertised goods by discussing the advantages of stocking advertised merchandise.

2. Discuss the National Advertising Program. The salesman representing a nationally advertised product should discuss his current advertising program and show how it increases the sales and profits of the merchant. The various media used in the campaign of national advertising should be described; full-sized proofs of individual advertisements should be shown and discussed and the schedule, coverage, and effectiveness of the advertising in terms of inquiries and sales presented. Each of these features, as described in the preceding pages, should be explained as fully as possible.

If the advertiser has been advertising for some time, the importance of this consistent effort should be emphasized to indicate the cumulative effect of continuous advertising in creating a demand for the product.

Exhibits, charts, and graphs illustrating the amount of the advertiser's investment and the resulting increase in sales volume and increased turnover for dealers are often used by salesmen in presenting national advertising.

The various features of the national advertising should also be explained to merchants. The specific objectives of the individual advertisements and the theme or dominant appeal of the campaign should be described. Every good advertising campaign has a theme such as "pink toothbrush" in a well-known toothpaste campaign or "halitosis" in a mouth-wash campaign, and this dominant idea should be described to dealers.

The specific action sought by the advertising, such as requests for a sample package, inquiries for a recipe booklet, or a telephone call to a dealer, should be described by the salesman in presenting his national advertising program.

Prepublication tests which are often made to measure the readership of the advertising may be described by the salesman as further proof of the value of the national advertising.

3. Discuss the Local Advertising. When a merchant understands the value and various features of the national advertising, a salesman should make a similar presentation of the manufacturer's advertising plan. The reasons why dealers should tie up their local advertising with the manufacturer's national advertising should be explained; the features of local advertising prepared by the manufacturer for dealers should be described; the local advertising media recommended by the manufacturer should be discussed together with the cost and the manufacturer's local advertising plan and assistance to dealers.

Each of the above features of local advertising may be discussed by a salesman at as great length as circumstances require. When a new dealer is appointed, it is usually necessary to explain in detail all particulars of local advertising; whereas an established dealer who is familiar with the manufacturer's local program is only interested in new advertising developments in the form of new types of local advertising and programs. Some feature of local advertising should be discussed on every call to keep the dealer sold on the local advertising program.

Examples of how other dealers are advertising the salesman's product successfully serve to stimulate interest in local advertising by dealers who are not taking advantage of the manufacturer's advertising cooperation.

4. Sell a Local Advertising Tie-up. A manufacturer's repeat orders depend upon the movement of merchandise from the dealers' shelves, and local advertising is the greatest accelerator of that movement. Therefore, the success of his salesmen depends largely upon their ability to induce dealers to tie up local publicity with the manufacturer's national advertising.

Outstanding salesmen are singularly successful in securing cooperation from dealers in planning their advertising efforts to take full advantage of a manufacturer's national and local program.

Starting with an analysis of a dealer's advertising needs and proceeding to a simple advertising plan involving the use of basic advertising media as described in the preceding pages, a salesman can step by step persuade distributors to adopt a program of local advertising

Sales Performance Rating Form

Presenting Advertising

Salesman————————————   Date————————————

Rated by————————————   Over-all Rating————————————

Score

I. *Salesman's Knowledge of his Company's Advertising*	Excellent 90–100	Good 80–90	Fair 70–80	Poor 60–70	Failure Below 60
A. Benefits of national advertising					
B. National advertising media and their values					
C. Features of advertisements					
D. Schedule of national advertising					
E. Coverage of national advertising					
F. Effectiveness of national advertising					
G. Cost of national advertising					
H. Why dealers should tie up with the company's national advertising					
I. The company's local advertising					
J. Local media and their values					
K. The cost of local advertising					
L. How to plan dealer advertising					

II. *Salesman's Use of Advertising Knowledge with Dealers*	Excellent 90–100	Good 80–90	Fair 70–80	Poor 60–70	Failure Below 60
A. Discovering Dealer's Attitude toward Advertising					
B. Discussing company's national advertising					
C. Discussing local advertising					
D. Securing tie-up between dealer and company's advertising					

Miscellaneous Comments————————————————————————

——

——

which ties up national advertising at the point of purchase, the merchant's store.

The effectiveness of a local tie-up with national advertising depends in a large measure on the follow-up of the salesman and his willingness to be responsible for some of the details that are incident to the production of the local advertising.

Problem I

Presenting Advertising to Dealers

Thomas P. Hanford, representing the Brilliant Lamp Corporation

The Brilliant Lamp Corporation, New York City, is a subsidiary of the Eastern Electric Company, manufacturers and distributors of electrical appliances, motors, transformers, generators, turbines, with 15 factories and branches throughout the world. The corporation specializes in the production of electric lamps, sold direct to hardware, electrical, variety, drug, and grocery stores through company salesmen operating out of branch offices in the principal cities.

To promote the sale of its lamps, the company advertises in national magazines to the extent of $500,000 annually and in addition supplies lithographed store, window, counter, and floor displays and display racks to retailers. These displays are distributed by company salesmen to dealers who pay a small charge for a monthly display service. A few small displays are distributed to dealers without charge.

One of the Brilliant salesmen, Thomas P. Hanford, operating out of the Boston branch, is calling in the following interview on the buyer of a chain of grocery stores. He is attempting to interest the buyer in the company's display advertising.

1. Salesman: We've got some nice basket counter displays I'd like to show you.
2. Buyer: One of your competitors has offered to install and service displays for us. They feel that they're in a position to service displays when they need it. They get around to all of our stores; these displays are new all the time.
3. Salesman: We'll do the same for you with no effort or expense whatever on your part. Here is our 1949 counter display (showing picture of display). This is one of the finest displays we've ever produced to help you sell more lamps. The illustration is by Russell Cartright, famous for his pictures of children. This display has a "sight-saving" appeal. Every mother wants to save the eyes of her children and will buy lamps to do it.

4. BUYER: Well, I want some of them but we won't promise to leave them up for long.

5. SALESMAN: That's just the story on this display. It's got to—

6. BUYER: It's got to what?

7. SALESMAN: It's got to be up some time to get results from it.

8. BUYER: Well, we'll leave it up long enough to get results from it, and if we take it down we'll keep it so that we can put it up later.

9. SALESMAN: With winter coming on, now is the time to feature lamps for the dark days ahead. I was wondering why it wouldn't be a good idea to have a display like this right up by the cash register to remind your customers to buy lamps as they go out.

10. BUYER: That's a good idea.

11. SALESMAN: That's 16 by 16 (pointing to dimensions of display). See? Now—I think this would be better than something of this type (showing picture of another display), or that type (showing pictures of displays)—any of these three types?

12. BUYER: Oh, I'd say in about a month maybe, if we will be promoting lamps. Possibly now, we should use this sign (pointing to picture of sign); do you think so—or don't you? When would you want them?

13. SALESMAN: No, I don't think so. For this reason: electric lamps are something different from anything you've got in your stores. People buy lamps when they see them, and they're reminded of them when they see them. Probably after hundreds of people have left your stores somebody would tell them when they got home that they forgot to buy lamps. If they happen to be shopping at five o'clock tonight and saw lamps, why they'd buy them.

14. BUYER: Why don't we take this counter basket and put it near the cash register in all of our stores?

15. SALESMAN: I'd like to have you try it.

16. BUYER: We'll see how they work. I'll be interested in watching them.

17. SALESMAN: That's just the idea. Now on this metal floor rack illustrated here—this is just the thing for a good floor display.

18. BUYER: I know we can use something like that—maybe not quite so often as other displays.

19. SALESMAN: Set one up near the front door, Mr. Buyer. These racks don't take much room.

20. BUYER: Yes, there is a limit to how much space we can give. Take a rack like that and I think we'd sell more lamps.

21. SALESMAN: Would you like the large rack or a small one?

22. BUYER: Which one would sell the most bulbs?

23. SALESMAN: Well, if you want a display for all lamps, I'd say the large rack would, but I don't think you would want to give it so much space. Take something like this (shows picture of small rack).

24. BUYER: You charge for those, don't you?

25. SALESMAN: They are charged to you but your money is refunded when you return them. We take them back.
26. BUYER: Your competitors are giving them away. Why are they furnishing them without charge?
27. SALESMAN: What are they giving away?
28. BUYER: Racks and displays.
29. SALESMAN: Well, we have some small racks we give away too, but you wouldn't want them.
30. BUYER: Your competitors are giving away metal stands, and maybe they are doing it to get in, I don't know.
31. SALESMAN: You can have the small rack free, but I wouldn't recommend it for stores of your size.
32. BUYER: Is the large rack the one shown on this paper here? (Looks at illustration of display rack.)
33. SALESMAN: Yep.
34. BUYER: Can we get one of those racks for each of our stores?
35. SALESMAN: You sure can. This is a large steel rack. We charge $2.50 for that and refund the cost when you return it.
36. BUYER: Well, we'll think it over. Come in and see me the next time you are around.

Questions

1. Criticize favorably or otherwise the salesman's discussion of his advertising in this interview. Cite special strengths or weaknesses.

2. Did the salesman discover the buyer's attitude toward advertising? What was the buyer's attitude?

3. Did the salesman know the buyer's advertising needs? Explain?

4. Did the salesman describe the displays satisfactorily?

5. Did he convince the buyer of the value of a tie-up using the company's local advertising?

6. Did the salesman recommend the proper displays?

Problem II

PRESENTING ADVERTISING TO DEALERS

Ralph H. Cox, representing the Randolph Oil Company

The Randolph Oil Company, Cleveland, Ohio, refines and distributes gasoline and lubricating oils as well as a line of petroleum specialties including fly killer, household oil, and window cleaner. A separate sales organization specializes in the sale of these products which are sold direct to wholesalers and chain stores.

The insecticide sold in pints and quarts is advertised to the extent of $400,000 annually in national magazines. The company is initiating a national radio broadcast featuring a well-known singer. Attached to each 25-cent can of insecticide is a coupon which entitles the buyer to a metal spray gun for 35 cents. The coupons are redeemed and the guns are shipped direct from the factory in Cleveland.

Ralph H. Cox is one of 10 salesmen selling Randolph specialties in greater New York City. In the following interview, he is discussing the advertising program behind the new Randolph insecticide "Bug-Go" with the buyer of a chain of small grocery stores located in the wealthier communities of suburban New York City.

1. SALESMAN: I've noticed you stock some well-known brands; you evidently think well of nationally advertised lines.
2. BUYER: Yes, we feel that we get some of the prestige from the old established, famous names. We're partial to fast-moving stuff. Advertising sure steps up turnover.
3. SALESMAN: Then you ought to be interested in our advertising for "Bug-Go," our new insecticide. We are using 10 national magazines, including *The Saturday Evening Post, Collier's, Life, Time, Good Housekeeping, Woman's Home Companion, Ladies' Home Journal, Better Homes and Gardens, McCall's* and the *Family Circle.* They are the best-read magazines in the country.
   Here are the proofs of the full-page ads. (Showing proofs.) Notice the humorous cartoon illustrations. Everybody likes cartoons. The colors attract attention. Every ad carries a coupon offering a 75-cent spray for 35 cents.
   One ad a month during May, June, July, August, and September in these 10 magazines is read by more than twenty million customers. In greater New York, your own market, over a half-million persons read these magazines every month.
4. BUYER: It's quite a premium offer. How much did you pay for the sprays?
5. SALESMAN: Twenty-five cents.
6. BUYER: You make money on those, don't you?
7. SALESMAN: We sell them at cost. We mail 'em out. The beauty of it is, it saves the hands from getting torn and scratched spraying rose bushes. This spray here (showing spray) is 35 cents with a 25-cent bottle of the liquid. The sprays are 75 cents in all hardware stores. This competitive combination is a special sale.
8. BUYER: Do you think it will sell?
9. SALESMAN: There is no question about it, with the coupon.
10. BUYER: The only thing I can say is that we'll keep our ears to the ground and see what we will get on call. I haven't heard anything yet. If

they get so they'll knock down the doors to try and get it, we'll have to see the results first; if it looks like it is working—

11. SALESMAN: We're backing up our national advertising with a strong local campaign to your own customers. Starting next week and for the next 16 weeks we are featuring Bertha Bayes, the famous singer, and Tom Clark's orchestra on a 15-minute daily broadcast over local stations W.O.L.K. and W.P.R.

What we'd like to do is to get you listed on the Bertha Bayes program and mention that you are stocking "Bug-Go" so that your stores would be identified with the product. They estimate that more than eight million listeners in greater New York are tuned to W.O.L.K. and W.P.R. every day. That will make a real demand on you for "Bug-Go."

A great many people in Blanktown and Homeville (where buyer's stores are located) are familiar with our products. We would like to tell it on the radio, get it in your *News* (weekly store circular) like we have been doing with Jones Market in Linkville. They've already hooked up with us; Morton Provision in Lawrence—the better markets. It's going to help a lot.

Then we attach a coupon to each can. The customer mails the coupon back to us with 35 cents and gets the Randolph Insecticide Spray. You will have calls for Randolph Insecticide.

12. BUYER: We've had calls in our main store here.

13. SALESMAN: Many stores stock just a small quantity.

14. BUYER: We operate a little different; we try to sell in large quantities and try to push out large quantities, but we do it on few items.

15. SALESMAN: You stock Blank Insecticide and we'd like to be in, too.

16. BUYER: Blank's is in and and yours isn't, and it's just absolutely impossible to change now. If there gets to be a demand, we'll carry it for demand.

17. SALESMAN: But, Mr. Buyer, you want to be ready for demand. When our radio program goes on the air, you'll get many calls.

18. BUYER: Do we make a good profit on it?

19. SALESMAN: There's a good profit in "Bug-Go." Don't let anybody tell you there isn't. Twenty per cent on the retail list price of 35 cents. It gives you seven cents a can profit. You say you haven't had a lot of requests for our product?

20. BUYER: No. Well, of course, the stores are supposed to report the calls. They don't report isolated calls, but they do continuous calls. We might try a case a store and see how it sells.

21. SALESMAN: I'm sure you'd be satisfied.

22. BUYER: Write it up on that basis and be sure to get our name on your broadcast.

Questions

1. Discuss the salesman's presentation of his advertising in this interview on the basis of the four-point routine.

a. Did the salesman discover the dealer's attitude toward advertising?

b. Did the salesman sell the general benefits to the dealer of the national magazine advertising? If not what should have been said?

c. Were proofs of the national media used and their values discussed? Satisfactorily?

d. Was the schedule of national advertising mentioned?

e. Was the national and local coverage of the advertising explained?

f. Did the salesman discuss the local advertising? How?

g. Did he sell a tie-up between the company and dealer's local advertising? How?

2. What are the weaknesses in this advertising presentation?

Reading References

J. R. DAUBMAN, "Salesmanship and Types of Selling," Chap. III, F. S. Crofts & Co., New York, 1939.

CHARLES H. FERNALD, "Salesmanship," Chap. XXI, Prentice-Hall, Inc., New York, 1945.

J. GEORGE FREDERICK, "Modern Salesmanship," Chap. XIX, Garden City Publishing Company, Inc., New York, 1937.

ALBERT W. FREY, "Advertising," The Ronald Press Company, New York, 1947.

H. W. HEPNER, "Effective Advertising," McGraw-Hill Book Company, Inc., New York, 1949.

PAUL W. IVEY, "Successful Salesmanship," pp. 483–484, Prentice-Hall, Inc., New York, 1947.

OTTO KLEPPNER, "Advertising Procedure," Prentice-Hall, Inc., New York, 1945.

C. H. SANDAGE, "Advertising Theory and Practice," Business Publications, Inc., Chicago, 1939.

HARRY SIMMONS, "A Practical Course in Successful Selling," Chap. XVII, Harper & Brothers, New York, 1939.

D. B. TANSILL, "So You're Going to Sell," Chap. IX, John C. Winston Company, Philadelphia, 1939.

EUGENE WHITMORE, "Helping People Buy," pp. 145–157, The Dartnell Corporation, Chicago, 1940.

CHAPTER IX

PRESENTING MECHANICAL SERVICE

I. IMPORTANCE OF MECHANICAL SERVICE
IN SALES PRESENTATIONS

The machine age has not only created new methods in industry and changed modes of life but has also produced a new problem for salesmen—the presentation of mechanical service.

Whether they purchase locomotives, mercury-vapor turbines, or tabulators for industry, electric shavers, oil burners, or automobiles for individual or home use, buyers desire more than mechanisms. They are buying results which can only be obtained from service. Salesmen of machines must make a dual sale, the product and the service.

Purchasers of mechanical products are primarily buying comfort, economy, performance, and durability, values which are obtained not only through the merits of the product but also through the mechanical service rendered by the seller. The customer is interested in motors, gears, or horsepower only as a means to an end. The salesman of machines, who sells a constructive program of service and maintenance as well as a high-quality machine, is doing a well-rounded job.

As the quality of many mechanical products becomes more or less standardized and prices uniform, buyers have so little choice in their selection that the character of mechanical service provided by a seller is often the deciding factor in a transaction.

Although many mechanical articles are today highly perfected, the need for regular adjustments, lubrication, replacement of worn parts, cleaning, tightening, and realignments is still necessary, if a buyer is to secure the satisfactory operation in which he is primarily interested. While the amount of service required to maintain mechanical devices in good operating order varies with the perfection and complexity of the mechanism, salesmen of every technical product have a maintenance story of significance to buyers.

The numerous benefits to be derived by a salesman from constructive service presentations to prospects include repeat sales to customers, valuable word-of-mouth advertising and testimonials from owners, increased sales of accessories and related products, names of of new prospects, satisfied users, fewer returns and repossessions, and increased service sales.

II. WHAT A SALESMAN SHOULD KNOW
ABOUT HIS MECHANICAL SERVICE

A salesman should have a comprehensive knowledge of each feature of his mechanical service, including (1) guarantee; (2) provisions of service policy; (3) service personnel; (4) accessibility of service; (5) maintenance requirements of product; (6) service equipment and facilities; (7) when service is available; (8) owner's experiences with service; (9) cost of service; (10) competitive service; (11) authorized service dealers.

1. Guarantee. A manufacturer's guarantee, or warranty, is a formal statement defining the seller's liability for defects in material and workmanship and describing satisfactory service. A guarantee usually limits the time for which the seller is responsible to the buyer for service and includes instructions for proper maintenance of the product. A liberal guarantee, properly presented by a salesman, may be a strong selling tool to win the confidence of prospects and to protect a seller against the competition of cheaper substitutes. Wholesale and retail distributors obtain for their customers the benefits guaranteed under the manufacturer's warranty.

Some machine industries have adopted a standard warranty which is subscribed to by a majority of manufacturers in the business. Typical of such warranties is that of the National Automobile Chamber of Commerce, which reads as follows:

We warrant each new motor vehicle manufactured by us, whether passenger car or commercial vehicle, to be free from defects in material or workmanship under normal use and service, our obligation under this warranty being limited to making good at our factory any parts or part thereof which shall within ninety days after delivery of such vehicle to the original purchaser be returned to us with transportation charges prepaid, and which our examination shall disclose to our satisfaction to have been thus defective; this warranty being expressly in lieu of all other warranties, expressed or implied, and of all other obligations or liabilities on our part, and we neither assume nor authorize any other person to assume for us any other liability in connection with the sale of our vehicles.

This warranty shall not apply to any vehicle which shall have been repaired or altered outside of our factory in any way so as, in our judgment, to affect its stability or reliability, nor which has been subject to misuse, negligence, or accident, nor to any commercial vehicle made by us which shall have been operated at a speed exceeding the factory rated speed, or loaded beyond the factory rated load capacity.

We make no warranty whatsoever in regard to tires, rims, ignition apparatus, horns or other signaling devices, starting devices, generators, batteries, speedometers, or other trade accessories, inasmuch as they are usually warranted separately by their respective manufacturers.

Salesmen should know all particulars of the warranties or guarantees covering their products and be able to discuss their features with prospects when the need arises. A straightforward guarantee is reassuring to a dubious buyer. It makes him feel that he is not taking a risk on mechanical quality.

2. Provisions of Service Policy. Manufacturers of mechanical products supplement their warranties with service policies describing gratuitous adjustments and inspections which the seller offers to customers to ensure satisfactory operation of the product.

To obtain service, manufacturers frequently require purchasers to register the serial number, date of purchase, name of dealer, and other information concerning the sales transaction. Separate registration by customers is often necessary on the principal mechanical accessories. In the case of automobiles, separate registration to obtain service from manufacturers is required on tires, batteries, radios, heaters, etc. To avoid misunderstandings, salesmen should be familiar with these special registration requirements and inform customers.

Manufacturers of mechanical products issue a service certificate which is delivered to the purchaser by the maker's or distributor's salesman when the product is transferred from seller to buyer. These service certificates describe the responsibilities of the seller to render specific services at certain periods following the date of purchase. Passenger automobiles are usually serviced free for 90 days or before the vehicle has been driven 4,000 miles. Tires are serviced gratis for 12 months, except for commercial vehicles, when the free service period expires in six months. Batteries are serviced for 90 days and in some cases for 18 months or 18,000 miles of use. Salesmen should know the duration of the free service period and use this as a selling point.

Some service certificates have coupons attached, entitling owners to specific free adjustments when the product has been in use for a certain time. The operations performed without charge are listed on each coupon which is detached by the buyer and presented to the seller to secure the service promised.

Service policies usually cover the following features: conditioning the product before delivery, necessary inspections and adjustments, warranty on parts and labor, transient service for change of user's residence during warranty period, inspection service after expiration of warranty period, regular maintenance, accessory replacements, and use of genuine parts. Salesmen must not only be. acquainted with all features of their service policies, but be able to interpret them to prospects so clearly that there will be no cause for the misunderstandings that may easily arise in regard to such promises.

3. Service Personnel. The experience and ability of service men may be a major selling argument. The efficiency of the mechanics who are available to service a product is an important consideration to the purchaser who wants to be sure that the adjustments promised in the service policy will be made satisfactorily. Successful salesmen discuss the competence of their service personnel.

The salesmen of one large motor-car manufacturer feature the "University of Service," where hundreds of mechanics take courses in service. The courses are one week to six months in duration and mechanics must demonstrate in service clinics their proficiency in every operation.

The salesmen of a milling-machine manufacturer discuss their servicemen who are trained mechanical engineers and university graduates, factory-schooled and experienced in technical problems.

Salesmen of an oil-burner producer discuss their traveling service schools, which are taught by expert instructors who keep dealers' servicemen up to date on correct methods. Customers are told how this instruction increases the efficiency of servicemen and cuts the cost of maintenance to owners.

The number of servicemen employed by the seller, the length of their experience, their training, specialized knowledge, background, and competence to make mechanical repairs are important selling points used by successful salesmen in personalizing their service.

Service department managers may be introduced by salesmen to prospects or may accompany them in making deliveries to new owners. In this way salesmen can establish valuable contacts between the service personnel and the customers.

4. Accessibility of Service. A salesman whose mechanical service facilities are conveniently located and readily accessible to customers has a competitive sales advantage in this respect. If the owner of a mechanical product requiring service must pay the cost of packing and shipping it to a service station and wait a long period for repairs, sales resistance is created. On the other hand, a salesman whose company can give overnight service in the neighborhood of the buyer has a selling advantage. Buyers expect convenient service and either demand that service be brought to them or made available in their vicinity.

A salesman of tires for a large oil company, with 14,000 service stations open 18 hours a day, has a distinct advantage over a competing mail-order house with no such facilities.

When a sale is made by a dealer who also gives service, the buyer should know where he can obtain service in the event that he moves out of the seller's area. In the case of service on automobiles, buyers who are touring should know where and how service may be obtained under their warranties.

Some sellers offer customers "call for" and "deliver" service; others list their authorized service stations in local telephone directories so that buyers may quickly summon servicemen by telephone. Salesmen whose firms make service easily accessible to customers capitalize this feature in their sales presentations.

5. Maintenance Requirements of Product. If a product is manufactured so well that it requires practically no service, a salesman should emphasize that feature. However, few mechanical articles have reached such a stage of perfection that they do not require occasional adjustment for wear. None are proof against the abuse of human inquisitiveness which impels people to investigate "what makes the wheels go 'round."

Accordingly, a salesman should know the amount of mechanical maintenance necessary to keep his product performing satisfactorily. The salesmen of an automobile manufacturer, for example, know and explain to buyers that the following special operations are necessary in the proper care of a car: every 1,000 miles, chassis lubrication; every 2,000 miles, lubrication of transmission and rear axle, filling shock absorbers, cleaning air cleaner; every 5,000 miles, lubrication of speedometer cable, cleaning and adjusting carburetor, general tightening, front wheel alignment, engine tune-up, and cleaning cooling system; every 10,000 miles, lubrication of steering gear, rear springs, hand-brake cable conduits, and shock absorbers.

Education of customers in the proper use and care of mechanical merchandise is a salesman's responsibility. Many salesmen fail to recognize that service education pays big dividends in repeat sales and good will. New prospects are often suggested by satisfied owners who have been instructed by salesmen to obtain regular inspections and adjustments.

It is a salesman's major responsibility to sell customers a constructive program of necessary maintenance to ensure continued satisfaction with a product. Salesmen are often to blame for unsatisfactory operation of a mechanical product because they do not know the service requirements of their product and do not convince buyers that it is necessary for them to give attention to maintenance.

Some salesmen promote the idea of regular care and attention to their products by selling new customers a continuous lubrication and adjustment program. Salesmen of one motor-car manufacturer offer owners a low-cost service-saver plan for systematic lubrication and regular inspection which ensures economical, satisfactory operation.

Many companies aid their salesmen in informing customers regarding proper maintenance by the publication of users' guides, operation manuals, and instruction sheets which give specific advice on the care of their product. Salesmen distribute these books to new owners and refer to them in discussing necessary maintenance.

6. Service Equipment and Facilities. The amount and character of a manufacturer's or dealer's service equipment and facilities may constitute a distinctive selling point to impress a prospective purchaser with the ability of the seller to render satisfactory service. A mechanic's work can be no better than his tools; a service department equipped with the latest testing devices, specialized equipment, and facilities with which to handle service has a distinct competitive advantage.

Salesmen can create interesting sales presentations around unique pieces of service equipment. The high degree of accuracy or precision with which modern service machines make adjustments is convincing proof of superior service. The amount of capital invested in service equipment, the number and types of testing devices in use, and the recent purchase of modern efficient tools are all excellent material for sales service presentations.

Prospects and customers interested in economy may be told how the use of improved service equipment saves time and reduces the expense of maintenance.

Service department equipment and facilities may be demonstrated by showing prospects and customers actual operations carried out with the latest equipment. A trip through the service department is an important part of the presentation of many salesmen of mechanical products. When prospects are unable to visit the service department, salesmen show photographs of the station and its equipment.

7. When Service Is Available. Buyers are often interested in knowing when or at what hours they can obtain mechanical service on a product. A salesman whose service department operates Sundays and holidays, as well as day and night, has a strong argument to convince prospects. Some types of mechanical product, particularly refrigeration, heating, and automotive devices, require 24-hour service. If they fail to operate, owners are seriously inconvenienced. Accordingly, salesmen of such equipment discuss the quick availability of their service.

Salesmen of mechanical products requiring regular lubrication and adjustments tell buyers when such maintenance operations are required. A salesman of electrical refrigerators failed to tell his customer when to oil the motor, with the result that the bearings burned out, the buyer was put to inconvenience and expense, and the salesman lost a satisfied customer. A personal or telephone call by a salesman to remind a customer to secure a periodic mechanical checkup pays dividends in good will and repeat sales.

8. Owners' Experience with Service. Customers' experiences with mechanical service are often excellent sales material. Salesmen question customers about their attitude toward the service rendered and ask them to write testimonial letters about their experience in this regard. These letters may be included in a salesman's portfolio and used in service discussions.

Every service department keeps records showing the character and cost of all service rendered to owners. Salesmen use these records as evidence of economical maintenance to show prospects the low cost of service furnished.

Salesmen should make occasional visits to their service departments for the purposes of meeting customers who are being served and of verifying their satisfaction with the service rendered. Such contacts give a salesman greater confidence in the character of his company's service and supply him with facts about service experiences which can be used in discussing these matters.

9. Cost of Service. Purchasers of mechanical articles are usually given a certain number of inspections and adjustments gratis. However, the cost of inspections after the expiration of the free-service period should be clearly understood and explained to prospects when necessary. Schedules of prices for replacement parts and labor rates are published by most service departments and should be in the hands of each salesman.

Continuous mechanical maintenance is provided by some companies on an annual or seasonal basis, whereby regular inspections and adjustments are included in a contract for a flat service charge. Salesmen who sell service contracts not only increase their market but secure customer satisfaction and good will.

Misunderstandings between buyers and sellers over service charges may arise unless salesmen make an effort to explain service costs clearly. Salesmen should leave no doubt in the minds of their customers regarding such charges.

A liberal amount of free service offered to purchasers is a strong selling point and is featured by the salesmen of a number of mechanical products. Low maintenance costs may be emphasized in service presentations.

10. Competitive Service. A salesman should know the principal provisions of the service policies and warranties of leading competitors. He should also be familiar with the amount of free service offered, the inspections and adjustments provided during and after the expiration of the warranty period, the places where service is rendered, and the amount of service equipment of competitors. This information may be obtained direct from competitors or by observation.

Familiarity with the character of a competitor's mechanical service enables a salesman, when called upon, to make favorable comparisons between his service and that of other companies, and also strengthens his confidence in his own company.

11. Authorized Service Dealers. Some manufacturers of mechanical products license certain dealers to service their products. A salesman should know the names and addresses of all such authorized stations in his territory. Authorized service stations are usually required to meet a manufacturer's standards for equipment, personnel, and workmanship. They often are supervised closely by his salesman and are trained by the salesman to give more efficient service than independent service companies.

The use of "gyp" unauthorized parts by service stations is a serious problem with some manufacturers of mechanical goods. Accordingly, wholesale salesmen are responsible for inducing such service stations to use bona fide parts and thereby ensure satisfactory operating results to customers.

By recommending that authorized service stations be patronized for adjustment and maintenance work, salesmen not only create good will with their customers and help them get the best service available, but they also cooperate with distributors in building up profitable service departments.

III. SALESMEN'S SERVICE RELATIONS WITH DEALERS

Consumers who buy machines or apparatus of any kind usually go back to the dealer from whom they made the purchase, if the device does not operate satisfactorily. It is most important, therefore, for salesmen to create an efficient, loyal dealer organization trained to provide mechanical service to owners.

Manufacturers' salesmen are responsible for interpreting service policies to dealers, for assisting authorized dealers in successfully conducting service departments, for keeping distributors and dealers supplied with replacement parts, and for educating dealers on the value of offering superior service to their customers.

Manufacturer's salesmen who interest dealers in giving good service sell more replacement parts, develop more profitable outlets, and secure larger orders. Dealers who give good service sell more merchandise and secure larger orders through contacts of the dealers' service men with consumers. The salesman in turn increases his sales to service dealers.

Some manufacturers offer larger discounts and greater profit opportunities to dealers for maintaining their own service departments. Dealers are graded on their service facilities, and salesmen have the added inducement of lower prices to offer those who will operate their own service departments.

Some manufacturers give mechanical service through factory branches, where customers may obtain service direct. In other cases, dealers return machines direct to the manufacturer for service. Salesmen should know how mechanical service is obtained so that they can cooperate with dealers in providing it to customers.

IV. SALESMAN'S RELATION TO HIS SERVICE DEPARTMENT

The task of salesmen and servicemen is identical in that both are working to make and keep satisfied customers. This mutual objective, however, is often overlooked in many organizations where service and sales departments do not cooperate to see that the interests of customers are best served.

A salesman should make a real effort to understand the functions, policies, and equipment of his service department. Close working relations between salesmen and servicemen are essential to secure maximum customer good will.

A serviceman can be of real assistance to a salesman by furnishing information about the needs of prospective customers. Servicemen are in a very favorable position to observe sales opportunities as they go about their work of inspecting and repairing mechanical equipment. They are often called upon for service when a problem arises in connection with the operation of a machine which can only be solved by the purchase of new or accessory equipment. A serviceman is credited by buyers with more technical knowledge than a salesman, and his recommendations may carry considerable weight with prospects. For these reasons, it is important that salesmen win the confidence and good will of servicemen to secure leads for sales.

In addition, service representatives can aid salesmen in keeping customers satisfied by making periodic inspections, instructing users on proper maintenance, and giving prompt, skillful service when the need arises. Repeat sales are largely a product of satisfactory service. By cultivating the good will of his servicemen, a salesman can gain their cooperation in building customer satisfaction.

Mechanical service reports made by servicemen are an excellent source of information about the needs of customers. When followed up by a salesman, these reports are often a source of profitable sales.

V. HOW A SALESMAN SHOULD DISCUSS SERVICE

Observation of the work of successful salesmen of mechanical products proves that an effective discussion of mechanical service is often a major factor in closing many sales. Mechanical service is an inseparable part of the value a user expects from a machine, and a good salesman is prepared to present his mechanical service facts to prospects.

The methods used by successful salesmen in discussing mechanical service with prospects may be summarized in a four-point routine, a practical plan which should be used by every salesman of mechanical goods in presenting service.

Routine for Discussing Mechanical Service

1. Discover the prospect's interest in mechanical service.
2. Discuss service features of interest to the buyer.
3. Minimize the buyer's need for mechanical service.
4. Show and discuss the service policy.

1. Discover the Prospect's Interest in Mechanical Service. It is a waste of both a salesman's and his prospect's time to engage in a long discussion of mechanical service, if this subject is of no interest to the customer. Therefore, a salesman should first discover his prospect's attitude toward mechanical service and previous experience with it before discussing the subject in detail.

Salesmen can readily determine whether or not a prospect is concerned with service by listening to his volunteered remarks or by asking tactful questions. If he is interested, he will often reveal it by a casual remark such as, "I've been disappointed with the service I have received on my present car," or "It took me more than a month to get repair parts for my old press." Sometimes, a prospect may also ask a direct question such as, "I'd like to know what repairs and maintenance will cost me." When a prospect reveals his interest or experience in these ways, he is indirectly inviting a discussion of mechanical service, and an alert salesman will not miss these cues to present service facts.

If a prospect fails to indicate his interest in mechanical service, a salesman should attempt to discover service interest by asking such tactful questions as, "Have you had good service on your present machine?" or, "Are you interested in mechanical service?" The answers to these or similar questions will quickly reveal a buyer's viewpoint on the subject and indicate those service features which should be discussed by the salesman.

On the other hand, if a prospect shows no interest in service, a salesman should subordinate his service discussion. After a salesman has made a complete product presentation, he may find it desirable to describe unique or competitive features of mechanical service and policy.

2. Discuss Service Features of Interest to the Buyer. After a buyer has shown an interest in mechanical service or the salesman has found that the buyer wishes information about it, the most interesting features should be fully described. With a knowledge of the various service features mentioned earlier in this chapter, a salesman can discuss them in as much detail as circumstances permit.

If a buyer is interested in the cost of service, the salesman should describe the free inspections and adjustments provided in the service policy as well as the cost of replacement parts and labor on specific repairs after the expiration of the free-service period. Examples illustrating the small amounts paid by customers for service may also be discussed.

As a salesman describes each feature of his service of interest to the buyer, he should observe the prospect's reaction and obtain commitments on each feature to ensure that the buyer is in agreement on each point presented. If a buyer refuses to commit himself favorably on a service feature or indicates by his response that he does not clearly understand the advantages presented, further explanation is essential.

3. Minimize the Buyer's Need for Service. When a buyer has indicated a desire to know about the character of service offered and the salesman has discussed the merits of his service, the prospect should not be left with the assumption that the product demands an unusual amount of service. A lengthy description of mechanical service may create the impression in the minds of some buyers that expensive and costly service may be necessary to maintain the product in good operating condition. To avoid this impression, it is good strategy for a salesman to minimize the need for extensive mechanical service.

First, convince buyers that the product has been so well designed and constructed that the amount of service necessary has been reduced to an absolute minimum. High precision in manufacture makes possible the production of machines which require almost no mechanical service. The working parts and control of many machines are now sealed against dirt and supplied with lubricant for the life of the product so that service is rarely necessary.

Second, many machines are now designed so that parts requiring attention are so accessible that it is possible for users to lubricate and adjust them without professional assistance or expense. Salesmen should be familiar with those construction features which minimize the need for mechanical service. Improved processes of manufacture, high quality of materials, skilled workmanship, and efficient design all combine to minimize the need for service, reduce cost of repairs, and ensure continuous operation of the equipment.

4. Show and Discuss the Service Policy. A salesman should supplement his discussion of mechanical service with the printed service policy or warranty of his company. Specific clauses in the policy covering the service features under discussion should be shown to the buyer so that he can verify the statements of the salesman.

The printed service policy also serves as a convenient reminder to the salesman to discuss various service features which might otherwise be overlooked in a service presentation. The policy is a full reservoir of service information which may be drawn upon as needed. Buyers will believe more readily what they read than what a salesman tells them about mechanical service. The printed service policy should be in the sales kit of every salesman of mechanical products.

VI. A SALESMAN'S SERVICE RESPONSIBILITIES TO CUSTOMERS

A salesman is responsible not only for discussing service with prospects, but also for seeing that customers secure the free mechanical service to which they are entitled after a sale has been made. Salesmen who "follow through" with customers on service, establish friendly relationships with them and secure repeat sales.

A successful salesman promotes service with a customer after closing a sale, in the following ways: (1) by delivering the service policy and going over its provisions with each new customer; (2) by convincing new customers of the need for regular inspections and good mechanical maintenance; (3) by seeing that each new customer secures the free service promised; (4) by instructing new owners in the operation and care of the machine.

At the time a machine is delivered to a new customer or shortly thereafter, a salesman resells him on service and discusses the service policy, which may not have been described before the sale was closed. A salesman then goes over the provisions of the policy and warranty and leaves a copy of it, issued in the owner's name, with the new customer. The customer's attention is called to the free adjustments offered during the "breaking-in" period.

Many users of mechanical products are not aware of the necessity for regular maintenance, lubrication, and adjustments required to ensure economical, efficient operation of new machines. By convincing new owners of the need for reasonable care and attention to mechanical articles, salesmen not only create good will and satisfied customers but also pave the way for much valuable word-of-mouth advertising and repeat sales. If purchasers are advised by salesmen to go to authorized service stations for inspections according to a regular maintenance schedule, breakdowns may be avoided and good will will be secured.

Many manufacturers of mechanical goods publish instruction books or guides describing proper maintenance procedure. These may be distributed by salesmen to new customers and serve as an invaluable aid in their education.

New customers often neglect to secure the inspections and adjust-

SALES PERFORMANCE RATING FORM

Presenting Mechanical Service

Salesman_____   Date_____

Rated by_____   Over-all Rating_____

Score

I. *Salesman's Knowledge of Mechanical Service*	Excellent 90–100	Good 80–90	Fair 70–80	Poor 60–70	Failure Below 60
A. Guarantee					
B. Provisions of service policy					
C. Service Personnel					
D. Accessibility of service					
E. Maintenance requirements of product					
F. Service equipment and facilities					
G. When service is available					
H. Customers' service experiences					
I. Cost of service					
J. Competitive service					
K. Authorized service dealers					

II. *Salesman's Use of Service Knowledge*	Excellent 90–100	Good 80–90	Fair 70–80	Poor 60–70	Failure Below 60
A. Discovering prospect's interest in service					
B. Discussing service of interest to prospect					
C. Minimizing prospect's need for service					
D. Showing service policy to prospect					

Miscellaneous Comments_____

_____

_____

ments to which they are entitled during a warranty period, with the result that the operation of their mechanical products is faulty and dissatisfaction results.

Alert salesmen make personal or telephone calls on new customers to ensure their taking advantage of the free inspections provided during the period of initial use.

Improper operation of a mechanical device is often responsible for excessive service and dissatisfied customers. Salesmen who instruct new owners in the correct operation of a machine create satisfied customers by preventing unusual wear or damage to the mechanism. Operating instruction sheets or tags are sometimes fastened to a product and salesmen call the attention of new owners to these directions and urge their observance. Personal instruction of new owners by salesmen, at the time of delivery or shortly thereafter, creates not only good will for the salesman but also repeat sales. When the operation of a product requires considerable skill, salesmen must know how to run the machine efficiently and be able to instruct new owners in its operation.

Problem I

John Walton, representing Braley Motor Car Company

The Braley Motor Car Company, established in 1918 in Providence, R.I., retails the Benton, a popular make of passenger automobile and commercial car selling in the $2,000 to $3,000 class. The company owns and operates a complete service station in connection with its salesroom, which is located on a traffic artery near the center of the city.

John Walton is one of six commission salesmen representing the company who sell in the city and surrounding trade territory. Each salesman is assigned to floor duty one day a week. The following interview took place in the Braley showroom on a day when salesman Walton was on duty:

1. SALESMAN: Good afternoon, sir, can I be of service to you?
2. PROSPECT: Yes, I believe you can. I dropped in to see the new Benton.
3. SALESMAN: Well, the Benton sure is a fine automobile this year.
4. PROSPECT: I live in Quebec, and when I'm home I have a car. However, now that I am living away, I am in need of a car, and I like a car that gives service. The car I have at home is in the same price range as the Benton, but I don't consider that it gave me good service at all.
5. SALESMAN: We hear this story quite often these days. Do you mind telling me what make the car is?

6. PROSPECT: No, it is the Medusa.

7. SALESMAN: Oh, the Medusa. I met a young fellow here just this morning with a Medusa convertible coupé he wants to trade. He also complained of service. Can you tell me some of the service troubles you found?

8. PROSPECT: Well, I often had to go back to my dealer for service, and his garage was so darned big that it was a big job just getting into the place for service. After fighting my way in, a group of supersalesmen would jump on my car and begin selling me their inspection plan, new seat covers, or a spring spray, even before they had asked what I wanted done to the car.

9. SALESMAN: Yes, many companies have adopted policies such as that. They build a huge garage and then rush the cars through. However, here we have a very thorough and efficient service crew. When you drive in, you can give your instructions to the shop-foreman and have any serviceman you prefer work on your car. We have been faced with the rapid expansion of our service trade and rather than find ourselves in the place of your Medusa dealer, we have divided our service stations so that on one side of the street we have our mechanical service and repairs, while directly across the street we have our new modern lubritorium equipped with the very latest equipment to lubricate any car. Having these two units in separate buildings eliminates a traffic jam at our door.

10. PROSPECT: Yes, the Medusa dealer had fine equipment too, but they still took all day to do a grease job on my little car. I think they could have painted it in less time than they took to grease it.

11. SALESMAN: Our lubrication department gives very quick service. When you bring your car in, just say what time you would like to have it, and we'll make every effort to have it for you at the appointed time. Of course, we do get some very busy days, when it is impossible to give our customers their cars when they want them, but then we tell you when you come in that we are overcrowded, and in this way we don't tie you up like some places would by taking your car and then delaying you a half hour till it is ready.

12. PROSPECT: How much does service cost on the Benton? It sure costs plenty to keep my Medusa on the road.

13. SALESMAN: With the new Benton, we give you free inspections at 300 or 400 miles, and again at 1,100 miles. We lubricate your car at these times and change the oil. All the service is free, but we ask you to pay for the oil—since you have used it.

14. PROSPECT: That sounds fair enough, but what happens if I am in Quebec city and need an inspection?

15. SALESMAN: Well, that is simple enough. Take your Benton to the Benton agency in Quebec city and they will service it for you. These

inspections can be had at any Benton dealer. This is much more convenient for you than if we insisted that you return to us for your free inspections. You see the dealer in Quebec city takes our name from the car and bills us for the labor.

16. PROSPECT: Now how about defective parts?

17. SALESMAN: Well, you know that your Benton is guaranteed for three months or 4,000 miles, whichever comes first. During this period we replace any defective parts, but since a Benton gives you more car for dollar value on the road you needn't worry about defective parts.

18. PROSPECT: And what happens when the guarantee has expired?

19. SALESMAN: Another Benton service feature is that in all the Benton agencies throughout the country they have standard prices for their parts. To replace the air filter, for instance, costs $5 all over the country. On other cars, this expense will range from $6 to $10.

20. PROSPECT: Well, those sound like good service features. I would like to have one of your catalogues and delivered prices of the Benton, and I shall drop in to see you again in a few days. Your name, sir, is?

21. SALESMAN: John Walton. Here is my card, and I wonder if I could have your name so I'll know you when you return?

22. PROSPECT: Certainly, Howard James, 18 Westwood Avenue. I thank you very much for your trouble. Good day.

Questions

1. Criticize the salesman's service presentation, stating specific strengths and weaknesses in his discussion of service.

2. Did the salesman discover the prospect's interest in service? How? Was it effective?

3. Was the prospect's need for service minimized? How?

4. What features of mechanical service were emphasized? What others should have been mentioned?

5. Did the salesman refer to the manufacturer's warranty or service policy?

Problem II

J. L. Kennison, representing the Long-Carter Appliance Company

The Long-Carter Appliance Company, Philadelphia, Pa., retails electric washers, ironers, freezers, refrigerators, vacuum cleaners, hotwater heaters, and other major appliances made by a well-known manufacturer of electrical equipment. A sales force of 12 men operates out of the Philadelphia salesroom and an additional five men sell from a branch sales office in Wilmington, Del. The company maintains well-equipped service stations in connection with both salesrooms.

J. L. Kennison, one of the salesmen in the Philadelphia office, has invited Mr. and Mrs. Mason, prospects for a vacuum cleaner, to visit the showroom. When the following interview opens, the prospects have entered the company's salesroom:

1. SALESMAN: Good evening, Mrs. Mason, I'm glad you came in.
2. MRS. MASON: This is Mr. Mason.
3. SALESMAN: How do you do, sir. Won't you both sit down?
4. MR. MASON: Mrs. Mason is interested in a new cleaner, so I thought we'd drive down and see what you have.
5. SALESMAN: I'll have a better idea of what to show you if you'll tell me a little about your home cleaning problems.
6. MRS. MASON: It certainly is a problem. That's why we came in to see what you might have to offer in cleaners.
7. SALESMAN: How many rooms do you have in your home?
8. MRS. MASON: It's a three-bedroom house.
9. SALESMAN: And is most of it carpeted?
10. MRS. MASON: No, just the livingroom, dining room, lower hall, and stairs. Upstairs we have bare floors and throw-rugs in the big bedroom and linoleum mats in the children's rooms.
11. SALESMAN: I see—and what type of cleaning equipment are you now using?
12. MRS. MASON: Oh, I'm using an Arco vacuum cleaner. I've had nothing but trouble with it. I called in the appliance man who sold it to me about two years ago and he took it away to service it. I waited and waited. It must have taken him three weeks. He said he had to send away for parts. Then when it did come back, he charged me nearly twenty dollars for repairs. I don't really think he knew how to fix it, for it has never worked right since. Just won't pick up the dirt.
13. SALESMAN: It is a real problem getting service on some cleaners. We happen to be an authorized service station for the Hancock cleaner. That means we are required to keep a full supply of parts on hand all of the time so you never have to wait for parts. Then our servicemen are factory-trained and know the Hancock thoroughly. We have three men who have been with us over ten years, who spend all of their time on cleaners, which means that we get the work out in a hurry. When we take a cleaner in for service, we tell you exactly when it will be finished, and if the work takes longer than we expect, we loan you a cleaner so you can go ahead with your cleaning.
14. MR. MASON: That's a good idea.
15. MRS. MASON: I don't want a cleaner that'll cost me $20 to have fixed after I've had it a few months.
16. SALESMAN: Our service charges are most reasonable. We have a standard rate for each operation. For example, a motor overhaul costs only $5 plus the cost of necessary parts which rarely runs over $1.50 to $2.

Before we start work, we make a thorough examination of the cleaner and tell you in advance what it will cost you to put it in good working order. That's reasonable, isn't it?

17. MRS. MASON: Yes, it is.

18. SALESMAN: While you're here, I'd like you to step out and see our service department. We're mighty proud of it. We employ 10 men in the department, servicing all types of electrical appliances—refrigerators, freezers, washers, hot-water heaters. We use the latest type of service equipment for testing and repairing. In fact there is more than $20,-000 worth of special equipment here in the shop.

19. MR. MASON: You seem to be set up to do a thorough job.

20. SALESMAN: From what you see here, you might get the idea that the Hancock requires a lot of service, but that's not the case. In fact, our customers spend an average of less than $1 a year for service on the Hancock. Here's one example, (showing customer service record) of a customer who bought a Hancock in 1940 and to date she has spent only $3.75 for service.

21. MRS. MASON: That's very little.

22. SALESMAN: The reason for the small amount of service is that the Hancock is precision made of the finest materials available. The motor is sealed in oil so that it never needs lubrication. It runs on self-oiling ball bearings.

23. MR. MASON: It's getting quite late now and I guess we'll have to be getting along.

24. SALESMAN: I would like to send out a Hancock for you to try for a week so you can see for yourself what a fine cleaner it really is. After you have used it in your own housework, I'd like to call by and tell you about its unusual features. Here is a copy of our service policy which confirms what I have been telling you.

25. MRS. MASON: I would like to try it.

26. SALESMAN: It will be out tomorrow.

27. MRS. MASON: I'll be looking for it. Good night.

28. SALESMAN: Thank you. Good-by.

Questions

1. How did the salesman discover the prospect's interests in service? What were the buyer's service interests?

2. Did the salesman discuss service features of interest to the prospect? What features were presented?

3. Was the need for service minimized? How?

4. Did the salesman use the service policy? How?

5. Was this service presentation satisfactory? How could it have been improved?

Reading References

CHARLES H. FERNALD, "Salesmanship," pp. 68–69, Prentice-Hall, Inc., New York, 1945.

J. H. FREDERICK, "Industrial Marketing," pp. 339–342, Prentice-Hall, Inc., New York, 1934.

R. F. ELDER, "Fundamentals of Industrial Marketing," Chap. XI, McGraw-Hill Book Company, Inc., New York, 1935.

HAROLD M. HAAS, "A Short Course in Salesmanship," pp. 134–137, Prentice-Hall, Inc., New York, 1939.

C. F. PHILLIPS, "Marketing by Manufacturers," pp. 207–225, Richard D. Irwin, Inc., Chicago, 1946.

HARRY R. TOSDAL, "Introduction to Sales Management," pp. 130–131, McGraw-Hill Book Company, Inc., New York, 1940.

CHAPTER X

CREDIT SALES PRESENTATIONS

I. IMPORTANCE OF CREDIT IN SELLING

Credit is so closely related to selling that a knowledge of it, skill in presenting it to customers, and a desire to cooperate with the credit department are fundamental to the success of a salesman. Salesmen are vitally concerned with credit because sales are not actually completed until the merchandise sold has been paid for in full. In the last analysis, a salesman is judged not only by the volume he sells but by the net profits he earns; and profits depend on sound credits. Furthermore, the credit department decides whether the orders which a salesman secures are acceptable.

A salesman who does not know how to determine the credit standing of a prospect wastes valuable time in attempting to sell a person or concern with no credit responsibility. A commission salesman receives no compensation for orders rejected because of poor credit; his commissions may be withheld until payment has been made in full by the buyer.

A liberal or competitive credit policy may be a salesman's most effective selling argument, enabling him to increase his sales and meet competition. Credit customers usually concentrate their purchases and buy in larger quantities from salesmen who offer liberal credit terms. A salesman who knows this subject can secure larger orders by advising his customers how to use credit to increase their purchasing power.

Salesmen must devote more time to credit investigations when business recessions and unstable economic conditions increase the danger of credit losses. Today profit margins of manufacturers and distributors are narrower and sellers are no longer able to absorb large credit losses and show profits. If the net profit of a wholesale grocer is 1.1 per cent, a loss of $100 is equivalent to the net profit on $9,090 in sales. Restricted margins of wholesalers and retailers have made it necessary for them to turn over their capital frequently.

Salesmen, by educating distributors and retailers to reduce outstanding accounts, to curtail long-term credits, and to abolish special terms, can aid their merchant customers in speeding up their capital turnover and increasing net profits. A customer who is making money buys larger orders and pays for them promptly.

Many companies, particularly those selling at wholesale and direct to consumers, depend upon their salesmen to make collections from customers. Through personal contact and friendliness, salesmen are often able to secure prompt payment of accounts. Credit managers, guided by the credit advice of salesmen, often authorize credit and pass shipments to customers who would otherwise not be extended credit accommodation.

Installment or time-payment sales increase a salesman's credit responsibilities and at the same time make it possible to sell many prospects whose accumulated wants are greater than their current incomes.

II. RELATION OF SALESMEN TO CREDIT DEPARTMENT

There is a long-standing misunderstanding between salesmen and their credit departments created by the natural optimism of salesmen and the cultivated conservatism of credit men. This misunderstanding often creates friction between salesmen and credit men detrimental to the work of both.

Some salesmen feel that credit men create ill will among customers by writing tactless collection letters and making arbitrary demands for payment of overdue accounts. This critical attitude of salesmen is often due to a lack of sales viewpoint by credit men but it also arises from salesmen's lack of understanding of the problems and responsibilities of credit men.

If salesmen will make a sincere effort to understand the work of credit men, they will acquire a more sympathetic understanding of the problems involved in extending credit to customers. Closer cooperation between salesmen and credit men is essential to the success of both.

A credit manager can be of great assistance to a salesman in selling to buyers with questionable credit standing, if the salesman wins the confidence and good will of the credit executive. A customer may ask a salesman for unusually liberal terms or an extension of time for payment. The salesman who has cooperated with his credit department can often secure the approval of special terms and close the sale.

A salesman who gives his credit department full, unbiased facts about a customer's financial situation is more likely to obtain the cooperation of his credit manager than a salesman who withholds information or reports misleading facts.

A credit manager will often increase the limits of small accounts or reopen closed accounts for salesmen who cooperate with the credit department by securing credit information and defending the position of the credit department.

A helpful credit manager can save a salesman much time and discouragement by supplying him with information about the credit position of present and prospective customers. Good teamwork between a salesman and his credit department pays big dividends.

III. WHAT A SALESMAN SHOULD KNOW ABOUT CREDIT

Every salesman selling on credit should be familiar with the essentials of credit procedure. Salesmen whose products arc sold for cash obviously have little need of credit information. However, since more than 90 per cent of the wholesale and retail business of the country is done on credit, it is necessary for most salesmen to be familiar with it.

A salesman should know: (1) nature and advantages of credit; (2) two types of credit; (3) what is a good credit risk? (4) sources of credit information; (5) how to determine the credit standing of a new account; (6) mercantile credit terms; (7) consumer credit terms; (8) discounts for prompt payment of mercantile credit; (9) penalty for slow payment; (10) account guarantee; (11) collections by salesmen; (12) credit service to merchants; (13) credit and collection policy and system; (14) competitors' credit policy.

1. Nature and Advantages of Credit. Credit has been defined as the ability to obtain goods or services immediately by promising to pay for them at a definite time in the future. The word "credit" is derived from the Latin verb, *credo*, which means, "I believe." Credit is the ability possessed by an individual or firm to buy without making an immediate cash payment. However, the seller or creditor is the final judge of whether or not the buyer or debtor possesses the ability to buy on credit. In exercising such judgment, the seller is said to be "extending credit" to the purchaser.

The function of a credit man, with the assistance of a salesman, is to determine whether a prospect or customer is able to buy without cash and in all probability will continue to have that ability until payment is due. It is the duty of the credit man and salesman to ob-

serve factors that affect each customer's credit. Because salesmen are
in frequent touch with customers, they are in the most favorable position to observe and report to their credit departments on the credit
standing of buyers.

Salesmen who sell on credit enjoy the following advantages: credit
secures customer good will by furnishing a convenient means of payment; it increases the amount of a sale; it creates repeat sales and
steady customers; it simplifies adjustments; it creates a demand for
quality merchandise; it overcomes price objections; it attracts a better
class of trade and increases sales volume.

2. Two Types of Credit. Salesmen are concerned with two general
types of short-term credit: (1) Mercantile credit, which is extended
by a manufacturer to a wholesaler or retailer or by a wholesaler to
a retailer on merchandise bought for resale; (2) Consumer or retail
credit, which is extended to users.

1. *Mercantile Credit.* Mercantile credit transactions are facilitated with credit instruments or legal documents recording the terms
of indebtedness. The principal types of mercantile credit instruments are (*a*) open-account or book credit; (*b*) promissory notes;
(*c*) commercial drafts; (*d*) trade acceptances; (*e*) letters of credit;
(*f*) trust receipts; (*g*) warehouse receipts; (*h*) consignment contracts.

A salesman should be familiar with each of these types of credit
instruments, particularly those which are used by his firm in extending credit to wholesale or retail merchants. Salesmen are obliged to
conform to the credit policy of their firm which describes the type of
credit or instrument used in extending credit to customers. The
credit instrument used varies according to the nature of the risk involved. For example, when a credit manager considers that a dealer's credit is satisfactory, the salesman may be instructed to sell the
merchant on an open-account basis. On the other hand, if the credit
of a dealer is considered questionable, the salesman may be instructed
to sell on a sight draft, attached to bill of lading, basis. In some
cases, salesmen are given responsibility to determine the type of
credit to be extended to various customers.

a. Open-account or book credit is the most common type of mercantile credit. The amount of the buyer's indebtedness is simply
recorded on the books of the seller. At the time of shipment of the
goods bought, a statement of the amount due is sent to the buyer,
who is expected to pay in full on or before the expiration of the
credit term. The duration of open-account terms ranges from 30 to 90
days. This plan stimulates sales and facilitates credit arrangements

by freeing customers from the detail of making and handling credit papers.

b. A promissory note is the written promise of the buyer to pay the seller a certain sum at a definite future time. This instrument is used occasionally in extending mercantile credit when the character of the risk does not justify open-account credit. A promissory note protects the seller as it is positive evidence of debt and affords a psychological advantage in bringing about payment through presentation at the buyer's bank. Promissory notes are not used as generally as book credit because they afford little more protection than an open account and involve more detail in handling, which slows up the extension of credit.

c. Commercial drafts, commonly used in mercantile credit transactions, are very much like checks. They are drawn by the seller against the buyer and mailed to the buyer's bank, ordering the buyer to pay through his bank the amount written on the face of the bank draft. Bank drafts, payable at sight, are usually sent to a buyer's bank accompanied by the bill of lading or shipping receipt of the transportation company carrying the merchandise purchased. The buyer's bank secures the acceptance of the draft by the buyer, releases the bill of lading to the buyer, and remits the amount of the draft to the seller. The use of a sight draft is comparable to selling on a cash-on-delivery basis with the exception that the transaction is handled through a commercial bank. The buyer usually arranges with his bank to charge the draft to his account.

A draft is sometimes used by sellers in collecting past-due accounts, in which case the seller draws a draft on the buyer and presents the draft to the buyer's bank for collection.

Drafts are commonly used in extending mercantile credit because their presentation through a bank is a more insistent method of collection than a direct demand on a buyer by a seller for the amount due.

d. Trade acceptances are negotiable certificates of indebtedness representing a particular sale of goods and are payable on demand at sight, or at the end of a stated time. For example, a salesman sells merchandise on trade acceptance. When the goods are shipped, the seller sends a trade acceptance with the invoice to the buyer. When the certificate is received by the buyer, he writes his acceptance on the face, agreeing to pay the face amount at his bank on the date specified, and returns it to the seller. The seller may discount the acceptance at his bank, giving him the immediate use of the money invested in the merchandise sold, or he may present it to the buyer's bank for payment on the date due.

Trade acceptance terms improve the credit standing of customers and thus enable them to buy more goods. These terms make possible sales to customers whose credit standing would not permit them to buy on ordinary terms.

e. Commercial letters of credit are used generally in export selling or in sales transactions when buyers and sellers are separated by long distances. Buyers arrange with their local banks to make available, by a letter of credit, a definite amount of money in a bank in the distant city where the seller is located. A copy of the letter of credit is sent to the seller who presents it to the bank in his city, which will honor his drafts covering shipments for a certain time up to the amount specified by the letter. For example, a merchant in San Francisco wishes to buy from a firm in London. The buyer goes to his San Francisco bank and arranges for a letter of credit on a London bank. A copy of the letter is sent to the London seller who presents it to his bank, which in turn makes payment to the seller for sales made to the buyer in San Francisco.

Commercial letters of credit establish a buyer's financial standing, facilitate payments, and aid salesmen in closing sales for larger amounts.

f. Trust receipts are a form of mercantile credit instrument sometimes used by manufacturers in financing sales to wholesalers or large retailers on sizable orders of seasonal merchandise. When a buyer does not wish to tie up a large amount of capital for an extended period, the customer may arrange with the seller, a bank, or finance company to take title to the goods and permit the buyer to hold them in his own warehouse in trust under a trust receipt. As the buyer resells the merchandise, he pays the title holder, plus interest from the date of the trust receipt agreement.

The seller or bank holding title makes a periodic inventory to see if the warehouse stock balances with the unpaid total on the trust receipt which is drawn for a specified time, usually four to six months. If all of the merchandise has not been sold by maturity of the receipt, the buyer pays for the balance.

This form of credit is extended to retailers and is sometimes referred to as a "floor plan" by which a merchant can secure a complete stock of new or seasonal merchandise for his display floor and pay for it under a trust receipt as the goods are sold to users.

g. Warehouse receipts are a common mercantile credit instrument used in financing large purchases by wholesalers and large retailers. The seller ships the merchandise to a designated public warehouse and bills a bank or finance company with whom the buyer has made arrangements to finance the purchase. The warehouse issues non-negotiable receipts for the goods placed in storage and the receipts are delivered to the bank. When the buyer desires to withdraw goods from the warehouse, he pays the bank, which issues a written order to the warehouse to release the merchandise to the buyer. If the buyer does not pay for all of the goods before the expiration of the agreement, the receipts may be made negotiable and the bank may dispose of them to another bank or financial company.

A similar form of credit is provided through field warehousing or storage of goods on the premises of the buyer, who leases space to a licensed warehouseman, who releases goods to the buyer as ordered by the bank or finance company which holds the merchandise as collateral.

h. Consignment selling is a form of mercantile credit used in the resale of perishable, quick turnover, seasonal merchandise for which there is considerable demand, and sales are automatic. The consignor ships the goods to the merchant consignee, who signs an agreement to report resales and pay at stated intervals for the goods which have been sold. The merchandise remains the property of the consignor until resold by the merchant.

2. Consumer or Retail Credit. This type of credit, which is extended to ultimate users, is an important factor in the sale of merchandise by manufacturers direct to consumers, and by retail stores, nearly one-half of which offer credit to customers. In addition, most services, such a laundry, automotive, and professional, are sold on credit. Manufacturers of automobiles, major appliances, and specialties sold by retail dealers have developed retail credit plans to stimulate sales to consumers.

Consumer purchases of merchandise and services are financed in three ways: (*a*) open-account or book credit, familiarly known as "charge accounts," (*b*) installment credit, (*c*) personal loans. A salesman selling direct to consumers for a manufacturer or retailer, and representatives of manufacturers offering consumer credit plans to retailers, should be familiar with these three forms of consumer credit.

a. Open-account or book credit is the most widely used and convenient form of consumer credit. The buyer takes possession of the merchandise, and the cost is entered on the books of the seller. Then the seller sends the buyer a statement, usually at the end of the month in which the purchase was made. Usually a credit limit is established by the seller which is often twice the weekly income of the customer.

A variety of open-account practices have been adopted by retail stores such as the "deposit account" in which customers make deposits, as in a bank account, and draw against their balances for purchases, receiving interest on the balance. Other stores use "deferred-payment" charge accounts, which are the same as open accounts except that the terms are more liberal, as one-third in 30 days, one-third in 60 days, and the balance in 90 days. Another variation is the "twenty payment" account on which payments are made over a period of 20 weeks.

b. Installment credit enables a consumer to borrow the full purchase price of an article and to liquidate the loan in successive fractions in the future. This form of credit is generally used by manufacturers and retailers in the sale of specialties to consumers and, to a more limited extent, in wholesale selling to distributors.

Installment, or time payment, credit enables a salesman to sell to customers whose wants cost more than their current incomes, to increase the amount of the average sale, to discount the effectiveness of competitive price advertising, to maintain regular relations with customers, and to reduce sales resistance.

It makes little difference to a salesman whether his sales are financed by his own company, the government, banks, or professional finance companies. The same steps, in general, must be taken by him to arrange for credit extension. On consumer installment sales, he usually must:

1. Have the customer fill out and sign Credit Application for Time Payment Terms giving information as to his residence address, occupation, references, etc.

2. Have customer sign Conditional Sales Contract or Chattel Mortgage. Conditional sales contracts vary according to the laws of the various states.

3. Advise customer when, where, and in what amounts payments on contract are due.

4. Collect initial payment.

When consumer installment credit papers have been executed by a retailer, they are assigned usually to a wholesaler, manufacturer, or finance company which credits the retailer with the principal of the unmatured installments, reserving the interest which is included in the face amount of the contract.

In some cases, salesmen make collections on installment contracts for the retailer as the agent of the wholesaler, manufacturer, or finance company, whichever happens to be carrying the paper. When a finance company buys consumer installment paper without recourse, retail salesmen are relieved of the responsibility of investigating an applicant's credit standing and of making collections from delinquent customers.

When a customer completes payments on a retail installment contract, it is returned by the finance company to the dealer who in turn gives it to the man who made the sale. The salesman delivers the paid-up contract to the customer. Having completed his payments, the customer is in an excellent position to purchase additional merchandise from the salesman.

Salesmen selling on installment terms usually carry a printed schedule showing monthly payments on principal and finance charges, including interest from date of purchase until maturity of the contract. Salesmen should know the minimum amount of initial payment required and the number of months in which the unpaid balance must be paid. Credit application forms and conditional sales contracts should be included in a salesman's equipment.

c. Personal loans are arranged by many consumers to finance their purchases of automobiles, home appliances, and furnishings. This financing is handled by industrial banks, Morris Plan banks, sales and personal finance companies, although some buyers borrow on life insurance or from friends or relatives. Money borrowed in this way is used to pay cash for purchases.

3. What Is a Good Credit Risk? To be able to judge and report on the credit position of prospects and customers for either mercantile or consumer credit a salesman must have a standard for determining the character of a credit risk. A firm or individual seeking credit recognition must have three basic qualities: (*a*) character; (*b*) capacity; (*c*) capital. Although all of these are important, credit is often extended on character alone, or on a combination of character and capacity. A banker may emphasize the importance of capital in weighing a credit risk; a merchant may favor character. There are numerous other factors that may have a bearing on a credit risk, such as the seasonal character of the buyer's business, the type of product being sold, current business conditions, and the amount of the sale.

a. Character, or the reputation of a buyer for fair dealing, is revealed by his honesty, personal habits, ethics, social standing, and integrity. It is a very important factor in granting credit. Salesmen must be continuously on the alert to observe indications of character, or the lack thereof, in prospects who desire credit for the first time and also in regular credit customers. Salesmen report these observations to their credit managers.

Character is often disclosed by a buyer's attitude toward competitors, his advertising, court record, and moral conduct. It may also be determined through inquiries of other salesmen, competitors, and customers.

b. *The capacity* of an applicant for credit is determined by his personal aptitude, his business knowledge, training, and experience. A salesman can determine largely the capacity of a retail or wholesale merchant through observation of the dealer's store, location, arrangement, lighting, and appearance. The type and quantity of merchandise stocked, the attitude of salespersons, the character of display advertising, the class of customer served, all have a bearing on the capacity of the prospect or customer. The capacity of an individual may also be gauged by his education, length of business experience, positions held, promotions, etc.

The line of business in which a buyer is engaged affects his capacity to pay. Some businesses are seasonal, others deal in perishable products; in some, the unit of sale is large and the demand limited. All these conditions must be taken into consideration in granting credit.

Salesmen, by observation and through conversation with prospects and customers, can discover the capacity of buyers and assist their credit managers in determining the soundness of credit risks.

c. *The capital* of a buyer is the third important factor to be considered in reaching a decision to grant, expand, or curtail credit. It is the most tangible and easiest to measure of the factors involved in the "3-C" formula. The amount, source, and nature of the finances of an individual or a business must be considered to determine whether or not a buyer can be expected to pay for his purchase when payment is due. Capital includes (1) quick assets, such as cash in hand, cash in bank, accounts receivable, and stock on hand, (2) fixed assets, such as store fixtures, furniture, and real estate. A credit applicant must have sufficient liquid or quick assets to meet his current obligations.

The source of a buyer's capital has an important bearing on his credit standing. If he earned, through his own efforts, the money to finance his operations, he may be entitled to more recognition than if he obtained his capital by inheritance or by borrowing.

4. Sources of Credit Information. There are several recognized sources of credit information usually consulted by salesmen and credit managers in making mercantile and consumer credit investigations.

These sources are (*a*) mercantile agencies; (*b*) other creditors; (*c*) credit interchange bureaus; (*d*) trade associations; (*e*) commercial banks; (*f*) business publications; (*g*) attorneys; and (*h*) salesmen.

a. Mercantile agencies, such as Dun and Bradstreet, Inc., are professional credit investigators with numerous offices in the principal cities and large staffs of credit reporters. These agencies publish quarterly credit-rating books giving the financial standing of large and small business organizations. Small pocket-sized sectional volumes are also published for the convenience of salesmen. These rating books are supplemented by special credit reports which include changes in the financial status of a business since the rating was last published.

Salesmen find these ratings and special reports invaluable in determining the credit standing of prospective customers. However, they must recognize that, since mercantile agency ratings are based on information collected several months before actual publication, it is unwise to place sole dependence upon them in determining a firm's credit standing. For the purpose of defrauding sellers, unscrupulous buyers sometimes adopt names similar to those of concerns that have satisfactory credit ratings. It is often impossible to detect these dishonest firms without a special credit inspection report.

In addition to obtaining credit information from the general mercantile agencies, salesmen may get similar data from numerous trade agencies which collect and report credit information for specific industries. Through close contact with buyers in their restricted fields, these agencies are often able to report more recent and reliable credit information than general agencies. Typical of trade agencies are the Credit Clearance Bureau of New England, serving the paper and allied trades, and the Shoe and Leather Mercantile Agency, Inc., serving the shoe and leather industry.

The financial responsibility of consumers is rated and reported by the Retail Credit Company, a national organization, and by retail merchants' credit associations in the principal cities of the country.

b. Other creditors are a recognized source of credit information. They are consulted by sellers to determine whether credit applicants are able and willing to pay their bills promptly and enjoy good credit standing. Such references usually provide quick, reliable, and up-to-date information on the credit of applicants.

Salesmen are usually expected to obtain references from new customers applying for credit. However, direct requests for references yield little more than the names of creditors who will recommend the applicant. Some applicants keep a few accounts paid in full to use as credit references. A dealer salesman may easily obtain references by observing a merchant's stock to discover the names of other suppliers who are extending credit accommodations. If a merchant is heavily stocked with the merchandise supplied by a manufacturer who enforces a strict credit policy, a salesman may infer that the merchant's credit is sound. Salesmen can usually obtain the most reliable references by observation. By questioning local attorneys, bankers, and competitors and by listening to their volunteered remarks, salesmen may also secure dependable credit information without resorting to direct inquiry.

c. *Credit interchange bureaus* for the exchange of information on the credit standings of firms and individuals have been established by creditors on local, sectional, and national bases. Creditors contribute their credit experience to a central bureau which makes this information available to other members. These bureaus, which have been established through the efforts of the National Association of Credit Men, maintain files showing payment habits, amounts owed, maximum credit allowed, and amounts overdue of many thousand debtors.

Salesmen, through their credit departments, may obtain much valuable information concerning the credit standing of prospects and customers from these interchange bureaus.

d. *Trade associations* in some industries have established credit interchange bureaus and salesmen may, through their credit departments, obtain reports on prospects and customers.

e. *Commercial banks* often possess valuable credit information about local merchants and manufacturers. However, credit information from banks should be obtained through the creditor's bank. Salesmen will meet with little success in securing credit information directly from banks, which are reluctant to reveal facts about their customers.

f. *Business publications* frequently publish news items or articles describing the financial condition of firms, changes in ownership or management, reorganizations, plant expansion, sales volume, and other information bearing directly on the credit standing of business organizations.

By reading business magazines, salesmen may secure valuable data about their prospects and customers.

g. *Attorneys* who specialize in collections may be of aid to salesmen and credit managers in obtaining information about the credit standing of firms and individuals.

h. *Salesmen* should be continuously on the alert for information about their customers and prospects. They are able to secure credit facts which cannot be obtained in any other manner. Several ways in which salesmen can obtain credit data have already been described. However, a salesman must guard against reporting biased information, colored by his optimism or sympathy for prospects or customers. The natural interest of a salesman in making sales must not influence him to magnify the favorable aspects and suppress the negative features of a prospect's or customer's credit standing. After a sale has been closed, a salesman must continue to keep his credit department informed regarding the financial status of the customer.

5. Determining the Credit Standing of a New Account. A salesman's credit responsibilities begin with his selection of prospects. Before approaching a prospective customer, a salesman should learn as much about his financial responsibility as the amount of the initial sale and future potential purchases justify. A few minutes spent by a salesman in observing and making inquiries about a prospect may save hours of time, discouragement, and embarrassment later when the order is rejected by the credit department because the buyer is a poor credit risk. All convenient sources of credit information should be investigated in advance of the first contact with a prospect. When a salesman has investigated and is satisfied that a prospect is able to pay for merchandise purchased, he can make his sales presentation without fear that the sale, if closed, will be rejected by his credit department. If, however, a salesman is unable to determine a prospect's credit rating in advance of a sales interview, it becomes necessary to obtain the information during the interview.

By asking tactful questions, a salesman can discover whether a prospect has the necessary capital, character, and capacity to pay his bills. Typical credit questions, which can be casually asked a prospect, are "How long has your business been established?" "Is this property owned or rented?" "Is your business operated on a cash or credit basis?" "Is your business growing?" "How often do you take inventory?"

By observing the condition of a buyer's property, its location, the number and type of employees, type of trade served, grade of merchandise carried, and other obvious conditions, a salesman can form very accurate conclusions on the character of a mercantile credit risk.

Salesmen are often required to complete a credit report on each new customer. These reports, which are studied by the credit department, call for answers to numerous questions concerning the financial status of a new customer. Some buyers are reluctant to answer questions concerning their financial situation and salesmen must use tact

---

SALESMAN'S REPORT FOR CREDIT APPROVAL
ON

Date_____

Name in Full

Trade Name   Address

Kind of Business

Form of Business   Single Ownership   Partnership   Corporation

If Partnership-Name of Partners
            Name of Treasurer

If Corporation-Name of Treasurer

Years in business   Length of Time at Present Location

Own, Lease or Rent Place Occupied   If owned, Approx. Value

Any Mortgages-If so, how many and what amounts

If Leased-Length of time   It rented, cost per month
       and yearly rent

Is Location? Good Fair Poor   Is Store Appearance? Good Fair Poor

No. of Employees

What do you Estimate Yearly Sales Our Line?

Trade Discount   Terms

        REFERENCES: Secure bank and at least five trade references with address
                      (Trade references should cover different lines of Merchandise)

Name_____ Address_____

_____

_____

_____

_____

Remarks: What is your opinion of this prospect?

                                          Salesman_____

Fig. 4. This credit report form is used by salesmen representing a large floor-covering manufacturer in reporting to their credit manager factors affecting the credit standing of a new retail customer.

in obtaining this information. Careful observation will provide answers to many of the questions listed, without antagonizing a new customer by direct questioning. If a new customer understands that credit information sought by a salesman is customarily obtained as a routine matter from every new customer, he is usually willing to speak frankly about his business and finances.

Salesmen, who open new accounts for large amounts, are often required to obtain from each new customer a balance sheet showing his financial condition and an operating statement reporting his sales activity. When a dealer objects to furnishing a financial statement, a salesman may explain that this request is no reflection upon the integrity or business ability of the customer. Customers who cooperate with creditors by furnishing financial statements obtain a broader knowledge of their own business operations as well as a more favorable credit standing.

In some companies, prospects to be solicited by salesmen are predetermined by the credit department, and the salesmen have no responsibility for credit investigations or for reporting on new customers.

6. Mercantile Credit Terms. Salesmen must be familiar with the terms upon which credit is extended. The length of mercantile credit terms varies widely. In the case of open-account credit, purchasers are usually allowed 30 days in which to make payment. In selling seasonal merchandise, longer terms are often extended to customers to enable them to pay in the season when they receive their income. Shorter terms prevail in the sale of staple articles which are turned over quickly and in large volume. The terms of payment also vary with different types of credit instruments. Promissory notes may be paid in 30, 60, 90 days or longer; bank drafts are payable at sight or in 30 days or longer; trade acceptances are usually payable in 30 or 60 days. The term of sale dates from the day the merchandise is shipped by the seller, although in special cases time extensions are granted to buyers.

The time when payment is due is sometimes extended by sellers who quote R.O.G. terms. By this arrangement, the term of payment dates from the time the goods are received by the buyer instead of the date of shipment by the seller. Similarly, E.O.M. terms are quoted whereby the term payment begins at the end of the month in which the purchase was made instead of from date of shipment.

Likewise, "prox terms" are quoted to buyers who make frequent

STATEMENT OF FINANCIAL CONDITION OF_____

At Close of Books on_____193___

Kind of Business_____ Address_____
(Corporation or Partnership)

TO_____ ←≡ { Name of firm asking for statement

[THIS FORM APPROVED AND PUBLISHED BY THE NATIONAL ASSOCIATION OF CREDIT MEN]

For the purpose of obtaining merchandise from you on credit, or for the extension of credit, we make the following statement in writing, intending that you should rely thereon respecting our exact financial condition.

[PLEASE ANSWER ALL QUESTIONS. WHEN NO FIGURES ARE INSERTED, WRITE WORD "NONE"]

ASSETS	Dollars	Cents	LIABILITIES	Dollars	Cents
Cash (On Hand)			Accounts Payable for Merchandise		
(In Bank)			Notes and Acceptances Payable for Merchandise		
Accounts Receivable (Not Due)			Notes to_____Bank		
(30 to 90 Days Past Due)			When Due_____(Secured) (Unsecured)		
(Over 90 Days Past Due)			Taxes, Interest, Rentals, Payrolls (Accrued)		
Notes and Acceptances (Not Sold or Discounted)			Notes Payable to Stockholders, Partners or Others		
Merchandise (Not on Consignment or Conditional Contract) (Valued at "Cost" ☐ or "Market" ☐, whichever is Lower)			Other Current Liabilities		
Other Current Assets (Describe):			TOTAL CURRENT LIABILITIES		
			Mortgage on Land or Buildings		
TOTAL CURRENT ASSETS			Chattel Mortgages on Merchandise or Equipment		
Land and Buildings (Present Depreciated Value)			Other Liabilities not Current		
Machinery, Fixtures and Equipment (Present Depreciated Value)			TOTAL LIABILITIES		
Due from Officers, Partners or Others not Customers			Net Worth { Capital		
Other Assets (Describe):			{ Surplus		
TOTAL ASSETS			TOTAL (NET WORTH AND LIABILITIES)		

STATEMENT OF PROFIT AND LOSS FOR PERIOD FROM_____**TO**_____

Sales for Period, cash		Salaries—owners		
credit		employees		
TOTAL SALES		Rent, Heat, Light, Insurance, Taxes		
Inventory, Start of Period		Advertising		
Purchases for Period		Delivery		
Total		Depreciation (Fixtures, Trucks)		
Less Inventory, end of period		Miscellaneous (other operation expense)		
COST OF GOODS SOLD		TOTAL OPERATION EXPENSE		
GROSS PROFIT		If incorporated, amount		
Less Expense of Operation		of dividends paid		
NET PROFIT FOR PERIOD				

BUY FROM THE FOLLOWING FIRMS:

NAMES	ADDRESSES	AMOUNT OWING

The foregoing statement and the information given on the reverse side of this statement has been carefully read by the undersigned (both the printed and written matter), and is, to my knowledge, in all respects complete, accurate and truthful. It discloses to you the true state of my (our) financial condition on the_____day of_____19____. Since that time there has been no material unfavorable change in my (our) financial condition, and if any such change takes place I (we) will give you notice. Until such notice is given, you are to regard this as a continuing statement.

Name of Individual or Firm_____

If Partnership, Name Partners }_____
" Corporation, " Officers }_____

How long established_____Previous business experience_____
_____Where_____

Date of Signing Statement_____Street_____ City_____ State_____

Witness _____ Signed by_____
Residence Address of Witness_____ Title_____

FIG. 5. Retail merchants often are required to complete this statement of financial condition. This is a typical form used by salesmen representing manufacturers in securing credit information from new accounts. The form is usually left with a merchant by a salesman. The dealer fills in the information requested and returns the statement to the creditor.

purchases. For example, a customer who purchases 10 items, each on a separate occasion during a month, ordinarily would receive as many separate invoices. If he paid for each purchase at the expiration of 10-day terms, to get a cash discount, he would be obliged to make 10 separate payments. To save the buyer the inconvenience of writing so many checks and the seller the added bookkeeping, prox terms are quoted. By this arrangement, payment by one check may be made, before the tenth of the following month, for all purchases made during a current month. Cash discounts usually are allowed on prox terms from payment before the tenth of the following month.

Mercantile credit terms also are extended by allowing certain buyers forward datings or deferred datings. Under these special terms a buyers invoice is dated as of 60 or 90 days after he has received the merchandise purchased. Salesmen sometimes are permitted to quote these special terms to secure advance orders or to make sales in off-seasons. Buyers sometimes abuse a forward-dating privilege, allowed on one occasion, by demanding that a similar time extension be regularly granted on all orders.

Other special terms are granted occasionally. C.B.D. terms require a buyer to pay cash before delivery and are similar to C.W.O., or "cash with order," terms.

7. Consumer Credit Terms. Consumer open accounts are usually payable within 30 days of the billing date, which is usually the last day of the month, except in case of cycle billing in which names of customers are divided into 25 groups and statements sent to a different group each day of the month.

8. Discounts for Prompt Payment of Mercantile Credit. To encourage merchant customers to pay their bills promptly, sellers commonly offer discounts for settlement of credit accounts before the expiration of the term of payment. These discounts, called "cash discounts," usually are given for payment of an account with 10 days from date of invoice or shipment by the seller. The amount of the discount varies from 0.5 to 5 per cent in various industries.

Salesmen should persuade buyers to take cash discounts for two reasons: (1) a salesman's firm profits by decreased credit losses, more rapid turnover of capital, strong liquid position, and curtailed credit and collection expense; (2) customers profit by taking cash discounts through increased earnings. A buyer who takes a 2 per cent cash discount for payment in 10 days on 60-day net terms earns the equivalent of 14 per cent a year on his accounts payable. This high rate of return is based on the assumption that a buyer keeps his money continuously employed. Under the terms of 2 per cent 10 days, net 60 days, a buyer receives 2 per cent for the use of his money for 50 days. And since there are more than seven 50-day periods in a year, a buyer receives seven times 2 or 14 per cent interest.

Customers who take cash discounts also benefit from superior credit ratings and by receiving special offers and allowances usually given only to preferred customers.

Salesmen occasionally must deal with customers who abuse the cash discount privilege by taking unearned discounts or deducting the amount of the cash discount when making payment after expiration of the cash discount period. To enforce a firm cash discount policy, salesmen may explain to customers who take unearned discounts that bills must be paid within the discount period to entitle the buyer to the discount. Abuse of the discount privilege may mean that cash discounts will be eliminated entirely.

Large customers sometimes demand unusually long terms or extra discounts, contrary to the credit policy of sellers. Salesmen should maintain a firm position on such demands for credit concessions. To accede to the demands of customers not only weakens a salesman's position with his employer, but buyers are quick to take advantage of a willingness to make special concessions.

9. Penalty for Slow Payment. Some sellers exact a penalty for slow payment of mercantile credit accounts by charging interest to buyers on past-due accounts. When the term for payment expires, an account becomes automatically an interest account and 6 per cent is charged up to the time the account is fully paid. Salesmen operating under this policy should explain clearly this penalty charge to customers and avoid misunderstandings and loss of business.

A customer who is slow in making payment may be required to sign a promissory note. This is a written acknowledgment of indebtedness and may be discounted by the seller at his bank, giving him immediate use of the money. A creditor who holds a promissory note has less difficulty in collecting interest charges from the buyer for the time an account is overdue.

10. Account Guarantee. When a buyer's credit standing does not justify an extension of credit on an open account, sellers sometimes require the buyer to give a guarantee of indebtedness signed by a financially responsible guarantor. Some sellers use a guarantee form, signed by the guarantor of the account, which permits the seller to make immediate collection from the guarantor if payment of the account is not made according to the terms of sale.

A salesman who obtains a guarantee of indebtedness from a customer should determine whether the person guaranteeing the account is financially responsible and legally authorized to issue a guarantee.

11. Collections by Salesmen. In some sales organizations, salesmen are required to make collections. Wholesale grocery, drug, and hardware salesmen, calling on retailers, usually are required to collect from their delinquent customers. House-to-house salesmen of low-priced, staple merchandise deliver and collect from buyers. Salesmen of high-priced specialties and services rarely make collections. Some salesmen are only required to collect large or long overdue accounts.

Responsibility for collections makes salesmen careful in investigating the credit standing of new accounts and accepting orders from old customers of questionable standing. Because a salesman meets his customers often and knows them well, he is in the best position to observe and report changes in their financial position. A salesman who is required to make collections is less likely to oversell his customers. He is able to hold their good will by tactful collection methods rather than risk losing their business by impersonal collection letters or undiplomatic collectors. Furthermore, a salesman who collects his accounts becomes more familiar with his customers' business problems and is able to serve them more effectively.

The task of collecting by salesmen who sell to merchants is fully detailed in the following sales-job description of a leading food manufacturer whose salesmen sell direct to retailers. Their duties and responsibilities in handling collections are as follows:

1. *Collect for previous order.*
   a. Arrange statements to correspond with route cards.
   b. Handle monies collected.
   c. Check statement against delivery slips or invoices.
   d. Educate customers to have check written out and ready at hand when the salesman calls. The customer usually knows how much he he owes.
2. *Follow up and collect slow accounts.*
   a. Make arrangement for payment.
   b. Explain terms of credit and salesman's inability to alter them.
   c. Determine reasons for failure to pay.
3. *Refer bad accounts to office for collection.*
   a. Follow credit limits set by branch manager or credit manager.
   b. Collect and submit all available facts on the case.
   c. Cooperate with office in making the collection.

4. *Make use of C.O.D. billing.*
   a. Determine when to use.
   b. Explain rules under which deliveryman operates.

12. Credit Service to Merchants. A salesman should give credit service to his merchant customers. Timely credit advice may save a merchant from bankruptcy. By giving credit service to dealer customers, a salesman obtains their good will and increases purchases by reason of their improved credit position. If a customer fails, the salesman loses the account and his firm often loses money. Credit service to customers includes: (*a*) buying service; (*b*) credit policy service; (*c*) collection service:

a. Buying Service. A merchant often weakens his credit position by poor buying. A salesman can help his dealer customers to maintain good credit standing by not overselling them and selling only merchandise which will resell readily.

b. Credit Policy Service. By advising dealer customers concerning their credit and collection policies, a salesman can aid them in improving their credit standing. A merchant who has a sound credit policy has few bad debts and strengthens his credit position with banks and suppliers.

A salesman who counsels his merchant customers in selecting credit risks carefully, establishing definite credit limits, keeping accurate and complete credit records, securing adequate initial payments, and obtaining reliable credit information is building buyers into preferred risks and regular customers.

c. Collection Service. The credit standing of a small merchant depends upon his ability to turn over his limited capital quickly so that he can have cash to buy more merchandise. If his capital is tied up in accounts receivable, he is a poor customer. A salesman who aids his dealer customers in collecting their outstanding accounts is building future business on a permanent foundation.

By advising merchant customers to send statements to debtors regularly, to follow up overdue accounts systematically, to resort to legal aid when necessary, and to use collection letters consistently, a salesman can help dealers to reduce the amount of their accounts receivable.

Salesmen should show customers that it is to their advantage to take cash discounts and comply with the credit terms of their suppliers. Customers in good standing buy larger orders and at more frequent intervals.

13. Know Your Credit and Collection System. A salesman should be familiar with the credit and collection system operated by his credit department. He should know how credit applicants are investigated, how credit limits are established, how credit lines are revised and collections made. The various credit investigating and reporting forms used by a salesman's credit department should be in his possession. A salesman should know the collection-letter sequence, including the statements, formal notices, and form letters used by his company in dealing with overdue accounts. The use of collection agencies, personal collectors, and attorneys should be understood.

14. Competitors' Credit Policies. Salesmen should also know the credit and collection policies of competitors, their terms of sale, special datings, and cash discounts allowed to customers. This knowledge often gives a salesman more confidence in his terms of sale and enables him, when necessary, to compare favorably the credit policies of his company with those of competitors.

HOW TO DISCUSS CREDIT WITH MERCHANTS

Successful salesmen have a definite plan for handling credit transactions with dealer prospects and customers. Although it is important that a salesman know the credit policy and procedure of his company, it is equally necessary for him to attain skill in discussing credit effectively. Many salesmen who know credit completely do not present it well to prospects and customers because they cannot impart their knowledge. Practical methods of presenting credit to buyers, used by successful salesmen of various types of products, have been combined into the following four-step routine, by means of which any salesman can discuss credit more effectively:

Routine for Discussing Credit with Merchants

1. Appraise the merchant as a credit risk.
2. Discuss credit terms.
3. Give credit service to merchant customers.
4. Advise credit department.

1. Appraise the Merchant as a Credit Risk. During the course of a sales interview, a salesman can discover by tactful questioning much worth-while information about the financial responsibility of a prospective customer, thus avoiding a lengthy and sometimes embarrassing process of direct interrogation later.

A salesman should show a friendly interest in the prospect's business by asking such questions as, "Is your business done largely on cash or credit?" or "How long has your business been established?" or "How often do you take stock?" Answers to these and similar questions reveal much information about the character, capacity, and capital of a dealer.

Salesmen should likewise determine the credit position of present customers by asking such questions as: "What is your turnover now?" and "How are collections?" These queries help to reveal illuminating facts about the ability and willingness of a merchant to pay his debts promptly.

By questioning a merchant about his assets and liabilities, a salesman obtains important credit information and at the same time determines the acceptable price, the quantity that may be bought, and whether or not continued solicitation is warranted.

2. Discuss Credit Terms. Misunderstandings between buyers and sellers over the payment of accounts are often caused by failure of salesmen to explain clearly the terms of sale. This should be done at the time a sale is closed. Good credit relations begin with the sale. Salesmen, selling on open-account, should make clear to each dealer customer when the net amount of an account is due. If deferred datings are allowed, the reason for these terms should be explained and the necessity for payment on or before the date specified emphasized.

A salesman whose firm uses various credit instruments, such as promissory notes, trade acceptances, letters of credit, and drafts should describe the use of these papers to customers and prospects if they are not clearly understood.

A salesman should describe clearly to merchants the amount of the discounts from the list price, the dates on which cash discounts may be taken, the penalties for delinquency in making payments, the date of maturity of the account, to whom payments shall be made, and other particulars of the terms of sale.

Some companies give salesmen authority to quote credit terms to suit the convenience of buyers. In such cases, salesmen must consider carefully the merchant's character, capacity, and capital before quoting terms.

3. Give Credit Service to Merchant Customers. Salesmen calling regularly on merchant customers have an excellent opportunity to become familiar with the operation of their stores and aid them in maintaining a good credit standing.

Successful salesmen can serve their dealers by giving the three-point credit service described previously: buying service, credit policy

SALES PERFORMANCE RATING FORM

Presenting Credit

Salesman_____ Date_____

Rated by_____ Over-all Rating_____

Score

I. *Salesman's Knowledge of Credit*	Excellent 90–100	Good 80–90	Fair 70–80	Poor 60–70	Failure Below 60
A. Types of credit					
B. Nature of credit					
C. Nature of credit risk					
D. Sources of credit information					
E. Determining credit standing of new account					
F. Mercantile credit terms					
G. Consumer credit terms					
H. Discount for prompt payment					
I. Penalty for slow payment					
J. Account guarantee					
K. Installment credit					
L. Collection by salesman					
M. Credit service to merchants					
N. Collection and credit policies					
O. Competitor credit policy					

II. *Salesman's Use of Credit Knowledge*	Excellent 90–100	Good 80–90	Fair 70–80	Poor 60–70	Failure Below 60
A. Appraise merchant's credit					
B. Discuss terms					
C. Give credit service					
D. Advise credit department					

Miscellaneous Comments_____

service, and collection service. A salesman can be of valuable assistance to customers by advising them regarding the quantity to buy which will not tie up an excessive amount of capital or consume their available credit.

Many small merchants want sound counsel regarding their credit policy. Through his contacts with many merchants, a salesman can be of substantial aid to his dealer customers in advising them on business conditions and questions of selling for cash only, charging for credit, limiting the amount of credit, and similar policies of vital importance to small merchants.

Collection of accounts receivable is a problem confronting every merchant who sells on credit, and a salesman who has made it a practice to learn about successful collection methods of retailers is able to pass along much worth-while experience to his merchant customers.

4. Advise Credit Department. A salesman, as a result of his appraisal of the credit of merchant prospects or customers, is able to furnish his credit department with much credit information regarding the character, capital, and capacity of buyers. Most credit departments provide salesmen with credit report forms to facilitate transmission of credit information. In the case of a large purchaser, financial statements are secured from buyers and forwarded by salesmen to their credit departments.

In addition to these reports on new accounts, salesmen should keep their credit departments informed regularly of any changes in the financial status of customers to enable credit managers to appraise the risk involved.

Problem I

Presenting Credit to a Prospective Dealer

Ray H. Butterfield, representing Sinton Radio Company

The Sinton Radio Company, Chicago, Ill., established in 1933, manufactures high-grade radio phonographs in 14 models, retailing from $200 to $900, which are sold direct to retail music, appliance, and department stores throughout the country.

Ray H. Butterfield has been associated with the company since 1938 as a wholesale salesman in the Los Angeles, southern California territory. He is one of a force of 40 salesmen who appoint new dealers and aid established customers to sell more Sinton radios.

In the following interview, salesman Butterfield is discussing the Sinton line with a prospective dealer in San Diego. In connection with the appointment of a new dealer, the company requires that the salesman make a complete credit report on the merchant concerned. In this interview, salesman Butterfield is appraising the credit of the dealer.

1. SALESMAN: Good morning. I'm Ray Butterfield of Minton Radio. Because of the recent merger of Electro-Appliance and Horner Electric Company we have an opportunity for another live dealer here in San Diego. As you are one of the better known music dealers in the city, I thought of you first as a logical outlet for our line here.

2. DEALER: Well, we're handling the Ramco line now and are doing a fairly good business on it. I doubt that we would be justified in taking on two competing lines. Our principal business is in pianos, and radios are just incidental. Radios are too competitive; the price cutters have chiseled all of the profit out of them.

3. SALESMAN: What line of pianos do you handle?

4. DEALER: The Baldwin. We have the quality trade in town. Last year we did a retail volume of better than $100,000.

5. SALESMAN: What part of that was cash and what credit?

6. DEALER: About 80 per cent of our business is on credit, but our losses are less than 1 per cent.

7. SALESMAN: Have you been in this location long?

8. DEALER: We moved here last year from down the street. Fortunately, we were able to buy this corner location at a very favorable price to close out an estate.

9. SALESMAN: I've noticed your advertising. It's certainly high-class.

10. DEALER: My partner writes it himself. He was formerly advertising manager of one of the big department stores in Los Angeles.

11. SALESMAN: I see you have a good stock of Ramcos.

12. DEALER: Yes, we're a little overstocked at present, but the Christmas trade will soon relieve us and the way things work now, we'll do a fine holiday business.

13. SALESMAN: I think you would do well with the Sinton line. Our exclusive tone-control system has made it impossible for even trained musicians to tell the Sinton tone from a live person's performance. We have a larger speaker and more power which produce a smooth, mellow tone. We have 14 console models with a new type, automatic record-changer and the silent diamond permanent point, with no needles to change.

14. DEALER: I know your line. And we might be interested in carrying it, if we could buy it on the right terms.

15. SALESMAN: Our terms are most liberal. We carry our best dealers on open-account, allowing you a trade discount of 60 per cent off list with 2 per cent for cash in 30 days, net 60. For instance, our DeLuxe model

retails at $600 list; with your discount of 60 per cent, you buy it for $240 net delivered; and with your cash discount, you get it for $235.20, which compares favorably with the price of leading competitors.

16. DEALER: Well, I'd like to talk it over with my partner. Do you have a retail credit plan for consumers?

17. SALESMAN: Yes, we have a subsidiary company, the Sinton Credit Corporation, which carries the consumer paper, a single installment note, paid off by a number of payments on a planned schedule, secured by a conditional sales contract. You draw up the contract, collect the first payment, and turn it over to our finance company which discounts the notes and sets aside a dealer's reserve of from 1 to 3 per cent of the initial amount of the contract to be released when the customer's obligations have been satisfied. The finance company collects the payments from the customer.

18. DEALER: We get R.O.G. terms on some of our lines which are shipped from the East.

19. SALESMAN: We ship from our Los Angeles warehouse and bill from there, so you receive the merchandise within 24 hours from time of shipment.

20. DEALER: Well, drop in and see me again within a week or 10 days and perhaps we can get together.

21. SALESMAN: Fine, I'll leave you this catalogue of our complete line and see you when I'm back next week. Do you have a recent financial statement?

22. DEALER: Yes, I'll be glad to let you have a copy.

23. SALESMAN: Thanks.

Questions

1. How did the salesman appraise the merchant as a credit risk? Explain.
2. What is your judgment of this risk on basis of the "3 C's"? Explain.
3. Did the salesman discuss the credit terms satisfactorily? Explain.
4. What is the length of the credit term?
5. Is a cash discount allowed? The amount?
6. Is consumer credit involved in this case? Explain.
7. Is the salesman in a position to advise his credit department on this risk? How?

Problem II

CONCERNING CREDIT OF AN ESTABLISHED DEALER

Kenneth G. Harvey represents the Maxon Motor Car Company, manufacturer of a popular make of six- and eight-cylinder automobiles, the Swift, retailing in the $1,500 to $2,500 price range in regular, special, and de luxe models in coupés, sedans, and convertibles. The company is represented by 90 wholesale salesmen, who appoint new dealers and serve established dealers throughout the country. Kenneth Harvey has represented his company as a wholesale salesman in northern Illinois for the past five years.

Salesman Harvey is interviewing Jack Nutter, a Maxon dealer in Freeport, Ill., who has sold Swift cars since 1938.

1. SALESMAN: Good morning, Jack. How are things going?
2. DEALER: Ken, business is slow with me for this time of year. How do you find it?
3. SALESMAN: The other day the company sent me a report by the Federal Reserve on consumer buying power that gave me the impression that the consuming power of the country is in a healthful condition. But prosperity is not evenly distributed. In fact, nine million families suffered a decline in their annual income last year. It is that group which is not buying new cars. That means to me that we have to be more selective in our selling—to work on those families which are able to keep ahead of the cost of living and increase their annual intake. You know the group here in town.
4. DEALER: I've noticed that cash sales have fallen off lately.
5. SALESMAN: Yes, that's a sign that more people are relying on credit to compensate for their lower incomes. You'll have to select your credit risks more carefully in the future, particularly on service and used cars. Analysis of your accounts will probably show that some of your customers are now exceeding their credit limits and you are going to have to apply the brakes.
6. DEALER: Yes, collections have been a little slow lately in the service end, and I've been wondering if something could be done to shake 'em up a bit.
7. SALESMAN: I ran across a collection system used by Ralph Clark, one of our dealers at Joliet, which you could use here to help you get in your accounts receivable. Ralph has worked up a series of four followup letters to overdue accounts which are certainly bringing home the bacon. If the customer fails to come across after these letters, Ralph uses the telephone to find out what is delaying payment. If you are interested in trying out those letters, Ralph will be glad to send you copies.
8. DEALER: I'll be glad to see what they'll do for us.
9. SALESMAN: How are you fixed for new cars?
10. DEALER: I could use three convertibles right now.
11. SALESMAN: Are they sold?
12. DEALER: No, but we expect to close 'em up this week.

13. SALESMAN: I didn't think there was much demand for convertibles in these parts.

14. DEALER: Ordinarily we don't sell a convertible a year, but there has been some interest lately.

15. SALESMAN: Don't you think it would be wise to hold off ordering convertibles until you book a firm order or two? You don't want to get stuck with cars that won't sell. It would be better to use your available credit to buy models that are moving.

16. DEALER: Maybe you're right. Have you seen our last monthly comparative operating statement? I'd like you to take a look at it. (Offering statement.)

17. SALESMAN: Although your sales have slipped since last month, gross is holding up well. Your promotion expense is down which may account for your drop in volume, and that new salesman you hired is running up your selling cost without bringing in more volume. Inventory is a little high in the parts department. There's nothing here that a little more volume can't correct.

Is that new salesman enrolled in the district training school to be held in Chicago the first of the month?

18. DEALER: No, I haven't thought about it.

19. SALESMAN: Might be a good idea to send him over for more training. When he gets better acquainted with the line, he should step up your volume.

20. DEALER: I'll give him a week in Chicago and watch him when he gets back.

21. SALESMAN: I'd like to send this statement in to our credit department. I know they'll be interested in your progress down here.

22. DEALER: Sure, send it along. If they have any suggestions, I'd be glad to get them.

23. SALESMAN: I'll have to be running along to Rockford. Will see you next week sometime.

24. DEALER: Good-by.

Questions

1. How did salesman Harvey give credit policy service to his dealer? Explain.

2. Did the salesman give collection service? Explain.

3. Was the dealer's credit conserved by buying advice? Explain.

4. How was the dealer appraised as a credit risk?

5. Did the salesman advise his credit department on the credit standing of the dealer? Explain.

6. Were the credit responsibilities of the salesman well handled in this case? Explain.

Reading References

J. C. Aspley, "What a Salesman Should Know about His Credits," The Dartnell Corporation, Chicago, 1926.

Roger W. Babson, "The Folly of Installment Buying," Frederick A. Stokes Company, New York, 1938.

J. T. Bartlett and Charles M. Reed, "Methods of Installment Selling and Collection," Harper & Brothers, New York, 1934.

B. R. Canfield, "Sales Administration, Principles and Problems," rev. ed., pp. 531–538, Prentice-Hall, Inc., New York, 1947.

E. Casey and R. L. Johns, "Salesmanship and Buymanship," pp. 425–426, H. W. Rowe Company, Baltimore, 1938.

J. R. Daubman, "Salesmanship and Types of Selling," p. 6, F. S. Crofts & Co., New York, 1939.

Charles H. Fernald, "Salesmanship," rev. ed., Chap. XXIII, Prentice-Hall, Inc., 1945.

Paul W. Ivey, "Successful Salesmanship," pp. 442–446, Prentice-Hall, Inc., New York, 1947.

H. H. Maynard and T. N. Beckman, "Principles of Marketing," pp. 469–486, The Ronald Press Company, New York, 1946.

H. C. Nolen and H. H. Maynard, "Sales Management," pp. 65–71, The Ronald Press Company, New York, 1940.

C. W. Pritchard, "Essentials of Selling," Chap. XVII, Prentice-Hall, Inc., New York, 1945.

D. B. Tansill, "So You're Going to Sell," pp. 125–128, John C. Winston Company, Philadelphia, 1939.

CHAPTER XI

ADJUSTING CLAIMS

CLAIM ADJUSTMENTS ARE SALES OPPORTUNITIES

Salesmen who have responsibility for settling claims of customers enjoy many opportunities to retain their patronage, create good will, and increase sales. By making adjustments promptly, cheerfully, and tactfully, a salesman establishes close relations with his customers and impresses them with his spirit of service and fair dealing. Claims give a salesman a chance not only to make friends for his firm, but also to discover, through criticisms, possible improvements in the quality of his product and the character of his service. A claimant who receives prompt, satisfactory adjustment service from a salesman is a source of valuable word-of-mouth advertising and prospects.

A salesman's attitude toward claims, in a large measure, determines his success in converting complaints into sales opportunities. If a salesman considers that claim adjusting is an objectionable duty, if he thinks that complaints prove the inferiority of his product or service and that all claimants are unreasonable, he is unlikely to succeed in this phase of his job. Salesmen should remember that it is easier to hold an old customer than to obtain a new one, and satisfactory adjustments are an important factor in keeping customers. A salesman should consider claims calmly, courteously, and cheerfully, with a spirit of kindliness. No doubt should remain in a customer's mind that a salesman is anxious to please even though he cannot fully comply with all the buyer's wishes in all cases. Claims are actually welcomed by successful salesmen, who believe that a dissatisfaction openly stated is much easier to correct than an unexpressed grievance which causes lost customers and ill will.

In his anxiety to please, a salesman must guard against a meek, excessively apologetic, and weak attitude in making adjustments. By firm, frank, sincere adherence to company adjustment policies, a salesman commands the respect of his customers and obtains adjustments that are fair to the seller and the buyer. Occasionally, claimants attempt to abuse adjustment policies by presenting unwarranted claims. When dealing with unfair complaints, salesmen must adhere courteously but firmly to their company's adjustment policies. Many claims may be forestalled by salesmen whose fairness and firmness discourage unjustified complaints by customers.

WHO SHOULD SETTLE CLAIMS?

Claims are considered so important in many companies that they are handled personally by the president or other executive heads. In some firms, claim adjustors are employed who are engaged exclusively in handling claims and making settlements. Frequently these men are assisted by a staff of correspondents, tracers, file clerks, and interviewers. Adjustment specialists, however, often lack a sales viewpoint. They are frequently not familiar with the background of a claim, the problems of the claimant, the way the product is used, and the human factors that give rise to a complaint. Adjustors frequently do not know the difficulties of overcoming sales resistance, meeting competition, answering objections, and securing signed orders, and accordingly often fail to recognize the value of a customer. For this reason, claim adjustors and correspondents are sometimes indifferent to the importance of keeping customers satisfied.

Salesmen who have the proper attitude toward adjustments are often better able to settle claims because they are acquainted with the customer, know his individual needs, problems, and attitude; they are able to give prompt attention to claims through frequent field contacts; they appreciate the importance of keeping customers; they have the right temperament, the courtesy, consideration, and cheerfulness to pacify claimants; they can render better service to customers and are in a position to make an additional sale or exchange rather than a refund. Customers believe that claims will be more intelligently handled by a salesman whom they know than by an adjustor or correspondent whom they have never seen. Salesmen who handle adjustments are made conscious of their errors and are less liable to make mistakes. Claims frequently may be settled more economically when salesmen make adjustments in conjunction with their regular sales work.

COST OF CLAIMS

Few salesmen appreciate the loss involved in returned goods and the necessity of giving more attention to preventing claims and making satisfactory adjustments. A silverware manufacturer analyzed his loss on a $100 shipment returned by a customer, as follows:

Selling cost	$10
Packing cost	2
Accounting cost	1
Transportation cost	1
Damage in shipping	2
Obsolescence	2
Rewrapping and placing in stock	2
Profit	30
Total loss	$50

In this case, one-half of the gross amount of the selling price of the goods is a definite loss to the manufacturer. The National Retail Dry Goods Association estimates that 14 per cent of all goods sold at retail are returned by buyers at an estimated loss of 20 per cent.

TYPES OF CLAIMS

Claims are inevitable in every business. The finest manufacturing methods and the most rigorous inspections sometimes fail to produce perfect products, and the most completely supervised service occasionally breaks down. The principal causes of complaints encountered by salesmen are as follows:

1. *Delivery complaints,* including late delivery, nondelivery, partial delivery, wrong goods delivered, excess delivery, substitutions, refusal to accept.

2. *Merchandise complaints,* including damage in shipment, damage in packing, damage before delivery, inferior workmanship, defective materials, faulty construction, shopworn merchandise.

3. *Charge complaints,* including overcharges, errors in invoice, wrong change, misunderstandings as to price, charges to wrong account.

4. *Returned goods complaints,* including disagreement over return policy of seller, wrong exchanges, no refunds or wrong refunds, and abuse of return privilege.

5. *Credit and accounting claims,* including unearned discounts, errors in bookkeeping, collection procedure, curtailment of credit.

6. *Service complaints,* including lack of attention, discourtesy, broken promises, clerical errors, and carelessness.

FIXING RESPONSIBILITY FOR CLAIMS

To determine the cause of a claim is the first duty of a saleman in making adjustments. It is important to discover who is at fault since the nature of the adjustment will vary according to the one responsible for the difficulty. The real causes of complaints are often not obvious to a casual observer. A salesman is sometimes obliged to investigate, ask questions, and listen to the explanations of several people before he can determine the real cause. For example, a case of canned milk is water-soaked, the labels on the cans are discolored, and the product is unsalable. The retail merchant who bought the milk protests to the manufacturer's salesman and demands an adjustment. Who is at fault in this instance? The situation demands that the salesman fix the blame and be guided accordingly in his adjustment of the claim.

In exceptional cases, it may be impossible for a salesman to determine who is at fault; usually responsibility may be fixed on (1) the buyer; (2) the seller; (3) a third party to the sales transaction; (4) joint responsibility.

1. Buyer's Responsibility for Claims. Mistakes made by customers are frequently responsible for claims. Some of the most common errors on the part of buyers are mistakes in ordering, misunderstandings as to price and terms, improper use of merchandise, wrong storage of stock, taking unearned discounts, and claims in violation of a guarantee.

Excessive returns by dealer customers form one of the most common difficulties that salesmen have to adjust. Dealers often return goods to manufacturers for the following reasons: the same goods can be bought for lower prices elsewhere; goods have been overbought; the buyer has changed his mind; the merchandise is out of season; the buyer is unable to resell the goods; the style has changed; the goods are shopworn; stocks are unbalanced in sizes, colors, prices, and models.

An analysis of 66,000 items, returned by customers to retail stores, showed that in 57 per cent of the cases the buyer was at fault. Returns, admittedly the fault of buyers, were attributed to wrong size ordered, change of mind, several items ordered on approval and returned, and wrong color ordered.

More than 90 per cent of the claims of customers are honestly made, but in many cases buyers are not conscious of their responsibility for mistakes. Before conceding that a customer is right, a salesman should consider the possibility that a buyer may be at fault and be guided accordingly in settling the difficulty.

2. Seller's Responsibility for Claims. A salesman or his firm is often responsible for complaints made by customers. Salesmen are sometimes responsible for claims in various ways described later. A frank acknowledgment of an error, on the part of a salesman, and a prompt adjustment are the surest ways to win the good will and further orders of customers.

Customer complaints may be the fault of a seller's shipping department. Common shipping mistakes are wrong goods shipped; shipment incomplete; wrong address; improper packing; wrong carrier used for shipment; and substitutions without buyer's authorization.

Bookkeeping mistakes account for many claims by buyers. Improper billing, wrong prices, excessive transportation charges, credit to wrong account, discounts not allowed, and numerous other errors are responsible for complaints.

Credit departments are sometimes at fault in antagonizing customers by curtailing credit, by writing tactless collection letters, or by injuring a buyer's pride through offensive credit investigating methods.

Defects in a product caused by poor materials, workmanship, or design are a factory responsibility and a source of many customer complaints.

A salesman should recognize the small, but often important, shortcomings of the various departments in his organization and admit their responsibility.

3. Third Party Responsibility for Claims. Sometimes a third party, usually a transportation company, is responsible for claims made by buyers. Carriers are principally at fault in damaging, delaying, and overcharging for shipments. If a shipment is delivered in good condition to a carrier by a seller, as indicated by the original bill of lading, and the buyer claims that the goods arrived in damaged condition, the responsibility of the carrier is clear. As shipments are well documented, it is not difficult to determine data of shipment, transportation charges, value, and condition of goods at time of shipment, thus fixing the blame for delays and damage.

4. Joint Responsibility for Claims. Sometimes more than one party is at fault when a claim is involved. A salesman may find, upon investigation of a claim, that the seller and buyer are both to blame. For example, an oil burner is sold to a homeowner. Three weeks later the customer claims that the burner is not working properly, that it is smoking badly. The salesman investigates, examines the burner, questions the customer, and finds that the burner was not regulated properly when installed and also that the owner is not burning the grade of oil recommended. Both conditions are responsible for the smoking and both buyer and seller are at fault.

Salesmen should recognize that sometimes several parties may be more or less responsible for a complaint and be guided accordingly in making an adjustment.

A SALESMAN'S RESPONSIBILITY FOR CLAIMS

While a salesman cannot control mistakes made by the factory, shipping, credit, or accounting departments of his company, he can avoid many errors that lead to complaints, returns, and customer dissatisfaction. When a salesman oversells a dealer whose capital and demand do not warrant large purchases, he is inviting excessive returns of shopworn, outmoded, or unseasonable merchandise. A dealer, who has been oversold and cannot dispose of his purchases, returns the goods and claims a refund or asks for a credit. The surplus merchandise returned to the seller is frequently in unsalable condition.

A salesman who fails to explain clearly the terms, prices, delivery charges, discounts, allowances, and rebates to customers is frequently responsible for misunderstandings and complaints. Salesmen can avoid claims by explicit explanations of all charges when sales are closed.

Sales of merchandise unsuited to the trade or the individual requirements of customers are responsible for many claims. Luxury goods sold to a merchant serving a low-income market are likely to be returned by the buyer; an expensive automobile sold to a man who cannot afford it will probably have to be repossessed.

Sales on approval, by which a customer is given the privilege of returning merchandise which he does not want to keep, are responsible for numerous returns and adjustments. Salesmen who promise, "We shall be glad to take back the goods if you do not want to keep them," or "I'll send out several models and you can take your choice," are inviting excessive returns.

Carelessness of salesmen in booking orders, by writing wrong quantities, sizes, colors, styles, prices, or terms, is a common cause of complaints which salesmen can easily correct. A salesman who makes promises which are not in conformity with the policies of his firm creates customer claims.

Salesmen can also reduce the number of complaints by instructing customers in the proper use and care of the product sold, to ensure its satisfactory operation. Dealers who are sold perishable merchandise should be advised how to store, refrigerate, and maintain the goods in sound condition for resale.

ADJUSTMENT POLICIES

The adjustment policy of the company represented by a salesman is the basis of his service to customers in adjusting complaints and settling claims. The aim of every adjustment policy is to satisfy the buyer and at the same time protect the interests of the seller. Policies range in liberality from "the customer is always right" to protect the company first and satisfy the customer last." The degree of liberality depends largely upon the policies of competitors, the amount of the sale, the resources of the seller, and the type of customer served. Some companies adhere firmly to a written adjustment policy which is distributed to buyers for their information; other concerns believe that it is practically impossible to follow a definite policy, so leave final interpretation in the hands of company executives or salesmen.

Most adjustment policies are liberal on the assumption that most customers are honest and that their complaints are genuine and represent a sincere grievance. They assume that the buyer is right until he is proved to be wrong. Although a small minority may attempt to take advantage of a liberal policy, the good will and advertising obtained thereby compensate the seller for his liberality.

A definite adjustment policy is necessary to guide salesmen in dealing uniformly with claims. The interpretation of an adjustment policy will vary, however, in every case according to its individual merit; it is here that the fairness and judgment of a salesman are tested. He must not let severity or lenience dominate his viewpoint. A buyer who is always fair in his complaints should be handled differently from a customer who seeks to take advantage of every opportunity to make unjustifiable claims.

A salesman should be familiar with every detail of the adjustment policies of his company. He should be aware also of the common abuses leading to customer complaints. The largest manufacturer and distributor of brushes in the world has a definite adjustment policy on claims, as follows:

What we will do:

1. If the bristles or hair fall out of a Blank brush under ordinary use, we will replace it free of charge.

Note to salesman: If the wire has been bent back or forth in some manner, or the brush has been crushed or abused, the bristles will fall out as the wire has been crushed or to some degree untwisted. This is through no fault of material or workmanship and the company should not be asked to replace the brush. Sell the customer a new one.

2. If the wire rusts, we will replace the brush free of charge.

Note to salesman: The water used in many localities, because of its chemical qualities, particularly iron, will put a coating on the best wire made. The coating looks brown like rust. Examine the coating carefully. Scrape the wire between the bristles with a knife and you will note that the coating comes off. Rust has a tendency to scale off, this coating does not. In such cases, an explanation should be made to the customer and the brush should not be returned for replacement.

3. If the wire of a Blank brush, under ordinary use, breaks, we will repair or replace the brush free of charge.

Note to salesman: Caution the customer against pounding the mop head against any solid material. Wire broken in this manner is due to abuse and not to defect in material and workmanship.

4. If the handle pulls off, we will re-cement it free of charge.

What we will not do:

1. Articles returned for adjustment which are found not to be our brushes will not be repaired or replaced, but returned to the customer.

2. Articles which have been worn out in service will not be replaced.

3. Articles which have been worn out or destroyed by abuse will not be replaced.

GUARANTEE IS BASIS FOR ADJUSTMENTS

The basis of every adjustment policy is a written guarantee to the buyer promising satisfactory performance of the product or service for a specified time. Claims frequently are made by customers to obtain the service promised in the written guarantee.

Guarantees are usually given to purchasers of new types of merchandise, of goods that a buyer cannot inspect before purchasing, and of all mechanical goods. Some guarantees are very broad, as the warranty of one manufacturer which states, "All products of the Blank Company are guaranteed as to materials and workmanship." Other guarantees are very specific, describing when, where, and what is warranted and the conditions whereby goods may be returned for adjustment.

Salesmen sometimes are called upon to interpret guarantees to customers. Many claims can be avoided if a salesman will interpret clearly a guarantee when closing a sale. If a buyer thinks that he has an inclusive guarantee and discovers later that it does not cover certain defects in materials or workmanship, he may be dissatisfied. When a customer makes a claim covered by a guarantee, a salesman must decide whether the buyer is abusing the guarantee or is making a just complaint. In making the adjustment, he must retain the good will of the customer and at the same time protect his firm.

Salesmen should be familiar with all specific stipulations of the guarantees of the products or services which they are selling. Guarantees of competitors should also be understood thoroughly by a salesman.

Wholesale and retail distributors often are called upon to adjust complaints on merchandise sold by them. The guarantees issued by manufacturers are the usual basis for distributors' adjustments.

Salesmen who represent manufacturers should discuss product and service guarantees with distributors so that they can interpret them correctly to their customers.

COMPLAINT ADJUSTMENT SYSTEM

A salesman should know the routine established by his firm for handling complaints and making adjustments so that he can settle claims and report adjustments systematically. When a salesman is given authority to make adjustments on his own responsibility in conformity with company policies, he is usually required to follow an established method in clearing the adjustment with his office. The adjustment system of a large canner of condensed and evaporated milk requires salesmen who make adjustments on spoiled canned milk to conform to the following system:

On small adjustments the salesman should:
1. Pay customer for cans not in good condition.
2. Take his receipt for payment.
3. Strip labels from all cans.
4. Forward cash receipt and labels from cans to home office with batch number which appeared on the cans in question.

On large adjustments, the salesman should:
1. Arrange with distributor delivering the damaged cans to pick up the stock and replace it with fresh goods.
2. Notify the broker in the territory.
3. Follow back defective goods to their source and see that additional quantities are set aside and further distribution is prevented.
4. Secure date of shipment and batch numbers and forward to broker with carbon copy of report to home office.

In some companies, salesmen are required to make a written report of each complaint received and the nature of the adjustment. Incomplete adjustments requiring further investigation are also reported. These reports are reviewed by the sales manager who passes on the decision made by the salesman and turns the report over to correspondents for writing the claimant a confirmation on the adjustment. Action is taken by the traffic department in the case of a transportation claim. If a product is defective, the difficulty is reported to the factory to prevent its recurrence.

A large manufacturer of packaged cheese and condiments, whose salesmen call on retail food merchants and institutions, describes the duties and responsibilities of salesmen for handling adjustments and complaints as follows:

1. *Handle all complaints promptly.*
    a. Get to complaining customers as soon as possible.
    b. If impossible to go immediately, write or call, depending upon seriousness of complaint.
2. *Get customer's or consumer's side of story.*
    a. Listen carefully and courteously and *do not argue.*
    b. In case of an unjustified claim, attempt to point out the irregularity, or if agreement cannot be reached, report fact to office. Do not set yourself up as the final authority as there may be conditions you do not understand completely and cannot control.
3. *Make adjustment promptly.*
    a. Do not postpone adjustment.
    b. Write proper credit before leaving store if the claim is justified.
4. *Determine cause of complaint.*
    a. Report findings of cause to office so that steps can be taken to forestall recurrence.

When salesmen are not given authority to make adjustments, they usually are required to refer claims to the company's adjustment department, which assumes full responsibility for settlement. It decides what adjustment, if any, should be made according to the product guarantee and the company policy.

A large company which follows this policy requires customers to return damaged goods direct to the factory adjustment department accompanied by an adjustment request card which is filled out by the salesman and signed by the customer. In addition, the salesman fills out a Customer Service Record card, reporting the adjustment, and mails it with his daily reports to his branch manager. The company adjustment department makes the settlement and returns the new or repaired article direct to the customer.

In some companies, responsibility for making adjustments is shared by the salesman in the field and the sales supervisor or adjustment department at the factory. Claims of a certain type or size are handled by a salesman exclusively; other complaints are referred by a salesman to his supervisor or to the factory for adjustment. The salesman must understand clearly his part in this routine to avoid confusion in handling claims and prevent customer dissatisfaction.

FORESTALLING CLAIMS

Salesmen can prevent many claims by educating customers in the proper use and care of the product. Instruction of buyers in the proper maintenance and service of mechanical products is particularly important. Salesmen of home appliances explain the necessity for cleaning and oiling; salesmen of tennis rackets tell how to take care of them in winter to prevent warping. There are few articles that do not need some attention if claims are to be avoided.

If customers are properly advised by salesmen concerning the merchandise best suited to their requirements, there will be fewer claims concerning returned merchandise. Assistance to customers and cooperation in determining the proper grade, quality, model, color, and price of an article will help to forestall adjustments and claims.

Many claims arise from extravagant promises made by salesmen to customers. Special delivery, price concessions, and extra allowances are often promised to overcome sales resistance and meet competition. Salesmen should avoid making extravagant promises, which only lead to customer dissatisfaction and complaints.

Customers should be told how to seek adjustments in the event they have complaints about a product or service. Delays and dissatisfaction are often caused when customers are unfamiliar with a seller's method of handling claims. Salesmen should explain to customers how they can obtain prompt adjustments on complaints.

Buyers who habitually return goods and make complaints secure a reputation for fault-finding which injures their standing. Salesmen should show customers who make unwarranted claims that abuse of adjustment privileges deprives them of the extra services and special concessions enjoyed by those who make few complaints.

HOW TO SETTLE CLAIMS OF CUSTOMERS

Observation of the work of salesmen of various types of products in settling claims and making adjustments shows that they follow similar methods. To aid salesmen in putting into practice the principles discussed in the preceding pages, the following six-step routine, incorporating the best practices of good salesmen, is recommended. This procedure will obviously have to be varied according to the circumstances surrounding each claim, but it can be profitably followed in most cases.

Routine for Settling Claims of Customers

1. Listen courteously and attentively to claimant.
2. Examine and verify the damage when possible.
3. Determine who is at fault and explain the facts.
4. Take prompt action on the claim.
5. Resell and educate the customer.
6. Report claim to company.

1. Listen Courteously and Attentively to Claimant. Claim adjusting begins when a customer first presents his complaint to a salesman. Then a salesman reveals his attitude toward claims and either puts the customer in a receptive frame of mind or creates irritation which makes a settlement more difficult. A salesman who is antagonistic and curt in dealing with claimants and handles claims in a routine, perfunctory manner is unlikely to have much success in making adjustments. A salesman, on the other hand, who is courteous, friendly, and sympathetic, who shows that he is interested in a customer's difficulties, can create good will even when refusing to make adjustments.

When a customer presents a claim, a salesman should permit the buyer to do most of the talking irrespective of the justice of the complaint. He should avoid interrupting or arguing with the buyer until his story has been completely told. While listening to a claimant, a salesman should think of the first six steps in this adjustment outline so that he can use this plan for handling the complaint. An attentive, sympathetic manner flatters a buyer and enables a salesman to get clearly full particulars of the difficulty.

After a claimant has told fully his version of the difficulty, the salesman should immediately "get in step" with the claimant by either (*a*) thanking him for bringing the claim to the attention of the sales-man, (*b*) regretting that the customer has been inconvenienced by the difficulty, or (*c*) appreciating the customer's position.

A salesman should first discuss with a claimant those obvious points on which he and the customer are in complete agreement, thus dis-arming the buyer and putting him in a receptive mood.

2. Examine and Verify the Damage When Possible. If the defec-tive or damaged merchandise is at hand, the salesman should ask the customer's permission to examine the difficulty so that he may deter-mine the extent of the claim and ascertain for his own information who is at fault. Examination of the goods in question should be made, when possible, in the presence of the customer. The salesman may explain that his inspection of the merchandise is not occasioned by any doubts as to the validity of the claim or the motives of the customer. Wherever possible a salesman should not accept a claim-ant's description of a difficulty without making a first-hand inspection of the damage.

Inspections will often reveal the circumstances responsible for a claim and indicate conditions which may be rectified by the salesman to prevent similar complaints in the future. If goods are stored improperly, a salesman can point this out and show a claimant his responsibility for the difficulty. If the merchandise was not shipped according to order, examination by a salesman can detect the extent of the error.

During the course of an examination a salesman should explain to his customer that he is not attempting to avoid or delay a settlement but is trying to inform himself more fully about the difficulty so as to be able to make a fair adjustment.

3. Determine Who Is at Fault and Explain the Facts. During the course of his inspection of a claim, a salesman can usually determine whether the fault lies with the seller, the buyer, a third party, or if there is joint responsibility. The examination also will reveal the necessity for further investigation to fix the blame. A salesman must be familiar with the various causes of complaints and how the parties to the sales transaction may be responsible for errors in delivery, service, charges, accounting, or merchandise. The numerous causes of claims are described in detail in the preceding pages of this chapter.

When a salesman knows who is a fault, he should explain his con-conclusions to the customer. He may admit that his firm shipped the wrong goods or billed them improperly, or he may tactfully explain how the customer failed to use the article properly and thus caused the difficulty. He may charge the transportation company with negligence. Whoever was at fault, the salesman should explain the causes of the claim clearly and fully so that the customer will understand the adjustment.

4. Take Prompt Action on the Claim. Customers appreciate prompt action on their claims. Delays in making adjustments give them the impression that the seller is attempting to avoid settlement and magnify the difficulty in the mind of the customer. Promptness in making an adjustment is fundamental in keeping a customer's good will.

However, in some cases, the responsibility for a difficulty may not be apparent. A salesman may be unable to fix the blame for a claim without further investigation. If an adjustment cannot be made immediately or if reference must be made to a sales executive or the home office adjustment department, the salesman should explain to the customer why settlement must be postponed. The customer should be assured that the claim is being investigated and that he will be informed promptly as soon as the adjustment is completed.

In most cases, however, a salesman can arrange immediate settlement. The method of making an adjustment will vary according to who is at fault and whether or not the claim is granted or rejected. Successful salesmen use the following methods in settling claims when (*a*) the buyer is at fault; (*b*) the seller is at fault; (*c*) a third party is at fault; (*d*) several parties are at fault.

a. Buyer at Fault. When a buyer is at fault and a salesman's investigation shows that the claim should not be allowed, the salesman has a choice of two courses: to grant the claim or refuse it. Which course the salesman should follow will be dictated by the adjustment policy of his firm, the importance of the customer, and other circumstances.

If a claim is refused, the salesman should explain to the buyer, in a straightforward, sincere manner, how the mistake was made, so that the decision will seem fair and reasonable. The salesman should appeal to the customer's sense of fairness and avoid criticizing him for the error. The refusal should be tactful; it may be implied and still be definite. The salesman should clear his firm of responsibility for the mistake rather than accuse the customer of error.

Sometimes, a salesman in refusing a claim may make an alternative settlement by offering to repair the damage or pay a portion of the sum in controversy. By such a partial settlement, the good will of a customer may be retained and the rights of the seller protected.

When a customer is at fault and the salesman decides that circumstances justify granting the claim, the salesman should tactfully explain that, even though the seller is not responsible, he is settling the claim to retain the good will of the buyer. The concession should not be made reluctantly to secure the maximum good will of the customer.

b. *Seller at Fault.* If a salesman decides that his firm is at fault, the claim should be settled promptly and the good will of the buyer obtained by emphasizing the desire to assure complete satisfaction. Lengthy apologies and a detailed explanation of how the mistake occurred are of no interest to the customer, who should, however, be assured that steps will be taken to avoid a repetition of the error. A salesman should not attempt to defend his firm's shortcomings by remarking that "Mistakes are bound to occur" or "This will never happen again," as these apologies are weak and unconvincing. Any suggestion that a customer might experience future difficulties or dissatisfaction should be avoided.

c. *Third Party at Fault.* If a third party, usually the transportation company, is to blame for a difficulty, a salesman will settle the claim according to the adjustment policy of his firm. Although a shipper's responsibility legally ceases when he delivers merchandise to a carrier for shipment to the customer, many companies offer to get a settlement for a buyer from a transportation company.

To aid his company in presenting a customer's claim to a carrier, a salesman should obtain from the buyer a bill for damage showing the amount of the claim. This bill should be presented to the carrier along with the original bill of lading showing that the goods were received by the carrier in good condition, the original invoice showing the value of the merchandise shipped, and the expense receipt from the carrier showing the amount paid for transportation.

Other companies require a customer to seek redress from carriers without their assistance. In such cases, a salesman should tell his customer how to secure settlement.

Some concerns permit their salesmen to offer allowances to customers on goods damaged in shipment, provided buyers retain the defective merchandise. Or minor repairs may be made by a salesman to put damaged goods in good usable or salable condition. A duplicate shipment may also be forwarded to a customer to avoid delay while redress is being sought from a carrier.

d. *Several Parties at Fault.* When investigation by a salesman shows that two or more parties are responsible for a claim, the salesman should decide promptly whether or not the buyer is to be relieved of responsibility for the difficulty. If the customer is not to be held accountable, the salesman should immediately grant the claim and seek redress from the other parties involved. A prompt settlement will create good will and assure the customer of the desire of the seller to give satisfaction.

When a salesman is unable to make settlement of a claim at once, because the cause of the difficulty must be investigated further to discover who is responsible for the mistake, the customer must be assured that the claim will be investigated promptly and the buyer notified of the seller's decision. Postponements of settlements should be avoided whenever possible as claimants are annoyed by delays and the difficulty of making a satisfactory settlement is magnified.

5. Resell and Educate the Customer. When a claim has been settled in favor of a customer, the salesman should capitalize the buyer's satisfaction resulting from the favorable adjustment by reselling him on the company's product or service. If a customer's confidence in the merchandise or service has been shaken by an unfavorable experience, a salesman should attempt to restore the faith of the buyer by describing the quality of the goods or service.

The quality of raw materials used, the improved processes of manufacture, the skilled labor employed, the frequent inspections, and technical research should be discussed with customers who have made claims for defective goods. Buyers who have found fault with service should be told of the supervision and care exercised in giving service to customers. If policies of a seller are the cause of a claim, the fairness of the firm's policies should be discussed.

When a delayed or damaged shipment leaves a customer short of merchandise, the salesman making the adjustment should seek another order.

When a claim has been settled, a salesman has an excellent opportunity to instruct the customer in the proper care and use of an article to avoid future complaints. In the preceding pages, methods for forestalling claims have been described. A few words of tactful suggestion will often prevent recurrence of a complaint and retain the good will of a customer. Particularly when a buyer has been at fault and the consequences of his error are fresh in his mind, he is more receptive to suggestions.

6. Report Claim to Company. After a salesman has settled a claim, he should promptly report the adjustment to his company in conformity with the procedure established for handling complaints. A complete report on a claim enables the firm to carry out the promises of the salesman to the customer in regard to replacements, allowances,

SALES PERFORMANCE RATING FORM

Claim Adjustment

Salesman ————————————   Date ————————————

Rated by ————————————   Over-all Rating ————————

Score

I. *Salesman's Knowledge of His Company's*

    A. Adjustment policy

    B. Guarantee

    C. Adjustment system

	Excellent 90–100	Good 80–90	Fair 70–80	Poor 60–70	Failure Below 60
A					
B					
C					

II. *Salesman's Attitude toward Claims*

	Excellent 90–100	Good 80–90	Fair 70–80	Poor 60–70	Failure Below 60

III. *Salesman's Method of Settling Claims*

    A. Listening and getting in step with claimant

    B. Examining and verifying damage

    C. Determining who is at fault and explain

    D. Taking prompt action on claims

    E. Reselling customer

    F. Reporting claim to salesman's company

	Excellent 90–100	Good 80–90	Fair 70–80	Poor 60–70	Failure Below 60
A					
B					
C					
D					
E					
F					

Miscellaneous Comments ————————————————————————

——

——

sales help, or an extension of time for payment. If the seller has been at fault, steps may be taken by the firm to prevent a recurrence of the difficulty. If a claim requires further investigation, a settlement can be expedited by a complete report by the salesman to his company.

Problem I

George H. Rice, representing the Braecox Tire and Battery Company

The Braecox Tire and Battery Company, Cleveland, Ohio, operates a chain of six service stations located in Cleveland, all retailing gasoline, oil, tires, batteries, and a complete line of automobile accessories. The company started in 1931 with a small capital and operated one station until 1935, when additional capital was obtained and five additional stations were established. The company sells only well-known, advertised products and features them in direct-mail advertising to car owners in the vicinity of each of its stations.

The company is the largest distributor of Butler batteries in the city. This is a well-known make of automobile storage battery which is sold, serviced, and charged at each of the company's stations.

George H. Rice is one of four salesmen employed at a Braecox station near the center of the city. On an early fall morning he greets a motorist who drives into the station and the following interview ensues:

1. SALESMAN: Good morning, sir. Can I help you?
2. BUYER: Good morning. This is the Butler battery station, isn't it?
3. SALESMAN: Yes, sir, it is. What can I do for you?
4. BUYER: Well, I want to know something. I've got a Butler battery in my car now which I bought in Toledo three or four months ago and it's gone bad on me. I went to a Butler battery dealer in my neighborhood and he told me that I would have to go back to Toledo, to the dealer who sold me the battery. Now I thought this battery was guaranteed at any Butler station.
5. SALESMAN: You're right. Your guarantee is good here. Let me see your guarantee. According to this policy, you bought this battery a little over six months ago. Your speedometer reading shows you've driven it 8,000 miles. Is that right?
6. BUYER: Why—I guess so. I didn't think I'd gone that far. I still have something coming though, haven't I?
7. SALESMAN: Yes, sir, you have. Your Butler battery carries an adjustment policy for 12 months or 12,000 miles. This battery went only

two-thirds that far, so you have a new one coming at two-thirds the regular price.

8. BUYER: Well, that's more like it. What is the regular price?

9. SALESMAN: Let's just step over to this battery display, and I'll show you another battery like yours—it sells for $8.95. One-third off is $3 and that makes it $5.95 to you.

10. BUYER: I see. Uh-huh.

11. SALESMAN: Yes, sir, your car is a Martin so any one of these batteries will fit your car. You're driving 8,000 miles in six months, that is 16,000 miles a year. Do you have any extra electrical equipment on your car?

12. BUYER: What do you mean?

13. SALESMAN: Heater, radio, fog lights, anything like that?

14. BUYER: No, I haven't.

15. SALESMAN: O.K. Then the battery you need is this Heavy Duty Butler with special insulation. This is the one you ought to have. (Pointing to battery on stand.)

16. BUYER: What's the price of this one?

17. SALESMAN: Only $12.95.

18. BUYER: Say, hold on. You were going to sell me a battery for $5.95. Now you're talking $12.95.

19. SALESMAN: Yes, sir, that's what I said, and that's what I'll do. If you want to buy another one like the one you had, I'll sell it to you for $8.95 less $3 adjustment on your old battery which would make it $5.95 and I'll be glad to do it. But remember, you're driving 16,000 miles a year. You really need a bigger battery. The one you have is a 13-plate, 80-ampere-hour job. This one is a 17-plate, 100-ampere-hour battery. It's really the one you ought to have.

20. BUYER: Yeh, and it costs $12.95.

21. SALESMAN: You've got $3 coming to you on another battery like your old one. I'll allow you $3 on this battery, too.

22. BUYER: That makes it $9.95. But that's more than I paid for my old one, in the first place.

23. SALESMAN: Yes, I know, but you ought to have a bigger battery, because of the miles you drive. A man usually drives about 12,000 miles a year. You're driving considerably more than that and therefore need at least a 100-ampere-hour battery. This model 100 does cost more than your old battery but it will give you a lot better service and last a lot longer, too.

24. BUYER: $9.95. That's a fair price on a $12.95 battery—but it sure shoots a $10 bill.

25. SALESMAN: Yes, it sure does. But it's better to pay $10 and get the battery you need. You can see by this chart that Butler 100's average more than 30 months of service—that's an average of better than two

and one-half years. If you keep on buying batteries like your present one, you'll wear them out in about eight months. That means you'll be buying three or four in the next two and one-half years. That way, you'll spend $18 to $24 instead of $10 and have all the trouble besides. You'll be saving yourself money, if you let me put this in your car now. It will take only a couple of minutes and you'll be on your way.

26. BUYER: O.K., put her in. It ought to wear longer than the old one.

Questions

1. Criticize favorably or otherwise the salesman's methods in handling the claim of the customer. Did the salesman follow the routine for adjusting claims as suggested in the text?

2. Did the salesman "get in step" with the claimant? How?

3. Did the salesman examine the difficulty? Explain the salesman's action on this point.

4. Who was at fault in this case? Was this determined?

5. Was action taken on the claim? What? Was this satisfactory?

6. Did the salesman resell and educate the customer?

7. What other action should have been taken by the salesman in this case?

Problem II

Lawrence J. Grable, representing the Henderson-Cook Motors Company

The Henderson-Cook Motors Company, Indianapolis, Ind., is one of 15,000 retail dealers of a well-known six- and eight-cylinder passenger automobile selling for less than $2,000. The company was established in 1924 and sells an annual average of 580 units. A complete service station adjoins the salesroom which is located on a main traffic artery of the city.

Lawrence J. Grable, one of the company salesmen, has recently sold a new two-door sedan to an Indianapolis businessman, L. O. Kane, who is calling on salesman Grable to make a claim for damaged seat upholstery.

1. SALESMAN: Good morning, Mr. Kane, what can I do for you today?
2. CUSTOMER: It's the upholstery in this car you sold me—it's all full of holes. The back of the front seat has five holes in it. They look like moth holes.
3. SALESMAN: I don't think it's old enough to have moths in it.
4. CUSTOMER: Then the back seat has a tear in the upholstery that looks like someone cut it with a knife.
5. SALESMAN: It wasn't that way when I delivered it.

6. Customer: Well, I thought I'd better report it to you so that you would know that it was in that condition when I bought the car. I didn't want you to think that I was responsible for the holes.

7. Salesman: Well, I know we didn't make them. You'd better see our serviceman, Mr. Jordan, and tell him about the holes. Drive the car into our service station and let our service manager look it over.

8. Customer: I'm pretty busy and I don't think I can take it in for a few days.

9. Salesman: I'd forget it if I were you. They don't amount to anything anyway.

10. Customer: I'm not satisfied with those seats and if I can't get action from you, I'll take it up with the manager.

11. Sales Mgr.: I overheard your remark. What can I do for you?

12. Customer: I just brought in this car to show you the holes in the upholstery. They look like moth holes to me. I'm dissatisfied with the looks of these seats.

13. Sales Mgr.: Let me see them.

14. Customer: The salesman argued with me when I told him they were moth holes.

15. Sales Mgr.: They might be at that if the material had been in stock for a long time before it was made up. But I think the real difficulty is a weakness in weaving in the material itself. Sometimes they drop a stitch and it soon develops into a hole. The factory is at fault for letting that material go out.

16. Customer: I should think they would catch it at the factory.

17. Sales Mgr.: Sometimes it gets by. If you can spare your car for a day, we'll take that fabric off and put new material on so the seats will be perfect.

18. Customer: That will be fine.

19. Sales Mgr.: To keep those seats in good condition, you need a set of the new plastic seat covers. You will never have any trouble with spots, wear, or tobacco burns with those covers. When we put new material on your seats, I would like to fit a new set of covers on the front and back seats.

20. Customer: What will they cost?

21. Sales Mgr.: Only $12.50 a set installed.

22. Customer: That's all right. I'll leave the car whenever you can work on it.

23. Sales Mgr.: Thank you. We'll be notifying you when the new material comes in.

Questions

1. Did the salesman listen attentively and courteously to the claimant in this interview? Explain.

2. Did the salesman examine the damage? Explain.

3. Did he take prompt action on the claim? Explain.

4. Did he resell and educate the customer? Explain.

5. Did the sales manager listen courteously to the customer?

6. Did he examine the upholstery?

7. Did he determine who was at fault? Who?

8. Was his explanation satisfactory? Why?

9. Did the sales manager take prompt action? How?

10. Did he resell the customer? Explain.

Reading References

E. G. Blackstone, C. C. Crawford, and E. Grinnell, "Selling," pp. 317–323, D. C. Heath and Company, Boston, 1942.

B. R. Canfield, "Sales Administration, Principles and Problems," rev., pp. 538–541, Prentice-Hall, Inc., New York, 1947.

Charles H. Fernand, "Salesmanship," pp. 448–453, Prentice-Hall, Inc., New York, 1945.

Paul W. Ivey, "Successful Salesmanship," p. 139, Prentice-Hall, Inc., New York, 1947.

Bernard Lester, "Sales Engineering," pp. 151–153, John Wiley & Sons, Inc., New York, 1940.

C. F. Phillips, "Marketing by Manufacturers," pp. 232–233, Richard D. Irwin, Inc., Chicago, 1946.

O. P. and C. H. Robinson, "Successful Retail Salesmanship," pp. 150–151, Prentice-Hall, Inc., New York, 1945.

CHAPTER XII

QUALIFYING PROSPECTS

WHAT IS A PROSPECT?

Salesmen commonly refer to potential customers as "prospects" and the process of searching for customers as "prospecting." Some salesmen have little difficulty in discovering logical prospects. Store reputation, prices, and policies attract prospects to salesmen in retail, specialty, and department stores. Salesmen, representing wholesale houses, and some manufacturers, selling standard goods to established dealers, have little difficulty in locating merchants likely to buy their merchandise. Likewise, salesmen of heavy industrial goods have no problem in finding concerns which should buy their products.

Many salesmen of consumer specialty goods and services, however, have considerable difficulty in determining the qualities or characteristics of those persons who are their best prospects. Salesmen cannot assume that everyone is a prospect for their commodities or services. One significant difference between a successful and a poor salesman is that the former sees the right people; the latter sees just anybody.

Like the gold miner who washes tons of sand and gravel in his search for nuggets, a specialty salesman must sift the qualifications of numerous persons in his search for genuine prospects. The process that a salesman follows in eliminating "suspects," or unlikely prospects, in his search for possible buyers is the important work of qualifying prospects.

The practical experience of many successful salesmen has produced a standard or measuring stick which can be used in determining the qualifications of persons and firms by salesmen of specialty products or services. This gauge for evaluating a prospect has five points, as follows: (1) a need; (2) ability to pay; (3) authority to buy; (4) accessibility; (5) right type for the salesman. A suspect who has all or most of these qualities may be classed as a prospect worthy of a salesman's time and effort.

In using this measuring stick for qualifying persons and firms, a salesman is making, in effect, a market analysis comparable to the research carried on by all progressive organizations to determine the group characteristics of a market.

Each of these five qualities described in Chap. IV is an important factor in gauging the worth of a firm or an individual as a potential customer.

1. A Need. The first qualification of a good prospect is that the person or organization have a definite need for the salesman's product or service. A prospect's need may be for safety and protection, comfort and convenience, satisfaction of pride and affection, or gain—all motives that impel individuals to make purchases.

A prospect may recognize his need, but more often he may not be conscious of his requirements. When a prospect recognizes his need, the task of a salesman is to persuade the buyer to satisfy his need with the product or service that the salesman is offering.

Some prospects have very definite knowledge of their needs. When the United States government buys supplies or equipment, sellers must comply with rigid specifications detailing the exact qualities of the commodity wanted. The needs of most consumers are not scientifically determined but arise as a result of desire for economy, comfort, convenience, satisfaction of pride, affection or safety.

Sales transactions that fail to satisfy actual needs are not economic and cannot prove ultimately profitable to either a salesman or buyer. A salesman who persuades a person to buy an article for which he has no real need may make a sale but often may lose that which is more important, the good will and continued patronage of the buyer. Successful salesmen attempt to sell only those persons or concerns having genuine needs for their products or services.

Every worth-while product or service satisfies certain needs with which a salesman should be familiar. An automobile satisfies needs for convenient, comfortable, safe, and economical transportation. It satisfies pride and affection. Life insurance satisfies needs for protection and gain and is also an expression of affection. Shoes satisfy needs for protection, comfort, and pride.

Some prospects have urgent needs for a salesman's product or service, others have little need. The degree of need is an important consideration in qualifying prospects. A wealthy man without dependents has less need for life insurance than a poor married man with children. A merchant who has just bought a heavy stock of merchandise obviously has less need for goods than a dealer whose stock is depleted.

The urgency of a prospect's needs is determined by his standards of living, environment, wealth, and other factors, all of which must be considered by a salesman in qualifying a suspect.

Most salesmen are "product" rather than "need" conscious. They customarily think and talk about the design, materials, or construction of their products and fail to relate these features to the needs of their prospects. The mechanical features or intrinsic values of a product are of interest to a prospect only in so far as they satisfy needs for comfort, convenience, safety, protection, gain, economy, pride, or affection. Customers are interested in results, not things. A salesman must discuss the needs of his prospects and describe the features of his product or service only in so far as they contribute to a satisfaction of specific needs.

A salesman should first ask himself, "What does this prospect need?" and automatically take the first step in qualifying him as a potential customer or a suspect.

2. Ability to Pay. The second qualification of a good prospect is that he have the ability to pay for the product or service that the salesman is selling. A suspect may have an urgent need, but he is not a prospect unless he can pay for his purchase. Salesmen of expensive articles often find that a large number of their suspects are worthless because they do not have the money to buy.

Just because a suspect says, "I have no money," it does not necessarily mean that he cannot pay. Many persons habitually resist salesmen by pleading their inability to pay, because they have not been convinced of their need. A salesman must be able to judge whether or not such a suspect is making excuses regarding inability to pay or is financially unable to make a purchase.

The selling price of a product or service determines the number of prospects a salesman can secure. A salesman of used automobiles can secure many more prospects than a salesman of new cars. Lack of purchasing power limits the prospects of personal aircraft salesmen.

In qualifying prospects, a salesman should determine the income range of the persons or concerns that can afford to purchase his product or service. By classifying them into income groups, it is possible to eliminate many whose purchasing power is insufficient to make them likely buyers. For instance, a salesman of oil burners may decide that persons with annual incomes of $2,500 and above are qualified to buy his burner. Many products formerly sold to wealthy prospects have been reduced in price to such an extent that millions of persons once considered as suspects are now actual prospects for the lower priced goods. Electric refrigerators, formerly bought by consumers with annual incomes in excess of $3,500, are sold now to families in the $1,500 income class. Salesmen who offer articles that have been reduced in price can tap the lower levels of purchasing power and increase their prospects.

Insurance salesmen have a formula for determining a prospect's ability to buy. If a man's annual earnings equal 100 times his age, he is considered an excellent prospect; if his earnings are from 75 to 100 times his age, he is a good prospect; but if his earnings are 50 to 75 times his age, he is only a fair prospect.

Installment buying has made it possible for many persons, formerly unable to afford many products or services, to purchase them out of income. A suspect who cannot qualify as a prospect on a cash basis may have no difficulty in paying on installment terms.

Closely related to a suspect's ability to pay, is his willingness to settle for his purchases. A miser may have the ability to pay his obligations but he would hardly be called a willing buyer. Many persons of lower purchasing power are more willing buyers and accordingly better prospects than some wealthier individuals. A salesman must be able to recognize a suspect who is financially able but by nature too "close" to be a qualified prospect.

3. Authority to Buy. The third important qualification of a prospect is that he have authority to buy. A person may have a definite need and the ability to pay and still lack moral or legal authority to enter into a sales contract. When two or more persons share in the purchase of an article or service, the problem of the salesman is to discover which individual has the authority to buy.

For example, a young man whose income is held in trust by a guardian may need an automobile. He has a definite need and the ability to pay, but the authority to buy rests with his guardian, who must be sold to the extent of giving his permission for the purchase. In this case, the young man lacks one of the qualifications of a prospect, the legal authority to buy.

Frequently a person has legal authority to buy but is morally obligated to consult another member of his family or a business associate before making a purchase. A housewife, for example, may need an electric range; her household budget can afford it but she is morally obligated to consult her husband, who makes the final decision in the matter. In this case, the housewife lacks the third qualification of a prospect, the moral authority to buy.

Every salesman is frequently confronted with the problem of determining who influences the final decision to buy. Sometimes several persons in authority must be interviewed before a sale can be made. Some buyers, in order to save their time, make it a practice to refer salesmen to subordinates who have no authority to buy. A salesman must discover the person or persons in authority and focus his selling effort on this individual or these individuals.

Ability to judge whether or not a suspect has sufficient authority can be gained by experience and by following the methods of outstanding salesmen described later in this chapter.

4. Accessibility. A person or corporation may need a product, have money to pay for it, and the authority to buy it but, at the same time, be so unapproachable or far removed that a salesman is not warranted in taking the time or making the effort to attempt a sale. Many major executives of large corporations who must conserve their time rarely see salesmen. They surround themselves with secretaries, clerks, and barriers to keep salesmen away. Even though a busy executive possesses all the other qualifications of a good prospect, the difficulty experienced by a salesman in gaining access to him may make him a poor prospect.

Persons or firms located at long distances from a salesman, even though they possess all the other qualifications of good prospects, may not be qualified. The time, effort, and expense necessary to reach such prospects are often out of proportion to the sales and profits secured by the salesman.

Some individuals are difficult to reach, not because they want to avoid salesmen but because their comings and goings are uncertain, their hours irregular, and their work so variable that they are rarely in their offices. Such men are often not qualified from the standpoint of accessibility.

Salesmen should consider the accessibility of suspects in deciding whether they are worthy of cultivation as prospects. In many instances the difficulty of getting face to face with a prospect is too great to warrant seeking interviews.

5. Right Type for the Salesman. The fifth qualification of a good prospect is that he be a type whom the salesman can meet and deal with agreeably. Buyers prefer to deal with salesmen who are familiar with their problems, understand their needs, and appreciate their viewpoints. Similarity of interests, age, education, and experiences creates mutual understanding and confidence between a buyer and a salesman. For this reason, a salesman should attempt to first select those prospects whose standards of living, social, religious, and racial viewpoints are similar to his own. When a salesman has the same background as his prospect, he appreciates the viewpoint of the buyer and is able to approach him more confidently and to deal more effectively with his needs.

A salesman can determine for himself the type of prospect with whom he is most effective by analyzing the characteristics of those prospects whom he succeeds in selling. Also, a salesman may analyze the relationship between his own characteristics and those of his customers. He should ask himself to what extent his own personal history, age, education, and income correspond with the characteristics of those to whom he sells.

6. Other Qualifications. There are other important qualities which prospects should possess depending upon the nature of the product or service being sold. Prospects for life insurance must be able to pass physical, occupational, and moral tests of acceptability. A man with a chronic heart ailment is not a prospect for life insurance irrespective of the fact that he needs insurance protection, can afford to pay for it, is accessible, has the authority to buy, and is the right type for the salesman.

Salesmen of electrical appliances operating exclusively on alternating current must reject as prospects those firms and individuals served entirely by direct current, even though they may possess all the other qualifications of a prospect.

Legal restrictions disqualify many persons residing in certain states as prospects for alcoholic beverages. Legal restrictions on the sale of certain drugs, drug sundries, gaming devices, foods, and other products eliminate numerous other individuals.

Various other factors including age, sex, skill, and occupation eliminate many persons as prospects for certain products.

"SPECIFIER" PROSPECTS

Some products or services are sold largely on the advice of professional "specifiers" including architects, engineers, and physicians who determine the user's need and create an acceptance by the person or concern using and paying for the goods recommended. Specifiers do not require ability to buy or personal need, but they should represent qualified consumers and have the authority to specify what shall be purchased by their clients.

The problem of qualifying good specifiers and eliminating the worthless is just as important as qualifying buyers. Specifiers are often the most important factors in the sale of drugs, building materials, technical equipment, and industrial supplies.

Some prospects buy but do not use or need the article or service purchased. Parents who buy for their children, husbands who buy for their wives, and women who purchase wearing apparel for men are in this classification. These persons qualify as prospects on all points except that of personal need.

WHY QUALIFY PROSPECTS?

Because salesmen want action and are impatient to be going places and seeing people, they often fail to stop and consider the kind of person or concern to whom they are most likely to sell.

By qualifying prospects, a salesman saves time calling on suspects. Time is a salesman's capital and his most important commodity. The way he uses his time determines in a large measure his success. If he spends valuable hours calling on worthless suspects, he has less time to devote to good prospects and customers.

A salesman who does not qualify his prospects wastes not only his own time but likewise the time of persons who have no need, ability to buy, or authority to purchase. Much of the indifference or antagonism of buyers may be traced to encounters with salesmen who have attempted to sell them something for which they had little need and no money.

A salesman who eliminates suspects saves himself or his firm considerable expense in traveling to see people who are not prospects. A salesman who earns $3,000 annually and averages an hour a day traveling to see worthless prospects is losing $380 a year in income.

Failure to qualify a prospect often causes numerous expensive repeat calls. Many salesmen continue to call on a person who shows some interest in their proposition regardless of the fact that the suspect has none of the qualities of a real prospect.

It is a discouraging experience for a salesman to spend much time and effort in attempting to sell a person who eventually proves to have a remote need, little purchasing power, or no authority to buy. Time spent calling on worthless prospects weakens a salesman's confidence and robs him of the enthusiasm which is the motive power of his work.

Another important reason why salesmen should qualify prospects is to enable them to sell more effectively. Unless a salesman knows the needs of his prospect, he cannot tell and show how his product or service will meet the buyer's needs or solve his problem. The best sales presentation is based on a knowledge of the exact physical and mental needs of a prospect.

Frequently a prospect may have several needs or uses for an article. However, one of these is likely to be more important and pressing than the others. A salesman should identify the most pressing need of a prospect and tell how his product satisfies that need.

A salesman cannot intelligently aid a prospect in reaching a wise buying decision unless he understands the buyer's real needs. A knowledge of a prospect's requirements is also fundamental to a salesman's decision as to what type or model and how much to sell.

HOW TO QUALIFY A PROSPECT

Before a salesman can effectively use the above five-point gauge in qualifying or determining whether a suspect has a need, financial responsibility, authority, accessibility, or agreeability, he must know how to recognize these qualities in an individual. A salesman cannot afford to spend any considerable amount of time in probing the qualifications of suspects unless the amount of the contemplated sale is large or there are repeat possibilities. Accordingly, some more or less obvious indicators of the five basic characteristics of a prospect must be relied upon by salesmen in qualifying suspects.

CHARACTERISTICS OF NEED

The needs of individual consumers are, to a large extent, determined by the following personal factors:

Age. A young man or woman has many more and diverse needs than an older person. The age of a prospect has a great bearing on the number and variety of his needs.

Sex. Women have many needs, both mental and physical, not common to men. Feminine needs for adornment, social prestige, and culture are characteristic.

Religion. Religious beliefs create needs for special foods, apparel, religious supplies, statuary, books, etc.

Dependents. Family responsibilities, including number and age of dependent children and number of relatives who must be supported by a prospect, create needs for housing, insurance, and many products.

Occupation. An individual's profession or business affects his needs for clothing, housing, food, books, transportation, and numerous other articles and services.

Disabilities. The physical disabilities of individuals determine their needs for eyeglasses, shoes, wheel chairs, artificial limbs, and similar goods, as well as for medical services.

Standards of Living. An individual's standard of living determines whether he needs numerous luxuries such as oriental rugs, airplanes, or pleasure boats, or whether his needs must be confined to necessities.

Recreations. A person's interest in sports creates needs for golf clubs, polo mallets, bathing suits, baseball bats, and other recreational equipment.

Home Ownership. A person who owns or plans to own his own home has many needs for home equipment and supplies such as coal, wallpaper, paint, etc.

Present Ownership of a Similar Product or Service. If an individual owns a product similar to the one offered by the salesman there may be no immediate need in this case. No previous ownership creates a sales opportunity. However, possession of a worn or an outmoded article creates an opportunity for a replacement sale.

The needs of industrial prospects are determined principally by the type, quantity, and quality of goods or services produced, as well as by the age, financial resources, and size of the company.

CHARACTERISTICS OF ABILITY TO PAY

The characteristics of an individual that have an important bearing on his ability to pay for his purchases are as follows:

Capacity. The knowledge, training, and experience of a prospect indicate, to a considerable extent, whether or not he has the ability to pay his bills.

Personal Habits. If an individual does not gamble, drink, or run heavily into debt, he is more likely to be able to pay for his purchases than one who is extravagant and improvident.

Family Responsibilities. The person who has an extravagant wife, a large family, or numerous relatives dependent upon him for support is often limited in buying power and not a good prospect.

Property Ownership. Ownership of a home, a business, real estate, and an automobile is evidence that a person has financial responsibility and probable ability to pay for his purchases.

Occupation. A person's position in business or a profession indicates his approximate income.

Social Position. The social strata in which a person moves may reveal to some extent his financial standing. Membership in exclusive clubs is a clue to purchasing power.

Personal Appearance. The dress of a person is sometimes an indicator of his ability to buy in reasonable amounts.

Credit Standing. The retail credit rating of an individual, the type of merchants from whom he buys on credit, and his reputation for meeting his obligations are all evidence of buying power.

The ability of a business concern to pay its bills may be determined by its financial rating, progressive management, physical resources, and demand for its product.

CHARACTERISTICS OF AUTHORITY TO BUY

A prospect's authority to buy may be estimated by one or more of the following characteristics:

Responsibilities. The amount of responsibility which an individual carries in home, business, or professional life is one indication of his authority to buy. Housewives who are responsible for home operation usually have the authority to buy all household equipment and supplies.

Business or Professional Position. In business and the professions, authority is usually designated by titles or ranks such as president, general manager, assistant foreman, or surgeon in chief according to the amount of authority commanded by each position.

Influence. Frequently a person may hold neither rank nor title nor carry large responsibilities, but may possess great personal influence by reason of his or her character, intelligence, charm, or beauty. These factors should be carefully considered in determining whether a suspect has authority to buy or to influence the purchases of others.

Wealth. A person of wealth often commands authority through control of purchasing power and can influence buying decisions.

Age. The amount of authority possessed by an individual usually increases with his age, within the sphere of his influence and responsibility. An older man is more likely to have authority to buy than a younger man with few responsibilities.

CHARACTERISTICS OF ACCESSIBILITY

Whether an individual may be approached with a minimum of time and effort can be determined to a large extent by qualifying him according to one or more of the following factors:

Physical Location. A person located in the same city with a salesman is a better prospect, all other qualifications being equal, than an individual living in another place.

Responsibilities. Numerous responsibilities of a home, social, business, or professional nature make persons inaccessible. Busy executives, society women, or physicians, hedged about by secretaries and maids, are not as desirable prospects from the standpoint of accessibility as others with few responsibilities.

Sociability. A person of a sociable nature may be approached by a salesman with less difficulty than an individual who lives in seclusion and avoids contacts with others.

Occupation. Persons in some occupations cannot be seen during business hours, such as office workers and mill hands; in other vocations, such as farming and selling, workers may be easily reached. Night workers, including watchmen and hotel clerks, can usually be visited at night without interruption.

CHARACTERISTICS OF RIGHT TYPE FOR SALESMAN

In determining whether a suspect is the right type, a salesman should find out if the suspect's situation is similar to his own in one or more of the following respects:

Standard of Living. If a suspect enjoys the same living comforts and conveniences as the salesman, he is in some respects a better prospect than a man who has a lower standard of living.

Education. If the salesman and prospect have had similar educational advantages, if both have graduated from college or traveled widely, they have like interests and a closer understanding.

Responsibilities. Similar family and business responsibilities give a salesman and a prospect mutual interests and enable them to meet under the most favorable circumstances. An executive may be more successful in selling another executive with similar responsibilities because he understands and appreciates the prospect's problems.

Religious and Political Beliefs. A salesman who seeks prospects with the same religious and political beliefs can meet them on a common ground without arousing the prejudices that sometimes stand in the way of making a sale.

Age. Similarity of age promotes mutual understanding and enables a salesman to win a prospect's confidence.

CHARACTERISTICS OF PROSPECTS FOR SPECIFIC
ARTICLES OR SERVICES

Each type of product or service is usually bought by a prospect with certain definite characteristics of need, ability to pay, authority, accessibility, and type. A salesman should select from the numerous characteristics, just described, those qualities which apply particularly to prospects for his commodity.

A young life insurance salesman, for example, might type his ideal prospects as follows: male; age thirty-three; married; with two children; annual income of ten thousand dollars; buying his home; good health; manager of small, prosperous business in same city with same education and standards of living as the salesman.

Although a salesman will have difficulty in finding prospects who can match his conception of an ideal prospect, better prospects will be obtained by establishing a standard of qualifications by which to measure each suspect.

HOW TO RECOGNIZE THE CHARACTERISTICS OF A PROSPECT

The characteristics of need, ability to buy, authority, accessibility, and right type, as previously described, must be recognized by salesmen in qualifying prospects.

Three general methods may be used by a salesman in determining whether his suspects possess the characteristics of prospects: (1) personal observation; (2) personal inquiry; (3) advertising inquiry.

1. Personal Observation. Prospect characteristics may be readily recognized in suspects in the course of a salesman's daily field work, provided he has a definite picture in mind of the type of prospect he seeks.

By observing people, their appearance, place of residence, automobile ownership, and other evidences of need and ability to buy, a salesman can quickly qualify many prospects. By listening to conversations at clubs and on trains, many clues to the qualifications of suspects will be secured. By reading newspapers and consulting public records, much valuable information of this kind may be obtained.

Many automobile, truck, tire, and battery salesmen make it a practice to observe the age, make, and condition of automobiles passed on the road and to record their license numbers and qualify their owners.

By observing the inventory, store appearance, and personnel of a prospective dealer, a salesman can determine whether a merchant has a need and the ability to pay for his purchases.

Salesmen selling to homeowners qualify their prospects for appliances, improvements, and building materials by observing the exteriors and interiors of houses for evidence of need and ability to buy.

Inspection of the equipment owned by individuals and firms enables salesmen of specialties and high-priced consumer and industrial equipment to qualify suspects. Salesmen of heating and ventilating equipment obtain permission from owners to survey the present equipment of their buildings to discover if there is a need for boilers, oil burners, or air-conditioning equipment.

2. Personal Inquiry. A salesman can qualify prospects by making direct personal inquiries or by indirectly questioning friends, relatives, neighbors, or business associates of suspects.

Direct inquiry is often the most reliable and quickest method of determining the suspect's needs, finances, and authority. Many salesmen open interviews by asking leading questions for the purpose of qualifying a prospect. The prospect is flattered by the interest shown by the salesman and often volunteers a complete account of his needs. Typical qualifying questions used by salesmen are: "Do you own your own home?" "Have you a large family?" "Do you have a charge account with the X company?" or "Are you a college man?"

Direct inquiries should be made casually and tactfully. If a salesman is a good listener, he need do very little questioning; most prospects, if given an opportunity, will qualify themselves.

Attentive listening by an alert salesman to the remarks of a prospect during the course of an interview will enable the salesman to determine the prospect's need, ability, and authority to buy.

Illustrations and charts picturing needs may be shown to suspects by a salesman to stimulate discussion and give the salesman a better understanding of the buyer's needs.

The telephone is used by some salesmen in qualifying suspects. Automobile salesmen frequently follow up passenger-car registrations by telephone to obtain facts about ownership.

Tactful questions put to friends, neighbors, competitors, and associates of a suspect will give a salesman much valuable information about the needs and other qualifications of the person or firm upon whom he is planning to call.

3. Advertising Inquiry. Suspects are sometimes qualified by direct-mail advertising. Letters or questionnaires with return cards are mailed by salesmen to selected lists of suspects who qualify themselves by their answers. The responses provide salesmen with a knowledge of the qualifications of each prospect. National magazine advertising, carrying coupons, is sometimes used for the same purpose.

WHEN TO QUALIFY PROSPECTS

When the amount of the sale is considerable salesmen should qualify prospects before seeking an initial interview in order to save time and effort in calling on worthless suspects. Advance qualification enables a salesman to deal more effectively with prospects. In selling articles of universal need and low unit price, however, there is little necessity for spending time qualifying suspects before calling upon them.

In selling high-cost products and services, several weeks or months may be spent by salesmen, aided by company engineers and technicians, in obtaining information about the needs of individual consumers or industrial prospects.

Salesmen of large unit-price mechanical specialties such as stokers, oil burners, air conditioners, and of intangible services such as life insurance, investments, and advertising frequently use a "two-call system" to qualify and secure information about prospects. By this method, a salesman makes an initial call exclusively for the purpose of qualifying a suspect. No attempt is made to present the product or service in the first interview. Sometimes permission is sought to make a survey or analysis of the prospect's needs.

On the basis of the information obtained in the qualifying interview, the salesman plans his presentation to suit the specific needs of the prospect and his ability to buy.

When the amount involved in a transaction does not warrant making qualifications in an initial interview, suspects must be qualified during a single sales interview. Direct inquiry by a salesman at the opening of an interview reveals the qualifications of the prospect and enables the salesman to present his product or service to meet the specific requirements of the prospect. Volunteered remarks by prospects during the course of an interview often give a salesman sufficient information to qualify his prospects and determine their needs.

HOW TO QUALIFY PROSPECTS

Observation of the work of numerous salesmen in qualifying prospects reveals that all follow a very similar method in securing facts about the need, ability to buy, authority, accessibility, and type of each suspect. Four simple and practical steps followed by outstanding salesmen in qualifying prospects have been described in the preceding pages. They are summarized here in a four-step routine to aid salesmen in putting into practice these methods.

Routine for Qualifying Prospects

1. Ask tactful questions.
2. Listen to voluntary remarks.
3. Use visual material to reveal needs.
4. Observe the prospect's situation.

1. Ask Tactful Questions. Indirect inquiry by a salesman among a prospect's friends, associates, neighbors, and acquaintances preceding a call and direct questioning of a prospect during a sales interview are the most common and resultful methods of obtaining information about a prospect's needs, buying power, and authority to buy. Tactful questions indicating the salesman's interest in a prospect's

SALES PERFORMANCE RATING FORM
Qualifying Prospects

Salesman _____ Date _____

Rated by _____ Over-all Rating _____

Score

I. *Salesman's Recognition of Prospect's*	Excellent 90–100	Good 80–90	Fair 70–80	Poor 60–70	Failure Below 60
A. Need					
B Ability to pay					
C. Authority to buy					
D. Accessibility					
E. Right type for salesman					
F. Other qualifications					

II. *Salesman's Method of Qualifying Prospects*	Excellent 90–100	Good 80–90	Fair 70–80	Poor 60–70	Failure Below 60
A. Asking questions					
B. Listening to prospect's remarks					
C. Using visual material to discover prospect's needs					
D. Observing prospect's situation					

Miscellaneous Comments _____

_____

problems are desirable. A salesman may prepare in advance a list of questions to ask the prospect and his acquaintances, which will bring out just the information needed to qualify him.

2. Listen to Voluntary Remarks. Most people like to talk about their problems and interests. If a salesman, by asking questions, can get a prospect and his friends to talk, he will secure much information helpful in deciding whether a prospect is the type who is likely to buy. A salesman who is a good listener is often able to qualify prospects with little effort.

3. Use Visual Material to Reveal Needs. Illustrations depicting needs may be shown by a salesman to a prospect to stimulate discussion of needs and to reveal qualifications of the buyer. Photographs, charts, graphs, diagrams, newspaper clippings—all may be used by a salesman to discover needs. A successful life underwriter shows his prospects a series of illustrations depicting the various needs for life insurance and asks the prospect to point out the one illustration which is of greatest interest to him.

4. Observe the Prospect's Situation. While driving to his office, riding on the train, walking on the street, at games or in church, a salesman who uses his eyes learns much about the needs, interests, hobbies, purchasing power, and authority of prospects. As he sits in a prospect's office, an alert salesman observes photographs, trophies, books, and furnishings which give him a clue as to the prospect's interests. Every hour of the day, a salesman who is observant identifies prospects in his field work.

Problem I

QUALIFYING PROSPECTS

Thomas J. Nolan, representing the Karper-Vaughter Agency of the Universal Life Insurance Company

The Karper-Vaughter Agency of the Universal Life Insurance Company, home office at Hartford, Conn., is one of three agencies of the company located in New York City. Thirty-nine full-time agents are under contract with the agency and operate in greater New York. One of these agents is Thomas J. Nolan, twenty-nine years of age, unmarried, in good health. His education consists of grammar and high school and one year of college.

When in his freshman year of college, he captained his class soccer team and managed the freshman crew, in addition to writing for the school paper. He is president of the young men's society at a Prot-

estant church. He enjoys reading, tennis, and music. He has been
in the insurance business for two years, having been previously connected with a brokerage house as auditing and billing clerk, with an
annual salary of $3,000.

Nolan carries $2,000 straight life insurance and has saved $350
which is invested in a local savings bank. His sales of insurance the
past year totaled $92,000. He was born in Brooklyn, N.Y., and
attended school there with the exception of one year spent in college
in Connecticut.

Suspect	Occupation	Age	Health	Marital Status	Home Ownership	Ins. Carried	Hobby	Education
1	Lawyer	40	Excellent	Married	Yes, $15,000	$ 60,000	Bridge	Law school
2	Doctor	28	Fair	Married; one child, 2 years	Yes, heavy mortgage	$ 12,000	Sports	Medical school
3	Draftsman	35	Under-weight	Single	No	$ 5,000	Cabinet-work	High school
4	Clerk	50	Kidney out 6 years ago	Married; boy, 23	Yes, small mortgage	$ 18,000	Music	Preparatory school
5	Clothing Salesman	30	Overweight	Single	No	$ 10,000	Books	College
6	Banker	45	Nervous	Married; two boys, 15 and 18	Yes, no mortgage	$100,000	Stamp collecting	College

One of Nolan's principal problems is locating and qualifying prospects. Most of them are obtained from old policyholders and friends.
He attempts to secure a minimum of 30 new prospects each month,
an average of one a day, in the course of his field work. In seeking
prospects, Nolan asks for information about their age, income, occupation, and other items of personal history, prefacing his request for
these facts by the following prospecting sales talk:

If you were a life insurance man you would be reminded constantly of the
need to find prospects who are genuine fighters, men who are doing things,
men, in other words, like yourself. You would need to know whether these
men had any money which could be diverted to life insurance. With these
facts in mind, if you had my job today, who are the first three men you
would try to sell?

Nolan has obtained from several of his own policyholders information about six persons living in the vicinity of New York City,
whom he considers as suspects. See the above table.

Questions

1. By what six factors should salesman Nolan qualify the six suspects in this problem?

2. Qualify each of the six suspects by this six-point standard of qualification and arrange them in order of value as prospects.

3. Describe an ideal prospect for this salesman, considering Nolan's background and experience.

4. Is salesman Nolan's method of prospecting likely to produce the type of prospect which would be most suitable for him?

5. How can salesman Nolan obtain more information about these prospects?

Problem II

QUALIFYING PROSPECTS

Marshall W. Hall, representing the Arkright Insulation Company

The Arkright Insulation Company, Providence, R.I., installs a nationally advertised brand of rock-wool insulation by hand and automatic blowing method in the side walls and over ceilings of old and new houses and commercial buildings. The company operates three mobile compressed air blowers and three three-man crews which cover Rhode Island, southern Massachusetts, and eastern Connecticut. Most of its installations are in houses over fifteen years old.

A sales organization of 10 commission salesmen calls on homeowners and owners of commercial properties, closing contracts for insulation ranging from $150 to $600 and averaging $200. Insulation is installed principally for excluding cold air as it effects savings of 10 to 15 per cent in fuel costs. It also contributes to comfort by repelling hot air in summer. It deadens noise and promotes health by excluding drafts and dust.

Insulation usually is installed in connection with air-conditioning equipment, in buildings of frame and stucco construction, in buildings in exposed locations vulnerable to cold and heat, in buildings with inadequate heating equipment, and in homes where children, aged, or sick make heating a problem.

Marshall W. Hall is one of the 10 sales representatives of the company. He has averaged annual earnings of $4,000 since he began work in 1937. He is thirty-eight years of age, a high-school graduate, and a former building material salesman. Hall owns his own insulated house in Pawtucket, R.I., which he occupies with his wife and three children.

Hall discovers many of his prospects by observing buildings likely to need insulation. He also cultivates old customers, neighbors, and friends and acquaintances who are likely to need insulation.

Salesman Hall has received the following information about five possible purchasers of insulation:

Suspect 1 has written the Arkright office asking a salesman to call. The inquirer gave the following information: Henry K. Lamson is general manager of a machine-tool company located in a town of 3,500, situated 40 miles from Providence. His house is of three-story frame construction, built in 1890, with 15 rooms, and valued at $20,-000. A new oil-heating system has just been installed but fails to heat the house comfortably. The house was inherited by the present owner from his father and is occupied by the owner, his wife, and a maiden daughter. The family spends five months of each winter in Florida with the exception of the father who lives at the local inn. A local insulation company has been asked to submit estimates.

Suspect 2 was referred to the salesman by a friend who gave the following information: Jacob Levy, fifty years old, a clothing salesman, owns jointly with his wife a two-story, two-family frame house in Providence. The owner and his family of two girls and a boy, aged eighteen, twenty, and twenty-two, respectively, live in six rooms on the first floor of the building, renting the second floor to tenants. The second floor has been vacant since the last tenants moved, complaining of the heat from the attic over the second-floor ceiling. Improvements must also be made in the bathroom and kitchen of the second-floor apartment before it can be rented. The house, which is 30 years old, is located in an old section of the city.

Suspect 3 was referred to the salesman by a customer who gave the following information: Mark L. Kane, forty-five years old, a printer, owns a two-story and attic frame house in a suburb of Providence. He is a widower and occupies a room on the second floor, renting the balance of the house to a family of three persons, a middle-aged man and wife and a daughter of eighteen years. The owner is considering remodeling the unfinished third floor for his own occupation. Plumbing and heating must be installed, a dormer window cut in the roof for light and air, and the interior finished in wall board. Insulation would be used for the ceiling. The estimated cost of the remodeling, exclusive of the insulation, would be $1,500. The house is valued at $8,500 and is 30 years old.

Suspect 4 was referred to the salesman by a customer who gave the following information: L. O. Tucker is a retired accountant, aged seventy, who supports his wife of the same age through a small life insurance annuity. They live in a nine-room frame house, heated by steam, and complain of the cost of fuel which averages $200 a winter. The house is owned by a local cooperative bank which leases the property to Mr. Tucker. The house is 40 years old and is located in a medium-class residential neighborhood.

Suspect 5 was referred to the salesman by a customer who gave the following information: Burton Christian is a clerk, employed by a Providence public utility. He has recently purchased and remodeled a colonial farmhouse, 150 years old, 20 miles from the city, where he lives with his wife and fourteen-year-old son. The house has 14 rooms and was bought for $8,500, of which amount a Providence bank holds a $7,500 mortgage. The owner has just spent $1,500 in improvements to the property, which amount was borrowed from Mr. Christian's father-in-law. Mrs. Christian is in poor health.

Questions

1. By what five factors should the salesman qualify the five suspects in this problem?

2. Qualify each of them on each of the five factors and arrange them in the order of their value as prospects.

3. Describe an ideal prospect for this salesman, taking into consideration his background and experience.

4. Is the salesman's method of prospecting likely to produce the type of prospect most suitable to him? Explain.

5. Does the salesman have enough information about these suspects? How can he obtain more information about them?

Reading References

E. G. BLACKSTONE, C. C. CRAWFORD, and E. GRINNELL, "Selling," Chap. V, D. C. Heath and Company, Boston, 1942.

J. R. DAUBMAN, "Salesmanship and Types of Selling," Chap. VIII, F. S. Crofts & Co., New York, 1939.

CHARLES H. FERNALD, "Salesmanship," 3d ed., pp. 127–144, Prentice-Hall, Inc., New York, 1945.

J. GEORGE FREDERICK, "Modern Salesmanship," Chap. XI, Garden City Publishing Company, Inc., New York, 1937.

PAUL W. IVEY, "Salesmanship Applied," Chaps. VII–VIII, McGraw-Hill Book Company, Inc., New York, 1937.

PAUL W. IVEY, "Successful Salesmanship," pp. 111–140, Prentice-Hall, Inc., New York, 1947.

N. KNEELAND, L. BERNARD, and G. B. TALLMAN, "Selling to Today's Customer," pp. 112–116, Ginn & Company, Boston, 1942.

DAVID R. OSBORNE, "Salesmanship for Today for Salesmanagers of Tomorrow," Chaps. V, VII, pp. 24, 33, Harper & Brothers, New York, 1939.

CHARLES B. ROTH, "Finding the Prospect and Getting the Interview," Chap. II, Prentice-Hall, Inc., New York, 1946.

FREDERICK A. RUSSELL and F. H. BEACH, "Textbook of Salesmanship," Chap. VI, McGraw-Hill Book Company, Inc., New York, 1949.

HARRY SIMMONS, "A Practical Course in Successful Selling," Chap. VI, Harper & Brothers, New York, 1939.

CHAPTER XIII

LOCATING PROSPECTS

NECESSITY FOR LOCATING PROSPECTS

When a salesman has determined the persons or firms who have the need, ability, and authority to buy his product or service, he must next find out where these individuals or concerns are located. He must first know exactly the type of prospect he wants—the age, income, marital status, and other characteristics of the person whom he believes will make a good prospect. With this picture before him, a salesman is ready to begin his search for prospects.

The problem of locating prospects varies with the type of selling, the nature of the product or service sold, and the breadth of the market or number of possible buyers. Salespersons in retail stores usually are not concerned with this matter. In a few progressive retail specialty stores, however, the salespersons do outside selling and are confronted with the problem of locating prospects. Salesmen who sell retail or wholesale merchants have little difficulty in discovering where possible customers are located. But salesmen selling specialties, luxuries, or intangible services to individuals or business concerns find that prospecting is one of their most important duties. A life insurance salesman's skill in locating prospects accounts for 80 per cent of his success in his work.

Competition compels specialty salesmen to search for prospects. Progressive business concerns can no longer wait for customers to seek them out. Buyers who do not recognize their needs must be sought by salesmen, and salesmen are faced with the necessity of maintaining a full reservoir of prospects to ensure a regular flow of orders and commissions. If consumers recognized their need for specialties and services and had a definite desire to purchase them, salesmen would not have to search for customers.

WHERE TO LOCATE PROSPECTS

"Where can I find customers?" is one of the first questions asked by most new specialty salesmen and it never ceases to be a problem to many experienced salesmen. Beginner salesmen are sometimes advised, "Prospects are everywhere. Everyone is a prospect." This advice often causes a salesman to minimize the importance of qualifying prospects, to discount the difficulties of prospecting, and sometimes to slight this significant phase of sales work. The greater the number of suspects, the more essential it is to qualify them.

Sources of prospects may be classified according to their importance to a salesman, as: (1) primary and (2) secondary. These sources may be explored in one or more of three ways: personal inquiry, observation, and correspondence.

Primary Sources of Prospects. A salesman is usually most successful in obtaining qualified prospects from those sources with which he is most familiar and which are most accessible to him. Those primary sources, which a salesman should develop first, are as follows:

1. *Immediate Family.* No source of prospects is so available, cooperative, and interested in aiding a salesman to locate prospects as his own immediate family. His wife, sisters, brothers, parents—all have friends, connections, associates, or employees who may be potential customers. By describing to adult members of his family the type of prospect in which he is interested, a salesman can enlist their most valuable cooperation in his search for customers.

2. *Friends, Distant Relatives, and Acquaintances.* Next to a salesman's own family, his friends and neighbors are most interested in helping him to succeed. A salesman should make a list of his closest friends, neighbors, and acquaintances, and call on each personally, discussing the product or service that he is selling. Friends may not only be prospects themselves but they can provide a salesman with information about their friends and relatives who may be prospects. Friends and acquaintances usually are not only willing but also in excellent position to help a salesman qualify the needs, ability to buy, and authority of suspects.

A salesman who may be reluctant to approach his friends and neighbors to buy can get their cooperation in qualifying and locating prospects.

A salesman must make friends and acquaintances to succeed in prospecting. Competent specialty salesmen participate in community affairs, religious, political, fraternal, and educational activities in their search for prospects.

3. *Suppliers, Tradesmen, and Professional Men.* The merchants from whom a salesman buys his food, clothing, and drugs are usually

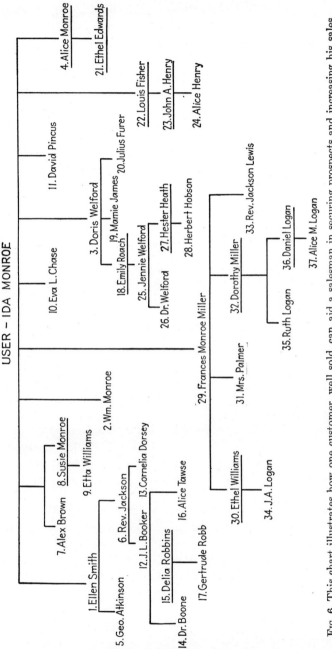

USER – IDA MONROE

1. Ellen Smith
2. Wm. Monroe
3. Doris Welford
4. Alice Monroe
5. Geo. Atkinson
6. Rev. Jackson
7. Alex Brown
8. Susie Monroe
9. Etta Williams
10. Eva L. Chase
11. David Pincus
12. J. L. Booker
13. Cornelia Dorsey
14. Dr. Boone
15. Delia Robbins
16. Alice Tawse
17. Gertrude Robb
18. Emily Roach
19. Mamie James
20. Julius Furer
21. Ethel Edwards
22. Louis Fisher
23. John A. Henry
24. Alice Henry
25. Jennie Welford
26. Dr. Welford
27. Hester Heath
28. Herbert Hobson
29. Frances Monroe Miller
30. Ethel Williams
31. Mrs. Palmer
32. Dorothy Miller
33. Rev. Jackson Lewis
34. J. A. Logan
35. Ruth Logan
36. Daniel Logan
37. Alice M. Logan

Fig. 6. This chart illustrates how one customer, well sold, can aid a salesman in securing prospects and increasing his sales. A Westinghouse Electric Refrigerator salesman of Washington, D.C., employing the "use the user" method of prospecting, followed up a sale made to Ida Monroe and secured **37** additional sales. The first sale produced **9** more sales, which in turn created **28** additional orders. Customers influence their relatives as indicated by this chart showing sales to four Monroes, three Welfords, four Logans, two Millers, and two Henrys.

willing to reciprocate for his patronage by furnishing him with information about prospects. A salesman's grocer, baker, landlord, doctor, and dentist can help him locate prospects by giving him facts about their friends and acquaintances.

4. *Business Associates, Employees, Stockholders.* A salesman's business associates, the employees and executives of his firm, are excellent sources of prospects. Many large companies reward nonselling employees who secure leads for salesmen. Stockholders can supply salesmen with names of prospects. Employees who meet the public, such as deliverymen, servicemen, and inspectors, are in an excellent position to aid a salesman in discovering potential customers.

5. *Customers.* A salesman's own customers are an excellent source of prospects for the reasons that they are acquainted with the salesman, know the merits of the product, and the quality of the service of the company. Customers like to show and discuss their purchases with friends, neighbors, and acquaintances. In this way customers meet other people who are interested in making similar purchases. A salesman who prospects among the friends and neighbors of his customers unearths many potential buyers.

In addition to his own customers, a salesman may obtain from his company a list of "orphan" users or owners who are not being actively followed up. These users should be solicited for names of prospects. Some companies furnish their salesmen with lists of customers arranged geographically so that they can be interviewed for prospects. Owner clubs are sponsored by several companies for the primary purpose of securing names of possible customers. Customers are supplied with mailing cards for reporting information about prospects. These are turned over to salesmen for follow-up. Customers are rewarded for their cooperation with cash or premiums in the event that prospects suggested by them are sold.

An annual national survey of automobile buyers reveals that owners are an important source of prospects. Twelve per cent of the annual purchases of one famous make of passenger automobile were made on recommendations of owners.

Policyholders are an excellent source of prospects for life insurance. A life insurance salesman wrote to eight of his policyholders for names of prospects, received eight replies nominating 92 prospects, of which number 20 were sold. Another insurance man obtains 75 per cent of his business through his policyholders. An electric refrigerator salesman closed eight sales in one block as the result of a single sale to a prominent resident of the neighborhood.

Secondary Sources of Prospects. After a salesman has exhausted his primary sources of prospects, there are numerous secondary sources which should be used.

1. *Canvassing.* In selling low-priced specialties consumed by many persons, canvassing is a common method of prospecting. Without advance knowledge of the needs or buying power of suspects, many salesmen call from house to house or office to office seeking interviews with prospects. Sometimes a limited amount of information is obtained in advance of the call from neighbors or office directories.

This method of prospecting depends for its effectiveness upon the exposure of a salesman to suspects and the law of averages to produce a worth-while number of prospects. If a salesman will expose himself to many suspects over a long period of time, he will automatically make some sales of almost any low-priced article. When a large number of suspects are canvassed, some are sure to buy. Canvassing serves to replenish a depleted supply of prospects and develops initiative, courage, and resourcefulness.

However, canvassing consumes much time and energy. It is often discouraging to a salesman to find that many suspects are not accessible or have little need, authority, or funds to buy. Many communities and office buildings prohibit canvassers, and consumers are often antagonistic to them. Canvassing is unprofitable for salesmen of high-priced specialties for which the demand is limited, the market restricted, and the need unrecognized. Canvassing for high unit-price products is often wasteful and expensive considering the cost of calling on worthless suspects.

For qualifying suspects, making appointments, and following up prospects, a telephone canvass may be used effectively. Many automobile salesmen use the telephone to canvass and to secure appointments, saying: "This is Mr. Salesman of the Jones Motor Company. We are checking our mailing list. Our records show that you own a 1939 Blank sedan. Is that correct?"

If the suspect no longer owns the car registered in his name, the salesman inquires about the make of car now owned and asks when it was bought. If the suspect still owns the car registered in his name, the salesman asks whether it was bought new or second-hand. He then thanks the suspect for the information and completes the call. No attempt is made to sell by telephone.

2. *The Endless-chain Method.* In using the endless-chain method of prospecting, a salesman secures from every person whom he interviews information about at least one other suspect. The merit of

this method is that one prospect leads to another, thereby creating an endless chain of prospects, from which the method takes its name. At the close of every sales interview, a salesman, using this method, asks the person interviewed for names, addresses, and facts about his friends who may be potential customers. This method may be used in connection with other primary methods of prospecting previously described.

Some advantages of endless-chain prospecting are the following: continuous rather than spasmodic prospecting is carried on; time is

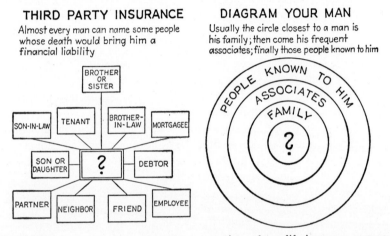

THIRD PARTY INSURANCE
Almost every man can name some people whose death would bring him a financial liability

DIAGRAM YOUR MAN
Usually the circle closest to a man is his family; then come his frequent associates; finally those people known to him

FIG. 7. Diagrams carried by salesmen representing a large life insurance company to remind them to secure names of prospects from friends, acquaintances, and other policyholders. These diagrams illustrate the endless-chain method of prospecting.

saved prospecting coincidentally with selling; a full supply of prospects may be obtained; ample information and references may be secured. On the other hand, prospecting by this method may be superficial, a large quantity rather than a good quality of prospects may be obtained, and persons interviewed may be reluctant to give an unknown salesman the name of a friend.

By listening attentively to remarks during interviews, an alert salesman will often pick up much information about the friends, relatives, or associates of a prospect. Many of these people may be potential customers. The salesman can ask for more information about them and call upon those who qualify as prospects.

By using the endless-chain method of prospecting, a Newark, New Jersey, life insurance man, from the sale of one $5,000 policy received recommendations that resulted in the sale of 50 policies. These varied in amount from $1,000 to $20,000 for a total of $446,000, an average case of $8,920 from a chain of 50 links.

Another Middle Western insurance man, using the endless-chain method of prospecting, sold a hardware merchant in his town a $3,000 life insurance policy. From this customer the salesman obtained the names of five of his friends and associates, each of whom bought policies ranging from $1,000 to $6,000 each. These five buyers in turn recommended other prospects until the salesman had made 37 sales for a total of $104,000 worth of insurance.

3. *The Center-of-influence Method.* By the center-of-influence method, prospects are sought from influential persons in a salesman's community or territory. Typical influential people whose assistance may be sought by a salesman are attorneys, officials of clubs, public officials, ministers, doctors, bankers, teachers, and heads of business organizations. Persons in these positions have many friends and acquaintances who may be good prospects.

If a salesman is acquainted with such influential people, he should have no difficulty in enlisting their aid. If he has no influential connections, he may make them through mutual friends. A salesman who does not know any public officials, bankers, or attorneys will experience little difficulty in making their acquaintance and securing their assistance if he presents his need for prospects in a friendly and candid manner. Most influential people are frequently called upon to do favors for other people and usually are willing to help an ambitious salesman representing a reliable product or service.

Centers of influence can do much more for a salesman than supply him with information. They can introduce him to their friends, make appointments for him, give him cards and letters of introduction, speak to their friends about him, and urge their acquaintances to buy from him.

The principal advantages of this method of prospecting are the following: the recommendation of an influential person carries weight with a prospective buyer; influential persons have a great many acquaintances and considerable information about them; the cooperation of centers of influence costs a salesman nothing and saves his time and effort. On the other hand, influential persons are sometimes inaccessible and reluctant to permit their names to be used by salesmen.

A salesman with an unselfish interest in serving other people will have little difficulty in winning the respect and active assistance of influential people. Participation by a salesman in charitable, frater-

nal, civic, and religious work in which influential people are engaged
will enable him to make their acquaintance and gain their cooperation.

An imaginative life insurance salesman applied the center-of-influence plan of prospecting by organizing an executive committee of
12 influential acquaintances in his community. In asking men to
serve on his committee, the salesman emphasized that his success depended upon their cooperation and that each would have no expense
nor obligation beyond a desire to aid him with his prospecting problem. Each committee member agreed to supply the salesman with
names of prospects and to permit the use of his name as a reference.
The salesman promised to report regularly to each member of the
committee on sales made and prospects discarded. Four other salesmen in the same office adopted this plan with the result that sales
increased 50 per cent, according to S. G. Dickinson.

4. *Sales Associate Method.* Sales associates usually are men and
women whose occupations bring them frequently in contact with
persons who are logical prospects for a salesman's product or service.
Associates are sometimes employed by salesmen to recommend prospects on a flat fee basis. Sales associates may be personal friends,
customers, or merely acquaintances of the salesman and are employed usually as telephone operators in hotels or apartments, information clerks, chain-store managers, barbers, beauticians, laundry-
truck drivers, service station attendants, policemen, postmen, and
hotel clerks.

Sales associates are usually compensated for supplying information
about prospects only when sales result. If information about a person or firm is already in the salesman's possession or if the prospect
has been canvassed previously by the salesman, the associate is not
remunerated. Amounts paid to informants vary according to the
sales price and return to the salesman. The compensation, however,
must be large enough to interest sales associates and to get their
active cooperation. The recommended remuneration for associates
on a popular make of six-cylinder automobile is $15 for each car
sold and on more expensive eight-cylinder models, $20. Salesmen
sometimes assume the full expense of paying their associates from
earnings or commissions. In other cases, compensation of associates
is shared on a 50-50 basis by the employer and the salesman. In some
companies the employer remunerates associates. In some cases an
associate is guaranteed payment by a letter from the salesman's employer.

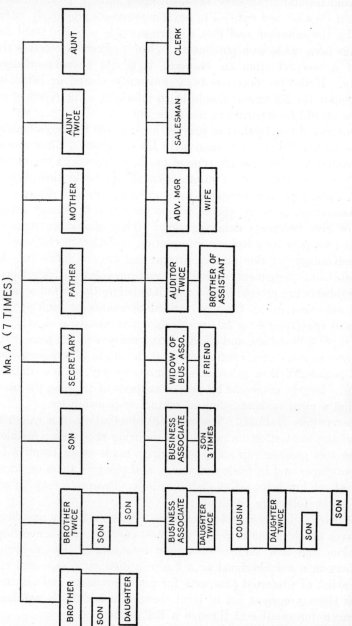

Fig. 8. This chart illustrates the "family tree" method of prospecting by an agent of the New England Mutual Life Insurance Company. Starting with Mr. A and following with his 7 relatives and secretary, 20 others were sold for a total of 41 sales.

To avoid misunderstandings, salesmen must make it clear to associates that they are not entitled to pay for prospects previously interviewed by the salesman and that compensation is not paid until delivery has been made to a purchaser. When a salesman receives the name of a prospect from an associate, it should be acknowledged promptly. If the prospect has been previously visited or listed by the salesman, the informant should be so informed. The result of an interview should be reported to the associate.

The success of this method of prospecting depends to a great extent upon the training that a salesman gives his associates. They should have a complete picture of the type of prospect desired. Current advertising, prices, and product information should be in their hands. Each should be given a complete sales presentation and demonstration. Associates, however, should not be permitted to do any actual selling or give prospects demonstrations. They should be required to report promptly by telephone information about prospects.

The advantages of this plan of prospecting are the following: An immediate and permanent source of good prospects is developed; many prospects are presold by the associate before the call of a salesman; a salesman has a force of trained assistants to multiply his efforts and effectiveness; a salesman's executive ability is developed; and he saves selling time and effort. The weakness of the plan is the indifference of associates, controversy over the origin of prospects, and lack of confidence in a salesman's promises to pay. These difficulties can be largely overcome by proper methods of training the associates and a clear understanding of mutual responsibilities.

5. *Observation Methods.* The personal observation of a salesman is one of the most effective methods of securing prospects. An alert salesman sees prospects in social gatherings, reads about them in his daily newspaper and in trade magazines, and observes them on trains and street, at luncheon, or at club meetings. Prospects may be observed in the following situations:

a. *Changes in business or home address.* When a family or a business leaves an old home or comes to a new one, old sales connections are broken and new sources of supply established. By observing newcomers in a neighborhood or a business district, a salesman can obtain a list of preferred prospects for many products and services. In some cities a current list of local changes in address is available to salesmen for small cost through a list service.

b. *Spotting old products.* Organized spotting of wornout, outmoded, or obsolete products reveals prospects for new equipment.

Old automobiles are observed by salesmen and the names of the owners are obtained from registration lists as prospects for tires, batteries, and new cars. One large tire company supplies its retail sales representatives with daily car-spotting quotas, tally sheets, and spotting prospect cards for their use. Local automobile license lists are obtained by salesmen from mailing list companies, police headquarters, or automobile clubs to use in identifying the names and addresses of owners of old cars.

An automobile salesman on Long Island, New York, carries a camera and takes pictures of old cars that he sees on the streets. The photographs are printed on post cards and mailed to the owners, whose names and addresses have been obtained from the local automobile registration list. The salesman follows up the mailing with calls and closes many deals.

Retail building-material salesmen obtain prospects by organized inspection of business and residential districts to locate houses and commercial buildings in need of remodeling, roofing, painting, insulation, side-walling, and other equipment.

c. New construction. The erection of new houses and commercial buildings creates numerous sales opportunities and supplies observant salesmen with many prospects for various kinds of building equipment, furnishings, and supplies. Dodge Construction Reports and city building permits provide a salesman with information about new projects.

d. Store displays and decorations. A salesman calling on dealers can qualify his prospect's needs and ability to buy by observing the appearance of his show windows, store arrangement, decorations, advertising signs, and merchandise.

e. Daily newspapers and magazines. A single issue of a daily newspaper is full of information about prospects for many products and services. News of accidents, death notices, birth announcements, business changes, engagements, marriages, real estate transfers, personals, and society news all reveal the names and addresses of persons and concerns with needs and ability to buy many things. Newspaper display and classified advertisements are an excellent source of prospects.

An indication of the number and quality of prospects that can be uncovered in one issue of a daily newspaper is found in the experience of a life insurance salesman in a city of 75,000 population who, according to S. G. Dickinson, read seven items in his morning newspaper and acted on them with the following results:

Cashier of store held up. Called on cashier, two clerks, and owner. Result, sold one clerk $2,000.

New chairman of own political party appointed. Offered services; sold no business; consider the man a good prospect.

President of town council resigned. Called on new appointee; sold no business; got three good leads; sold one $3,000.

Young man killed in automobile crash. Called on attending physician, no sale; called on six pallbearers; sold two a total of $3,000.

Financial report for successful month for distributor of nationally advertised coffee. Got name of salesman from local grocer; found he lived in the city; sold $1,000.

Owner of small chain of stores died. Company paid small claim; called on manager of each of five stores; sold one $2,500.

Small bank reopened on an unrestricted basis. Called on cashier who had lapsed a policy two years before; sold him $3,000.

The total sales made within 30 days to prospects found in one issue of the newspaper was $14,500, nearly 50 per cent more than the salesman's previous monthly average. Within three months this method of prospecting increased this salesman's volume 40 per cent.

Professional clipping services for a small cost can supply salesmen with selected news items from a large number of newspapers and trade magazines. These items report significant business changes, deaths, liquidations, new incorporations, and other happenings, invaluable information for a salesman in locating and qualifying prospects.

f. Conversation. By keeping his ears open, a salesman can learn much about prospects from conversations at club meetings, conventions, parties, religious and social gatherings.

6. *Advertising Methods.* Advertising is an effective method of prospecting because it reaches many more people than a salesman is able to see in the same time at a fraction of the cost of a personal call. Advertising alone, however, is insufficient to keep salesmen continuously supplied with an adequate number of prospects. Accordingly, advertising is useful in supplementing other methods.

Names and addresses of thousands of interested prospects are secured by many concerns in response to national consumer, trade or professional magazine, newspaper, and radio advertising. Advertising inquiries received, in the form of coupons or requests for samples and booklets, are turned over to salesmen for personal follow-up. Although many inquirers are good prospects, some are merely curious and have no authority or ability to buy the product or service advertised. Accordingly, advertising inquirers should be carefully qualified by salesmen. Some salesmen qualify advertising inquirers by telephone to determine whether or not they are legitimate prospects.

Many concerns aid salesmen in prospecting by sending suspects direct-mail advertising in the form of folders, letters, and booklets designed to produce interested inquiries. The mailing lists are usually furnished by salesmen from their own lists of suspects. Inquiries received by the advertiser are forwarded to the salesman to follow up.

One large automobile manufacturing concern cooperated with its salesmen in a facetiously named "Foot in the Door" campaign to obtain prospects. Two illustrated folders and return cards were mailed by the company once a week to 20 suspects whose names were supplied by the salesmen, who were charged with the cost of postage. The printing and mailing costs were assumed by the company.

The effectiveness of company direct-mail advertising in aiding salesmen to obtain prospects is illustrated by the experience of one representative of the Massachusetts Mutual Life Insurance Company who precedes every call with a prospecting letter furnished by this company. In one year this salesman averaged one sale to every 10 prospects produced by the advertising and sold a total of $245,776 worth of insurance.

If a salesman does not receive direct-mail advertising assistance from his company, he may write and mail his own prospecting letters. With the assistance of a typist or a letter shop, he can mail five individually typed one-page, hand-signed letters a day and follow them up promptly for maximum results. When prepaid postage return cards are enclosed, replies are facilitated. No attempt is made to close a sale by mail but merely to secure an expression of interest and qualifying information.

The following prospecting letter is mailed by a Cleveland, Ohio, insurance salesman to a list of suspects:

Mr. A. Doe,
Cleveland, Ohio.
Dear Mr. Doe:

The Social Security Act has made the population of the United States conscious of the fact that incomes are necessary during the "sunset of life" just as they are during the more productive years.

My message to you this morning is not to offer ideas as to whether the Social Security Act is right or wrong, but to point out the fact that the maximum income which may be derived is $85 monthly.

Income is derived from only two sources, labor and property; when

we reach the retirement age and income from labor ceases, then we must
turn to property for income, and that income will be governed by the
kind and amount of property we have accumulated.

I have in mind a type of property which may not be swept away by
floods, fires, or depressions, and which has stood the test of one hundred
years without interruption.

I shall call you by 'phone for an appointment whereby we may discuss the details.

Cordially yours,

From 20 of these letters typed on personal stationery and addressed
to persons in a position to buy retirement insurance, the salesman
received 16 interviews and wrote $47,500 worth of insurance, an
average of $2,375 a letter.

Advertising premiums or novelties are sometimes offered by salesmen to suspects to discover those who are interested and to qualify
them as prospects. Salesmen, representing a well-known electric refrigerator, personally distributed to housewives more than 1,500,000
cold gauges and obtained many qualified prospects. Tire salesmen
have distributed thousands of key cases and handy pocket screw
drivers to motorists to secure the names of prospects. Representatives
of several life insurance companies secure the names of prospects by
offering gratis leather memorandum books with the prospect's name
stamped in gold on the covers.

7. *Lists of Prospects.* Published lists and directories of firms,
organizations, and individuals are excellent sources of prospects for
many products and services.

Municipal, county, state, and national records are frequently used
by salesmen as a source of prospects in practically every line of business. A county assessor's list, for example, contains the name, address,
and assessed valuation of every property owner in the county. City
tax lists, building permits, voting registration lists, automobile licenses,
marriage licenses, vendor's licenses, and similar lists contain the names
of persons and firms with specific needs.

Organization membership lists are excellent sources of prospects.
Civic organizations such as chamber of commerce, Lions, Rotary,
Kiwanis, and advertising clubs have on their rosters the names and
addresses of leading businessmen. Rosters of professional organizations, such as medical, architectural, engineering clubs and societies
of nurses are sources of names of prospects with specific needs for
many products. Social and fraternal group membership lists, direc-

tories of school and college graduates, and similar lists usually can be obtained from members or upon application to club secretaries.

City, telephone, trade, social, and professional directories contain many names of firms and individuals who are qualified prospects for many articles and services. A complete list of manufacturers appears in Thomas's "Directory of Manufacturers." The names of officials and directors of large corporations are listed in Poor's "Directory of Directors," and there is published in every major industry a directory of firms and officials in the trade.

Mailing-list concerns compile, from directories and other sources, special lists of firms and individuals brought up to date and guaranteed to be 95 to 98 per cent accurate. The experience and facilities of such list companies as Buckley, Dement, and Company, Chicago, and R. L. Polk and Company, Detroit, enable them to supply quality lists of prospects to salesmen.

By exchanging lists of suspects with salesmen of noncompetitors calling on a similar class of trade, a salesman can obtain quantities of names of possible buyers.

In using a list or directory of any kind, the correctness of the names and addresses should be verified. The mortality in consumer lists, on account of deaths and changes of address, is often as great as 30 to 40 per cent annually, depending upon the type of individual and occupation. Verification of reliability of all lists is necessary to avoid wasted postage.

8. *Miscellaneous Methods of Prospecting.* There are numerous miscellaneous methods of locating prospects which have been used successfully by salesmen. Some salesmen obtain many names of suspects at exhibits, fairs, conventions, and industrial shows where their companies have displays.

Consumer guessing and voting contests are often productive of names of good prospects. A home-appliance retailer offered a washing machine to housewives who would come nearest to guessing the motor number. Women who competed in the contest were required to enter their guesses on entry blanks which provided space for recording their names, addresses, ownership, and age of their electrical appliances. Complete information about the appliance needs of several hundred desirable prospects was obtained in this way and turned over to salesmen.

Demonstrations by salesmen before civic clubs and women's groups also serve as sources of prospects for salesmen of home appliances.

Salesmen selling aluminum utensils direct to consumers serve luncheons and dinners gratis and obtain the names and addresses of the suspects who are invited to the meals.

9. *Surveys and Programing.* In selling high-priced specialty goods and services, including industrial installations, domestic heating and

DOMESTIC HEATING PLANT DATA Date_____

Name:_____ Address:_____

Electric Current: AC ☐ DC ☐ Volts:_____ Cycle:_____ Phase:_____

BOILER DATA	FURNACE DATA
Steam ☐ Vapor ☐ Gravity Hot Water ☐ Forced Hot Water ☐	Gravity ☐ Forced Warm Air or Air Conditioning ☐
Cast Iron ☐ Steel ☐ Made by_____ No._____	Cast Iron ☐ Steel ☐
Number of Sections:_____ Height of Base:_____ Floor to Crown:_____	Made By:_____ Cat. No._____
Round Boiler Outside Diameter:_____ Grate Diameter:_____	Grate: Diameter:_____ Height Above Floor:_____
Rect. Boiler Width:_____ Length:_____ Grate Width:_____ Grate Length:_____	Firebox Diameter:_____ Casing Dimensions or Diameter:_____
Does Boiler Have Curtain Section?_____ (If so, Make Sketch Showing Dimensions)	Ash Pit Door: Width_____ Height_____
	Center Line or Firebox to Furnace Front_____

RADIATION DATA

Type of Radiator	Height Inches	No. Tubes	No. Sections	Sq. Ft. Per Section	Sq. Ft. Per Radiator	No. Radiators	Sq. Ft. of Radiation

1. Total Direct Radiation

2. Allowance for Piping and Pick-up_____ (Item 1) = _____
   over 3

3. Domestic Hot Water Load _____ × (1.5 Steam) (2 Hot Water) = _____
   (Tank Gallons)

Equivalent Direct Radiation = 1 + 2 + 3 = _____

Recommended E.D.R. Load for _____ Boiler = _____

E.D.R. Capacity No. (Lb. Per Hour) (BTU Per Lb.) (Est. Eff.)
Stoker:_____ × _____ × _____ = _____
(240 Steam) or (150 Gr. Hot Water) or (200 Forced Hot Water)

RETURN AIR DUCTS (Gravity)

Size Inches	Number	Area Each Duct	Total Area Square Inches

Total Return Duct Area

WARM AIR DUCTS (Gravity)

Diameter Inches	Number	Area of Each Duct	Total Area Square Inches
8		50.3	
9		63.6	
10		78.5	
12		113.1	

Total Warm Air Duct Area—Sq. In.

BTU's Required_____ × (140 Gravity) (240 Forced) = _____
(Warm Air Duct Area)

BTU Capacity No.
Stoker_____ × _____ × _____ = _____
(Lbs Per Hr.) (BTU Per Lb.) (Eff.)

FIG. 9. Survey form used by salesmen of a domestic coal stoker in determining the needs of a prospect, preparatory to submitting a written proposal. Information to complete this survey form is obtained by a stoker salesman by inspection of a prospect's heating system.

air-conditioning equipment, life insurance, and securities, suspects may be qualified by surveys of present equipment or services. An inspection shows the amount and type of equipment or service required and whether the person or firm is actually a prospect. If the suspect qualifies as a prospect, a program or plan based on the investigation is next presented by the salesman.

A salesman usually selects his most likely suspects and first secures their permission to inspect their equipment or examine their insurance policies or securities. In making the examination, the salesman is often assisted by a technical adviser or engineer who aids him in qualifying the prospect in respect to need.

This method of prospecting is now widely used in selling life insurance and other specialty services and equipment because it enables a salesman to get a complete picture or information about a prospect's needs, ability to buy, and acceptability. The prospect is flattered by the consideration given his problem and impressed by the helpfulness of the salesman. A salesman is in a better position to tell and show definitely how his product or service fits the prospect's exact needs. On the other hand, surveys and programs consume much time and effort with no assurance that the prospect will act upon the recommendations and buy. Prospects may not want to be troubled to give a salesman information about their needs and they may question the value of his recommendations as biased and superficial.

OCCUPATIONAL PROSPECTING

By seeking prospects engaged in the more prosperous occupations, salesmen are able to concentrate their efforts on buyers with greater purchasing power. If economic conditions are favorable, persons in industry and professions are fully employed and earning a good income. When farm prices are high, farmers are in the best position to buy. In periods of inflation, salaried workers whose wages do not keep pace with price increases suffer from curtailed purchasing power. The increase in government employment has created opportunities for salesmen cultivating this class of workers.

In periods of business depression, workers in basic, repeat, and essential industries, such as food, clothing, drugs, and shelter, are usually better able to buy than those employed in specialty lines. In prosperous times, employees connected with luxury services enjoy increased buying power.

By personal observation and by reading business reports and magazines, a salesman can easily discover those occupations and industries which are prospering and confine his efforts to prospecting in those lines.

A specialty salesman may classify his prospects according to their ability to buy, as follows:

Class A. Business and semiprofessional men, executives, professional men, proprietors and partners of large businesses.

Class B. Factory superintendents and supervisors, government officials, small jobbers and dealers, small merchants, professional women, specialty salesmen, college teachers, tradesmen.

Class C. Chain-store managers, skilled factory employees, farm owners, female clerical workers, housewives, salesmen of staples.

Class D. Laborers, domestic servants, clerks, farm tenants, waiters, unskilled workers.

Unit sales of life insurance vary in amount with each of these classifications, as follows:

Class	*Average Sale*
A	$8,320
B	3,670
C	3,130
D	1,620

This illustrates one reason why salesmen of certain types of specialties should use occupational prospecting.

SEASONAL PROSPECTING

Just as economic conditions favor prospecting among certain occupations, so seasonal changes create special needs and make some firms and people better able to buy at certain times of the year.

In the fall, most farmers have been paid for their crops and are in a better position to buy than at any other time. Retail merchants are most active during the fall and early winter months. An enterprising life insurance salesman found that jewelers do about half their annual business in the last two months of the year; by making luncheon and evening appointments with jewelers, he paid for four months' business in 60 days.

Another insurance man found that many teachers are employed at summer camps and schools during the summer. He started with a list of 25 teachers working at summer school and sold five a total of $27,000 worth of insurance during the season.

Prospecting in season, among employees of such industries as fuel, beverages, ice, and sporting goods, not only produces immediate sales, but also creates prospects to carry over to off-seasons.

SELECTING METHODS OF PROSPECTING

Successful prospecting involves the use of not one but several of the methods described previously. A salesman should take into consideration his own preferences and experience and select those methods most suitable to his way of working and best applicable to his situation. Experiments with several prospecting methods will soon indicate to a salesman which plans are most effective for him. Good prospecting demands diversification of method. The most important consideration is not so much what method a salesman should use in prospecting but that he should employ *some definite plan* for locating and qualifying possible customers.

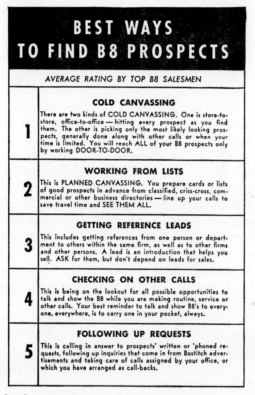

BEST WAYS TO FIND B8 PROSPECTS

AVERAGE RATING BY TOP B8 SALESMEN

1

COLD CANVASSING

There are two kinds of COLD CANVASSING. One is store-to-store, office-to-office — hitting every prospect as you find them. The other is picking only the most likely looking prospects, generally done along with other calls or when your time is limited. You will reach ALL of your B8 prospects only by working DOOR-TO-DOOR.

2

WORKING FROM LISTS

This is PLANNED CANVASSING. You prepare cards or lists of good prospects in advance from classified, criss-cross, commercial or other business directories — line up your calls to save travel time and SEE THEM ALL.

3

GETTING REFERENCE LEADS

This includes getting references from one person or department to others within the same firm, as well as to other firms and other persons. A lead is an introduction that helps you sell. ASK for them, but don't depend on leads for sales.

4

CHECKING ON OTHER CALLS

This is being on the lookout for all possible opportunities to talk and show the B8 while you are making routine, service or other calls. Your best reminder to talk and show B8's to everyone, everywhere, is to carry one in your pocket, always.

5

FOLLOWING UP REQUESTS

This is calling in answer to prospects' written or 'phoned requests, following up inquiries that come in from Bostitch advertisements and taking care of calls assigned by your office, or which you have arranged as call-backs.

FIG. 10. Methods of prospecting used by most successful salesmen of model B8 stapling machines for Bostitch, Inc. Sales are made direct to stores and offices.

QUOTA OF PROSPECTS

A salesman will be more successful in obtaining a sufficient number of prospects if he establishes a daily, weekly, or monthly quota of prospects. Such a definite quota will give him an objective and will ensure him an adequate supply. An experienced salesman can easily determine from past performance the number of prospects that he must secure to maintain a desired volume of sales. By determining the ratio of prospects secured to the number of units or dollar volume sold, a salesman can quickly establish the number of prospects which he must obtain to sell a certain volume. Then by multiplying his total sales expectancy in dollars or units by his prospect ratio, he can quickly determine his prospect quota. If a salesman averages 10 prospects to a sale and he desires to make five sales a month, he must secure a total of 50 prospects a month to obtain his sales quota. Ten new prospects must be secured for every prospect converted into a customer.

Life insurance salesmen sometimes use a 50-name monthly prospect quota plan. On the first day of each month, the names and addresses of 50 suspects who must be seen during that month (an average of two every business day) are listed on a suspect sheet. As the suspects are contacted during the month, their names are either "killed," or "sold," or "transferred" to the 50-name sheet for the succeeding month. By beginning each month with a definite list of names, a salesman is insured a full reservoir of prospects. Analysis of the disposition of prospects, as shown on the sheet, indicates strengths and weaknesses of a salesman's methods.

Prospecting must be a continuous activity if a salesman is to replace those who buy or are disqualified for lack of needs, funds, or authority to buy. When a salesman has exhausted his supply of prospects, it may be necessary for him to take time out from selling to devote one day a week to replenishing his supply of possible customers. Sales momentum is lost when a salesman must stop sales presentations and devote his time exclusively to prospecting. If a list of prospects is accumulated continuously by the addition of one or two new names a day, a salesman never lacks prospects to convert into customers.

"REFERRED" PROSPECTS

The highest grade prospects are often those to whom a salesman is sent or referred by a friend of the prospect. These "referred" prospects are usually obligated to give a courteous hearing to a salesman who has been directed to them by a friend. A salesman who can open an interview by referring to a friend of the prospect establishes his prestige with the buyer and puts the interview on a more friendly basis. The person referring the salesman to the buyer may be willing to arrange an appointment or introduce the salesman with a telephone call or letter of introduction. A salesman usually can secure from his informant much advance information about a referred prospect.

Some salesmen call only on referred prospects. A life insurance salesman who used various methods of prospecting decided that he would make no calls except on persons to whom he had an introduction. In two years he increased his sales from $250,000 to $290,000, a gain of about 16 per cent, with more pleasant working conditions, according to S. G. Dickinson.

However, in interviewing referred prospects, salesmen are often obliged to protect their sources of information. The informant's name must not be disclosed without his permission. A salesman should put the transaction on a business rather than on a friendship basis by requesting that his proposition be considered on its merits rather than out of regard for the prospect's friend who referred the salesman to the buyer.

HOW A SALESMAN SHOULD PROSPECT

Although most experienced salesmen are familiar with the various sources of prospects described previously, few employ these methods skilfully and acquire good prospecting habits. Many salesmen know what constitutes a good prospect, but few have the ability to develop prospects from known sources.

Observation of the methods of good salesmen reveals a successful technique for obtaining prospects from owners, centers of influence, friends, neighbors, and other sources. The six practical steps taken by successful salesmen in locating prospects are summarized here in a six-step routine which, if memorized and practiced by salesmen, will simplify the problem of seeking prospects.

Routine for Securing Prospects

1. Justify your request for prospects.
2. Describe type of prospect wanted.
3. Secure permission to use informant's name.
4. Promise to keep information confidential.
5. Get complete information.
6. Limit the number of names requested.

1. Justify Your Request for Prospects. An influential acquaintance, neighbor, or customer will readily supply a salesman with names of prospects, if the salesman will explain his need for prospects and show the informant how he can aid the salesman and at the same time help his friends. Most people are eager to help salesmen and to have their friends enjoy good products and services.

A salesman should point out that one of his principal problems is locating persons who can profitably use his product or service. To find prospects, he must seek the cooperation of those who are willing

to give him information about people who need the product which he
is selling. A salesman should emphasize that he is not just interested
in increasing his own sales and earnings, but is primarily seeking an
opportunity to be of service to others. If a salesman is genuinely
motivated by a desire to benefit others, he will have little difficulty in
getting the cooperation of his friends and influential persons in locating prospects.

Informants may be told human interest anecdotes illustrating the
profit and satisfaction to be gained from buying the salesman's product. A successful life insurance salesman subordinates his self-
interest and uses human interest anecdotes in prospecting by relating
the following experience:

> Not so long ago one of my friends died, leaving a wife and three small chil-
> dren. His wife came to me for advice. This chap left his family a savings
> account of $800. There was no other estate. The children were two, five,
> and seven years old. What would you have advised her?
>
> Among your friends is a man whose death would practically leave his wife
> and small children dependent upon charity for support. Out of regard for
> his family and their future, it is your duty as a friend to acquaint him with a
> safe, inexpensive way to provide for his loved ones. I would like to meet
> such a man. Will you put me in touch with him?

2. Describe the Type of Prospect Wanted. A salesman should
describe the type of persons whom he is seeking. By painting a word
picture of the qualifications of a desirable prospect, a salesman makes
it possible for his informants to suggest persons who have a genuine
need, ability to pay, authority, accessibility, and of the right type for
the salesman.

For example, an automobile salesman may describe a desirable
prospect as one now owning a car more than two years old in the
same price class as the car sold by the salesman; a person with a
regular income in excess of $3,000 annually; one who uses his car
in business or for pleasure trips; preferably a man with a family; one
who is socially ambitious and desirous of keeping up appearances.

Informants may be given a description of typical prospects whom
the salesman has sold—their age, sex, occupations, number of dependents, home ownership, wealth, standards of living, hobbies, and
other characteristics which reveal the type of persons whom the salesman is seeking.

One life insurance salesman describes the kind of prospect he is
seeking, as follows:

My own experience has taught me that I can operate best by calling on a certain type of person whom I have pictured clearly in mind. I have in mind a man in an executive position of some kind, earning good money, ambitious, and likely to get on; preferably a man who has a family; a man who is in good health and one whom I can approach.

3. Secure Permission to Use Informant's Name. A referred prospect is a preferred prospect, and a salesman should attempt in all cases to secure permission from informants to use their names in contacting prospects. Some informants may refuse to do this for fear of annoying their friends. However, if an informant has confidence in the salesman and is convinced of the merit of a product or service, he is not likely to object to the use of his name.

Many salesmen secure letters of introduction and business cards from informants to facilitate contacts with prospects. Customers and close friends of a salesman may be induced to make personal or telephone calls on prospects to pave the way for his call.

4. Promise to Keep Information Confidential. A salesman may secure from his sources much valuable information about prospects. However, informants should be assured that the salesman's source of information will not be divulged. If an informant does not wish his name to be used, his wishes should be respected. By treating the suggestions confidentially, a salesman secures more information from him as well as his continued cooperation. A good salesman, like an able news reporter, protects his sources of information.

5. Get Complete Information. Good prospecting demands that a salesman secure more than names and addresses of possible buyers. It is necessary to obtain information about a prospect's ability to pay, his need, and his authority to buy.

Tactful inquiries by a salesman bring out much information about possible buyers. A home-appliance salesman obtains information about prospects by questioning his friends about their neighbors. The following dialogue is typical of this salesman's methods:

SALESMAN: Fred, how long have you lived in Brookdale?

FRIEND: Oh, about nine years.

SALESMAN: I suppose you know the families in your block pretty well.

FRIEND: Yes, I know 'em all.

SALESMAN: There are probably several who have had hard luck during the war. If you were to pick out the one family that has suffered least during the war, who would it be?

FRIEND: Why, the Martins. Frank Martin.

SALESMAN: What kind of a business is he in?

FRIEND: He's in the public utility business, the electric company.
SALESMAN: What's his job in the company?
FRIEND: Why, Frank is purchasing agent.
SALESMAN: Do they have a large family?
FRIEND: Yes, his mother and three boys live with them.

In this way the salesman develops facts about suspects to enable him to qualify them as prospects. This method may be used by salesmen of numerous types of products and services. The nature of the questions asked by a salesman will be determined by the type of product which he is selling.

6. Limit the Number of Names Requested. Quality is rather to be desired than quantity in securing prospects. By limiting the number of names requested and getting more facts about each prospect, a salesman can improve the quality of his prospects. An informant rarely will be able to supply adequate information about more than

SALES PERFORMANCE RATING FORM

Locating Prospects

Salesman_____ Date_____

Rated by_____ Over-all Rating_____

Score

I. *Salesman's Method of Securing Prospects*	Excellent 90–100	Good 80–90	Fair 70–80	Poor 60–70	Failure Below 60
A. Justify request for prospects					
B. Describe type of prospect wanted					
C. Get informant's permission to use his name					
D. Offer to treat suggestions in confidence					
E. Obtain complete facts about prospect					

Miscellaneous Comments_____
_____
_____

one or two prospects in a single interview; and a salesman should not impose on the generosity of his friends by asking them for long lists.

A customer or an acquaintance who supplies a salesman with facts about prospects should be thanked for the information and informed as to the outcome of the efforts to sell the persons or firms suggested.

Problem I

Locating Prospects

George M. Tyler, representing Eastern Reserve Life Insurance Company

George M. Tyler, thirty years old, has been associated with the Eastern Reserve Life Insurance Company for two years in the Indianapolis, Ind., agency. He concentrates his sales efforts on young men with vision, intelligence, ambition, and good possibilities of making more money in the future. He has two objectives on every call, to sell and to prospect.

In the following interview, Tyler is calling upon William B. Boulter, single, a university graduate, about twenty-six years of age, who is employed in the research department of a manufacturing concern. Tyler obtained Boulter's name and information about him from Tom Maxon, a policyholder and friend of Boulter.

Tyler calls without appointment at Boulter's office. Boulter meets the salesman in the lobby and the following conversation ensues:

1. SALESMAN: Good morning, Mr. Boulter, my name is George Tyler of the Eastern Reserve Life Insurance Company. I didn't come here to talk business now because I know we can only have a few minutes. The other day Tom Maxon and I were talking about plans to help us young men to become successful financially. He thought my ideas worth while and suggested that I meet you. I called to find out when I might see you outside of your business hours to bring you these ideas.

2. PROSPECT: I just bought $6,000 worth of insurance last month and can't think of more insurance for a while. I'm glad to have met you and if you're around this way again sometime drop in and see me. I won't need any more life insurance for some time.

3. SALESMAN: Mr. Boulter, I can see your position clearly. You are well taken care of and are not a prospect for me now. However, Bill, there is something I want to ask you. If it is asking too much, don't mind telling me. Tom Maxon seemed to think you knew a number of young men who are worth while. Are there any men from your college class who are working in Indianapolis? (Salesman takes a pencil and paper from his pocket and prepares to write down names and information.)

4. PROSPECT: I can't think of anyone who would be interested.

5. SALESMAN: That may be true but I want to meet these young men as I have met you. As we go along, it is a pleasure to have a wide acquaintanceship. I have enjoyed meeting you and as time passes, we may be of service to each other.

6. PROSPECT: I can't think of anyone right now. Everybody I know has plenty of life insurance.

7. SALESMAN: It's hard to think of names out of a clear sky and I don't expect you to know anybody who is ready to buy. I do want to meet these young men anyway for future service. Are any of the fellows who went to school with you working here?

8. PROSPECT: No.

9. SALESMAN: Are any of your old schoolmates working at the Horton Manufacturing Company or the Dixon Tool Works or Silby, Wilcox, and Company?

10. PROSPECT: I don't like to send anyone to my friends. I don't know anything about their personal affairs.

11. SALESMAN: I know how you feel. However, I operate this way. After I have met a man, I never call again unless he asks me to. He will not be bothered and I may be of real service to him. It hasn't been unpleasant to talk to me, has it?

12. PROSPECT: No, I've just received a letter from a friend of mine living here in town who might be of interest to you.

13. SALESMAN: I'll be glad to meet him.

14. PROSPECT: His name is Jack Turner, and he is connected with the First National Bank.

15. SALESMAN: I certainly appreciate your help. What about new men and those who have had recent raises in the plant here? I'd like to know something about their age, whether they are single or married, and their approximate salaries.

16. PROSPECT: I've only been here a short time and don't know much about the men in the works.

17. SALESMAN: I see. At any rate, I appreciate your giving me Turner's name. So long.

18. PROSPECT: Good-by.

Questions

1. What method of prospecting is the salesman using in this case? Is this method in general, not referring to the way it is used here, effective? Why?

2. Did the salesman justify his request for prospects? How?

3. Did he describe the type of prospect wanted? How?

4. Did he secure permission to use Boulter's name?

5. Did he promise to keep informant's information confidential?

6. Did he limit the number of names requested?

Problem II

LOCATING PROSPECTS

Martin Crocker, representing Federal Insurance Company

The Federal Insurance Company, Pittsburgh, Pa., established in 1860, has assets in excess of one billion dollars and more than eight billion dollars' worth of insurance in force. It is represented by 10,000 part and full-time life underwriters. The average life policy sold is $3,500. The average earnings of three-quarters of the company's representatives are in excess of $200 a month. More than 3,000 representatives have been with the company over five years.

Martin Crocker is one of 30 salesmen associated with the Clyde Linton Chicago agency of the company, which he joined in 1928, after five years of sales work. Crocker uses the programing method of selling, auditing the life insurance carried by influential persons, and making recommendations for more effective coverage of their insurance needs. He asks each of his prospects, for whom he has made an audit, to write him a letter of recommendation, stating the value of the services which he has been able to render. These letters are used by Crocker in approaching men to whom he has no introduction and in answering objections.

The following interview illustrates Crocker's method of obtaining information about prospects and a letter of recommendation from a policyholder or prospect for whom he has prepared a program. This interview is a verbatim account of the conversation between salesman Crocker and Joseph Connelly to whom Crocker recently has sold a $20,000 life policy.

1. SALESMAN: Joe, from what you have said, I know you have profited from my work. I am glad that you do like it and I am sure you know someone else who can also profit from the same kind of information. Whom do you know who is making progress in his work, or who seems to be in line for further advancement? Perhaps there are such men in your organization, in your neighborhood or your club, or right here in your own office. Who comes to your mind first?

2. POLICYHOLDER: Martin, I just can't think of anybody right offhand, but I will certainly keep you in mind and let you know when I do think of someone.

3. SALESMAN: Well, Joe, how about the fellow who was holding that meeting in here Saturday morning? He seemed to be telling the fellows what it was all about.

4. POLICYHOLDER: Oh, you mean Ned Powers. Yeah, he's a swell guy—his bite isn't as bad as his bark.

5. SALESMAN: What position does he hold?

6. POLICYHOLDER: He's field service manager of the company. He's right on his toes and doing a good job.

7. SALESMAN: Is he married?

8. POLICYHOLDER: Yes, he's married.

9. SALESMAN: Any children?

10. POLICYHOLDER: Yes, two girls, one sixteen and one thirteen, I believe.

11. SALESMAN: Does he seem to be in good health?

12. POLICYHOLDER: Yes.

13. SALESMAN: Well, Joe, anybody who could tell 'em like that boy did would have to be in good health. He certainly built a fire under them. About what income bracket is he in?

14. POLICYHOLDER: Well, I don't exactly know. I would say reasonably well above the $5,000 figure.

15. SALESMAN: Does he own his own home?

16. POLICYHOLDER: I believe that he rents.

17. SALESMAN: How about his habits? Does he golf? What does he do, Joe?

18. POLICYHOLDER: I think he plays golf.

19. SALESMAN: Is he a college man?

20. POLICYHOLDER: Yes, but I'm not sure about the school he attended.

21. SALESMAN: Well, if he has impressed you so favorably he certainly is the type of man I would like to know. I'm going to stop in to see him sometime soon. It may be a little while before I have an opportunity to do so. I'll tell you what I would like to have you do, write a letter to Ned Powers telling him what you think of my work. This letter will help us to get acquainted when I do call.

22. POLICYHOLDER: I would like very much to do it for you, Martin, but frankly I don't like to refer a salesman to my friends.

23. SALESMAN: Well, Joe, your unwillingness to refer salesmen to your friends is certainly understandable. I'd probably feel much the same way were I in your position. Let's go back to the time when I introduced myself to you through the medium of my friend and client, Jack Brothers. It would have been impossible then for me to have won your confidence, as I needed to have it, without the recommendation of Mr. Brothers. I would have stood before you as just another life insurance man. You can easily see now how vital a part your confidence has played in my correct interpretation of your problem and recommendations for its solution. In giving me the information you have about Ned Powers, you have furnished me with a great deal of background I need. I am sure that you can see now that in order for me to properly maintain my professional standing, it is imperative

that I borrow temporarily the confidence that Mr. Powers has in you, until I have had the opportunity to develop his confidence in me.

24. POLICYHOLDER: Martin, you've got me on the fence.

25. SALESMAN: Joe, let's put it another way. If Mr. Powers were to walk in this office right now, would you hesitate to introduce me to him and tell him what you have just told me about the quality of my work? That is all I want you to do by means of this letter of recommendation—simply introduce me to Ned Powers in a way that I will merit his attention. I recognize that it is up to me then to serve him as I have served you, in order to obtain his full confidence. So, won't you call your secretary in and give her this letter?

26. POLICYHOLDER: Well, I'll make an exception in this case, because I believe your plan really has merit, and we'll see how it works.

27. SALESMAN: I certainly appreciate your help and am sure you won't regret it.

Questions

1. What method of prospecting is the salesman using in this case? Is this method in general, not referring to the way it is used here, effective? Why?

2. Did the salesman justify his request for prospects. How?

3. Did he describe the type of prospect wanted? How?

4. Did he promise to keep the information confidential?

5. Did he get complete information?

6. Did he limit the number of names requested?

7. Is the letter of recommendation a sound device to use in contacting the prospect? Give your reasons for or against.

8. Should the salesman have used other methods of prospecting? What? Why?

Reading References

J. R. DAUBMAN, "Salesmanship and Types of Selling," pp. 136–138, F. S. Crofts & Co., New York, 1939.

CHARLES H. FERNALD, "Salesmanship," pp. 458–459, Prentice-Hall, Inc., New York, 1945.

HAROLD M. HAAS, "A Short Course in Salesmanship," Chap. XI, Prentice-Hall, Inc., New York, 1939.

PAUL W. IVEY, "Successful Salesmanship," pp. 230–231, Prentice-Hall, Inc., New York, 1947.

W. A. MATHESON, "The Selling Man," pp. 49–55, Keating Publishers, Inc., New York, 1947.

DAVID E. OSBORNE, "Salesmanship for Today for Salesmanagers of Tomorrow," Chap. IV, Harper & Brothers, New York, 1939.

CHARLES B. ROTH, "Finding the Prospect and Getting the Interview," pp. 20–39, Prentice-Hall, Inc., New York, 1946.

FREDERIC A. RUSSELL and F. BEACH, "Textbook of Salesmanship," Chap. VII, McGraw-Hill Book Company, Inc., New York, 1949.

HARRY SIMMONS, "A Practical Course in Successful Selling," Chap. V, Harper & Brothers, New York, 1939.

DONALD K. SMITH, "Essentials of Selling," Chap. IV, Prentice-Hall, Inc., New York, 1945.

CHAPTER XIV

PLANNED SALES PRESENTATIONS

Napoleon was seated in his tent; before him lay a map of Italy. He took two pins, stuck them in the map, measured, moved the pins, and measured again. "I shall meet him there," he said, pointing to Marengo. By skillful planning, Napoleon crossed the Alps, led his army onto the Plains of Lombardy, surprised Melas, the Old Fox of Austria, and inflicted a crushing defeat, deciding the Italian campaign by a single plan of action.

Because he planned his battles on paper months before they were fought, Napoleon achieved victories so habitually that it has been said that he won his battles before he fought them. Similarly, salesmen who plan their sales presentations before they deliver them are invariably more successful than men who rely upon inspiration when face to face with prospects.

Successful salesmanship is 90 per cent preparation and 10 per cent presentation. However, many salesmen confuse planned sales presentations with the much-maligned memorized presentations or "canned" sales talks breathlessly delivered in a mechanical monologue by inexperienced salesmen. This common conception of prepared sales presentations has brought planned selling into disfavor with many salesmen. However, there are four types of planned presentations, each of which, when properly used and intelligently applied, has many advantages.

Unplanned sales presentations cause salesmen to lack confidence, substitute oratory or personality for sound arguments, misstate and exaggerate, ramble, discourse illogically, omit important sales points, waste time, and tell an incomplete story.

Before a lawyer faces a jury he spends many hours preparing his case, reading, accumulating evidence, and interviewing witnesses, because he knows that the better his preparation, the greater his chances of convincing the jury of the justice of his plea. Like a good lawyer, a successful salesman prepares his arguments in advance of his interviews; he acquaints himself with the needs of his prospect; he assembles ideas, illustrations, and facts to meet these needs and arranges them in the most effective order; he anticipates possible objections and has answers ready. A salesman may adopt the tested presentations of the successful salesmen in his company and use them in interviewing prospects.

Planned sales presentations are more essential today than ever before as buyers demand that salesmen be better informed and render superior service. Keen competition is forcing salesmen to prepare for sales interviews by knowing in advance what they are going to say and how they are going to say it.

TYPES OF PLANNED SALES PRESENTATIONS

There are four distinct types of planned sales presentations, each of which has its particular usefulness according to the type of product and customer, the experience of the salesman, and the objective of the interview. These four types are: (1) standard sales presentation; (2) outlined sales presentation; (3) survey or program presentation; (4) work-sheet presentation.

These four types of planned presentations are valuable for beginners as well as experienced salesmen of many kinds of products and services. When properly used by a beginner salesman, they enable him to have something worth while to say, to start producing in a shorter time, and to train himself. When used by experienced salesmen, they prevent visiting and casual conversations with customers and prospects, keep a salesman on the track, result in more interesting interviews with prospects, and make for a more logical order of presentation of the significant facts.

1. STANDARD SALES PRESENTATION

A standard sales presentation or "canned" sales talk is the most maligned and common type of planned interview. It is a complete sales presentation written and memorized in advance and repeated verbatim to buyers.

A standard presentation is based on observations and recordings of the most effective statements of successful salesmen. Statements used by salesmen in approaching, demonstrating, meeting objections, presenting facts, and closing sales are incorporated into a single presentation. The sales arguments are presented in logical order leading up to a conclusion and represent the "one best way" to make a sales presentation for a particular article or service.

The originator of the standard sales presentation was the late

John H. Patterson of the National Cash Register Company who, fifty years ago, visited 51 sales agencies in 50 days and had a stenographer take down the sales talks of the best salesmen in the organization. From these notes, Mr. Patterson prepared a standard presentation for approach and demonstration which all salesmen were and still are required to memorize and use in selling cash registers to merchants.

A standard sales presentation is a complete discussion of all of the features of a product and usually includes (1) an opening to get the attention and arouse the interest of a prospect in a specific need for the product or service; (2) a description of how the product meets the prospect's needs or solves his difficulties; (3) proof or evidence of how the product has satisfied the needs of other persons through substantiated facts in the form of statistics, testimonials, references, tests, and guarantees; (4) a conclusion that motivates a prospect to buy through special inducements.

A standard sales presentation may include a demonstration presentation for mechanical products involving the following steps: (1) creating anticipation by arousing the interest of the prospect in features to be demonstrated; (2) showing how the product meets the prospect's needs; (3) getting the prospect to take part in the demonstration; (4) requesting an order.

When prospecting is an important function of selling, a standard prospecting presentation may be used involving the following steps: (1) securing the interest of an informant in aiding the salesman; (2) painting a picture of the type of prospect desired; (3) obtaining information from the informant about his friends and acquaintances; (4) getting an informant's permission to use his name as a reference.

Salesmen who use standard memorized sales presentations that are based on the work of successful salesmen are less likely to make exaggerated statements and claims, use better and more forceful English, emphasize the most important sales points, always have something worth while to say, and tell a more complete story in a shorter time.

The principal weaknesses of a standard presentation are the following: it is not adaptable to individual prospects, it embarrasses a salesman, it destroys his originality and initiative, and it may not suit his personality. Interruptions and digressions by a prospect disconcert a salesman using a memorized presentation and disrupt the continuity of his talk. A salesman has no opportunity to discover the motives and interests of his prospects. A sales interview becomes a monologue and a prospect has little chance to participate in the conversation. A salesman is likely to tell too much or discuss features of no interest to a prospect and create ill will by forced delivery. The chief complaint against a standard memorized sales talk is that it cannot be delivered naturally. The average salesman delivers it rapidly, in an artificial and monotonous voice, which irritates or amuses prospects and holds a salesman up to ridicule.

When the advantages and weaknesses of standard memorized presentations are considered, it must be admitted that few salesmen have the ability to repeat a standard presentation effectively. The average salesman who attempts to deliver a memorized sales talk is self-conscious, ill at ease, and awkward. He is thinking of words foreign to his vocabulary and his discussion sounds unnatural.

However, if a standard presentation is rewritten by a salesman in his own words, it is more natural and effective. When a salesman does not have the benefit of a standard presentation prepared by his management, he can write his own sales talk to suit his own ideas and methods. If he originates his own talk or rewrites a standard presentation prepared by his company, he usually has more confidence in it and delivers it more naturally than if he repeats it verbatim.

All salesmen would benefit by memorizing a standard presentation. In the process of memorizing, many product facts are learned and a logical method of presenting them acquired. For this reason all salesmen should memorize a standard sales talk whether or not they use it in sales interviews.

A salesman who memorizes a standard talk acquires a knowledge of the principal sales points of his product, the answers to many common objections, more confidence, and an adequate supply of reasons why prospects should buy.

A standard presentation written by a salesman or his company is of particular value to salesmen in the following situations:

1. A memorized presentation will get beginner salesmen, who are unfamiliar with a product, into early production.

2. Salesmen of simple, inexpensive products, such as books, hosiery, cosmetics, corsets, vacuum cleaners, or brushes, sold direct to consumers, can find in a standard presentation many valuable sales points.

3. Salesmen selling life insurance or investments for a single need, such as retirement, education, or family income.

Although a salesman may never deliver a standard presentation to buyers, it is important to memorize a good sales talk. The importance of memorizing a standard presentation is emphasized by the sales training director of a large electric refrigerator manufacturer, who says:

The number of salesmen who will use a verbatim talk in the presence of prospects will be extremely low. However, under no circumstances would I ever give up recommending that every salesman in a specialty sales organization be forced to memorize a standard presentation. We have proved conclusively that a salesman who has memorized a standard canvass will unconsciously adopt much of the phraseology from the standard talk and tend to follow the sequence of the points outlined.

Memorized standard sales presentations have been used extensively in life insurance selling. Three hundred salesmen representing one large life insurance company successfully use a standard sales talk. In another life insurance company salesmen using standard sales presentations produced twice as much business per man in their first year as men not using them. The representatives of one large insurance company who use standard sales talks remain with the company twice as long as those agents who extemporize in their sales interviews. Salesmen who do not use standard presentations suffer a 25 per cent decrease in sales their second year with the company; those using memorized presentations increase their sales in the second year.

Routine for Making a Standard Presentation

1. Adapt to needs of prospect.
2. Deliver naturally.
3. Allow prospect to participate.
4. Secure action.

1. Adapt to Needs of Prospect. Standard presentations are built around a particular need for a product or service. It is essential that the prospect interviewed have the need discussed in the standard presentation. One great weakness in the use of standard presentations is that they are often delivered to persons who do not need the product for the purpose discussed by the salesman.

If there are several major needs for a product, a salesman should have a standard presentation for each need so that the presentation can be adapted to the need of each individual buyer. For example, an insurance salesman interviewing a father who is planning to send his children to college can logically use an "educational fund" standard sales presentation. But in the case of a nurse without dependents, a "retirement income" standard presentation would be more logical.

Select prospects with the specific need featured in the standard sales presentation.

2. Deliver Naturally. Unless a standard presentation can be delivered naturally, it should not be used. Mechanical, rapid, and artificial delivery of a standard presentation immediately identifies it as a memorized or "canned" sales talk, and prospects lose interest or discredit the salesman's presentation. By rewriting a presentation and committing it thoroughly to memory, it is possible for a salesman to make a presentation such an integral part of his thinking that it can be naturally delivered.

3. Allow Prospect to Participate. A standard presentation which is delivered as a monologue bores most buyers who want an opportunity to express their views about their needs and the product under discussion. By pausing from time to time to allow the buyer to ask questions, or raise objections, a salesman gives consideration to the prospect's opinions and avoids the impression of high-pressure tactics.

4. Secure Action. A standard presentation, like every good sales interview, should lead to definite action by the prospect in the form of a signed order, appointment for return call or demonstration, appraisal of a trade-in, or other action leading to an eventual sale.

2. Outlined Sales Presentations

An outlined sales presentation involves a short summary in the form of heads and subheads of the most significant features of the sales talk. Each heading in the outline is memorized by the salesman in the order in which it is to be presented and the supporting material is spoken extemporaneously.

A sales-presentation outline usually is developed by a company after observation and analysis of the interviewing methods of its successful salesmen. Or a salesman may prepare his own outline of his procedure in making a sale, arranging each step in logical order from the introduction to the close of the interview.

The advantages of an outlined presentation compared with a standard canvass are that a salesman is free to vary his presentation according to the needs and motives of the prospect; he can return to his train of thought more easily than if he departs from a memorized talk; he is more natural, conversational, and therefore more interesting and convincing; the opinions and viewpoints of the prospect are considered; there is no tension or domination by the salesman.

In addition, a salesman who uses an outlined presentation is clear and coherent; he avoids irrelevant ideas, emphasizes the most important sales points, saves time, and has definite interview objectives.

The principal objections to an outlined presentation are as follows: salesmen who lack knowledge are unable to amplify the major steps in an outline; words and ideas chosen on the inspiration of the moment are often unconvincing; salesmen may grope for elusive ideas and lose the attention of prospects.

Outlined presentations are most effective in selling products or services of a complex character which satisfy a variety of needs and appeal to a variety of buying motives. High-priced consumer specialties and industrial goods are often sold with an outlined presentation. Experienced salesman, who are thoroughly familiar with all features of their products and who are resourceful in expression can use an outline presentation effectively.

Sales-presentation Outlines. Outlined sales presentations used for various types of products illustrate how a sales interview outline is prepared. Salesmen of a well-known make of automobile memorize and base their sales presentations on the following five-point outline:

1. Begin every interview by locating and appealing to the prospect's needs.
2. Tell how the product fits the prospect's needs.
3. Show how the product fits the prospect's needs.
4. Look for the first opportunity to get an order.
5. Attempt to close a sale in every interview.

Retail salesmen of a famous make of automobile tire use the following six-step presentation outline, which is based on the sales methods of numerous successful retail salesmen of this product:

1. Greet each prospect promptly and courteously.
2. Carefully analyze each customer's driving needs.
3. Demonstrate outside and inside story of quality.
4. Explain the complete year-round service.
5. Quote prices.
6. Close the transaction so that satisfaction is assured.

Salesmen of this company are given suggestions and advice for carrying out each step in the above presentation.

Retail salesmen of a well-known brand of electric refrigerators are trained to follow tested sales-presentation methods by using the following five-point outline:

1. Get the favorable attention of the prospect in the opening sentence.

BLUEPRINT OF B8 SELLING

THE PROPOSITION	THE PRESENTATION
	SELLING PLANS AND IDEAS YOU CAN USE TO MAKE MORE B8 SALES

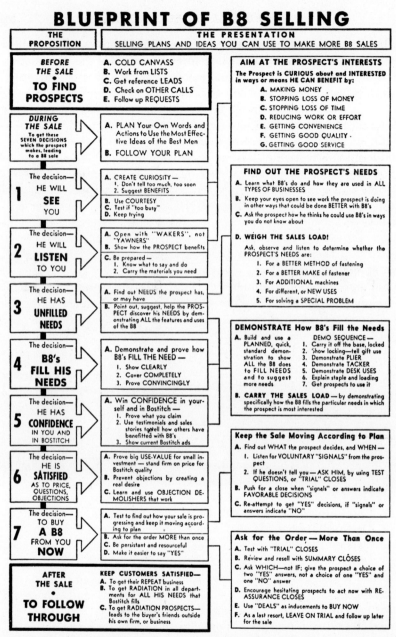

BEFORE THE SALE
•
TO FIND PROSPECTS

A. COLD CANVASS
B. Work from LISTS
C. Get reference LEADS
D. Check on OTHER CALLS
E. Follow up REQUESTS

AIM AT THE PROSPECT'S INTERESTS
The Prospect is CURIOUS about and INTERESTED in ways or means HE CAN BENEFIT by:
A. MAKING MONEY
B. STOPPING LOSS OF MONEY
C. STOPPING LOSS OF TIME
D. REDUCING WORK OR EFFORT
E. GETTING CONVENIENCE
F. GETTING GOOD QUALITY
G. GETTING GOOD SERVICE

DURING THE SALE
To get these SEVEN DECISIONS which the prospect makes, leading to a B8 sale

A. PLAN Your Own Words and Actions to Use the Most Effective Ideas of the Best Men
B. FOLLOW YOUR PLAN

1 The decision— HE WILL SEE YOU

A. CREATE CURIOSITY —
1. Don't tell too much, too soon
2. Suggest BENEFITS
B. Use COURTESY
C. Test if "too busy"
D. Keep trying

FIND OUT THE PROSPECT'S NEEDS
A. Learn what B8's do and how they are used in ALL TYPES OF BUSINESSES
B. Keep your eyes open to see work the prospect is doing in other ways that could be done BETTER with B8's
C. Ask the prospect how he thinks he could use B8's in ways you do not know about

2 The decision— HE WILL LISTEN TO YOU

A. Open with "WAKERS", not "YAWNERS"
B. Show how the PROSPECT benefits
C. Be prepared —
1. Know what to say and do
2. Carry the materials you need

D. WEIGH THE SALES LOAD!
Ask, observe and listen to determine whether the PROSPECT'S NEEDS are:
1. For a BETTER METHOD of fastening
2. For a BETTER MAKE of fastener
3. For ADDITIONAL machines
4. For different, or NEW USES
5. For solving a SPECIAL PROBLEM

3 The decision— HE HAS UNFILLED NEEDS

A. Find out NEEDS the prospect has, or may have
B. Point out, suggest, help the PROSPECT discover his NEEDS by demonstrating ALL the features and uses of the B8

DEMONSTRATE How B8's Fill the Needs
A. Build and use a PLANNED, quick, standard demonstration to show ALL the B8 does to FILL NEEDS and to suggest more needs

DEMO SEQUENCE—
1. Carry it off the base, locked
2. Show locking—tell gift use
3. Demonstrate PLIER
4. Demonstrate TACKER
5. Demonstrate DESK USES
6. Explain staple and loading
7. Get prospects to use it

B. CARRY THE SALES LOAD — by demonstrating specifically how the B8 fills the particular needs in which the prospect is most interested

4 The decision— B8's FILL HIS NEEDS

A. Demonstrate and prove how B8's FILL THE NEED —
1. Show CLEARLY
2. Cover COMPLETELY
3. Prove CONVINCINGLY

5 The decision— HE HAS CONFIDENCE IN YOU AND IN BOSTITCH

A. Win CONFIDENCE in yourself and in Bostitch —
1. Prove what you claim
2. Use testimonials and sales stories to tell how others have benefitted with B8's
3. Show current Bostitch ads

Keep the Sale Moving According to Plan
A. Find out WHAT the prospect decides, and WHEN —
1. Listen for VOLUNTARY "SIGNALS" from the prospect
2. If he doesn't tell you — ASK HIM, by using TEST QUESTIONS, or "TRIAL" CLOSES
B. Push for a close when "signals" or answers indicate FAVORABLE DECISIONS
C. Re-attempt to get "YES" decisions, if "signals" or answers indicate "NO"

6 The decision— HE IS SATISFIED AS TO PRICE, QUESTIONS, OBJECTIONS

A. Prove big USE-VALUE for small investment — stand firm on price for Bostitch quality
B. Prevent objections by creating a real desire
C. Learn and use OBJECTION DEMOLISHERS that work

7 The decision— TO BUY A B8 FROM YOU NOW

A. Test to find out how your sale is progressing and keep it moving according to plan
B. Ask for the order MORE than once
C. Be persistant and resourceful
D. Make it easier to say "YES"

Ask for the Order — More Than Once
A. Test with "TRIAL" CLOSES
B. Review and resell with SUMMARY CLOSES
C. Ask WHICH—not IF; give the prospect a choice of two "YES" answers, not a choice of one "YES" and one "NO" answer
D. Encourage hesitating prospects to act now with RE-ASSURANCE CLOSES
E. Use "DEALS" as inducements to BUY NOW
F. As a last resort, LEAVE ON TRIAL and follow up later for the sale

AFTER THE SALE
•
TO FOLLOW THROUGH

KEEP CUSTOMERS SATISFIED—
A. To get their REPEAT business
B. To get RADIATION in all departments for ALL HIS NEEDS that Bostitch fills
C. To get RADIATION PROSPECTS— leads to the buyer's friends outside his own firm, or business

FIG. 11. Blueprint of planned sales presentation used by 250 salesmen of Bostitch Inc. in selling B8 model stapling machines to industrial concerns. This planned presentation is largely credited with increasing sales 100 per cent in 1948 with 10 per cent additional salesmen employed. This presentation can be applied to the sale of all types of specialties.

2. Arouse interest by answering his question, "Why bring that up?"

3. Build up desire by appealing to one or more of the five following buying motives: comfort and convenience, safety and protection, gain and economy, satisfaction of pride, or satisfaction of affection.

4. Prove the advantages to gain the following five buying decisions: the need, the brand, the source, the price, and the time.

5. Ask for action to close the sale.

Salesmen representing a large brush manufacturer, selling direct to consumers, use the following eight-point sales-presentation outline:

1. Place gift cards.
2. Redeem gift cards.
3. Give free brush.
4. Parade brushes in sets before the prospect.
5. Demonstrate brushes in which the prospect is interested.
6. Attempt to close on brushes that the prospect needs.
7. Use illustrated portfolio to increase size of order.
8. Get the order.

Product-Point Outlines. Outlines of the principal selling points of a product or service are helpful to salesmen in presenting product features. A large linoleum manufacturer has prepared sales-point outlines for each product in its line. These outlines are fixed so firmly in a salesman's mind that the sales features are recalled every time a product is mentioned in a sales interview. However, when a salesman has memorized a product-point outline, the major product features immediately come to his mind, arranged in logical order and ready to enable him to make a worth-while presentation.

An example of a typical sales-point outline for one type of linoleum follows:

1. Special "super-key" construction.
2. Extra cost of linoleum mix.
3. No loss in thickness.
4. Smoother surface.
5. Superior marbling.
6. Outstanding patterns.

The following product-outline of the exterior features of a popular make of electric refrigerator is used by refrigerator salesmen in interviewing prospects:

1. Designed by famous stylist.
2. New high-crowned door.
3. Ionic column fluting.

4. New embossed name plate.
5. Lifetime porcelain finish.
6. New satin-finished finger-tip latch.
7. New piano-type hinge.
8. New stainless-steel base grill.

Memorizing Presentation Outlines. If a sales-presentation outline is thoroughly memorized, a salesman can move logically and unhesitatingly from one step in the sale to another.

Some salesmen write their sales-presentation outline on the back of a business card and refer to it during interviews with prospects. This serves as a reminder of steps to be taken during an interview.

The value of outlined presentations is illustrated by the experience of a life insurance salesman who outlined his interviews in advance of calls and increased his sales 60 per cent in nine months. Another man in the same business decided to make only three points in each sales interview and increased his sales volume 30 per cent in 60 days.

Routine for Making an Outline Presentation

1. Adhere to outline.
2. Amplify each point in outline.
3. Get prospect participation.
4. Secure action.

1. Adhere to Outline. An outlined sales presentation is effective because it represents the logical organization of the most convincing sales arguments based on the experience of successful salesmen of a particular product or service. Because it has been proved effective, each part should be presented in the same logical order as in the original outline if it is to be used successfully. Some salesmen carry a small card listing the principal outline headings as a reminder to follow the outline in making sales presentations. An outline is easily memorized and when committed to memory should be followed closely in presentations. Only by adhering to the accepted outline can the full advantages of this type of presentation be secured.

2. Amplify Each Point in Outline. Outline headings merely suggest subject matter to be presented. It is essential that salesmen familiarize themselves thoroughly with the needs of buyers and product or service features so that the outline can be amplified to the fullest in making outline presentations. Supplementary outlines of product points are helpful in providing facts about such product features as raw materials, processes of manufacture, and design.

3. Get Prospect Participation. A good outline presentation is a dialogue in which a prospect has an opportunity to ask questions and to participate. The outline is merely a guide for discussion in which the buyer should be encouraged to express himself to the fullest.

4. Secure Action. As in all good sales presentations, the salesman should secure an order or get the buyer's permission to consider the salesman's proposition further.

3. Survey or Program Presentation

A survey or program sales presentation is a written plus oral proposal to a buyer based on a survey or analysis of the prospect's needs and ability to buy the product or service recommended. The process of making a survey or program presentation has been compared to the two primary steps in photography: taking the picture and developing the negative. In a survey presentation, a salesman first obtains a clear impression or picture of a prospect's requirements and then develops a plan involving the product or service in the solution of the prospect's problem. The written proposal which is prepared for the prospect usually is discussed orally by the salesman.

A survey or program presentation usually consists of five steps, as follows: (*a*) selling the survey; (*b*) getting the facts; (*c*) diagnosing the facts; (*d*) building a proposal or program; (*e*) selling the proposal.

a. Selling the survey to the prospect is the first step to be taken by a salesman in making a survey presentation. Frequently one or more interviews are devoted to this purpose. The initial interview is designed to sell the survey, reduce sales resistance, make a prospect conscious of his need, obtain consent to an analysis of his situation, and secure his agreement to carry out the proposed program if feasible. In selling a survey a salesman may show a prospect examples of other surveys which he has conducted and testimonials from satisfied customers who have carried out the programs recommended.

b. Getting the facts about the prospect's problem is the second step in a survey presentation. This may be done at the initial interview or, if the situation of the prospect is complex, several interviews may be necessary. The salesman may require the assistance of engineers, technicians, analysts, and other specialists to diagnose the prospect's difficulty. Extensive study of the properties, existing equipment,

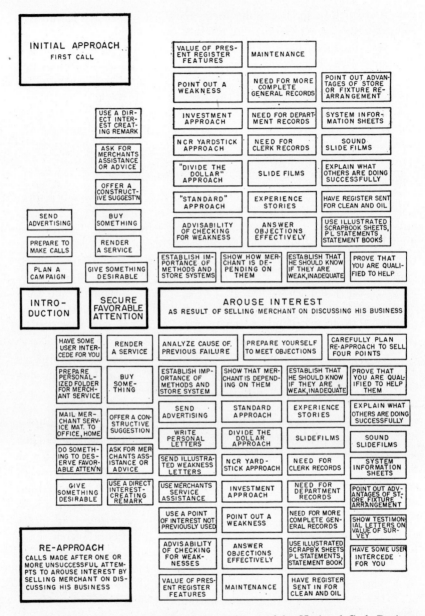

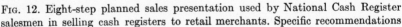

Fig. 12. Eight-step planned sales presentation used by National Cash Register salesmen in selling cash registers to retail merchants. Specific recommendations

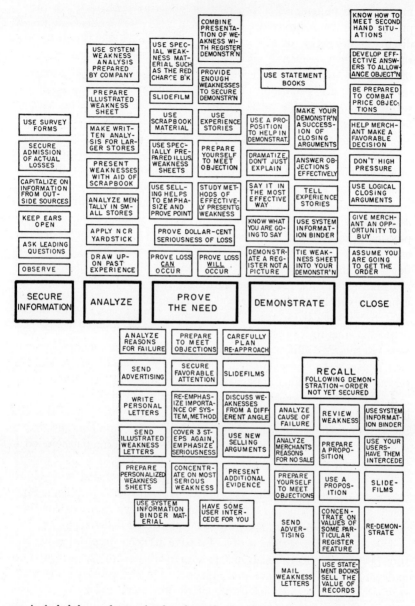

are included for each step in the planned sale which may be profitably used by salesmen of all types of specialties to merchants as well as consumers.

methods, or policies of a prospect is sometimes necessary before a proposal can be submitted. A salesman may use a questionnaire to discover the needs of the prospect. Facts may be obtained also through direct personal observation of the prospect's methods or problems or through interviewing employees, neighbors, or others familiar with his situation. The more information a salesman can secure, the better able he is to prepare a good program or offer an acceptable solution.

c. *Diagnosing the facts* is the next step to be taken by a salesman. This may be done in case of simple needs in the presence of the prospect, but is usually undertaken for complex needs in the salesman's office. Frequently the facts obtained by the salesman in his survey are turned over to analysts or engineers for diagnosis. A salesman is in a position similar to that of a doctor who makes a physical examination of a patient, considers all the facts that his examination has revealed, and determines their significance. In making a diagnosis of a prospect's situation, some salesmen use a survey or "plan sheet" for listing the data obtained. Although considerable time is involved in collecting and analyzing facts for complex needs, this groundwork is essential if a salesman is to make intelligent recommendations to a prospect.

A salesman's ability to diagnose a problem and recommend a solution depends, to a great extent, on his knowledge of his product or service and its various applications to the prospect's situation.

d. *Building a proposal or program* involves a written description of the prospect's current situation, present equipment, or facilities plus the salesman's recommendations for service or equipment needed to solve the problem. A full statement of cost and terms is included in the proposal.

The proposal, usually typewritten, may be illustrated with charts or diagrams to picture the solution of the prospect's problem. Since every prospect's situation differs in numerous ways from that of every other prospect, each proposal obviously must be "custom-made."

The following description of a six-page written proposal submitted to a prospect by a life insurance salesman illustrates the typical form and content of a program presentation. On the first page is a description of the present insurance of the prospect and how it will be paid in case of death. On page two is a list of recommendations. On page three a complete program is described with minimum cash and monthly incomes and the extent to which present holdings satisfy the prospect's needs. On the fourth page retirement income features are described. On page five are shown the cost of the prospect's existing insurance and the additional cost necessary to provide the recommended income and cash. On page six is a compromise minimum program which is offered by the salesman in the event the prospect is unable to undertake the original plan recommended.

e. Selling the proposal is the final and most important step. The salesman undertakes to close the sale of the program recommended at a separate interview, preferably on appointment at a time when the prospect can give careful consideration to the salesman's proposal. A successful method of presenting a program to ensure its being properly understood by a prospect is described in detail in the following routine:

Routine for Making a Survey or Program Presentation

1. Thank prospect for survey opportunity.
2. Control the presentation.
3. Get prospect to participate in the discussion.
4. Commit prospect on the proposal.
5. Secure prospect's implied consent or offer a compromise.

1. Thank Prospect for Survey Opportunity. The prospect has given liberally of his time and may have been put to some inconvenience in furnishing the salesman with information about his needs and situation. The salesman in making his presentation should recognize the contribution of the prospect and express appreciation for his assistance and cooperation in making the survey possible. A salesman who expresses his appreciation makes a favorable impression on the prospect and prepares the way for a fair consideration of the proposition.

By speaking sincerely in praise of the steps which may have been taken by the prospect toward a solution of his problem, the salesman prepares the way for his proposal. If the salesman recognizes the value of competing products or services used by the prospect, the good will of the prospect is secured.

2. Control the Presentation. Care should be taken by the salesman to control the typewritten material, charts, and diagrams used in his program presentation. The prospect should not be handed the proposal in its entirety to read at his leisure. Rather each page or illustration should be introduced separately by the salesman and completely discussed before turning to another feature of the program.

The salesman should preferably sit by the side of the prospect keeping the material in his own hands until it has been discussed. Significant phrases or features of illustrations may be pointed out with a pencil by the salesman. The material should be placed before the prospect in such a position that he does not have to turn his head to see it comfortably.

The salesman should not attempt to read the material verbatim but should develop his own comments and anecdotes to illustrate the written recommendations in the proposal.

3. Get Prospect to Participate in the Discussion. The presentation should not be a monologue with the salesman doing all the talking. The prospect should be encouraged to ask questions, raise objections, and make comments on the program recommended. Unless the prospect enters into the discussion, the salesman is unable to discover his attitude toward the proposition, to meet his objections, and to convince him of the merit of the proposal. By asking such questions as, "What do you think of this idea?" or "Is this a reasonable assumption?" a salesman encourages a prospect to express his opinions and thereby put the interview on a more friendly basis.

4. Commit Prospect on the Proposal. So that the salesman may test the prospect's interest in the program proposed, definite commitments should be sought from the prospect on the major points in the proposal. The buyer may be asked directly if he agrees to the points made by the salesman, or his remarks may indicate whether he confirms, denies, or desires to modify the suggestions made. If the prospect objects to the recommendations, the salesman should present additional advantages. If he concedes that the proposal is satisfactory, the salesman can ask for the order. Several favorable commitments by a prospect put him in agreement with the salesman and lead to a final favorable decision to act.

5. Secure Prospect's Consent or Offer a Compromise. The salesman may determine, if the prospect is ready to give his consent, to carry out the proposal by asking for minor decisions on some of the details of the transaction. "Do you prefer to pay cash or would you rather make time payments?" an automobile salesman asks. "Do you want these securities registered?" is a typical question which an investment salesman asks to imply that the prospect is ready to buy.

If a prospect does not agree to the salesman's original proposal, a compromise proposal should be offered. An alternate program is usually prepared in advance by a salesman and held in reserve. It is not discussed during the original presentation and is introduced only when a prospect refuses to accept the first proposal. The compromise plan, which usually involves less expense, is presented in the same manner as the original program.

Advantages of a Survey or Program Presentation. A survey presentation enables a salesman to deal understandingly with a prospect's needs and assist him to buy to the best advantage. Sales resistance is reduced, the good will of prospects is secured, and considerable word-of-mouth advertising, names of prospects, and repeat sales often result. Although a prospect may not accept a salesman's proposal, the buyer is favorably disposed toward the salesman who has made a serious study and submitted sound recommendations for a solution of his problems.

Survey selling puts the work of a salesman on a professional basis. He becomes a counselor to his prospects and his efforts are dignified. He is welcomed by his prospects as a helpful assistant in the solution of their personal or business problems.

A salesman who uses a survey presentation usually sells a larger amount of merchandise or service because the prospect fully understands his requirements and recognizes the extent to which he needs the services, materials, or equipment offered.

A salesman saves his own time and effort by being able to qualify his prospects better through an intimate knowledge of their needs, their ability to buy, and their ownership of competitive products.

Objections to a Survey or Program Presentation. The most common objection to a survey presentation is that it requires too much time to prepare. A salesman must spend time in investigating, analyzing, and preparing a proposal, with no assurance that his recommendations will be accepted and a sale will result. Burdened with survey detail, a salesman makes fewer calls and presentations and may secure less business.

There are usually only a limited number of prospects who are able to buy enough of the salesman's goods or services to justify enough time and effort to cultivate them so intensively. In many cases their needs have been largely satisfied. The competition for the patronage of large buyers is keen.

Many salesmen have not had enough experience or knowledge to make reliable surveys, diagnoses, and sound recommendations. Prospects have little confidence in the recommendations of salesmen with little experience and knowledge of their needs.

Some prospects feel that the recommendations of salesmen are biased and designed to sell goods and services rather than to solve their problems. It is difficult for a salesman to forget that his live-lihood depends on sales made, and his recommendations may be col-ored accordingly.

Considering the advantages and objections to survey or program presentations, this type of sales approach is being used more gener-ally today than ever before by salesmen of high unit sales price spe-cialty products and intangible services. The growing popularity of the survey presentation may be accounted for by the fact that selling is now conceived of as primarily a service to buyers. Through a pro-gram approach, a salesman is enabled to offer maximum service to his prospects.

The survey or program presentation is widely used in the sale of life insurance. It is generally used in selling industrial installation equipment, office appliances, heating and air-conditioning equipment, and specialties and services of complex character with numerous ap-plications and high unit sales value.

This type of presentation is most effectively used by experienced salesmen. However, beginner salesmen are sometimes trained to sell by performing the first two steps in a program presentation, selling the survey and gathering the facts. The diagnosis, preparation of a proposal, and sales presentation are made by an experienced salesman.

A large office-equipment concern trains all its new salesmen in this way. Beginner salesmen interest prospects in an "obsolescence sur-vey" of their equipment. Then an experienced salesman analyzes the needs of the prospect and presents a program for efficiency and sav-ings in office equipment.

The value of a survey or program presentation is illustrated by the experience of a Detroit life insurance salesman who uses this method of selling exclusively. During a four-month period this salesman secured 46 "pictures," or obtained information about the life insur-ance situations of 46 prospects. He prepared programs for 32 quali-fied prospects. Sales resulted in 22 cases for a total of $241,500. The closing ratio was two sales to every three program presentations.

4. Work-sheet Presentation

A work-sheet sales presentation involves the preparation of a chart or "work sheet" showing the situation, needs, and product application of an individual customer. On the basis of this work sheet, a presen-tation is made.

A salesman draws up a work sheet ruled vertically into four col-umns, one headed, "Name of Prospect"; the second, "Prospect's Picture"; the third, "Resulting Needs"; and the fourth, "Proposal and Selling Points."

In the first column, the salesman writes the name of a prospect believed to have a need for the salesman's product or service. In the second column is written all the available information about the prospect. In the third column are listed the various reasons why the prospect should buy and in the fourth column the selling points that the salesman plans to use in presenting the product or service.

To illustrate how a typical work sheet is prepared, an investment trust salesman prospects for men who are likely to need money for retirement. He obtains advance information on the prospect and draws up a work sheet, as follows:

WORK SHEET

Name of Prospect	Prospect's Picture	His Needs	Proposal and Sales Points
John K. James	A physician, age forty; married, three boys aged three, five, and nine years; owns his home; is member of country club; owns $2,000 life insurance and $4,000 U.S. bonds.	Regular savings plan. Retirement fund. Protection of family in event of death.	Ways to provide funds: a. Hoarding cash. b. Savings account. c. Building and loan. d. Investment trust. Accumulation by each method. Security of funds. Principle of diversity. Compound earnings.

The salesman prepares a work sheet as above showing the buyer's situation, needs, and the sales points to be discussed. The work sheet is referred to by the salesman during the sales presentation and serves as a reminder of sales points and needs.

Preparing a work-sheet presentation before approaching a prospect, a salesman is forced to obtain as much information as possible about a buyer in advance of an interview. This saves the salesman's and the prospect's time. When he uses this method, a salesman knows the buyer's needs and he does not waste time in idle conversation. He knows what sales points he is going to discuss and has a definite interview objective.

The work-sheet presentation is effective in training beginner salesmen to organize their presentations and to develop sound selling habits. Experienced salesmen are able to develop a work sheet while interviewing a prospect.

Planned Sales Presentation

Salesman_____   Date_____

Rated by_____   Over-all Rating_____

Score

I. *Salesman's Use of a "Standard Presentation"*

	Excellent 90–100	Good 80–90	Fair 70–80	Poor 60–70	Failure Below 60
A. Adapt to needs of prospect					
B. Natural delivery					
C. Prospect participation					
D. Securing action					

II. *Salesman's Use of an Outlined Presentation*

	Excellent 90–100	Good 80–90	Fair 70–80	Poor 60–70	Failure Below 60
A. Adhere to outline					
B. Amplify each step in outline					
C. Prospect participation					
D. Securing action					

III. *Salesman's Use of Survey Presentation*

	Excellent 90–100	Good 80–90	Fair 70–80	Poor 60–70	Failure Below 60
A. Thanking prospect					
B. Controlling presentation					
C. Prospect participation					
D. Committing prospect					
E. Securing consent					

Miscellaneous Comments _____

_____

_____

A work-sheet presentation is a form of outline to guide salesmen who know their products and uses in making better organized presentations. The method takes considerable time and is not applicable to the sale of low-priced consumer goods.

Problem I

STANDARD SALES PRESENTATION

Ralph E. Weeks, representing the Levering Typewriter Company

The Levering Typewriter Company manufactures the Monarch Typewriter, sold direct to industrial and commercial concerns by 125 salesmen operating out of 25 branch offices located in the principal industrial cities of the country.

Ralph E. Weeks is one of eight salesmen employed in the Cleveland, Ohio, branch, who calls regularly on office managers and purchasing agents of business concerns in northern Ohio. He uses the standard sales presentation which the Levering Company requires all salesmen to use in demonstrating the Monarch to prospective customers.

In the following interview, salesman Weeks is presenting a Monarch to Miss Eddy, private secretary to the treasurer of a large machine-tool manufacturer in Cleveland. Ralph Weeks has arranged with the company treasurer to demonstrate the Monarch to Miss Eddy, who has been given full responsibility for selecting the typewriter for her own use. Miss Eddy has been considering three well-known makes. She is now using a Speedwell which has given satisfactory service for 10 years, but must now be replaced.

Salesman Weeks's standard presentation follows:

SALESMAN: Good morning, Miss Eddy. I've brought over the new Monarch for you to try. If you have a few moments, I'd like to demonstrate its outstanding features to you.

MISS EDDY: Thank you very much. Will you set it on this desk, please?

SALESMAN: Miss Eddy, typewriters have generally been designed from the viewpoint of the mechanic. They have probably been sold to you as a mechanical instrument. But I want to present to you a new typewriter designed from the viewpoint of the operator and the business executive and show you some of the most radical improvements in the entire history of the typewriter business. This new Monarch gives you more exclusive features than any other typewriter.

Have you ever had the pleasure of looking at a more beautiful writing machine? I am going to prove to you, and I know you will agree when I get through, that the operating mechanism of this typewriter is as good as the appearance of the machine itself. It is without doubt the greatest writing-machine value on the market today.

First, let's consider its appearance. This nonglare finish completely eliminates all light reflections. It is easy to clean and extremely durable.

You will notice that these metal parts are chromium plated. They will not rust or tarnish from contact with the fingers. Chromium stays bright without polishing throughout the entire life of the machine. All the metal parts of the interior and the metal underneath the nonglare finish are treated with a rust-resisting process. This new Monarch is streamlined and symmetrical and for the first time on any typewriter gives a complete enclosure of the entire operating mechanism.

The new top design, an exclusive Monarch feature, the complete enclosure on the four sides and bottom, new carriage ends, cylinder knobs, and paper table, all make it a finer looking typewriter, one that harmonizes with the furnishings of your office and does not look like a piece of machinery.

In designing this new typewriter, we have introduced greater convenience into every one of the operations that constitute typing. During the day, the operator does several things when she types. For instance, she sets the margins, inserts the paper, line-spaces, touches the keys, shifts for capital letters, removes the paper from the machine, erases, changes ribbons. In every one of these operations the Monarch saves time and effort for her. You will see as I go along how this is accomplished.

MISS EDDY: The Monarch certainly is beautiful in appearance. Will you demonstrate its operation?

SALESMAN: Yes, of course. As you insert the paper, a flip of your finger pulls forward this lever, and this is the first of the many time- and effort-saving features I am going to show you. It is called the Automatic Paper Lock. When the paper lock is returned, notice how the rubber rollers strike the paper a little below the place where they finally come to rest, thus ironing out the bulge that ordinarily prevails on other makes of typewriters and hugging the paper tightly to the cylinder. This subdues the striking of the type, gives a clearer cut impression and better and more uniform carbon copies. The paper lock holds the paper securely like an additional set of feed rolls. It permits you to write to the extreme left and right edges of the paper and from the top to the bottom of any size sheet within the carriage range without a single adjustment. Notice that the paper lock provides complete visibility of the entire writing line. Here is another Monarch advantage: When you pull the paper out of the machine, the paper lock automatically is thrown forward and you are ready to insert a new sheet of paper without touching the paper lock.

MISS EDDY: That *is* an improvement over the ordinary paper feed roll.

SALESMAN: You're right! Now note this long feed roll in the rear of the cylinder. This gives perfect adhesion of the paper to the cylinder and uniform pressure clear across.

Other machines have several individual rollers and you know it is difficult to keep the tension uniform when using several rollers. When I rotate the cylinder, the paper feeds in straight, eliminating the adjustment which is ordinarily necessary. I have now put in operation the greatest paper feed of any typewriter. As I hold this cylinder, will you grasp the paper and try to pull it out of the typewriter?

Miss Eddy: The paper was certainly held tightly! It tore but didn't slip out.

Salesman: That's right! Perfect, accurate, uniform tension of the single feed roll makes it impossible for paper to slip.

Miss Eddy: I have had trouble with paper feeding in crooked. I have to adjust it almost every time.

Salesman: That annoyance is completely eliminated on the Monarch and in addition, this machine will feed letters, invoices, envelopes, and cards—in fact, anything down to a postage stamp with equal facility.

Now notice how I insert this small calling card, and as I do so, raise these disappearing card fingers. You can write on the top, sides, and bottom of the card; also reverse it with ease. Special attachments or adjustments are not necessary.

Miss Eddy: What is the Monarch Automatic Margin I've heard so much about?

Salesman: I was just about to demonstrate that. First, let's insert a sheet of paper as you would do before you begin to type. Now, as the sheet of paper is in the machine, you want to determine margins. This is done very easily. You move the carriage to the point where you want your left-hand margin, flip this Automatic Margin lever and it's set.

Notice that as I move the carriage back and forth against the margin stop that the setting is positive and accurate.

Miss Eddy: Why that's just like an electric light switch. Click—it's set!

Salesman: You're right, Miss Eddy, Automatic Margin is the most amazing feature ever presented on a typewriter. It does away completely with the setting of margin stops by hand. Watch me as I set margins more slowly.

Let's suppose that you have typed several paragraphs and want to indent a quotation. You simply move the carriage to the point where you want your margin. There are no scales to read, no figuring to do. You pull this lever forward and push it back and that's all there is to it. The margin stop automatically sets and locks itself in position.

To return to a *narrower* margin, simply pull the lever forward, move the carriage to the right and push the lever back. The right-hand margin is set just as easily. Automatic Margin is an exclusive Monarch feature. There is nothing like it on any other typewriter. On other machines, you must reach somewhere for the margin stops, and push them across by hand. Automatic Margin eliminates all this. It is the greatest time- and effort-saving convenience introduced on any typewriter in the last 20 years. It will help you in every letter you write—and enable you to set up better-looking letters. Don't you think so?

MISS EDDY: I certainly do! One thing I dislike to do is to stretch and strain to reach inaccessible margin stops.

SALESMAN: Now, Miss Eddy, occasionally it is necessary to erase. Suppose you have written down to the center of the sheet and an erasure is necessary. On the Monarch, you simply move the carriage to one side or the other and the erasure grit which, incidentally, is made of a very sharp abrasive, drops on these erasure-protecting shields and does not fall into the working parts of the typewriter. This also is an exclusive feature of the Monarch.

Even should you erase directly over the printing point, there are hoods inside the machine to prevent the erasures from getting into the bearings. Monarch is the only manufacturer to make a sincere effort to reduce maintenance. Erasure grit, if permitted to fall into a typewriter, will clog up operating parts and cause wear. Keeping it out will save you two cleaning jobs during the life of the machine, approximately twenty-five dollars, and yet the Monarch is priced no higher than competitive machines which do not give you this important protection.

When erasing is necessary, the paper lock can be thrown back, making it easy to erase on carbon copies.

When you have made the erasure, the paper lock falls into position, and when it is returned, it hugs the paper to the cylinder in the same way as before.

Every feature of this new Monarch has been made entirely for your convenience and speed of operation.

Let's consider tabulating for a moment. Monarch has added to the keyboard two keys which eliminate the old-fashioned method of setting tabulator stops by hand and permit you to both set and clear the stops without having to reach to the rear of the machine. By merely depressing this set key, you can set tabulator stops at any desired point, and you can instantly clear them by depressing this clear key and moving the carriage either to the right or left. Here is another feature: A single stop may be cleared by tabulating to it and depressing the clear key—this is a great convenience.

MISS EDDY: That is easier. It seems as though I'm always losing the old tabulator stops which must be removed to reset tabulator spaces. If the boss buys this Monarch, I won't have to think about that any more.

SALESMAN: Very often, you have occasion to refer to the scales on the typewriter for various operations. Every scale on the Monarch is synchronized—in other words, the scale on the paper guide, the scale on the automatic paper lock, and the scales on the bottom of the carriage are uniform, number for number, and have white numerals against black for instant visibility.

You use the scales at the bottom of the carriage to indicate its position and the position of the paper. Now suppose you want to center a heading and you see that the paper comes to number 84 on the scale. Half of 84 is 42. Strike a period here. As you fold the paper, you will notice the period is exactly in the center.

Now suppose you want to center a word like "typewriter." Press down the backspacer for the letter "t," release it for "y." Press it down again for "p" and raise it for "e," etc. You will find the word is exactly centered. This is a great convenience made possible by the uniform scales of the Monarch.

MISS EDDY: I like that. That's quick and easy.

SALESMAN: All other operating features are equally convenient. For instance, touch the backspacer. The backspacer on this machine is as easy to operate as the letter keys. The margin-release key has been placed on the keyboard for greater speed and comfort. The line-space lever is very long and sturdy. It is shaped to fit your fingers. When you return the carriage, your hand drops naturally to the writing position on the keyboard. Notice how the levers for moving the carriage back and forth, for releasing the paper, and for disengaging the ratchet are accessible and easy to handle.

For instance, you have a single ruled line on a form and you want to write something on that line and then return to your original spacing. All you do is raise this lever to take the cylinder out of click, roll the paper so that the ruled line is exactly at the top of the type guide scale, and write.

When ready to return to the original spacing, just push back the lever and you go right back where you were. Suppose you want to fractional-space and start your spacing from that line. A simple movement of the hand accomplishes it. Press the palm against this button on the left cylinder knob and turn the paper to the point where you want to write. Release it, and your machine is back in spacing. On other typewriters if after pulling out the fractional line spacer, you forget to return it, your machine won't space. You write over the same line again and your letter is ruined. On the Monarch, the cylinder is never out of spacing.

MISS EDDY: The Monarch really is designed from the viewpoint of the operator, isn't it? (Laughingly.) Typing is almost fun instead of work.

SALESMAN: Yes, thousands of operators are just as enthusiastic. And here's another exclusive Monarch improvement I'd like to show you—Touch Adjustment. This is one of the most important easy-writing conveniences on the typewriter. Do you see this little dial and pointer at the side of the typewriter? That is the Touch Adjustment dial. On the new Monarch you can control the touch to suit yourself. Stenographers are not of uniform weight and physical strength. Before Monarch invented Touch Adjustment, typewriters had always been made with a uniform key tension. One girl might have a light touch, another a heavy one. If it were not possible to personalize the key tension, each operator would be handicapped by having to use a typewriter that was not adjusted to her physical strength. On the Monarch, any operator can adjust the tension instantly to suit herself. This dial tells you just what the degree of tension is. When you turn the knob so that the pointer moves to the higher numbers, you are increasing the tension. If you want a light touch, turn it to the lower numbers. Both the dial and knob are conveniently located at the side of the machine where they can be set and read easily from the normal typing position. Touch Adjustment is another feature developed by Monarch for easier and faster typing.

Miss Eddy: I notice the shift, tabulator, and back space keys are rectangular in shape. What is the reason for that?

Salesman: That's another Monarch feature designed and engineered for your convenience and to save you strain and effort. These keys provide greater finger surface, more convenience and accuracy in shifting, tabulating, and back-spacing operations. They make for a pleasing, new typing comfort, greater speed, and smooth rhythm; you will type with less fatigue, more naturally, more beautifully.

And the entire Monarch keyboard is just as modern. The new keys have been designed with the idea of protecting the eyes as well as the fingers. They have no curves to break the fingernails and injure the delicate nerves of the finger tips. Your fingers glide naturally from one key to another, increasing your speed. The new key surfaces are concave to exactly fit the fingers and are made of lucite which is practically indestructible, withstands all forms of wear, and is easy to clean. The key cards are scientifically designed with white letters on a black surface to eliminate glare. The Monarch protects your eyes from every possible source of strain.

Miss Eddy: Yes, the keys are pleasing to the touch and there isn't any glare.

Salesman: Speaking of eyestrain, on other makes of typewriters you constantly see the type bars flashing up and down before your eyes as they approach the printing point. This flashing movement is known as "type-bar blur." It is a dangerous source of eyestrain and fatigue. The moving type bars constantly distract your attention from your copy and send little sparks of light up and down before your eyes. On this new Monarch, we have eliminated "type-bar blur" by designing a top mask that conceals the movement of the type bars as they approach the printing point. The Monarch is the only typewriter that protects you from strain, fatigue, and slowed-up work.

This top design, in addition to guarding your eyesight, is a very important convenience feature. You have, perhaps, wondered how you clean type and change ribbons on this new Monarch. Simply raise the top like this and the type and ribbon are instantly and easily accessible. Type cleaning is only a moment's work and changing the ribbon takes hardly any longer.

I once asked an executive of a company using another make of machine how long it took his stenographer to change the ribbon and I was surprised when he told me 20 minutes. I asked him how he figured 20 minutes for so simple an operation. He said that it probably took about 10 minutes to make the actual change, but that the stenographer got herself so tangled up in the ribbons, and got her hands so dirty, that she had to go to the washroom to clean up. So that the actual time for changing the ribbon was 20 minutes.

Notice that while talking to you I made the entire ribbon change and did so without soiling my fingers. Isn't this new top a real timesaver, Miss Eddy?

MISS EDDY: Well! The hand is almost quicker than the eye. That was easy to do all right.

SALESMAN: Incidentally, the Monarch features the only postive two-color device on the market. Most typewriter companies supply machines with a single-color ribbon because they have no positive bichrome device. Will you move this lever back and forth and notice as I type that there is no bleeding of color?

MISS EDDY: I'll certainly appreciate that. Sometimes I type a letter and the appearance is spoiled by the little bits of red showing here and there, especially on the capitals.

SALESMAN: That's impossible on the Monarch. I have left one of the most important features about this new Monarch until now because it is a feature I want to impress upon you most strongly. We have developed and incorporated in it the principle of easy shifting. It is one of the chief reasons why the Monarch is the operator's own typewriter. Operators occasionally have a headache at the end of the day, a pain at the back of the neck, or a touch of neuritis. They are at a loss to account for it and blame everything but the typewriter. The ordinary typewriter causes eyestrain, which in turn causes other disturbing conditions, interfering with your work and your good health.

Notice how I take this sheet of paper and move it up and down behind this pencil. This strains your eyes and is unpleasant. Yet it is exactly what the old-fashioned typewriter does. Every few strokes you shift for a capital letter and you have that white paper bobbing up and down in front of your eyes. The shifting carriage, Miss Eddy, is a thing of the past. It is just as obsolete as the blind typewriter of yesterday. The Monarch's easy shifting has relegated it to the graveyard.

MISS EDDY: Well, exactly what is easy shifting?

SALESMAN: It is simply this. The carriage does not bob up and down any more. When you write capital letters with a pencil, you do not move the paper, you move the pencil. The Monarch does the same thing—it does not move the paper, it moves the type. Notice when you press down the shift key, the carriage does not move. It is rigid. Only the type segment moves.

Now, will you press on the type bars yourself and notice that you can't push them down.

MISS EDDY: Why, yes, they seem to be permanently fastened in place.

SALESMAN: That's because they're positively locked in position in both upper and lower cases, and this is one reason for the wonderful quality of work this Monarch produces. But press the shift key. Do you notice that the slightest touch of your finger drops the type into a capital letter position? On the Monarch, the segment is locked and free at the same time. That's easy shifting.

MISS EDDY: I can see that it's easier and more natural to drop the segment when shifting than to push up the heavy carriage.

SALESMAN: Right! Faster too!

I am going to take the draw band off this carriage and show you something in connection with easy shifting which is most important. First, I'll insert this pencil under the paper lock to hold the carriage-release lever down. Now note how easily the carriage moves from left to right. It glides so smoothly because it is riding on case-hardened steel inserts in the carriage rails. Running between these inserts in the upper and lower rails there are ball bearings, positively guided by gears. If you look closely, you can see these bearings as I push the carriage all the way over.

MISS EDDY: Oh, yes, I see them.

SALESMAN: Now I want you to notice that the same thing is true of the Monarch segment. It moves up and down less than three-eights of an inch, against cushioned metal stops on case-hardened rails with upper and lower guided ball bearings. If you will look at this spot, you can see them— here, in back, just above the carriage rail.

MISS EDDY: Oh yes, the construction is the same as on the carriage.

SALESMAN: That's right—and this means perfect type alignment throughout the life of the typewriter, and ease of operation as well as speed. It is such a remarkable feature that there is nothing on any typewriter on the market to compare with it. It eliminates vibration, assures longer life and perfect press work.

I think you will agree, Miss Eddy, that in every feature of operating convenience and operator protection, this new Monarch is supreme. There are, of course, two other qualities which interest you and your employer. One of these is the length of life of your typewriter, and I think I have pointed out to you many of the reasons, such as protection against erasure grit and the encasing of the machine at top, sides, and bottom, which contribute to longer life.

Now I know you're interested in speed, and this new Monarch is the fastest typewriter on the market and I can prove this to you. It is so because it incorporates one of the earliest principles of Monarch manufacture, the Speedup Type Bar. Notice when I touch the key, the type bar flashes to the paper and returns so fast that you cannot see it strike. Incidentally, the key stroke of each key on the Monarch is identical—9/16 inch throughout the keyboard.

Michael Maderia, operating a Monarch with this famous type-bar action, set a new all-time world's typing record in winning the title of World's Champion Typist, writing for one hour at the amazing rate of 141 net words per minute. This record has never been equaled or even approached. The contests were sponsored by the International Commercial Schools Contests Committee, a group of impartial educators.

Miss Eddy: That *is* fast typing! (Laughingly.) I'd only have to work half a day if I could do that.

Salesman: Well, you may not be able to attain such record-breaking speed, but on the Monarch you will find you type faster, easier, and with less fatigue.

I believe I have shown you, Miss Eddy, that this new Monarch with its automatic margin, easy shifting, touch adjustment, finger-comfort keys, and all of the other conveniences and improvements is the ultimate in typewriters.

In addition, you are getting a typewriter which is quieter, which is easier to operate, which will turn out more work because it speeds your work, and will last longer because it is designed to last longer.

The work of this machine is even better than any of the previous Monarch models.

Wouldn't you like to use one?

Miss Eddy: Yes, and I'd like to own one.

Salesman: I want you to, and I'm sure your boss will buy it for you when he sees how enthusiastic you are, and the advantages and benefits the new Monarch offers to both you and himself.

Questions

1. Does this standard presentation gain the attention and interest of the prospect?

2. Does it describe how the product meets the prospect's needs?

3. Does it prove how the product has satisfied the needs of other persons?

4. Is the buyer induced to act by this presentation?

5. Is the presentation adaptable to the buyer in this case?

6. Do interruptions by the prospect distract the salesman?

7. Does the salesman give the prospect an opportunity to participate in the interview?

8. Does the salesman discuss features which do not concern the needs of the prospect?

9. Criticize this standard presentation in general?

10. Should another type of planned presentation be used in this interview? What?

Problem II

Frank L. Harlan, representing the Standard Vacuum Cleaner Company

The Standard Vacuum Cleaner Company, Toledo, Ohio, sells domestic vacuum cleaners direct to homes through 3,000 commission salesmen operating out of 300 branch offices located in the principal cities of the country. The Standard Cleaner is nationally advertised and is made in several models, the largest of which retails for $85. A majority of the sales are made by demonstration in homes. A liberal time payment plan is offered.

Frank L. Harlan represents the company in Milwaukee, Wis., where he has averaged earnings of $3,100 annually for the past four years. He has consistently followed an outlined sales demonstration prepared by the company and based on the successful methods of outstanding company representatives. The demonstration has 10 main points and an introduction which salesman Harlan has memorized.

The standard outlined sales presentation follows:

Introduction:
    Make a courteous entrance.
    Timely remarks.
    General observations.
    Mental investigation.
    Have prospect seated.
    Lay out dusting tools.

1. *Set Up Cleaner; Review Mechanical Features:*

Appearance.	Bag.
Finish.	Tilting device.
Cord.	Switch.
Handle.	Motor.
	Adjustment.

2. *Demonstrate Dusting Tools:*
    Explain tools.
    Cheesecloth test.
    Shelves, corners, etc.
    Benefits of blowing.
    Mica test.

3. *Clean Half of Rug:*
    Have prospect operate cleaner.

Explain agitation of grit.

Reerected nap.

Restored colors.

Discuss rug beating.

4. *Explanation of Dirt:*

Spread newspaper.

Remove bag.

Lay out soda, kapok, and sand.

Describe each.

Embed sand with hand broom.

Rub up dead nap.

5. *Empty Dirty Bag:*

Make three piles on newspaper.

Analyze dirt.

6. *Explain Storage Capacity:*

Use Wilton swatch.

Compare with prospect's rug.

Embed soda.

7. *Explain Difference between* Standard *and Other Vacuum Cleaners:*

Remove agitator.

Operate as vacuum cleaner.

Beat out sand with screw driver.

Upside-down demonstration with green ingrain.

Describe agitator.

8. *Explain and Demonstrate the Absence of Rug Wear:*

Use georgette crepe test.

Millions of users.

Standing guarantee.

9. *Make Dirt Spread:*

Prepare prospect's mind.

Make spread.

Explain what spread represents.

Summarize benefits of Standard.

Endeavor to close.

10. *Clean Balance of Rug:*

If close is not made, clean balance of rug.

Repeat the many benefits.

Empty bag.

Close the sale.

Salesman Harlan amplifies each point in this outline by discussing facts, reasons, illustrations, and examples which he has learned from the company and from his experience.

Questions

1. Criticize favorably or otherwise this outlined sales presentation. Support your criticism with specific reasons.

2. Is this type of presentation best suited to the type of product, buyer, and salesman in this case?

3. Should any other type of planned presentation be used in selling this product? What? Give reasons in your answer.

4. Would a product sales-point outline be desirable in this case? Why?

Reading References

CHARLES H. FERNALD, "Salesmanship," Chap. VIII, Prentice-Hall, Inc., New York, 1945.

J. GEORGE FREDERICK, "Modern Salesmanship," Chap. XIV, Garden City Publishing Company, Inc., New York, 1937.

H. M. HAAS, "A Short Course in Salesmanship," Chap. VII, Prentice-Hall, Inc., New York, 1939.

PAUL W. IVEY, "Successful Salesmanship," pp. 191–196, Prentice-Hall, Inc., New York, 1947.

DAVID R. OSBORNE, "Salesmanship for Today for Salesmanagers of Tomorrow," pp. 83–87, Harper & Brothers, New York, 1939.

HARRY SIMMONS, "How to Get the Order," pp. 37–38, Harper & Brothers, New York, 1937.

HARRY SIMMONS, "A Practical Course in Successful Selling," Chap. VIII, Harper & Brothers, New York, 1939.

ELMER WHEELER, "Tested Sentences That Sell," Prentice-Hall, New York, 1940.

F. A. RUSSELL and F. H. BEACH, "Textbook of Salesmanship," pp. 305–313, 348–353, McGraw-Hill Book Company, Inc., New York, 1949.

PERCY H. WHITING, "The Five Great Rules of Selling," Chaps. 10–11, McGraw-Hill Book Company, Inc., New York, 1947.

CHAPTER XV

ORGANIZING SALES EFFORTS

IMPORTANCE OF SYSTEMATIC SALES ACTIVITY

The way a salesman uses his time, plans his work, and organizes his efforts is often more fundamental to his success than unusual ability in making sales presentations. Lack of systematic and consistent effort is responsible for the failure of more salesmen than any other factor.

Success in selling, as in any other business, depends upon good management methods. A salesman is the general manager of his own business. If he is a good manager, his business prospers; if he cannot manage himself, he fails.

The unusual liberty of action and freedom from supervision which the average salesman enjoys make his problem of self-management serious. Unlike men in other vocations, a salesman does not sit at a desk and find work automatically accumulating before him. He must make his own work.

A salesman must force himself to keep business hours, arrange his work in advance, keep records of his activity, plan his time, route his calls, provide time for self-improvement, establish work objectives, and analyze his performance. If a salesman is a good self-manager, he will drive himself to perform these essential tasks and accomplish the goals in sales and earnings that he has set for himself.

Hard work alone, however, is not enough to make a salesman successful. His efforts must be controlled and directed into the right channels. To avoid waste effort, each day's work must be planned systematically, travel must be curtailed, prospects must be selected carefully, interviews must be arranged, and customers must be followed up at the proper time. Efficient organization of these varied sales activities ensures a methodical development of a salesman's territory and maximum results from the efforts expended.

THE CASE OF SALESMAN RED AND SALESMAN BLACK

The value of well-managed sales efforts as a factor in successful selling is illustrated by the actual work records of two salesmen representing a large life insurance company. These men shall be known by the fictitious names of Mr. Red and Mr. Black. They are of approximately the same age, experience, and personal qualifications. The striking difference in their working methods accounted largely for the successful performance of Mr. Black and the mediocre work of Mr. Red. Their work methods for one year, as taken from their daily activity reports, have been compared on a basis of: (*a*) hours spent in the field; (*b*) total sales contacts; (*c*) total contacts resulting in progress; (*d*) total new prospects; (*e*) number of first, second, and third interviews; (*f*) number of customer service calls; and (*g*) their sales accomplishment.

AVERAGE NUMBER OF HOURS IN THE FIELD DAILY

Salesman	Monday	Tuesday	Wednesday	Thursday	Friday	Saturday
Red............	5.7	5.2	5.3	4.8	4.6	0.7
Black..........	6.2	8.0	10.5	7.9	6.0	1.6

Analysis of the field work of these two men shows that Red averaged 4.3 hours per working day in the field daily against 6.7 hours for Black. Black spent more hours daily in the field than Red. However, Black's field activity was irregular; he was slow getting under way each week and after his peak of activity on Wednesday, his effort declined sharply. Red was more consistent in his effort each day although his effort also declined after Wednesday. Sales effort of both men was lowest on Saturday.

AVERAGE NUMBER OF SALES CONTACTS MADE DAILY

Salesman	Monday	Tuesday	Wednesday	Thursday	Friday	Saturday
Red............	3.5	2.9	3.1	3.0	2.2	0.4
Black..........	7.0	7.9	6.7	6.3	5.3	2.3

Salesman Black averaged 5.9 contacts a day, more than twice as many as Red, who spent about 64 per cent as much time in the field and made only 42 per cent as many sales contacts as Black. Obviously Black wasted less time in travel and planned his time so that he could make more contacts. Both salesmen began the week strong, but their day-to-day effort declined steadily, indicating poor planning of daily calls. The number of their sales contacts should have been more uniform throughout the week.

AVERAGE NUMBER OF SALES CONTACTS RESULTING IN PROGRESS DAILY

Salesman	Monday	Tuesday	Wednesday	Thursday	Friday	Saturday
Red............	2.3	2.2	2.1	2.0	1.6	0.3
Black..........	5.6	6.6	5.4	5.3	4.8	2.4

A good salesman makes productive contacts. Salesman Black averaged five productive contacts daily compared with an average of only 1.7 for Red. The quality of Black's effort was higher than Red's.

AVERAGE NUMBER OF PROSPECTS SECURED DAILY

Salesman	Monday	Tuesday	Wednesday	Thursday	Friday	Saturday
Red............	0.8	0.9	0.5	0.6	0.3	0.1
Black..........	5.6	4.1	5.5	4.9	2.6	2.3

A salesman must have a full reservoir of prospects to convert into customers. Salesman Black averaged more than eight times as many prospects a week as did salesman Red.

AVERAGE NUMBER OF FIRST INTERVIEWS DAILY

Salesman	Monday	Tuesday	Wednesday	Thursday	Friday	Saturday
Red............	0.8	0.6	0.6	0.5	0.6	0.1
Black..........	2.2	2.6	2.0	2.2	1.7	0.3

Salesman Black planned his work to get more interviews. He averaged 11 first interviews in a week compared with Red's three. With the exception of Friday and Saturday, Black averaged two or more first interviews a day.

AVERAGE NUMBER OF SECOND INTERVIEWS DAILY

Salesman	Monday	Tuesday	Wednesday	Thursday	Friday	Saturday
Red............	0.2	0.3	0.3	0.2	0.2	0.1
Black..........	0.4	0.1	0.1	0.8	0.7	0.2

A good salesman saves time and energy by closing as many sales as possible in one interview. However, all buyers cannot be sold in one interview. Although salesman Black averaged twice as many second interviews a week as Red, he made three times as many initial interviews and had a lower ratio of second interviews to first contacts.

AVERAGE NUMBER OF THIRD INTERVIEWS DAILY

Salesman	Monday	Tuesday	Wednesday	Thursday	Friday	Saturday
Red............	1.0	0.7	0.7	0.8	0.5	0.1
Black..........	0.2	0.3	0.4	0.3	0.2	0.1

One of the greatest wastes of time in selling is caused by repeated calls upon worthless prospects. These take time that might better be spent in interviewing more desirable prospects. Salesman Red showed a weakness in closing by averaging 2.4 third interviews a week; Black averaged only 1.2.

AVERAGE NUMBER OF INTERVIEWS DAILY

Salesman	Monday	Tuesday	Wednesday	Thursday	Friday	Saturday
Red............	2.1	1.7	1.5	1.5	1.2	0.2
Black..........	3.0	3.7	3.7	3.5	2.8	0.7

It is necessary that a salesman make an adequate number of presentations to prospects. Salesman Black averaged 2.9 interviews a day, compared with 1.3 by Red. Black began the week strong and increased his number of interviews daily until Friday, maintaining a quota of three a day except on the last two days of the week. Poor management is evident in Red's interviewing record.

AVERAGE NUMBER OF CUSTOMERS CULTIVATED DAILY

Salesman	Monday	Tuesday	Wednesday	Thursday	Friday	Saturday
Red............	0.05	0.03	0.08	0.05	0.10	0.02
Black...........	0.80	0.80	0.50	0.40	0.80	0.40

Methodical sales work demands that customers be followed up regularly. Salesman Black did about twelve times as much service work as his associate. He planned his time so that he saw a customer every other day.

SUMMARY OF ANNUAL SALES EFFORTS OF RED AND BLACK

Average time and effort expended	Salesman Red		Salesman Black	
	Daily	Weekly	Daily	Weekly
Hours in field......................	4.4	26.3	6.7	40.2
Sales contacts......................	2.5	15.1	5.9	35.5
Contacts resulting in progress..........	1.7	10.5	5.0	30.1
New prospects......................	0.5	3.2	4.1	25.0
First interviews.....................	0.5	3.2	1.8	11.0
Second interviews...................	0.2	1.3	0.4	2.3
Third and subsequent interviews.......	0.6	3.8	0.2	1.5
All interviews......................	1.3	8.2	2.9	17.4
Customer cultivation................	0.05	0.33	0.6	3.7

A comparison of the work methods of these two salesmen for a year clearly shows the greater quantity and quality of effort expended by salesman Black. He spent 36 per cent more hours in the field daily, made twice as many sales contacts, secured eight times more prospects, and conducted more than twice as many interviews as salesman Red.

COMPARATIVE SALES ACCOMPLISHMENT

As a result of his planned activity, salesman Black sold during the year more than twice as much life insurance as salesman Red and

closed more than four times as many sales. Red's sales averaged
$7,627 monthly and Black's, $15,332. In number of contacts closed,
Red averaged 1.6 monthly; Black averaged 6.5.

It is clearly evident that salesman Black's good self-management
was responsible for his success. By systematic effort he was able to
spend more hours in the field, make more contacts, conduct more interviews, secure more prospects, and follow up more customers than

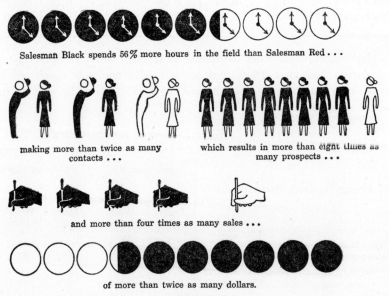

Salesman Black spends 56% more hours in the field than Salesman Red . . .

making more than twice as many   which results in more than eight times as
contacts . . .   many prospects . . .

and more than four times as many sales . . .

of more than twice as many dollars.

Fig. 13.

his associate. His accomplishment shows what can be done by any
salesman who will plan his work and work his plan.

VALUE OF SELLING TIME

Manufacturing is accelerated by time saving machines and time is
recorded and observed on every operation. However, time saved in
manufacturing is often wasted in selling because salesmen have not
become conscious of the importance of conserving time.

Time is a salesman's greatest asset. It is his working capital and,
when properly invested in interviews and demonstrations, yields hand-
some dividends in orders and earnings. "The management of a salesman's time is often the cause of his success or failure," said Alfred C.
Fuller, one of America's greatest salesmen.

The value of a salesman's time in terms of income is illustrated in the following table prepared by a salesmanager to show the importance of saving selling time.

Yearly income	Value of half hour	Half hour a day for a year	Hour a day for a year
$1,500	$0.31	$ 93	$186
2,000	0.43	123	246
3,000	0.63	189	378
4,000	0.83	249	498
5,000	1.04	312	624
7,500	1.56	468	936

HOW A SALESMAN SPENDS HIS TIME AND ENERGY

A salesman's working time and energy are spent in the following activities: (1) traveling; (2) calling, waiting and interviewing; (3) planning and routine work; (4) self-improvement; (5) prospecting; (6) cultivating customers; (7) miscellaneous.

The time spent by an average life insurance salesman during the course of a year is illustrated by the following figures:

In a year a salesman has only 2,336 hours of working time, of which 350 hours are spent face to face with prospects, 467 hours waiting to see prospects, 935 hours traveling between prospects, and 584 hours in clerical work and planning. The balance of his time, devoted to sleep, meals, and recreation, is 5,840 hours; Sundays take up 416 hours, on the basis of an eight-hour day, and holidays, 168 hours. This analysis illustrates that actual selling time is short—only about an hour and a half a day.

1. TRAVEL TIME

Traveling consumes time in proportion to the extent of a salesman's territory. Rural salesmen spend nearly 40 per cent of their time in travel; city salesmen spend more than 25 per cent of their time; suburban salesmen average 32.4 per cent of their time en route between calls.

The type of product sold and customer served by a salesman affects the amount of his travel time according to studies made of the travel time of salesmen. A food salesman, contacting wholesalers and working in rural areas, averaged 44.1 per cent of his time in travel; an industrial equipment salesman working in the same area spent only **36.7** per cent of his time in travel. A city salesman of office equipment traveled only **28.7** per cent of his time. The average travel time of **26** country salesmen representing six wholesalers was **20.4** per cent of their total work time, according to H. C. Nolen.

Many salesmen in city and suburban areas travel more on foot than by automobile. There is a definite relationship between the number of miles that a salesman walks and his sales production.

To compare the foot travel of successful salesmen with that of mediocre sales producers, a number of salesmen were equipped with pedometers and the mileage walked each day was recorded. It was found that successful salesmen walk, on the average, **11** per cent farther than poor salesmen. Good city salesmen walk an average of **4.15** miles daily; mediocre salesmen average only **3.7** miles.

How to Control Travel Time. To control travel time, a salesman must know how much time he is spending in travel. By keeping a simple record of starting time in the field, time spent traveling between stops, and stopping time each day for a week or two, he can see how his travel time is being used.

The following automobile travel time record of a grocery specialty salesman calling on wholesalers in New England shows how a salesman spends his time in travel:

Day	Total time in field, hours	Travel time, hours	Percentage travel to total	Travel interval, minutes	Starting time	Stopping time
Monday..........	13.96	4.13	29.5	17	8:05	10:02
Tuesday..........	Holiday					
Wednesday......	14.91	4.98	33.4	18	7:25	9:05
Thursday........	14.49	6.66	45.9	28	8:05	9:55
Friday..........	11.25	5.70	50.7	31	8:20	7:35
Average..........	13.65	5.37	44.9	23		

Every salesman should make an analysis of his travel record to discover opportunities to reduce travel. Then he should reduce the amount of travel time shown by the record by planned travel.

Reducing Travel Time. Practical methods of planned travel used by salesmen to conserve travel time are:

1. By centralizing calls in a limited area or section, travel time is conserved.

2. By routing calls in order of coverage and by arranging them by location, time is saved in traveling from one call to another. A daily route list should be prepared, taking into consideration the number of calls to be made, the average time per call, and the time interval between calls.

3. The elimination of needless calls results in a great saving in travel time. By using a telephone and making advance appointments, a salesman can eliminate many useless contacts.

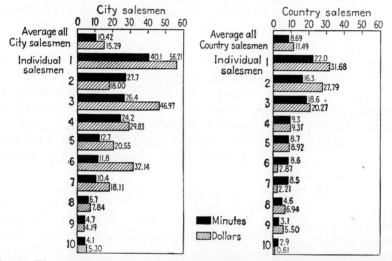

SALES EFFORTS IN MINUTES AND RESULTS IN DOLLARS

Fig. 14. The relationship between the average time per call and the dollar sales volume of city and country salesmen is graphically illustrated by this chart, reproduced through the courtesy of Herman C. Nolen, who has made extensive studies of the selling time of wholesale salesmen. The salesmen with the highest selling time sell the greatest dollar volume.

4. Selection of the method of transportation best adapted to the area to be covered saves travel time. The use of an automobile in congested metropolitan areas sometimes wastes travel time.

2. CALLING, WAITING, AND INTERVIEWING TIME

Next to time spent in traveling, the greatest part of a salesman's time is devoted to calling on prospects, waiting for interviews, and interviewing. A sales call is a visit to a prospect for the purpose of conducting a sales interview. Many calls, however, do not result in interviews because prospects are busy, absent, or unwilling to be interviewed. A sales interview is a more or less complete sales presentation.

The amount of time devoted by a salesman to calling, waiting, and interviewing varies widely according to the area covered and the type of product sold. As a general average, manufacturers' salesmen make 10 calls a day and spend 45 minutes on each call. Salesmen traveling in rural areas average 7 calls a day; suburban salesmen, 11 calls.

A successful grocery salesman calling on wholesalers averages 13 calls a day and 35 minutes to a call. A packing-house salesman calling on retailers averages 16 calls a day and 19 minutes to a call. A salesman of office equipment who sells business concerns averages 5 calls a day but spends an hour on each call. A typical life insurance salesman averages 6 calls a day and takes 60 minutes for a call.

Waiting for interviews consumes an average of only 2.12 minutes of a salesman's time according to a study of the waiting time of 895 manufacturers' salesmen. Although some salesmen were observed to wait as long as 23 minutes to see prospects, others secured interviews in 28 seconds. City wholesale salesmen wait an average of 5.2 minutes a call; those in the country wait 5.1 minutes a call, according to H. C. Nolen.

Time spent by salesmen in face-to-face contact with prospects averages only 7½ minutes an interview, according to a time study of 900 sales interviews of manufacturers' salesmen. A study by H. C. Nolen of the time spent by a wholesaler's salesmen in sales interviews shows that city salesmen average 5 minutes a call and country salesmen 8 minutes. The average salesman does about 63 per cent of the talking during interviews.

How to Control Calling, Waiting, and Interviewing Time. To effectively conserve contact time, a salesman should know the amount of time he is spending in calling, waiting, and interviewing. A record of time consumed in calling, waiting, and interviewing prospects can be easily kept along with the travel time record previously described.

The next step in conserving a salesman's contact time is to analyze his calling, waiting, and interviewing records. By comparing his contact record with his sales record, a salesman can discover the exact mathematical ratio between the number of calls and interviews which he makes and the volume of sales he closes. If a salesman averages one sale to 20 calls and 10 interviews, then in 40 calls and 20 interviews he should complete two sales; in 60 calls and 30 interviews, he should close three sales.

By analyzing his contact record, a salesman can determine the number of calls and interviews which he must make to sell a certain volume. For example, a salesman may find it necessary to spend 48 hours in the field, make 50 calls, hold 20 interviews, and close 2 sales a week in order to sell the volume necessary to earn the income needed to maintain his standard of living at the level to which he is accustomed. Every salesman must establish his own daily call and interview objectives which take into account his own ability, territory, and product. Such a definite objective will give a salesman a basis for conserving his time and effort.

WEEKLY SUMMARY																
	No. of Sales	Amount Closed	New Pros-pects	Effec-tive New Con-tacts	Sales Contacts			Interviews				Service Calls Deliv-eries, etc.	Hours			
					Total	Progress	Ineffec-tive	Total	First	Second	3rd and over		Field	Plan-ning	Study	Total
Mon.																
Tues.																
Wed.																
Thur.																
Fri.																
Sat.																
Total																

Fig. 15. Weekly summary of sales activity form, used by salesmen of a large life insurance company in reviewing their progress and comparing their activity with their standards of performance.

Increasing Contact Time. When a salesman has determined his daily call and interview objectives, he next adopts methods of reaching these goals. Calling, waiting, and interviewing time can be conserved in the following ways:

1. Advance cards may be mailed to prospects informing them of the salesman's call. They pave the way for interviews and reduce waiting time.

2. Advance appointments made by telephone or letter save waiting time, enable a salesman to get past buffers, ensure interviews, and enable him to find sufficient time for a complete sales presentation. A salesman who represents a large manufacturer made 12 personal calls a day and found many prospects out of their offices. He sought appointments by telephone and increased his interviews 100 per cent, obtained 25 appointments, and avoided 10 unnecessary calls a week.

3. Secure 9 A.M. and 1 P.M. appointments to ensure effective use of the early morning and afternoon hours when prospects are difficult to see.

4. Plan evening work when selling products or services for personal or home use. When purchases are made jointly by a husband and wife, evening interviews are productive. Many prospects are more accessible at home in the evening than during the day. Few home-appliance or life insurance salesmen succeed without doing evening work.

5. Plan each day's calls in advance by making a time schedule of interviews, listing the names and addresses of prospects to be called upon each hour during the day. An emergency call schedule should be prepared also, listing the names of prospects who may be seen in the event that prospects on the original list are not available.

6. Determine the most suitable hour of the day and the day of the week to call upon certain types of prospects. Many physicians make calls during morning hours; salesmen are rarely found in their offices in the morning; merchants are usually too busy to be interviewed on Saturdays. If a salesman discovers the best time to interview prospects in certain vocations and professions, he can conserve his own calling and waiting time.

Observation of nearly 900 manufacturers' salesmen showed that approximately 21 per cent call on Monday, 22 per cent on Tuesday, 22 per cent on Wednesday, 16 per cent on Thursday, 12 per cent on Friday, and 6 per cent on Saturday. By concentrating his calls in the latter part of the week, a salesman can avoid congestion in reception rooms and save his waiting time.

7. A prepared sales presentation saves the time of both a salesman and his prospects. A salesman who is prepared avoids irrelevant conversation and visiting with prospects. If he has advance information about a prospect's needs and situation, interviewing time is reduced. Well-organized sales equipment also enables a salesman to save interviewing time.

8. Digressions from a daily plan, including attendance at theaters and ball games or playing golf, disorganize a salesman's work. Salesmen are often tempted to stop work on account of the weather or because a successful sale has been concluded.

9. Many salesmen believe that no sales can be made on Saturdays, on the days before or after a holiday, and on rainy days. Such misconceptions are responsible for time lost which could be profitably used for calling on prospects.

10. The late morning start, the long lunch hour, and the early quitting are responsible for much lost selling time. If a salesman will spend an additional hour a day in the field for a week, he will increase his sales and earnings through the added calls and interviews. The best selling hours of the day, from 9 A.M. to noon and from 2 to 5 P.M., should be filled with appointments and interviews.

3. PLANNING AND ROUTINE WORK TIME

To conserve time and energy in selling, proper planning is necessary. By careful organization, a salesman's time devoted to planning and routine work may be minimized. The amount of planning that a salesman must carry on depends on the complexities of his work. Some men can plan their day's work in 10 minutes; others may require an hour or more. Planning and record-keeping are of value only in so far as they contribute to increased sales. A salesman should neither work haphazardly nor devote so much time to routine planning that little time is left for making sales presentations.

How to Control Planning Time. The first essential in the conservation of planning time is adequate records of traveling, calling, interviewing, waiting, study, and planning. Every salesman should keep the following records of his work: *daily activity records,* showing names and addresses of firms or individuals called upon, with the results of the calls and remarks; *prospect records,* listing the names, addresses, source, occupation, present ownership, age, and other pertinent information about prospects; *customer records,* listing dates and amounts of purchases, names, addresses, and other necessary data; *summary records,* for totaling, by the week or month, the hours worked, the number of calls, sales, prospects secured, presentations, demonstrations, lost orders, time employment, etc.

Routine planning is also simplified by the use of printed forms for laying out daily call and appointment schedules, route lists, weekly and monthly summaries of interviews, demonstrations, surveys, and other sales activities.

Time, activity, prospect, customer, and summary records are necessary to enable a salesman to review the results of his past efforts, locate his shortcomings, and plan his future work. These records enable him to establish contact objectives. By consulting his records, a salesman can tell the number of calls necessary to secure an interview, the ratio of presentations to sales, and the amount of time that must be spent in the field to obtain a profitable volume of sales.

Salesman's Record-filing System. So that information contained in a salesman's activity records is readily available for planning field work, a simple filing system is necessary. A simple filing system aids a salesman's memory, frees him from routine work, and gives him more time for field activity.

FIG. 16. Salesman's prospect-card filing system prepared by the Berkshire Life Insurance Co. showing cards filed from front to back as follows: alphabetical index section which provides for a general pool of prospect cards; geographical section in which prospect cards are filed by sections of a city or by towns; current month section in which prospect cards to be followed up the current month are filed; monthly tickler section in which prospect cards are filed for the month in which they should be followed up, and a customer section where record cards of present customers are filed. This system may be used as effectively by all types of salesmen of specialties, including advertising, office equipment, and appliances.

Records of contacts with prospects and customers may be kept most conveniently on 3- by 5-inch cards, which may be filed in a 4- by 6-inch file box, obtainable at any stationery store, or in a card-filing section found in the upper drawer of many standard office desks.

This prospect and customer record file is divided into three principal parts. The first section is reserved for live or current prospects and divided by days of the month indicated on guides numbered from 1 to 31. Behind these daily guides are filed the cards of prospects and customers who should be seen by the salesman on certain days of the current month. This is the active working section of the file and is used in planning daily contacts and making up call schedules for each day of the month.

The second section is for record cards of inactive prospects. This section is divided into months, indicated by guides reading from January to December. This monthly section is for cards to be given attention a month or more ahead of the current date. On the first day of each month the cards for the month are distributed through the daily guides in the first or daily section of the file. The monthly section facilitates planning by providing an automatic reminder to call on prospects and customers who should be interviewed in future months.

The third section of the file is for customer record cards. It is divided alphabetically by guides lettered from A to Z. The cards in this section are examined monthly and cards of certain owners are selected for calls and distributed among the daily guides of the current month.

A fourth section of the file may be arranged by geographical location for records of prospects and customers. Guide cards listing the counties, towns, or sections covered separate the record cards of prospects or users located in each area. This section of the file aids in routing calls and saves travel time and energy.

A fifth section may be reserved for special types of prospects such as institutional prospects, professional men, and evening prospects which require special follow-up.

This prospect and customer record filing system can be readily used by salesmen of various products and services. It can be maintained in a few minutes a day and provides invaluable aid in recalling appointments, timing call backs, and scheduling each day's calls.

A larger vertical file of the same type, or a desk drawer file, may be used for keeping time records, daily activity records, and daily, weekly, or monthly work summaries.

Daily Sales Work Planning. Daily work planning usually includes the following activities:

1. Recording results of day's work, including:
   a. Number of calls made.
   b. Number of presentations made.
   c. First, second, third interviews made.
   d. Service calls on customers.
   e. New prospects secured.
   f. Demonstrations made.

    g. Volume of sales made.

    h. Lost orders.

2. Keeping time records of day's work, including:

    a. Travel time.

    b. Calling time.

    c. Interviewing time.

    d. Total hours spent in field.

    e. Planning time.

    f. Study time.

3. Filing prospect and customer cards.

4. Completing summary records of the day's, week's, or month's activities.

5. Planning the following day's work, including:

    a. Preparation of a daily time schedule of calls and interviews, routed and zoned.

    b. Preparation of an emergency daily time schedule of calls.

    c. Securing appointments for a nine and a one o'clock call the following day.

    d. Set daily time and energy objectives of hours for field, travel time, interviewing time, number of calls, number of new prospects, number of old prospects, number of old customers, balancing activity among these objectives.

    e. Prepare selling equipment and written proposals.

    f. Plan presentation and answers to objections.

6. Write and answer sales correspondence.

Every salesman should have a similar description of his daily planning duties.

Conserve Planning Time. Planning time can be conserved by the following practices:

1. Planning is done best at a slack time of day or in the evening when it is not a desirable time to call on prospects or customers. The best times to plan usually are early in the morning before prospects can be interviewed, late in the afternoon when they have left their offices, or at home in the evening when business interruptions can be avoided.

2. A filing system such as the one previously described simplifies the work of planning and makes it possible for a salesman to reduce planning time to a minimum.

3. If a salesman spends little time at his desk he avoids time consuming routine duties. By following a definite planning routine and observing a definite time each day for planning, a salesman conserves his time in handling office routine.

4. By planning in advance on a long-range basis, a salesman has a

better perspective of his work and can simplify each day's planning. Some salesmen find it profitable to budget their time a year ahead by establishing weekly and monthly activity objectives on calls, interviews, new prospects, sales, etc.

A successful life insurance salesman lists monthly on a one-page ruled form the names and addresses, ages, occupations, and sources of 50 prospects whom he plans to interview during the current month. In a space beside each name is recorded the result of each contact. If a prospect proves to be worthless, his name is killed. If a buyer postpones action, his name is transferred to the prospect sheet made up at the end of the month for the succeeding month. If a sale results, the amount of the transaction is recorded. This system provides a monthly visual inventory of prospects and enables a salesman to analyze the results of his activities, locate his strengths and weaknesses, and increase his efforts to secure greater production.

4. SELF-IMPROVEMENT TIME

Salesmen should regularly spend time in study and self-development. Increasing competition is forcing salesmen to acquire a better knowledge of the needs of buyers and a more complete understanding of their own products. Successful salesmen devote at least an hour a day to personal improvement.

Numerous opportunities for self-education are available to ambitious salesmen. Planned reading is a fundamental source of information about a salesman's product, service, advertising, and selling methods. The following sources of information provide excellent opportunities for a salesman to improve his knowledge:

1. Company publications including manuals, policy books, engineering data, house organs, bulletins, and advertisements.

2. Professional or trade publications, association organs published in the field in which a salesman is engaged, as well as sales magazines including *Printer's Ink* and *Advertising & Selling*.

3. Business service publications dealing with current economic conditions and business trends, including United Business Service, Babson's Reports, and Kipplinger's Letters.

4. Collateral reading related to a salesman's business, such as current books on economics, labor, and management.

5. Inspirational publications dealing with selling and personal efficiency, such as "How to Win Friends and Influence People," by Carnegie; "The Knack of Selling Yourself," by Mangan; "Press On," by Hill; "Step Out and Sell," by Holler.

Additional sources of information are company sales meetings, trade or professional association meetings, adult evening educational courses in selling or related subjects. Membership in salesmen's organizations, such as the National Association of Life Underwriters for life insurance salesmen, provides opportunities for a salesman to exchange experiences with others and learn new sales methods. Correspondence courses in salesmanship, prepared by manufacturers, trade associations, and extension departments of recognized educational institutions, also provide helpful information. The American College of Life Underwriters, established in 1927 by the life insurance business, has trained and awarded the degree of Certified Life Underwriter to nearly five thousand life insurance salesmen.

A salesman should analyze his own needs for self-improvement and plan to set aside a certain time each day for study. One salesman may be weak in his knowledge of product, prices, or advertising. Another may be having difficulty in locating prospects or securing interviews. Still another may be weak in meeting objections. Personality weaknesses, a critical attitude, poor appearance, and argumentativeness handicap some salesmen. Planned study can correct these weaknesses and enable a salesman to increase his sales and earnings.

A salesman may profitably use time spent on trains, buses, or in waiting for buyers for business reading and self-improvement.

5. Prospecting Time

Much valuable time is wasted by salesmen in a fruitless search for possible buyers. When a salesman has no proven method of prospecting, he wastes many hours that might otherwise be spent more profitably in closing sales.

By making prospecting a daily activity and setting up an objective of one or two new prospects a day, a salesman does not have to take time out to look for potential buyers. Prospecting time is conserved when a salesman employs one or more of the following methods of locating buyers:

1. Secure one or more prospects on each call by using the endless-chain method of obtaining prospects from each person interviewed.

2. Use the telephone to qualify suspects and select prospects in advance of calls.

3. Rely upon informants or sales associates to suggest names of prospects so that a salesman will not have to take time to locate them.

4. Follow scheduled calls on customers or live prospects with one

or more calls on "suspects" in the same neighborhood, in the next office, or across the street.

6. Customer Cultivation Time

Time spent in cultivating customers pays big dividends to salesmen in repeat sales, word-of-mouth advertising, names of new prospects, letters of recommendation, accessory and service sales, and good will. Fifty-three per cent of the sales of a popular make of automobile are repeat sales to old customers. Motor-car manufacturers advise their salesmen to make not less than three calls a year on new owners. From 40 to 50 per cent of the sales of automatic refrigerators are said to be made to old customers. In view of these facts, salesmen should plan to spend more time in contacting old customers.

If analysis of a salesman's daily call report shows that he is not calling on old customers, a daily or weekly objective of customer contacts should be established. The number of customer calls to be made weekly depends upon the amount of the original sale, frequency of repeat orders, and service requirements of the product.

A large electric refrigerator sales organization requires all salesmen to make their first call each day on an old customer. Successful life insurance salesmen average a service call a day on policyholders.

By including one or two old customer contacts in each day's schedule of calls, a salesman ensures that his clients will receive the attention they deserve.

7. Miscellaneous Time

Salesmen selling to wholesale and retail distributors have numerous miscellaneous duties which consume much time. A time study of wholesale drug salesmen, made by H. C. Nolen, showed that an average of 4.7 per cent of a country salesman's time was spent in collecting and 2.3 per cent of his time in making adjustments. City wholesale salesmen devoted only 1.8 per cent of their time to collecting and 1.7 per cent to making adjustments. Missionary duties, including dressing windows, checking inventories, and preparing advertising, consume a considerable portion of the time of salesmen who call upon dealers.

A salesman should keep a daily record of the time spent in these miscellaneous activities to discover whether he is devoting too much time to nonselling work.

HOW A SALESMAN SHOULD ORGANIZE HIS DAY'S WORK

Successful salesmen organize their time by taking the five following steps which constitute a practical program for good personal management. If a salesman will learn and practice these five routine points in systematizing his activities, he will experience more profitable sales results.

Routine for Organizing a Salesman's Activities

1. Set daily contact quotas.
2. Schedule daily calls and interviews.
3. Keep records of daily, weekly, and monthly sales performance.
4. Review and analyze each day's work.
5. Plan next day's work.

1. Set Daily Activity Quotas. Establish a definite number of calls and interviews based on the number of calls, interviews, and hours in the field necessary to obtain the volume of sales desired. These quotas should provide for a well-balanced expenditure of sales time and effort for each day, as follows:

1. Daily quota of hours in field.
2. Daily quota of calls on:
   a. New prospects.
   b. Old prospects.
   c. Old customers.
3. Daily quota of interviews.
   a. First.
   b. Second.
   c. Third and over.
4. Daily quota of sales volume.
5. Daily quota of new prospects.
6. Daily quota of demonstrations.
7. Daily quota of planning time.
8. Daily quota of studying time.
9. Starting time.
10. Stopping time.
11. Hours of travel.

From his call and interview records a salesman can set these objectives accurately and establish the correct number of calls, interviews, and sales. Quotas must be changed to meet variable business conditions. In periods of depression a greater number of calls and hours in

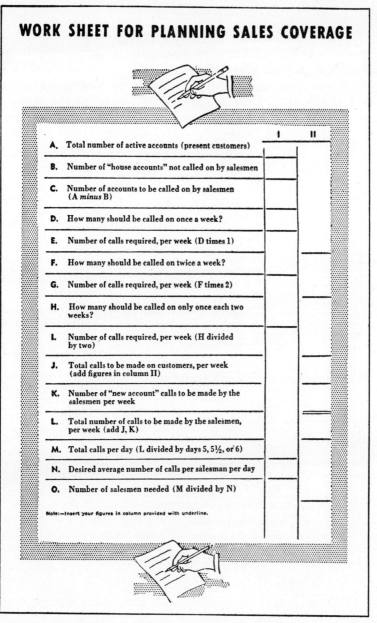

WORK SHEET FOR PLANNING SALES COVERAGE

		I	II
A.	Total number of active accounts (present customers)		
B.	Number of "house accounts" not called on by salesmen		
C.	Number of accounts to be called on by salesmen (A *minus* B)		
D.	How many should be called on once a week?		
E.	Number of calls required, per week (D times 1)		
F.	How many should be called on twice a week?		
G.	Number of calls required, per week (F times 2)		
H.	How many should be called on only once each two weeks?		
I.	Number of calls required, per week (H divided by two)		
J.	Total calls to be made on customers, per week (add figures in column II)		
K.	Number of "new account" calls to be made by the salesmen per week		
L.	Total number of calls to be made by the salesmen, per week (add J, K)		
M.	Total calls per day (L divided by days 5, 5½, or 6)		
N.	Desired average number of calls per salesman per day		
O.	Number of salesmen needed (M divided by N)		

Note:—Insert your figures in column provided with underline.

FIG. 17. To aid salesmen who call on merchants in organizing the coverage of their territories, this work sheet has been prepared by the Distribution Committee of the National Confectioner's Association. By classifying customers according to call frequency, a salesman can determine the total number of calls a day and a week which must be made and plan route and territory travel to save time, expense, and effort and increase sales effectiveness.

the field are necessary if a salesman expects to accomplish the same sales results as in good times. By keeping the proper balance between calls on old prospects, new prospects, and owners, a salesman can create a well-rounded work program and secure maximum results.

2. Schedule Daily Calls and Interviews. A list of the names and addresses of prospects and customers to be contacted should be pre-

PLAN YOUR WORK				WORK YOUR PLAN			

List below Calls you propose to make today.   Remember, Lost Order Reports aid the management and you.

Date _____   Salesman _____

TO DO TODAY

	FIRM	ADDRESS OR DEPT.	PARTY TO SEE	SALES TOOLS NEEDED	NEXT CALL DATE	AMOUNT SOLD
1						
2						
3						
4						
5						
6						
7						
8						
9						
10						
11						
12						
13						
14						

ADDITIONAL CALLS · NOT PLANNED

1					
2					
3					
4					
5					
6					
7					

REMARKS

NO. CALLS	RECORD FORM ITEMS SOLD	NO. OF INSPECTIONS			PROSPECTS DEVELOPED						DISPOSITION				
TO-DAY	STOCK	SPL.	VIS.	VER.	L.L.	S.C.	FIL.	LED.	SAL.	STK.	FURN.	SER.	R.AS.	TOTAL	SOLD	LOST	DROP'T	DEF.	TOTAL

Turn into office each night with day's prospect follow-up, and inspection slips attached.

Fig. 18. Daily plan sheet used by salesmen of a large office equipment manufacturer in recording names of companies and individuals to be contacted each day. Space is provided for an emergency list of concerns to visit in the event prospects who are listed at top of sheet cannot be interviewed.

pared daily to provide for contacts each hour of the day. A supplementary list of prospects should be prepared also in the event that some prospects listed on the original schedule cannot be interviewed. Sales interviews for personal products or services may be scheduled after 7 P.M.

To make a call schedule effective, appointments should be secured in advance whenever possible and the work habits of prospects considered in planning calls.

In making up a daily call schedule, the contacts planned should be grouped in one locality and routed in order of coverage to save a salesman's time and energy.

3. Keep Records of Daily, Weekly, and Monthly Sales Performance. A daily call report, listing the names of prospects or owners called upon, with the results of each call; the hours spent in the field, in the office, and in studying; the number of new prospects secured; starting and stopping time; time spent in interviews; waiting and traveling time—all should be completed at the close of each day and summarized for each week or month. Daily and monthly records kept regularly will enable a salesman to set accurately his future activity objectives, check his time employment, and measure the effectiveness of his work.

Cards recording information about each prospect and owner called upon and the results of each call should be prepared and kept in an adequate file for future reference and follow-up.

4. Review and Analyze Each Day's Work. By studying his call reports, a salesman can quickly get a clear picture of his progress. When compared with each day's quotas on calls and interviews, the record will frequently show a need for more calls that might otherwise never be made unless the facts were known.

5. Plan Next Day's Work. With the aid of a prospect and customer file, a salesman can quickly select record cards which can be zoned, routed, and listed on his call schedule for the following day. Appointments may be secured for the first call in the morning, and a luncheon interview may be arranged. Adjustments, collections, and service calls may be scheduled. Sales presentations may be prepared, proposals written, information collected, and sales equipment organized for the following day's work.

Problem I

Time Employment

Robert Maiden, representing the Holmes Apparel Corporation

The Holmes Apparel Corporation, established in 1930 in Louisville, Ky., sells an annual volume of $10,000,000 worth of men's and women's hosiery, underwear, and men's neckties and shirts. They sell direct to consumers through 7,500 full- and part-time commission representatives operating out of branch offices in the principal cities

SALES PERFORMANCE RATING FORM

Organization of Sales Activities

Salesman_____   Date_____

Rated by_____   Over-all Rating_____

Score

I. *Daily Contact Quota Established*	Excellent 90–100	Good 80–90	Fair 70–80	Poor 60–70	Failure Below 60
A. Daily calls					
B. Daily interviews					
C. Daily demonstrations					
D. Daily new prospects					
E. Number of first interviews					

II. *Daily Schedule of Calls Followed as Planned*	Excellent 90–100	Good 80–90	Fair 70–80	Poor 60–70	Failure Below 60

III. *Sales Records*	Excellent 90–100	Good 80–90	Fair 70–80	Poor 60–70	Failure Below 60
A. Daily					
B. Weekly					
C. Monthly					
D. Prospects					
E. Customers					

IV. *Planning Daily Work*	Excellent 90–100	Good 80–90	Fair 70–80	Poor 60–70	Failure Below 60
A. Maintain file					
B. Regular planning time					
C. Starting time planned					
D. Stopping time planned					

Miscellaneous_____

_____

_____

of the country. The company advertises in national magazines, read by 4,500,000 people monthly, to create a demand for its trade-mark "Glossy."

Operating out of the Providence, R. I., office of the company is Robert Maiden, twenty-five years of age, who has been with the company two years. He owns and operates his own automobile. The following record of three typical days' activities of salesman Maiden, as written by himself in his own words, describes his procedure and illustrates how he uses his time in selling:

1. Wednesday: Left home about 8:30 A.M. Didn't go to the office, but drove to the Telephone Company. Got there about 9 A.M.

2. Made my first demonstration; showed her why she wore so many stockings by asking her questions. Showed her just why we had such and such a feature and sold her a box of hosiery. Showed her underwear but couldn't make any further addition to her order. She said that I was quite lucky to have sold her at all, as in the past other salesmen had tried but without results.

3. Next girl was too poor; perhaps in a month, but she wouldn't place her order now.

4. Girls were getting busy as their work began to pile up, so, seeing I couldn't sell if I stayed on, excused myself and told them I would call back when they wouldn't be so busy.

5. Next called on an insurance man and, as I presented my goods, a funny thing happened. I was able to sell him a box of socks and not only that, but he wanted me to come to work for him, and he commenced to give me a talking-to, of how much I could make selling insurance, if I was able to sell socks the way I did. He talked with me for quite a while. Near 11 o'clock, as I noticed as I went out.

6. He had certainly used a lot of my time, of course, but he too had been willing to give me his time in order for me to sell him socks, so I guess that I shouldn't say that he imposed on his sale.

7. Made one other call before lunch on a doctor. He talked with me and asked me questions about socks. Why I thought I could save him money, etc. The interview lasted until 12 noon. Finally he said that he was convinced about the wearability and that his next order would be with me, but that right now he had plenty, but he was glad to have seen them.

8. Called on Mr. T. Waited in reception room for 15 minutes, but he finally decided when I was announced that today was too busy to bother with socks and ties, etc.

9. Called on another doctor and sold him a box of socks.

10. Next I saw an office girl. I explained our hosiery to her, but only got a "too poor" answer and the girl stuck to her guns, convincing me too

that she was sincere. This is so often used as a source of escape from sales-people.

11. Made four more presentations with no results. Some were too poor or overstocked with stockings; will order in the fall, if I call again. Stopped work about 5:25 P.M. and went to supper.

12. Went out after supper and made one call and a good sale. Sold the husband, wife, and daughter. Home by 9:30 P.M.

13. Thursday: Got up early, took my suits in to be cleaned and pressed. Called on first prospects at 9 A.M.

14. Mrs. V. had appointment. Sold her a box of silk hose and added some anklets also. Called on Miss F., the girl who had to ask her mother. Her mind was quite made up. She had talked to a friend who had advised her not to try them so she used her friend's judgment. Next called on an executive in one of our large companies. Waited 15 minutes to see him and had a very interesting interview. Talked about his hobbies for a while, then he got into our line, and I was able to sell him a good sized order.

15. Went to a photographer next. Gave one of our mending kits to the lady in charge. She was very busy now but asked me to call back, as she knew us and would like to see them soon.

16. Called next on a foot doctor, who was very busy peeling corns now, and so couldn't stop.

17. Saw another photographer and sold his secretary a set of our pajamas.

18. Went next into the Girl Scout office. Girl there acted quite irritable and wouldn't even grant me a minute of her time.

19. Called next on Mrs. S. She was sorry that I had bothered to call as she couldn't buy now. I assured her that it was all right, and that I would call at another time.

20. Called next on Miss F. Got her exchange—then decided to go to Sea Point. I was disgusted with the city for today.

21. On the way out I stopped and called on a customer. She was well supplied in hosiery but I sold her some underwear. Saw Mr. H. at the same time. He was not interested.

22. Called on Miss R.; sleeping; call back in half an hour. Called back and sold her an order for September delivery. Called on Mrs. R. Call back later in the summer. Called on Mrs. G. who wants me to call back later in the season.

23. Saw Mr. C. Mrs. C. was out. Talked with him for one half an hour about his travels this past winter in South Africa. Will want socks this fall or late summer. Left the Point and went home about 7 P.M.

24. Friday: Left home about 8:30 A.M. Went to the office. Called back at 9:30 on Miss F. Gave her some mending kits and some perfume. She gave me her New York address, and she told me to call any time I was in the city, that she would be glad to see me.

25. Called next at an electric company. Mr. C. was too busy. Called on

girl in insurance office. Busy now. Made an appointment for the last of the week. Made a call on another stenographer and sold her an order.

26. Next made a call on a stenographer in motor vehicles office. Made her a snap presentation, and sold her a box of hosiery. Called on Miss M. Busy, call back. Called on Miss B. "Too busy, see me later." Called on attorney. Too busy, See him later. Made one more call. Made one sale before I quit in disgust at 3:30. Everyone today seemed busy.

Questions

1. Analyze salesman Maiden's time employment for *each* of the three days described in his diary by charting his:

  a. Starting time.

  b. Stopping time.

  c. Total hours in the field.

  d. Number of calls (no presentation made).

  e. Number of interviews (presentation made).

  f. Number of sales.

  g. Number of old customer calls.

2. Did salesman Maiden use his time effectively on the three days described in his diary? Criticize each of the seven items analyzed in Question 1 favorably or otherwise. Cite specific instances of wasted time.

3. Prepare a daily time and effort objective program for salesman Maiden indicating ideal goals on each of the seven items listed in Question 1.

4. What records should salesman Maiden keep of his daily activities? How should he use these records?

5. What steps should Maiden take to conserve his time?

Problem II

TIME CONTROL

Clyde R. Pritchard, representing Furbush Mayonnaise Company

The Furbush Mayonnaise Company, established in Philadelphia, Pa., in 1916, manufactures and distributes a line of mayonnaise, salad dressing, cheese, pickles, and condiments direct to retail food stores and delicatessens through an organization of 300 driver-salesmen who sell and deliver from company trucks in one operation. Distributing branches, where warehouse stocks are maintained, are located in the principal markets throughout the country.

Each salesman operates over a weekly route, calling on individual and chain-store customers once every six days. He writes orders, makes collections, delivers from his truck, cleans and rearranges his customers' stocks, exchanges, keeps route books to record sales and

STARTING TIME 7:35 A.M.

Stop	Type of stop	Time of arrival	Travel time, minutes	Time wait, minutes	Time leave	Remarks
1	Restaurant	7:45	10	0	8:00	Breakfast
2	Grocery	8:10	10	0	8:20	Order
	Battery trouble—Phoned repair man			65	9:25	
3	Chain Grocery	9:30	5	0	9:47	Order
4	Restaurant	9:48	1	0	9:49	Nothing
5	Chain grocery	9:50	1	0	10:10	Order
6	Chain grocery	10:10	0	0	10:40	Order
7	Chain dairy	10:40	0	0	10:55	Order
8	Delicatessen	10:55	0	0	10:56	Out
9	Restaurant	10:56	0	0	11:00	Nothing
10	Restaurant	11:02	2	0	11:04	Nothing
11	Market	11:05	1	0	11:15	Collect
12	Delicatessen	11:19	4	0	11:25	Collect
13	Market	11:28	3	0	11:47	Order—collect
14	Market	11:50	3	5	12:10	Advertising—collect
15	Chain grocery	12:10	0	20	12:45	Order
16	Restaurant	12:45	0	0	12:47	Nothing
17	Market	12:50	3	0	12:55	Nothing
18	Grocery	1:00	5	0	1:04	Order
19	Market	1:06	2	0	1:12	Order
20	Chain grocery	1:13	1	0	1:17	Out
21	Spa	1:18	1	0	1:40	Exchange order
22	Restaurant	1:40	0	0	1:50	Eat
23	Market	1:53	3	5	2:15	Order
24	Chain grocery	2:15	0	0	2:30	Order
25	Grocery	2:35	5	0	2:55	Order
26	Grocery	3:00	5	0	3:10	Order
27	Market	3:10	0	0	3:35	Exchange order
28	Market	3:40	5	0	3:50	Nothing
29	Chain grocery	3:50	0	0	3:51	Out
30	Delicatessen	3:55	4	0	3:57	Nothing
31	Market	3:57	0	0	4:00	Nothing
32	Hospital	4:12	12	0	4:20	Order
33	Grocery	4:35	15	0	4:45	Delivery
34	Return trip to branch, arriving at 5 P.M.					

collections, loads truck, places store and window display advertising, and drives his truck.

Clyde R. Pritchard is one of 10 salesmen-drivers operating out of the Boston branch of the company and has been selling Furbush products for two years. A typical day spent in the suburbs of Boston by him is illustrated on the time and activity report as shown on page 386.

Questions

1. Compute the travel time, waiting time, number of calls, number of sales, number of hours in the field, and interviewing time of salesman Pritchard on the day described in the case. What is the percentage of each item to total hours in field?

2. Criticize favorably or otherwise the activity of the salesman, citing specific instances of wasted time or good use of time. How else could he have saved time? In what other ways should he spend his time?

3. Did the salesman apparently zone and route his calls to conserve his selling time?

4. What was salesman Pritchard's efficiency ratio of calls to interviews, interviews to sales? Set up a daily objective in calls and interviews to enable him to increase his number of sales 10 per cent.

Reading References

B. R. CANFIELD, "Sales Administration, Principles and Problems," rev. ed., Chaps. XVI, XVIII, Prentice-Hall, Inc., New York, 1947.

E. CASEY and R. L. JOHNS, "Salesmanship and Buymanship," Chap. XVI, H. W. Rowe Company, Baltimore, 1938.

J. R. DAUBMAN, "Salesmanship and Types of Selling," pp. 140–142, F. S. Crofts & Co., New York, 1939.

P. S. FASSETT, "Essentials of Selling," Chap. XXII, Prentice-Hall, Inc., New York, 1945.

CHARLES H. FERNALD, "Salesmanship," Chap. XXV, Prentice-Hall, Inc., New York, 1945.

J. GEORGE FREDERICK, "Modern Salesmanship," Chap. XXVIII, Garden City Publishing Company, Inc., New York, 1937.

HAROLD M. HAAS, "A Short Course in Salesmanship," Chap. XII, Prentice-Hall, Inc., New York, 1939.

PAUL W. IVEY, "Successful Salesmanship," pp. 252–256, Prentice-Hall, Inc., New York, 1937.

BERNARD LESTER, "Sales Engineering," pp. 188, 191, John Wiley & Sons, Inc., New York, 1940.

ROBERT E. MOORE, "Man Alive," Chap. XX, Harper & Brothers, New York, 1947.

DAVID R. OSBORNE, "Salesmanship for Today for Salesmanagers of Tomorrow," Chap. XII, Harper & Brothers, New York, 1939.

CHAPTER XVI

SENSORY SALES PRESENTATIONS

APPEALING TO THE FIVE SENSES

A salesman has five avenues of approach to a prospect's conviction —through sight, touch, taste, smell, and hearing. One or more of these senses are appealed to in making a sensory sales presentation of a product or service. Salesmen usually appeal to only one sense, the auditory or sense of hearing. The other four, equally keen, responsive, and important senses are often ignored in making sales presentations, with the result that a weak impression is made on prospects.

The forcefulness of a salesman's presentation is determined by the number of sensory appeals that he makes. If he appeals only to the ear of a prospect by spoken words, the sales impression is weak. Buyers are so accustomed to listening to the verbal claims of salesmen that they are often indifferent to what salesmen say. However, if in addition to appealing to the sense of hearing, a salesman also appeals to a buyer's sense of touch, by asking him to feel the product, a dual sense impression is made. If he also shows the prospect a picture or a working model of the product, the sense of vision is affected. By appealing to touch and sight, a multiple sensory impression is made which is three times as strong as the impression made on a prospect by speech alone.

Some products and services are especially adapted to multiple-sense selling. In presenting a breakfast food to merchants, for example, a salesman can describe its merits and reach the buyer's ear; he can offer the buyer a prepared sample and thus appeal to taste; by calling the dealer's attention to the delicious aroma of the product, the sense of smell is affected; by asking the buyer to feel the product, the sense of touch is reached; and finally the buyer's sight may be impressed by the appearance of the product.

Intangible services, such as travel, life insurance, and securities, do not lend themselves so completely to multiple-sense selling as tangible goods. However, salesmen of intangibles can make a dual sensory presentation appealing to hearing by oral description and to sight through the medium of charts, graphs, and pictures of profits, and benefits. If a salesman's product or service is complex or difficult to explain, there is greater need for appealing to several senses of prospects.

A salesman who appeals to several senses is like a dramatist who reaches not only the ears of his audience by the spoken words of the actors but also their eyes through effective stage settings and costumes. He who relies upon speech alone in making sales presentations is sacrificing other equally important means of communication which can help him to reach his objective more quickly and effectively.

Multiple-sense selling is effective because it emphasizes sales points through repetition, by words, illustrations, and demonstrations. Details may be amplified by repeating them, picturing them, and showing them to prospects. This method of repetition is more effective than repeating a sales point by word of mouth until it becomes boring.

A prospect secures a clearer understanding of the values of a product when he learns about them through his eyes, hands, or mouth as well as his ears. Some persons can comprehend more readily through one sense than another, and sensory selling creates ready understanding.

The interest of a prospect is gained and retained by appealing to his sight as well as to his hearing; a newspaper clipping, a check, or a diagram secures attention because it arouses curiosity and causes a prospect to listen more attentively.

The value of multiple-sense selling was first recognized by the late John H. Patterson, president of the National Cash Register Company, who advocated that his salesmen appeal to several senses in making a sales presentation, as follows:

I hold that one cannot rely on speech alone to make himself understood or to gain and hold attention. A dramatic supplement is needed. It is better to supplement whenever possible with pictures which show the right and wrong way; diagrams are more convincing than mere words; and pictures are more convincing than mere diagrams. The ideal presentation of a subject is one in which every subdivision is pictured and in which the words are used only to connect them. I early found that in dealing with men a picture was worth more than anything I could say.

APPEALING TO A PROSPECT'S EYES

Visual presentation is the oldest and almost universal method of conveying ideas from one person to another. According to an ancient

Chinese proverb, "One picture is worth ten thousand words," and in Mesopotamia archeologists have found pictographic tablets dating from 3000 B.C.

Graphic illustrations are effective because pictures are entertaining and induce a receptive mood on the part of the observer. Appeals to the eye are a welcome change to buyers who are accustomed to oral sales presentations.

Ideas received by the eye are remembered longer than those that are heard. Scientists say that the average man remembers one-tenth of what he hears, three-tenths of what he sees, and five-tenths of what he both sees and hears. Twenty-five times more attention is given to eye impressions than to appeals to the ear. The nerves that lead from the eye to the brain are many times larger than those leading from the ear.

Not only are sales points received through the eyes retained longer than other sense impressions, but the sense of sight is by far the fastest to register images in the mind. Vision accounts for 83 per cent of acquired knowledge; the other senses accumulate only 17 per cent. In other words, the eye outdistances all the other senses combined by at least four to one. Pictures make it possible for a person to understand in a few seconds what would otherwise take many minutes of explanation.

Ideas that are pictured are usually believed more readily than those which are spoken. Illustrations give an impression of reality and genuineness not associated with the spoken word. Leonardo da Vinci, the famous painter, once said, "The eye giveth to man a more perfect knowledge than doth the ear. That which is seen is more authentic than that which is heard."

The use of visual material in sales interviews saves the time of both salesman and prospect by speeding up the transfer of ideas and often making it possible to conclude a sale in one interview. Illustrations keep a sales presentation on the right track and prevent time-killing interruptions.

Pictures help a salesman to obtain a complete interview. When illustrative material is placed before a prospect, the buyer is more inclined to give a salesman a full hearing than when he presents his proposition orally.

A prospect's attention is held and concentrated on a sales presentation when pictorial material is used. If a sales interview is interrupted, the thread of the salesman's story can be more quickly picked up with illustrations.

A beginner salesman can quickly acquire knowledge of his proposition and attain confidence more rapidly when he uses illustrative material. Pictures acquaint him with an abundance of facts and evidence of the merit of his product so that he can make an impressive presentation to a prospect.

Visual sales material is indispensable in making sales presentations to groups, boards of directors, or committees. The attention of groups is secured and held more effectively by pictures than by verbal arguments.

Visual Selling Aids. There are numerous subjects for illustrations which a salesman can use in sales presentations. A salesman should use the following types of pictorial sales material:

Product or Service Illustrations:

1. Illustrations of the product itself, including phantom, cross section, X-ray, or detail of a single feature.

2. Illustrations of a product in use create interest and enable a prospect to visualize the ways he may be able to use the product. If the product is used for a variety of purposes, a series of illustrations may be necessary.

3. Illustrations of results of a product's use or consequences of failure to use a product carry conviction. "Before and after" pictures are of this type.

4. Illustrations of well-known users of a product or service are strong evidence of satisfactory service.

5. Illustrations of laboratory tests and field demonstrations show unique sales features.

The Company, Organization, Personnel, and Equipment Illustrations: .

1. Illustrations of company properties, plants, and branches impress prospects with company stability.

2. Illustrations of production equipment, tools, and machines show facilities to make a quality product.

3. Illustrations of workers, executives, and directors of a company show the personnel producing the product.

Illustrations of Service Facilities:

1. Illustrations showing location and size of warehouses and branches indicate ability to provide quick service and cut transportation costs.

2. Illustrations of truck fleets, steamships, and other transportation facilities can be used to sell good delivery service.

3. Illustrations of mechanical service depots, service schools, serv-

ice personnel, and equipment show the availability and reliability of mechanical service to buyers.

Illustrations of Advertising and Merchandising Aids:

1. Illustrations of national and local advertising media used in promoting sales of a product show the character of the advertising.

2. Illustrations of advertising copy in magazines, newspapers, outdoor, and other media show appeals and quality of advertising.

3. Illustrations of advertising schedules show dates of appearance of various advertisements and enable distributors to read, listen to, and see advertising when it appears.

4. Illustrations of the coverage of advertising aid in proving the effectiveness of the media used in reaching the customers and prospects of distributors.

5. Illustrations of advertising effectiveness, fan mail, coupons, and inquiries received show the resultfulness of an advertising program.

6. Illustrations of dealer cooperative advertising and window and store displays aid in inducing dealers to tie up local with national advertising.

Illustrations of Costs:

1. Graphs of price trends show comparative product costs over a period of years and prove values.

2. Charts showing returns to customers on their original investment expressed as dividends and earnings are convincing evidence to prospects of profit possibilities.

3. Charts of operating-cost comparisons show relatively low costs of operation and are convincing arguments for low operating expense.

Visual Selling Tools. The foregoing illustrations are excellent visual sales tools in the form of: photographs, retouched photographs, pen-and-ink drawings, cartoons, charts, graphs, diagrams, motion pictures, slide films, and maps. Many companies supply their salesmen with illustrative sales tools; otherwise, salesmen must prepare their own pictorial sales material.

Pictorial sales materials are collected and arranged in the most effective sequence for presentation in various types of visual sales interview portfolios, including pictorial kits, loose-leaf binders, and books. Salesmen coordinate oral presentations with the illustrations in visual portfolios to make both oral and visual appeals to customers.

Tablets or figuring pads of notebook size, with sheets of printed diagrams, sketches, or figures, are frequently used by salesmen in making visual sales presentations. The illustrations on these tablets are often printed incompletely so that a prospect's situation can be filled in with the pertinent facts by the salesman during an interview. The pages are usually arranged in logical sequence to parallel the oral presentation of the salesman. Blank scratch-pads, upon which a salesman can make sketches, figure costs, or write sales points with a soft pencil or crayon are also good visual sales tools.

Visual presentations are also prepared in miniature size to be carried in a salesman's coat pocket. Loose-leaf, accordion-fold, and other types of binders for visual sales material may be obtained in pocket size.

Advertising portfolios are usually prepared by advertisers to aid salesmen in visualizing advertising programs to distributors. Advertising portfolios picture advertisements appearing in current publications, testimonials of effectiveness, illustrations of inquiries received, specimens of direct mailings, photographs of premiums, charts of circulation coverage, graphs showing response, diagrams of schedules, maps indicating locations of radio broadcasting stations, and other features of an advertising and sales-promotion program.

By showing the actual product, a sample or a miniature model, a salesman can make a strong visual sales appeal. The realism gained by introducing the product itself in a sales interview is a definite selling advantage. When the size of the product permits, it may be carried by a salesman on all calls.

Sight appeals may also be made with special testing or demonstrating devices furnished by many manufacturers to their own as well as wholesalers' and dealers' salesmen. These demonstrating devices show dramatically one or more product advantages.

APPEALING TO A PROSPECT'S TOUCH

Scientists estimate that more than five thousand sensory nerves terminate in one square inch of finger-tip surface to receive touch impressions and flash them to the brain. A salesman who asks buyers to touch the smoothness of surfaces, to handle various parts of products, and to feel the texture of materials creates a strong impression of value.

By putting a package or a product into the hands of a prospect, a salesman creates a sense of ownership. A buyer who feels an article appreciates more clearly and quickly its smoothness, softness, strength, or suppleness. He receives a much stronger impression than he would gain from hearing about these qualities.

When a salesman asks a prospect to try on a pair of shoes to feel their comfort; when he urges a buyer to slip on a glove to feel its flexibility and fit; when he invites a buyer to touch an electric heating pad to enjoy the warmth, he is putting into action thousands of sense nerves to make strong sales impressions.

Prospects prefer to experience by personal and direct impression the benefits of a product rather than to hear about them secondhand from a salesman. By giving prospects an opportunity to learn for themselves, a salesman capitalizes on the universal instinct to experience satisfactions.

Certain types of products are particularly well suited to selling by touch. Textile fabrics, paper, fruits, and commodities with pronounced surface characteristics should be sold by appealing to a prospect's sense of touch. The finish of furniture, the texture of cloth, and the skin of a peach, all have characteristics that make strong touch appeals to prospects. The balance of a golf club or a tennis racket has a strong appeal to buyers of these products. The snug set of a coat collar imparts a feeling of comfort which may be a clothing salesman's strongest selling appeal.

By asking a prospect to feel an article, a salesman can keep the buyer's attention from wandering and focus it on the specific product feature under discussion. Interruptions and distractions are avoided if a prospect is given an opportunity to feel a product.

A buyer's confidence in an article is gained when he experiences for himself, through his sense of touch, the values claimed by the salesman.

Touch Selling Tools. Many progressive companies prepare touch selling tools for their salesmen. Otherwise, a salesman should develop his own touch selling aids. A salesman who uses his imagination can devise numerous ways to appeal to a prospect's sense of touch. One successful tire salesman shows his prospects how heat is generated in an automobile tire by giving them a piece of crude rubber. The prospect is asked to stretch it several times, then to touch the hot rubber quickly to his upper lip. By feeling the rubber heated by the stretching process, the prospect understands how heat is generated in a tire on the road.

An automobile salesman appeals to the sense of touch of prospects who are interested in safety by asking them to hammer a square of safety glass and then feel how the glass cracks but does not shatter from the blow.

A salesman of automobile lacquer uses a piece of zinc coated with lacquer, a hammer, and a bottle of acid to illustrate the hard finish of the product. Prospects are asked to hammer the surface of the lacquer and feel that it is unmarred by the beating. Next they are asked to pour acid on the lacquer and feel that the acid has no effect on the surface.

A rock-wool insulation salesman appeals to the sense of feeling of his prospects by placing a 4-inch thickness of rock wool on a lighted gas range burner. The prospect is asked to place his hand on top

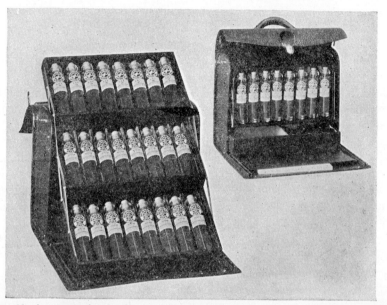

Fig. 19. A strong visual sales appeal is made by salesmen representing a lubricating oil company, who carry this attractive extension tray sales case filled with samples of various grades of the product. This case is typical of similar sample kits which afford excellent visual display of a product.

of the insulation and feel that no heat from the fire penetrates the material.

A salesman can appeal to a prospect's sense of touch by inviting the buyer to feel the product itself, its package, a sample, or a part thereof. If a product is small and light in weight, it may be carried by a salesman. Otherwise a part may be carried to make touch impressions. When products or samples are too bulky or heavy to be carried, a miniature model is sometimes used. If it is impracticable to carry a product to prospects a model is the most effective device to give buyers an opportunity to feel its surface and shape. Many

companies furnish their salesmen with miniature product models of
the following types: operating models, nonoperating models, cross-
sectional models, and toy models. Models are valuable in securing
interviews, holding the attention of prospects, arousing interest, and
explaining technical features.

Typical models used by salesmen include miniature hot-air furnaces, oil burners, fire extinguishers, electric motors, plumbing fixtures, washing machines, valves and fittings, and many other articles.
Automobile tire salesmen use cross sections of casings and miniature
models of tires.

Touch selling tools including samples, actual products, and models
are housed and transported in carrying cases which are usually made
to order to fit a specific product or sample, to provide a convenient
arrangement of all materials, to ensure an attractive display, and to
give maximum protection. Frequent inspection is necessary to keep
samples fresh and clean and materials and cases in good order.

APPEALING TO A PROSPECT'S TASTE AND SMELL

Salesmen of food products, drugs, cosmetics, and beverages make
sensory sales presentations by appealing to prospects' senses of taste
and smell. A perfumery salesman who puts a drop of his product
on the handkerchief of a prospect is making the strongest sales appeal
to the buyer. A confectionery salesman who asks prospects to taste
his chocolate creams is appealing to the one sense most likely to
influence a buyer's decision to purchase.

Taste appeals can be used in selling many products. Tastes may
be either sweet, bitter, acid, or salty, although many taste sensations
are a combination of touch, warmth, cold, or pain. A dentifrice may
have a "biting" taste which is a combination of pain and taste.

The sense of smell rather than taste gives many products their characteristic flavor. Coffee owes its appeal to the sense of smell; its taste
is bitter. Cider would taste the same as onion juice if it were not for
the sense of smell. By emphasizing the taste and smell appeals of
his product, a salesman can make strong sales impressions on prospects.

Although many taste sensations are combined with smell, there
are six primary odors: spicy, found in pepper, cinnamon, etc.; flowery,
found in gardenias, etc.; fruity, found in oranges, lemons, etc.;
resinous, found in balsam needles, pine gum, etc.; foul, found in rotten
eggs; and scorched, found in tar. There are many compound odors

such as peppermint, which smells both fruity and spicy. The sense of smell is a fundamental sales appeal for food, beverages, flowers, and perfume.

The sale of some products possessing no natural odor is often stimulated by perfuming them. Personal writing paper is perfumed with flowery odors; lingerie is scented with lavender; fiction books have been scented to create an atmosphere conforming with the plot. Products that give off disagreeable natural odors are often made more salable by disguising their smell with pleasing odors.

A salesman of sandwich spread appeals to the sense of taste of grocers. He first buys a loaf of bread from the dealer, slices the bread, makes a sandwich with the spread, and offers the dealer the sandwich, proving by taste appeal the quality of the product.

A ginger ale salesman buys a bottle of his own product and a bottle of competing ginger ale from the dealer whom he is trying to sell. Then he asks the buyer to taste both beverages. Eight out of ten dealers prefer the taste of the salesman's ginger ale. The salesman doubles his sales for each dozen calls when he uses this taste comparison sales appeal.

A salesman of electric refrigerators appeals to the taste of prospects, who come to the showroom for demonstrations, by serving them frozen desserts and ice cream from the cold compartment of a refrigerator. To his word-of-mouth presentation the salesman adds an effective taste appeal.

Some salesmen appeal to the taste and smell of prospects by carrying prepared samples. A soup salesman, calling on retailers, carries a thermos bottle filled with hot soup and a supply of paper cups and spoons for serving the soup to buyers. A canned goods salesman carries cut cans of his fruits and vegetables, which make their own taste appeal to buyers.

APPEALING TO A PROSPECT'S HEARING

Usually the only sense appeal made by a salesman is to the hearing of buyers. A buyer's ears may be compared to a piano with over twenty thousand strings which are set in vibration by the sound waves of a salesman's voice. Just as the strings of a piano can be thrown into sympathetic vibration by the skilled fingering of a pianist, so can the membrane of a prospect's ear be set to vibrating in harmony by the trained voice of a salesman. By proper tone control, a salesman can produce a harmonious sensation in the ears of his prospects.

A good voice is an important factor in appealing to buyers. The three fundamentals of voice control which enable a salesman to make a more effective appeal to the ears of his prospects, are: change of pitch, variation of rate, and change of volume of tone.

A salesman who speaks in a monotonous voice with a dull, level pitch of tone hypnotizes his prospects. By changing pitch, his voice runs up and down the tone scale from high to low and back again and, by variety, commands the attention of prospects. By suddenly lowering or raising pitch, an important word or phrase can be made to stand out and register.

Enthusiasm often causes salesmen to speak too loudly and rapidly. This confuses prospects as much as an excessively slow and deliberate rate of speaking annoys them. A salesman's rate of speaking should range from slow, when discussing important ideas, to fast, when mentioning insignificant details. By changing his rate of speaking, pausing before and after important ideas, a salesman can hold the attention of a prospect.

Volume of tone is an important factor in making a sales presentation. A loud, overemphatic tone not only annoys prospects but also others who may be in the vicinity. A salesman who changes the volume of his conversational tone emphasizes important ideas loudly and subordinates details in whispers. Variety in voice volume is necessary to hold the attention of prospects and to emphasize vital sales points.

Pause before important sales ideas. Silence can be just as emphatic as speech. Prospects become attentive and listen to hear the next words of a salesman when he pauses in his presentation. A pause after a vital point lets the idea sink into the consciousness of a prospect. Silence is sound selling strategy.

A salesman's oral delivery offers many opportunities for improvement. Because conversation is a commonplace, everyday method of communication, most salesmen give little consideration to the impression which it makes on buyers. By practicing to vary pitch, rate, and volume of voice, a salesman can improve his oral presentations and make a better auditory impression on prospects.

HOW TO MAKE A SENSORY SALES PRESENTATION

The finest visual sales portfolio, album, sample, or model loses its value as a sales aid unless it is used with skill. There is a proved technique in using sensory sales tools just as there is a best way to fell a tree or pull a tooth. From the experience of many salesmen who make effective sensory sales presentations, five principles of making a sensory appeal have been observed and combined into a single routine. If a salesman will memorize and practice this simple procedure, he will soon acquire skill in making sensory presentations.

Routine for Making a Sensory Sales Presentation

1. Time introduction of material.
2. Apply to buyer's needs and motives.
3. Keep control of material.
4. Get buyer to participate.
5. Leave with prospect.

1. Time Introduction of Material. When a salesman begins an interview, the buyer is often preoccupied with affairs quite foreign to the salesman's proposition. So that the buyer may have an opportunity to adjust himself to the salesman's presence and personality, sensory sales material should not be introduced immediately but should be prefaced by general remarks or pertinent conversation. Timing the introduction of sales tools is important as there is a point in the sales presentation where they can be used most effectively.

Sometimes sales material is used as an "entering wedge" in opening a sales interview. In that case its introduction need not be prefaced by general remarks.

An automobile salesman prefaces his introduction of a chart of buying motives by saying, "I realize that you are a very busy man, Mr. Prospect, and it was considerate of you to allow me the few minutes that I asked. Of course, I don't know what you look for in buying an automobile, but I believe that I am safe in assuming that you want to get the most for your money. Your automobile dollar is divided into eight parts." Here the salesman lays before the prospect a pie chart showing the automobile dollar divided into the eight parts of beauty, safety, performance, economy, service, reputation, dollar value, and comfort.

Sales material may be withheld until the interview has progressed to a point where the salesman wishes to clarify a sales point or prove an advantage. Then he reaches for his portfolio naturally, saying, "Let me illustrate that point. This picture tells the whole story clearly and quickly." Here the salesman lays before the prospect a picture of the product.

Visual materials are useful sales tools but they can lose much of their effectiveness if they are not used at the time when they can best supplement oral presentation.

2. Apply to Buyer's Needs and Motives. Sales material should be applied by a salesman to the specific needs or interests of the buyer. To bore a buyer with illustrations or other sales material which have little or no relation to his needs or buying motives is usually a waste of time. After he has discovered a buyer's needs and motives by asking questions, listening, or observing, a salesman should introduce only those illustrations or sales tools which relate to the customer's needs or motives. When a salesman adheres to a standard picture presentation, beginning at the first page and closing with the last, the prospect usually becomes bored and is not interested in pictures of no significance to him. It is essential that a salesman select certain illustrations which relate to the needs of each prospect.

As a salesman discovers the needs and interests of a prospect, he may supplement his spoken presentation with illustrative material. Eye appeal should supplement ear appeal, and both appeals should be unified in a convincing single impression on the eyes and ears of a prospect. A good oral presentation may be planned or written to accompany each illustration or sales tool.

A salesman should be so familiar with the contents of his picture portfolio and other sales tools that he can quickly refer to any particular picture or feature and relate it to the needs of the prospect. By thumb-indexing a portfolio, a salesman can save his time and create a better impression on prospects by quickly finding illustrations pertinent to the needs of buyers.

3. Keep Control of Material. Unless a salesman keeps control of his visual material, demonstrating equipment, or samples, the prospect may handle illustrations or equipment in such a way as to destroy the salesman's continuity, causing him to lose control of the presentation. By sitting on the right side of a prospect, a salesman is in the best position to control the pages of a visual portfolio and at the same time give the prospect an uninterrupted view of the illustrations. An easel-back portfolio keeps illustrations out of the hands of a buyer and facilitates control by a salesman.

By pointing out features of illustrations, parts, or samples, with a pen or pencil, a salesman can focus the eyes of a prospect on those details of greatest importance and prevent his attention from wavering.

If the prospect takes illustrations, samples, or demonstrating devices into his own hands for closer inspection, the salesman may regain control of the material by asking for its return on the pretext of pointing out another feature.

No attempt should be made by a salesman to read text material to a prospect. Many people resent being read to out of a book—a parrot process that bores them. Prospects should be permitted to read without interruption any text accompanying pictures. Instead of a humdrum reading of the text, the salesman should supplement it with his own stock asides or anecdotes on definite selling points illustrated in the portfolio.

In introducing visual material, a salesman should place it squarely in front of the prospect, laying it on the desk or table before which the buyer is seated. The pages should lie under the prospect's eyes so that he does not have to turn his head to see everything comfortably. If the prospect is obliged to stretch or get into an uncomfortable position to see the illustrative material, his attention is hard to hold and he may not see some of the pictures or charts. A salesman should seat himself beside the prospect so that his face will be on the same plane with that of the prospect's. An easel portfolio keeps illustrations on the eye level of a prospect and makes them easier to see.

4. Get Buyer to Participate. In using samples, illustrations, or demonstrating equipment to make sensory appeals, a salesman should make every effort to get the buyer to touch, taste, smell, see, and experience the benefits which the sales materials are designed to prove.

Multiple-sense impressions can only be made if the prospect is given an opportunity to use his hands, nose, eyes, and ears in a sales interview. By getting a prospect to handle a part of the product, taste a sample, or smell its aroma, a salesman provides the strongest evidence of quality.

At the same time the buyer feels that he is buying and not being sold. His full attention is secured and his play instincts are satisfied by being given a chance to "see what makes the wheels go round." He becomes a participant rather than a bystander in the presentation and reveals his attitudes more readily.

Salesmen can encourage participation of buyers by simply inviting them to hold the product, feel its texture, see its design, and examine other features or manipulate a demonstrating device.

5. Leave with Prospect. When the salesman has covered the salient points in his presentation, he should not close his portfolio or put away his illustrations to signalize the end of the interview, but should leave his portfolio or pictures open before the prospect at a page illustrating an important sales point. If he is unable to close a sale, he may leave his portfolio, advertising, or other visual material with the prospect to be examined at leisure in the salesman's absence. Not only does this give a prospect an opportunity to sell himself, but it leaves the door open to the salesman to make a return

SALES PERFORMANCE RATING FORM

Use of Sensory Selling Aids

Salesman_____   Date_____

Rated by_____   Over-all Rating_____

Score

I. *Salesman's Appeal to Prospect's*	Excellent 90–100	Good 80–90	Fair 70–80	Poor 60–70	Failure Below 60
A. Sight					
B. Touch					
C. Taste or smell					
D. Hearing					

II. *Salesman's Method of Making a Sensory Presentation*	Excellent 90–100	Good 80–90	Fair 70–80	Poor 60–70	Failure Below 60
A. Time introduction of material					
B. Applying to needs and motives					
C. Controlling material					
D. Get buyer to participate					
E. Leaving with prospect					

Miscellaneous Comments_____

_____

_____

call to pick up his portfolio or sales tools. Some salesmen keep several portfolios in the hands of prospects all of the time.

Problem I

Using Visual Sales Materials

Arthur Ostrow, representing Talbot Tire and Accessory Company

The Talbot Tire and Accessory Company, Boston, Mass., established in 1925, retails a complete line of automobile accessories including tires, batteries, horns, radios, heaters, speedometers, headlights, and other accessories. Well-known brands of nationally advertised products are sold through the company's two stations located on main traffic arteries of the city. Local newspaper advertising is used weekly.

Arthur Ostrow, one of the two inside salesmen in the company's main store, has just sold a customer a set of four tires and while they are being installed, the following interview ensues between them:

1. Salesman: I imagine you do a great deal of traveling?
2. Prospect: Yes, I do. I travel about 350 miles every week between Boston and Connecticut.
3. Salesman: While you're waiting for your tires to come down from the stock room, I would like to show you a short moving picture about a new kind of safety tube that I believe will interest you.

(The salesman seated the prospect before a small portable motion-picture projector located in a darkened corner of the salesroom. A sound motion picture was projected, illustrating traffic hazards and demonstrating various safety devices such as hydraulic brakes, shatter-proof glass, and knee action. The danger of blowouts was pictured by showing automobiles turning over when blowouts occurred. The film concluded by showing a new type of inner tube which permits a driver to come to a slow safe stop when blowouts occur. Testimonials by famous racing drivers and police officials advised the use of the tubes to prevent accidents. The picture featured the Safe T tubes made by a well-known tire company and sold by the Talbot Company.)

   Salesman (at conclusion of picture): Well, what did you think of that picture?
4. Prospect: Those new tubes are quite an idea.
5. Salesman: Here in this scrapbook (salesman shows prospect a scrapbook containing newspaper clippings) are newspaper clippings telling about various accidents which were caused by tires blowing out. Aren't they convincing?
6. Prospect: Exactly how does this new tube work?
7. Salesman: In reality, the Safe T tube is a tube within a tube. When

the outer tube bursts as it does when a blowout occurs, the tube within the tube carries sufficient air to permit the driver to slow down and come to a stop safely. The same thing happens when a tire is punctured. Now here is a cross section of one of these tubes (handing cross section of tube within a tube to prospect) with a nail driven through the outer tube. Now force that nail into the inner tube and see what happens. (Prospect follows directions.) You see that the inner tube does not puncture. The car runs on the tube within the tube.

8. PROSPECT: The tube may be all right but blowouts happen so rarely that I do not see why I should invest my money in Safe T tubes.

9. SALESMAN: Well, that's just like locking the barn after the horse is stolen. We never know when blowouts will occur and it is certainly a grand feeling to know that you are protected against blowouts. Don't you agree with me?

10. PROSPECT: Yes, I do. But a month ago I bought some regular tubes and it would be a financial loss to me if I threw away the regular tubes and brought Safe T's.

11. SALESMAN: No, we are in a position to give you full return value on your regular tubes.

12. PROSPECT: What is the price of these Safe T tubes?

13. SALESMAN: They list for $11.50 each, but in view of the fact that you operate a fleet of trucks, we are able to offer you a fleet discount on these tubes which will bring them down to $6.45 each.

14. PROSPECT: The price seems reasonable but I do not expect to keep my car much longer than the first of the year.

15. SALESMAN: We can take care of that very easily. When you trade in your car in the spring, bring it in here first, and we will take out the Safe T tubes and put in some regular tubes. When you receive your new car, bring it in here and we will put in your set of Safe T tubes.

16. PROSPECT: Yes, that may be so, but the new car may use a different size tube than my present car does.

17. SALESMAN: We will give you a new set of Safe T tubes to fit your new car for the difference in price between the Safe T set which I'd like to put in your present car and a new set.

18. PROSPECT: How will I know that these tubes will work under actual conditions?

19. SALESMAN: If you had been in here two weeks ago, I would have taken you to the traveling show the Safe T Tire Company put on here in town. They drove cars over spikes and the Safe T tubes permitted the drivers to slow down and come to a stop without endangering their lives.

20. PROSPECT: Well, I have to get out of town tomorrow. When can you put them in?

21. SALESMAN: It'll only be a matter of a few minutes until we can put them in your new tires. (Salesman fills out order blank and hands it to prospect to sign.)
22. PROSPECT: O.K. Put 'em in.

Questions

1. What senses does the salesman appeal to in this interview? How?

2. Criticize favorably or otherwise the salesman's use of graphic materials in this presentation?

3. What advantages does the salesman gain through the use of a graphic presentation in this case?

4. What additional graphic appeals might have been made by the salesman in this presentation?

5. How could the salesman make a strong appeal to the hearing of the prospect in this case?

Problem II

A SENSORY SALES PRESENTATION

Robert G. Redmon, representing Lockhart and Benchley, Inc., Dealers in Monton Motor Cars

Lockhart and Benchley, Inc., have retailed Monton six- and eight-cylinder automobiles in Brooklyn, N. Y., since 1924. The Rex Six manufactured by the Monton Motor Car Company, one of the "big three" automobile producers, retails for $1,800 up and is made in sedan, coach, coupé, and convertible models. The Royalty Eight retails for $2,200 up and is made in all models. The dealer is represented by 11 salesmen, one of whom, Robert G. Redmon, has been associated with it for five years. Previously he was connected with a large investment house as a bond salesman.

Each of the company's salesmen takes his turn in selling on the showroom floor. On a Saturday afternoon, salesman Redmon is on floor duty when a young man and woman, evidently a newly married couple, whom he has never seen before, enter the showroom. The following conversation ensues:

1. SALESMAN: How do you do? My name is Redmon.
2. PROSPECT: My name is Martin and this is my wife. We'd like to see something in a convertible.
3. SALESMAN: A sedan or a coupé?
4. PROSPECT: We're rather interested in something small.
5. SALESMAN: Well, I think we have a coupé out in back. Will you just step out here, please. (Salesman leads way to garage and points out a coupé.) Is this what you had in mind?

6. Mrs. Prospect: Oh, no. That's a Rex, isn't it? We want to see a Royalty.

7. Salesman: Oh, I see. We have one on the floor. (Salesman leads couple back to showroom and points out a convertible eight-cylinder car in dark green.)

8. Prospect (turning to wife): Well, what do you think of this, Jean?

9. Mrs. Prospect: It's nice but I think that there isn't much room in those back seats for your legs.

10. Salesman: I'd like to have you look at this chart which shows the relative room in the front and back seats of the leading cars. (Shows chart.) Isn't that proof of the room in the Royalty?

11. Prospect: Yes, it does have more room than the others.

12. Salesman: Then, the seat moves forward about 6 inches. (Salesman moves seat forward.)

13. Mrs. Prospect: I like this color, dear.

14. Prospect (getting out of car): Yes, but I'll bet it shows dust. (Prospects walk around to back of car.)

15. Salesman (opening up luggage compartment): In case you're interested in color, the Monton people have just completed some fade tests on the Royalty. This bulletin shows that the green stands up better than any other color. That's convincing, isn't it?

16. Mrs. Prospect: I like green.

17. Prospect: We're going on a trip to Michigan in June.

18. Salesman: That's a long trip and you want a comfortable car so you won't get tired. The Royalty has a new type of rear spring. This model (showing model of spring) illustrates why it rides so well. Just press down on that spring. It's very flexible, isn't it?

19. Prospect: Yes, it is.

20. Salesman: This car also steers very easily. Just get behind the wheel and try it. (Prospect gets behind wheel.)

21. Prospect: Hmm. Awfully crowded in here.

22. Salesman: But you can move the seat back. (Prospect attempts to move seat back but cannot locate lever.) Down in front. (Prospect fumbles in front of seat looking for shift lever.) No, on your right side. (Prospect locates lever and moves seat.)

23. Prospect: That's better.

24. Salesman: Yes.

25. Mrs. Prospect: How much is the car?

26. Salesman: Why, this one is $2,400.

27. Prospect: I thought you made a cheaper coupé, without rear seats. How much is that?

28. Salesman: We don't make that any more. It sold for $1,700.

29. Prospect (examining top): This top looks pretty hard to get down.

30. Salesman: No, it's very simple. Just turn this switch on the dash and it comes down automatically.

31. Prospect (looking at top): Oh, I see.
32. Salesman: We have a fine eight-cylinder motor. (Lifts hood and prospects look inside.)
33. Mrs. Prospect: Does it get your feet hot on long drives?
34. Salesman: No, you see those air vents on the side? (Salesman points to ventilators.) And there is a complete partition between the motor and the front of the car inside. That keeps the heat out.
35. Prospect (blowing horns): I like those horns.
36. Mrs. Prospect (to husband): You wouldn't buy a car without a nice horn, would you, dear?
37. Prospect: That's right. Has to have that quality sound, you know.
38. Mrs. Prospect: This car seems a little short. I wonder if it rides as well as a larger car.
39. Salesman: Oh, yes, it does. It has a 122-inch spring wheel base.
40. Prospect: What do you mean "spring wheel base"?
41. Salesman (stooping down and indicating springs): That's the distance from the end of one spring suspension to the other.
42. Prospect: I've heard that these cars use a lot of gas.
43. Salesman: Here is a letter from one of our owners which says he gets over 18 miles to a gallon. (Prospect reads letter.)
44. Mrs. Prospect: That's pretty good for a big car. It's a nice car, all right.
45. Salesman: Sure is. We'd like to sell you one.
46. Prospect: Well, we want to think it over.
47. Salesman: I understand. Here is a new booklet which describes all of the features of the Royalty. Take it along with you.
48. Mrs. Prospect: Before we go, what other colors do you have?
49. Salesman: Just a minute, I'll get you a color chart. (Salesman gets color chart and hands to prospects.) Here are the colors.
50. Prospect: I'll be able to let you know the first of the week what we're going to do.
51. Salesman: All right, I'll call you the first of the week.
52. Prospect: Good-by.

Questions

1. Did the salesman time the introduction of his material? Explain.
2. Did he apply sales material to the buyers' needs and motives? How?
3. Did he control his visual material? Explain.
4. Did he get buyer to participate? How?
5. Did he leave any sales material with the prospects? What?
6. What senses did the salesman appeal to in this interview? What other senses might have been appealed to?
7. How could the salesman appeal more effectively to the prospect's sense of touch?
8. What other appeals might have been made to sight in this interview?

Reading References

R. C. Borden, "How to Make a Sales Point Hit," Prentice-Hall, Inc., New York, 1938.

B. R. Canfield, "Sales Administration, Principles and Problems," rev. ed. Chap. X, Prentice-Hall, Inc., New York, 1947.

J. George Frederick, "Modern Salesmanship," Chap. XV, Garden City Publishing Company, Inc., New York, 1937.

Kenneth Goode and Zenn Kaufman, "Showmanship in Business," Chap. 13, Harper & Brothers, New York, 1939.

C. B. Larrabee and H. W. Marks, "Tested Selling Ideas," McGraw-Hill Book Company, Inc., New York, 1936.

Bernard Lester, "Sales Engineering," pp. 133–137, John Wiley & Sons, Inc., New York, 1940.

Robert E. Moore, "Man Alive," Chap. XI, Harper & Brothers, New York, 1947.

H. C. Nolen and H. H. Maynard, "Sales Management," Chap. XIV, The Ronald Press Company, New York, 1940.

David R. Osborne, "Salesmanship for Today for Salesmanagers of Tomorrow," Chap. IX, Harper & Brothers, New York, 1939.

F. A. Russell and F. H. Beach, "Textbook of Salesmanship," pp. 317–333, McGraw-Hill Book Company, Inc., New York, 1941.

Harry Simmons, "A Practical Course in Successful Selling," Chap. XVIII, Harper & Brothers, New York, 1939.

CHAPTER XVII

SECURING SALES INTERVIEWS

THE PROBLEM OF GETTING A HEARING WITH BUYERS

A salesman must first gain admission to a prospective buyer's home or office before he can make a sales presentation. Salesmen ordinarily have no difficulty in getting face to face with buyers by simply asking for interviews. However, specialty salesmen frequently experience considerable opposition. Many experienced salesmen particularly encounter difficulty in getting in to see buyers.

A study based on the reports of 100,000 soliciting hours of salesmen, representing a large life insurance company, shows that these salesmen must make an average of two calls for every interview that they secure; in other words, their effectiveness in obtaining interviews averages 50 per cent. A leading life insurance salesman, producing $500,000 annually, averages 2.8 calls for each interview secured. During a period of eight months, a Pittsburgh life insurance salesman averaged an interview effectiveness of 58.1 per cent, or out of 43 calls he was able to interview 25 prospects.

A salesman's difficulty in securing interviews varies with the type of buyer approached, the kind of product sold, and the reputation of the company which he represents. Professional purchasing agents and buyers for wholesale and retail stores are readily accessible to salesmen. Qualified salesmen are welcomed by professional buyers as important sources of price and product information. Ultimate consumers buying for individual or home consumption, who do not recognize their needs, are often unwilling to grant interviews to salesmen. The problem of securing interviews also increases in difficulty in proportion to the responsibilities of a business executive prospect.

If a salesman is selling a specialty, novelty, or luxury item about which a prospect knows little and for which he has felt no need, the salesman has more difficulty in securing an interview than if he were selling a staple necessity. Salesmen of intangibles and services find more difficulty in getting to see prospects than do salesmen of tangible goods.

If a salesman represents a well-known company, he has less difficulty in getting face to face with his prospects than the representative of an unknown firm. A vacuum cleaner salesman working for a well-known local department store or public utility is more successful in getting interviews in homes than if he represented a manufacturer with no local identity.

Salesmen meet resistance in getting interviews for numerous reasons. If a salesman understands why some buyers refuse to see him, he is better able to solve this problem. Many persons instinctively resist anything that is novel or different. An unknown salesman, bringing new ideas, experiences this natural opposition in securing interviews with prospects.

Many prospects are so busy with business or personal matters that they are reluctant to interrupt their work and to give their time to listening to salesmen. Business executives holding responsible positions are particularly difficult to interview for this reason.

Many buyers have had unpleasant experiences with discourteous or persistent salesmen and seek to avoid such annoyance by refusing interviews to all salesmen. House-to-house salesmen often have difficulty interviewing housewives who have experienced the offensive tactics of peddlers. Some persons are strongly prejudiced against all salesmen because of unpleasant experiences with a few.

Buyers obviously cannot patronize all salesmen. When a prospect is satisfied with his sources of supply, he is reluctant to take the time to hear arguments of other salesmen. If a buyer is committed by contract or other considerations to purchase from one source, he is not interested in buying elsewhere.

A prospect who is not conscious of his need for a product or service is naturally reluctant to listen to reasons why he should buy something that he does not want.

For these reasons buyers protect their privacy with subordinates, including maids, information clerks, custodians, office boys, and secretaries. One of the duties of these barriers to salesmen is to conserve the time of their employers by admitting only those salesmen whom they think are worthy of an interview.

METHODS OF OBTAINING INTERVIEWS BEFORE CONTACTING PROSPECTS

Before seeking an interview with a buyer, a salesman should first determine the place where the prospect can be interviewed to the best advantage. Prospects who cannot be interviewed by salesmen during business hours must be visited at their homes. Buyers of products or services for individual or home use are usually interviewed at home; buyers of industrial goods are interviewed at their offices. Many interviews are secured for the sale of both industrial and personal goods on golf courses, in club rooms, at card parties, theaters, and conventions.

As there is a best place to hold every sales interview, so there is also a best time to get a hearing with every buyer. The occupation of a prospect often determines the time of day when he can be interviewed to the best advantage. Interviews with physicians are often difficult to obtain during morning hours when they are calling on patients or engaged in hospital duty; stockbrokers rarely grant interviews to salesmen during stock exchange hours; retail merchants usually are too busy to buy on Saturdays; professional purchasing agents generally interview salesmen on certain days of the week and at definite hours.

Instead of seeking appointments on the full, half, and quarter hours, salesmen should try to secure interviews at such odd times as 10:50, 11:20, and 3:40 to avoid appointment conflicts with other salesmen. Since many business and professional men make appointments on the hour and half hour, it is often easier to arrange for calls at such times. When a salesman asks for an interview at 11:50, he also gives the impression that his call will be short.

If a salesman will obtain advance information about the best time and place to interview a prospect, he can usually secure appointments without difficulty. Customers, friends, centers of influence, and sales associates can give a salesman information about the best places and times to arrange interviews with prospects. By asking tactful questions and observing the habits of buyers, a salesman can secure more interviews at the right time and place.

After a salesman has decided when and where to interview a prospect, he may use one of several proved methods to aid him in getting face to face with his potential customer. A salesman may seek interviews with prospects by (1) using third parties; (2) sending advance cards or letters; (3) offering gifts; (4) using the telephone; (5) sampling.

1. Using Third Parties. A salesman's customers, relatives, friends, and acquaintances can help him to gain access to prospects. These persons can cooperate with a salesman in three ways: by suggestions, by letters or cards of introduction, and by their personal intercession.

A salesman's customers or friends are often well acquainted with buyers whom the salesman would like to interview. By making inquiries among his friends, a salesman discovers those who are acquainted with a particular prospect. He asks them for their suggestions as to when, where, and how to secure an interview with the prospect.

An automobile salesman desired an interview with the president of a large corporation who was very busy and difficult to approach. He asked a friend of the big executive for suggestions as to the best way to secure an interview with the prospect. The salesman's informant suggested, "Go and see his mother." The salesman called on the prospect's mother, demonstrated his car to her, returned to her son's office, and presented his business card with the following notation, "Your mother expressed a desire for my car. So will you when you know more about it." The salesman got the interview and the order.

A third party can aid a salesman in getting an interview with a prospect by furnishing him with a personal letter of introduction. If the person who refers the salesman to the prospect is well and favorably known to the buyer, a letter of recommendation may be very effective in paving the way for a sales interview. Formal impersonal letters of introduction, however, have become commonplace and carry little weight with many buyers. A personal note written on the reverse side of a business card by a friend of the prospect is often sufficient to secure a favorable reception for a salesman. A letter of introduction from the president or manager of a salesman's own firm is sometimes used successfully by salesmen in getting interviews.

Instead of a written recommendation, a salesman usually can secure a customer's or friend's permission to use his name in obtaining an interview with a buyer. A salesman has an advantage when he can announce himself to the "barrier" in the buyer's office by saying, "Please tell Mr. Prospect that a friend of Dick Hare is calling."

Or a friend or customer may be willing to make personal arrangements with a prospect for an interview for the salesman. A salesman's friends may be willing to telephone their friends and ask that the salesman be granted an interview. Or a friend of a salesman may arrange for the salesman to meet a prospect informally at luncheon or at a dinner party. By giving helpful service to customers and friends, a salesman can gain their active cooperation in securing interviews with inaccessible prospects.

2. Sending Advance Cards or Letters. Direct-mail advertising is a valuable aid to salesmen in securing interviews with prospects. When mailed in advance of calls, cards, letters, folders, and telegrams arouse interest and stimulate curiosity in a salesman's proposition. Advertising sent to a prospect may cause him to postpone buying until he has had an opportunity to see the salesman's product or hear his story.

Many salesmen, calling on merchants, mail a printed advance card announcing their coming and timed to reach the buyer a few days before the salesman's arrival. Many of these advance cards are illustrated with a photograph of the salesman and refer to his visit by saying, "Your many past courtesies have been appreciated and I am looking forward to seeing you about (date) with a full line of samples."

A salesman may prepare his own advance cards at little cost by using government postal cards and a small hand-stencil-type duplicator.

Engraved reference cards, signed by references, have been used by house-to-house salesmen of a large direct sales organization in gaining admission to homes in wealthy neighborhoods.

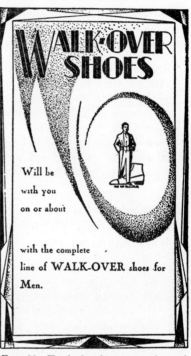

Individually typed personal letters are used by many salesmen of specialty products and intangible services in seeking interviews. Many progressive companies cooperate with their salesmen by processing form letters for securing

Fig. 20. Typical advance card used by wholesale shoe salesmen in paving the way for interviews with dealer customers and prospects.

interviews with prospects. A typical advance letter, signed by the sales manager of an investment house, follows:

Dear Mr. Prospect:
    Each day we ask our salesmen to call on certain carefully selected people of this and other communities.
    We want you to know more about this pioneer financial institution, founded over eighty-four years ago.

For this reason, we have asked our salesman, Mr. John Doe, to call on you next Wednesday, to personally lay before you a very specific idea which will unquestionably prove of interest to you.

We want to thank you in advance for the courtesy you will extend Mr. Doe and please be assured that there will be no obligation on your part and no importunity on ours.

Most sincerely yours,

When a salesman calls and fails to secure an interview, some companies follow up the call, asking for another appointment at a future time, as in the following letter over the signature of the sales manager of an industrial specialty company.

DEAR MR. PROSPECT:

We are sorry that you were unable to grant an interview to our representative, Mr. Smith, when he called yesterday to tell you about the new product we have just perfected.

Could Mr. Smith call next Thursday afternoon to see you? If not, please designate the hour and day that would be most convenient to you and drop the enclosed card in the mail—no postage is required. We promise that you will be glad you did.

Cordially yours,

Many salesmen compose and mail their own letters to precede their calls on prospects. The following is a successful letter used by an oil-burner salesman:

DEAR SIR:

"We have forgotten our heating plant."

"Our house is always heated perfectly."

"My wife does not shovel coal any more."

"Most comfortable winter we have ever spent and best of all it costs less than coal."

"It is a pleasure to deal with a concern like yours."

That's what experienced owners say about their Blank Oil Burners.

Tomorrow—or the next day—I shall call at your home to tell you more about this wonderful modern heating method, how it does away with all the labor and dirt of old-fashioned heating, how it makes winter warmth as automatic as June sunshine, and even more dependable.

Will you give me a few minutes to explain the marvelous convenience of the Blank Oil Burner and its reasonable cost?

Yours for better heating,

A Savannah, Georgia, life insurance salesman found the way to an interview with a railroad executive blocked by the prospect's secretary. He wrote a personal letter to the prospect and within a few days the secretary telephoned the salesman to call, and a $2,500 sale resulted. Another life insurance salesman, who uses letters to precede his calls on prospects, obtained interviews with 85 prospects to whom he sold $245,776 worth of insurance in one year.

3. Offering Gifts. An inexpensive gift is another effective medium for opening doors of prospects to salesmen. Typical gifts offered by salesmen to prospects in return for the privilege of an interview, are ash trays, paperweights, memorandum books, automatic pencils, sewing kits, letter openers, and similar novelties. When a prospect accepts such a gift, he obligates himself to give the salesman an opportunity to present his proposition.

Leather-covered pocket memorandum books have been used by thousands of life insurance salesmen in gaining access to prospects. The books are sold to the agents at cost by the insurance companies. They usually are offered to prospects in a form letter such as the following mailed to prospects by salesmen of one large life insurance company:

DEAR MR. PROSPECT:

A high-grade real leather-covered pocket memorandum book with a renewable filler is being reserved for you. Your name will be stamped in gold on the cover and the book forwarded immediately to you upon receipt of the enclosed card.

Just take out your pencil and indicate on the card how you want your name gold-stamped. You are placed under no obligation.

Frankly, we are taking this means to bring to your attention the valuable services that we can render to you in the important matter of estate analysis.

Just send along the card and the memorandum book will be delivered to you in a few days. Remember it places you under no obligation.

Cordially yours,

Several thousand salesmen, representing a large hosiery and ready-to-wear manufacturer selling direct to consumers, secure interviews with women prospects by giving free mending kits which contain silk thread in several shades, mending needle, and run arrestors to stop runs in hosiery. This gift is featured in cards of introduction, pictured on page 416, signed and distributed to prospects by the salesmen in advance of solicitations.

Salesmen, representing a large brush company, obtain interviews with housewives with the aid of a gift brush. A salesman distributes from 30 to 40 gift cards, offering a free brush, to homes of prospects between 5:30 and 6:00 P.M. A day or two later, the salesman returns to the homes where cards were left, asks for the card, and usually obtains an interview by saying, "Just get the card for me and I will step inside and give you your free brush. To secure interviews in foreign districts, gift cards are printed in 17 foreign languages. In rural districts, gift cards are delivered by mail and followed up by salesmen. No other "door opener" has been so widely and successfully used as this free brush.

Automobile salesmen, representing a popular make of car, distributed a miniature rubber model of the automobile, useful as a paperweight or toy for children, to secure interviews with prospects. Two

Fig. 21. Gift announcement card which is presented to women prospects by salesmen of a direct to the consumer sales organization, to aid them in securing sales interviews.

folders illustrating the gift were prepared by the manufacturer and mailed by the salesmen to their best prospects in advance of calls. Thousands of models were delivered by salesmen to prospects who were given demonstrations of the automobile.

Washing-machine salesmen representing a large manufacturer of washers used toy models of washing machines to secure interviews with housewives. The gift was featured by the salesmen in their introductions as a plaything for children.

Mechanical pencils, imprinted with the names of prospects, desk memo pads, calendars, and similar novelties have been used successfully in getting interviews with businessmen. The small cost of these gifts is justified by the savings in time and energy enjoyed by salesmen in getting interviews with prospects.

4. Using the Telephone. The telephone is an effective device for securing interviews. Some salesmen never call on a prospect without first making an appointment by telephone.

Prospects with whom interviews are sought by telephone should be carefully selected as to need, ability to buy, and authority to purchase. If a prospect has been sent letters and advance advertising by a salesman, appointments may be obtained by telephone with little difficulty. In seeking interviews by telephone, a salesman should not attempt to discuss his product or service or seek an order from the prospect over the telephone.

If a salesman has been referred to the prospect by a third party, interviews are easily secured over the telephone by using the name of the reference. A life insurance salesman who telephones for interviews obtains an appointment from every three telephone calls and eventually sells one out of every four persons interviewed. He uses the following telephone conversation:

Mr. Prospect, my name is Jones. Mr. Smith, a mutual friend of ours, has suggested that I ought to make your acquaintance. I am going to be down your way at three o'clock this afternoon. Could you see me for 5 or 10 minutes then?

A standardized telephone talk to secure interviews is used by many salesmen. From experience they have found the most effective combination of words to speak over the telephone for this purpose. The following standardized telephone conversation has been used by electric refrigerator salesmen in seeking interviews with housewives. Experienced salesmen average 15 appointments out of every 100 calls when they use this telephone talk:

Good morning, is this Mrs. Smith? This is Mr. Salesman of the Bateman Company, refrigeration specialists.

Mrs. Smith, several of your neighbors have given us permission to call at their homes and answer their questions about electric refrigeration. You do not have an electric refrigerator at present, do you, Mrs. Smith?

(If the prospect has a refrigerator, the salesman determines its age and whether the buyer may be interested in a replacement. If the prospect does not have a refrigerator, the salesman continues.)

Then I am sure that you would like to know more about this modern method of food preservation, because you know it's something that concerns the health and comfort of every member of the family.

I will be on your street again this week, Mrs. Smith, and I'll be glad to stop in for just a few minutes to explain its advantages. What day would be most convenient for you to have me call, Mrs. Smith? I'll need only a few minutes of your time.

Tuesday? That will be fine. Say about 10 o'clock? Thank you. Good-by.

In seeking interviews by telephone, a salesman who does his calling at the hours most convenient to prospects gets the greatest number of appointments. The highest percentage of appointments is usually secured on calls made between 9:15 and 11:15 A.M. and 1:15 and 4:15 P.M.

Courtesy, tact, and consideration aid a salesman in telephoning to prospects. A pleasant voice, the ability to inspire confidence, and mental alertness are helpful to a salesman in getting appointments by telephone.

Appointments for interviews obtained by telephone may be followed up by a salesman with a letter confirming the day and hour and thanking the prospect for the interview.

Some salesmen are assisted by their wives, sisters, or secretaries in getting interviews with prospects by telephone. A vacuum cleaner salesman in Chicago arranged with his sister to make telephone calls to suspects to secure appointments for interviews. In 30 days, his sister obtained 51 appointments with buyers who bought 38 cleaners, 6 washing machines, and 5 ironers.

Salesmen associated with a retail motor-car dealer in Chicago made 1,532 telephone calls for appointments in one month and obtained 917 interviews with prospects, many of whom were converted into customers.

In telephoning for interviews, some salesmen deliberately avoid mentioning their product or service in an effort to overcome the natural resistance of buyers to granting interviews to salesmen. One life insurance salesman telephones for appointments, as follows: "Mr. Prospect, I have a plan for that boy of yours which I would like to discuss with you tomorrow afternoon. Which time will be most convenient for you, 1:40 or 2:35?"

After making appointments by telephone, salesmen should be punctual in keeping their engagements. If a salesman asks for 10 or 15 minutes of a prospect's time, the buyer expects him to keep his promise and not stay longer. When a salesman cannot keep an appointment, a prospect is entitled to a telephone call explaining the delay.

5. Sampling. Some salesmen secure interviews by leaving their product or a sample with the prospect's secretary or maid with the understanding that the buyer will give it a trial. The salesman returns at another time to pick up the product or sample and secures an interview with the prospect.

Salesmen who sell small home appliances to housewives use this method of getting past maids and securing interviews. They leave the product with a maid at the door, saying, "Will you please ask Mrs. Prospect to try this for a few days and tell her that I shall call for it next Monday afternoon, if she will be home at that time."

The same method may be used to get interviews with industrial buyers. A salesman leaves with the secretary of the buyer a part or sample of his product to arouse the prospect's curiosity and cause him to become interested in learning more about the device.

METHODS OF SECURING INTERVIEWS ON FIRST CONTACT WITH BUYERS

When a salesman has had no opportunity, before calling at a prospect's home or place of business, to secure an advance appointment for an interview, he has to employ other methods of obtaining an interview on first contact with the buyer. Successful methods used by salesmen to gain immediate access to prospects are: (1) good personal impression; (2) cultivation of barriers; (3) interviewing subordinates; (4) positive introduction; (5) meeting excuses.

1. Personal Impression. The personal impression which a salesman makes in seeking an interview often determines whether or not he gains admission to the prospect's home or office. If a salesman has a good appearance, poise, and dignified bearing, the secretary of the buyer or other intermediary associates these qualities with the importance of the salesman's mission and the value of his product or service.

A confident manner, springing from a sincere conviction of his ability to serve, aids a salesman in creating an impression that his call is important. If a salesman establishes himself on a plane of equality with prospects and barriers rather than assuming an attitude of superiority, arrogance, and self-importance, he is more successful in securing interviews. By acting as though he anticipates no opposition and expects to be granted a hearing by a prospect, a salesman often obtains interviews without difficulty.

Courtesy and consideration to secretaries and associates of buyers are important personal characteristics in securing interviews. Salesmen who wisecrack, talk loudly, smoke, and wear their hats in anterooms create poor impressions and arouse resistance in getting interviews.

2. Cultivation of Barriers. Many prospects who are very busy are obliged to conserve their time by protecting themselves from interruptions with receptionists, secretaries, office managers, maids, information clerks, and office boys. These subordinates often have authority to determine whether or not a salesman shall be granted an interview by their employers. A conscientious private secretary who has the responsibility of admitting salesmen to her superior's office is usually anxious to see that every salesman with a worth-while proposition secures an interview with her employer.

When a secretary or receptionist asks a salesman, "What is your business?" she is attempting to judge whether or not her superior would be interested in the salesman's proposition. A salesman who ignores barriers' questions, gives an evasive answer, becomes facetious, turns aggressive, resorts to flattery, or is condescending and noncommittal defeats his own objective of securing an interview.

Successful salesmen show respect for secretaries and maids and win their favor and cooperation by consideration and courtesy. Frankness, confidence, a good appearance, and an earnest and pleasant manner aid a salesman in securing the good will of subordinates.

If a salesman explains briefly to a barrier the merits of his product or service and convinces her of the worth of his proposition, he usually experiences no difficulty in gaining access to the prospect. However, a barrier should not be expected to sell the buyer, a salesman should do his own selling to ensure that it is well done.

A favorable impression may be made on a secretary or receptionist by calling her by name. One salesman secures the name of a prospect's secretary from other employees and greets her as follows: "Good morning, Miss Jones, I should appreciate it greatly if you would secure an interview for me with Mr. Prospect. If he cannot see me conveniently now, I shall be glad to come back later."

Salesmen who anticipate difficulty in securing interviews with busy prospects sometimes interview the buyer's secretary. They explain to her their reasons for wishing to interview her employer and persuade her to arrange an appointment with the prospect.

3. Interviewing Subordinates. Instead of attempting to gain immediate access to a busy prospect, a salesman may choose first to seek interviews with a prospect's assistants or business associates. From these subordinates the salesman secures information which aids him in obtaining a subsequent interview with the subject who has authority to buy.

Interviews are sought with subordinates principally for the purpose of obtaining facts about the needs of the buyer. Usually no attempt is made by a salesman to sell subordinates. When a salesman has secured information about the situation of a buyer, he has little difficulty in getting an interview to present a specific solution to the buyer's problem.

A successful adding-machine salesman always interviews statisticians, accountants, and office managers before seeking an interview with the purchasing agent or other buyer in authority. He obtains facts on the number of cash and credit transactions, the amount of computing done, when statements are rendered, how often a trial balance is taken, and similar information from the bookkeepers before approaching the buyer. The salesman then estimates the savings that his equipment will effect. With this information in hand, the salesman seeks an interview with the buyer in authority, saying, for example, "I have a reliable estimate based on a study of your bookkeeping methods that our equipment can save you $8,600 in your accounting department next year." The salesman usually gets an appointment by this method.

The same strategy can be used in securing interviews with homeowners who are prospects for oil burners, insulation, gas heating, air conditioning, refrigeration, and other household products. Information obtained in preliminary interviews with housewives, maids, and custodians is not only helpful in securing interviews but also in making sales presentations.

4. Positive Introduction. The wording of a salesman's introduction to a receptionist, secretary, or maid should not be left to chance but should be phrased to create the impression that the salesman's call is expected or is important. Many salesmen show by their negative introductions that they expect to be refused an interview. A salesman who says to a barrier, "Mr. Prospect doesn't want to see anybody today, does he?" or "I hate to bother Mr. Prospect, but I'd like to see him for a minute," is inviting a refusal. Equally poor is the trite introduction, "I was going by and thought I'd drop in and see if Mr. Prospect would see me." Weak introductions of this character reveal a salesman's lack of confidence and make an unfavorable impression on secretaries and receptionists.

A positive introduction, such as, "Please tell Mr. Prospect that Mr. Salesman is here, ready to discuss his investment program," creates a favorable impression. If a salesman represents a well-known company and product, they may be mentioned in his announcement, as follows: "Please tell Mr. Prospect that Mr. Salesman of the Mammoth Automobile Company is here to see him." Both of these positive introductions create the impression that a salesman confidently expects to be invited into a prospect's home or office.

If a salesman is seeking an interview with a referred prospect, he should announce himself to the information clerk in the outer office, as follows: "Please tell Mr. Prospect that Richard Roe, a friend of Mr. Doe, is calling."

When a salesman mails buyers personal letters in advance of his calls, he should say to the barrier, "Please tell Mr. Prospect that Mr. Salesman is calling in regard to the subject of his recent letter." This introduction arouses the curiosity of the prospect and often secures an interview for the salesman.

5. Meeting Excuses. A salesman frequently encounters numerous excuses from barriers and prospects who do not want to grant interviews. If a salesman is prepared to deal with these excuses, he usually experiences no difficulty in getting face to face with prospects. A prospect or barrier makes these pretexts in the hope that a salesman will accept them as facts and not persist in seeking an interview.

One of the most common excuses encountered by salesmen seeking interviews is the statement of a barrier that the prospect is "busy." Salesmen handle this excuse by saying, "May I see him later in the day, say at 3:30 o'clock this afternoon?" or "Can you tell me how long he will be engaged?" or "Please tell Mr. Prospect that another appointment prevents my waiting now, but I shall return this afternoon at 2:40."

Another excuse frequently met by salesmen seeking interviews is, "Not interested." One salesman answers this excuse by saying, "That's just why I called to see you. I believe that if you know more about this service you'll be interested." A life insurance salesman says, "Please tell Mr. Prospect that a few minutes at his desk will be sufficient to show him that I can be of real service to him in an important matter."

Prospects sometimes ask a salesman for more information about his proposition before granting him an interview. If a salesman does not wish to reveal the purpose of his call, he may evade the buyer's inquiry and arouse his curiosity with an indefinite reply. An investment salesman, when asked by a prospect, "What do you want to see me about?" writes the words "Financial Independence" on a slip of paper and asks the buyer's secretary to carry it to the prospect. This salesman finds that it is more effective to write his message than to depend upon the secretary or telephone operator to repeat his reply orally. An insurance salesman handles this situation by saying, "Mr. Buyer, I am here to give you, first, information, and second, a word or two of suggestion."

Successful salesmen meet these common excuses of prospects and barriers with standard answers based on responses which they have found most effective. Instead of relying upon momentary inspiration to dispose of the excuses of prospects, salesmen who are prepared with ready responses have little difficulty in securing interviews.

WAITING FOR INTERVIEWS

If a prospect is busy or absent when a salesman calls for an interview, he is confronted with the problem of waiting or returning later to see the buyer. A long wait for a buyer not only means a loss of time but often prevents a salesman from keeping an appointment with another prospect. Some buyers deliberately keep a salesman waiting for the purpose of "wearing him down."

Unless a salesman is granted an interview within a reasonably short time, it is usually not advisable for him to wait for a prospect. Some salesmen definitely limit the time which they will wait for prospects to five or ten minutes. Before deciding to wait, they ask the receptionist, "Can you tell me how long it will be before I can see Mr. Prospect?" If the waiting time does not exceed their limit, these salesmen wait until the buyer may be interviewed. The distance traveled by a salesman in reaching a prospect and the importance of the interview also determine the amount of time that may be spent in waiting.

If a prospect is absent or engaged for a longer time than a salesman feels he should wait, he may attempt to get an appointment for an interview at a future time by asking the secretary or receptionist, "Please tell Mr. Prospect that another engagement makes it impossible for me to wait, but I shall return at 2:40 this afternoon if that time is convenient." Usually this strategy secures another appointment.

If a salesman gives a prospect the impression that his time is valuable, he is less likely to be kept waiting long for interviews.

Some prospects prefer to interview salesmen in reception rooms, in the presence of third parties, or while engaged with other work. A salesman cannot get proper consideration of his proposition under these conditions. By asking for a private interview or by getting an appointment for a return call at a more opportune time, a salesman ensures a favorable hearing.

When a salesman is faced with a reception-room interview, he should seek a private interview by saying, "May we step into your private office?" or "I should like to speak to you about a matter that can best be discussed in private." Prospects usually accede to these requests.

When a salesman meets a prospect who continues working on other matters or is talking to a third party, he can handle the situation by saying, "I see that you are busy now. Would it be possible for you to see me privately at 4:25 this afternoon?" The third party usually takes the hint and leaves, and the prospect grants the salesman an interview at another time or gives his full attention to the salesman's presentation.

USING BUSINESS CARDS IN SECURING INTERVIEWS

The advisability of using a business card in seeking access to prospects, depends upon the reputation of the salesman's firm, the type of product or service sold, and the type of buyer. A representative of a famous electrical equipment manufacturer, selling generators to purchasing agents of public utilities, can capitalize on the reputation of his company by presenting a business card, thus identifying himself with a reputable firm. It is a common practice in many companies for receptionists to ask salesmen seeking interviews for their business cards.

However, a representative of a little-known company seeking access to business executives or professional men might find that a business card would not be helpful in securing interviews. The name of an unfamiliar firm on a business card carries no prestige with a prospect. When a buyer learns from a business card what a salesman is selling, he may refuse to grant an interview on the grounds that he does not need the product or service.

In general, the use of business cards in obtaining interviews is advisable in selling to professional buyers. However, in selling specialties and intangible services for individual or home consumption, business cards are of little assistance or may be a handicap in gaining access to buyers.

On the other hand, after a salesman has completed his presentation, it is good strategy to leave a business card with the prospect as evidence of the identity of the salesman and as an aid to the buyer who wishes to communicate with him.

AVOID TRICKERY IN SECURING INTERVIEWS

Deception or trickery to obtain interviews with prospects is never justified. The subterfuges and fraudulent practices of a few unscrupulous salesmen in obtaining interviews have made it difficult for salesmen to gain access to buyers. The house-to-house salesman who puts his foot in a buyer's door or poses as a meter reader, inspector of home appliances, or an investigator making a market survey to gain entrance to homes or offices of prospects creates ill will and resentment which are detrimental to his efforts.

Sincere, honest efforts to obtain interviews are, in the long run, far more effective than trickery in getting face to face with buyers.

HOW TO SECURE SALES INTERVIEWS

To aid salesmen in putting into practice some of the practical methods used by successful salesmen in securing interviews, as described in the preceding pages, the following five-step routine is recommended. By following these simple steps, a salesman can increase his ratio of interviews to calls, save selling time and improve sales volume.

Routine for Securing Interviews with Buyers

1. Prepare the way for interviews.
2. Make good first impression.
3. Use a positive introduction.
4. Deal effectively with excuses.
5. Cultivate barriers.

1. Prepare the Way for Interviews. The problem of securing interviews is often solved by a salesman who cultivates prospects in advance by one or more of the several methods previously described. The small expense involved in mailing interview-seeking letters and advance cards or in offering gifts is amply repaid in time and effort saved in securing interviews. Telephone calls to prospects also save much time and travel expense. Customers, friends, and influential informants are usually willing to permit a salesman to use their names in securing interviews.

If a salesman will experiment with several of these methods, he will soon discover which are the most effective for him. By preparing for interviews in advance, a salesman can obtain them at the best time and place and avoid interruptions. Instead of depending on fortunate circumstances or high-pressure aggressiveness to open prospects' doors, a salesman can get interviews more successfully by one of the indirect approaches described previously.

2. Make Good First Impression. If a salesman looks attractive to a receptionist or secretary, his chances of securing an interview with a buyer are greatly increased. Prospects prefer to meet salesmen who are neat, clean, and well groomed. A shave, haircut, clean nails, fresh linen, and polished shoes combine to make a good personal appearance which is one of the most important factors in getting past barriers to an interview.

A prospect knows nothing about a strange salesman seeking an interview except what he appears to be by his dress and manner. If his appearance is good, a salesman has overcome the first hurdle to an interview. Until a salesman has an opportunity to present product advantages, the buyer must take a salesman at his face value. A kindly face and a friendly smile have opened many doors to salesmen.

If a salesman has complete confidence that his product or service will give profit and satisfaction to a buyer, he has the right mental attitude to secure interviews. When a salesman knows that his product or service will save buyers time or energy, enable them to make more money, or enjoy life more completely, he can be enthusiastic about his proposition and his enthusiasm creates a good first impression that opens doors which are closed to many salesmen.

3. Use a Positive Introduction. A salesman should avoid apologetic or negative introductions which create the impression that he does not expect to be successful in securing a hearing. Trite, commonplace salutations give buyers and barriers little confidence in the importance of a salesman's mission. Facetious introductions cause buyers to doubt a salesman's sincerity. Usually these weak, social preliminaries to securing sales interviews are evidence of a salesman's embarrassment and lack of confidence.

A salesman who prepares the way for interviews by using third-party references, advance letters, and telephone appointments can make a positive introduction for he has something of significance to say. Advance knowledge of a buyer's needs enables a salesman to refer to a prospect's problem in seeking an interview.

The wording of a salesman's opening statement should reveal his confidence and expectation that he will get a hearing. By saying to a receptionist or secretary, "Please tell Mr. Buyer that John Salesman is calling at the suggestion of his friend Richard Roe," a salesman has little difficulty in getting face to face with the buyer.

4. Deal Effectively with Excuses. Many buyers habitually make excuses for not giving interviews to salesmen. Many buyers use excuses deliberately to discourage salesmen from persisting in their efforts to obtain interviews. These excuses are sometimes evidence of natural sales resistance arising from a prospect's belief that he does not need or cannot afford the salesman's product or service.

In dealing with these excuses many salesmen ignore them entirely or agree with them and pass on to discuss a need or benefit to be gained by buying the product or service.

Successful salesmen have routine methods of handling all of those common excuses. If a prospect refuses to see a salesman on the pretext that he is "too busy," the salesman may seek an appointment for an interview at a later time. If a buyer denies an interview because he is not interested, a salesman may arouse interest by discussing benefits which the prospect would receive from ownership of the product or show how the salesman can serve the buyer profitably.

It is essential that a salesman anticipate the common excuses for refusing interviews by preparing a number of responses rather than relying on inspiration of the moment to get hearings with prospects.

5. Cultivate Barriers. Most salesmen give too little consideration to the buyer's secretary, information clerk, or receptionist, who is often the most important factor in determining whether or not they

SALES PRESENTATION RATING FORM

Securing Sales Interviews

Salesman_____   Date_____

Rated by_____   Over-all Rating_____

Score

I. *Salesman's Method of Securing Interview*	Excellent 90–100	Good 80–90	Fair 70–80	Poor 60–70	Failure Below 60
A. Advance preparation to secure interview					
B. Make good first impression					
C. Use positive introduction					
D. Deal effectively with excuses					
E. Cultivate barriers					

Miscellaneous Comments_____

will gain access to the prospect. Successful salesmen employ a proved
technique in getting the cooperation of these barriers. Instead of
overriding barriers with bluff, flattery, or arrogance, wise salesmen
greet them courteously and by pleasant persuasiveness win their aid
in establishing contact with buyers.

Good appearance, frankness, a positive introduction, ready answers
to objections, and a sincere interest in the buyer's problem enable
a salesman to deal effectively with subordinates and secure their
cordial cooperation in securing interviews.

Problem I

Obtaining Interviews with Business Executives

Cornhill, Daley, and Waters, Advertising Agency

The Cornhill, Daley, and Waters Advertising Agency, organized in
1901, with headquarters in New York City and branch offices in Chicago, San Francisco, Boston, and St. Louis, plans, produces, and places
an annual volume of advertising in excess of $5,000,000 for 40 na-
tional and sectional advertisers using magazines, newspapers, radio,
outdoor, and other advertising media.

Sales representatives of numerous magazines, newspapers, and other
advertising media call at the agency offices to make sales presentations
to the agency account executives, who recommend various advertising
media to the clients served by the agency.

The Boston office of the agency receives numerous calls from advertising media salesmen and the receptionist of the agency has kept a
verbatim record of the conversations of a number of these salesmen
who are seeking interviews with the agency executives. The records
follow:

1. Salesman A (selling advertising space in a magazine, telephoned in ad-
    vance of his call and asked for Mr. Wiley, an agency executive. He
    was told by the receptionist that Mr. Wiley would return at 2:00 P.M.)
2. Salesman A (calling at 2:15): Is Mr. Wiley back yet?
3. Receptionist: No, but we expect him any minute now.
4. Salesman A: He hasn't called in to say he would be late, then?
5. Receptionist: No, I think he will be right along.
6. Salesman A: I'll wait a few minutes. (Salesman waits 10 minutes and
    rises to leave.) I think I'll try him a little later. Please give him my
    card and tell him I'll be back tomorrow at 2:00 o'clock.
7. Receptionist: All right, good-by.

* * * * *

1. SALESMAN B (selling advertising space in a magazine): My name is Hawkins, *Thursday Night Magazine.* I want to see Mr. Garfield in regard to our correspondence on the Martin account.
2. RECEPTIONIST: Mr. Garfield is in a meeting which may last for some time.
3. SALESMAN B: Could you see if he can see me at 3:00 tomorrow?
4. RECEPTIONIST: Yes, I'd be glad to.
5. SALESMAN B: Thank you.
6. RECEPTIONIST: He will be glad to see you at 3:00 tomorrow.
7. SALESMAN B: Thank you. Good-by.

* * * * *

1. SALESMAN C (selling advertising space in a magazine): I'm Jim Harvey of *Sport Review.* Is Mr. Garfield in this afternoon?
2. RECEPTIONIST: Yes, he is.
3. SALESMAN C: I want to see him in regard to the Blank Manufacturing Company account.
4. RECEPTIONIST: He's in conference and can't be seen now.
5. SALESMAN C: Can you ask him to come out so I can see him?
6. RECEPTIONIST: Yes, what was your name please?
7. SALESMAN C: Here's my card.
8. RECEPTIONIST: He wants to know what you want to see him about on the Blank account.
9. SALESMAN C: Their Fall schedule.
10. RECEPTIONIST (returning to the reception room and speaking to the salesman): Just come with me, please.

* * * * *

1. SALESMAN D (selling time on radio network): Hi, is Mr. Wiley in?
2. RECEPTIONIST: Yes.
3. SALESMAN D: Will you tell him I wait without?
4. RECEPTIONIST: Without what?
5. SALESMAN D: I'll tell you that after I see him.
6. RECEPTIONIST (announces Salesman D to Mr. Wiley who says that there will be a half-hour wait): He says that you will have to wait about a half hour.
7. SALESMAN D: Tell him that I'll be glad to wait a half hour, will you?
8. RECEPTIONIST: Yes.
9. SALESMAN D: Thank you.
10. RECEPTIONIST: You're welcome.

* * * * *

1. SALESMAN E (selling space in a national magazine, enters).
2. RECEPTIONIST: Good morning.
3. SALESMAN E: Good morning. I'm Bill Stout, representing *Tiny Tots.* I want to talk with Mr. Grace in regard to the Genter Hosiery account.
4. RECEPTIONIST: Mr. Grace happens to be out of town today.

5. SALESMAN E: Then I'd like to see Mr. Spencer about the Watson Under-
    wear account.

6. RECEPTIONIST: Mr. Spencer has a man waiting to see him already.

7. SALESMAN E: I see. Is Mr. Barton in? I would like to see him if I could.
    (Salesman hands his card to receptionist and she delivers it to Mr.
    Barton.)

8. RECEPTIONIST (returning to the reception room): Mr. Barton will see
    you in a few moments.

9. SALESMAN E: Thank you.

10. RECEPTIONIST: Yes.

* * * * *

1. SALESMAN F (a salesman of advertising in a magazine; is well acquainted
    with the receptionist as he is a regular caller): Hi, May.

2. RECEPTIONIST: Hello, Mr. Gorton.

3. SALESMAN F: Are any of the boys in? (In undertone he adds quickly)
    I hope not.

4. RECEPTIONIST: Not today.

5. SALESMAN F: Good, where are the rest of the girls?

6. RECEPTIONIST: Mr. Gorton, what a cutting remark! Won't I do?

7. SALESMAN F: No, I've got to have all five of you. Come on now, gather
    around. (Salesman tells humorous stories until he hears footsteps
    without and reaches for his hat.) So long, girls. (With a flourish of
    his hat he disappears out the door.)

* * * * *

1. SALESMAN G (selling advertising space in a magazine): Hello, how are
    you? Please tell Mr. Blake that Mike Todd of *Style* is here to discuss
    the Royal account.

2. RECEPTIONIST (announces Salesman G and returns to the reception
    room): Mr. Blake will be out in a minute.

3. SALESMAN G: Here's a new booklet on the late fashions we have just pub-
    lished. You might be interested.

4. RECEPTIONIST: Yes, I would like to see it.

5. SALESMAN G: Will you tell Mr. Pope I was in today?

6. RECEPTIONIST: I'd be glad to.

7. SALESMAN G: Thanks, I'd like to make an appointment with him at 2:00
    Wednesday.

8. RECEPTIONIST: I am sure he can see you then. Just phone before you
    come in.

* * * * *

1. SALESMAN H (salesman of newspaper space): Is Mr. Barton in?

2. RECEPTIONIST: Yes, he is.

3. SALESMAN H: If he's not busy, I'd like to see him.

4. RECEPTIONIST: May I have your name please?

5. SALESMAN H: Mr. Jackson of the *Daily Eagle*.

6. RECEPTIONIST: Thank you. (She announces salesman to Mr. Barton.) Mr. Barton is busy now.

7. SALESMAN H: Thank you. I'll come back again some other time.

Questions

1. Which one of the eight salesmen used the best strategy in securing a sales interview?

2. Who, if any of these salesmen, attempted to secure an interview before calling at the office of the advertising agency? What method did he use?

3. What methods might have been profitably used by these salesmen in paving the way for interviews in advance of their calls?

4. Who, if any of these salesmen, cultivated the receptionist most effectively? Who was least effective in this respect? How should the barrier have been cultivated?

5. Which one of the men used the best worded introduction? Who had the poorest introduction? What introductory statement might have been used by these men?

6. Did any of these salesmen encounter "excuses" from the barrier? Who answered these excuses most effectively?

7. Who showed the poorest strategy in waiting for an interview? Which salesman handled the problem of waiting most effectively? How?

Problem II

SECURING INTERVIEWS WITH GIFTS

James T. Diamond, representing the Hill Washer Company

The Hill Washer Company, established in 1920 in Baltimore, Md., is one of the largest manufacturers of household washing machines. More than 3,000 distributors represent the company in selling direct to housewives in all parts of the country. In addition to the main factory in Baltimore, the company operates branch plants in St. Louis, Cleveland, Atlanta, and San Francisco.

One of the problems of the distributors is to gain access to homes and then present and demonstrate their line of washing machines to housewives.

To aid its representatives in securing interviews, the company sells them at cost small bags containing three dozen new-type plastic clothespins which are given to housewives who give salesmen home interviews.

James T. Diamond has sold Hill washers for five years in Binghamton, N. Y. He solicits orders daily from housewives in that city and on Saturday of each week he works in the branch office mailing out gift cards to suspects.

To secure interviews with housewives, salesman Diamond mails weekly 100 gift announcement cards which read as follows:

> Save This Card. It entitles you to a Hill Free Bag
> of Clothespins
>
> FREE
>
> I will call in a day or two and exchange this card
> for a Hill bag of plastic clothespins—free.
>
> So keep this card.
> Signed.......................
> Your Hill Washer Man.

Sometimes salesman Diamond delivers the gift cards in person and says:

Good afternoon. I am from the Hill Washer Company. (Hands housewife gift card.) Keep this card and I will be back in a day or two and do just what the card says. Will eight o'clock be convenient for you to receive your gift? Thank you.

If a prospect does not answer the door promptly, salesman Diamond leaves the card in the door.

The following day, he calls at all homes where he left cards the previous afternoon to redeem them. His conversation follows:

Good morning, Mrs. Prospect. You have one of these cards? (showing copy of gift card.) Just get the card for me and I will step inside and give you your free bag of plastic clothespins. (Here the salesman starts to walk in.)

If the card has been left in the door by the salesman, he says:

Good morning. You received one of these certificates from the Hill Washer Company (showing card) entitling you to a free bag of clothespins. Just get the card for me and I will step in and give them to you.

If a prospect says that she does not have the card, the salesman says:

Sometimes it is lost. It announces my coming, you see. (Holding up card.) I'll step inside and give you your free clothespins.

If a prospect says that she does not want to buy, the salesman replies:

That's all right. You don't need to buy unless you wish. Just get the card for me, please.

When the salesman has gained admittance to the prospect's home, he presents her with a free bag of clothespins, saying:

This is your free bag of new plastic clothespins, Mrs. Prospect. Aren't they attractive? You will find them real handy when you do your washing. Do you own a washer, Mrs. Prospect? If you do your own washing, you will be interested in the new Hill Automatic Washer which cuts washing time in half.

To secure interviews in wealthy neighborhoods, salesman Diamond hands gift cards to the maid in charge of laundry. In foreign districts, gift cards are printed in the appropriate languages.

Questions

1. Criticize favorably or otherwise the gift method of securing interviews as described in this case.

2. What other methods of securing interviews might be used effectively by salesman Diamond? Describe them in detail.

3. Assuming that the salesman is confronted by a maid when he calls to redeem the gift card, what tactics should he use? What should he do if confronted by a husband?

4. What is the importance of personal impression in securing interviews in this case? What personal qualities are particularly desirable?

5. What do you think of salesman Diamond's introduction?

Reading References

E. Casey and R. L. Johns, "Salesmanship for Colleges," Chap. 10, H. N. Rowe Company, Baltimore, 1938.

J. R. Daubman, "Salesmanship and Types of Selling," Chap. X, F. S. Crofts & Co., New York, 1939.

Charles H. Fernald, "Salesmanship," Chap. X, Prentice-Hall, Inc., New York, 1945.

Harold M. Haas, "A Short Course in Salesmanship," Chap. VI, Prentice-Hall, Inc., New York, 1939.

Paul W. Ivey, "Salesmanship Applied," Chap. XVIII, McGraw-Hill Book Company, Inc., New York, 1937.

Paul W. Ivey, "Successful Salesmanship," pp. 270–279, Prentice-Hall, Inc., New York, 1947.

David R. Osborne, "Salesmanship for Today for Salesmanagers of Tomorrow," Chap. VI, Harper & Brothers, New York, 1939.

Charles B. Roth, "Finding the Prospect and Getting the Interview," pp. 61–90, Prentice-Hall, Inc., New York, 1946.

Frederic A. Russell and F. H. Beach, "Textbook of Salesmanship," Chap. IX, McGraw-Hill Book Company, Inc., New York, 1949.

HARRY SIMMONS, "A Practical Course in Successful Selling," Chap. VII, Harper & Brothers, New York, 1939.

D. B. TANSILL, "So You're Going to Sell?" pp. 43–45, John C. Winston Company, Philadelphia, 1939.

PERCY H. WHITING, "The Five Great Rules of Selling," Chap. XXIV, McGraw-Hill Book Company, Inc., New York, 1947.

CHAPTER XVIII

OPENING A SALES INTERVIEW

IMPORTANCE OF A GOOD OPENING

In delivering a sales presentation, the initial remarks made by a salesman to a prospect are the most important of the interview. A prospect's interest is often won or lost by the first half-dozen sentences spoken by a salesman. If the opening sentences appeal to the buyer's needs, self-interest, or motives, he is likely to listen attentively to the entire sales presentation. If, on the other hand, a salesman's opening remarks are trite and uninteresting, a buyer will pay little attention to the balance of the salesman's message.

The first few remarks of a sales interview offer a salesman an unusual opportunity to impress the buyer whose mind is fresh and receptive to ideas. It is a moment of too much consequence to be left to chance, as is often the case. A vague, trite, or irrelevant introduction puts a prospect in a negative mood which is difficult to overcome by any subsequent amount of skillful persuasion. If the first impression made by a salesman is negative, it is almost impossible to alter that impression in a prospect's mind throughout the interview.

Sales presentations are often poorly launched because the importance of a good introduction is not appreciated by many salesmen. Opening remarks are made usually on the inspiration of the moment. The opening of a sales interview, just like the introductory remarks of a good speech, should be carefully planned in advance to appeal to the interests of the listener.

ATTITUDE OF A TYPICAL PROSPECT

The attitude of a typical buyer toward a salesman at the opening of a sales interview is often one of indifference and sometimes even antagonism. Although he may be courteous, a prospect is usually on the defensive. Figuratively, some buyers are frozen in a cake of ice, coldly determined to resist any efforts to melt their resolution not to buy. Frequently a buyer does not know the salesman and is suspicious of his motives. Many prospects are noncommittal and inhospitable or disposed to sit back and wait until a salesman shows by what he is, what he says, and how he says it that his proposition is worthy of consideration.

When approached by a salesman, the typical buyer is not listening attentively, eager to catch every word of the salesman. Rather, he stifles a yawn, sinks back passively in his chair, resigned to spending a boring time until the salesman leaves. When not indifferent, a buyer busies himself devising excuses for dismissing the salesman or discouraging him to such an extent that he will depart voluntarily.

A salesman often finds a buyer preoccupied with subjects or activities quite foreign to the subject of the interview. He may be thinking about a complaint from a customer, a telephone call that he must make, a luncheon appointment, the temper of his mother-in-law, or the illness of his wife. A prospect's mind must be diverted from these preoccupations before he can give full attention to the salesman's proposition. The first task of a salesman is to build a bridge between the island of the buyer's interests and the salesman's proposition.

A prospect may give shallow attention to a salesman's story. Natural curiosity may cause a buyer to look at the salesman for a minute or two at the opening of an interview; unless the salesman quickly establishes a bond of common interest, the buyer's attention wavers and he becomes indifferent.

Salesmen encounter indifference because most persons instinctively resist new ideas and oppose changes in customs and habits. Some buyers have been annoyed by salesmen and these experiences have made them antagonistic toward all salesmen. Other prospects are satisfied with their existing sources of supply and do not want to spend time interviewing salesmen representing other suppliers. Still other prospects do not recognize a need for a salesman's product and are not interested in considering it. These are the principal reasons for the apathy which a salesman experiences in his efforts to establish contact with prospective purchasers.

ATTITUDE OF A SALESMAN IN OPENING INTERVIEWS

The first impression that a salesman makes on a buyer whom he has never met before is very important for it frequently determines the buyer's attitude during the balance of the interview. Before a salesman has an opportunity to say a word, he unconsciously creates an attitude in the mind of the prospect. A strange salesman is only as good as he appears to be in the eyes of the buyer.

A salesman's poise, appearance, and bearing combine to make a positive or negative initial impression. If a salesman is motivated by a sincere desire to help a buyer satisfy his needs, the prospect subconsciously senses this attitude and adopts a favorable attitude toward the salesman.

If a salesman approaches a prospect alertly, with an air of confidence which suggests he has important business to discuss, the buyer is favorably impressed. On the other hand, if a salesman approaches a buyer with a swagger to cover up embarrassment or a feeling of inferiority, if he tiptoes in timidly, if he strides in pompously with head held high and chest thrown out, or if he dashes in nervously with excessive animation, the buyer senses the salesman's attitude and is not favorably impressed.

When a salesman stands silently before a prospect, pausing for a few seconds before he speaks, he commands attention and gives the buyer an opportunity to make the transition from his previous work. Some salesmen breeze in impetuously to greet a prospect, losing their self-possession in a burst of enthusiasm and giving the buyer an impression that he is being swept off his feet.

An effective salesman is direct in manner; he looks directly into the eyes of his prospect and establishes a cordial, personal contact with him. Such a salesman gives an impression of frankness and sincerity which is lacking in the approach of the shifty-eyed, furtive salesman who seems to be hiding something.

The Chinese have a proverb, "He who cannot smile ought not to keep shop." A salesman who approaches prospects with a sincere, friendly smile gains their confidence and good will. If a salesman genuinely likes people and enjoys his work, his cordiality radiates in a genial smile which comes from his heart and inevitably prospects respond by being friendly. But a smile must be sincere; an affected smirk is worse than no smile at all.

A well-groomed, immaculately attired salesman creates an impression of quality that is inseparably associated with the caliber of his product and proposition. A salesman who looks successful not only impresses prospects favorably but also gains increased confidence from his appearance. Prospects prefer to deal with salesmen who are clean-shaven, have their hair trimmed, shoes shined, suits pressed, and wear clean linen.

To impress automobile salesmen with the importance of making a good impression on prospects, a large motor-car manufacturer urges them to give attention to the "three twelves," referring to the first 12 inches from the top of a salesman's head to his vest line, the first 12 steps he takes toward a prospect and the first 12 words that he speaks. If a salesman qualifies on each of these "three twelves," he is prepared to make a favorable start with new prospects.

SOCIAL PRELIMINARIES TO AN INTERVIEW

A sales interview between a salesman and a new prospect calls for the customary social preliminaries incident to the meeting of two strangers. The usual social amenities include introductory greetings, handshaking, seating, disposal of coat, hat, and equipment. Many experienced salesmen perform these preliminaries naturally and instinctively. However, beginners sometimes find it difficult to make an initial social contact with new prospects. An inexperienced salesman is often embarrassed, awkward, ill at ease, and makes a poor impression on a buyer. However, by following a planned routine of social preliminaries, sales interviews will get off to a better start.

A good salutation enables a salesman to begin his presentation naturally and fluently. The correct pronunciation of a prospect's name is ascertained before a salesman enters a home or office. A buyer is often annoyed by a thoughtless mispronunciation of his name. Mr. Smythe does not want to be called "Mr. Smith" and neither does Mr. Wood like to be referred to as "Mr. Woods."

A salesman may avoid embarrassment, resulting from mistaking the identity of a prospect, by verifying the name and position of the buyer in his opening remarks, as follows: "You are Mr. Sloan, buyer of the house furnishings?" If the salesman has been misdirected or finds his way into the wrong office, the prospect can quickly correct the mistake and confusion is avoided.

In wording his salutation, a salesman is guided by custom and the type of buyer addressed. Some buyers must be approached with dignity; others may be addressed familiarly. In introducing himself, a salesman mentions his name and that of the company which he represents. The customary formal introduction of a salesman is, "I am John Brewer, representing the Central Electric Company." A less formal greeting would be, "I'm the Central Electric man."

After a salesman has introduced himself, he is next confronted with the question of whether or not he should shake hands with the prospect. There is much difference of opinion among salesmen about the desirability of offering to shake hands with a prospect. Some salesmen believe that they should shake hands with every prospect just as they would greet a friend. They think that handshaking injects cordiality and friendliness into an otherwise cold business transaction.

Other salesmen contend that a salesman should not offer to shake hands unless a buyer first extends his hand in greeting. They believe that handshaking should be initiated by a buyer if he feels so disposed. Some buyers are reluctant to shake hands with a salesman and nothing is more embarrassing to a salesman than to have his extended hand refused by a prospect.

To avoid an awkward situation, it is the best practice for most salesmen to withhold their hands until a buyer shows a desire to shake hands by offering his hand. Reserve on the part of a salesman is usually more highly regarded by buyers than effusive handshaking.

The next decision confronting a salesman in opening an interview is whether or not he should stand or sit. Some salesmen feel that they can sell better and dominate the situation more effectively on their feet. However, if a salesman and the prospect are both seated, they are in a more natural, comfortable position to give full consideration to the salesman's proposition. When a salesman remains standing during an interview, he may distract the prospect's attention by his movements. Also, he may be more easily dismissed by the buyer. Some buyers discourage lengthy sales presentations by removing all seats from their offices. If a salesman uses visual material, he can control it most effectively when seated by the side of the prospect.

When a salesman is comfortably seated beside a prospect, he is in the best position to carry on a sales interview. Many prospects naturally invite a man to be seated; other buyers intentionally or otherwise allow a salesman to remain standing. If he is not invited to be seated, a salesman may indicate his desire to be seated with a motion of his hand toward a chair and the buyer will usually say, "Have a chair." Or a salesman may request permission to sit down, by saying, "May I sit down here?" and the buyer usually will nod his permission. A prospect rarely refuses a salesman's courteous request for a seat.

When a salesman is encumbered with an overcoat, hat, brief case, samples, and other equipment, these materials should be placed on the floor beside the salesman so that they will be accessible if needed in the interview and at the same time not interfere with the presentation. Many prospects are annoyed by salesmen who use their desks as depositories for hat, portfolio, and samples. If a salesman finds it necessary to place his sales materials on a prospect's desk, permission may be readily secured by asking, "May I use this space on your desk?"

If a salesman's hat, overcoat, overshoes, and umbrella are left in the reception room, they do not interfere with his presentation. However, if they must be brought into a buyer's office, they are best deposited on a vacant chair or on the floor beside the salesman and out of sight of the prospect. Most salesmen remove their overcoats before entering a buyer's office. If a salesman attempts to wear a heavy overcoat in a heated office during a long interview, he soon becomes uncomfortable and loses his effectiveness.

Although these suggestions may be unnecessary for many salesmen, others become careless in carrying out these commonplace social preliminaries to an interview and ignore the fundamental courtesies necessary to launch a sales presentation successfully.

OPENING STATEMENTS

The first 15 words which a salesman says to his prospect are the most important in his presentation. A salesman's opening remarks as well as his manner and appearance cause a prospect instinctively to form a positive or negative opinion of the salesman and his proposition that vitally affects the success of the interview. A buyer instinctively responds to the attitude of a salesman. If a salesman is courteous, sincere, and pleasant, a prospect usually will act in a similar manner.

In opening an interview, a salesman who directly discusses the needs of the buyer and benefits of ownership secures preferred attention. Simple, direct opening statements are best. A long, rambling, indefinite, vague introduction, designed to keep a buyer in ignorance of a salesman's objectives, annoys many prospective purchasers.

Failure to plan opening remarks results in introductions which are trite, irrelevant, timorous, vague, and negative.

Typical negative introductions to sales interviews are apologetic remarks, "You don't want to buy any steel today, do you?" or "I'm sorry to take up your time because I know you're busy," or "I won't stay but a minute but I'd like to show you our new product." These openings make it easy for a prospect to say, "No." They lack vitality, are hackneyed and commonplace.

Equally poor are negative introductions, such as, "What if you should die tomorrow—what would your family do then?" These unpleasant suggestions are hard to erase from a prospect's mind and handicap the salesman in getting favorable action on his proposition. Although openings of this sort get attention, they create a negative impression which is often detrimental to a salesman in securing orders.

Irrelevant introductions confuse a buyer and weaken a salesman's presentation. For example, a chewing-gum salesman who begins interviews with grocers by saying, "How would you like to have a year's vacation with pay?" uses an irrelevant opening. It has no relation to his proposition. An investment salesman who asks prospects, "Do you know that slavery exists in 17 nations in the world today?" arouses their curiosity by a question that has a remote relation to the subject of securities. These irrelevant openings are so remote from the objective of a salesman's interview that they confuse prospects and weaken a sales presentation.

Generalized, indefinite, and exaggerated introductions fail to arouse the interest of prospects in a salesman's product. An automobile salesman who opens his presentation by remarking, "This car is the best, most stupendous value on the road today, surpassing all others in quality and distinction," has exaggerated and said nothing specific to interest a prospect or to inform him of the real merits of the product. If the salesman had used a more specific opening such as, "This car averages 25 miles to a gallon of gasoline and accelerates from a standing start to 50 miles an hour in 10 seconds," the prospect would comprehend quickly and clearly the value of the automobile.

In planning an opening statement, select an appeal to the selfish interests of the prospect. If a salesman knows a buyer's needs and motives, he can discuss benefits which will gain the buyer's attention. An automobile salesman can open an interview by appealing to a prospect's interest in economy, comfort, beauty, performance, service, and reputation. A food-products salesman can appeal to the taste, health, appearance, or desire of prospects to save money. In selecting an opening for an interview, a salesman should be guided by his knowledge of the interests of a prospect or by his experience and judgment of the motives of buyers in general.

An oil-burner salesman opens interviews by appealing to the desire of prospects to save money, as follows: "If you could buy an oil burner that would heat your home for one-third the cost of operating your present heating system, you would be interested, wouldn't you?"

An automobile salesman opens many interviews, as follows: "Do you realize the comfort to be derived from 74-inch leg room in the front compartment of an automobile?"

TYPES OF INTERVIEW "OPENERS"

Successful salesmen have found that the favorable attention of prospects may be secured by using one or more of the following 10 types of "openers," including: (1) question; (2) significant fact; (3) curiosity; (4) anecdote; (5) reference; (6) gift; (7) survey; (8) service; (9) exhibit; (10) resale. A salesman can experiment with several of these types of opening methods and select one or more which suit his product, personality, and the type of prospect approached.

1. Question Opening. Questions that relate to the needs of a buyer and can be answered in the affirmative are effective in launching a selling interview. Salesmen of a well-known make of electric refrigerator open interviews with the following questions: "Have you ever stopped to figure how much time you spend waiting for the iceman and then cleaning up after him?" "Mrs. Prospect, do you know that you can have an electric refrigerator at a cost of less than 25 cents a day?"

A question arouses curiosity; it stimulates the thinking of a prospect and makes him want to hear more about a salesman's proposition. The following question asked by a salesman of investments in opening interviews starts a train of thought, "Would you sacrifice a year's interest on ten $1,000 4 per cent securities?"

An opening question, however, must be worded so that it cannot be answered in the negative. The following question opening is weak: "You enjoy a good turnover on kitchen clocks, don't you?" If the dealer prospect says "No," the question has proved a boomerang for the salesman.

2. Significant-fact Opening. The favorable attention of a prospect can be secured by stating facts related to his special interest: Prospects are selfishly interested in facts relating to their health, children, homes, hobbies, profits, and occupations. This type of opening takes the point of view of the prospect and makes a favorable contact for a salesman.

A salesman of business equipment uses the following significant-fact opening in interviewing prospects: "As an auditor, you will be interested to know that the Mason Manufacturing Company is saving $50,000 this year through the installation of our equipment in the auditor's office."

A salesman of golf equipment appeals to the interest of his golfer prospects in a significant-fact opening, "Did you see that Tommy Andrews, the famous professional, drove 400 yards in the Texas Open the other day? He was using our new liquid center ball."

3. Curiosity Opening. Every person is more or less curious; an opening statement which appeals to that trait causes a prospect to give attention and want to hear more. A storage battery salesman opens interviews by saying, "The other day I met a man walking down a country road carrying a little black box." The prospect's curiosity is aroused and he gives favorable attention. The buyer naturally wants to know, "Who was the man? What did he have in the black box? Where was he going?" The salesman explains that the box was a dead battery and the man was a motorist walking to a battery station to get a new battery because he failed to buy a reliable battery.

A plastic salesman opens interviews with prospective customers, appealing to their curiosity by asking, "Have you ever heard of invisible eyeglasses?" Then he explains how a new plastic material of water-white resin, half as heavy as glass, is being used for contact lenses. The curiosity of the prospect is aroused and the salesman is off to a good start in the interview.

4. Anecdote Opening. Under certain conditions and with some prospects, a leisurely opening is desirable. In opening leisurely sales interviews, a brief and relevant story is an excellent way to secure a prospect's attention. If an anecdote relates to a salesman's product or service or the needs of the buyer, it may be used effectively in opening a sales interview. An anecdote, if well told, puts a prospect in a receptive buying mood. A good story not only secures attention but sustains the interest of a prospect, arouses his curiosity, and makes him want to hear more about the salesman's proposition.

A story from a salesman's personal selling experience illustrating the need for the product is an effective type of anecdote for opening an interview. A North Carolina life insurance salesman opens interviews with many prospects by relating the following true story from his experience:

In 1932 I sold a $5,000 policy to a young bank teller who had recently married. Soon after he bought the policy, a baby came along, he lost his job in the bank and moved to another town. He began sending checks for his quarterly premium with the request that they be held for a period, then deposited. At first the checks were taken care of. Then they began to come back. Finally his father sent in the money. Eventually no checks came at all and the policy lapsed in December, 1947.

In February, 1948, I received the following note from the father, "After all my struggle to hold my son's insurance in force, it turned out that I and his family lost it. He is dead."

Recently I met the widow on the street and inquired about her situation. Here is what she told me.

"All my husband left was a $2,500 policy. We had no home and just a little furniture. The last expenses took several hundred dollars and since I am expecting another child, I dare not use the balance of the money. I drew out $900 to buy a little cottage on the edge of town and obtained a job in a small café waiting on tables, but yesterday the café changed hands and I am out of a job."

A story opening is often useful in simplifying the explanation of a complex subject which prospects may have difficulty in comprehending. A young woman who represents the Penn Mutual Life Insurance Company in New York City and specializes in selling insurance to women used a story opening effectively in selling a Cuban woman who had come to New York City to live. Her knowledge of English was limited and the saleswoman could not understand much Spanish, so she told the following story to explain a retirement income policy:

You have a grandmother, her name is Penn Mutual. She lives in Philadelphia. She makes this arrangement with you. You send her $100 a month until you are fifty-five years old. When you are fifty-five years old, she will write you a letter reading as follows:

DEAR DOLORES:
    You need not send me any more money. From now on I am going to send you $200 a month as long as you live.

That is the way life insurance works.

The prospect understood clearly this story explanation and a sale resulted.

5. Reference Openings. In calling on a referred prospect, a salesman usually opens the interview by referring to the friend of the buyer. By naming the prospect's friend, a salesman secures recognition and prestige and puts the interview on a more personal and friendly basis.

A salesman of a well-known electric refrigerator uses the following reference opening: "Mrs. Prospect, your friend Mrs. Brown asked me to call and tell you about our new plan that gives you all the ice you need, for years to come, in one delivery."

An insurance salesman, who calls only on referred prospects, uses the following reference opening: "Mr. Prospect, a mutual friend of ours, Tom Dockum, has suggested that I ought to make your acquaintance. I would like to go into your insurance situation with you just as I did with Mr. Dockum without caring in the least whether or not you need my services." This introduction enables the salesman to average one sale from every four persons interviewed.

6. Gift Opening. Many salesmen obtain interviews with prospects by offering a gift, such as a memorandum book, mechanical pencil, or novelty. When delivering a gift, representatives of a large brush company use the following gift opening: "This is your utility brush, Mrs. Prospect, made for so many different uses. Isn't that a clean-looking brush? All our brushes are made on this sanitary principle."

The salesman of a well-known electric refrigerator presents a recipe book to prospects in opening interviews, as follows: "Mrs. Jones, may I present you with this useful recipe book as a reminder of the services we have to offer you? My name is Mr. Salesman. I am with the Blank Electric Company."

Another gift opening, employed by the salesman of the same company in distributing, gratis, savings banks to housewives, is: "No doubt you are busy this morning, but I would like to leave this bank with you and come back tonight and tell you about our new thrift plan whereby you can buy a refrigerator for only 10 cents a day." The salesman calls in the evening and attempts to sell a refrigerator.

7. Survey Opening. Salesmen of specialty products who use a "two-call system" of selling, devoting an initial interview to making a survey of the prospect's needs, employ a "survey opening." The same type of introduction also may be used in securing facts about a buyer's situation in opening a single-call sales presentation.

A "program opening" is used by many life insurance salesmen to procure information about the insurance needs of prospects. A successful insurance man uses the following program approach: "Mr. Prospect, I am not here to suggest the acquisition of additional life insurance. Such a suggestion would seem impracticable in view of the fact that I don't know much about your circumstances. I am here to offer a service, without obligation, which I would like to have you consider in the light of a diagnosis. I am here because I want to learn from you some of the things in which you are interested."

Salesmen representing a manufacturer of domestic water softeners use the following survey introduction in interviewing housewives: "Mrs. Prospect, I want to deliver to you 1,000 gallons of completely conditioned water, free. I simply connect a small tank temporarily to your water supply. There's absolutely no obligation, no inconvenience. When I take it out, everything is left just as before. I believe you'll enjoy this new special water, but mainly I want your frank opinion about it."

After the water softener has been on trial for five days, the salesman returns to the prospect's home, demonstrates the softener, and seeks a favorable buying decision.

A survey approach made by an electric refrigerator salesman selling to housewives is: "We are making a survey for the Blank Electric Company of the electrical appliances in this neighborhood. Would you mind answering just three questions? Do you have an electric refrigerator? If so, how old is it? What appliance do you intend buying next?"

8. Service Opening. In selling mechanical products that require occasional inspection and service salesmen frequently use service introductions. This method of approach secures the good will of users and enables a salesman to inspect the equipment in use and determine the need for replacement or accessories.

Retail salesmen of electrical and gas appliances who sell to housewives use a service introduction as follows: "Mrs. Prospect, do any of your electrical appliances need attention? If so, I will be glad to see what is required. May I look them over?"

A similar opening is: "Mrs. Prospect, I have come to inspect your radio. We are checking up on all Blank radio users to make sure that they are receiving the proper service. Is your radio working all right? May I look it over for a moment?"

Salesmen of office and industrial equipment who are trained to make small adjustments and repairs use a service opening to gain access to users of their equipment and through them discover needs for additional equipment or accessories.

9. Exhibit Opening. One of the easiest ways for a salesman to gain the attention of prospects in opening a sales interview is to use an exhibit. The object used to attract attention should relate to the needs of the prospect or show how his needs may be satisfied by the salesman's product.

Salesmen representing a famous pharmaceutical house open interviews with retail druggists by rolling a large pair of white plastic dice across the counter toward the buyer. The merchant picks up the dice, reads the name of the product and its profit-making possibilities, and the sales interview is under way.

In selling flat silverware, the wholesale representatives of a large manufacturer open interviews by placing before buyers a cross section of an automobile tire. The salesmen explain that the wear points on their product are reenforced with extra silver just as an automobile tire is reenforced with extra rubber on the tread to ensure long wear.

Salesmen of an electric refrigerator open sales interviews by showing prospects two small magnets. One magnet is moved along on the surface of a piece of paper by the second magnet held beneath the paper. Salesmen explain the purpose of the demonstration by saying, "These magnets are a part of one of the latest developments of our research engineers and are another example of how research keeps us years ahead. These magnets are used in the control that automatically starts and stops the refrigerator."

A salesman can use pieces of metal, glass, lead, and other product parts as exhibits in opening sales interviews to secure the attention of prospects. Miniature models, charts, advertising proofs, clippings, photographs, and letters also may be used effectively in opening interviews.

10. Resale Opening. Salesmen, representing manufacturers and wholesalers selling to retail merchants, use resale openings offering suggestions for the resale of merchandise to consumers. A resale opening may suggest window, counter, and floor displays; newspaper or handbill advertising; or sales-promotion ideas such as a one-cent sale, combination sale, or premium promotions to stimulate sales for dealers.

Salesmen representing a large manufacturer of cosmetics use the following resale opening with druggists: "You can increase your sales of sunburn lotion 15 per cent with this new counter display which we will give you free with the purchase of a half gross."

A representative of a well-known soap manufacturer used the following resale opening to get the attention of dealers in local newspaper advertising, "Do you know that this little 2-inch space showing the package and price of Beautee Soap sold more than 10 cases for the Somerville Market over in Wrightstown? A similar space in your next newspaper ad can do the same for you."

Merchants are always interested in profit-making suggestions, and a resale opening is an effective way to begin interviews with dealer customers.

After a salesman has secured attention with a forceful opening statement, his next problem is to arouse the buyer's interest by telling him how the product or service will satisfy his needs. However, to bring a prospect to a recognition of his needs, a salesman must understand a prospect's needs and be familiar with his situation. To obtain a knowledge of needs, salesmen qualify prospects either in advance or in the opening stages of a sales interview. Methods of qualifying prospects are described in detail in Chap. XII on Qualifying Prospects.

Failure to discover the needs of a prospect early in a presentation makes it impossible for a salesman to present his product or service intelligently. Without a knowledge of a buyer's needs, a salesman does not know what type, model, or size to recommend; what sales points to emphasize; or what features to demonstrate. A salesman who is not familiar with a prospect's situation is like a marksman shooting blindfolded at a target. To attempt a sale without a clear idea of a prospect's requirements confuses the buyer with meaningless generalities and handicaps the salesman in securing a favorable buying decision. The opening stages of an interview provide an excellent opportunity for a salesman to discover and discuss the needs of the buyer.

A prospect may not recognize his need for a product or service, and a salesman may be obliged to convince the buyer of his need early in an interview. If a prospect does not feel a need for a salesman's product or service, there is little to be gained in discussing product features.

ESTABLISHING THE NEED OF THE PROSPECT

Direct questioning is the quickest and one of the most effective ways for a salesman to discover if a prospect recognizes his needs. A direct question by a heating-equipment salesman establishes a prospect's need for heating comfort:

"Was your home comfortably heated last winter?" The buyer's response to this question indicates whether he recognizes his need for comfortable heat.

Other direct questions such as, "Do you own your home?" or "How many children in your family?" help a salesman establish the needs of buyers. A more tactful statement is: "If you have children in your home, you'll be interested in this feature."

Many prospects recognize their needs but do not know how to satisfy them. They look to the salesman for advice. Because many buyers do not know the type of product they need, it is useless to ask such questions as, "What model or size of refrigerator do you want to buy?" or "Do you prefer a four-ply or a six-ply tire?" A more effective question for determining the needs of a tire buyer would be, "Do you tour long distances or just drive around town?" A salesman's questions should be worded so as to aid the buyer in reaching decisions rather than to force him to make his own decisions.

If a salesman asks too many questions about a prospect's needs, the buyer may feel that he is being cross-examined and become irritated. After asking a buyer a question about his requirements and receiving an answer, a salesman should discuss the information received in relation to the buyer's needs before asking additional questions. By avoiding a long series of interrogations, and encouraging a prospect to volunteer information, a salesman does not use offensive "third-degree" methods in getting facts about buyer's needs.

By a helpful manner, a salesman quickly gets the cooperation of a prospect in securing an understanding of his requirements. An oil-burner salesman asks prospects such helpful questions as, "There are several types of oil burners for different kinds of heating systems. I can help you find which one you need if you'll tell me how many rooms there are in your home."

A successful life insurance salesman establishes the needs of his prospects. "Mr. Prospect, I find few business and professional men who have had the time to devote to the study of insurance options, trusteeships, and annuity provisions. I have built my business by rendering this detailed service. I want to render this service to you. In order to do that, I would like to ask you some personal questions." The salesman then asks the prospect a number of pertinent questions about his insurance situation.

A leading automobile-tire manufacturer advises retail tire salesmen to analyze each customer's driving needs in opening a sales interview by asking the following questions: (1) What is the make and model of your car? (2) What has been the service given by your present tires and tubes? (3) How many miles do you expect to drive your car? (4) Over what kinds of roads do you drive? (5) At what speeds do you drive? (6) How often do you take long trips? (7) Is extra protection needed for the family car against punctures and blowouts? (8) Are the utmost in comfort and safety desired?

Salesmen of an electric refrigerator ask prospects the following questions: (1) What is the size of your family? (2) How much entertaining is done? (3) Are there small children in the family? (4) Is the refrigerator intended for a house or an apartment? (5) How much ice is used now? (6) Does the family spend much time away from home?

A salesman should decide upon the questions to ask in analyzing needs of buyers for his product and use them in opening interviews.

OBSERVING NEEDS

If a salesman keeps his eyes open, he will observe many things about a prospect's situation which will obviate the necessity for asking questions to fix the buyer's need. When talking to a prospect in his factory, office, or home, where the product or service represented by the salesman will be used, a salesman can observe the kind and condition of the buyer's present equipment, the circumstances surrounding its use, and the need for new equipment.

Some salesmen determine needs by making a formal survey or inspection of a prospect's property and equipment. Salesmen of mechanical stokers usually inspect the heating plants of prospects, check up on the amount of radiation used, and observe the number of rooms, the space available for equipment, the number of persons in the family, and similar pertinent facts.

Some prospects have a definite idea of the type of product or service that they need. If a salesman will encourage a prospect to talk by asking a few questions, many buyers will describe their requirements. If a salesman listens attentively, he can often hear the buyer's specifications and is enabled to make an intelligent recommendation and effective sales representation.

DEALING WITH DIVERSIONS

In opening an interview, a salesman occasionally must contend with such diversions as the presence of a third party, inattention on the part of the prospect, or interference from telephone calls. These interruptions of a sales interview distract the attention of a prospect and obstruct the progress of a presentation. The undivided attention of the buyer must be secured if a salesman expects to secure an order.

When a salesman discovers that a prospect is engaged with a third party, the best strategy is to ask for an appointment for an interview at another time when the buyer can be seen alone. Or a salesman may offer to withdraw from the prospect's office and wait until the buyer is at liberty. A prospect may not be willing to talk freely about his needs in the presence of a third party and it is inadvisable for a salesman to attempt to carry on an interview under these circumstances. However, when two or more persons are jointly interested in buying, a salesman makes his presentation to the group as a matter of course.

Some prospects deliberately attempt to discourage a salesman by carrying on other work, signing letters, reading reports, and writing at the time a salesman is making his presentation. A salesman may deal with an inattentive prospect by offering to withdraw and return at another time when the buyer is not busy. Or he may offer to wait until the buyer has finished his work. A courteous request for the full attention of the prospect usually is sufficient to enable a salesman to overcome this difficulty.

When telephone calls or secretaries interrupt the opening of an interview, a salesman who waits patiently for the attention of the prospect is usually rewarded with the buyer's full attention in a few minutes. A salesman may be obliged to recapture the attention of a prospect and renew his interest in the subject under discussion by asking a question, introducing an exhibit, or summarizing the discussion up to the point that it was interrupted.

HOW TO OPEN A SALES INTERVIEW

To aid salesmen in planning openings to sales interviews, the methods used by qualified salesmen are described in detail in the following four-step routine which is based on the principles described in the preceding pages. If a salesman will memorize these simple steps, practice them, and use them in opening interviews, he will soon experience little difficulty in getting the favorable attention of prospects and launching interviews successfully.

Routine for Opening a Sales Interview

1. Make a favorable social contact.
2. Use an attention-getting opening.
3. Establish the prospect's need.
4. Deal with diversions.

1. Make a Favorable Social Contact. Good appearance, erect carriage, and confidence are important personal qualifications in opening a sales interview. Friendliness, a genuine desire to serve, and a direct, sincere manner combine to give a salesman a favorable start in interviewing new prospects.

A self-introduction conforming to the personality of the salesman and type of prospect approached is a standard greeting with successful salesmen. The name of the buyer is verified to avoid mistaken identity and embarrassment. Many salesmen do not initiate hand-shaking in greeting prospects although the practice varies in different sections of the country. Seek a chair by the side of the prospect to provide a natural, comfortable position for carrying on an interview. A salesman's coat, hat, and equipment are laid aside to avoid interference with his sales presentation.

To create a favorable impression on prospects, able salesmen plan their social preliminaries to interviews. A qualified salesman knows definitely what he expects to say to a prospect and exactly how he hopes to adjust his personality to suit the individuality of each buyer approached.

2. Use an Attention-getting Opening. After a salesman has opened an interview with a favorable social contact, his next task is to secure the attention of the prospect by means of an attention-getting opening in the form of a question, significant fact, curious statement, anecdote, reference to a friend of the prospect, a gift offer, service, or an exhibit. The type of opening used depends on the nature of the product or service sold, the type of buyer, and the personal preference of the salesman. Experimentation with several types of introductory statements will enable a salesman to discover which kind of opener will serve him most effectively. A salesman's introductory remarks must be sufficiently interesting not only to get momentary attention but to intensify that attention into continuous interest. Openings that are closely associated with the product or service presented and at the same time related directly to the personal interests of the prospect are usually the most effective.

3. Establish the Prospect's Need. Once a prospect's attention has been secured by a good opening, a salesman should next establish the buyer's need. The need may have already been recognized by the buyer. Or it may be a need which is not apparent to the prospect, and the first task of a salesman is to convince the buyer of his need. Whether the need is large or small, evident or unrecognized, it is necessary for a salesman to establish the need before a sale can be made.

If a prospect's need is not evident to him, a salesman may find it necessary to discuss all phases of the buyer's need until it becomes so apparent that the prospect recognizes it and is genuinely desirous of doing something about it. For example, many men are not aware of their need for accumulating funds for educating their children, providing for retirement in old age, or creating an estate for their families. Life insurance salesmen discuss these needs with prospects, point out their importance, and impress on prospects the urgency of meeting them by means of life insurance.

Until a prospect recognizes his need, a salesman can gain nothing by urging the purchase of his product or service. The need must be recognized and admitted by the prospect in the opening of a sales interview.

In determining the nature of a prospect's needs a salesman asks tactful questions, makes inspections, conducts surveys, and observes until he is thoroughly familiar with the circumstances and is in a position to advise the buyer intelligently in regard to the satisfaction of his needs.

4. Deal with Diversions. In opening sales interviews, salesmen are frequently confronted with interruptions by third parties, telephone calls, or inattention of buyers. These interferences should be anticipated and strategy planned to dispose of them. Otherwise, they may spoil a good sales presentation. A salesman should not attempt to proceed with his sales presentation in the face of competition for

SALES PRESENTATION RATING FORM

Opening a Sales Interview

Salesman _____   Date _____

Rated by _____   Over-all Rating _____

Score

I. *Salesman's Method of Opening Interview*	Excellent 90–100	Good 80–90	Fair 70–80	Poor 60–70	Failure Below 60
A. Personal impression					
B. Salutation					
C. Self-introduction					
D. Handshaking					
E. Seating					
F. Disposal of equipment					
G. Attention-getting opening					
H. Establish prospect's needs					
I. Dealing with diversions					

Miscellaneous Comments _____
_____

the attention of the customer. It is better to retire and try for another interview at a future time than to compete with diversions.

Various ways to deal with interruptions have been discussed previously, and salesmen who have made definite plans to dispose of these diversions can get interviews off to a good start.

Problem I

OPENING DEALER INTERVIEWS

The following introductions to sales interviews were used by salesmen calling on the buyer of a chain of grocery stores located in Portland, Me. In some cases the salesmen are acquainted with the buyer and are making return calls; in other cases the salesmen are making their initial contacts. Various kinds of grocery specialties are represented by the salesmen.

1. Opening of a sales interview by a salesman of cookies produced by a large wholesale bakery:

1. SALESMAN: How are you?
2. BUYER: Pretty good.
3. SALESMAN: My name is Jack Tolman of Sanitary Bakeries. How would you like to make 25 per cent profit on a new brand of Crispy Cookies?
4. BUYER: We're always interested in making money.
5. SALESMAN: You make more profit on our line than you make on any other brand of cookies.
6. BUYER: There's so much price cutting that no one makes a profit.
7. SALESMAN: We price maintain this brand so that you are guaranteed your profit. You get no price cutting on this cookie.
8. BUYER: That's fair enough.

2. Opening of interview by a salesman of a food packer selling chicken, fruits, and vegetables packed in tin and glass:

1. SALESMAN: Hello, Tom. Have you ever heard of orange slices in glass?
2. BUYER: No, it's new to me.
3. SALESMAN: Well, here are the finest California oranges packed in delicious wine sauce.
4. BUYER: How do they taste?
5. SALESMAN: Here, have a slice. They're delicious.
6. BUYER: Can you book us a demonstration?
7. SALESMAN: The last of next month, Tom. The week of the twenty-third is all right, isn't it?

3. Opening of interview by a salesman of bottled carbonated beverages;

1. SALESMAN: How are you? I'm the Snookie man.
2. BUYER: How is Snookie going these days?
3. SALESMAN: Good.
4. BUYER: Say you reminded me of something. We had a meeting of our store managers last night and talked about beverages, but we didn't talk about your drink because I forgot to put it down.
5. SALESMAN: Yeah?
6. BUYER: Black, one of our store managers, ordered one case of Snookie, but I couldn't get any interest from the other managers.
7. SALESMAN: Oh, you couldn't? That's not so hot, is it?

4. Opening of interview by a salesman representing a manufacturer of candy specialties:

1. SALESMAN: I'm representing the Case Candy Company. You wouldn't be interested in five-cent bars, would you? We've got some fancy numbers. Our line is very high grade; it isn't junk like a lot of those bars.
2. BUYER: We're not interested.
3. SALESMAN: This piece is five cents; this is 10; these are five; fruit centers are 10.
4. BUYER: What were you telling me about the last time you were here?
5. SALESMAN: Chocolate mints.
6. BUYER: We weren't talking about peanut bars, were we?
7. SALESMAN: Yes, I was wondering what you did about ordering some.

5. Opening of interview by a salesman of peanut butter packaged in glass:

1. SALESMAN: I'm Robinson of Tasty Foods. I'd like to give you one of our new automatic pencils to write an order with.
2. BUYER: About all I use a pencil for these days is to figure prices.
3. SALESMAN: We can now pack our Plantation brand under your own private label.
4. BUYER: Is that right?
5. SALESMAN: You get a longer profit and good turnover. Let me sell you a few cases, just as a start-in.

6. Opening of interview by a salesman of shoe preparations and polishes:

1. SALESMAN: I've a new shoe whitener, I'd like to show you.
2. BUYER: What kind is it?
3. SALESMAN: It comes in bottles, that's what it is.
4. BUYER: Is it liquid or cream polish?
5. SALESMAN: The liquid would be in the white bottle, but it's called "Cream Polish."

6. BUYER: Cream color?

7. SALESMAN: Well, it's called cream but it's white liquid.

8. BUYER: Have you ever sold us any other items in your line?

  7. Opening of a salesman of gelatin dessert and ice-cream mixture:

1. SALESMAN: Manton of Easy-Make Desserts. I'll only take a minute here. I wondered if it would be possible to get an order from you around the first of June or the last of May?

2. BUYER: I doubt it. I'm busy on the 'phone now.

3. SALESMAN: Sorry to bother you. I was wondering if we could sell you. We have quite a few new products out. There's our gelatin and ice-cream mix. You've heard about it?

4. BUYER: No, what's the story?

5. SALESMAN: Say, I've got about a dozen reactions from different people.

6. BUYER: I don't know anything about it except we had it in one year and it didn't sell and we cut it out last year.

Questions

1. Criticize, favorably or otherwise, each of the seven openings of the sales interviews on each of the following points:

  a. Attitude of the salesman.

  b. Attention-getting opener.

  c. Establishing the buyer's needs.

  d. Dealing with diversions.

2. Which of the seven openings is the most effective? Give specific reasons.

3. Write a new opening for Number 7.

Problem II

OPENING CONSUMER INTERVIEWS

The following introductions to sales interviews were used by consumer salesmen in greeting buyers at offices and homes in greater Boston. In only one case is the prospect acquainted with the salesman. Various types of products are being sold by specialty salesmen calling on buyers.

  1. Opening of interview by a salesman of heating equipment who is calling on a customer who has bought a hot-water heater:

1. SALESMAN: I'm Tom Drake of Dutton Appliance Company, where you bought your hot-water heater.

2. PROSPECT: How do you do?

3. SALESMAN: May I inspect your water heater?

4. PROSPECT: Sure.

5. SALESMAN (after inspecting heater): The heater seems to be in good shape.

6. PROSPECT: Yes, we get plenty of hot water.
7. SALESMAN: I noticed that your boiler has sprung a leak.
8. PROSPECT: Yes?
9. SALESMAN: I would like to have our engineer look over that boiler.
10. PROSPECT: O.K.

2. Opening of interview by an automobile salesman with a prospect and his wife in their home:

1. SALESMAN: How do you do, sir?   I'm Jack Lind of Cook Motors.   Mr. Spaulding at your office told me you were considering a new car.
2. MR. PROSPECT: Yes, we were thinking about it.
3. SALESMAN: Is there any special model you would like?
4. MRS. PROSPECT: We have not definitely decided upon any particular model as yet. If we look around maybe we can decide on one that is comfortable.
5. SALESMAN: I've driven out our new Blank six convertible coupé and would like you to see it.
6. MRS. PROSPECT (inspecting car in drive): This is a very good-looking car.
7. SALESMAN (walking over to car and opening door): Will you step inside and see how roomy and comfortable it is?

3. Opening of an interview by a salesman of radios with a young married couple at home:

1. SALESMAN: How do you do, sir? You received my letter about the new Tilson Radio?
2. PROSPECT: Yes, we've been considering something in the way of a console model radio.
3. SALESMAN: What type of program do you prefer?
4. PROSPECT: Oh, I don't know. We like classical music.
5. SALESMAN: Well, sir, here is a picture of the Tilson Console, favored by music lovers.
6. PROSPECT: What is the exclusive feature of this particular set?
7. SALESMAN: The melody tone arm is exclusive with the Tilson radio for the next two years because they own all the patent rights on it.
8. PROSPECT: How much is this radio?
9. SALESMAN: $159.

4. Opening of an interview by a salesman of automobile tires with a prospect in his office:

1. SALESMAN: Mr. Prospect, I'm Bill Tate of Thompson Tire Company. I noticed that your tires are showing fabric on the tread.
2. PROSPECT: Yes, soon I'll be in the market for a new set of tires.
3. SALESMAN: Do you drive much?
4. PROSPECT: About 30,000 miles a year.

5. SALESMAN (drawing out a miniature model of a tire): This is our J-73 model, the best tire we make. This tire is guaranteed for 25,000 miles against blowouts under any conditions.

5. Opening of an interview by a salesman of luggage with a prospect in his office:

1. SALESMAN: My name is Dickens of Putnam Luggage. I got your 'phone call and brought along my catalogue.
2. PROSPECT: I intend to take a long trip this summer so I thought that I would call about luggage. What do you suggest?
3. SALESMAN: Do you have a two-suiter bag? They are much better on a long trip than a grip.
4. PROSPECT: No, I don't have one. As a matter of fact, I have never owned one and hadn't thought about purchasing one.
5. SALESMAN: A two-suiter bag will hold much more clothing and accessories than a grip. If you are planning a trip, you will want a bag that will carry a lot of clothing. Here is a picture of our best two-suiter. This bag is constructed of top grain leather and finely finished. It will carry two suits, several shirts, and accessories. It is priced at $50.

6. Opening of an interview by a service station salesman with a motorist in the driveway of a station operated by a large oil company:

1. SALESMAN: Hello, Mr. Jones. Have you seen the new-type sun visors?
2. MOTORIST: No.
3. SALESMAN: They are a big help in driving in the late afternoon.
4. MOTORIST: Yes. You know I'm getting sick and tired of dodging the sun on my way home from work. I think the best thing to do is get a pair of sun glasses.
5. SALESMAN: Why don't you buy one of these sun visors?

Questions

1. Criticize, favorably or otherwise, each of the six openings of the sales interviews on each of the following points:
  a. Attitude of the salesman.
  b. Evident social preliminaries to the interview.
  c. Type of "opener" used.
  d. Establishing the buyer's needs.
  e. Dealing with diversions.
2. Which of the six openings is the most effective? Give specific reasons.
3. Reword openings for 1, 4, and 5.

Reading References

B. F. BAKER, "Effective Retail Selling," Chap. X, American Technical Society, Chicago, 1947.

E. CASEY and R. L. JOHNS, "Salesmanship for Colleges," Chap. XI, H. W. Rowe Company, Baltimore, 1938.

C. H. FERNALD, "Salesmanship," Chap. XI–XII, Prentice-Hall, Inc., New York, 1945.

J. GEORGE FREDERICK, "Modern Salesmanship," Chap. X, Garden City Publishing Company, Inc., New York, 1937.

HAROLD M. HAAS, "A Short Course in Salesmanship," Chap. VII, Prentice-Hall, Inc., New York, 1939.

J. M. HILL and R. G. WALTERS, "Success through Salesmanship," Unit XII, South-Western Publishing Company, Cincinnati, 1940.

PAUL W. IVEY, "Salesmanship Applied," Chap. XIX, McGraw-Hill Book Company, Inc., New York, 1937.

PAUL W. IVEY, "Successful Salesmanship," Chaps. XIX–XXI, Prentice-Hall, Inc., New York, 1947.

N. KNEELAND, L. BERNARD, and G. B. TALLMAN, "Selling to Today's Customer," pp. 128–136, Ginn & Company, Boston, 1942.

DAVID R. OSBORNE, "Salesmanship for Today for Salesmanagers of Tomorrow," Chap. VI, Harper & Brothers, New York, 1939.

CHARLES B. ROTH, "Finding the Prospect and Getting the Interview," pp. 91–151, Prentice-Hall, Inc., New York, 1946.

FREDERICK A. RUSSELL and F. H. BEACH, "Textbook of Salesmanship," Chap. IX, McGraw-Hill Book Company, Inc., New York, 1949.

CHAPTER XIX

CONDUCTING SALES DEMONSTRATIONS

THE IMPORTANCE OF DEMONSTRATIONS

Demonstrating is showing with proof and example how a product benefits the buyer. A demonstration gives a prospect an opportunity to experience for himself the benefits or profits to be derived from the ownership of a product. It directly affects a buyer's judgment or feelings through personal impressions, and prospects can best understand the merits of a product by personal use or observation. When a prospect is given an opportunity to hear the music of a great orchestra through a radio receiving set, or to feel the quick acceleration of a powerful motor car, desire for ownership is aroused to its highest intensity. A salesman who demonstrates his product satisfies the universal desire to taste, touch, smell, feel, and experience benefits rather than to hear about them.

A demonstration makes it possible to emphasize product features in new and interesting ways without boresome oral repetition. A demonstration also relieves the natural sales resistance of prospects by taking their minds off the business of buying and focusing them on the satisfactions that result from ownership of a product. When a prospect experiences the benefits of an article, he sells himself on its merits.

The confidence of a prospect may be secured more readily by a demonstration that proves by test and satisfies an instinctive desire for evidence supplied directly by the senses.

Furthermore, a demonstration secures the attention of prospects and prevents distractions and interruptions. When a hat salesman asks a prospect to try on a new hat, he secures the undivided attention of the buyer and at the same time demonstrates comfort and style.

Demonstrations make it possible for a salesman to practice sensory selling to impress the sales message on a buyer's taste, touch, sight, hearing, or sense of smell. By appealing to several senses a salesman forcefully impresses the prospect with the benefits of his product. A demonstration also appeals to the desire of prospects to excel and causes them to want to try their skill at operating the product or taking part in the demonstration, thereby selling themselves on its merits.

Intangible services, however, cannot be demonstrated and many heavy, bulky industrial products are difficult to demonstrate because of their size and weight. A salesman, however, can demonstrate the benefits of intangibles and bulky goods by means of diagrams, models, or miniature parts which are light and easily manipulated.

WHEN TO DEMONSTRATE

A demonstration should be given along with an oral sales presentation. After the buyer recognizes his need, a demonstration shows how the product satisfies the need. A prospect should not be rushed into a demonstration in the opening stages of a sales interview, nor is it desirable to reserve a demonstration as a climax to a sales presentation. A demonstration which is used as a last-resort method of convincing a prospect is rarely successful.

A demonstration should be introduced into a sales presentation naturally as the best method of showing that a product meets a prospect's needs. After a salesman has discovered a prospect's requirements, a demonstration should follow in the presentation as the next step in showing how a product will bring profit or satisfaction to the buyer.

A salesman should never stop his oral presentation and say, "Now I shall demonstrate this radio," as that separates and formalizes the demonstration so that it ceases to be a natural part of the sales presentation. Nothing is to be gained by making a prospect aware that he is experiencing a selling stratagem.

By asking a prospect, "Would you like to have me give you a demonstration?" a salesman invites a refusal. A prospect may claim that he does not have time or is already familiar with the operation of the product. Demonstration should be coincidental with description as a fundamental part of a sales presentation.

Under some circumstances, it is impracticable to demonstrate a product during an initial sales interview. An adding-machine salesman, for example, cannot conveniently carry his product into the office of a prospect on the first call and it may be necessary to arrange a second interview when a complete demonstration can be conducted. Certain features of bulky products, however, can usually be demonstrated in the home or office with miniature models, parts, and accessories.

HOW TO PREPARE FOR A SALES DEMONSTRATION

Successful demonstrations require careful preparation if they are to make a favorable impression on prospects. The product to be demonstrated or the demonstrating equipment to be used, including models, parts, or accessories, should be in good operating order; a logical, convincing sales talk should be written or outlined to accompany each step in the demonstration; and the place where the demonstration is to be staged should be selected and put in readiness. Sometimes an appointment with a prospect is necessary before a separate demonstration is given. If a salesman plans each of these elements, his demonstrations will yield maximum results.

Preparation of Demonstrating Equipment. Nothing is more fatal to the success of a demonstration than a breakdown in the operation of the product or the demonstrating equipment. By checking the operation of product or demonstrating devices in advance, a salesman ensures that they are in good working order. Periodic overhauling of a demonstrator by the service department will save a salesman not only embarrassment but lost orders.

The exterior appearance of product or demonstrating devices and carrying cases require frequent attention to ensure that they are polished, clean, and freshly painted, in order to make a favorable impression on prospects.

When demonstrating equipment is carried by a salesman, it should be packed so that parts are arranged in the order in which they are to be used so that they are readily accessible, avoiding delay and confusion.

A salesman should be so familiar with the operation of his product or demonstrating devices that he can carry out a demonstration efficiently and without hesitation. Awkwardness or fumbling in conducting a demonstration weakens a prospect's confidence in the knowledge of the salesman and sometimes in the merit of the product.

Preparation of Demonstrating Sales Talk. Each step in a demonstration requires oral explanation and every feature shown should be related by the salesman to the specific needs of the prospect. A brief oral presentation may be written or outlined by a salesman or prepared by his company to accompany each step in a demonstration. Such a presentation may be memorized for use in demonstrating. It is very essential, however, that a standard demonstrating talk be adapted to the individual needs of a prospect to avoid a lengthy, mechanized, factual recitation which may be of no interest to the buyer.

A typical demonstrating sales talk used by salesmen of a well-known make of automobile tire illustrates how a demonstration can be related to a prospect's needs in a friendly, informal conversation.

SALESMAN: Mr. Prospect, you told me that you want a tire that will wear. (Salesman rolls a miniature tire over surface of prospect's desk, pressing down jerkily to bend out the side walls.) When your car is riding along on ordinary roads, your tires act as shock absorbers. The side walls continually flex, stretching and compressing the cord at the shoulder as you see by this demonstration.

In balloon tire service nothing is more important than the ability of a tire body to stretch and come back millions of times, and that's why our tire has greater durability. Doesn't that seem reasonable?

The body of our tire is made of a specially designed and patented cord for greater flexibility. It stretches 61 per cent farther before it breaks. Don't you think this tire will wear?

Preparing a Place for Demonstrating. A showroom is usually the most satisfactory place to demonstrate heavy, bulky products. When a prospect is interviewed at the showroom, the demonstration may be conducted most conveniently with the complete equipment available, interruptions are avoided, and the salesman is working on familiar ground.

Some salesmen of installation equipment plan to interview prospects and demonstrate in the plants or homes of customers. Permission is first secured from cooperating owners to demonstrate their equipment. A salesman may also arrange with owners to be present at demonstrations so that a prospect can hear from a satisfied customer about the favorable features of the product.

Salesmen of automobiles and real estate carefully plan the routes over which prospects are driven on demonstrations. Automobile salesmen, representing a large motor-car company, lay out routes so that the various features of the car can be tested and demonstrated to prospects. Several demonstration routes are laid out near the salesroom and in different parts of a salesman's territory to include the following features:

1. A smooth street or highway to begin the ride quietly.
2. A heavily traveled street for showing flexibility, pickup, and easy handling.
3. A stretch of rough road for demonstrating comfort features.

4. A moderate downgrade where braking may be demonstrated.

5. One or more steep grades for demonstrating hill climbing.

6. A straight, well-paved road, with little traffic, for demonstrating speed.

Appointments for Demonstrations. When a separate demonstration is planned, an appointment must be arranged for a time and place convenient to the buyer. By making an appointment, a salesman ensures that he has adequate time to make a complete presentation.

Preparing the Prospect for a Demonstration. Before demonstrating a specific feature, successful salesmen prepare the mind of the prospect by creating anticipation for the evidence they plan to present.

A salesman may arouse the interest of a prospect in a forthcoming demonstration by displaying a piece of demonstrating equipment. Or, a salesman may stimulate a prospect's curiosity by remarking, "In a few minutes, I am going to show you, with this little device, how you can save 10 per cent on your annual purchases."

Automobile salesmen build up their demonstrations by preparing prospects for a drive in a new car with a planned preview, which includes the three following steps: (1) a walk around the car to view it from all sides and admire its beauty; (2) seating the prospect comfortably in the rear seat to show roominess; (3) inviting the prospect to sit behind the wheel. Another purpose of this preview is to make sure that all important features of the car are covered at a time when their merits are not overshadowed by the demonstration ride.

Salesmen of household brushes prepare prospects for demonstrations by spreading before them an attractive display cloth which bears the company trade-mark; upon this background the various sets of brushes are laid out.

A prospect may be mailed direct advertising in advance of a product demonstration. A large insulation manufacturer aroused the curiosity of building material dealers in a novel demonstration of a new product by sending them a folder announcing, "A new principle in insulation, different from any now employed in the building field. Our salesman will soon call and demonstrate this new principle in insulation to you."

Prospects may be prepared for a demonstration by an anecdote about the advantages of the product to be shown. A relevant question may be asked to arouse a prospect's curiosity in a demonstration, as, "Have you ever seen wool that will not burn?" asked by salesmen of rock-wool insulation.

WHAT FEATURES OF A PRODUCT TO DEMONSTRATE

Few buyers have the interest or patience to see a demonstration of all features of a product. It is a mistake to bore a prospect by a mechanical recitation of facts in which he is only remotely interested. The prospect has little opportunity to take part in the discussion, which soon degenerates into a monologue, with the prospect becoming a disinterested listener.

Successful salesmen select the one or two features of the product which are most likely to appeal to a prospect's needs and motives and concentrate on those. The attention and interest of the prospect are secured and the demonstration is much more effective.

Sales resistance is reduced when a demonstration is related to the needs of a buyer.

When a salesman establishes the needs of the prospect in the opening of the interview, he is able to focus the demonstration on those needs. Unless a salesman is familiar with the prospect's needs, a demonstration loses much of its effectiveness.

For example, an automobile salesman asks a prospect, "Do you drive much—make long trips?" The prospect replies, "Yes, I'm a salesman on the road most of the time and I've got to have a car that's comfortable." From the buyer's answer, the salesman knows that the need of this prospect is "comfort." So the salesman demonstrates comfort by asking the prospect to get in the front seat to experience the roominess, the depth of the cushion, and the adjustable seat. The salesman next drives over a route planned to show other comfort features such as ride control over a rough road, easy steering, and elimination of wheel fight.

The salesman, in this case, concentrated his demonstration on the one feature of comfort which was the principal need of the prospect. As the prospect was chiefly interested in comfort, the salesman wisely avoided a demonstration of many other features of the car and did not confuse the prospect by talking about its performance, safety, beauty, and other advantages.

However, during the course of the demonstration drive, the prospect remarked, "My expense allowance is only five cents a mile. How many miles can I get on a gallon of gas?" From this remark, the salesman immediately recognized that the prospect also needed economy of operation. The salesman replied, "I'm going to prove right now with this gasoline consumption tester how economical this car is to operate." Then the salesman swung into a demonstration and discussion of low gasoline consumption, concentrating his test and presentation on economy. He did not yield to the temptation to display his knowledge by telling the prospect all about the automobile.

After a salesman has demonstrated his product in relation to the principal needs of a prospect and the buyer is still unready to make a decision, other outstanding or exclusive features may be selected and demonstrated until the prospect is ready to buy.

GETTING A PROSPECT TO PARTICIPATE

It is important that a prospect experience and prove for himself the satisfactions resulting from ownership of a product. To experience product benefits a buyer must take part in a demonstration. Participation creates in a prospect's mind a sense of ownership.

When a prospect takes part in a demonstration, he gives his full attention to the product. He forgets his objections and becomes interested in what the product will do for him. He convinces himself by his own experience that it meets his needs and he visualizes it as serving him.

As he demonstrates, a salesman should ask the prospect to assist him in conducting the demonstration.

Salesmen of a fire extinguisher demonstrate the liquid used in the device by asking a prospect to hold a small aluminum cup into which some of the liquid is poured. The salesman next ignites a match which the prospect is asked to hold over the cup and observe how the vapor, rising from the liquid, extinguishes the flaming match.

Salesmen for a leading make of electric refrigerator ask prospects to participate in a demonstration of the cleanliness of the chromium shelves in the cabinet, as follows:

SALESMAN: Mrs. Prospect, the shelves in this cabinet are chromium. That means that they are fit to use as receivers for any food. Here is a clean cloth. Just rub the surface of that shelf with it. Will you rub it hard? Now examine the cloth. You see, the cloth shows no sign of stain.

An automobile salesman who discovers that a prospect is interested in comfort, drives him to a rough stretch of road and says, "Now, take the wheel and feel for yourself how comfortably this car rides over this rough road."

Salesmen of vacuum cleaners get a prospect to participate in a demonstration by moving the cleaner toward her, implying that they expect her to try it, and say, "I would like to have you run it yourself and see how easily it operates."

By placing the product within easy reach of a prospect so that he can easily turn the control knobs, switch on the current, or operate any feature with a minimum of inconvenience, prospect participation in a demonstration is encouraged.

GETTING A COMMITMENT FROM THE PROSPECT

After a salesman has demonstrated a product feature with the cooperation of the prospect, it is important that the salesman know whether or not the prospect has been favorably impressed by the demonstration. If a prospect understands and agrees with a demonstrated feature, the salesman knows that he is progressing satisfactorily toward a favorable buying decision.

If a buyer comments favorably about a feature that has been demonstrated, the salesman knows that he has convinced the buyer on that point. If the buyer is not convinced, the salesman must repeat the demonstration. The commitment of a prospect may be secured by asking such questions as, "Does that brake test prove this car is safe?" or "Isn't this stainless porcelain easy to keep clean?" or "Isn't this vacuum cleaner the lightest you have ever operated?" By asking these test questions, a salesman can find out whether or not a prospect is in agreement on the point which has been demonstrated.

Committing questions should be asked tactfully so as not to put a prospect on the defensive but to secure a sincere expression of his viewpoint.

Demonstrations involving technicalities may not be clearly understood by prospects with little mechanical sense. Rather than reveal technical ignorance, a prospect may commit himself favorably on a salesman's proposition. Accordingly, a salesman has to judge whether or not such an agreement is made with understanding. If a salesman believes that a buyer does not understand a technical demonstration, it may be necessary to repeat the important points in the demonstration several times to ensure that they are clearly understood and that the prospect is in agreement.

The interest of prospects in a demonstration may also be tested by encouraging them to ask questions about some technical feature. By pausing and saying nothing, a salesman encourages a prospect to talk and so reveal whether he has understood the demonstration clearly and is in agreement.

Some prospects who are convinced by a demonstration appear unresponsive. They cultivate natural sales resistance and refuse to encourage a salesman by agreeing with him on points demonstrated.

This type of buyer will usually reveal his real attitude if asked directly for an order.

Frequently prospects will voluntarily give commitments by remarking, "There's a lot of leg room in this front seat," or "That thermostatic control should save a lot of steps," or "There shouldn't be any service with that sealed-in mechanism." When a prospect indicates voluntarily that he is convinced, the salesman can select another need and continue the demonstration.

A prospect may show by his physical reactions or by nodding his head, by smiling broadly, by relaxing, or by an agreeable attitude, that he accepts a product demonstration. These physical manifestations of acceptance, if detected by an observant salesman, are among the surest evidences that a prospect has been convinced.

Frequently a prospect will refuse to agree with a salesman and give a negative answer to a committing question. A salesman seeks a commitment by asking, "Mr. Prospect, isn't that a money-saving feature?" The prospect objects, saying, "I don't know that it is." Or a prospect, who does not understand a demonstration, may make a negative response.

These negative replies do not mean that the sale has been lost. The salesman has merely failed for the moment to establish conviction on the particular point demonstrated. To go on and demonstrate other features and ignore the prospect's misunderstanding or lack of conviction is poor sales strategy for, as the prospect continues to think about his objection, it is magnified out of proportion to its real importance.

If a prospect is sincere in an objection or does not clearly understand a point demonstrated, a salesman should repeat every step of the demonstration slowly, speaking distinctly, avoiding technicalities, and mentioning the important points several times.

Prospects, who object to some feature of a demonstration but do not make their objection clear, should be asked, "Just what is your objection to that feature, Mr. Prospect?"

When a buyer states the reason why a demonstration fails to convince him, a salesman can repeat that portion of the demonstration which did not impress the prospect and again attempt to obtain agreement.

Successful salesmen always seek a definite agreement from a buyer that he is convinced of the merit of each product feature demonstrated. By securing a number of commitments from a prospect during the course of a demonstration, a salesman creates in the buyer's mind an attitude of acceptance which is helpful in securing a final decision to buy.

To record the favorable reactions of prospects during a demonstration, a salesman may use a check chart listing the various points demonstrated. The reaction of a buyer to each point may be checked on the chart as the demonstration proceeds. A large automobile manufacturer provided retail salesmen with a printed demonstration check chart upon which were recorded the commitments of a prospect. At the close of a sales demonstration, the buyer is confronted with this chart which shows his agreement to numerous product features. Faced with these admissions, it is not difficult to secure a decision to buy. A similar check sheet can be prepared by any salesman by listing product features on paper and checking off each feature as favorable commitments are secured.

USING DEMONSTRATING DEVICES

To aid salesmen in carrying on demonstrations, many manufacturers have created ingenious demonstrating devices for use in interviewing prospects in homes, offices, and retail showrooms. These devices are useful in dramatizing a presentation, explaining special product features, presenting exclusive features, and getting buyers to participate in a demonstration. They enable a salesman to clarify technical explanations with simple, familiar objects designed to illustrate applications and principles of operation. Variety is introduced into a demonstration and the attention and interest of a prospect are focused on results or uses of a product with the aid of these demonstrating aids.

Effective demonstrating devices to show the merits of almost any product can be made by a salesman from pieces of metal, hardware, wood, and glass. Salesmen of a mechanical stoker demonstrate its screw principle of conveying coal from bin to stoker by means of a ¾-inch auger bit.

Retail washing-machine salesmen use a piece of heavy rope, shoelaces, a glass eye dropper, and three bottle corks to demonstrate the superior operation of a well-known home washer. The three corks are used to show the water agitation in washing. The corks float on the surface of the water in competing washers but circulate all through the water in the demonstrated washing machine. A "listening rod" is used to enable a prospect to hear the grinding and groaning of her present machine and to compare it with the quiet operation of the washer being demonstrated.

In selling industrial goods, similar demonstrating devices are used. Salesmen representing a shellac manufacturer demonstrate the quality of their product with three small hourglasses. Each glass contains a different cut of shellac: one, heavy body; one, medium body; and one, light body. The salesman asks the buyer whether he can tell which is which. Neither the buyer nor an expert can identify the quality by sight alone. Then the salesman turns the three hourglasses upside down and asks the prospect to watch the shellac fall into the lower half of each. The difference in body of the shellac is clearly evident as the glasses fill. The glass which fills first contains shellac with the lightest body; the glass filled last contains the best product. This demonstration shows a buyer that it pays to buy from a shellac manufacturer of good standing whose product can be depended upon.

A waterproof asphalt roof coating is demonstrated dramatically by covering a handkerchief with the product. The handkerchief is next filled with water to show that a roof coating which can make a porous handkerchief waterproof can repair a leaky roof.

TRIAL SELLING DEMONSTRATIONS

A form of sales demonstration is trial selling. A product is installed in a prospect's home, office, or factory for several days' free trial. Properly controlled, trials are successfully used by many appliance salesmen in closing sales. If the credit of the buyer is satisfactory and the product is not allowed to remain in the prospect's possession longer than the time actually needed to prove the advantages claimed by the salesman, trial selling is very effective.

Definite time limits usually are established for trial demonstrations, the length of time depending upon the nature of the product. In selling home appliances the following time limits have been found practical: water softener, five days including washday; refrigerators, 15 to 30 meals; washing machines, one washing; cleaners, overnight to three days; and radios, 24 hours. The experience of those who use this method in selling shows that a majority of sales are closed within three days after the product has been installed on trial.

Many industrial products which can be easily installed may also be sold on trial. A trial removes a buyer's hesitation by convincing him that the product can meet his requirements. A prospect is more easily persuaded to try a product than to purchase because he does not obligate himself to buy until he has found the article satisfactory.

HOW TO CONDUCT A DEMONSTRATION

The methods used by successful salesmen in conducting a demonstration are similar. The basic principles of good demonstrating are summarized in the following five-point demonstrating routine. If a salesman will study these fundamentals, several of which are explained in the preceding pages, memorize, and rehearse them, then practice their use in interviews with prospects, his demonstrations will yield better results in sales and earnings. Demonstrating by these five simple rules is a simple and natural procedure for even the most inexperienced salesman.

Routine for Conducting a Sales Demonstration

1. Prepare for demonstration.
2. Concentrate demonstration on prospect's needs.
3. Get prospect to participate.
4. Commit prospect on each point demonstrated.
5. Watch for opportunities to close the sale.

1. Prepare for Demonstration. To ensure the success of a demonstration, thorough preparation of the time, place, equipment, and accompanying oral presentation is essential. If the product is portable, a demonstration can be conveniently introduced at the appropriate time in every sales presentation. When the product is heavy and bulky, demonstrations must be arranged in advance at a showroom, testing ground, or in the plant, office, or home of a cooperative customer. The place selected should afford opportunity to show the operation of the product under actual working conditions. An appointment must be arranged for the showing.

The product itself may be used for demonstrating purposes or a miniature model or demonstrating device can be employed. Demonstrating equipment should be examined in advance of sales interviews to ensure that it is in good working order. The salesman should be prepared to operate the equipment skillfully by practice in handling each part.

An oral presentation to accompany the demonstration of each product feature should be prepared in advance and practiced until it can be delivered naturally.

The prospect may be prepared for the demonstration by being given a "preview" of the features which will be shown. The buyer's curiosity and interest should be aroused in the advantages which will be demonstrated. Advertising to pave the way for a demonstration may be sent to a prospect.

2. Concentrate Demonstration on Prospect's Needs. By qualifying a prospect in the opening stages of a sales interview, by asking questions, by listening to volunteered remarks, and by observing, a salesman can quickly determine the buyer's specific needs, then demonstrate the particular product features that satisfy the needs of the buyer.

Demonstrating all the features of a product, regardless of a prospect's needs and special interests, has been compared to target-shooting with a shotgun. Although some of the shot may hit the target, a majority will go wild. By singling out a buyer's needs and demonstrating features that satisfy those requirements, a salesman has a better chance of hitting the bull's-eye of a prospect's interests.

A demonstration that attempts to prove the merits of every feature of a product often bores a prospect and commands only shallow attention. Few buyers are interested in listening to a recitation of features of no significance to their needs. The demonstration which covers all product features is usually an impersonal monologue which becomes a mechanized and unnatural presentation.

Concentrate the demonstration on the specific needs of the prospect, covering one need at one time, until his requirements have all been covered and the buyer has been shown how the product solves his "problem."

3. Get Prospect to Participate. One of the easiest ways to secure a prospect's interest in a demonstration is to invite him to participate. His hands and mind are put to work; his curiosity is satisfied; he experiences the benefits of ownership; and his instinctive desire to exercise his skill is gratified. All these advantages, in addition to the fact that he learns quickest and easiest by his own personal experience, make it desirable to get him to participate in a demonstration.

If a buyer is asked to turn a control knob, switch on the current, operate a part, open a door, listen to the operating noise, feel a surface, or smell a liquid, he satisfies his craving for evidence supplied directly by his senses. Any doubt which may have been in his mind as to the truth of the salesman's statements is removed by his own experience.

A more natural interview results when the buyer is drawn into the sales discussion. He is encouraged to express his views, thereby giving a salesman an opportunity to meet objections and more clearly understand his requirements. A mechanized presentation is avoided.

Prospects usually are eager to take part in a demonstration. A salesman can invite them to participate by saying, "Just see for yourself how easily this door opens," or "I'd like to have you try this, if you will," or "You simply pull this handle down—try it yourself, won't you?" When a buyer accepts these invitations, he takes another step toward signing an order.

4. Commit Prospect on Each Point Demonstrated. To determine whether or not a demonstration is convincing, seek commitments on each feature demonstrated. If a demonstration has not been clearly understood or has failed to convince, there is little to be gained by continuing the demonstration. When a prospect does not understand or agree, redemonstrate the feature in question more clearly and completely and again attempt to obtain the prospect's favorable reactions. On the other hand, if a buyer admits that he has been convinced by a demonstration, swing back into the presentation of other needs, demonstrate other features, and close the sale.

A salesman, like a good physician, periodically takes the temperature of a prospect to see whether or not he is responding to treatment. If a demonstration fails to convince, the salesman should know it immediately. If a buyer has not been convinced on a demonstrated feature, his attention will waver, his interest die, and the salesman may eventually lose the sale.

By securing a prospect's commitment on each product feature, a salesman, in effect, wraps up the sales points and puts them on a pile of favorable decisions which he is accumulating to win the final consent of the prospect. Some salesmen call this process "buttoning up" each point in the demonstration. A salesman should leave no unburned bridges behind him on his march to the order.

If a salesman makes sure that a prospect understands and agrees with him on each point, all obstructions are removed in the way of closing a sale. Such questions as, "Doesn't that refrigerant seem absolutely safe?" or "Can't you see the convenience of this feature?" easily and quickly enable a salesman to secure commitments from prospects.

5. Watch for Opportunities to Close the Sale. When a prospect has been favorably impressed with a demonstration, he is often ready to buy. A salesman can determine a prospect's willingness to purchase by seeking minor decisions with such questions as, "Now that you feel this feature will save you money, would you prefer to pay cash or take advantage of our easy payment plan?" or "It's so easy to keep clean. Would you prefer the enamel or Dulux finish?" or "Since you've agreed that this machine is so easy to operate, shall I send our serviceman the first of the week to make the installation?" A prospect's responses to these questions will indicate his willingness to buy. If he says, "Hold on now, I'm not ready to buy yet," the salesman merely continues to demonstrate other features which satisfy the prospect's needs and again seeks a commitment. Several features may have to be demonstrated before a buyer is convinced that the product

SALES PRESENTATION RATING FORM

Conducting a Sales Demonstration

Salesman _____ Date _____

Rated by _____ Over-all Rating _____

Score

I. *Saleman's Conduct of Demonstration*	Excellent 90–100	Good 80–90	Fair 70–80	Poor 60–70	Failure Below 60
A. Condition of demonstrating equipment					
B. Preparation for demonstration					
C. Arousing anticipation of prospect					
D. Concentrating on prospect's needs					
E. Getting prospect to participate					
F. Getting commitments from prospect					
G. Attempt to close					
H. Use of demonstrating devices					
I. Use of nontechnical terms					

Miscellaneous Comments _____

_____

fills his needs. A salesman loses nothing by making a "tryout" close after each feature has been demonstrated; frequently a decision is reached by this method.

Problem I

Sales Demonstration

J. P. Tuckerman, representing Butler Electric Company

The Butler Electric Company operates a large retail electric specialty store in a wealthy residential suburb of Philadelphia. The company carries a complete line of electric lighting fixtures and appliances, including electric refrigerators, radios, electric ranges, washing machines, ironers, and small appliances, including toasters, waffle irons, hair curlers, driers, etc. The appliances sold by the company are nationally advertised and made by well-known manufacturers.

In addition, the company operates an electrical contracting department employing three full-time electricians engaged in house wiring, electric repairs, installation of fixtures, and servicing of oil burners, refrigerators, etc.

J. P. Tuckerman is one of two salesmen who divide their time between selling in the showroom and soliciting prospects for appliances in the suburb in which the store is located. Upon the invitation of salesman Tuckerman, a prospective customer for an electric sun lamp called at the showroom. The following conversation ensued:

1. Prospect: Good morning, Mr. Tuckerman.
2. Salesman: Good morning, Mr. Prospect, I'm glad to see you.
3. Prospect: I have been thinking about that sun lamp you were talking to me about. How do they run in price?
4. Salesman: The good ones are $39.50. Others are as low as $19.50. This one is $39.50 (pointing to a sun lamp on display).
5. Prospect: What do you mean by good ones?
6. Salesman: The ones that have a good ultraviolet lamp and a good transformer to supply the right voltage.
7. Prospect: You mean that the poor ones do a person no good?
8. Salesman: Yes, you might just as well sit up against a radiator, as all they give off is heat.
9. Prospect: What good does this one do?
10. Salesman: The rays are beneficial in deep-seated localized infections, sluggish healing wounds, sinuses, ulcers, burns, and almost all skin infections.
11. Prospect: Are they beneficial for children?
12. Salesman: It has been proved that they cure impetigo in babies.

13. PROSPECT: This $39.50 lamp is pretty expensive, don't you think?

14. SALESMAN: You might think so, but when you consider that each lamp must have its own transformer and the bulb is made of a special glass which transmits ultraviolet radiations and the base and shade are especially designed for the purpose, they are reasonable in price.

15. PROSPECT: Will it give you a good sun tan?

16. SALESMAN: This sun lamp emits ultraviolet radiation which is effective in producing erythema or reddening of the skin in seven minutes at a distance of 30 inches.

17. PROSPECT: Do the lamps burn out easily?

18. SALESMAN: This lamp has an average laboratory-rated life of 400 hours.

19. PROSPECT: How does this ultraviolet lamp work, exactly?

20. SALESMAN: This is really a small arc lamp and the arc discharge takes place within a small tube of quartz. The quartz tube transmits the ultraviolet radiation. The outer bulb is merely a protective container.

21. PROSPECT: Could I use this lamp on A.C. current?

22. SALESMAN: Yes, it operates on A.C.

23. PROSPECT: I've heard reports that these are dangerous and that they are liable to break.

24. SALESMAN: I don't think so.

25. PROSPECT: I've also heard that you can get a severe burn with them.

26. SALESMAN: That's true. You've got to be pretty careful because they are pretty powerful. Now to give you a good tan, you should not sit under it over seven minutes. Here, turn on this switch and try it. Notice how your skin is reddening. Isn't that good?

27. PROSPECT: That's good.

28. SALESMAN: O.K. When do you want it delivered?

29. PROSPECT: Oh, send it up tomorrow.

30. SALESMAN: Thank you.

Questions

1. Criticize favorably or otherwise the salesman's demonstration of the sun lamp on each of the following points:

  a. Preparation for the demonstration.

  b. Concentration on the prospect's needs.

  c. Prospect participation.

  d. Commitment of prospect.

  e. Taking opportunities to close.

Indicate how each of these steps might have been taken more effectively by the salesman.

2. When should the demonstration have been started by the salesman? How should it have been introduced?

3. In what ways could the salesman have prepared himself for a better demonstration?

4. How could the prospect have been prepared for a demonstration?

5. What features of the product should the salesman have demonstrated?

6. In what other ways could the prospect have been made a party to the demonstration?

7. What demonstrating devices might have been used by the salesman?

Problem II

FIELD SALES DEMONSTRATION

M. F. Langdon, representing the Millbury Motors Company

The Millbury Motors Company, established in Cleveland, Ohio, in 1928, are retail dealers of the Progress, a popular make of six- and eight-cylinder motor car. The company sells 300 cars annually in Cleveland and suburbs, in sedan, coach, coupé, and convertible models. The automobiles range in price from $1,900 to $3,000 plus freight from the factory. The company maintains an attractive showroom on one of the main traffic arteries of the city and advertises extensively in the local papers and over the radio.

A separate used-car department is maintained for the display, servicing, and sale of used cars taken in on sales of new models, and a separate sales force specializes in the sale of used cars.

M. F. Langdon has been connected with the Millbury Company for five years as one of its new-car salesmen. He is assigned to showroom duty several days a month. Salesman Langdon by appointment is calling on a family in the Shaker Heights section of Cleveland. The following interview ensues:

1. SALESMAN: How do you do? I'm Mark Langdon of Millbury Motors. I would like you to see the Progress convertible coupe I have outside.

2. FATHER: We'll have a look at it.

3. SALESMAN (following prospects to car and opening front door): Won't you step in?

4. MOTHER: Oh, son, this isn't the kind you want. I don't like to ride in the open, do you?

5. YOUNG MAN: Why, yes, mother, that's the best part of it. If you don't like to sit out in the open, you can put the top up.

6. SALESMAN: That's right. You see we have discontinued this model in our old line, and put it into the Progress line, because we have found that many people like convertibles very much. You see the convenience of this automatic top is remarkable. It is very easy for a lady to let it down. Just push this button. That's easy, isn't it?

7. MOTHER: Yes, but it doesn't seem to me that back seat would be very comfortable. It is so small.

8. SALESMAN: That's very true. It is smaller than the usual run of back seats, but it is used mostly for a short drive. You must remember that this car combines many of the advantages of a convertible coupé and a sedan. Besides having all the occupants under one roof, it has the advantage of a quickly collapsible top. Won't you two sit in the back seat to try it out?

9. MOTHER: Yes, you go in, son. If your long legs fit in there, I guess almost anyone would be comfortable.

10. YOUNG MAN (sits in back seat): This seat is very comfortable.

11. SALESMAN: Many favorable comments have come to us on this new model.

12. MOTHER: One really can't see much on the side of the road. This canvas top obstructs the view.

13. SALESMAN: Our designers have tried to provide as much comfort and enjoyment in this model as possible. They have tried to make vision as perfect as they can by providing a large windshield in the front. Although some people look out the side occasionally, the greater percentage use the windshield because it is more restful. I know you (salesman addresses young man) and your mother are most interested in obtaining an automobile which is distinctive. Do you travel much?

14. FATHER: Why, yes, in the summer we go up to Canada quite often.

15. SALESMAN: You will have ample space in the big luggage compartment in the rear to carry all your extra luggage without messing up the front of your car.

16. YOUNG MAN: How much does this car sell for just the way it is now?

17. SALESMAN: Our new convertibles deliver for $2,200. If you want white side-wall tires, it will cost $15 more. Would you want white side-wall tires on your car?

18. YOUNG MAN: Well, I don't know, I have them on my present car. They are very hard to keep clean.

19. SALESMAN: I would like to show you how comfortably this car rides.

20. YOUNG MAN: I should like very much to have a ride.

21. SALESMAN (to mother and father): You might like to sit in back and determine the riding qualities in our new automobile. I'll drive out the boulevard.

22. SALESMAN: Notice how comfortable the back seat is on this rough stretch.

23. FATHER: How does this car compare with a Blank convertible as far as wheel base and horsepower are concerned?

24. SALESMAN: This car is made 4 inches longer to secure greater riding comfort and it has eight additional horsepower to give it more pickup.

25. MOTHER: Two of our friends have just purchased Progress cars and they like them so much they won't even drive their big cars now. One has a Blank and the other a Super, and they leave them in the garage.

26. SALESMAN: Yes, many of our old customers have discovered that this new model fits their demands for comfort, beauty, dependability, and economy better than their large cars. (Addressing young man.) I'd like you to take the wheel. Turn up here to the right and test the power on this incline. You will notice that this automobile takes this hill smoother than most cars of its size.

Slow down here now. This cop is standing at the beginning of a speed trap.

27. FATHER: You mean to say that they have one here on a main street?

28. SALESMAN: Yes, there have been several severe accidents right near this school. These two policemen clock the motorists as they pass.

29. FATHER: Progress cars all have automatic gearshift, don't they?

30. SALESMAN: Yes, they do. They're a big convenience.

(Young man drives car back to his house. All get out and walk into house.)

31. YOUNG MAN: What colors does this car come in? I don't like that red. It's too bright.

32. SALESMAN: Just a minute, sir, I'll show you our color book. (Salesman shows color book.) Won't you all come over here to the light so that you really can appreciate the tone quality?

33. YOUNG MAN: I wonder if you'll give me an estimate on my car which is out in the garage?

34. SALESMAN: Why, yes, I'd be glad to. Do you have your registration with you?

35. YOUNG MAN: Yes, it is on the steering column of the car.

36. SALESMAN: Will you pardon me for a moment while I check up on it? (Salesman takes young man's keys, goes out to appraise car, and returns.) You really have a very nice automobile there.

37. YOUNG MAN: I have always kept it in good repair.

38. SALESMAN: The blue book quotes your car for $810. We will allow you $850.

39. YOUNG MAN: Mother, what do you think about the color? I like light green.

40. MOTHER: Yes, green is very nice, but I don't like a black top with light colors, do you?

41. YOUNG MAN: Yes, I think it really makes a good contrast.

42. FATHER (to salesman): How soon could we get delivery on this car?

43. SALESMAN: I can give you immediate delivery. Would you want to pay cash or use your credit?

44. FATHER: Credit, I believe.

45. SALESMAN: Then I'll ask you a few questions about credit and fix up the details.

46. FATHER: That's all right.

Questions

1. Criticize favorably or otherwise the salesman's demonstration of the automobile on each of the following points:

a. Preparation for the demonstration.

b. Concentration on prospect's needs.

c. Prospect participation.

d. Commitment of prospect.

e. Taking opportunities to close.

Indicate how each of these steps might have been taken more effectively.

2. Was the demonstration started at the proper time by the salesman?

3. In what ways could the salesman have made better preparation for the demonstration?

4. Could the prospects have been prepared more effectively for the demonstration?

5. What other features of the product should the salesman have demonstrated?

6. In what other ways could the prospect have been made a party to the demonstration?.

7. What demonstrating devices might have been used by the salesman?

Reading References

R. C. BORDEN, "How to Make a Sales Point Hit," Prentice-Hall, Inc., New York, 1938.

J. R. DAUBMAN, "Salesmanship and Types of Selling," Chap. XI, F. S. Crofts & Co., New York, 1939.

C. H. FERNALD, "Salesmanship," pp. 276–277, Prentice-Hall, Inc., New York, 1945.

J. GEORGE FREDERICK, "Modern Salesmanship," Chap. XV, Garden City Publishing Company, Inc., New York, 1937.

J. M. HILL and R. G. WALTERS, "Success through Salesmanship," Unit XIV, South-Western Publishing Company, Cincinnati, 1940.

PAUL W. IVEY, "Successful Salesmanship," pp. 361–373, Prentice-Hall, Inc., New York, 1947.

DAVID R. OSBORNE, "Salesmanship for Today for Salesmanagers of Tomorrow," pp. 101–110, Harper & Brothers, New York, 1939.

F. A. RUSSELL and F. H. BEACH, "Textbook of Salesmanship," Chaps. X, XI, XII, McGraw-Hill Book Company, Inc., New York, 1949.

HARRY SIMMONS, "How to Get the Order," Chap. II, Harper & Brothers, New York, 1937.

HARRY SIMMONS, "A Practical Course in Successful Selling," Chap. XVIII, Harper & Brothers, New York, 1939.

ELMER WHEELER, "Tested Direct Selling," Chap. XII, Prentice-Hall, Inc., New York, 1942.

CHAPTER XX

ANSWERING OBJECTIONS

WHY PROSPECTS OBJECT

In every sales interview prospects raise objections which are one of the major problems confronting a salesman. Actually a salesman does not begin to sell until a prospect has raised an objection. If no objections are raised by a buyer, the salesman is merely an order taker. It has been aptly said, "All there is to salesmanship is disposing of objections to buying."

If a salesman understands the various reasons why prospects raise objections, he can deal with them more effectively. Prospects often raise objections because of their natural aversion to new and unfamiliar ideas and things. When the first railroads were built, reactionary citizens tore up the tracks; riots accompanied the introduction of the cotton gin. Such instinctive aversion to change causes many buyers to instinctively oppose the purchase of new products or services. A housewife who has always cooked with gas naturally objects to adopting an unfamiliar method of cooking by buying an electric range.

Many prospects object to a salesman's product or service because they do not appreciate the benefits which it will bring to them. Until a salesman has convinced a prospect that a product is worth more than the money involved in the transaction, the buyer is going to raise objections. If a salesman ignores the satisfactions which come from using a product and discusses construction features or ingredients, a prospect who is interested in results is likely to object to hearing about things in which he has no interest.

Prospects often object because they do not clearly understand a salesman's presentation. Rather than reveal their ignorance or lack of understanding by asking, "Please say that again, I don't understand you," they may take refuge behind the commonplace excuse, "Not interested." Prospects with little technical training who do not clearly understand mechanical features often raise objections when salesmen of technical products or complex services fail to make themselves clear. Simple, nontechnical sales presentations forestall objections of this character.

To test a salesman or his proposition, a prospect may raise an objection. Rather than reveal his interest, he may raise an objection to induce the salesman to present additional advantages.

Prospects sometimes raise objections so that they can compare the advantages of one product with those of other products with which they are familiar. Rather than ask a salesman, "How does the cost of operating your compressor compare with the operating cost of the X compressor?" a prospect may make an adverse comment, as, "Your compressor costs too much to operate." The buyer expects that he will receive information to enable him to answer the question of operating cost.

A prospect may have no valid objection to a salesman or his product, but poor health or a recent unpleasant experience may prejudice a buyer's consideration of a salesman's proposition.

If a person is not a qualified prospect because of lack of finances, need, or authority to buy, he may be sincere in his objections. By qualifying a prospect, a salesman will be able to recognize the buyer's excuses regarding his need and ability to buy.

Prospects who have been solicited by unscrupulous salesmen and subjected to trickery or annoyance are often prejudiced against all salesmen and instinctively object to any sales proposition. If a buyer is on the defensive, a salesman must use tact and sincerity to reduce or remove this opposition.

SALESMAN'S ATTITUDE TOWARD OBJECTIONS

Many salesmen are discouraged by the objections of prospects and fear that they have missed an opportunity to close a sale. When confronted with an objection, they retreat in confusion and lose the confidence of the prospect. Some salesmen discouraged by an objection become indifferent. Other salesmen consider that an objection is a challenge to combat and that a prospect who objects is an antagonist to be defeated by clever repartee or high-pressure tactics.

Successful salesmen, however, welcome objections as opportunities to discover the needs and requirements of a buyer, to clarify sales points, to review advantages, to offer more information, to meet competition, and to determine the interest of the prospect.

The objections most difficult to deal with are not those that are spoken, but the unexpressed criticisms hidden in the prospect's mind. If a buyer can be persuaded to reveal his objections, a salesman can deal with them intelligently and effectively. Experienced salesmen, accordingly, encourage prospects to state their objections freely. One of the most difficult prospects to sell is the person who raises no objections to a sales proposition.

The majority of prospects who raise objections are actually seeking more information about a salesman's product or service. A prospect who raises objections is usually interested and is trying to justify his interest in buying. The buyer may not be clear on some points made by the salesman and he may merely want more facts.

If a prospect does not have an opportunity to voice his objections, a salesman is working in the dark. A salesman who does not get a reaction from a buyer cannot aid him in satisfying his needs and assist in solving his problems. A sincere objection gives a salesman a chance to secure a better understanding of the buyer's needs.

Objections offer an opportunity to a salesman to create more value for his product in the mind of a buyer. They are an invitation to explain more clearly and describe more fully the advantages and profits of ownership. Objections may also be indicators of poor selling tactics and show the necessity for more constructive salesmanship. If a salesman sells effectively, he never worries about objections because they rarely occur.

ANTICIPATING OBJECTIONS

Successful salesmen do not wait for prospects to raise objections. They anticipate possible resistance by taking the offensive and presenting counterarguments before a prospect has an opportunity to object. Before a prospect can object to the noise of an oil burner, a good heating salesman says, "This oil burner has been certified by the Blank laboratories as the quietest oil burner on the market." In this way, the salesman forestalls a prospect's objection by presenting the features of the product before the prospect has an opportunity to object to them.

By taking the offensive against objections, a salesman often avoids the necessity of defending his product or service against the adverse comments of prospects. By forestalling objections, he beats his opponent to the draw and dominates a sales interview; he gains confidence and courage by using offensive strategy.

Once a prospect has advanced an objection, his self-respect demands that he defend his criticism against the arguments of a salesman. After a prospect has raised an objection, a salesman has much greater difficulty in overcoming it, as the buyer has "gone on record" against the product. Accordingly, difficulties which are anticipated by a sales-man and satisfactorily disposed of before a buyer has had an oppor-tunity to express them rarely become serious obstacles.

In selling a specific product or service, certain common objections may be expected. Salesmen of high-priced articles often hear the criticism, "It's too expensive"; on the other hand, salesmen of low-priced articles must answer the objection, "It's poor quality." Prospects for life insurance often say to salesmen, "I have enough life insurance now," and buyers of automobiles raise the objection, "I'd like to look around and get a better trade-in offer." An experienced salesman knows the principal objections he may expect to hear from prospects.

A salesman can prepare to forestall objections of prospects by making a list of the criticisms or objections which he encounters most frequently in sales interviews. These may be classified as product, competitive, price, quality, service, and company obstacles.

When the most common objections have been listed, the best an-swers to these criticisms next should be gathered and put in writing. A common objection, encountered by an electric refrigerator salesman, may be, "The design is too extreme—too modernistic to suit me." This difficulty may be anticipated by discussing the following advan-tages, before the buyer has had an opportunity to raise the objection:

This refrigerator is the most beautiful you have ever seen. The lines of the cabinet, the finish, the fittings, even the name plate, are just right. This is a one-piece cabinet, without joints, cracks, or seams, which adds to its ap-pearance. The chromium door opener adds to the beauty of the exterior. Notice this freezer door, with its blue and gold insignia and its white and polished-metal color scheme. And notice how this color combination is con-tinued in the hydrator, the whole interior harmonizing with the blue and white of the door and door casing. Both the exterior and interior of this cabinet are the work of one of the nation's most famous designers and color experts, and I am sure you will agree with me that he has certainly done a beautiful job.

Similarly, other arguments can be prepared to anticipate possible objections to any product or service. By including sound answers to objections in a sales presentation as strong reasons for buying, a sales-man can forestall many difficulties.

QUALIFYING OBSTACLES

To meet effectively the criticisms and objections that arise in every interview, a salesman should first qualify them. By qualifying an obstacle, a salesman determines whether or not the objection is genuine and sincere. Many obstacles raised by prospects are merely excuses or pretexts which have no foundation in fact. Until a salesman discovers a prospect's real purpose for voicing an objection, he cannot deal with it effectively. Obstacles to a sale fall into two clearly defined classes: excuses and genuine objections.

Excuses

An excuse is commonly used by prospects for hiding their real reasons for not buying. Excuses are a smoke screen behind which a buyer takes refuge to evade the decision of purchasing. Like a chameleon, which changes the color of its skin according to the surroundings, prospects make excuses to disguise their sincere objections.

Buyers make excuses for numerous reasons. Rather than admit that he cannot afford to buy, a poor but proud prospect may say, "I want to look around and see what other companies have to offer." A kind-hearted buyer, who has no authority to purchase but does not want to disappoint a salesman, may say, "I can't afford it now, see me later." A prospect who does not recognize his needs may remark, "I have all I need." And a buyer who has more important business demanding his attention may camouflage his real reason for not buying by saying, "I'm not interested now." These are but a few of the many excuses raised by prospects in sales interviews to hide their real reasons for not buying.

Some of the most common excuses encountered by salesmen are: "I'd like to think it over," "Business is bad," "I want to talk it over with my wife," "I have other better plans," "It costs too much," "My wife has money of her own," "I want something else," and "I have enough." Behind each of these pretexts are sincere reasons for not buying, and it is a salesman's major problem to discover the actual objections so as to be able to deal with them effectively.

Excuses are easily recognized by an experienced salesman. An inexperienced salesman soon learns to distinguish between excuses and objections. A salesman has no difficulty in qualifying an obstacle if the person interviewed has been effectively qualified on his need, ability to buy, and authority to purchase. Any objections that a qualified prospect may raise on these grounds are obviously insincere pretexts. When a salesman is confident that a prospect has ability to buy, the comment, "I can't afford it," is readily recognized as an excuse.

A prospect's attitude often reveals his sincerity in making an objection. A casual tone of voice, a furtive manner, and an attitude of indifference characterize those who are making excuses. A sincere objector, on the other hand, is commonly more positive in his manner of offering objections.

Most excuses are made early in a sales interview before the buyer knows enough to raise a real objection. Furthermore, most of the obstacles raised by prospects are excuses, not objections.

Although a salesman can never be altogether sure in qualifying an obstacle as an excuse or a sincere objection, the time in the interview when the resistance is expressed, the way an objection is worded, the obvious qualifications of the buyer, and his manner in raising the objection, all combine to identify the criticism as an excuse or as a sincere objection. The fact that a great majority of objections are merely excuses further simplifies a salesman's problem of qualifying them.

Disposing of Excuses. When a salesman is confronted with an excuse, nothing is to be gained by discussing it with a prospect. Discussion only serves to magnify its importance in the mind of the prospect, who instinctively rushes to the defense of his pretext, and a major argument ensues. A salesman who debates excuses with prospects makes a mountain out of a molehill and creates greater opposition. When a salesman discusses excuses, his presentation is detoured over a by-pass that leads to a dead end.

Successful salesmen often ignore excuses completely. They make no response to pretexts of prospects and continue with their discussion of the buyer's needs. By this strategy, the resistance of a prospect is not aroused, the pretext is soon forgotten, and the interview is not sidetracked by meaningless distractions.

Rather than ignore an excuse entirely, a salesman may prefer to comment on it briefly and continue with his sales presentation. If a buyer interrupts with the excuse, "Business is too bad to buy now," a salesman may simply say, "Yes, business could be better," and go on with his presentation, making no further reference to that subject. If a prospect remarks, "I have enough now," a salesman may pass over the pretext by saying, "Yes, almost everyone feels the same way." To avoid antagonizing a buyer, a salesman may make a sympathetic answer, as, "That's too bad," or a similar evasive reply that arouses no discussion, and the buyer's excuse is quickly forgotten. Answers to excuses also may be postponed by a salesman by saying, "I'm coming to that later," and in the course of conversation the excuse is forgotten by both salesman and prospect.

Before a salesman has had an opportunity to present his product, many buyers say, "I'm not interested." Some salesmen handle this excuse by replying, "I understand why you are not interested now, but in a few minutes I believe that I can show you why it would be to your interest to consider my proposition."

A common excuse of many prospects is "I'm too busy now." Without attempting to argue the matter, the strategy of good salesmen is to ask the buyer for an appointment at a later time when the salesman can return and make his presentation. Some salesmen ask, "May I see you tomorrow afternoon at 2:40?" This response usually disposes of this excuse and the prospect gives the salesman an appointment to continue his presentation at a later time.

A prospect's excuse may be turned frequently into a reason for buying by resorting to the "boomerang method." If a prospect says, "I haven't any money," a salesman can throw the excuse back at the buyer phrased as a selling point by saying, "That's just the reason why I am recommending this investment to you." Then the salesman continues with his presentation, ignoring the buyer's excuse. Or a prospect may say, "My business is different," an excuse which can be handled with the reply, "Because your business is different, you need this unique equipment."

Postponements are common excuses, as "I'd like to think it over," or "See me next month," or "I'll let you know later." Excuses of this character may be valid obstacles when the prospect definitely lacks the authority, a need, or ability to buy. However, in most cases they are merely subterfuges to avoid buying. Qualified salesmen meet these evasions by saying, "If I have failed to make myself clear, I shall be glad to explain more fully," or "I shall be glad to help you explain my proposition to your partner," or "I can give you the information you want right now."

A salesman who refuses to consider excuses seriously, usually has little difficulty in side-stepping them without offending a prospect. As many of the objections advanced by buyers are merely excuses, a salesman has little difficulty in recognizing and minimizing them.

Answering Valid Objections

Buyers often have sincere, valid reasons for objecting to the purchase of a product or service. These fundamental objections are usually: (1) price objections; (2) need objections; (3) product objections; (4) service objections; (5) company objections.

1. Price objections are the most common and difficult sales objections for many salesmen to answer. A typical comment of many buyers is, "Your price is too high." If a salesman has anticipated this objection by demonstrating and discussing the quality features of his product, this criticism may never arise.

When a prospect raises a price objection, a salesman should attempt to secure a better understanding of the buyer's point of view on price. When a buyer says, "Your price is too high," one successful salesman asks, "Too high when compared with what?" Other questions which may be asked to discover a prospect's concern with price are, "What would you consider a fair price?" and "What would you be willing to spend?" By asking such questions, a salesman can discover what is going on in the prospect's mind in regard to price so that he can deal with it intelligently and justify his price on grounds of quality, performance, style, durability, and other factors, thus giving the buyer a chance to talk about price.

Successful salesmen answer price objections by using one or more of the following appeals:

a. Terms of payment are easy, with small initial payment, small monthly installments, and a long period to make payment, as well as low financing costs.

b. Direct comparisons between high-priced and low-priced articles establish the quality of high-priced products and minimize the price. By comparing the features of a low-priced article with the superior advantages of his higher priced product, a salesman can justify its greater cost.

c. By reducing the cost of an article to small amounts, a salesman can minimize the initial cost. This can be done by quoting the small daily, weekly, or monthly payments required to purchase a product on the installment plan. The cost of a piano may be compared to the price of a package of cigarettes a day over a five-year period.

d. Savings in operating costs may be compared with the prospect's present costs. A prospect may be shown how operating economies are sufficient to absorb a higher initial cost.

e. Quick turnover, price protection, and advertising assistance frequently are used to answer price objections when selling merchandise for resale to wholesale and retail merchants.

f. A salesman may refer to the fact that a prospect owns many high-priced articles as evidence of his willingness to pay more for quality goods.

g. By showing the limitations of a lower priced article, a salesman may convince a prospect of the desirability of paying a higher price.

h. By discussing and demonstrating the benefits of ownership, a salesman can make product value outweigh price in the mind of a buyer.

2. Need objections are frequently raised by prospects who believe that they have no real need for the product offered; or they insist that their need has been satisfied; or the article does not satisfy their requirements as well as do competing products.

Frequently a prospect does not recognize that he needs an article or service because the salesman has failed to convince him that such a need exists. When a prospect has not been convinced of his need for an article, his normal objection is, "I don't need it." If a prospect has been properly qualified as to his need, it remains for the salesman to convince him of his requirements.

Successful salesmen convince prospects of their needs by resorting to one or more of the following methods:

a. Survey evidence obtained by a salesman in an inspection or inventory of the prospect's property may provide conclusive proof of the existence of a definite need for the product. If the survey has been conducted by engineers or other experts, it carries added weight.

b. Testimonials of other persons in a similar position are often effective in proving to a prospect his need for a product or service.

c. Description of the benefits of ownership, the comfort, safety, economy, with emphasis on the motives of the buyer, will establish a need.

d. Objections of wholesale or retail merchants that there is no demand for a product may be answered with records of sales, inquiries of consumers, and other evidence of demand. By offering assistance to merchants in creating demand, through store and window displays, local advertising, and store sales, a salesman may overcome the objection that there will be no demand for the merchandise.

e. By showing a prospect the inadequacy of his present equipment or service, a salesman may overcome a need objection. One of the common objections met by life insurance salesmen is, "I have all the life insurance I need." By showing that the proceeds of a prospect's life insurance, in terms of monthly income, are inadequate to support his family, an insurance salesman answers this objection.

3. Product objections are raised by prospects to quality, design, construction, size, raw materials, color, and performance of a product. Likewise, objections may be made to the features of a service. A life insurance contract, for example, may be criticized on such features as loan provisions, waiver of premiums, participation in surplus, repayment of loans, exchange or conversion options.

An analysis of the product objections encountered by retail salesmen of underwear showed that buyers objected to the following: shrinkage, flap button in wrong place, crotch chafes, collar stretches, cuffs too small, legs too long, sleeves draw up, top button on collar too tight, and buttons break off easily.

Many product objections can be forestalled by a salesman if he will anticipate them by demonstrating and discussing product features clearly, completely, and convincingly. When a prospect objects to a product, it is often an indication that the salesman has failed to show him how the product meets his needs.

The following methods of answering product objections are used by good salesmen:

a. Discover a prospect's real reason for raising a product objection by asking questions to draw out the prospect's real objections. If a buyer says, "I don't like the quality," a salesman inquires, "Just what don't you like about the quality?" In this way a salesman is able to answer the objection more effectively by clarifying an obscure objection. Or a salesman may say, "I do not believe I fully understand what you mean. Please explain." Sometimes a prospect is unable to give a sound reason for his objection and the obstacle is automatically eliminated.

b. When a prospect favors a rival product, a salesman may set up a standard by which the features of the competing product may be judged. For example, a prospect for an automobile says, "I prefer the Blank car because it is safer." The automobile salesman can establish a standard of safety features for making specific comparisons with a competing car on such features as top, body, headlights, braking system, steering apparatus, front-wheel stability, glass, and ventilation. The salesman can compare exclusive features of his own product with each feature of the competitor's.

c. Quality objections may be answered by discussing raw materials, processes, inspection, and labor which ensures quality. If product quality is high, a salesman can answer complaints concerning it with proof in the form of testimonials or demonstration.

d. Product objections can be overcome with demonstrations. The actual performance of the product itself is one of the best answers to criticisms. Laboratory test reports may be shown to buyers to answer objections; or a trial of a product may be offered.

e. Testimonial proof, in the form of local references, letters of recommendation, statements of authorities, and guarantees, is frequently used to answer product objections.

4. Service objections, or criticisms of deliveries, adjustments, mechanical repairs, and maintenance, are sometimes raised by buyers of repeat essentials and mechanical appliances. By inquiring about the service experience of a prospect with similar products, a salesman can deal more intelligently with objections to service. Tactful questions enable a salesman to determine quickly whether or not a buyer has had difficulty in securing satisfactory service from other sellers. For example, a salesman asks a prospect, "Have you had satisfactory mechanical service on your present car?" If the prospect has no objection to the service he has received, it is unlikely that he will raise a service objection.

If a buyer criticizes the service of a salesman's house by saying, "Your company is very slow in making deliveries," a salesman can meet this and similar objections in the following ways:

a. Obtain a clear understanding of the difficulty by inquiring and listening to the explanations of the buyer. By asking "Why?" and "How?" a salesman can discover the real reasons behind a service objection and can answer it convincingly.

b. By describing the satisfactory service experiences of well-known customers, a salesman can overcome many such objections. Unusual services that have been rendered to buyers and examples of low service costs are excellent material for answering this type of criticism.

c. Demonstrations of prompt service may be used to overcome these objections of prospects. An oil-burner salesman, calling at a buyer's house, demonstrated the promptness of his mechanical service by asking the prospect's permission to use the telephone to call a mechanic. The salesman did not disclose his identity to his office. In 30 minutes the mechanic called at the prospect's home, demonstrating to the buyer's satisfaction the prompt service rendered by the salesman's organization.

d. Illustrations of service facilities, including trucks, distributing stations, service equipment, and personnel are used by many salesmen in answering objections to delivery and mechanical service.

5. Company objections, or criticisms of the financial stability, resources, size, age, personnel, policies of a salesman's organization are sometimes raised by prospects. Merchants considering the resale of a specialty usually raise objections of this nature. Industrial buyers of large quantities of supplies or technical equipment are interested in the resources of their suppliers.

Many of these objections can be forestalled before they are raised if a salesman convincingly presents his company and organization to buyers. However, if company objections are raised, a salesman may take one or more of the following courses:

a. Persuade a prospect to air his complaint completely. Frequently, an objection to company policy or stability is the result of rumor or gossip and is not founded on fact. If such is the case, a salesman can state the facts and quickly correct the misunderstanding.

b. A common objection met by salesmen is that a buyer prefers to deal with another concern. If a salesman will persuade a buyer to reveal his reasons for preferring to buy from competitors, the buyer's objections can usually be met effectively. However, many buyers who are reluctant to break established connections, or family or corporate relationships, prefer not to discuss this objection. A salesman may meet the objection by discussing the importance of having more than one source of supply, the weakness of "putting all eggs in one basket," the value of variety in merchandise, and the disadvantage of doing business with friends.

c. Charts or graphs of company growth, financial stability, and volume of sales are frequently used by salesmen to answer objections as to the reliability of their organizations.

Genuine objections to price, product, company, and service should be anticipated, but when raised should be answered immediately after discovering the real reason for the objection.

Some objections cannot be answered. The best strategy is to admit the truth of the objection but point out other offsetting advantages that outweigh the unanswerable objection.

HOW TO ANSWER OBJECTIONS

In answering objections of prospects, it is important that a salesman know not only what to say but also how to say it. A salesman may have a formidable array of facts and figures to answer a buyer's objection but, unless these reasons are expressed with tact and conviction, the buyer may not accept them as conclusive. Various techniques are used by salesmen in answering objections.

The "Yes, but" Method. One effective way to phrase answers to objections is called, in the vernacular of salesmen, the "Yes, but" method. When a prospect raises an objection such as, "I prefer to invest in bonds because they are safer," a salesman, using the "Yes, but" method, replies, "Yes, Mr. Prospect, that is one way to look at it, but did you ever consider it from this viewpoint?"

Everyone likes to have his opinion respected. When a salesman uses the "Yes, but" method, he disarms a prospect by agreeing with him before attempting to answer his objection. Argument is avoided as a prospect is not called upon to defend his objection. The buyer is conciliated when he recognizes that the salesman is in at least partial agreement with him. A salesman who uses this method gives the impression that he is fair and courteous.

It is immaterial how a salesman's response is phrased as long as it concedes to some extent the justice of the prospect's objection. For example, a prospect for an electric range says, "Doesn't that range cost a lot to operate?" Using a variation of the "Yes, but" response a salesman can reply, "I can see why you would feel that way. In fact, only a few years ago electric ranges were very expensive to operate. However, costs of current have been reduced and the heating coils so improved that this range costs only a few cents a day to operate."

If a salesman emphatically denies a buyer's objection by saying, "No, you're wrong, this range only costs a few cents a day to operate," this blunt contradiction may precipitate an argument. Nothing is to be gained by irritating a prospect in this way, as the buyer's mind becomes closed to the salesman's answer. By conceding that a buyer has brought up a point worth considering, a salesman has less difficulty in inducing him to accept another point of view.

By ignoring a prospect's objection, a salesman only magnifies its importance in the mind of the buyer. If a buyer's objection is minimized, he may become irritated. Recognize fairly an objection for what it is worth.

The "Why" Method. Frequently an objection is obscurely stated so that its meaning is not clear to a salesman. For example, a buyer may say, "I prefer the Blank radio." Before a salesman can effectively answer vague or indefinite objections such as the above, he must clarify them. The most effective strategy for clarifying obscure objections is the "Why?" method.

When a prospect raises an obscure criticism such as, "If I bought any, I'd buy a Thompson mixer," a salesman can ask, "Just why do you prefer a Thompson?" By this inquiry a salesman resorts to the "Why?" strategy to clarify the objection. In many cases, a prospect cannot give a convincing reason why he prefers another product and the objection is automatically eliminated. If a buyer has a good reason for objecting, the salesman, by getting more information, can deal with the obstacle more intelligently.

In responding to a salesman's "Why?" a prospect may give some minor reason for favoring a competing product, as, "The Thompson mixer has an inverted fan." A salesman can smoke out this objection by asking another question, "What can be the advantage of anything like that?" and the objection is often minimized and forgotten by the buyer.

Objections are frequently obscurely stated because a prospect is not clear in his own mind concerning his opposition to a product. He may say, "I just don't like your refrigerator." In this case the "Why" strategy fails because the buyer has no concrete objections to offer. A salesman, when confronted with such an indefinite objection, can do one of three things: (1) change the subject and take the prospect's mind off his doubts; (2) review each of the sales points that have been made; or (3) select a feature that the prospect has approved and discuss it thoroughly with the expectation that the prospect may forget his objection.

Although excuses may be dismissed without comment and forgotten, sincere objections should be answered immediately. If a salesman fails to answer an objection immediately, a prospect assumes that the salesman is unable to reply or that he is unfamiliar with his product. These assumptions weaken a buyer's confidence in the salesman and the proposition. A prospect keeps thinking about an unanswered objection and pays little attention to what a salesman is saying about other features. And the longer an objection remains unanswered, the more important it becomes to the buyer and the more difficulty a salesman experiences in answering it.

HOW TO OVERCOME OBSTACLES TO SALES

Obstacles to sales can be handled easily and effectively if a salesman is prepared to dispose of them. A knowledge of common objections and effective answers is first necessary; secondly, a plan for making responses to objections is equally important. Observation of the practices of hundreds of successful salesmen in many lines has shown that they all follow six simple practices in answering objections and disposing of excuses in sales interviews.

These six tried and proved practices for overcoming objections have been combined into a six-step routine for the convenient use of salesmen of all types of goods and services. If a salesman will memorize and practice the six steps in this routine, he will experience little difficulty in answering objections and closing sales.

Routine for Overcoming Sales Difficulties

1. Welcome objections.
2. Qualify obstacles.
3. Restate objection.
4. Answer briefly.

5. Commit objector.
6. Swing back into selling.

1. Welcome Objections. A salesman, who understands the reasons why prospects raise objections and realizes the opportunities which they afford to secure a better understanding of the buyer's point of view, sincerely welcomes objections. By calmly, cheerfully, and respectfully listening to objections, a salesman impresses a buyer with his confidence and ability to dispose of the obstacle satisfactorily.

Many successful salesmen favorably impress prospects by sincerely answering objections, saying, "I'm glad you brought that up." Hesitation, annoyance, and embarrassment weaken a salesman's effectiveness in answering objections. A salesman who ignores objections or ridicules criticisms antagonizes prospects and places himself at an immediate disadvantage.

If a salesman takes the attitude that he is an assistant to the buyer, desirous of giving him the facts so that he can make his own decisions and enjoy greater satisfaction and profit, little difficulty will be experienced in disposing of objections. Prospects will answer objections themselves if given the facts. The problem of answering objections is not a battle of wits but an opportunity to serve.

2. Qualify Obstacles. When a buyer has raised an objection, a salesman qualifies it as (1) an excuse or (2) a sincere objection. Obstacles are qualified to determine the method of dealing with them. Experienced salesmen have little difficulty in deciding whether a prospect is making excuses or is voicing sincere objections. Inexperienced salesmen soon learn to recognize such common excuses as, "I haven't any money," "I have enough," "I don't need it," "I want to talk it over with my wife," "See me later," and similar pretexts. By ignoring, deferring answering, or passing over excuses with a brief reply, a salesman has little difficulty in disposing of them.

If a buyer has been thoroughly qualified as to his ability to buy, his need, and his authority, a salesman can quickly recognize as excuses any protests that the prospect may make on these grounds.

Valid objections to the seller's price, product, service, or organization may be readily recognized by the attitude of the buyer and his qualifications. Few sincere objections are raised early in a sales interview. Real objections normally appear when a salesman is well along in his presentation; excuses are usually made by a buyer in the opening of an interview to confuse and discourage a salesman.

If a salesman does not understand a prospect's objection, he can clarify the subject by asking "Why?" the buyer objects to a product feature.

When several objections are raised, it is important to recognize the principal objections and deal with them first.

A salesman who accepts excuses as real objections dissipates his time and effort in a futile effort to answer pretexts and loses the attention and interest of the buyer. A salesman who cannot recognize sincere objections fails to grasp the real issues in the situation and misses opportunities to close sales.

3. Restate Objections. Genuine objections should be restated by a salesman for several reasons. First, a buyer is favorably impressed by the fact that a salesman who repeats a criticism is not attempting to dodge the objection. For example, a prospect says, "I think that is a larger machine than we need." The salesman restates the objection in his own words, as follows: "Now as I understand it, your objection to this machine is that it is larger than you need."

Another advantage of restating an objection is that the prospect's criticism is often minimized by repetition. A salesman may reword an objection to make the criticism seem immaterial, as, "Your only objection to this refrigerator is that the food compartment is 1 inch narrower than in the Blank refrigerator?"

If an objection is obscure, it may be clarified by repetition so that both buyer and salesman definitely understand it. A salesman may ask, "If I understand you correctly, you do not like the size of this cabinet. Is that right?"

4. Answer Briefly. If answers to objections are stated briefly and to the point, they may be disposed of quickly and minimized. A lengthy answer gives a prospect the impression that an objection is important. Wordiness dissipates the force of a salesman's response and often confuses a buyer.

If a salesman's answer is stated positively and vigorously as though it admitted of no argument or contradiction, a buyer may not be encouraged to debate the matter. A hesitant answer gives a prospect an impression that a salesman lacks confidence and sometimes invites a discussion.

In striving for brevity in answering objections, successful salesmen do not sacrifice completeness or omit fundamental reasons for buying. An inadequate answer often fails to convince a prospect. The "Yes, but" strategy of answering objections avoids direct contradictions and arguments.

5. Commit Objectors. After a salesman has conclusively answered a sincere objection, he can determine whether or not the buyer has been convinced by seeking his agreement. If the prospect accepts the salesman's answer, the latter may continue with his sales presentation, assured that he has left no unanswered objections to block the way to a sale. If, on the other hand, a prospect is not satisfied with a salesman's answer to his objection, it is important that the salesman recognize that the buyer still objects and he should attempt to answer the objection in another way.

For example, a refrigerator salesman answers a prospect's objection to the current consumption of a refrigerator. To determine whether or not his answer is acceptable to the buyer, the salesman says, "Doesn't it seem to you that this refrigerator would be very economical to operate?" If the prospect says, "Yes," the salesman knows that he has overcome the objection and proceeds with his sales presentation. If the buyer says, "No, it doesn't seem economical to me," the salesman makes another atttempt to answer the objection and again seeks a commitment.

A salesman should try to secure the agreement of a buyer on every major objection. "Buttoning up" each objection, by checking the buyer's reaction, makes it possible for a salesman to proceed confidently to a favorable conclusion.

In addition to serving as a check upon a salesman's progress, favorable commitments give a salesman a psychological advantage in securing the final "yes" from a prospect. A prospect who has admitted that a salesman has satisfied each of his major objections cannot logically refuse to give his favorable consent to signing an order.

6. Swing back into Selling. After a salesman has answered an objection and secured the favorable commitment of the prospect, he does not pause but swings back into his sales presentation. By hesitating, a salesman invites further objections. If he continues his presentation, a salesman takes the prospect's mind off of the objection and it is soon forgotten.

Problem I

ANSWERING OBJECTIONS OF INDUSTRIAL BUYERS

Clyde L. Chilton, representing the Industrial Supply Company

The Industrial Supply Company, Rochester, N.Y., manufactures and distributes, direct to industrial concerns throughout the country,

Sales Presentation Rating Form

Answering Objections

Salesman_____   Date_____

Rated by _____   Over-all Rating_____

I. *Salesman's Method of Answering Objections*	Excellent 90–100	Good 80–90	Fair 70–80	Poor 60–70	Failure Below 60
A. Welcoming objections					
B. Anticipating objections					
C. Qualifying obstacles					
D. Disposing of excuses					
E. Restating objections					
F. Using the "Yes, but" response					
G. Clarifying objections asking "Why?"					
H. Promptness in answering objections					
I. Brief yet complete answers to objections					
J. Committing the objector					
K. Swinging back to selling					

Miscellaneous Comments _____
_____
_____

a complete line of cleaning compounds and janitor's supplies, including washing powders, soaps, disinfectants, disinfecting machines, mops, and brushes for use in office buildings and factories. The company maintains warehouses and sales offices in Chicago, New York City, New Orleans, Boston, and Los Angeles out of which travel 20 salesmen who call on purchasing agents.

One of the leaders in the industrial line is No-odor, a disinfectant packaged in pint and 2-quart cans. Another product featured by the company is Cleanup washing powder. Noxem insecticide is widely sold for exterminating purposes. Company salesmen are instructed to push these specialties in their interviews with industrial buyers.

From the branch office in New Orleans works Clyde L. Chilton, who has represented the company in Louisiana, Mississippi, and Alabama for five years. In the following interview, salesman Chilton is interviewing the purchasing agent of a large public utility company in New Orleans. This company has bought small quantities of several products from salesman Chilton in the past and he is trying to secure a larger share of their business.

1. SALESMAN: Nice and cool, isn't it?
2. BUYER: Yes, it is.
3. SALESMAN: Have you bought disinfectant recently? I'm with the Industrial Supply Company.
4. BUYER: No, we haven't. We're not interested now. Maybe in the Fall we could use some.
5. SALESMAN: What kind do you buy? Do you remember?
6. BUYER: A commercial disinfectant put up in pint and in 2-quart cans.
7. SALESMAN: Was it for use in that quantity?
8. BUYER: Yes. Now, all I can say is that occasionally we put out inquiries on it, and when we do, I'll see that your name is on the list.
9. SALESMAN: You wouldn't consider disinfecting machines, would you? You wouldn't see the necessity of them?
10. BUYER: Our machines are already under contract with the Doe Company. They've got a better machine than yours.
11. SALESMAN: Oh, I see. Oh, is that so?
12. BUYER: We've got them in a number of our washrooms so that we're not in a position to talk with you one bit on that.
13. SALESMAN: I see. Ever hear of Cleanup, our famous cleaner?
14. BUYER: Well, we're not in position to buy that, I don't believe. We're using a soap powder and that's about all we can do.
15. SALESMAN: You don't mind if I leave you those Cleanup samples, do you?
16. BUYER: Well, I don't know as they are of any real value to me. They'd

be of some value probably to somebody who is actually going to use them. I couldn't do much with them.

17. SALESMAN: Yeah. That cleaner has been used since 1901. It absolutely cleans everything off. It's a wonderful cleaner.

18. BUYER: Well, we have been using a better cleaner. It's easier on painted surfaces. We don't use very much of it; and to tell you the truth, I wouldn't be inclined, for the volume involved, to disturb it right at the minute. If there's nothing wrong with it, why change it? That's the point. There isn't enough involved.

19. SALESMAN: Do you have any trouble with roaches?

20. BUYER: Yes, we use a roach powder. But yours isn't powerful enough for us.

21. SALESMAN: The Swift Steamship Company uses our roach powder on their boats. The United Gas Company, Mr. Jones, in town here, uses it in their buildings.

22. BUYER: Well, we're using one now and—

23. SALESMAN (interrupting): You don't use it in a box do you?

24. BUYER: No box whatsoever. No, sir. I think we'd better just stick to the disinfectant and do what we can—

25. SALESMAN (interrupting): By the way, what's the story on germicide? Will you be needing any more of that stuff?

26. BUYER: No, sir, we don't use it.

27. SALESMAN: O.K. Well, I'll see you again.

28. BUYER: All right, yes, sir.

Questions

1. List the "excuses" offered by the buyer in this interview.

a. Did the salesman recognize them as pretexts?

b. Did the salesman dispose of these excuses effectively? If not, how should they have been handled? Write your answer to each excuse.

2. List the sincere objections of the buyer in this interview.

a. Did the salesman recognize them as real objections?

b. What was the salesman's attitude toward objections? If not sound, what should it have been?

c. What features of the salesman's proposition did the buyer object to: price, need, product, service, company?

d. Did the salesman answer these objections effectively? If not, how should they have been answered?

e. Did the salesman use the best strategy in answering these objections? If not, what should he have said?

f. Did the salesman follow the six-point routine in answering objections? If not, what steps should have been taken?

3. How should this salesman improve his methods of answering objections?

Problem II

ANSWERING OBJECTIONS OF MERCHANTS

H. G. Gilson, representing the Acme Specialty Company

The Acme Specialty Company, Cincinnati, Ohio, manufactures and distributes direct to wholesalers, chain stores, and large direct buyers a line of shoe polishes and dressings sold to consumers in 10- and 25-cent packages. The line is branded Amco and is advertised in small space in national magazines. Sales offices are maintained in New York City and Pittsburgh, Pa., out of which work eight salesmen who call on the buyers of large distributing organizations.

One of the three salesmen operating out of the New York office is H. G. Gilson, who contacts buyers in New York and Philadelphia. He has been representing the Acme Company for two years. In the following interview, he is attempting to sell a new shoe whitener to the buyer of a chain of specialty grocery stores located in several wealthy residential suburbs surrounding New York City. The product is made in paste form and packed in tubes as well as in liquid form which is sold in bottles. The buyer has bought shoe polish from the company in the past.

1. SALESMAN: I represent the Amco Shoe White.
2. BUYER: What did you say you sell?
3. SALESMAN: Amco Shoe White.
4. BUYER: We've never sold it before. I don't believe we're interested.
5. SALESMAN: All of the big chains in the country stock Amco and enjoy good sales. There is a lot of advertising behind it.
6. BUYER: If we bought some, do you think we should have the white paste in 10- and 25-cent sizes or the white liquid in 10- and 25-cent sizes?
7. SALESMAN: Both, then you will have a complete line of cleaners.
8. BUYER: What's your price?
9. SALESMAN: That will be $2 a dozen. All your quarter items are $2 and all your dime items are 80 cents.
10. BUYER: I think that price is a little high. Now, I wonder what deal you have. A summer deal, or something?
11. SALESMAN: None other than that you get a dozen free with a gross.
12. BUYER: You are not making a special to me?
13. SALESMAN: No, the regular deal.
14. BUYER: What's your deal you have open to everybody?
15. SALESMAN: A dozen free with a gross.

16. BUYER: A dozen free with a gross.

17. SALESMAN: That's right.

18. BUYER: What are we going to do with our old merchandise? I can't buy any new cleaner as long as the old stuff is on hand.

19. SALESMAN: I'm glad you mentioned it. As I understand it, your objection to stocking Amco is that you have other cleaners in stock.

20. BUYER: That's right.

21. SALESMAN: Well, of course, on your black polish assortment, you can always sell that for it's always in demand. You don't anticipate any difficulty on that, do you?

22. BUYER: Well, it's in good condition and we probably can sell it.

23. SALESMAN: Now, Amco gives you a better discount than other brands.

24. BUYER: Unquestionably.

25. SALESMAN: And the package is more attractive.

26. BUYER: Is the sale guaranteed? If it doesn't sell, we'll be stuck.

27. SALESMAN: Well, I see what you mean. You want us to take back what does not sell. I will check with the office as to whether or not we'll take unsold stuff on whole credit or some sort of a credit basis and you will not be stuck with it. Is that fair?

28. BUYER: Well, can you find out about the returned goods credit?

29. SALESMAN: Of course, as I say, it's our instructions to avoid selling you the wrong items because it's very costly, and we realize it's just going to lie on your shelves—it's not going to sell. That's, of course, what the company would like to have you do—sell it and get away from taking it back. It's 100 per cent loss to us. We have to throw it away when it gets over there.

30. BUYER: How many tubes do we need?

31. SALESMAN: Well, two cases in Brownsville and five in Smithtown and three in Blakesley and six here.

32. BUYER (examining list): You've got listed, paste a quarter, tube a quarter, liquid a quarter. Which is the paste, this one (examining bottle of paste)?

33. SALESMAN: No, the paste you have is in the tube. Well, I'll check with the office, Mr. Buyer. Will it be convenient to see you later today, or—

34. BUYER: Well, give me a ring if you're coming any distance to make sure I'm here.

35. SALESMAN: Well, we're just over in Manhattan, see, the branch is—so I don't know, but I'll check this anyway. All right, thank you, Mr. Buyer.

36. BUYER: I'll be glad to see you, too.

37. SALESMAN: I hope we can take back that unsold stock.

38. BUYER: O.K.

39. SALESMAN: Good-by.

Questions

1. What were the buyer's pretexts or excuses in this interview?

a. Did the salesman recognize them as excuses?

b. Did the salesman dispose of these excuses effectively? If not, how should they have been handled? Write your method of handling each excuse.

2. List the sincere objections of the buyer in this interview.

a. Did the salesman recognize them as real, sincere objections?

b. What was the salesman's attitude toward the buyer's objections? If he did not have the right attitude, what should it have been?

c. Did the salesman answer these objections effectively? If not, how should they have been answered? Describe in detail.

d. Did the salesman use the best strategy in answering these objections? If not, what should he have said?

e. Did the salesman follow the six-point routine in answering objections? If not, what steps should have been taken?

3. What, in general, should this salesman do to improve his methods of answering objections?

Reading References

CHARLES H. FERNALD, "Salesmanship," Chaps. XVII–XVIII, Prentice-Hall, Inc., New York, 1945.

J. GEORGE FREDERICK, "Modern Salesmanship," Chap. XVI, Garden City Publishing Company, Inc., New York, 1937.

HAROLD M. HAAS, "A Short Course in Salesmanship," Chap. VIII, Prentice-Hall, Inc., New York, 1939.

J. M. HILL and R. G. WALTERS, "Success through Salesmanship," Unit XV, South-Western Publishing Company, Cincinnati, 1940.

PAUL W. IVEY, "Successful Salesmanship," Chap. XI, Prentice-Hall, Inc., New York, 1947.

DAVID R. OSBORNE, "Salesmanship for Today for Salesmanagers of Tomorrow," Chap. X, Harper & Brothers, New York, 1939.

F. A. RUSSELL and F. H. BEACH, "Textbook of Salesmanship," Chaps. XIII–XIV, McGraw Hill Book Company, Inc., New York, 1949.

HARRY SIMMONS, "A Practical Course in Successful Selling," Chap. IX, Harper & Brothers, New York, 1939.

FRANK S. WARD, "Essentials of Selling," Chap. VIII, Prentice-Hall, Inc., New York, 1945.

PERCY H. WHITING, "The Five Great Rules of Selling," Chaps. XXI–XXIII, McGraw-Hill Book Company, Inc., New York, 1947.

CHAPTER XXI

SECURING ACTION IN SALES INTERVIEWS

IMPORTANCE OF SECURING ACTION

Interviews are conducted by salesmen for the purpose of persuading prospects to make favorable buying decisions. If a prospect refuses to buy or defers action, a salesman has failed to accomplish his mission. Salesmen sometimes forget to seek action and spend their time and effort "creating good will," "dropping in to get acquainted," "keeping contact," and other pleasant but pointless diversions which have little to do with securing signed orders.

To remind salesmen to ask prospects to buy, sales managers have devised unique ways to get salesmen to "ask for the order." A large automobile manufacturer furnished thousands of its retail salesmen with a pocket piece resembling a gold nugget and called a "closing stone," which salesmen were asked to carry in their vest or coat pockets. When salesmen put their hands into their pockets during the course of a sales presentation and touched the "closing stone," they were reminded to ask the prospect for the order.

Another company whose salesmen were order-shy furnished its representatives with giant-size order books about 2 feet square bearing a large label, "Order Book." Salesmen were required to carry these books on all calls as reminders to ask for orders.

When a salesman understands that his success depends on his ability to get some action in every interview, he does not have to tie a string around his finger to remind himself that he must ask for an order.

On the other hand, it may not always be necessary or even advisable for a salesman to seek a signed order in every interview with a prospect. In some cases a salesman's presentation may be interrupted by a third party; the buyer may not have time to hear the salesman's story; the prospect may share the authority to buy with a second party who must be consulted before the sale can be closed; the salesman may be merely seeking information as a basis for a complete presentation at another time; or the buyer may want to make comparisons with other products. These and many more legitimate reasons make it impracticable for a salesman to attempt to get an order in every interview.

However, a salesman should always attempt to secure some favorable action from the buyer in every interview. It may not be decisive or final but it should, at least, lead toward eventual acceptance of the salesman's proposition. A salesman can attempt to induce a prospect to act in one or more of the following ways: (1) make an appointment for a return call; (2) make an appointment for a demonstration; (3) get permission to make a survey or inspection of the buyer's needs; (4) make an appointment for a showroom visit; (5) get permission to interview a prospect's associates or subordinates; (6) get permission to submit additional facts, figures, or proof; (7) get a prospect to agree to visit the installation of some satisfied customer.

A salesman can usually get a prospect to "do something" in every sales interview. An interview that fails to get some concession from the buyer is a waste of a salesman's time. If a salesman does nothing more than secure an appointment for a future demonstration, he retains the interest of the prospect and paves the way for a favorable decision. Before seeking an interview a salesman should plan to get one or more specific courses of action from the prospect.

Many sales can be closed in a single interview if a salesman is determined to sell a prospect in the shortest possible time and concentrates his efforts on accomplishing that objective. By concluding a sale in a single interview, a salesman saves his time and avoids the possibility that a prospect may be approached by competing salesmen.

An analysis of 1,000 life insurance sales by S. G. Dickinson showed that 732, or more than 73 per cent, were closed on the first and second interviews; 17 per cent were closed on the third call; 8 per cent were concluded on the fourth; and the balance on subsequent interviews. The type or size of policy sold had no effect on the number of calls necessary to make the sale.

Prospects for specialties, luxuries, or intangibles rarely say, "I'll buy that insurance policy," or "Just send me out an air-conditioning system." They usually postpone their buying decision unless urged by a salesman to take definite action. This natural reluctance of many prospects to make buying decisions makes it necessary for a salesman to persuade prospects to buy. When a buyer says to a salesman, "Wrap it up, I'll take it," the salesman is merely taking an order.

Most prospects are not easily convinced of their need for a product or service; unless a salesman persuades them to take some definite action, no sale results.

SALESMAN'S ATTITUDE TOWARD CLOSING

A salesman's attitude toward closing is probably the most important factor in securing favorable buying decisions. Mental attitude often makes the difference between success and failure in closing sales interviews. If a salesman has faith in himself, and confidence in his ability to persuade a prospect to buy, he will have little difficulty in closing sales. Self-confidence, courage, and persistence are more essential in closing than in dealing with any other problem of selling.

A salesman's attitude of self-confidence and assurance is unconsciously communicated to the buyer whose doubts about the wisdom of buying are dispelled by the faith of the salesman.

The greatest handicap of many salesmen in their effort to close sales is their fear of failure and conviction that the buyer will refuse to buy. Unless a salesman at least expects to secure favorable action, he is unlikely to close many sales. A negative attitude of fear must be supplanted by a firm, positive conviction of success. A salesman must expect to be refused, but remember that most refusals are rarely final.

Confidence in closing arises from a thorough knowledge of the needs of the prospect and how the product or service will satisfy the buyer's requirements. It comes from the mental and physical stimulation of good health and the realization that the salesman's appearance makes a favorable impression.

If a salesman is mentally alert, he quickly senses when prospects are ready to buy. By paying close attention to their remarks, observing their reactions, and noting their evident interest in his proposition, a salesman readily recognizes when the desire of a buyer has reached the buying point.

Reasonable aggressiveness is required by a salesman to persuade hesitant prospects to decide to buy. Many people lack confidence in their own judgment; they procrastinate and defer action unless a salesman dominates the interview and urges them to make a favorable decision.

A placid, self-possessed manner aids a salesman in securing the confidence of a buyer. Nervousness and hesitation in closing a sale give a prospect the impression that a salesman is inexperienced and lacking in confidence.

WHEN TO SECURE ACTION IN A SALES INTERVIEW

The act of securing an affirmative buying decision from a prospect is not a separate function in a sales presentation. It may take place at any time in a sales interview and is not distinct from demonstrating, answering objections, offering proof, citing facts and figures, or meeting competition.

A convincing answer to an objection and an enthusiastic demonstration offer equal opportunities to a salesman to seek a favorable decision. Closing should be considered as a component part of each of these elements in a sales interview, any one of which may serve as a terminus to a sales presentation.

At one time salesmen were advised to watch for the "psychological moment" in a sales interview or the ideal time to ask a prospect to buy. Since a prospect may be ready to make a favorable buying decision several times during the course of a sales presentation, there may be numerous "psychological moments" when a salesman should ask for an order.

To determine when to seek buying action, a salesman should listen attentively to the comments, questions, and asides of a prospect, since they reveal interest in the salesman's proposition. If a prospect asks, "How soon can I get delivery?" an alert salesman knows that the buyer is ready to sign an order. If a prospect comments favorably about the product or service, saying, "That's a mighty fine-looking car," a salesman knows that the buyer may be ready to make a favorable decision. Sometimes a prospect expresses himself as an owner, "That oil burner will save me from carrying out ashes next winter," and thus signifies his receptiveness.

These voluntary remarks are like a red stop light on the road to an order, a signal to a salesman to stop his presentation and arrange the closing details. If a salesman ignores these closing signals, he misses a buying opportunity which may never occur again during an interview.

Another practical indication of a prospect's readiness to buy is his response to committing questions. If a salesman says, "Now that we've reviewed these advantages, don't you think that this refrigerator is a good buy?" and the buyer responds, "Yes, it suits me all right," the salesman knows that the prospect is ready to buy and proceeds to get his signature.

A salesman may seek a buying decision from a prospect at practically every stage of a convincing sales presentation. When a salesman has discovered a prospect's need, has given several convincing reasons why the product satisfies that need, and has tested the buyer's reaction and found it favorable, he is justified in seeking a favorable decision. For example, an automobile salesman finds that a woman prospect is interested in beauty in a motor car. He convincingly discusses styling, streamlining, color, chromium trim, interior fittings, hardware, and upholstery and secures the buyer's commitment on these features. He next tries for a favorable decision on beauty by asking, "Would you prefer the blue or the red car?" Then he tries for a major decision by asking, "Shall I deliver the car tonight or will tomorrow be satisfactory?"

Instead of waiting until a prospect is exhausted with facts or bored with figures before asking for an order, successful salesmen make several attempts to close a sale during the course of a presentation. Closing attempts may logically be made after demonstrating, after answering a major objection, or after presenting a testimonial from a customer. Closing is coincidental with selling and is not a separate process. It is a natural sequel to a sales point well presented, a convincing answer to an objection, or competition convincingly met.

METHODS OF SECURING A FAVORABLE BUYING DECISION

Observation of the strategy of many successful salesmen reveals a number of tried and proved practices to secure favorable acceptance of a sales proposal. One or more of these methods may be used by a salesman in closing a sale. Eight methods commonly used are (1) tryout close; (2) committing questions; (3) implying ownership; (4) getting basic buying decisions; (5) emphasizing a distinctive feature; (6) summarizing principal advantages; (7) offering a special inducement; (8) implying consent; (9) asking directly for an order.

1. Tryout Close. To discover whether or not a prospect is favorably impressed with a salesman's proposal and ready to buy, a tryout close may be used. This method has been compared to the practice of aviators in attempting two or three landings before making the final descent. In making a tryout close, a salesman asks a prospect for a decision on a minor point. For example, an automobile salesman applies a tryout close by asking, "Which car would you prefer, the red or the blue?" An insurance salesman, selling a retirement income policy, inquires, "When would you wish your retirement income to begin, at age sixty or age sixty-five?" A salesman of refrigerators may ask, "If you decided to buy this refrigerator, would you prefer to pay cash or buy on time?"

This method is effective because it minimizes resistance by asking a buyer to make only a minor decision. Minor decisions may be individually of little consequence. However, when a prospect has made several of them, they are conclusive evidence of his desire to buy. If a buyer has responded favorably to several tryout closes, it is easier to induce him to make a major buying decision.

If a salesman does not get a favorable response to a tryout close from a prospect, he has not blocked the way to a sale, but can continue his presentation by offering additional reasons why the prospect should buy.

2. Committing Questions. By securing an affirmative response from a prospect on each point made during a sales presentation, a salesman leads the buyer step by step toward an order. To make sure that a prospect understands and accepts each important point presented, he is asked to commit himself favorably. The interest of a prospect should be tested several times during an interview by asking casual questions worded to get an affirmative response, as, "Having considered these favorable features, don't you agree that this article meets your needs?" or "This is a reasonable conclusion, isn't it?"

Prospects often resent blunt, committing questions which, in effect, command the buyer to concede a sales point. If a salesman asks a buyer, "You agree with me, don't you?" or "That's right, isn't it?" the prospect receives the impression that he is being forced to agree with the salesman. No one likes to be told what to say, and prospects resent being coerced. By asking tactful questions, a salesman has little difficulty in determining the attitude of a prospect on a sales point.

After a prospect has agreed with a salesman on several fundamental points, it is much easier to persuade him to sign an order.

If a buyer answers a salesman negatively by saying, "I don't know that I agree with you on that point," the salesman simply continues his presentation, clarifying and explaining his arguments, and attempts to get another commitment from the buyer.

3. Implying Ownership. By implying that a prospect is already the owner of the product, a salesman creates in the mind of a buyer a feeling of possession that puts him in a buying mood. A successful domestic coal-stoker salesman suggests ownership to prospects by saying, "Think of the comfort you will have all over your home next winter with this stoker." An automobile salesman uses the same strategy when he tells prospects, "You'll be mighty proud to have

your neighbors see this beautiful car standing in front of your home."
Similar questions visualizing the satisfactions, profits, or pride of
ownership may be used in closing sales of all kinds of commodities
or services.

By instructing prospects in the proper operation of a product as
though they were already owners, some salesmen subtly suggest ownership. An automobile salesman uses this method of implying ownership by instructing prospects in operating the automatic gearshift.
He says, "Now, sit behind the wheel, start the engine, set the ride
control to neutral, and put your foot on the accelerator." After a
prospect has learned to automatically shift gears in this way, he has
a feeling of ownership which stimulates buying action.

If a prospect rejects a suggestion of ownership by saying, "Wait a
minute, who said I was going to buy?" a salesman continues to demonstrate or present additional facts and again tests the buyer's interest with a tryout close.

4. Getting Six Basic Buying Decisions. Before reaching a final
buying decision, a prospect must make six secondary decisions on
need, price, product, source of supply, service, and time to buy. Before a buyer signs an order, he must be satisfied that the article or
service is needed, that the price is fair, that the product will adequately meet his needs, that the seller is reliable, that he will receive
efficient service, and that now is the right time to buy.

By seeking definite commitments from a prospect on these six basic
decisions, a salesman can determine which of these decisions have been
made and which must still be made before a prospect is ready to buy.
To help a buyer decide these questions, a salesman should offer additional facts and demonstrate the value of his product or service, the
reliability of his company, and the fairness of the price.

When a prospect has made these secondary decisions, a salesman
may assume that the buyer is ready to sign an order.

Salesmen representing a large distributor of electric appliances are
trained to close sales by persuading prospects to make secondary buying decisions on the need, the brand, the source of supply, the price,
the service, and the proper time.

5. Emphasizing a Distinctive Feature. Every product or service
has one or more distinctive features which excel those of competing
articles. The feature may be a technical superiority, a unique ingre-
dient, distinctive design, or an unusual method of operation. By focusing a prospect's attention on this unique feature and emphasizing

that it alone justifies the purchase price, a salesman may secure a buyer's decision to buy.

A life insurance salesman, for example, may choose to concentrate his closing efforts on the liberal disability and indemnity features of his contract. A refrigerator salesman may focus his sales presentation on the hermetically sealed compressor unit which is a unique feature of his product.

When a salesman makes an enthusiastic and convincing presentation of some distinctive feature by demonstrating, using visual aids, quoting the experiences of others, and submitting references and statements of authorities, he can often persuade a prospect to buy on the strength of that one feature alone.

6. Summarizing Principal Advantages. By summarizing the principal advantages of his product, a salesman presents such a convincing array of reasons that a buyer is often persuaded to buy. When confronted with a long list of product features, a prospect has difficulty in saying "No."

A domestic water-softener salesman uses the summary method of closing by reviewing the principal advantages of his product, after a home demonstration, as follows: "In our discussion, Mr. Prospect, you told me about the delightful baths you had with soft water; you admitted that shaving was easier and more pleasant; you conceded that your drinking water tasted better; your wife says that soft water makes easier washdays and clothes are softer and whiter. Now, in view of all these advantages, don't you feel you need a water softener in your home?"

If a buyer does not respond favorably to such a summary of benefits, a salesman can then discover the prospect's real objections by inquiring or by listening to his remarks. When a buyer's actual objections have been revealed, a salesman tries to remove them by presenting additional reasons for buying.

7. Offering a Special Inducement. An excellent method of closing a sale is by offering a special inducement to act at once. Typical special concessions which may be offered are: a small initial payment, longer terms, free delivery, or an extra trade-in allowance. These concessions must, of course, be approved by company policy.

Buying action may be stimulated by announcing an increase in price after a certain date, as, "After January 1, these coats will be sold at the regular price of $300. At the present price you are saving $100. Or a closing date may be set for the expiration of a special offer, as, "Our offer to include a heater free with this car expires on May 14. For that reason you should make an immediate decision."

By making it difficult for a prospect to secure a product or service, the desire to buy may be stimulated and an immediate sale result. If a prospect for life insurance is told that many persons find it difficult to pass the necessary physical examination, his desire for insurance may be intensified and he may make immediate application.

Similarly a prospect may be induced to buy immediately if he is told that there is a limited supply of the product available, as, "Mr. Prospect, there are only 100 sets of these books on the market and when this supply is exhausted no more will be printed." Limited facilities may also induce a prospect to act, as, "Mrs. Brown, there is only one first-class cabin available on the South American cruise sailing January 1. I suggest that you make your reservations now."

A premium may be offered to prospects to encourage them to buy at once, as, "With each refrigerator bought this week, we are including, free, a set of covered refrigerator dishes worth $10.50."

A trial order is often sought by a salesman who cannot persuade a prospect to buy a full quantity at once. However, a trial order should be accepted only as a last resort because the cost of selling and shipping often exceeds the profit to the seller; competition is given an opportunity to supply the balance of the buyer's needs; a small quantity is often inadequate to establish a buying habit or to secure an adequate display; and distributors often resort to substitution when the limited supply is exhausted.

On the other hand, a trial order may be the first of a long and profitable series of future sales; it often requires less time and effort to sell a repeat order to an established customer than to obtain an initial order from a prospect; and a satisfied customer is often the source of other customers.

8. Implying Consent. In selling luxuries and intangible services, a salesman may frequently assume that a prospect is ready to buy without securing his express consent. If a buyer indicates by his comments and questions that he is ready to buy, it is often unnecessary for a salesman to ask directly, for example, "Do you want to buy this automobile?" A salesman can take it for granted that the buyer is going to buy, and say, "May I phone the garage and get them busy on servicing your car for you?"

Many buyers are doubtful and wavering and look to the salesman to help them make a positive buying decision.

If a salesman assumes that a prospect accepts his proposition and proceeds to fill out the order blank without waiting for the buyer to give his consent, the transaction may be closed without further discussion.

9. Asking Directly for an Order. Instead of using one or more of the eight preceding methods of securing a favorable buying decision, it is sometimes desirable to ask directly for an order. Some buyers prefer direct action and like to be asked to buy. Some salesmen always make a minimum of three direct requests for an order in every presentation. By asking directly for an order, a salesman will close more sales than the salesman who makes many contacts without asking prospects to buy. Make it a rule to ask for an order after every presentation.

HANDLING THE ORDER BLANK DURING THE INTERVIEW

While a purchaser's oral promise to buy is acceptable to some sellers, a majority of buyers and sellers require a written contract of sale or order signed by the buyer and accepted by the representative of the seller. Some industrial purchasers do not give salesmen signed orders but give their promise to buy and confirm it with a purchase order mailed to the salesman's firm.

If a salesman has made a convincing presentation, has tested a prospect's interest, and secured his commitment, the buyer has ordinarily no reluctance to signing an application or order. However, when faced with the necessity of making a written commitment, some prospects procrastinate and shy away from signing an order.

Many salesmen prefer to get a prospect accustomed to the sight of an order blank early in a sales interview. One specialty salesman uses an order book as a pointer when demonstrating his product to a prospect. Another salesman keeps an order form before a prospect at every stage of the interview to record the minor decisions on such questions as color, accessories, quantities, sizes, and other details. When the final decision is reached, the order form is completely filled in ready for the buyer to sign.

Other salesmen, however, prefer to keep an order form or application out of sight but readily accessible during a sales interview so that it can be turned to in a natural way when needed. If a salesman is submitting a written proposal or survey, an order form may be inserted as a last page in the proposal. Salesmen who use visual material, portfolios, or figuring pads, include an order form in the visual presentation at the point where the buyer probably would be ready to sign.

Many salesmen carry order forms in their inside coat pockets where they can be easily reached when the time comes to secure a buyer's signature. However, if a salesman draws an order form out of his pocket with a flourish, like a highwayman pulling a gun, a prospect may be taken by surprise and stiffen his resistance to signing.

There is positive suggestion value in keeping an order form before a prospect, as well as added utility to a salesman in using it to record any minor decisions. By keeping an order form before him during an interview, a salesman is continually reminded of the real purpose of a sales interview. Some salesmen have an order form partially filled out before approaching a prospect to save time and possible embarrassment in handling the closing details.

EXECUTING AN ORDER

Completeness and accuracy in handling the details of a sales transaction is very important if a customer is to receive the product or service in good order; nervous with anticipation that a buyer may alter or revoke his decision to buy, a salesman may hastily prepare an order, overlook important details, and make mistakes that create customer misunderstanding and ill will.

Carelessness by a salesman in writing orders is often responsible for poor service to customers; delays in granting credit; tardiness in delivery; shipment of wrong quantities, colors, sizes, and styles; delivery to wrong address; excessive transportation charges; and similar mistakes which can be easily avoided by greater care in writing the original order.

Salesmen are provided with printed order forms or application blanks, listing information necessary to enable a shipper to complete delivery of the material ordered. Spaces are provided for the name and address of the purchaser, method of shipment, date of shipment, product ordered, quantity, price, and other items depending on the product or service. Order forms usually are executed in quadruplicate, one for the buyer, another for the salesman, a third for the sales office, a fourth for the shipping department. Special order forms are often prepared for certain types of products, methods of delivery, or classes of customers.

Such a small detail as the correct name and address of a buyer on the order form is an important matter if the order is to be filled properly. If a shoe salesman, for example, writes an order for J. K. Jones, and the correct name of the purchaser is John Jones Shoe Company, correction notices have to be sent to various departments of the

SALESMAN & NO.		SOLD TO						ORDER NUMBER		
DATE SOLD		Town & State								
TERMS		SHIP To For				ATTENTION OF		DIST. NO.		
		R. R. Station				Freight	Express	P. P.		

Ack.	Quan.	Diam.	Thickness	Hole	Face or Shape	Grain	Grade	Remarks

Name of Part   Size

Size of surface ground   If int. grinding No. of keyways

Finish required   Excellent- - Commercial – Not Important

Material   Hard – Soft – Chilled – Annealed

If steel – Kind   Carbon Content   Alloying Metals

Operation   Stock removed   Wet or Dry

Preceding & Succeeding operations

Number of Passes   Limits   Feed

Machine   Condition   Straight In   Traverse

Wheel Speed   RPM SFPM   Work Speed   RPM SFPM   Table Traverse   Feet per min.

If necessary, illustrate this information with sketch on reverse side.

Competing Product

Approximate Yearly Consumption

Object of Test

Mark Tags & Invoice

CREDIT STAMPS	SPECIAL ATTENTION	RECEIVING STAMP

FIG. 22. Order blank used by salesmen of a manufacturer of grinding wheels and abrasives sold direct to industrial concerns. In filling out this order blank, it is necessary for a salesman to give accurate and complete information to ensure that the product will meet the customers' requirements.

firm handling the order and numerous changes must be made, causing expense, confusion, and delay. Plain, legible handwriting prevents misunderstandings.

If an order is written by a salesman in the presence of the customer mistakes will be reduced. Some salesmen ask a prospect to fill in the order form or read the written order to ensure its correctness. The practice of writing orders several days after they have been taken usually creates errors and dissatisfaction. Orders should give complete information. Skeleton orders, without sizes, delivery dates, and other details, are not actual orders.

GETTING THE BUYER'S SIGNATURE

Many buyers must be asked for their signature to an order. It is natural for people to dawdle and procrastinate in making decisions. The same reluctance causes buyers to hesitate and postpone signing. In many cases a salesman is obliged to help a prospect make up his mind to sign. However, prospects resent being coerced into signing orders. The problem of securing a prospect's signature, therefore, calls for skill, initiative, and tact on the part of a salesman.

A prospect who is making a buying decision may be very susceptible to a salesman's suggestion but resentful of a direct command. A thoughtless statement by a salesman may cause the prospect to postpone his decision to buy. For this reason, many salesmen in seeking a buyer's signature prefer to use indirect suggestions in the form of tactful statements rather than direct commands. Instead of commanding a prospect to "Sign this order blank here," or "Just write your name on this dotted line," many salesman prefer the suggestions, "Now, Mr. Prospect, will you please complete these arrangements by signing your name here?" or "So that we will have a mutual understanding on this matter, please write your name here."

Some salesmen ask for the correct spelling of a prospect's name or the corporate name of his firm and write it on the order or application blank. They then ask for his signature, by saying, "Please write your name here just as I have written it above." By asking for a signature in this way, a salesman avoids directly commanding a buyer to sign an order.

To suggest signing an order, some salesmen keep a fountain pen or pencil in sight throughout an interview. The prospect becomes accustomed to them and may accept the subtle suggestion that they be used in signing an order. Oversized pens and pencils have been used by salesmen to attract the attention of prospects and subtly suggest that buyers sign orders. A pen or pencil may be used by a salesman as a pointer in showing features of his product or in emphasizing ideas in charts or illustrations.

A prospect should not be expected to use his own pen or pencil in signing an order. If a buyer lays aside the pen or pencil proffered by a salesman, another may be offered later when the salesman believes that the buyer is ready to sign. The proffer of a pen is a suggestion that a prospect sign the order and at the same time makes it easy for him to affix his signature.

SECURING PAYMENT WITH THE ORDER

In selling many products or services, a salesman is required to collect all or a part of the purchase price with the order. When a sale is made on an installment payment plan, a salesman secures the initial payment and prepares the finance papers. When a prospect has been well sold, the initial payment is easily secured. If a salesman acquires the habit of asking for a check with an order, he experiences little difficulty in getting an initial payment or deposit.

Salesmen should suggest the benefits of ownership in securing initial payment. An electric refrigerator salesman says, "I am sure that you want to enjoy the delicious desserts from this refrigerator right away, so please make out your check for $——." A life insurance salesman says, "You will feel more secure when you go home tonight to know that no one can take your insurance away from your wife. If you will let me have your check for $—— right now, that satisfaction will be yours."

If a prospect objects to making an initial payment, a salesman can minimize the amount by comparing it with the cost of an inexpensive article like a cigar or a daily paper.

PREPARING FOR FUTURE RELATIONS WITH PROSPECTS

If a salesman is unsuccessful in securing an order from a prospect, he can further his future contacts by expressing his appreciation for the prospect's time and the opportunity of presenting his product or service. A salesman may also attempt to obtain an appointment for another interview, seek permission to submit additional samples, try to arrange for a demonstration, leave a visual portfolio to be picked up at a future time, or secure the buyer's consent to interview a subordinate or a business associate. One of these methods may be used to "keep the door open" for a later interview with a prospect.

A salesman who shows annoyance at being refused an order or criticizes a buyer for his lack of judgment has difficulty in getting favorable consideration from the prospect in the future. A salesman who persists good naturedly in his efforts to sell often is rewarded with an order at another time.

LEAVING AFTER SECURING ACTION

When a salesman has succeeded in securing an order, he closes the interview promptly by thanking the buyer and explaining briefly the details of delivery or installation. He creates good will by promising to return later to determine the buyer's satisfaction and render any necessary service.

Salesmen usually leave a customer quickly upon the conclusion of a sale. The buyer is busy and wants to get back to his work. A salesman does not want to give the buyer an opportunity to change his mind and cancel all or a part of the order. If he lingers after an interview, the customer has an opportunity to ask for special concessions. By leaving promptly, a salesman does not risk talking himself out of an order.

If a buyer does not appear to be completely sold, a salesman should summarize the advantages of his product or service and resell the customer before leaving. Salesmen representing a manufacturer of aluminum kitchen utensils (sold direct to housewives) immediately after closing sales, place their samples on the kitchen stove of each customer, show her how the utensils appear in use, and briefly review their advantages. Advertising material may be left with a customer to aid her in justifying her purchase and to explain the advantages of the product to her friends and neighbors.

HOW TO SECURE ACTION IN A SALES INTERVIEW

Successful salesmen use a proved strategy, based on the principles described in the preceding pages, in securing favorable buying decisions from prospects. To assist salesmen in applying these principles successfully in closing sales, a simple five-step plan or routine, which can be adopted by a salesman of any type of commodity or service, is described here. By committing these five points to memory, practicing their use, and applying them at every opportunity, a salesman can easily increase his ratio of sales to presentations.

Routine for Securing Action in a Sales Interview

1. Watch for indicators of acceptance.
2. Get minor decisions.

3. Commit the prospect frequently.
4. Use a reserve selling point.
5. Ask for the order often.

1. Watch for Indicators of Acceptance. At all stages of an interview, successful salesmen are alert for evidence that a prospect is ready to buy. The most obvious signs of interest are the buyer's comments or questions, as, "How soon can I get delivery on this car?" or "That's an excellent location for a home." Statements such as these reveal that a prospect is convinced of the merit of a salesman's proposition and has already made up his mind to buy.

Objections raised by a prospect are frequently evidence of his sincere interest in a salesman's proposition. When a prospect objects, he often means, "I want to know more about that," but he does not wish to show his interest by asking for additional facts.

Without saying a word, a buyer often reveals by his attitude that he is interested and perhaps ready to buy. Although these indicators are not infallible evidence of a prospect's desire to buy, they frequently give a salesman assurance that a prospect is ready to sign an order.

2. Get Minor Buying Decisions. By attempting to get a favorable decision on minor points, a salesman gradually brings a prospect to a final decision to buy. Every purchase is the result of a number of favorable decisions on minor features. Before placing an order, a prospect must make six minor buying decisions. He says to himself, "I need it," "The price is right," "The product is satisfactory," "The service looks adequate," "I believe the company will stand back of it," and "Now is the time to buy."

If a salesman neglects to get these minor decisions, he cannot hope to receive an order. When a buyer's attitude on each decision is tested by tactful questions and a salesman is assured that the prospect is in agreement, an order is to be expected.

A salesman must, in effect, close several sales: one on need, another on source, and the other decisions before he can secure an order.

3. Commit the Prospect Frequently. To make sure that a prospect understands and agrees with him on each point, a salesman tests a buyer's interest frequently by asking questions worded to provoke a favorable response. Typical committing questions are: "That advantage is very apparent, don't you think?" and "Isn't that the way it should be considered?" When worded tactfully, these questions permit a salesman to "take a prospect's temperature" and determine whether or not he is ready to buy.

Prospects often reveal their agreement with a salesman by their voluntary remarks, as, "I think that this automobile is the best looking car I've seen on the road." A buyer may also reveal his receptiveness by his attitude and attentiveness.

Sometimes a prospect does not understand a salesman's explanation yet does not want to show his lack of knowledge, so he nods his head in agreement or says "Yes" to a committing question. A salesman should learn to distinguish between genuine commitments and insincere responses by the manner in which they are made. To discourage a salesman, a prospect may agree with everything he says. Experienced salesmen handle "yes men" by attempting to "smoke out" their objections or discover their real resistance. If a buyer continues to "yes" a salesman in responding to committing questions, the prospect may be asked a definite "No" question, as "Would you ride in an automobile with faulty brakes?"

If commitments are sought after each important sales point or minor buying decision has been made, a salesman saves time and ensures satisfactory progress toward an order.

4. Use a Reserve Selling Point. Some salesmen keep one or more sales points in reserve to use in the event that a prospect hesitates to buy. The reserve point may be a unique or distinctive feature of the product calculated to make a strong impression. A buyer should be convinced of the advantages of a reserve feature, and the sale should be closed on that one feature.

A reserve selling point may also be a distinctive appeal or product feature which may not have been discussed previously in the salesman's presentation.

5. Ask for the Order Often. Many salesmen are reluctant to give a prospect the opportunity to say "No" for fear that a sale cannot be consummated. As a consequence, they fail to ask for an order and lose sales to competitors who are not afraid to ask prospects to buy. "Not one salesman in five makes a habit of asking his prospects to buy during the first interview," says David R. Osborne.

Confidence and courage are indispensable characteristics in getting favorable buying decisions. If a salesman has made a thorough presentation of his product, answered objections convincingly, and demonstrated clearly, he need not fear to ask a prospect to buy.

Some salesmen follow a policy of asking for an order at least four times during an interview. Salesmen who ask prospects to buy during the first interview, close a greater number of sales on the first call.

Sales Presentation Rating Form

Securing Action

Salesman_____   Date_____

Rated by_____   Over-all Rating_____

Score

I. *Salesman's Method of Securing Action*	Excellent 90–100	Good 80–90	Fair 70–80	Poor 60–70	Failure Below 60
A. Alertness for signs of acceptance					
B. Using "try out" closes					
C. Committing prospect					
D. Implying ownership					
E. Securing basic decisions					
F. Emphasizing single feature					
G. Summarizing benefits					
H. Offering inducements					
I. Implying consent					
J. Using reserve point					
K. Handling order form					
L. Securing signature					
M. Securing payment					
N. Requesting order					
O. Preparing for future relations					
P. Leaving					

Miscellaneous Comments_____

_____

_____

Problem I

SECURING ACTION IN AN INDUSTRIAL SALES INTERVIEW

Parker Nettleton, representing Carter Paint Company

The Carter Paint Company, Cleveland, Ohio, manufactures and distributes a complete line of paints for interior, exterior, marine, and industrial purposes. The company separates its sales organization into two divisions: one sells paints to wholesale and retail hardware and paint stores; the other sells industrial paints direct to industrial concerns and mill-supply firms.

The industrial division employs 20 salesmen who sell direct to large users of paint and work with mill-supply salesmen. Eighty per cent of the production of the company is sold by this division. A competing company makes about 25 per cent of the total industrial paint sold in the country, and the Carter Company manufactures about 10 per cent of the industrial paint sold, approximately the same volume as two other paint manufacturers.

Carter salesmen call from three to four times a year on the principal industrial concerns in their territories. The competitive situation is severe and there is much price cutting. As a result, industrial buyers usually secure estimates from several paint companies before ordering large quantities.

In the following interview, salesman Nettleton, who has represented the Carter Company in New England for five years, is discussing a quotation with the purchasing agent of a large Boston public utility. This is the third call made by Nettleton on this buyer within a week. On previous calls he has secured favorable decisions on the product, need, service, and source, and in this interview he is seeking a decision on price and time.

1. SALESMAN: Hello, Mr. Buyer, getting colder this morning.
2. BUYER: Yes, it was chilly this morning.
3. SALESMAN: I've been working on that quotation now for a week and I just finally got an answer this morning. We had to go into quite some detail to get it, but we got it. We went into several short cuts in manufacturing and larger quantities and things of that sort, saved a few pennies here and there, and I just got an answer this morning from Mr. Blank, our general manager; so he told me to come in and see you about it and find out about the contract.
4. BUYER: Well, of course, I don't know what we're going to do. I know we are going to do over those two buildings in Springfield.

5. SALESMAN: Yes, what are you going to do, make a one-coat job or two? Do you know?

6. BUYER: Two coats from what I understand over there and two coats from what they're doing in the other plants.

7. SALESMAN: I see. What do they figure to use?

8. BUYER: They figure about 5,000 gallons for a two-coat job. About 3,000 gallons for the first coat and about 2,000 for the second.

9. SALESMAN: Do you want to write that up on the basis of 5,000 gallons?

10. BUYER: We'll be glad to consider it.

11. SALESMAN: We can give it to you in drums or gallon cans. Which would you prefer? (Telephone rings and buyer engages in conversation.)

12. BUYER: We want it in the drums.

13. SALESMAN: Yes, that will be O.K.

14. BUYER: That price, now, is what?

15. SALESMAN: Yesterday, when I went back to the office trying to chisel that price, our manufacturing costs at that time, I don't mind telling you, were 84½ cents.

16. BUYER: Yes.

17. SALESMAN: Well, that's why I'm back with a price of 90 cents a gallon. It positively couldn't be any cheaper as we didn't want to change the materials.

18. BUYER: Yes.

19. SALESMAN: Now, we went all through the whole thing and we've had the factory on the line and everybody else all the way through the line on raw materials, and we've chiseled a penny here and there so that we could hold that 90-cent price. That's quite a job on account of the oil it takes and that fluctuates like a "son of a gun," but now it happens to be a fairly nominal price.

20. BUYER: Yes.

21. SALESMAN: Well, that's why they wanted me to get a contract on it right now, because there's no doubt that everything is going to increase.

22. BUYER: I guess that's right.

23. SALESMAN: All I've been doing for the last month is going around to all my customers, trying to get contracts through on stuff. What do you think of that price? Are you ready to buy?

24. BUYER: I guess it would be cheaper now than later.

25. SALESMAN: All right. I'll fix up the details right now so you can get this low price while you can.

26. BUYER: O.K. What colors did we discuss?

27. SALESMAN: Dark green for the outside and grey inside. I suggest that you order everything you need right now. I'd like to get this order in right away before we get this notice of higher prices.

28. BUYER: O.K. All right, we'll go along with you.

29. SALESMAN: I'll tell them to draw up that contract for 5,000 gallons. We got that settled.

30. BUYER: Yeah. Send that in, right away.
31. SALESMAN: O.K. Good-by. Much obliged. Now I'll get out of your way.
32. BUYER: Good-by.

Questions

1. What type of close did the salesman use?

2. At what stage of the interview did the salesman secure a decision? Was it the proper time?

3. Was it necessary for the salesman to secure a signed order? Explain.

4. Did the salesman prepare the way for future relations? How?

5. Did the salesman leave the buyer properly? Explain.

6. Did the buyer give the salesman any indicators of acceptance? What?

7. Did the salesman secure any minor decisions? What?

8. Was the prospect committed during the interview? How?

9. Did the salesman ask for action more than once? Explain.

10. Was a reserve selling point used? What?

Problem II

GETTING ACTION IN A DEALER INTERVIEW

Benton J. Fuller, representing Farnsworth Fish Company

The Farnsworth Fish Company, established in Boston, Mass., in 1901, packs and distributes dried and canned fish, including mackerel, herring, lobster, and codfish, direct to institutions, wholesalers, large direct buyers, and chain food stores throughout the country. The company does little advertising and relies on the quality of its product to secure sales volume and meet the keen competition of several larger fish packers serving the same market.

Benton J. Fuller is one of 10 salaried wholesale salesmen, employed by the Farnsworth Company. These men are located in the principal wholesale food markets and cover that trade regularly. Salesman Fuller's headquarters are in Albany, N. Y., and his territory includes the entire state of New York, except New York City, and Pennsylvania excluding Philadelphia.

In the following dialogue, salesman Fuller is interviewing in Buffalo the buyer of a small chain of five high-class specialty food stores located in Buffalo, Rochester, Syracuse, and Utica, N. Y. This chain has never bought Farnsworth products.

1. SALESMAN: I'd like to interest you in fish cakes. I see that you've got Doe's (a nationally advertised brand) in stock.

2. BUYER: Well, we're selling it two for 29 cents right now.

3. SALESMAN: We've got fish cakes at two cans for a quarter the same size and just as good as Doe's. (Of course, Doe's advertise a little bit more than we do.)

4. BUYER: Well, we put Buxton's (a nationally advertised brand) in. They thought they had better ones than Doe's. We didn't think so though. 'Course, they've got a price about like yours.

5. SALESMAN: I really think ours comes right up to Doe's fish cakes, positively, because I know, in fact; I've got three ex-chain-store managers who have opened up stores of their own and tried them out and say they're just as good as Doe's.

6. BUYER: Uh, huh.

7. SALESMAN: I think that's a pretty fair advertisement if chain-store men will say it.

8. BUYER: Of course, there's only one way to tell those things and that's to open them up and eat them.

9. SALESMAN: Yes, sure. Well, listen—

10. BUYER: But unless we thought your brand was an awful lot better than Doe's we might not be interested in them, as fish cakes are a relatively small item with us. Doe's got the advertising and they're in demand.

11. SALESMAN: I see that one of your competitors had Doe's advertised for a dime.

12. BUYER: Well, we don't mind.

13. SALESMAN: No, I don't imagine you worry about them. Say, I'd like you to buy a couple of cases a store and try them out.

14. BUYER: Yeah, but we have a lot of Doe's on hand.

15. SALESMAN: You want a quality product, don't you?

16. BUYER: Yes, definitely.

17. SALESMAN: Would you prefer to buy through a jobber or direct?

18. BUYER: We always buy direct on fish.

19. SALESMAN: Our codfish is caught off Newfoundland and packed right on the shore for freshness.

20. BUYER: Yes, that sounds good.

21. SALESMAN: Well, listen, the best proof of quality is the taste. I want you to sample some of our codfish cakes—I've got 'em downstairs now.

22. BUYER: Well, take a can down to the fry cook in our store restaurant, ask him to fry a couple, and I'll sample them for you.

23. SALESMAN: All right, I'll bring them in when they're done.

24. BUYER: I'd like to taste them.

25. SALESMAN: Oh! You'll find 'em delicious.

26. BUYER: Just bring them in when they are ready.

27. SALESMAN: The proof is in the tasting you know.

28. BUYER: That's right. If they taste good, I'll take six cases.

Questions

1. Did the salesman watch for indicators of acceptance? **How?**

2. Did he get minor decisions? What?

3. Did he commit the buyer? How?

4. Did he use a reserve selling point? What?

5. Did he ask for the order often? How?

6. Did the salesman "leave the door open" for future dealings with the buyer? How?

7. Did the salesman have the right personal characteristics for securing buying action? If not, what characteristics did he need?

Reading References

R. C. Borden, "How to Deliver a Sales Presentation," Harper & Brothers, New York, 1938.

Norman J. Collister, "Essentials of Selling," Chap. IX, Prentice-Hall, Inc., New York, 1945.

J. R. Daubman, "Salesmanship and Types of Selling," Chap. XII, F. S. Crofts & Co., New York, 1939.

Charles H. Fernald, "Salesmanship," Chaps. XV–XVI, Prentice-Hall, Inc., New York, 1945.

J. George Frederick, "Modern Salesmanship," Chap. XVIII, Garden City Publishing Company, Inc., New York, 1937.

Harold M. Haas, "A Short Course in Salesmanship," pp. 314, 317, 325, 333, Prentice-Hall, Inc., New York, 1939.

J. M. Hill and R. G. Walters, "Success through Salesmanship," Unit XVII, South-Western Publishing Company, Cincinnati, 1940.

Paul W. Ivey, "Successful Salesmanship," Chap. X, Prentice-Hall, Inc., New York, 1947.

N. Kneeland, L. Bernard, and G. B. Tallman, "Selling to Today's Customer," Chap. VIII, Ginn & Company, Boston, 1942.

David R. Osborne, "Salesmanship for Today for Salesmanagers of Tomorrow," Chap. XVI, Harper & Brothers, New York, 1939.

Charles B. Roth, "Secrets of Closing Sales," Prentice-Hall, Inc., New York, 1947.

F. A. Russell and F. H. Beach, "Textbook of Salesmanship," Chap. XV, McGraw-Hill Book Company, Inc., New York, 1949.

Harry Simmons, "A Practical Course in Successful Selling," Chap. XXIII, Harper & Brothers, New York, 1939.

Percy H. Whiting, "The Five Great Rules of Selling," Chaps. 15–20, McGraw-Hill Book Company, Inc., New York, 1947.

CHAPTER XXII

CULTIVATING CUSTOMERS

I. CULTIVATING USERS

"Never forget a customer and never let a customer forget you," says the general sales manager of a large automobile manufacturer. And his opinion is emphasized by the president of a prominent public utility, who says, "Don't forget the people who made you in the days of your prosperity; they can break you."

Many salesmen overlook their old customers in their efforts to get new accounts. Many customers, secured at a considerable expenditure in time and effort, are disregarded or treated with indifference while salesmen scramble madly for new business.

To illustrate the importance of retaining and cultivating old customers, the value of a customer has been estimated for various types of retail businesses. The annual purchases of an average clothing customer make him worth $85 to a clothing retailer; the average shoe customer is worth from $35 to $68 a year, depending on the size of his family; the average furniture customer is worth $87 a year, after he has made his main purchase; the average department store customer is valued at $362 a year; and the average Ford automobile owner is worth $251 a year to the dealer from whom he originally bought a car.

These estimates are an indication of the annual retail purchases of a typical consumer. They do not take into consideration the cost of selling and advertising to secure the customer originally.

The turnover of customers of retail establishments is large. Analysis of the purchases of 2,000 retail charge customers of a large department store showed that 60 per cent had lapsed or were inactive. A similar study of the charge accounts of a successful retail store showed that 27 per cent were inactive for at least a year or more. The turnover in consumers is a more serious problem than the turnover in merchandise.

A large majority of consumers discontinue buying because of neglect by salesmen. A questionnaire sent to inactive customers by a large retail store showed that 70 per cent drifted away for no particular reason; 5 per cent were influenced by friends to buy elsewhere. Only 15 per cent of them stopped buying because of grievances and 10 per cent were influenced to buy elsewhere by lower prices of competitors.

A salesman who maintains contact with customers has many opportunities to make repeat sales. A satisfied customer is his best prospect for additional purchases. It is easier to retain an old account than to get a new customer. A salesman of repeat essentials can make more sales and earnings by cultivating his present customers than by seeking new ones. A survey of the owners of a well-known make of automobile showed that 43.3 per cent had bought the same make of car two or more times and 58.5 per cent were planning to buy the same make again.

The good will of customers created by consistent, friendly cultivation is an intangible but invaluable asset to a salesman. A salesman cannot be successful in the long run if he fails to win and keep the good will of his customers. Owners can be helpful in recommending a salesman and his product to their friends and associates. From 40 to 50 per cent of the sales of a well-known electric refrigerator are made through the influence of present owners.

A satisfied customer is the best advertisement for a product or service. Every owner is proud of his possessions and is eager to discuss them with others. Around luncheon tables, at bridge parties, or wherever people congregate, the conversation often turns to praise of various products or services. Customers who have been kept well informed by salesmen of the distinctive features of a product can discuss it most effectively with their friends and acquaintances. A famous motor-car manufacturer recognizes the importance of customer recommendations by advertising, "Ask the man who owns one."

Satisfied customers are an excellent source of new prospects for salesmen. Many companies have developed special plans to secure the cooperation of owners in locating possible buyers. A salesman can use customer references as an excellent entering wedge in opening interviews with prospects.

Dissatisfaction of customers can be forestalled if a salesman will call regularly to make adjustments, explain proper operation, and see that proper mechanical service is secured.

Selecting Users to Be Cultivated

Certain customers should be given more attention than others. A salesman who serves a large number of customers must obviously select certain ones for preferred cultivation. Those selected for development should have the greatest buying potential, be the most influential, and be able to assist a salesman. New customers should be given preferred attention to ensure their understanding of the use of the product and, in the case of mechanical products, the importance of proper maintenance.

To ensure systematic cultivation, complete and accurate card files of customers must be maintained by a salesman. Owner record cards should be filed alphabetically and distributed in a daily follow-up file for regular attention. Customer records should show the customer's name, address, products used and dates of purchase, mechanical service received, and the calls by the salesman who sold the customer.

WHEN TO SERVE USERS

Owner cultivation should first begin when a sale is closed and end only when a buyer no longer needs a salesman's product or service. When a salesman receives an order for a mechanical product or complicated service, he should briefly show the new customer how to use the product or service. A large manufacturer of cooking utensils instructs its salesmen, "The first service call is to be made immediately at the time of sale in order really to clinch your order. Be sure that your customer knows and understands the five rules on the new method of cooking."

Many salesmen of home appliances and industrial equipment arrange to be present when a purchase is delivered to a new customer to be sure that it is in good condition and as ordered. A customer should be resold briefly at time of delivery, reminded of the importance of regular maintenance, and instructed in proper operation.

If a salesman cannot be present when a product is delivered to a new customer, he should call the next day to see if the product arrived in good order and is operating satisfactorily. Salesmen representing a well-known make of electric refrigerator are instructed to follow up new customers, as follows:

Let it be your unchanging rule to make your first call on a new customer on the next day after the refrigerator is delivered. Your whole purpose during this call should be to create a favorable impression by letting the customer know that you are interested in her satisfaction with the refrigerator and in seeing that she is entirely satisfied with the service rendered by you and your company.

Another follow-up call should be made on a new customer from two weeks to 30 days after delivery of a product costing $100 or more. The purpose of this call is to determine whether or not the product is rendering satisfactory service to the buyer and to enable the salesman to begin capitalizing on the good will which has resulted from the satisfactory performance of the product.

After the first two cultivation calls, the number of calls to be made on a new owner depends on the response received from the customer, the amount of the sale, and the repeat sales possibilities. A customer may easily become annoyed by too many service calls. However, a salesman who has a helpful attitude, a reason for calling, and renders the customer a definite service is always welcome. A leading automobile manufacturer advises retail salesmen to make cultivation calls at a frequency of 7, 21, and 42 days after delivery of a new car. Owners are given helpful information for the care and operation of their cars on each call.

When sales are made on the credit installment plan, salesmen should follow up customers as soon as all partial payments have been completed. At that time the buyer has available the amount of his monthly payments to apply on the purchase of another product. Through arrangement with the finance companies serving the customer, salesmen are notified automatically as soon as a buyer has completed his payments. Some salesmen follow up a customer who has made six monthly payments and explain to him that he is now privileged to buy another article without making a down payment and that his new, adjusted monthly payments will be only slightly higher because of the extended time the new installment contract has to run.

Regular contact should be made with all customers at least once a year and at more frequent intervals if the nature of the product and the cooperativeness of the customer justify more attention.

METHODS OF SERVING USERS

A salesman can serve customers by instructing them in care and operation, by making adjustments, by checking on service, by informing about improvements, by introducing new products or accessories, by showing other ways to use a product. If a salesman serves his customers in these ways, good will and cooperation will result.

Instructing in Operation. Owner satisfaction and freedom from service expense depend largely on the proper use or operation of a mechanical product. If the buyer of a mechanical product has never owned a similar article before, use instruction is fundamental. Customers who have previously owned similar products should be reminded of the proper way to operate them to ensure fullest satisfaction. Salesmen sometimes find it necessary to give a new customer a short course of instruction in operation. Operating handbooks are provided by most manufacturers of mechanical appliances for the guidance of customers. These books may be used effectively by salesmen in instructing new owners in proper operation. The "breaking-in" period in the life of most mechanical appliances calls for special care in operation which should be explained by a salesman. Some sellers of mechanical products maintain training schools for the instruction of the operators employed by customers.

Making Adjustments and Minor Repairs. If a salesman of mechanical appliances is prepared to make small adjustments, he can save his customers service expense and secure their good will and cooperation. The sales representatives of a large manufacturer of cooking utensils are provided with service kits containing small parts and tools for making minor repairs to customers' utensils. Salesmen of this company call on customers and offer to service their old utensils free of charge. As a result of this service, these salesmen secure repeat orders, names of prospects, and valuable testimonials.

A salesman's prestige is increased if he is able to make minor adjustments without calling for the assistance of the service department. A customer learns to look to a helpful salesman for mechanical aid and a close and permanent relationship is established which pays big dividends in good will and future sales.

If a salesman can make small adjustments, he is able not only to give a customer immediate satisfaction but to prevent future major dissatisfaction. A small but persistent rattle in a motor car, if uncorrected, may prejudice an owner against a repurchase of the same make. Through contact with owners, a salesman has an unusual opportunity to prevent small dissatisfactions from becoming major obstructions to repeat sales.

Ensuring That Owners Receive Service. By reminding buyers of mechanical products to secure the free mechanical service to which they are entitled during the "breaking-in" period, a salesman ensures that the life of the product is prolonged and that the buyer obtains maximum satisfaction from its use. Proper and regular maintenance of a mechanical product is vital to its efficient operation. By advising owners in preventive maintenance, a salesman can help his customers to avoid unnecessary and costly repairs. Many owners of mechanical products do not recognize the importance of preventive maintenance and are forgetful of and indifferent to periodic inspections. A salesman who reminds his customers to secure necessary service paves the way for repeat sales.

Many salesmen of mechanical products telephone their new customers at regular intervals for several weeks after delivery to remind them to have the product properly serviced. By checking service department records, a salesman can keep himself informed regarding the amount of service received by customers and follow up those who require service.

Following the installation or delivery of a mechanical product, a personal call is made by many salesmen to deliver and explain the service policy to the new customer.

Acquainting Customers with Improvements. To ensure that customers get the fullest satisfaction from products, a good salesman informs them of the latest product improvements. New product developments make it possible for an owner to effect economies in operation, secure added comfort, speed up performance, improve appearance, or enjoy greater safety. Improvements are being made frequently in the design and construction of many products, which give a salesman an excellent opportunity to bring greater profit and satisfaction to customers and at the same time secure orders for replacement or accessory equipment.

Good salesmen circularize customers regularly with advertisements describing the new product features. Owners are invited to come to the salesroom to see a demonstration of product improvements. Salesmen also deliver accessories or new models to old customers for free trial use to show them the benefits of product improvements.

A product improvement gives a salesman a valid excuse for making a cultivation call on an old customer who is usually interested in knowing how he can get greater use or profit out of the product.

Increasing the Number and Variety of Applications. A customer may be using a product exclusively for one purpose, whereas there are many other possible applications that would bring the user greater satisfaction or profit. By discovering how a customer uses a product, a salesman can make suggestions for new and more profitable uses and so win the good will of the owner.

A salesman of visible record systems, for example, sold an installation to a manufacturer to control collections and to reveal past-due accounts. The salesman later studied the customer's business and found that the system could be used also for sales control or for measuring the accomplishment of salesmen. By suggesting this additional application, the salesman doubled the utility of the product to the customer and received an order for additional equipment.

Salesmen of electric refrigerators aid customers in using them in various ways by distributing free recipe books describing how to use an electric refrigerator in the preparation of frozen desserts and other foods.

Supplying Helpful Information. A salesman may cultivate a customer by supplying him with helpful information to aid in the general conduct of his business and in his professional or home activities. The sales representatives of a large life insurance company, selling industrial insurance to housewives, distribute to customers numerous booklets dealing with such home problems as first aid, food preparation, and family finances.

Miscellaneous Methods of Cultivating Customers. Numerous miscellaneous methods of cultivating customers are used by salesmen. One electrical appliance salesman staged an essay contest among his customers; another salesman ran a competition to determine the oldest user of his product in his territory; another asked users for suggestions for the improvement of his product or service. A life insurance salesman persuaded policy holders to buy life insurance for their children and succeeded in selling 19 out of a total of 42 contacted.

Some salesmen cultivate customers regularly by sending them a company magazine and writing them letters asking for names of prospects.

How Users Can Aid Salesmen

A salesman who cultivates customers secures not only good will and repeat orders but he also receives: (1) names of prospects; (2) testimonials and references; (3) recommendations to friends and neighbors; (4) assistance in demonstrating the product.

1. Names of Prospects. Customers are in a very favorable position to provide a salesman with names of prospects. Customers usually discuss purchases with friends and acquaintances who are also considering similar purchases. By asking customers three questions: "Do you know of anyone who might be interested in a ————?" or "Have you any friends, neighbors, or relatives who have shown an interest in your ————?" or "Who among your neighbors or business associates is not using a ————?" a salesman can usually secure from each owner the names of one or more possible customers.

Many companies provide their salesmen with special plans for securing the cooperation of customers in locating prospects. One manufacturer aids salesmen in cultivating users with an "owner-booster plan"; another features a "use the user campaign." Many of these plans compensate customers for the names of prospects who are eventually sold by salesmen. One oil-burner company pays a customer $5 in cash for the name of each prospect who buys the product. An electrical appliance company rewards customers with gifts for their cooperation in providing salesmen with prospects. A home insulation manufacturer gives each new customer a $100 bond which carries 20 coupons representing $5 each. Coupons are filled in by customers with the names of prospects and turned over to a salesman for solicitation. If the salesman succeeds in selling a prospect, the customer receives $5.

2. Testimonials and References. A satisfied customer is an excellent source of reference. If a salesman is alert for profitable or satisfactory experiences of customers, such as low current consumption, low service expense, or unusually long life of a product, he can secure much valuable sales ammunition from users in the form of testimonial letters.

A large electric refrigerator manufacturer supplied retail salesmen with an attractive book titled, "My Refrigerator Friends." Salesmen asked their customers to write their comments about the product in the book. In this reference book are listed the names and addresses of the salesman's customers with the dates of their purchases. This book provides an easy way to get comments from customers and is useful as a source of testimonials and references in closing sales.

Customers may also aid by permitting photographs to be taken of their installations or equipment in use. Pictures of the homes or plants of well-known users are excellent material for sales portfolios.

Good customers usually permit a salesman to use their names as references in seeking interviews and convincing prospects of the merit of the product. An owner list of impressive length and quality is an excellent selling tool.

3. Recommendations to Friends and Neighbors. A satisfied customer is an excellent advertisement for a product and for the services rendered by a salesman. Buyers enjoy discussing their possessions with friends and neighbors. The recommendations of owners are more readily accepted by prospects than are the claims of a salesman. A satisfied user will often recommend a product to his friends who may be in the market.

PERMUTIT USERS EXPERIENCE REPORT

What features about Permutit appeal to you and your family most? Please check below.

Luxurious soap lather_____	No more ring around tub_____
Delightful baths_____	Vegetables and pastries tastier_____
Better shampooing_____	Tea and coffee tastier_____
Makes shaving easier_____	Saves food otherwise wasted_____
Smoother skin_____	Better for drinking_____
Better for care of baby_____	Saves soap_____
Easier washdays_____	Keeps pipes scale-free_____
Makes clothes softer, whiter_____	Plenty of hot water_____
Makes clothes last longer_____	Saves fuel_____
Cuts down housework time_____	Any others?_____

Owners report that Permutit water softeners save them money in many ways. How much do you **think it saves** you **per week?** (Just use check marks)

CHECK ESTIMATED SAVINGS **PER WEEK**

	25c	50c	$1.00	$1.50	$2.00	$3.00	Over $3.00
SOAPS, SHAMPOOS, CLEANERS (By eliminating soap curds, soft water cuts down soap and cleanser expenses —often more than half)							
FUEL (Soft water ends hard-water boiler scale, allows boilers to heat faster, saves 10% fuel bills sometimes)							
PLUMBING REPAIRS (No more scale to choke pipes, heaters, boilers. This saves plumbing repair bills)							
CLOTHES, LINENS (No more soap curds to damage fabrics, no more harsh scrubbing. So washables last 25-50% longer)							
COSMETICS (Soft water often saves as much as 25% on creams and lotions by ending hard-water skin troubles)							
BOTTLED WATER (A soft water filter ends need for bottled water. So put down all you used to spend for this)							
OTHER SAVINGS (Faster cooking? Savings on razor blades? Anything else?)							
TOTAL							

Perhaps you have noticed a saving in household duties because of soft water's faster cleaning. About how many hours a week do you save? (Just check)

1 hour_____ 2 hours_____ 4 hours_____ 6 hours_____ 8 hours_____ 12 hours_____ any more_____

REMARKS:_____

_____

_____

Signed_____Address_____

Fig. 23. Salesmen of a domestic water softener follow up customers and secure reports of the experiences of owners on the above report form. These reports are excellent sales ammunition in selling prospects. This is one way consumer customers can cooperate with salesmen.

Enthusiastic owners sometimes cooperate with a salesman by distributing samples or advertising to their friends and associates. Sometimes customers will telephone or write their acquaintances or associates seeking interviews for a salesman. A friendly owner may be willing to write letters of recommendation to prospects at the request of a salesman. Owners are usually willing to aid salesmen by giving buyers information by telephone or correspondence about their experiences with products or services.

Owners can aid a salesman by supplying him with reports detailing their experience with his product. Salesmen of home water softeners ask customers to fill out forms, as shown above, reporting their experience with the product; these reports are then used in interviewing prospects.

4. Assistance in Demonstrating the Product. Customers can aid a salesman in demonstrating to prospects. Industrial users often permit salesmen to bring prospects to their plants to see the operation of equipment bought from the salesman. Homeowner customers frequently aid salesmen by demonstrating oil burners, air conditioning, and other home equipment to prospects. Salesmen representing a large cooking-utensil manufacturer arrange with housewives to serve demonstration dinners or luncheons in their homes. Friends of customers are invited to the luncheons and are later solicited by the salesmen to buy utensils.

Salesmen representing a manufacturer of rock-wool insulation for homes send direct-mail advertising to all homeowners in the neighborhood of a home in which the product is being installed. The salesmen personally follow up prospects who have received the advertising referring to the installation in the neighborhood.

Demonstrations carried on by salesmen in the homes, factories, or stores of customers bring users and prospects together and afford an opportunity for potential customers to hear directly from owners about their favorable experiences with a product.

How to Service a User of Major Products

In cultivating users, successful salesmen apply the principles described in the preceding pages, following a simple three-point plan involving service contacts at the time delivery is made, and following the delivery. These points are incorporated in the following routine which can be applied by a salesman of any product or service in securing the cooperation of customers.

Routine for Servicing Users

1. Make delivery call and instruct in operation.
2. Make postdelivery call to explain service and sell maintenance.
3. Make periodic calls to ensure continued satisfaction.

1. Make Delivery Call and Instruct in Operation. A few minutes taken by a salesman when a major product is delivered to instruct a new customer in its proper operation, will ensure that it will give maximum satisfaction to the new owner. Use instruction creates a favorable impression on a new customer by showing him that the salesman is interested in having the product give satisfaction.

Salesmen representing a large automobile manufacturer, when delivering a new car, instruct buyers by presenting them with a "User's Guide," saying, "This book was prepared by the factory to help you get the greatest amount of pleasure and service out of your new car. Such subjects as driving economy, care of your car, starting in cold weather, and suggestions for night and winter driving are covered fully. This book will be of tremendous help to you and I suggest that you read it carefully."

Helpful operating suggestions made to a new customer by a salesman often pay big dividends in good will and future business.

When a new customer takes delivery of a product, he may notice small scratches, soiled spots, or needed adjustment. Although these deficiencies are often insignificant, they mar his complete satisfaction at a time when he is particularly conscious of the product. By calling on a new user when he takes delivery, a salesman can easily adjust these small complaints and ensure the customer's complete satisfaction.

If a salesman quickly corrects mistakes that may have occurred in delivery, the good will of a new customer is secured. The customer experiences no delay, loss of service, or expense in calling a serviceman or in sending the product to a service station, if the salesman makes the adjustment.

2. Make Post-delivery Call to Explain Service and Sell Maintenance. Salesmen of mechanical products can ensure satisfaction to new customers by explaining the importance of proper maintenance and regular inspections. The service policy should be delivered, features of the service policy emphasized, and new owners advised as to the correct way to prolong the life of their purchase. By explaining service to a new customer, a salesman can establish a service habit which will not only give a customer maximum satisfaction but also produce profitable service sales by keeping the customer in frequent contact with the seller.

3. Make Periodic Calls to Ensure Continued Satisfaction. By calling on one or more customers each day, a salesman can keep in contact with owners, make repeat sales, sell accessories, secure names of prospects, and enjoy the cooperation of loyal customers. The number of such contacts to be made by a salesman depends on the amount of the sale, the repeat possibilities, and the attitude of the customer. A good salesman always plans to perform a definite service for each customer on cultivation calls.

II. CULTIVATING WHOLESALER AND RETAILER CUSTOMERS

SERVING DEALERS

The same fundamental reasons which make it essential for consumer salesmen to cultivate users apply also to manufacturers' salesmen selling wholesale and retail merchants. The prosperity of manufacturers whose products are sold through wholesale and retail stores depends on the success of these distributors and dealers.

Progressive manufacturers recognize their responsibility to aid their distributor and dealer customers. "The present and future success of any manufacturer in the automotive business must be directly measured and limited by the success of that manufacturer's dealer organization," says the president of a large motor-car corporation. "We have a problem. The problem consists of improving the profit position of all dealers, particularly those who, for some reason or other, are in an unfavorable operating position."

A modern concept of the responsibility of a manufacturer's salesman for the success of his dealers is expressed by the sales manager of a large drug sundry manufacturer, "We have a new sales philosophy which is summarized in a slogan, 'Sell out of the store rather than into the store'."

A manufacturer of household electrical specialties estimates that a retailer customer is worth $1,200 a year. In one year this concern lost 400 customers out of a total of 2,000 active accounts.

Many retailers become inactive and buy only a small portion of their requirements from manufacturers whose salesmen neglect to cultivate their dealers.

A survey of the purchases made by retailers from a well-known manufacturer of ten nationally advertised food products, showed that 18 per cent of the dealers stocked only one item; an additional 16 per cent stocked only two items; 12 per cent more stocked as many as three. Over 20 per cent of the manufacturer's accounts were inactive, or had not bought for six months, and 20 per cent of the rest were considered lapsed.

Salesmen have many opportunities to increase sales through sound dealer cultivation. A large dry goods wholesaler, through the efforts of its salesmen, restored more than 75 per cent of the "dead" accounts from a list of 1,600. In another campaign, salesmen of distributors, aided by advertising, restored a total of 1,739 accounts and added 2,981, a total of 4,720 new customers.

By assisting wholesale and retail customers, a manufacturer's salesman ceases to be "just another salesman." His helpful suggestions make it easier for him to obtain more of a dealer's time and to increase his sales.

The cooperation of a wholesaler or retailer in pushing the sale of a manufacturer's line is readily secured by salesmen who aid their customers by preparing local advertisements, arranging window displays, setting up floor and counter displays, and conducting store sales.

A salesman who gives dealers sales assistance, advertising aid, or management advice not only wins their good will but automatically secures larger and more regular orders for a greater number of items in his line. Competition is met more effectively, and merchants are more successful reselling the products of salesmen who give constructive aid to dealers.

Selecting Merchants for Cultivation

Although every customer is entitled to a salesman's assistance, practical necessity demands that a salesman spend his time and effort with those merchants who are potentially able to distribute the largest profitable volume of his product.

Dealers and distributors are selected for special cultivation according to the following factors: (1) present volume of sales of the product; (2) potential volume of sales of the product; (3) willingness to cooperate with the salesman; (4) store location on streets that carry the greatest volume of vehicular and pedestrian traffic; (5) merchandising ability of the store; (6) the type of store according to principal line carried; (7) the size of store; (8) the merchant in greatest need of assistance; (9) progressiveness of the merchant; (10) type of store according to service offered, such as cash-and-carry, delivery, credit, etc.; (11) competitive lines carried; (12) location of competing out-lets; (13) length of time store has been a customer.

By qualifying retailer customers for cultivation on the preceding factors, a salesman can readily determine which deserve special atten-tion and concentrate his efforts on selected outlets. In addition to giving all customers a minimum amount of assistance, certain selected outlets should be chosen for more complete cooperation.

Salesmen of a well-known soft drink, sold through thousands of re-tail outlets, are instructed in cultivating dealer customers, as follows: "Your present service to all dealers should be maintained, but the dealers on busy streets can be further developed by means of added sales effort, more dealer help, advertising material, and close coopera-tion at all times." The salesmen of this company are also advised to concentrate on dealers who have clean, attractive stores, who make an effort to sell the product, who feature attractions to bring cus-tomers inside the store, and who are sold on the value of the product.

By carefully selecting merchant customers for development, a sales-man can avoid competitive jealousies between dealers, secure maxi-mum cooperation, and obtain larger and more frequent sales.

WHEN TO CULTIVATE MERCHANTS

Dealer development begins when a customer places his initial order or signs a franchise. A new dealer is usually enthusiastic about stock-ing a new line; he is most receptive to a salesman's suggestions con-cerning newspaper announcements, store displays, and other merchan-dising aids to resell the product.

Salesmen usually call on a new dealer shortly after the first ship-ment arrives to see if the goods were received in good condition and adjust any mistakes which may have been made in filling the order. The salesman can see also that the new stock is well displayed and that the merchant and his salespeople are informed and enthusiastic about the new line. An advertising program may be discussed and an introductory retail sale may be planned.

After a merchant customer has been initiated in the best methods of marketing a new line, a good salesman calls at frequent intervals to make sure that the merchant maintains sales effort behind the prod-uct. When a new account has been well established, the frequency of a salesman's calls depends on the potentialities of the customer and the 13 factors previously named. A good salesman makes some defi-nite resale suggestions on every call.

Merchandising Score Card

KEEP THIS RECORD!

MERCHANDISING . . . is selling to the retailer plus helping him to sell.

√ = Yes	Tally if done by Salesman				
✕ = No	A	B	C	D	E
1 Checked stock by examining or counting (not just by "glancing at it")					
2 Straightened up stock					
3 Replenished stock on shelves or counters or in showcases					
4 Set up any newly delivered stock that had not yet been placed on shelves, etc.					
5 Installed some store advertising material (cards, posters, etc.)					
6 Gave store advertising material to dealer					
7 Set up a display					
8 Suggested displays that the dealer should make					
9 Suggested ways for dealer to improve sales of slow-moving items					
10 Gave the dealer selling ideas or promotional ideas					
TOTAL MERCHANDISING SCORE					

FIG. 24. The 10 tasks listed on this Merchandising Score Card describe the missionary work of a salesman to retail merchants. This score card was prepared by the Distribution Committee of the National Confectioner's Association to enable salesmen to score their merchandising activities and improve their service to customers. It may be profitably used by salesmen of all types of goods and services sold through retail outlets.

Methods of Cultivating Distributors and Dealers

Salesmen can help dealer customers in three general ways: (1) sales assistance and counsel; (2) advertising assistance and counsel; (3) management assistance and counsel. It is best practice to concentrate efforts to develop customers by specializing on one of these three phases of retailing or wholesaling. Inexperienced salesmen ordinarily confine their assistance to selling and advertising; experienced men are competent to advise customers on management problems as well. The average salesman, however, can give most useful assistance to retailer customers on sales and advertising problems.

Many progressive companies have specific programs of dealer development. The dealer development plan of a large manufacturer of electric lamps is called a "four-step plan" and includes: (1) making window displays; (2) making store displays; (3) educating clerks to ask customers to buy; (4) educating dealers to do outside selling. The salesmen of this company help dealers by aiding them with these four merchandising methods.

Salesmen of a large manufacturer of home heating equipment concentrate their assistance to dealers on the four following activities: (1) making personal calls on prospects for the dealers; (2) selling the dealer on direct-mail advertising; (3) selling the dealer on doing local newspaper advertising; (4) selling the dealer on installing store and window displays.

Advertising materials created by manufacturers usually are distributed to dealers by salesmen to carry out the advertising plans recommended.

Determining a Customer's Need for Assistance

When a salesman is provided by his company with a development plan for dealers, he must decide on the application of the plan to each customer. A salesman must answer, in regard to every dealer, the question, "What does this dealer need to help him make money selling my goods?" A salesman must first discover the merchandising, advertising, or management difficulties of each dealer. Next he ranks these problems in the order of their importance. Then he selects the most important problem, the one on which he can offer the greatest assistance, and gives suggestions for solving it. The salesman who concentrates on the fundamental problem and ignores the other difficulties until he is ready to deal with them, is most successful in dealer development.

To determine a dealer's problems, a salesman asks tactful questions about the merchant's difficulties, methods, or objectives. A salesman may also discover many weaknesses by observation, or the customer may volunteer information about his problems. For example, a salesman asks a customer, "How are collections coming in?" and discovers that the merchant may need suggestions for collecting accounts receivable. By observing a customer's window displays, a salesman may find that the dealer is not making the best use of his windows and needs display suggestions. When a merchant customer remarks, "My clerks are missing a lot of sales," an alert salesman recognizes that here is an opportunity to instruct the merchant's salespersons in better selling methods.

RECOMMENDATIONS AND ASSISTANCE TO CUSTOMERS

After a salesman has analyzed a customer's needs for sales, advertising, or management assistance, he next makes specific suggestions for solving the most important difficulties.

The recommendations proposed by a salesman may involve one or more of the following activities which may be either carried out, supervised, or planned by the salesman.

1. *Sales Assistance and Counsel.*
   Special sales suggestions, as combination sales, one-cent sales, premium sales, store-wide sales, etc.
   Compensating salespeople.
   Selection of salespeople.
   Training salespeople.
   Conducting consumer sales.
   Consumer calls with dealer's salesmen.
   Independent selling for dealer.
   Outside selling by dealer's salespeople.
   Telephone-selling suggestions.
   Sales contests.
   Supervising salesmen.
   Stimulating salesmen.
   Personal conferences with salesmen.
2. *Advertising Assistance and Counsel.*
   Determining advertising appropriation.
   Planning advertising campaigns.
   Preparation or planning of the following local advertising media:
   Newspaper advertising.
   Direct-mail advertising.
   Radio advertising.

Store and window displays.
Outdoor posters and signs.
Novelty or premium advertising.
Directory advertising.
Car card advertising.
Preparation of mailing lists.
Publication of publicity stories.
Arranging for product demonstrations.
Handling cooperative advertising.
Arranging distribution of handbills.
Management Assistance and Counsel.
Figuring selling prices.
Store organization and personnel.
Buying policies.
Interior store arrangement and equipment.
Store lighting.
Delivery service.
Stock control and sizing.
Credits and collections.
Accounting methods.
Adjustment policies.
Store records and system.
Inventory turnover.

In advising a merchant customer on one or more of the above activities, a salesman usually takes advantage of the assistance of his sales promotion department. Many manufacturers cooperate with distributors through sales promotion or special dealer service departments, such as the Merchants Service Division of the National Cash Register Company, which has assisted thousands of merchants in all parts of the world with their operating problems. Publications of dealer development departments are effectively used by many salesmen to excellent advantage in cultivating dealers.

A large electrical appliance manufacturing company has prepared six manuals for training retail salespersons of electrical appliances. Many other progressive companies have published similar excellent dealer development materials which can be used by salesmen in cultivating dealers.

Salesmen also can secure valuable material for developing dealers from worth-while publications treating of retail problems and methods. The U.S. Department of Commerce has published numerous booklets relating to retailing, including "Retail Store Problems," "Measuring a Retail Market," and "Retail Store Planning." The National Cash Register Company publishes "Better Retailing, a Handbook for Merchants," filled with proved solutions to merchandising problems. These booklets may be distributed by salesmen to their customers.

Business magazines, serving every industry, are packed with practical plans for aiding merchants. Some salesmen read and clip worthwhile articles from trade magazines and send them to selected customers for their information.

How to Cultivate a Merchant-Customer

In developing dealers, successful salesmen put into practice the principles previously described by following a simple plan of cultivation which can be applied by a salesman of any product sold through wholesale and retail merchants. This plan of dealer development includes four simple steps which have been incorporated into a four-point routine which may be memorized and practiced by salesmen in aiding their merchant-customers to increase their sales and profits.

Routine for Servicing Merchant-Customers

1. Select best accounts for development.
2. Analyze the resale needs of selected customers.
3. Present a resale plan.
4. Aid the customer in carrying out the plan.

1. Select Best Accounts for Development. By selecting those customers who are most likely to be receptive to assistance, and who offer the best possibilities for sales volume, a salesman concentrates his development efforts where they will be most effective. Since volume and profit do not permit a salesman to spend the same amount of time on all his customers, he must choose for development those dealers most likely to respond to his efforts.

Some companies classify dealer customers, according to credit standing, progressiveness, volume possibilities, and other factors, into A, B, and C groups. A salesman whose customers are identified in this way has no difficulty in determining which justify special development efforts. When a salesman uses his own judgment in selecting customers for cultivation, he can make his selections according to the 13 factors described previously.

In selecting certain dealers for development, a salesman must be careful to avoid antagonizing competing customers serving the same area.

RATING SHEET FOR RETAIL EMPLOYEES

NAME OF EMPLOYEE_____ POSITION _____

RATED BY _____ POSITION _____, DATE _____

1. What is the effect of his personality upon people? Does he handle customers well?	◯ Generally well liked.	◯ Makes favorable impression	◯ Liked by intimate friends only.	◯ Unfavorable impression.	◯ Generally disliked.
2. How industrious is he? Does he stay on the job? Is he easily interrupted or does he have power of concentration?	◯ Very industrious, conscientious.	◯ Steady worker, good concentration.	◯ About normal.	◯ Requires constant supervision.	◯ Too much loafing.
3. Does he know his line, its selling points, and have sufficient trade knowledge?	◯ Exceptional knowledge well applied.	◯ Good training and experience	◯ Fair knowledge.	◯ Requires constant coaching.	◯ Knowledge inadequate.
4. Does he learn new duties quickly and retain this knowledge?	◯ Requires little teaching, quick to grasp new ideas.	◯ Retains instructions fairly well.	◯ Average coaching required.	◯ Requires great deal of instructions.	◯ Slow to learn, poor memory.
5. Does he think intelligently and make logical decisions?	◯ Thinks quickly and logically.	◯ Judgment usually sound.	◯ Makes a few errors in judgment.	◯ Inclined to be illogical.	◯ Generally mistaken.
6. Does he have initiative and creativeness?	◯ Offers many good ideas	◯ Above average	◯ Shows initiative occasionally.	◯ Waits to be told.	◯ Needs to be pushed.
7. Does he cooperate with others?	◯ Goes out of way to cooperate.	◯ Gets along well with associates.	◯ Acceptable.	◯ Reluctant to cooperate.	◯ Stubborn.
8. Is he in good health?	◯ Has lots of energy.	◯ No noticeable handicap.	◯ Normal health.	◯ Lacks vigor.	◯ Poor health handicaps work.
9. Does he take full advantage of selling opportunities?	◯ Successful in making extra sales.	◯ Usually alert to opportunities.	◯ Occasionally suggests other items.	◯ Needs constant reminders.	◯ Waits for customers to ask.
10. Is he willing to accept responsibility?	◯ Seeks it.	◯ Usually anxious to try.	◯ Willing to accept it.	◯ Accepts it reluctantly.	◯ Refuses responsibility.
11. Does he enjoy his work?	◯ Very happy in his job.	◯ Likes most of his duties.	◯ Satisfied.	◯ Would prefer other work.	◯ Dissatisfied.

Fig. 25. Salesmen representing the International Shoe Company aid retail shoe merchants to improve the efficiency of their sales personnel by providing merchants with this form to rate their sales employees. After rating a salesperson, a merchant then holds conferences with the employee to discuss ways of improving his personal efficiency.

2. Analyze the Resale Needs of Selected Customers. Although some self-sufficient customers may resent a salesman's efforts to help them, most merchants are flattered by a salesman's interest and willingness to assist them in making more money. Accordingly, an alert salesman has little difficulty in discovering the problems of his customers by asking tactful questions, listening to their complaints, and observing their methods. A qualified salesman who has the respect of his customers is usually taken into their confidence on many business matters and has an opportunity to become familiar with their merchandising needs.

By becoming interested in the problems of his customers, a salesman discovers many practical solutions for resale needs and can apply them to similar problems of other customers.

If he concentrates his attention on the fundamental problems of each customer and on those difficulties with which he is most familiar, a salesman can render the most effective service to his customers. If he has little knowledge of retail management methods, he will be more successful in confining his efforts to studying and attempting to solve the advertising or selling problems of his dealers.

Most salesmen can call in expert assistance to aid them in analyzing and solving the difficulties of a merchant-customer. A large automobile manufacturer operates a business management department, as one section of its sales organization, which collects and analyzes, monthly, the financial statements of its retail dealers. This information reveals a dealer's difficulties and gives the company's salesmen an opportunity to aid in solving them. A manufacturer of floor covering operates a department of retail management and merchandising to aid its salesmen in analyzing and overcoming the difficulties of its customers.

The profit and volume on a product determine the amount and type of assistance that a salesman can render a dealer. A chewing-gum salesman, for example, cannot be concerned with his customers' problems of store lighting or accounting; he may, however, logically aid his customers in improving their counter or window displays.

Outstanding salesmen who are successful in cultivating dealer-customers prepare a list of the principal difficulties of each selected customer and then attempt to aid each customer in solving his fundamental problems. Wise salesmen do not attempt to scatter their service efforts over many problems.

3. Present a Resale Plan. After a salesman has selected a customer's fundamental problem, he next suggests a practical resale plan for solving the difficulty. The solution suggested may call for a simple counter display or it may involve a plan for the complete reorganization of a customer's finances and management methods.

In presenting resale suggestions to a customer, a good salesman organizes his recommendations so that the dealer will be interested in the proposal and understand clearly the points brought out in the plan. Proofs of advertisements, actual examples of counter and window dis-

SALES PRESENTATION RATING FORM

Cultivating Customers

Salesman_____   Date_____

Rated by_____   Over-all Rating_____

Score

I. *Salesman's Methods of Cultivating Users*	Excellent 90–100	Good 80–90	Fair 70–80	Poor 60–70	Failure Below 60
A. Make delivery call and instruct in operation					
B. Make post-delivery call, explaining service					
C. Make periodic calls discussing improvements					
D. Secure sales cooperation of customers					

II. *Salesman's Methods of Cultivating Dealers*	Excellent 90–100	Good 80–90	Fair 70–80	Poor 60–70	Failure Below 60
A. Select best accounts for development					
B. Analyze dealer's resale needs					
C. Aid dealer in carrying out plan					

Miscellaneous Comments_____
_____
_____

plays, photographs of displays in the stores of other customers, copies of direct-mail pieces and handbills, charts and diagrams, training booklets, motion pictures, and slide films are used to dramatize the recommendations of a salesman.

The presentation of merchandising ideas is arranged at a time and place when the merchant can give his full attention to the proposal, which may be submitted in writing. Salesmen of a large oil company use an automobile trailer for merchandising conferences with dealers so that customers will not be interrupted by the details of their business.

After securing the acceptance of a resale plan, a salesman secures a signed order from the dealer for the advertising materials, signs, direct-mail pieces, manuals, or other materials necessary to put the plan into operation.

4. Aid the Customer in Carrying Out the Plan. When a dealer has accepted the suggestions of a salesman and has committed himself to an advertising program, store sale, or other merchandising effort, the salesman follows up his recommendations on subsequent calls to ensure that the plan is carried out as agreed upon. A merchant may lack the ability to execute a development plan or become so engrossed in other details of his business that the proposals of the salesman are forgotten. Accordingly, a salesman may have to install a window display, take copy for a handbill to a printer, or write a newspaper advertisement to ensure that an advertising program which has been planned is put into operation. In persuading a merchant to initiate a direct-mail advertising program, it is often necessary for a salesman to see that a good mailing list of the customer's prospects is prepared so that the folders, letters, or mailing cards can be sent.

Problem I

Cultivating Dealer Customers

Thomas C. McAdams, representing Eastern Specialty Manufacturing Company

The Eastern Manufacturing Company, Syracuse, N.Y., manufactures and distributes a complete line of packaged food specialties including baking powder, dog food, spices, desserts, and condiments. The Eastern line is sold direct through wholesale and retail drug, department, grocery, and delicatessen merchants who are contacted by a sales organization of 40 men. These salesmen operate out of the company branch offices located in the principal cities of the country.

The Eastern Company invests $400,000 annually in national advertising and window and store display materials which are distributed by its salesmen to retail merchants carrying the Eastern line. Salesmen are instructed to aid dealers by persuading them to use the store advertising produced by the company.

Thomas C. McAdams represents the company in New York City and calls principally on chain stores and large retail buyers. He has been connected with the company five years and previously was associated with a competing food manufacturer.

In the following interview salesman McAdams is calling on the buyer of a chain of 30 specialty grocery stores, the Gem Stores, which have sold a good volume of the Eastern line of foods for four years. The salesman calls regularly on the buyer every 30 days.

1. SALESMAN: Hello, Tom. Have you played golf lately?
2. BUYER: I played last night—nine holes; that's enough for a while.
3. SALESMAN: Yeah.
4. BUYER: Well, what have you got on your mind?
5. SALESMAN: I've been looking over your dog food stock and see you have a big inventory. You should do something to move it. A good display will stimulate sales. Here are two good store displays. (Shows two displays.) Now, some of our other displays might be used instead. I'd like to show you the others. Now that display (pointing to display) certainly could be used in some of your stores.
6. BUYER: These are your latest displays, is that it?
7. SALESMAN: Yes. They are distributed the same as all of our line, on consignment so that you are protected in the event of return if they don't sell. A new price on dog food was fixed on April 1. The discount for all sizes was 20 per cent on that date.
8. BUYER: You mean we can return any unsold dog food without question?
9. SALESMAN: Well, that's what I mean. The displays are free. This illuminated display here (pointing to display) I think is particularly attractive. The markets in Blanktown, Brownville, Sackstown use that. The Jonesboro Market uses it with great success. You can move it around to various parts of the store. It holds all the different types.
10. BUYER: Will the lamps light up?
11. SALESMAN: Yes, sir. You light those up there. You can light it to attract the attention of customers. I don't hesitate in recommending these displays to you and if you decide to use them, we will be perfectly willing to do all the work as far as packing up the stock and installing the displays.
12. BUYER: They may have a tendency to wake us up a little. It's something the customer can get a hold of and see what we've got on display.

13. SALESMAN: You use displays like these for other products, don't you?

14. BUYER: We do from time to time, although our stores aren't display places like public markets and a lot of others. They have lots of room and our space is very little. We don't have time to look for a loop-hole; there are lots of times when we don't have the space.

15. SALESMAN: Dog food is a good profitable item; you'll find that just by pushing it you will make some money on our dog food. It'll be worth while to start. Please sometime take just a Saturday and question each customer on the 'phone. Here is the order blank for 30 displays, one for each store.

16. BUYER (signing the order): There's not much difference on these dog foods anyway.

17. SALESMAN: They are all pretty much the same, but we feel that our merchandising devices are a little superior. Will you give this advertising to Miss Blue (supervisor of telephone sales)? Thanks very much. I hope the displays work out to your satisfaction. I'll bring them along and install them on my next trip.

18. BUYER: I'm sure they will. Good-by.

Questions

1. In what way did the salesman cultivate the dealer in this interview? Was his method of development satisfactory? Criticize it favorably or otherwise.

2. Was the salesman wise in cultivating the Gem stores? Why?

3. Did the salesman analyze the dealer's need for assistance? How did the salesman discover the needs of the buyer?

4. Did the salesman present a plan for resale? What? Was it desirable?

5. Did he aid the dealer in carrying out the plan? How?

Problem II

CULTIVATING USER CUSTOMERS

Lawrence D. Davis, representing the Oxford Home Appliance Company

The Oxford Home Appliance Company, Hartford, Conn., distributes direct to homeowners a complete line of major electrical appliances, including washers, ironers, refrigerators, and oil burners made by famous manufacturers.

The company has sold and served consumers in central Connecticut since 1920. It is a large local advertiser. Ten outside retail salesmen of the Oxford Company spend much of their time calling on home-owners selling appliances.

Lawrence D. Davis has been associated with the company for the past five years. Salesman Davis makes a practice of following up all customers at the time of delivery as well as six months later to determine if the customer is satisfied with his purchase. In the following interview, Lawrence Davis is calling on a new customer who has recently bought an electric refrigerator. Davis is accompanying the deliveryman who is delivering the customer's purchase.

1. SALESMAN: Good morning, Mrs. Roberts, I'm calling to deliver your new Coldmaster. Shall we bring it in the side door?
2. BUYER: Yes, that will be fine.
3. SALESMAN: If you have time, I'd like to step in and give you a few suggestions which will help you get greater satisfaction from your new Coldmaster.
4. BUYER: Come right in.
5. SALESMAN: You are going to really save money with the Coldmaster with its big super-freezer chest here at the top (salesman opens door to freezer compartment) which keeps 50 pounds of foods frozen at zero degrees. You can buy frozen foods in quantities at lower prices and store them here until you're ready to use them. My wife buys a gallon of ice cream and stores it in our super-freezer and it's always ready to use.
6. BUYER: Can we freeze our own food in there? We have a few berry bushes and my husband was wondering if he could freeze some raspberries for next winter?
7. SALESMAN: Yes, you can freeze up to 10 pounds of berries at one time by putting the boxes around the walls of the chest.
8. BUYER: What about ice cubes?
9. SALESMAN: There are six trays of ice cubes in the freezer chest which give you ample supply for the hottest day or biggest party.
   Another feature of this 8-cubic-foot model is the full-width Hydrator which provides moist cold storage for fruits and vegetables so that you can keep them garden fresh.
10. BUYER: Does this refrigerator have to be oiled?
11. SALESMAN: No, the sealed-in refrigerating system is airtight and oiltight and never needs a drop of oil for the life of the refrigerator.
12. How often does it have to be defrosted?
13. SALESMAN: This Coldmaster never has to be defrosted. There is no bother with removing trays of water as in the old-fashioned refrigerators.
   Does Mr. Roberts like desserts?
14. BUYER: He is very fond of them.
15. SALESMAN: Then I know you'll be interested in this new booklet on "Delicious Frozen Desserts," which describes many new ways to make ice cream, sherbet, and other delicious frozen desserts. My favorite is frozen custard.

16. BUYER: What's that rattle I hear?

17. SALESMAN: Sounds like a loose shelf fitting. Let me see. (Salesman opens refrigerator and examines shelves.) By tightening up these small nuts, I've stopped the vibration. Sometimes dishes or bottles on the shelves will make an annoying rattle unless they are firmly set and separated so that they can't knock together. That sounds all right now, doesn't it?

18. BUYER: Yes, the noise has disappeared. What if the refrigerator should stop sometime?

19. SALESMAN: Simply call Lafayette 6–9330 and our serviceman will come within an hour and take care of any difficulty. You know that you have free service for five years, which includes regular annual inspections. I'll drop around soon and deliver your service policy which describes the Coldmaster guarantee and service provisions.

20. BUYER: Do I have to keep the dishes covered?

21. SALESMAN: No, it is not necessary to keep the dishes covered to retain the moisture in your food as the new moist cold-storage compartment keeps the humidity just right for all foods.

Here is a folder that explains that feature which is one of the greatest conveniences in the modern Coldmaster.

Your friends will probably be interested in seeing your new Coldmaster and I would appreciate an opportunity of meeting those who are seriously thinking of buying a new electric refrigerator in the near future. After they have seen your new box, I am sure that they will want one just like it.

22. BUYER: I'll be glad to have you know about any of our friends who may be interested in a new refrigerator.

23. SALESMAN: Many of my users have been very helpful in referring me to their friends, and I'll certainly appreciate your cooperation.

24. BUYER: Another thing, I wanted to ask you about the finish—will it wear off?

25. SALESMAN: No, it is made of life-time porcelain enamel on steel and keeps its high lustre for years. You need never worry about its wearing off and you can clean it with a damp cloth as it has no large pores in the surface to absorb the dirt.

If there is anything else you may want to know about your new Coldmaster, just call me at the office. Here's my card. (Hands customer business card.)

26. BUYER: I'll call you if anything comes up.

27. SALESMAN: Thank you, Mrs. Roberts. Good-by.

Questions

1. What did the salesman do on his delivery call? Explain what was done? Was this desirable? Why?

2. Did the salesman handle the matter of mechanical service satisfactorily? Explain.

3. Did the salesman seek reciprocal aid from the customer? What? Was this desirable?

4. Is there any indication that the salesman will make a postdelivery call? For what purpose?

5. Were the salesman's methods of user cultivation satisfactory? What else might have been done?

6. What benefits does the salesman derive from serving users in this way?

Reading References

E. G. BLACKSTONE, C. C. CRAWFORD and E. GRINNELL, "Selling," Chap. 10, D. C. Heath & Company, Boston, 1942.

B. R. CANFIELD, "Sales Administration, Principles and Problems," rev. ed., pp. 479–489, Prentice-Hall, Inc., New York, 1947.

E. CASEY and R. L. JOHNS, "Salesmanship for Colleges," Chap. 15, H. M. Rowe Company, Baltimore, 1938.

C. H. FERNLAND, "Salesmanship," Chap. XXII, Prentice-Hall, Inc., New York, 1945.

J. M. HILL and R. G. WALTERS, "Success through Salesmanship," Unit XVIII, South-Western Publishing Company, Cincinnati, 1940.

BERNARD LESTER, "Sales Engineering," pp. 161–163, John Wiley & Sons, Inc., New York, 1940.

HARRY SIMMONS, "A Practical Course in Successful Selling," Chap. XXIV, Harper & Brothers, New York, 1939.

D. B. TANSILL, "So You're Going to Sell," Chap. XII, John C. Winston Company, Philadelphia, 1939.

INDEX